BARRY FRIEDMAN, Ph.D.

The **MMPI:**

Use with Specific Populations

ROGER L. GREENE, Ph.D.
*Professor,
Department of Psychology,
Texas Tech University*

Grune & Stratton
Philadelphia, San Diego, London, Toronto, Montreal, Sydney, Tokyo

Library of Congress Cataloging-in-Publicaton Data

The MMPI: use with specific populations.
   1. Minnesota Multiphasic Personality Inventory.
I. Greene, Roger L.
RC473.M5M63   1988   616.89'075   88-1649
ISBN 0-8089-1913-X

Grune & Stratton
Philadelphia, PA 19106

Library of Congress catalog Number 88-1649
International Standard Book Number 0-8089-1913-X

Printed in the United States of America

88 89 90   10 9 8 7 6 5 4 3 2 1

To Mary Sharon and Holly

CONTRIBUTORS

ROBERT P. ARCHER
Department of Psychiatry and Behavioral Sciences, Eastern Virginia Medical School, Norfolk, Virginia

J. D. BALL
Department of Clinical Psychology, Highland Hospital, Asheville, North Carolina

WILLIAM D. BARLEY
Department of Counseling Psychology and Guidance Service, Ball State University, Muncie, Indiana

WILLIAM E. BELL
Veterans Administration Medical Center and The University of Texas Health Science Center, Dallas, Texas

JANE C. DUCKWORTH
Department of Counseling Psychology and Guidance Service, Ball State University, Muncie, Indiana

STEPHEN P. FARR
Department of Psychiatry, Health Sciences Center, Texas Tech University, Lubbock, Texas

ALLAN FINKELSTEIN
Veterans Administration Medical Center and The State University of New York Medical School at Albany, Albany, New York

D. ROBERT FOWLER
Veterans Administration Medical Center and The University of Texas Health Science Center, Dallas, Texas

WILLIAM N. FRIEDRICH
Mayo Clinic, Rochester, Minnesota

ROBERT D. GARVIN
Department of Psychology, Texas Tech University, Lubbock, Texas

ROGER L. GREENE
Department of Psychology, Texas Tech University, Lubbock, Texas

TERENCE KEANE
Veterans Administration Medical Center and Tufts University School of Medicine, New England Medical Center, Boston, Massachusetts

PAULETTE MARTIN
Department of Psychiatry, Health Sciences Center, Texas Tech University, Lubbock, Texas

LESLIE C. MOREY
Department of Psychology, Vanderbilt University, Nashville, Tennessee

DAVID S. NICHOLS
Dammasch State Hospital, Wilsonville, Oregon

WALTER E. PENK
Veterans Administration Medical Center and Tufts University School of Medicine, New England Medical Center, Boston, Massachusetts

CHARLES K. PROKOP
Department of Psychology, University of North Carolina at Asheville, Asheville, North Carolina

RALPH ROBINOWITZ
Department of Psychology, East Texas State University, Commerce, Texas

MARCIA R. SMITH
Department of Psychology, Vanderbilt University, Nashville, Tennessee

GLENN D. WALTERS
Psychology Services, United States Penitentiary, Leavenworth, Kansas

ACKNOWLEDGMENTS

I would like to express my appreciation to a number of persons who made this book possible. The authors were extremely cooperative in following the suggested outline for the chapters and the table formating. They also responded quickly and positively to the editiorial changes that needed to be made. Their MMPI expertise is well known and will be readily apparent in their chapters.

Holly A. Greene checked each published reference in the manuscript against the original source. Mary Sharon Greene performed the thankless task of proofreading the galleys. Their diligent work helped to make the text as accurate as possible.

I appreciate the permission to reproduce copyrighted materials. Specific citations occur wherever such material is used in the book.

PREFACE

This book is intended to assist the clinician in addressing the issue of how specific populations should perform on the MMPI. Clinicians are prone to think that a specific MMPI codetype exists for each diagnostic classification. For example, it is likely for a patient with a *6-8/8-6* codetype to be described as manifesting some type of schizophrenic process without considering the multitude of factors such as profile validity, ethnicity, education, social class, and base rates for both the diagnosis and codetype that may affect this relationship. This book will summarize both the standard validity and clinical scales as well as the more frequently scored special scales of the MMPI in a number of specific populations. Even a quick perusal of any of the chapters will show that there is not a typical codetype for any of these specific populations. Unfortunately, the data are more complex then clinicians would like to think.

Since it is difficult for a single person to be conversant with all of the MMPI data for a variety of populations, a group of experts were assembled to provide a comprehensive overview of the major populations in which the MMPI is used. The Table of Contents will illustrate both the specific populations that are to be reviewed as well as the MMPI expert(s) that wrote each chapter. A chapter on the use of the MMPI in prison populations was intended, but it was not possible to obtain an expert who could meet the time constraints necessary for publication. The reader also may note that there is not a chapter specifically on anxiety disorders. This diagnositic catergory surprisingly has received little attention from MMPI researchers.

Most of the data that are summarized in this book are based on DSM-II categories. Despite the appearance of DSM-III in 1980 and DSM-III-R in 1987, most MMPI research which is published currently still is based on earlier diagnostic systems. It will be a number of years before the increased diagnositic specificity provided by DSM-III is manifested in MMPI research.

CONTENTS

Chapter 1

Introduction

ROGER L. GREENE

This chapter provides an overview of the issues that are raised when the Minnesota Multiphasic Personality Inventory (MMPI: Hathaway & McKinley, 1967) is used in a variety of specific populations. It is assumed that the reader is familiar with the general interpretation of the MMPI so the issue to be addressed is improvement of skills in the interpretation of the MMPI in specific populations. This chapter begins with a discussion of the general issues that arise in trying to organize and synthesize the vast amount of research that exists on the MMPI. Next, the reliability and validity of psychiatric diagnosis using the Diagnostic and Statistical Manual of Mental Disorders (DSM-III: American Psychiatric Association, 1980; DSM-III-R: American Psychiatric Association, 1987) are reviewed briefly, since accurate diagnoses will be critical for evaluating how the MMPI performs within a specific group. Then the effects of base rates (the frequency with which a given diagnosis/ behavior occurs in a specific group/setting) on overall accuracy of diagnosis are covered. The chapter concludes with a schema for organizing the data within each specific group to facilitate comparisons among the various groups.

GENERAL ISSUES

The MMPI is the most widely used and researched objective measure of psychopathology in professional psychology (Lubin, Larsen, Matarazzo, & Seever, 1985). This wealth of information makes it virtually impossible for a single person to be conversant with the entire field; consequently, it is necessary to organize this research into meaningful categories so that it can be assimilated and used appropriately. This text is organized by specific populations, since it is assumed that the reader is interested in learning about the use of the MMPI in a particular group or setting. That is, the clinician is interested in how one patient's MMPI compares with that of similar patients or settings and/or what behaviors and correlates of MMPI performance can be expected. The clinician is less interested in the results of a single scale or index except as they relate to the overall profile. Once data are organized by specific group or setting, the only question that remains is how many categories should be employed. A perusal of the table of contents will reveal the decisions made on the number of categories to be reviewed in this text.

VARIABILITY IN MMPI PERFORMANCE

Experienced MMPI users are well aware of the variability in MMPI performance that occurs in any group or setting. Clinicians who are just becoming acquainted with the MMPI, however, frequently are surprised by the amount of variability in MMPI performance both within and between various diagnostic groups. Such variability in MMPI performance can be obscured when the "mean" profile for a group of patients is reported. For example, Profile 1–1 provides the mean profile for a group of schizophrenic patients that is an 8-6 codetype (Davies, Nichols, & Greene, 1985). On the basis of data such as these, clinicians

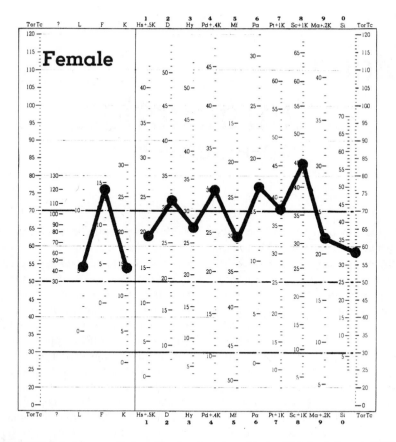

PROFILE 1–1. Mean profile for schizophrenic patients (Davies, Nichols, & Greene, 1985).

might assume that all patients within such a diagnostic group in a specific setting produced exactly the same profile. It is more likely, however, that only a small portion of the patients have the same codetype as the mean profile and that few, if any, have a similar configuration (patterning of the validity and clinical scales) on the entire profile. This point can be illustrated by looking at the variety of codetypes that were produced by this group of schizophrenic patients. As can be seen in Table 1–1, a total of 30 different codetypes occur in these 99 patients, all of whom met DSM-III criteria for Schizophrenic Disorders (Davies et al., 1985). Fourteen (14.1 percent) of these patients had within-normal limit (*WNL*) profiles, i.e., no clinical scale elevated to a *T*-score of 70 or higher, and consequently they were not classified in Table 1–1. These 14 patients, despite their presence in a state hospital and meeting all DSM-III criteria for schizophrenia, did not elevate any clinical scale to a *T*-score of 70. (See Chapter 11 for a discussion

TABLE 1–1.   FREQUENCY OF CODETYPES IN SCHIZOPHRENIC PATIENTS

Highest Clinical Scale	Second Highest Clinical Scale										Total
	1	2	3	4	5	6	7	8	9	0	
1	1	0	0	0	0	0	0	1	0	0	2
2	0	2	0	1	0	0	0	6	0	0	9
3	0	0	1	1	0	0	0	0	0	0	2
4	0	1	1	7	0	6	1	8	2	0	26
5	0	0	0	0	0	0	0	0	0	0	0
6	0	1	0	2	0	2	1	4	0	0	10
7	0	1	0	0	0	0	0	2	1	0	4
8	2	6	1	2	0	17	2	1	0	0	31
9	0	0	0	0	0	0	0	0	1	0	1
0	0	0	0	0	0	0	0	0	0	0	0
Total	3	11	3	13	0	25	4	22	4	0	85

Davies, J., Nichols, D.S., & Greene, R.L. (1985, March). *A new schizophrenia scale for the MMPI.* Paper presented at the 20th Annual Symposium on Recent Advances in the Use of the MMPI, Honolulu. With permission.

Note: When the highest and second highest clinical scale are identical, the codetype is a Spike profile. For example, there is one Spike *1* profile in these schizophrenic patients.

of *WNL* profiles in psychopathologic samples.) Scale *8* (*Sc*) was the most frequently elevated clinical scale in 31 patients (31.3 percent) and the second highest clinical scale in 22 patients (22.2 percent). Thus, a majority (53.5 percent) of these patients had Scale *8* as their highest or second highest clinical scale, which is one measure of the construct validity of this scale. The most frequent codetype was *8-6*, occurring in 17 (17.1 percent) patients; if *6-8* codetypes are combined with *8-6* codetypes, then 21 (21.2 percent) patients fall within this category (see Table 1–1). Thus, less than one-quarter of these patients had the same codetype as the mean profile of the group. The next most frequent codetype in this group of schizophrenic patients was a *WNL* profile. It is to be hoped that these data will alert clinicians to the high degree of variability in MMPI performance even within the same diagnostic category. Space precludes the presentation of all of the individual profiles for patients with the same codetype to illustrate their variability. Profile 1–2 provides an

example of the variability in performance for three of these schizophrenic patients who had *8-6* codetypes. The reader might review a sample of profiles within the same codetype in his or her setting to get a better appreciation of this type of variability in MMPI performance.

Hathaway and Meehl (1951) provided the observed codetypes for a number of DSM-I diagnoses (see pp. xxx–xxxvi). In their sample of 161 schizophrenic patients, 8 (5.0 percent) patients had *6-8* codetypes and 12 (7.2 percent) patients had *8-6* codetypes; these were among the most frequent codetypes. Nine (5.3 percent) patients had *2-7* codetypes, the second most frequent codetype. Again it is apparent that schizophrenic patients produce a variety of MMPI codetypes.

Schizophrenic patients are not the only patients whose profiles are characterized by variability in MMPI performance; Profile 1–3 and Table 1–2 present similar variabilities in a group of 101 bipolar disorder, manic patients who responded positively to psychopharmacologic treatment with

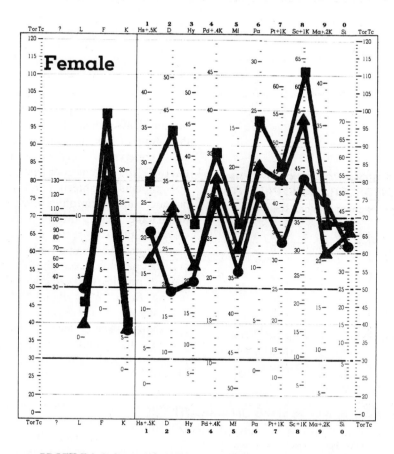

PROFILE 1–2. Examples of three *8-6* profiles in schizophrenic patients.

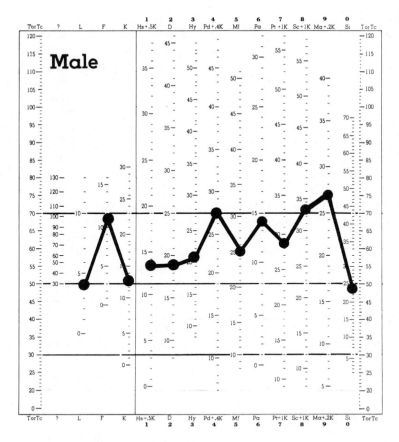

PROFILE 1–3. Mean profile for bipolar disorder, manic patients (Davies, Nichols, & Greene, 1985).

TABLE 1–2.   FREQUENCY OF CODETYPES IN BIPOLAR DISORDER, MANIC PATIENTS

Highest Clinical Scale	Second Highest Clinical Scale										Total
	1	2	3	4	5	6	7	8	9	0	
1	0	0	0	1	0	0	0	0	1	0	2
2	0	1	0	1	0	0	1	0	0	1	4
3	0	0	0	0	0	1	0	0	0	0	1
4	0	2	0	6	0	1	1	3	6	0	19
5	0	0	0	0	0	0	0	0	0	0	0
6	0	0	0	1	0	0	0	2	3	0	6
7	0	1	0	0	0	0	0	0	0	0	1
8	1	1	0	2	0	4	0	0	6	0	14
9	0	0	1	7	0	7	1	10	10	0	36
0	0	0	0	0	0	0	0	0	0	0	0
Total	1	5	1	18	0	13	3	15	26	1	83

Davies, J., Nichols, D.S., & Greene, R.L. (1985, March). *A new schizophrenia scale for the MMPI.* Paper presented at the 20th Annual Symposium on Recent Advances in the Use of the MMPI, Honolulu. With permission.

Note: When the highest and second highest clinical scale are identical, the codetype is a Spike profile. For example, there is one Spike 2 profile in these bipolar disorder, manic patients.

lithium (Davies et al., 1985). The mean profile for this group of bipolar disorder, manic patients was a *9-8* codetype. As can be seen in Table 1–2, a total of 28 different codetypes occurred in these 101 patients. Eighteen (17.8 percent) of these patients had *WNL* profiles and were not classified in the table. Scale *9* (*Ma*) was the most frequently elevated clinical scale in 36 (35.6 percent) patients and the second highest scale in 26 (25.7 percent) patients. Excluding the 10 patients with Spike *9* profiles who are counted in Table 1–2 as having Scale *9* as their highest and second highest scale, 52 (51.5 percent) patients had Scale *9* as their highest or second highest clinical scale. The fact that slightly over half of this diagnostic group had Scale *9* as their highest or second highest clinical scale attests to the construct validity of this scale. Still, nearly half of these patients had other scales as their highest or second highest clinical scale. The 18 (17.8 percent) *WNL* profiles were the most frequent codetype in this sample of patients. Spike *9* profiles and 9-8 high-point pairs were the two next most frequent codetypes, each of which occurred in 10 (9.9 percent) patients, followed by 9-4 and 9-6 high-point pairs in 7 (6.9 percent) patients each. Thus, a total of 34 (33.7 percent) patients were classified in the four most frequent codetypes, if WNL profiles are not included. Profile 1–4 provides an example of the variability in three of these bipolar disorder, manic patients who had 9-8 codetypes.

Hathaway and Meehl (1951) found similar variability in codetypes in their manic-depressive, manic type patients who are the DSM-I equivalent of bipolar disorder, manic patients. Fourteen (30.0 percent) patients had a 9-4 codetype, which was the most frequent codetype among Hathaway and Meehl's 47 manic depressive, manic type patients. Eight (16.0 percent) patients had a 9-8 codetype, which was the second most frequent codetype. Only one patient had a WNL codetype in contrast to the rather high frequency of this codetype in Davies et al. (1985) reported above.

Mean profiles for a specific group of patients can serve as a general source of information about MMPI performance that will be seen in specific groups of patients and can serve to document the construct validity of specific scales on the MMPI. Clinicians should be more confident in using the MMPI if they are aware that groups of schizophrenic patients score higher on Scale 8 (Sc) than do groups of bipolar disorder, manic patients, and conversely that groups of bipolar disorder, manic patients score higher on Scale 9 (Ma) than schizophrenic patients. The most useful information to be obtained from these mean profiles are the differences among the profiles from various groups. Thus, if the reader contrasts the mean profile for schizophrenic patients (Profile 1–1) to the mean profile for bipolar disorder, manic patients (Profile 1–3), a number of differences should be apparent. The schizophrenic patients tended to elevate more of the clinical scales to a T-score of 70 or higher. They also elevated Scales 1 (Hs), 2 (D), and 3 (Hy) (the neurotic triad), and

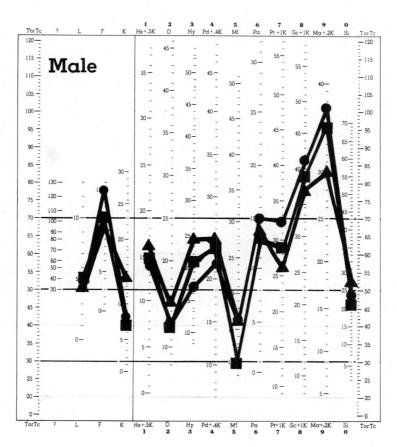

PROFILE 1–4. Examples of three 9-8 profiles in bipolar disorder, manic patients.

particularly Scale *2* and Scale *0* (*Si*) higher than the bipolar disorder, manic patients. In fact, the most reliable method for discriminating these two groups of patients was on the basis of their scores on Scales *2* and *0*, with the schizophrenic group higher on both scales. Lanyon (1968) provides mean profiles for 297 different diagnostic and behavioral groups for similar information.

The other side of the issue of the inherent variability in MMPI performance for patients within a specific diagnostic group involves the number of psychiatric diagnoses found in patients with the same codetype. For example, Marks, Seeman, and Haller (1974) reported that 68 percent of adult patients with a *6-8/8-6* codetype were diagnosed as being psychotic (schizophrenic or paranoid were the most frequent diagnoses), 18 percent as having a personality disorder (paranoid), and 14 percent as having chronic organic brain syndrome. Gilberstadt and Duker (1965) reported that the diagnosis for their *8-6* codetype was paranoid schizophrenia; since they reported prototypic codetypes, they did not provide information on the frequency with which *8-6* codetypes were diagnosed as being schizophrenic. Hathaway and Meehl (1951) found that 16 (46 percent) of their 35 patients with *6-8/8-6* codetypes had some form of schizophrenic diagnosis. Their patients also were twice as likely to be diagnosed as schizophrenic when they had an *8-6* codetype as compared with a *6-8* codetype. It appears that patients with a *6-8/8-6* codetype have a significant probability of receiving a schizophrenic diagnosis, although a number of other diagnoses also are encountered.

Marks et al. (1974) found that 70 percent of adult patients with a *8-9/9-8* codetype were diagnosed as being psychotic (schizophrenic or mixed were the most common diagnoses), 17 percent as being neurotic (depression), and 9 percent as having an acute organic brain syndrome.[1] These diagnoses are very different from those reported above for the bipolar, manic patients who had *8-9/9-8* codetypes since more of the patients of Marks et al. were described as being schizophrenic. It also is apparent from the mean profile reported by Marks et al. that Scale *0* is much more elevated (over ten *T*-points) in their *8-9/9-8* codetypes than in the bipolar, manic patients reported above, which could account for the higher

probability of schizophrenic diagnoses in the patients of Marks et al. Gilberstadt and Duker (1965) reported that the diagnosis for their prototypic *8-9* codetype was schizophrenic reaction, catatonic type, with alternative diagnoses of "schizo-manic" psychosis and paranoid schizophrenia. Hathaway and Meehl found that three (37.5 percent) of their eight patients with *9-8* codetypes were diagnosed as manic-depressive, manic type. Only five patients had *8-9* codetypes and none were diagnosed as manic-depressive, manic type. Thus, it appears that bipolar disorder, manic diagnoses may be common in *8-9/9-8* codetypes, but such diagnoses occur less than half the time at best, probably closer to one-quarter.

Regardless of whether the clinician is concerned about specific diagnoses within a particular codetype or the codetypes encountered in a specific diagnosis, it is imperative that certain basic issues be considered. Careful attention must be paid to the validity of this administration of the MMPI. The procedures for assessing the validity of a specific administration of the MMPI have been examined elsewhere in great depth (cf. Duckworth & Anderson, 1986; Graham, 1987; Greene, 1980) and they will not be reiterated here. Nevertheless, researchers need to be very sensitive to this issue. Similarly, the reliability and validity of the psychiatric diagnosis must be evaluated; this is discussed below. Unless appropriate consideration is paid to both of these issues, it is difficult to reach any definitive conclusions about the relationship between MMPI performance and psychiatric diagnosis.

Another issue that needs to be considered is the frequency with which various codetypes are found on the MMPI. Tables 1–3 and 1–4 provide the frequency with which codetypes occurred in a large sample of male and female psychiatric inpatients and outpatients (Hedlund & Won Cho, 1979). Several conclusions can be drawn quickly even from a cursory review of Tables 1–3 and 1–4. First, it is apparent that all codetypes did not occur equally often. Some codetypes are very common (Spike *4*, *8-6*, *9*, *4-9*, *8-7*, etc.) while other codetypes are very rare (*1-0*, *3-0*, *5- 0*, *9-0*, *0-1*, *0- 3*, etc.). Second, Scale *4* is the most frequent highest (males: 1,747, 28.4 percent; females: 676, 26.3 percent) and second highest clinical scale (males: 1,332, 21.6 percent; females: 523, 20.3 percent). If

---

[1]The careful reader may have noted that these percentages do not total 100 percent; they also do *not* total 100 percent in the original article.

**TABLE 1–3. FREQUENCY OF CODETYPES
IN MALE PSYCHIATRIC INPATIENTS
AND OUTPATIENTS**

Highest Clinical Scale	Second Highest Clinical Scale										Total
	1	**2**	**3**	**4**	**5**	**6**	**7**	**8**	**9**	**0**	
1	66	151	104	46	4	10	12	49	23	1	466
2	148	188	75	210	19	40	218	149	6	40	1093
3	40	18	18	17	1	2	3	3	1	0	103
4	66	263	71	561	72	141	104	214	245	10	1747
5	6	21	10	27	70	10	9	17	26	1	197
6	6	18	5	51	9	48	13	104	19	3	276
7	15	76	1	36	6	14	24	80	13	6	271
8	111	192	10	232	20	337	262	35	126	6	1331
9	15	7	10	148	23	50	20	93	255	1	622
0	2	16	0	4	1	0	5	1	1	18	48
Total	475	950	304	1332	225	652	670	745	715	86	6154

Hedlund & Won Cho, 1979.
Note: When the highest and second highest clinical scale are identical, the codetype is a Spike profile. For example, there are 66 Spike *1* profiles in these psychiatric patients.

the Spike *4* codetypes are subtracted from these two numbers, since they are counted twice, 2,518 male (1,747 + 1,332 - 561, 40.9 percent) and 1,008 female (676 + 523 - 191, 39.2 percent) patients had Scale *4* as their highest or second highest clinical scale. No wonder clinicians get the impression that Scale *4* is being interpreted in every profile. The frequent occurrence of codetypes that include Scale *4* indicates that such codetypes are an excellent starting point for identifying common subgroups that should have different treatment interventions and outcomes. Third, Scale *0* is the least frequent highest (48, 0.08 percent) and second highest (86, 1.4 percent) clinical scale in men. Scale *0* also is infrequently the highest or second highest clinical scale in women, although Scale *5* is the highest or second highest clinical

scale even less frequently. The relative infrequency of Scale *0* as one of the two highest clinical scales no doubt reflects the restricted range of *T*-scores on Scale *0* when compared with other clinical scales. Fourth, the frequency of the various codetypes tends to correspond to the amount of clinical literature available. For example, Greene (1980) states that no interpretive information is available on *1-0/0-1*, *3-0/0-3*, and *6-0/0-6* codetypes, which occurred infrequently in either male or female patients. Conversely, Spike *4* codetypes occur frequently in male and female patients, and hence a large amount of interpretive information is available. It would be instructive for clinicians to construct tables such as these in their own settings so that frequent codetypes can be identified. Such codetypes could be examined

**TABLE 1–4. FREQUENCY OF CODETYPES
IN FEMALE PSYCHIATRIC INPATIENTS
AND OUTPATIENTS**

Highest Clinical Scale	Second Highest Clinical Scale										Total
	1	**2**	**3**	**4**	**5**	**6**	**7**	**8**	**9**	**0**	
1	10	19	61	6	2	4	2	9	3	0	116
2	31	43	57	63	1	22	74	61	1	38	391
3	36	22	26	22	0	9	8	13	4	2	142
4	22	71	58	191	10	95	17	112	86	14	676
5	1	2	1	4	43	1	0	2	4	0	58
6	6	7	6	71	1	54	3	102	34	7	291
7	1	24	4	4	1	6	9	29	2	4	84
8	19	61	15	114	2	143	80	19	38	14	505
9	5	4	5	44	5	29	2	52	93	1	240
0	2	17	2	4	2	3	2	3	0	36	71
Total	133	270	235	523	67	366	197	402	265	116	2574

Hedlund & Won Cho, 1979.
Note: When the highest and second highest clinical scale are identical, the codetype is a Spike profile. For example, there are 10 Spike *1* profiles in these psychiatric patients.

more closely to determine whether specific subgroups are apparent, which should enhance treatment interventions and outcomes. Finally, there are few gender differences in the frequency of codetypes, although some codetypes are more frequent in men (e.g., *1-2*, *2-1*, *4-2*) and some are more frequent in women (e.g., *2-3*, *6-4*, *6-8*).

The final issue considered is the frequency with which low points among the clinical scales are encountered in frequently occurring codetypes. Codetype interpretation of the MMPI emphasizes the high point(s) among the clinical scales and consequently pays less attention to low-point scales. Since the low-point scale already is available in the standard profile, clinicians can make use of this information without any additional work. For example, a low point on Scale *9* in conjunction with a high point on Scale *2* should alert the clinician to the presence of significant depressive symptoms. Meehl and Hathaway (1951, pp. xxvii–xxix) provided data on the frequency with which low points occur with each high-point scale, but they did not report low points for codetypes. Table 1–5 provides the frequency of low points on the clinical scales for the 27 most frequent codetypes for men (Table 1–3) and women (Table 1–4). Scale *9* is a common low point when Scale *2* is the highest clinical scale in both male and female psychiatric patients. However, Scale *9* is much less often the low point when Scale *4* is the highest clinical scale; instead, Scale *0* is a frequent low point. As might be expected, Scale *5* is the most common low point in female psychiatric patients, and Scale *0* is the most common low point in male psychiatric patients. Interestingly, Scale *7* is rarely a low point with any codetype in either males or females. The clinician could consult Table 1–5 with every profile to determine whether the person's low-point scale is a common one and could incorporate that information into the profile interpretation.

RELIABILITY AND VALIDITY OF PSYCHIATRIC DIAGNOSIS

This review of the reliability and validity of psychiatric diagnosis will be limited to the consideration of the *Diagnostic and Statistical Manual of Mental Disorders* (DSM-III: American Psychiatric Association, 1980; DSM-III-R: American Psychiatric Association, 1987), even though a

large part of the research on the MMPI was conducted while DSM-I (American Psychiatric Association, 1952) and DSM-II (American Psychiatric Association, 1968) were in use. It is beyond the scope of this chapter to review the history of psychiatric diagnosis and the rationale for each revision of the manual. Also, this chapter will be limited to a general discussion of the use of DSM-III and DSM-III-R in adults, particularly their impact on the MMPI; issues related to a specific mental disorder or diagnostic group will be covered in chapters devoted to them. Finally, the reader is cautioned to keep in mind that frequently there is not a direct translation for specific diagnoses from the earlier versions of the diagnostic manual to DSM-III and DSM-III-R.

One of the initial issues dealt with in DSM-III was a definition of mental disorders:

> A mental disorder is conceptualized as a clinically significant behavioral or psychological syndrome or pattern that occurs in an individual and that is typically associated with either a painful symptom (distress) or impairment in one or more important areas of functioning (disability). In addition, there is an inference that there is a behavioral, psychological or biological dysfunction and that the disturbance is not only in the relationship between the individual and society. (When the disturbance is *limited* to a conflict between the individual and society, this may represent social deviance, which may or may not be commendable, but is not by itself a mental disorder) (American Psychiatric Association, 1980, p. 6).

This definition was reworded slightly in DSM-III-R:

> A mental disorder is conceptualized as a clinically significant behavioral or psychological syndrome or pattern that occurs in a person and that is associated with distress (a painful symptom) or disability (impairment in one or more important areas of functioning) or with a significantly increased risk of suffering death, pain, disability, or an important loss of freedom. In addition, this syndrome or pattern must not be merely an expectable response to a particular event, e.g., the death of a loved one. Whatever its original cause, it must currently be considered a manifestation of a behavioral, psychological, or biological dysfunction in the person (American Psychiatric Association, 1987, p. xxii).

No assumption was made in DSM-III or DSM-III-R that each mental disorder was a discrete entity with definitive boundaries from other mental disorders or "normality." A number of other changes

TABLE 1–5.   FREQUENCY OF LOW-POINT SCALES FOR 27 FREQUENT CODETYPES BY GENDER (%)

Codetype	Low-Point Scale									
	1	2	3	4	5	6	7	8	9	0
1–2										
Male	–	–	2.0	2.0	27.8	9.3	4.6	6.6	26.5	21.2
Female	–	–	0.0	5.3	52.6	10.5	5.3	0.0	26.3	0.0
1–3										
Male	–	1.0	–	0.0	18.3	2.9	2.9	1.9	17.3	55.8
Female	–	1.6	–	4.9	42.6	6.6	1.6	0.0	31.2	11.5
Spike 2										
Male	10.1	–	2.7	3.2	14.4	14.9	1.6	17.6	28.7	6.9
Female	7.0	–	2.3	11.6	30.2	9.3	0.0	4.7	32.6	2.3
2–1										
Male	–	–	0.0	4.7	22.3	12.2	0.0	9.5	39.2	12.2
Female	–	–	0.0	0.0	38.7	6.5	3.2	0.0	51.6	0.0
2–3										
Male	0.0	–	–	0.0	12.0	8.0	1.3	1.3	40.0	37.3
Female	0.0	–	–	0.0	63.2	0.0	0.0	0.0	33.3	3.5
2–4										
Male	13.3	–	1.4	–	16.7	8.6	0.0	6.2	33.8	20.0
Female	1.6	–	0.0	–	71.4	4.8	1.6	0.0	20.6	0.0
2–7										
Male	6.4	–	4.1	2.3	19.7	8.3	0.0	1.4	52.3	5.5
Female	0.0	–	0.0	1.4	64.9	1.4	0.0	0.0	32.4	0.0
2–8										
Male	7.4	–	3.4	1.3	28.2	4.0	0.7	–	43.6	11.4
Female	6.6	–	3.3	1.6	63.9	1.6	0.0	–	21.3	1.6
Spike 4										
Male	9.5	2.1	3.6	–	16.9	9.1	4.6	4.3	8.0	41.9
Female	10.9	6.3	3.7	–	34.0	6.8	6.8	3.1	6.8	21.5
4–2										
Male	16.4	–	2.7	–	20.5	4.9	2.3	5.7	16.4	31.2
Female	9.9	–	0.0	–	60.6	0.0	0.0	0.0	18.3	11.3
4–3										
Male	0.0	0.0	–	–	5.6	4.2	0.0	1.4	12.7	76.1
Female	1.7	1.7	–	–	51.7	1.7	1.7	0.0	6.9	34.5
4–6										
Male	26.2	3.6	3.6	–	16.3	–	4.3	1.4	2.1	42.6
Female	23.2	6.3	2.1	–	48.4	–	4.2	0.0	7.4	8.4
4–7										
Male	26.9	1.0	2.9	–	19.2	5.8	–	1.0	7.7	35.6
Female	17.7	0.0	0.0	–	47.1	0.0	–	0.0	23.5	11.8
4–8										
Male	18.7	0.5	6.5	–	20.6	3.3	2.8	–	7.0	40.7
Female	14.3	1.8	3.6	–	57.1	0.9	0.9	–	8.9	12.5
4–9										
Male	15.1	5.7	5.7	–	10.2	3.7	2.5	0.4	–	56.7
Female	11.6	7.0	2.3	–	36.1	0.0	3.5	0.0	–	39.5
Spike 6										
Male	31.2	4.2	12.5	0.0	10.4	–	8.3	4.2	8.3	20.8
Female	16.7	0.0	18.5	3.7	33.3	–	3.7	1.9	11.1	11.1
6–4										
Male	17.7	5.9	9.8	–	13.7	–	5.9	2.0	7.8	37.3
Female	8.5	1.4	5.6	–	59.2	–	4.2	0.0	9.9	11.3
6–8										
Male	20.2	5.8	12.5	1.0	20.2	–	2.9	–	11.5	26.0
Female	10.8	5.9	13.7	1.0	59.8	–	1.0	–	1.0	6.9
8–1										
Male	–	0.0	0.0	0.9	41.4	4.5	0.9	–	9.9	42.3
Female	–	0.0	0.0	0.0	89.5	0.0	0.0	–	5.3	5.3

(Continues.)

TABLE 1–5 *(Continued.)*

| Codetype | Low-Point Scale | | | | | | | | | |
	1	2	3	4	5	6	7	8	9	0
8–2										
Male	10.4	–	8.9	1.6	30.7	3.7	0.0	–	31.8	13.0
Female	4.9	–	3.3	0.0	70.5	1.6	0.0	–	19.7	0.0
8–4										
Male	17.2	1.7	10.8	–	23.3	1.7	0.0	–	8.2	37.1
Female	9.7	3.5	0.9	–	64.0	0.9	0.0	–	6.1	14.9
8–6										
Male	11.6	1.5	11.3	0.9	37.7	–	0.6	–	6.5	30.0
Female	4.2	4.2	9.8	5.6	68.5	–	0.7	–	2.1	4.9
8–7										
Male	11.5	3.4	9.5	1.9	32.4	2.3	–	–	13.4	25.6
Female	8.8	0.0	5.0	1.3	78.8	0.0	–	–	5.0	1.3
8–9										
Male	10.3	7.1	20.6	0.0	17.5	0.8	0.0	–	–	43.7
Female	2.6	15.8	21.1	5.3	42.1	0.0	0.0	–	–	13.2
Spike 9										
Male	13.3	13.7	13.3	1.6	9.8	6.3	2.4	2.8	–	36.9
Female	19.4	23.7	12.9	0.0	16.1	2.2	4.3	2.2	–	19.4
9–4										
Male	12.2	11.5	8.1	–	10.1	4.1	2.7	0.7	–	50.7
Female	0.0	20.5	6.8	–	25.0	2.3	0.0	0.0	–	45.5
9–8										
Male	7.5	20.4	14.0	0.0	10.8	5.4	1.1	–	–	40.9
Female	11.5	26.9	13.5	1.9	30.8	0.0	0.0	–	–	15.4
Total										
Male	11.6	3.0	6.3	0.8	20.6	5.2	1.9	2.7	15.4	32.5
Female	8.7	5.0	5.1	1.4	51.8	1.9	1.9	0.6	11.3	12.4

were incorporated into DSM-III that have been perpetuated in DSM-III-R. First, a descriptive approach was utilized that was "atheoretical with regard to etiology or pathophysiological process except for those disorders for which this is well established and therefore included in the definition of the disorder" (American Psychiatric Association, 1980, p. 7). Consequently, DSM-III attempted to describe the manifestations of the mental disorders comprehensively, and only rarely attempted to account for *how* the disturbances came about, unless the mechanism was included in the definition of the disorder. Each disorder was described at the lowest order of inference necessary to provide its characteristic features, although it was recognized for some disorders, and particularly the personality disorders, a much higher level of inference was necessary. Second, specific criteria were provided for each mental disorder as guides for clinicians in making the diagnosis. It was anticipated that these specific criteria would enhance the reliability of the system. Third, a system of multiple dimensions or axes was proposed to record additional information that may have etiologic significance or play a role in treatment

planning and prognosis. This multiaxial system was intended to ensure that certain mental disorders would not be overlooked, particularly the personality disorders, since attention is likely to focus on the more florid disorders diagnosed on Axis I, and to focus attention on environmental factors and other areas of functioning. Fourth, a hierarchical organization of the diagnostic classes was developed so that a disorder higher in the hierarchy may have features that are found in disorders lower in the hierarchy, but not vice versa. This hierarchical system made it possible to present the differential diagnosis of major symptom areas in a series of decision trees (see Appendix A [pp. 339–349] in DSM-III or Appendix B [pp. 377–387] in DSM-III-R). Fifth, a systematic description of each disorder was made in the following areas: essential features, associated features, age at onset, course, impairment, complications, predisposing factors, prevalence, sex ratio, familial pattern, and differential diagnosis. Finally, it was recognized that behavioral or psychological problems may be the focus of treatment even though they are not attributable to a mental disorder. These problems constitute the *V* codes, which also are listed on Axis I. DSM-III did *not* attempt to classify disturbed dyadic, family, or other interpersonal relationships.

There are five axes in DSM-III and DSM-III-R on which each patient is to be evaluated, although the first three axes constitute the official diagnostic assessment. These five axes and their corresponding class of information are listed below.

Axis I
    Clinical syndromes
    Conditions not attributable to a mental disorder
        that are a focus of treatment (*V* Codes)
    Additional codes
Axis II
    Personality disorders
    Specific developmental disorders
Axis III
    Physical disorders and conditions
Axis IV
    Severity of psychosocial stressors
Axis V
    Highest level of adaptive functioning past year

Probably the most controversial aspect of DSM-III was the omission of any reference to diagnoses of neurosis as part of the emphasis on a descriptive approach. Since there was limited consensus on whether the concept of neurosis is used descriptively or to imply a specific etiologic process, the term *neurotic disorder* was coined to refer to:

> a mental disorder in which the predominant disturbance is a symptom or group of symptoms that is distressing to the individual and is recognized by him or her as unacceptable and alien (ego-dystonic); reality testing is grossly intact; behavior does not actively violate gross social norms (although functioning may be markedly impaired); the disturbance is relatively enduring or recurrent without treatment and is not limited to a transitory reaction to stressors; and there is no demonstrable organic etiology or factor (American Psychiatric Association, 1980, pp. 9–10).

The interested reader should consult Bayer and Spitzer (1985) for the history of this controversy. The term *neurotic disorder* thus was used descriptively without any implication of etiologic process, and these disorders were spread across five categories within DSM-III: Affective; Anxiety; Somatoform; Dissociative; and Psychosexual Disorders. Since the MMPI groups the neurotic scales (Scales *1*, *2*, and *3*) together, it is inconvenient for the clinician to have to leaf

through five different areas of DSM-III or DSM-III-R when exploring the relationship between MMPI performance and these neurotic disorders. Also problematic is the redefinition of some terms in DSM-III, changes that eliminate the direct relationship between MMPI performance and a specific neurotic disorder. For example, Scale *1* (Hypochondriasis) no longer bears a direct relationship to the Somatoform Disorder of Hypochondriasis since that diagnosis now requires an "unrealistic interpretation of physical signs or sensations as abnormal, leading to preoccupation with the fear or belief of having a *serious* disease" (American Psychological Association, 1980, p. 251; 1987, p. 261, emphasis added). Patients with the variety of vague and nonspecific complaints about bodily functioning that are assessed by Scale *1* now are likely to be diagnosed within the Somatoform Disorders as Somatization Disorder or Psychogenic Pain Disorder. It remains to be seen whether separating these patients into multiple diagnostic categories facilitates treatment and intervention.

The emphasis on specific diagnostic criteria was intended to increase the overall reliability of the multiaxial system. The interrater reliability for the diagnostic classes in adults, expressed as a kappa statistic, was .72, .64, .66, and .80 for Axes I, II, IV, and V, respectively (American Psychiatric Association, 1980, pp. 470–472). The kappas for the specific Personality Disorders on Axis II were quite low, ranging from .26 to .75. In general, the kappas ranged from .65 to .85 for most of the major classes and specific categories within Axis I. Subsequent research has substantiated these ranges of reliabilities (cf. Mellsop, Varghese, Joshua, & Hicks, 1982; Williams, 1986).

The issue of whether monothetic or polythetic criteria are more appropriate for classifying mental disorders has not been resolved in DSM-III. Monothetic criteria detail the necessary and sufficient features for making a diagnosis, while polythetic criteria require only that a minimal number of the features be present. Consequently, polythetic criteria are likely to recognize a number of diverse features that are thought to overlap in the disorder, but they are not mutually exclusive. It is possible in a disorder defined by polythetic criteria to have two patients who share few, if any, features. Livesley suggested (1986) that, in disorders defined by polythetic criteria, not all patients are equally good representations of the

TABLE 1–6. DIAGNOSTIC CRITERIA FOR SCHIZOID PERSONALITY DISORDER

Schizoid Personality Disorder

The following are characteristic of the individual's current and long-term functioning, are not limited to episodes of illness, and cause either significant impairment in social or occupational functioning or subjective distress.

    A. Emotional coldness and aloofness, and absence of warm, tender feelings for others.

    B. Indifference to praise or criticism or to the feelings of others.

    C. Close friendships with no more than one or two persons, including family members.

    D. No eccentricities of speech, behavior, or thought characteristic of Schizotypal Personality Disorder.

    E. Not due to a psychotic disorder such as Schizophrenia or Paranoid Disorder.

    F. If under 18, does not meet the criteria for Schizoid Disorder of Childhood or Adolescence.

American Psychiatric Association. (1980). *Diagnostic and statistical manual of mental disorders* (3rd ed., p. 311). Washington: Author. With permission.

disorder and that prototypic behaviors and/or patients could be identified to facilitate agreement among clinicians in making the diagnosis of the disorder. Livesley (1986) also provided examples of the prototypic behaviors in personality disorders that could serve as a basis for identifying such characteristics within this area of DSM-III. Polythetic criteria do reflect the overlap among various diagnostic categories with few firm boundaries that are seen clinically, although such criteria also result in more heterogeneous diagnostic categories. Despite the fact that the primary emphasis in DSM-III has been placed on monothetic criteria, a number of disorders reflect more polythetic criteria. Schizoid and Borderline Disorders are good examples of this issue within the Personality Disorder section of DSM-III, the diagnostic criteria for which are provided in Tables 1–6 and 1–7, respectively. The diagnosis of Schizoid Personality Disorder (Table 1–6) requires that *all* criteria (monothetic) be met,

while the diagnosis of Borderline Personality Disorder (Table 1–7) requires that *any five of these eight* criteria (polythetic) may be met. It follows that groups of patients who are diagnosed as having a Schizoid Personality Disorder should be more homogeneous than a group of patients with the diagnosis of Borderline Personality Disorder. Hence, it would seem that patients with a diagnosis of Borderline Personality Disorders would have a lower probability of exhibiting common codetypes, demonstrate larger variances on the special and research scales, and have a lower reliability coefficient on a scale specifically designed to assess it (Morey, Waugh, & Blashfield, 1985). These anticipated relationships will be examined in more detail in Chapter 5. This same pattern of relationships would be expected to be seen between other diagnostic groups that reflect monothetic and polythetic criteria such as Hypochondriasis vs. Somatization Disorder or Psychogenic Pain Disorder (see Chapter 2),

TABLE 1–7. DIAGNOSTIC CRITERIA FOR BORDERLINE PERSONALITY DISORDER

Borderline Personality Disorder

The following are characteristic of the individual's current and long-term functioning, are not limited to episodes of illness, and cause either significant impairment in social or occupational functioning or subjective distress.

    A. At least five of the following are required:

      (1) impulsivity or unpredictability in at least two areas that are potentially self-damaging, e.g., spending, sex, gambling, substance use, shop lifting, overeating, physically self-damaging acts.

      (2) a pattern of unstable and intense interpersonal relationships, e.g., marked shifts of attitude, idealization, devaluation, manipulation (consistently using others for one's own ends).

      (3) inappropriate, intense anger or lack of control of anger, e.g., frequent displays of temper, constant anger.

      (4) identity disturbance manifested by uncertainty about several issues relating to identity, such as self-image, gender identity, long-term goals or career choice, friendship patterns, values, and loyalties, e.g., "Who am I?", "I feel like I am my sister when I am good."

      (5) affective instability: marked shifts from normal mood to depression, irritability, or anxiety, usually lasting a few hours and only rarely more than a few days, with a return to normal mood.

      (6) intolerance of being alone, e.g., frantic efforts to avoid being alone, depressed when alone.

      (7) physically self-damaging acts, e.g., suicidal gestures, self-mutilation, recurrent accidents or physical fights.

      (8) chronic feelings of emptiness or boredom.

    B. If under 18, does not meet the criteria for Identity Disturbance.

American Psychiatric Association. (1980). *Diagnostic and statistical manual of mental disorders* (3rd ed., pp. 322–323). Washington: Author. With permission.

Phobic Disorder vs. Posttraumatic Stress Disorder (see Chapter 7), and so on.

This problem of polythetic criteria has become more pronounced in DSM-III-R since all of the personality disorders require that a limited number of criteria are needed to make the diagnosis. For example, the diagnosis of Schizoid Personality Disorder in DSM-III-R now requires that the patient display any four of seven criteria.

BASE RATES

A consideration of base rates, the relative frequency with which given behaviors occur in a specific setting, is an important part of any diagnostic process. The general issues that arise as a function of base rates will not be summarized here, since there are a number of excellent papers on this topic (Arkes, 1981; Meehl, 1973; Meehl & Rosen, 1955; Wiggins, 1973, pp. 240-274). Instead, the MacAndrew Alcoholism Scale (*MAC*: MacAndrew, 1965) will be used to illustrate the issues that arise in the classification of patients as a function of changes in base rates. MacAndrew (1965) developed his scale to separate male alcoholic outpatients from male nonalcoholic psychiatric outpatients. He also suggested that a cutting score of 24 was optimal in this setting for identifying the alcoholic patients. It should be

noted that MacAndrew excluded any patient whose raw score on Scale *F* was greater than 16, and that the alcoholic patients were older (41.8 years) than the psychiatric patients (34.7 years). The potential effects of gender, age, and profile validity on classification accuracy must be kept in mind when these data are generalized to other settings, since the base rates potentially will change. For example, the classification accuracy of the *MAC* in women has been reported to improve with different cutting scores (cf. Rich & Davis, 1969; Schwartz & Graham, 1979). In order to pursue the issues raised when considering the base rates of a given behavior, it will be necessary to define some terms. Table 1–8 summarizes the data from MacAndrew's original standardization sample. MacAndrew created a base rate of alcoholism of 50 percent in his study by including equal numbers of alcoholic outpatients and nonalcoholic psychiatric outpatients; the effects of changing this base rate of alcoholism will be examined in Table 1–9. A cutting score of 24 or greater on the MAC correctly classified 165 alcoholic patients (true positives) and incorrectly classified 35 (false negatives). This cutting score also correctly classified 162 psychiatric patients (true negatives) and incorrectly classified 38 (false positives) for an overall hit rate or classification rate of 81.75 percent. The sensitivity rating, the number of alcoholic patients who were classified correctly, was

TABLE 1–8. EXAMPLE OF THE CLASSIFICATION ACCURACY OF THE MACANDREW ALCOHOLISM SCALE

| | | MacAndrew Alcoholism Scale | | |
		Alcoholic (MAC > 24)	Nonalcoholic (MAC<24)	Base rate
Patient Type	Alcoholic outpatients (N = 200)	True positives 165 (82.5%)	False negatives 35 (17.5%)	50%
	Non-alcoholic psychiatric outpatients (N = 200)	False positives 38 (19.0%)	True negatives 162 (81.0%)	50%

$$\text{Hit rate} = \frac{\text{true positives} + \text{true negatives}}{\text{total number of cases}} = \frac{165 + 162}{400} = \frac{327}{400} = 81.75\%$$

$$\text{Sensitivity} = \frac{\text{true positives}}{\text{true positives} + \text{false negatives}} = \frac{165}{165 + 35} = \frac{165}{200} = 82.50\%$$

$$\text{Specificity} = \frac{\text{true negatives}}{\text{true negatives} + \text{false positives}} = \frac{162}{162 + 38} = \frac{162}{200} = 81.00\%$$

Data are from MacAndrew (1965).

**TABLE 1–9. ANOTHER EXAMPLE OF THE CLASSIFICATION
ACCURACY OF THE MACANDREW ALCOHOLISM SCALE**

		MacAndrew Alcoholism Scale		
		Alcoholic	Nonalcoholic	Base rate
Patient Type	Alcoholic patients (N = 40)	True positives 32 (79.6%)	False negatives 8 (20.4%)	20%
	Medical patients (N = 160)	False positives 60 (37.3%)	True negatives 100 (62.7%)	80%

$$\text{Hit rate} = \frac{\text{true positives} + \text{true negatives}}{\text{total number of cases}} = \frac{32 + 100}{200} = \frac{132}{200} = 66.0\%$$

$$\text{Sensitivity} = \frac{\text{true positives}}{\text{true positives} + \text{false negatives}} = \frac{32}{32 + 8} = \frac{32}{40} = 80.0\%$$

$$\text{Specificity} = \frac{\text{true negatives}}{\text{true negatives} + \text{false positives}} = \frac{100}{100 + 60} = \frac{100}{160} = 62.5\%$$

Note: No actual cutting score was used in this hypothetical example.

82.23 percent, and the specificity rating, the number of psychiatric patients who were classified correctly, was 81.28 percent. These ratings indicate that the cutting score of 24 or greater was not biased toward over- or under-classification of either group in this study, which can also be seen by noting the relationship between the percentage of false negatives (17.5 percent) and false positives (19.0 percent). The *MAC* did an excellent job of improving on the classification rate of the alcoholics in this study since it produced an overall classification rate of 81.75 percent in comparison with the base rate of 50 percent. MacAndrew appropriately cross-validated his scale and found that classification accuracy only shrank to 81.5 percent, which is phenomenally small shrinkage. MacAndrew's success in identifying alcoholics in this study was followed by a deluge of research investigating various aspects of the *MAC*; these studies will be reviewed in Chapter 6.

Observing the changes in classification accuracy as the base rates of alcoholism and the probability of a false positive and/or a false negative outcome are changed can be very informative. As noted above, MacAndrew created a base rate of 50 percent by using equal numbers of male alcoholic outpatients and psychiatric outpatients. Since the prevalence of alcoholism varies widely depending on the type of setting, a number of different base rates could be explored. In the interests of brevity only a single specific example will be provided.

It is important for the clinician to identify the presence of alcoholism or alcohol-related problems in individuals who may be unwilling to do so; this issue is confronted in most medical settings. If it is assumed that 20 percent of the patients seen in a medical setting are alcoholic or have alcohol-related problems (Robins et al., 1984), a base rate of 20 percent can be used with the *MAC* to examine its accuracy of classification. Table 1–9 provides the same information as Table 1–8 except that the base rate has been changed to 20 percent, the false positive rate has been changed to 37.3 percent, and the false negative rate to 20.4 percent. The latter two figures are the median of the false-positive and false-negative percentages reported for the *MAC* (see Table 6–12 in Chapter 6). A drastic change in classification accuracy in this new setting is immediately apparent—the hit rate is now 66.0 percent. A reasonable probability of identifying the alcoholic patients in this hypothetical medical setting would still exist, since the sensitivity rating is 80.0 percent. However, a substantial number of medical patients would be classified as potential alcoholics with a specificity rating of 62.5 percent. These rather substantial differences in the performance of the *MAC* resulted from the appreciable change in the probability of a false-positive and a false-negative outcome, as well as the base rate of alcoholism. In this hypothetical example no cutting score has been used; optimizing the cutting score would increase the accuracy of classification. The clinician, in deciding whether to use the *MAC* in this medical setting, should consider the hit rate of 66.0 percent when the base rate for alcoholism is only 20 percent, as well as the high percentage of false positive outcomes. The relative cost of misclassifying 37.3 percent of the medical patients (false positives) in order to classify correctly 80.0 percent of the alcoholics (true positives) becomes the crux of the issue that must be decided. The clinician may be tempted to conclude that predicting that all medical patients are not alcoholic (predicting from the base rate) would produce a hit rate of 80.0 percent and consequently that using the *MAC* has produced a *decrease* in the accuracy of classification, which is not totally accurate. This apparent disparity will be explained below.

The effects of varying the probability of false-positive and false-negative outcomes in conjunction with the change in the base rate are summarized in Table 1–10. It can be seen that when the base rate is 50 percent there are significant improvements over the base rate, even when the false-positive and false-negative percentages are as high as 25 percent. However, as the base rate decreases to 25 and 15 percent or increases to 75 and 85 percent, there is limited improvement over the base rate, and in some cases there appears to be an actual decrease in the accuracy of classification. The clinician should realize that if the base rate decreases below 15 percent or increases above 85 percent, these problems only become worse. Hence, the repeated cautions against trying to predict low and high base rate behaviors are apparent (Meehl, 1954). The relatively small improvements over the base rate as the base rate decreases to 25 and 15 percent or increases to 75 and 85 percent quickly raise the issue of the cost involved in making these classifications. It is possible that such small improvements in classification accuracy are not worth the cost in clinical time and expense. Since this latter issue would require extensive discussion, it will not be pursued further here. The clinician must realize, however, that it is imperative to have some reasonable estimate of the base rate of the behavior being classified and the percentage of false-positive and false-negative outcomes that can be tolerated when using any scale and its cutting score in a new setting. Even a small change in these variables can have an appreciable effect on the accuracy of classification, as can be seen in Table 1–10. The clinician also should investigate whether another cutting score in this new setting might enhance the accuracy of classification. Procedures for deriving a cutting score will be discussed below.

Wiggins (1973, p. 252) noted that any test or predictor whose validity coefficient is greater than .00 cannot result in a decreased proportion of correct decisions when compared with prediction from the base rate since predicting from the base rate sets the false positives at 0 percent. Thus, the negative signs in Table 1–10 when the hit rates are compared with the base rates assume that the same percentage of false positive and false negatives would occur in both cases, which is an inaccurate assumption. For example, if the base rate for alcoholic patients is 15 percent and false positives and negatives are equal to 25 percent, the hit rate is 75 percent, which is a 10 percent decrease from the base rate (see last row of first section of Table 1–10). Any classification made from the base rate would set the false positives equal to 0 percent and false negatives to 15 percent, which produces the apparent differences in hit rate. Rather than focusing on hit rate, however, which is technically lower in several instances in Table 1–10, it is more relevant to consider the relative cost of false-positive to false-negative outcomes since the base rate predicts all negative outcomes so that the only errors are false negatives, while the cutting score will classify accurately some percentage of the alcoholic patients (true positives) and classify inaccurately some percentage of the psychiatric patients (false positives). In most clinical settings, false negatives tend to be more serious errors than false positives since failure to provide treatment is a more serious error than the identification of someone for treatment who may not need it. Such clinical realities must not obscure the primary issue here, which is the variations in the accuracy of classification as determined from base rates and false-positive and false-negative percentages.

The final issue to be discussed is the procedure for deriving the most appropriate cutting score for a given scale in a specific setting. The optimal cutting score can be determined fairly easily by plotting the frequency distribution for both groups on

TABLE 1–10. CHANGES IN HIT RATE AS A FUNCTION OF BASE RATES AND PERCENTAGE OF FALSE POSITIVES AND FALSE NEGATIVES

Base Rate (%)	False Positives (%)	False Negatives (%)	Hit Rate (%)	Improvement Over Base Rate (%)[a]
15	10	10	90	5
15	10	20	89	4
15	10	25	88	3
15	20	10	82	−3
15	20	20	80	−5
15	20	25	79	−6
15	25	10	77	−8
15	25	20	76	−9
15	25	25	75	−10
25	10	10	90	15
25	10	20	88	13
25	10	25	86	11
25	20	10	83	8
25	20	20	80	5
25	20	25	79	4
25	25	10	79	4
25	25	20	76	1
25	25	25	75	0
50	10	10	90	40
50	10	20	85	35
50	10	25	83	33
50	20	10	85	35
50	20	20	80	30
50	20	25	78	28
50	25	10	83	33
50	25	20	78	28
50	25	25	75	25
75	10	10	90	15
75	10	20	83	8
75	10	25	79	4
75	20	10	88	13
75	20	20	80	5
75	20	25	76	1
75	25	10	86	11
75	25	20	79	4
75	25	25	75	0
85	10	10	90	5
85	10	20	82	−3
85	10	25	72	−13
85	20	10	89	4
85	20	20	80	−5
85	20	25	76	−9
85	25	10	88	3
85	25	20	79	−6
85	25	25	75	−10

[a]See text for explanation of negative signs in this column.

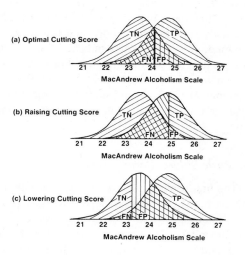

(a) Optimal Cutting Score

MacAndrew Alcoholism Scale

(b) Raising Cutting Score

MacAndrew Alcoholism Scale

(c) Lowering Cutting Score

MacAndrew Alcoholism Scale

FIGURE 1–1. Changes in cutting score and the effect on true negatives (TN), true positives (TP), false negatives (FN), and false positives (FP).

the same axes (illustrated in Figure 1–1a)—the point at which the two frequency distributions overlap is the optimal cutting score. These examples will assume that the variances of the scores in both groups are equal and sample sizes are equal. Rorer and Dawes (1982) provide information on how to select the optimal cutting score when these assumptions are not met. They also demonstrate how the optimal cutting score can be estimated even when the base rate in the local setting is not known. As can be seen in Figure 1–1a, the alcoholic patients who fall above this cutting score are true positives and the medical patients are false positives; likewise, the alcoholic patients who fall below this cutting score are false negatives and the medical patients are true negatives. By raising (Figure 1–1b) or lowering (Figure 1–1c) this cutting score the percentage of patients classified in each category will change. Thus, it is possible not only to identify the optimal cutting score, but also to investigate the relative effects of different cutting scores on false positives and false negatives. Since the hit rate may not be as important as the relationship between the number of false-positive and false-negative outcomes in most clinical settings, clinicians can consider all of these variables in selecting the most appropriate cutting score for

this scale in their particular setting. It is important to note that a statistical test of the differences between the means of the two distributions provides much less information than the data on the relative numer of false positives and false negatives and the base rate of the behavior. As few as 100 patients in each group are sufficient to provide reasonable estimates of the base rate of the behavior and the frequency of false positives and false negatives (Meehl, 1973), and a smaller number of patients will provide approximations of these variables while more data are being collected. This type of information is generally available in most clinical settings, although most clinicians do not realize its importance.

The issue of base rates and the optimal cutting score also applies directly to the use of DSM-III and DSM-III-R. Finn (1982) demonstrated that the polythetic criteria used to define many diagnoses in DSM-III (such as Borderline Personality Disorder described above) resulted in different rates of false positives and false negatives as functions of the base rate of the disorder in the setting because more or less criteria are required to be met in order to make the diagnosis. For example, if the number of criteria to be met for the diagnosis of Borderline Personality Disorder were changed to four or six, the percentage of false-positive and false-negative errors as well as the base rate of the disorder in the setting would change proportionally. As the number of criteria to be met are increased, the percentage of false positives would decrease, and conversely as the number of criteria are decreased, the false positives would increase. Because DMS-III-R does not provide information on the influence of criteria requirements on the rate of false positives and false negatives for particular diagnoses, clinicians using the manual are unable to determine the amount of influence these factors have on the base rate of a specific disorder in a setting. As noted above, DSM-III-R uses polythetic criteria for all of the personality disorder diagnoses, which makes this issue even more salient.

ORGANIZATION OF EACH CHAPTER

In order to make it easier for the reader to compare and contrast the information among the ensuing chapters, a standard format will be followed. Each chapter will be organized along this outline:

1. OVERVIEW

2. SPECIFIC POPULATION GROUP

A description of the diagnostic group will be provided with information on base rate issues, demographic and/or moderator variables that affect MMPI performance, and a "typical" patient.

3. DIFFERENTIAL DIAGNOSIS

Issues that exist within DSM-III for the diagnosis of this specific group will be raised as will questions on how this group can be differentiated reliably from other diagnostic groups.

4. PROTOTYPIC STUDY

A prototypic study will be outlined to apprise the reader of how research is conducted in this specific group, the usual procedures that are followed, and the potential problems that may arise. The presentation of a single prototypic study for each specific group eliminates the need to describe in great detail one study after another. Instead the focus can be on integrating the empirical data from these studies into a comprehensible format.

5. STANDARD VALIDITY AND CLINICAL SCALES

The empirical data from each specific group on the standard validity and clinical scales will be summarized as much as possible in tabular format. The frequency with which the various codetypes are encountered will be provided as well as other pertinent information on each specific group's performance on the various validity and clinical scales. Again, the focus will be on integrating the entire data base rather than reporting one single study after another.

In summarizing MMPI performance in the various specific groups, several methodologic issues will be raised that can potentially affect the interpretation of any differences found. These methodologic issues will be categorized into nine areas that will serve as the basis for comparing the studies being reviewed. The headings used to label each area within this section also correspond to the column headings in the tables throughout the chapters in order to facilitate the appreciation of these issues across the entire area of research on MMPI performance in various groups. Thus, a + sign in column A of Table 2–1 (see page 29 in Chapter 2) for Beals and Hickman (1972) indicates that basic information about the subjects in the study such as age, gender, and education were reported. A − sign would indicate that the study did not provide this information. For example, the − sign in column C of Table 2–1 for Beals and Hickman (1972) indicates no specific mention was made of the criteria used to define group membership.

A. Basic Subject Parameters

The first general issue is whether the authors reported basic information on the number of subjects, their age, gender, education, type of setting (VA hospital, state hospital, mental health clinic, etc.), and in- or outpatient status. In most cases, it also is important to provide information regarding the chronicity and severity of the illness, whether the patients were medicated when evaluated, and other complications of treatment such as concurrent illnesses, dual diagnoses, atypical symptoms, history of brain injury/damage, and so on. Occasionally an article is encountered that merely contrasted the MMPI performance of a small number of persons from two diagnostic groups on the traditional MMPI validity and clinical scales without specification of any characteristics at all of the sample.

B. Specific Group Membership

Researchers need to be very explicit in reporting the criteria used to specify membership within the diagnostic group whose MMPI performance is being evaluated. Thus, researchers should report the diagnostic system used (e.g., DSM-III, DSM-III-R), the training and expertise of the persons who made the diagnostic decisions, and whether information from other sources (family members, behavior rating scales, etc.) was used to confirm the diagnoses. The issue of whether the MMPI contributed to the diagnostic process also should be specified.

C. Profile Validity

Some attempt should be made to assess profile validity prior to the comparison of the specific groups. The question of whether the validity criteria that are employed may differentially include or exclude members of a specific group must be considered. For example, a very stringent criterion on the F scale would tend to limit the elevations on Scales 4 (Pd), 7 (Pt), and 8 (Sc) because of the item overlap and correlations among these scales.

D. Role of Moderator Variables

The potential confounding effects of many moderator variables, such as chronicity, ethnicity, education, socioeconomic status, education, and intelligence, which if not controlled or analyzed may preclude making any conclusions about real differences between the specific groups, must be given careful consideration. For example, if a study compares members of one group from a lower class with members of another group from a middle or upper class, it makes little sense to interpret any obtained differences as reflecting solely group membership. The consideration of the role of moderator variables becomes particularly difficult when differences on these variables are intrinsic to the diagnostic groups being compared. For example, patients with affective disorders tend to attain higher levels of education and socioeconomic status than patients with schizophrenic disorders; equating these two groups on these variables would serve to limit the representativeness of the diagnostic groups.

E. Appropriate Statistical Analysis

Because the MMPI consists of a number of moderately intercorrelated scales (cf. Butcher & Tellegen, 1978), a number of issues arise in statistical analysis. The most frequently encountered error involves the use of an univariate design to analyze multivariate data. For example, a researcher may report the results of 13 independent t-tests without apparent consideration of the problem of experiment-wise error rate. Although there currently is a tendency to favor multivariate designs, researchers should understand that the real issue involves controlling the experiment-wise error rate rather than the precise method of data analysis.

F. Adequate Sample Size

A corollary of the issue of an appropriate statistical analysis involves adequate sample size. Although there are no absolute guidelines on the exact sample size required with multiple dependent variables, it is generally agreed that from 10 to 15 subjects per variable is minimal. Thus, at least 130 subjects are needed in each group if a researcher is interested in examining for differences in performance on the standard validity and clinical scales. This minimal requirement for sample size also needs to be met after the researcher has eliminated any invalid profiles and considered the influence of any moderator variables.

G. Scores Analyzed

It is important to know whether raw scores, K-corrected T-scores, or non-K-corrected T-scores were analyzed. Raw scores will generally be the most appropriate when the researcher wants to compare the performance of two specific groups without consideration of the K-correction process. In a sample of males and females where gender differences are *not* of interest, non-K-corrected T-scores would eliminate any gender differences in the frequency of item endorsements if the assumption is tenable that this transformation process produces the same distribution of scores in each group. In any case, the question of what scores are analyzed should be carefully considered and then reported explicitly.

H. Effect Size

The meaningfulness of the obtained effect size always must be considered when the performance of two specific groups is being compared on a specific scale from the MMPI. Researchers may report that a statistically significant difference was found between the two groups on a given scale and then state that the obtained difference was 3 T-points. Little consideration is given to whether a difference of 3 T-points has any clinical significance, i.e., whether the clinical interpretation of that scale would change as a function of that small difference. If a moderate effect size is required (cf. Cohen, 1977) to ensure that any obtained difference has some probability of being manifest clinically, then a T-score difference of at least 5 points is necessary. Requiring a difference of at least 5 T-points also seems consistent with clinical interpretation of the MMPI since differences smaller than one-half of a standard deviation are unlikely to have any clinical relevance. Consequently, a minimum difference of at least 5 *T*-points between the two specific groups rather than actual statistical significance will be used as another criterion in evaluating the studies reviewed here. (It should be noted that a study could *not* be evaluated on this criterion if no differences were found between the two diagnostic groups. In such circumstances, columns H and I were left blank.)

I. Empirical Correlates

The final criterion to be used in evaluating these studies will be whether the obtained differences between the two specific groups have any empirical correlates. Although it is an important first step to demonstrate that two specific groups differ on a specific scale, which indicates a base rate difference in the frequency of item endorsement, it also is necessary to determine whether this difference in the frequency of item endorsement is manifest in the external correlates of the scale, i.e., does this difference have any empirical correlates? This last step—determining whether the obtained differences actually have any empirical correlates— is rarely ever considered in research into MMPI performance as a function of specific group membership. Since this last step is the basic issue in determining whether specific group membership affects MMPI performance, the reasons why such research is almost nonexistent are unclear, other than the difficulty and time involved. (Again, it should be noted that a study could *not* be evaluated on this criterion if no differences were found between the two groups. In such circumstances, columns H and I were left blank.)

6. SPECIAL/RESEARCH SCALES

This section will summarize the empirical data on the special/research scales that are scored frequently in each specific group. These data also will be integrated and summarized in tabular form to facilitate comparisons among the various groups.

7. SUMMARY

A concise summary of the data that have been presented will be provided with suggestions for future research. Emphasis will be placed on the issues that need to be addressed in each diagnostic group to facilitate the use of the MMPI.

8. REFERENCES

REFERENCES

American Psychiatric Association. (1952). *Diagnostic and statistical manual of mental disorders*. Washington: Author.

American Psychiatric Association. (1968). *Diagnostic and statistical manual of mental disorders*. (2nd ed.). Washington: Author.

American Psychiatric Association. (1980). *Diagnostic and statistical manual of mental disorders*. (3rd ed.). Washington: Author.

American Psychiatric Association. (1987). *Diagnostic and statistical manual of mental disorders* (rev. 3rd ed.) Washington: Author.

Arkes, H. R. (1981). Impediments to accurate clinical judgment and possible ways to minimize their impact. *Journal of Consulting and Clinical Psychology, 49,* 323–330.

Bayer, R., & Spitzer, R. L. (1985). Neurosis, psychodynamics, and DSM-III. *Archives of General Psychiatry, 42,* 187–196.

Butcher, J. N., & Tellegen, A. (1978). Common methodological problems in MMPI research. *Journal of Consulting and Clinical Psychology, 46,* 620-628.

Davies, J., Nichols, D. S., & Greene, R. L. (1985, March). *A new schizophrenia scale for the MMPI.* Paper presented at the 20th Annual Symposium on Recent Advances in the Use of the MMPI, Honolulu.

Duckworth, J. C., & Anderson, W. (1986). *MMPI interpretation manual for counselors and clinicians* (3rd ed.). Muncie, IN: Accelerated Development.

Finn, S. E. (1982). Base rates, utilities, and DSM-III: Shortcomings of fixed-rule systems of psychodiagnosis. *Journal of Abnormal Psychology, 91,* 294–302.

Gilberstadt, H., & Duker, J. (1965). *A handbook for clinical and actuarial MMPI interpretation.* Philadelphia: W. B. Saunders.

Graham, J. R. (1987). *The MMPI: A practical guide* (2nd ed.). New York: Oxford University Press.

Greene, R. L. (1980). *The MMPI: An interpretive manual.* Philadelphia: Grune & Stratton.

Hathaway, S. R., & Meehl, P. E. (1951). *An atlas for the clinical use of the MMPI.* Minneapolis: University of Minnesota Press.

Hedlund, J. H., & Won Cho, D. (1979). (MMPI data research tape for Missouri Department of Mental Health patients). Unpublished raw data.

Lanyon, R. I. (1968). *A handbook of MMPI group profiles.* Minneapolis: University of Minnesota Press.

Livesley, W. J. (1986). Trait and behavioral prototypes of personality disorder. *American Journal of Psychiatry, 143,* 728–732.

Lubin, B., Larsen, R. M., Matarazzo, J. M., & Seever, M. (1985). Psychological test usage patterns in five professional settings. *American Psychologist, 40,* 857–861.

MacAndrew, C. (1965). The differentiation of male alcoholic outpatients from nonalcoholic psychiatric outpatients by means of the MMPI. *Quarterly Journal of Studies on Alcohol, 26,* 238–246.

Marks, P.A., Seeman, W., & Haller, D. L. (1974). *The actuarial use of the MMPI with adolescents and adults.* Baltimore: Williams & Wilkins.

Meehl, P. E. (1954). *Clinical versus statistical prediction.* Minneapolis: University of Minnesota Press.

Meehl, P. E. (1973). MAXCOV-HITMAX: A taxonomic search method for loose genetic syndromes. In P. E. Meehl (Ed.), *Psychodiagnosis: Selected papers* (pp. 200–224). Minneapolis: University of Minnesota Press.

Meehl, P. E., & Rosen, A. (1955). Antecedent probability and the efficiency of psychometric signs, patterns, or cutting scores. *Psychological Bulletin, 52*, 194–216.

Mellsop, G., Varghese, F., Joshua, S., & Hicks, A. (1982). The reliability of Axis II of DSM-III. *American Journal of Psychiatry, 139*, 1360–1361.

Morey, L. C., Waugh, M. H., & Blashfield, R. K. (1985). MMPI scales for DSM-III Personality Disorders: Their derivation and correlates. *Journal of Personality Assessment, 49*, 245–251.

Rich, C. C., & Davis, H. G. (1969). Concurrent validity of MMPI alcoholism scales. *Journal of Clinical Psychology, 25*, 425–426.

Robins, L. N., Helzer, J. E., Weissman, M. M., Orvaschel, H., Gruenberg, E., Burke, J. D. Jr., & Regier, D. A. (1984). Lifetime prevalence of specific psychiatric disorders in three sites. *Archives of General Psychiatry, 41*, 949–958.

Rorer, L. G., & Dawes, R. M. (1982). A base-rate bootstrap. *Journal of Consulting and Clinical Psychology, 50*, 419–425.

Schwartz, M. F., & Graham, J. R. (1979). Construct validity of the MacAndrew alcoholism scale. *Journal of Consulting and Clinical Psychology, 47*, 1090–1095.

Wiggins, J. S. (1973). *Personality and prediction: Principles of personality assessment.* Reading, MA: Addison-Wesley.

Williams, J. B. W. (1985). The multiaxial system of DSM-III: Where did it come from and where should it go? II. Empirical studies, innovations, and recommendations. *Archives of General Psychiatry, 42*, 181–186.

Chapter 2

Chronic Pain

CHARLES K. PROKOP

OVERVIEW

Chronic pain is a serious health and economic problem in the United States. The National Institutes of Health (1979) estimated that 15 million persons in the United States suffer from low back pain, and the annual cost of medical care for these patients is $5 billion. Other figures suggest the cost may be higher. Brena, Chapman, and Decker (1981) estimated that the total cost to society of one million pain-disabled patients is $20 billion per year. The difference between the total costs to society and the medical care costs of chronic pain patients is due, in part, to the risk for psychological dysfunction and the losses of social, vocational, and financial supports often associated with the chronic pain experience. Psychological factors also may intensify the experience of pain due to documentable physiological damage, may affect response to medical/surgical intervention, and in some cases may be the primary cause of the pain.

The costs of chronic pain, in conjunction with the probability of psychological involvement in symptom presentation and treatment response of the pain patient, have led to extensive involvement of psychologists in the diagnosis and treatment planning of chronic pain patients. Hickling, Sison, and Holtz (1985) reported that 85.5 percent of the comprehensive pain clinics they surveyed employed psychologists, a higher percentage than for any other discipline including medical fields such as anesthesiology, neurosurgery, and orthopedics. Hickling et al. also found that the MMPI was the most commonly used assessment tool in the pain clinic, used by 77.7 percent of all clinics. The second most common technique, the clinical inter-

view, was cited by only 33.3 percent of the clinics responding. The MMPI clearly plays a major role in the assessment of chronic pain patients.

This chapter reviews the applications of the MMPI in chronic pain populations with an emphasis on the chronic low back pain (LBP) population. Back and hip pain patients represented almost half of the clinic population in the Hickling et al. (1985) survey, while the next most common pain site was the lower extremities, accounting for only 11.9 percent of the patients. Particular attention will be paid to the use of the MMPI in describing the psychological characteristics of chronic pain patients, attempting to determine the etiology of the pain problem itself, and predicting response to medical/surgical and psychological intervention.

THE CHRONIC PAIN POPULATION

Chronic pain patients are members of a heterogeneous population unified by a single characteristic: the presence of pain, usually of 6 months or more duration. In most cases, the pain has not responded to conventional medical/surgical treatment, or the pain is in excess of what would be normally expected based on physiological findings. Moderator variables likely to be viewed as relevant to MMPI performance include patient gender and pain chronicity or intensity.

A quick review of the published studies of the MMPI and LBP suggests that there are no predominant gender differences, although if a study concerns LBP patients of only one gender, the patients are most likely to be male. This potential

THE MMPI: USE WITH
SPECIFIC POPULATIONS

© 1988 by Grune & Stratton.

ISBN   0-8089-1913-X

bias is probably related to sample availability, as many such studies are conducted in Veterans Administration hospitals. Although there is no apparent predominance of males or females in the LBP literature, gender does appear to be a variable demanding attention. As will be seen later in this chapter, profile differences based on gender have been reported, most commonly involving a greater probability of the conversion "V" profile (elevations on Scales *1* [*Hs*] and *3* [*Hy*] with an intervening valley on Scale *2* [*D*]) in females and a corresponding increase in the likelihood of elevations on Scales *1*, *2*, and *3* in males.

The importance of pain chronicity as a moderator variable influencing MMPI performance is less clear. Although there have been reports suggesting that pain of longer duration is associated with more elevated MMPI profiles (Cox, Chapman, & Black, 1978; McGill, Lawlis, Selby, Mooney, & McCoy, 1983), other studies have failed to find such a relationship (e.g., Armentrout, Moore, Parker, Hewett, & Feltz, 1982; McCreary, 1985). It is generally found, however, that pain of greater intensity is related to more elevated MMPI profiles. For example, all of the studies just noted, except Cox et al. (1978), reported such a relationship, and they did not investigate pain intensity.

Two questions on base rate are of primary interest when the MMPI is used with chronic pain patients. First, what is the base rate of diagnosable physical pathology in the pain population? This question often is expressed as the percentage of pain patients whose pain and disability is functional (without a clear physical basis or out of proportion to the degree of physical pathology) as opposed to organic (with a clear physical basis and consistent with the degree of physical pathology). The presence or absence of physical pathology has obvious implications for the selection of appropriate treatment strategies.

The second base rate question flows naturally from the first. What percentage of chronic pain patients typically respond to treatment? An accurate answer requires the specification of both treatment and patient characteristics, and is complicated by the need to identify the treatment response measures of interest and the length of time that gains must be maintained in order for the intervention to be judged a success. The primary treatment modalities for chronic pain

patients may be loosely categorized as either medical/surgical or conservative. Conservative treatments typically involve a heterogeneous mix of behavioral and psychotherapeutic interventions, physical therapy, medication reduction, and patient education. A conservative treatment strategy incorporating all of these elements often is referred to as a comprehensive treatment program. Patients in comprehensive pain treatment programs frequently are those who have not responded to medical/surgical intervention or who have no such options available.

The functional vs. organic distinction may be difficult to draw due to the subjectivity involved in judging the appropriateness of complaints of pain and disability. The distinction is further complicated by the need to determine when sufficient physical diagnostic work has been completed and the less-than-perfect reliability of medical diagnostic procedures. Watson and Buranen (1979) reported that 25 percent of male patients diagnosed as hysterical were later found to be suffering a physical disorder related to their physical symptoms.

Estimates of the percentage of LBP patients without demonstrable organic pathology have been reported to range from 60 to 78 percent, with an average of approximately 70 percent (Loeser, 1980). A survey of the studies discussed in this chapter that reported the percentages of patients judged as functional or organic yielded a median of 52.5 percent functional diagnoses. This figure includes patients classified as "mixed" in the functional diagnostic category. A patient with a mixed diagnosis generally has pain or disability out of proportion to the degree of physical pathology or contradictory findings on medical and physical examination. Several of the studies surveyed were not specific as to the chronicity of the patients' pain problems. It is therefore difficult to arrive at a functional diagnosis base rate specific to chronic pain patients, but the evidence suggests that a figure near 60 percent is not unreasonable.

The second base rate question is probably the more crucial of the two for the practicing clinician. Loeser (1980) estimated that approximately 60 percent of pain patients respond positively to surgical procedures. The range of positive responses reported in the literature is generally from 50 to 95 percent, although more pessimistic figures have also been cited (Gottlieb et al., 1977). It also should be noted that pain complaints subside within 6 months in approximately 50 percent of pain patients where rest is the only treatment (Loeser, 1980).

Responses to comprehensive pain treatment programs, which usually include a large operant or other behavior modification component, also vary significantly. Linton (1982) reviewed operant and comprehensive treatment programs for pain other than headache and found a median improvement rate of 57 percent with a range from 14 to 86 percent. These figures were for all outcome measures reported and included follow-up periods from immediately following discharge to 8 years later.

Clinicians attempting to use the MMPI to predict treatment response or pain etiology are in some ways in a favorable position, as the base rates noted above are near 50 percent. However, the variability in the figures indicates that it would be important for the individual clinician to gather base-rate data for her or his particular setting.

One of the best descriptions of the "typical" LBP patient may be found in Gentry, Shows, and Thomas (1974), to which the interested reader may refer for a more complete description. In summary, the typical LBP patient is in the mid 30s to mid 40s, and has suffered from pain for 7–8 years. Several unsuccessful surgical procedures have been attempted, and the patient is experiencing significant impairment in the ability to work, to be sexually active, and to participate in leisure activities. The patient's marriage may be beginning to show the strain of altered sexual and financial conditions, although the presence of marital distress may be denied due to a perceived need to acknowledge the support of spouse and family. The patient is likely to have 12 years, or slightly less, of education and to have worked at a job requiring physical exertion. Depression and/or anxiety are likely to be acknowledged; the patient commonly attributes these symptoms to living with his or her pain. The patient may be somewhat resistant to psychological intervention and may thus question the reasons for completion of an instrument such as the MMPI. The patient is likely to cooperate, however, if the reality of the pain is acknowledged and the evaluation is not perceived as an attempt to prove that the pain is "all in the head."

DIFFERENTIAL DIAGNOSIS

Several DSM-III diagnostic categories are relevant to chronic pain, and the clinician may have difficulty determining the most appropriate psychiatric diagnosis for the individual patient. The most likely Axis I diagnoses to be considered include Psychological Factors Associated With Physical Condition and the Somatoform diagnoses of Psychogenic Pain Disorder, Conversion Disorder, and Somatization Disorder. Factitious Disorder and Malingering also are considerations in some cases, as are Affective Disorders and Schizophrenia. Axis II diagnoses that may be appropriate in some chronic pain patients include Histrionic Personality Disorder and Dependent Personality Disorder. As will be discussed later, the selection of the appropriate diagnosis is based on a number of factors, including the presence or absence of demonstrable organic pathology, the magnitude of pain complaints and disability, the presence or absence of somatic complaints other than pain, and the nature of any goals the symptoms allow the patient to meet. The MMPI alone is unlikely to provide sufficient information for making the diagnosis.

The following discussion will not review all the criteria necessary for DSM-III diagnoses, but instead will focus on issues likely to arise in the consideration of chronic pain patients. The assets and liabilities of the DSM-III in diagnostic work with chronic pain patients and the utility of the MMPI in DSM-III diagnosis will be discussed after the nomenclature itself is reviewed.

Psychogenic Pain Disorder is the appropriate diagnosis when pain is the only or predominant complaint and no physical findings are present, the pain is inconsistent with anatomic principles, or the pain is out of proportion to physical findings. There must be evidence that psychological factors are important in the etiology of the pain complaints. Operantly controlled pain may satisfy this criterion, since the pain is reinforced by environmental or interpersonal support or by the avoidance of unpleasant stimuli. Pain related to psychodynamic conflict also is diagnosed appropriately as Psychogenic Pain Disorder. For example, the onset of LBP may be associated with the birth of a child, since the patient may be concerned about the ability to support the new family. In cases where all of the above criteria are met but pain is only one of the presenting symptoms, Conversion Disorder is the appropriate diagnosis. However, Conversion Disorder should not be diagnosed when many symptoms are present—Somatization Disorder should be considered instead. DSM-III lists 37 symptoms, including pain, that are relevant to Somatization Disorder. Female patients must have experienced 14 of these symptoms and male patients 12 for Somatization Disorder to be diagnosed. The symptoms must have been of sufficient magnitude that life activities are disrupted, medical care was sought, or nonaspirin medication was taken.

Many chronic pain patients possess documentable organic pathology, but psychological factors appear to affect the waxing and waning of pain complaints. For these patients, a diagnosis of Psychological Factors Affecting Physical Condition is indicated. Consider the case of the new parent presented above. If this patient was diagnosed as suffering from degenerative disc disease and the pain increased whenever financial matters were discussed at home or when monthly bills arrived, Psychological Factors Affecting Physical Condition should be diagnosed. However, the choice between these two diagnoses may be quite difficult in cases where the pain and disability is judged to be in excess of the level expected from the severity of physical pathology. DSM-III demands that Psychological Factors Affecting Physical Condition not be diagnosed when Psychogenic Pain Disorder might be a possibility, but the subjectivity involved in judging the appropriate degree of pain to be associated with a specific organic symptom is likely to make a clinician uncomfortable with this diagnostic decision. This dilemma is particularly cogent in view of the pejorative connotations that may be attached to a psychogenic diagnosis and the impact this diagnosis may have on later medical care provision.

The diagnoses likely to arouse the most conflict in the clinician are Factitious Disorder and Malingering. Both of these diagnoses require that the presenting symptoms be under the voluntary control of the patient, such as cases where pain complaints and performance in physical therapy are deliberately controlled by the patient in order to simulate the appearance of a disorder. DSM-III acknowledges that these diagnoses require a subjective judgment by the clinician, particularly in the case of the chronic pain patient, since the diagnostician must maintain that the patient is not experiencing pain despite the presence of pain complaints. Such an inference concerning the sensory experience of another individual is clearly difficult to draw. Therefore, these diagnoses should be used with great caution and with a recognition of the difficulty of making such a discrimination.

Factitious Disorder and Malingering are differentiated by the nature of the goals of the symptoms. Reinforcers in Factitious Disorder are related to the individual patient's psychological needs. When complaints of pain allow the patient to maintain a dependent relationship with the medical establishment or allow for the indirect expression of hostility about perceptions of medical care mismanagement, Factitious Disorder is the appropriate diagnosis. In such cases, symptoms are voluntary in the sense that they are purposeful, but they may not be controllable in the sense that they are used consciously to reach a goal. Instead, the patient is likely to feel driven to complain of pain but be unable to express the reasons for this behavior. Factitious Disorder is therefore commonly associated with other forms of psychopathology. Malingering is diagnosed when an examination of environmental circumstances provides clear evidence for the reinforcer. For example, pain complaints to gain admission to a hospital in order to avoid being arrested for writing bad checks or to gain disability income would indicate a diagnosis of Malingering.

Chronic pain often is associated with depression (Romano & Turner, 1985). Thus, Major Depression and Dysthymic Disorder may be appropriate diagnoses in some chronic pain patients. It is noted in DSM-III that patients suffering from Affective Disorders may complain of pain, although it is seldom the dominant complaint in the clinical picture, and that prolonged physical illness may predispose an individual toward depression. Chronic pain patients with documentable organic pathology, particularly those whose medical treatment options are limited or exhausted, may experience understandable depression secondary to their physical condition. In these patients, a Somatoform diagnosis is not appropriate if DSM-III criteria for an Affective Disorder are met. Instead, the physical disorder relevant to the pain problem is coded on Axis III, and the appropriate Affective Disorder is coded on Axis I.

Pain patients satisfying criteria for Somatization Disorder present a more complicated diagnostic problem. Since mild depression is common in Somatization Disorder, this diagnosis receives precedence over a diagnosis of Dysthymic Disorder. However, if Major Depression is present and may be distinguished from the patient's customary condition, then Major Depression should be diagnosed in addition to Somatization Disorder.

Some schizophrenic patients suffering from somatic delusions may complain of pain. In these cases, the appropriate schizophrenic diagnosis takes precedence over a diagnosis of Psychogenic Pain Disorder. However, Somatization Disorder and Schizophrenia may coexist, and in such cases both diagnoses should be made.

Those Axis II diagnoses most likely to be considered in chronic pain patients are Histrionic Personality Disorder and Dependent Personality Disorder. Hysterical personality features historically have been associated with somatic symptoms through the mechanism of conversion, and DSM-III notes Conversion Disorder and Somatization Disorder as complications of Histrionic Personality Disorder. The self-dramatization and dependent behavior characteristic of histrionic individuals may affect the presentation of pain and disability complaints. In cases where organically based pain is presented in a dramatic fashion, Histrionic Personality Disorder, but not Somatoform Disorder, should be considered.

The social role of the chronic pain patient may prove reinforcing to an individual suffering from Dependent Personality Disorder. Dependent individuals may be at greater risk for the development of an operantly maintained pain problem due to the reinforcement value of the patient role. DSM-III notes that chronic physical illness may predispose children and adolescents to the development of Dependent Personality Disorder.

Finally, it is important to remember that some chronic pain patients may not be experiencing sufficient psychological distress to justify a DSM-III diagnosis. Such patients are likely to be experiencing pain related to documentable physi-

cal pathology and to be limiting the degree to which the pain interferes with normal activities. The absence of a DSM-III diagnosis should not preclude the use of psychological or behavioral techniques in treatment. Fordyce, Brockway, Bergman, and Spengler (1986) have reported that behavioral management methods may be more effective than traditional methods in preventing the development of a chronic pain problem in acute pain patients.

Several facts are clear from a review of the DSM-III diagnostic issues discussed above. First, a major issue in the selection of the appropriate diagnosis is the presence or absence of diagnosable physical pathology and the match between pain complaints and the degree of pathology. These emphases on physical pathology largely reflect the medical heritage of the DSM-III, in that the presence of physical pathology is a crucial point in the selection of a medical/surgical intervention. This tradition has led to abundant research on the personality characteristics of functional and organic pain patients and the ability of the MMPI to distinguish between these categories.

Second, the DSM-III has not only separated pain from other conversion disorders, but it has separated the somatoform and the dissociative aspects of the DSM-II category of Hysterical Neurosis. Psychogenic Pain Disorder previously would have been labeled Hysterical Neurosis, Conversion Type, and the diagnosis would have carried implications for general personality style not contained in the DSM-III diagnosis. The wisdom of the separation of Psychogenic Pain Disorder and Conversion Disorder has been questioned (Watson & Tilleskjor, 1983), as has the diagnostic utility of the "Conversion V" MMPI profile (Leavitt, 1985). Much of the research on this profile, and the development of the Scale 3 (Hy), occurred prior to the advent of DSM-III and may have limited application to DSM-III diagnosis. The role of the MMPI in DSM-III diagnosis thus may be limited, even though the MMPI may provide information useful in personality description and treatment planning. Third, DSM-III diagnosis may or may not carry specific implications for treatment. Most psychologists would consider pain that is a symbolic expression of unconscious conflict and pain that is developed and maintained through operant mechanisms will require different treatment approaches. However, both types of pain would be diagnosed as Psychogenic Pain Disorder according to DSM-III criteria. In a similar vein, a diagnosis of Major Depression implies a need for a relatively specific treatment, but if the depression is secondary to chronic pain due to physical pathology, the pain problem and the need for treatment may be missed in the diagnosis even though the physical disorder should be noted on Axis III. The ability of the MMPI to aid in treatment planning and to diagnose coexisting affective disorder in chronic pain patients also has received research attention (cf. Beutler, Ensle, Oro'-Beutler, Daldrup, & Meredith, 1986; Pheasant, Gilbert, & Herran, 1979; Romano & Turner, 1985).

THE PROTOTYPIC CHRONIC PAIN INVESTIGATION

The focus of a particular study will naturally affect the structure of the investigation, but all projects must deal with certain core issues. The most common research goals in chronic pain studies include psychological description of the chronic pain population, often in an attempt to associate psychological status with pain etiology, and the search for psychodiagnostic predictors of treatment response. A composite study including the major issues in the area is presented below, followed by a discussion of the choices that must be made in the study's design and the potential assets and liabilities of these choices.

A group of chronic pain patients, defined as patients experiencing pain for at least 6 months, receives a comprehensive medical and psychological evaluation at the time of admission to a pain treatment program. Patients may report pain with a single locus, such as the lower back or head, or with multiple loci. The etiology of the pain problem also is usually quite variable; it may be attributable to a documentable injury or disease or it may be due to unknown causes. Males and females are likely to be included in the patient sample, although all-male samples are common, particularly when the study is conducted in a VA clinic or hospital. All-female samples are rare. If the investigation is concerned with patient description or the relationship between

psychological and physiological status, data collection stops at this point. If treatment response prediction is at issue, it continues.

Treatment planning decisions are made based on the results of the evaluation, although the nature of the treatment provided and the type of data receiving primary weight in the decision process varies as a function of the setting. Treatment may be inpatient or outpatient and may include medical/surgical intervention, physical therapy, and psychological or behavioral approaches. Following treatment, MMPI predictors of successful or unsuccessful treatment are determined. Success is most commonly defined by pain relief, a return to gainful employment or normal daily activity, and/or medication reduction. Treatment response data are gathered at the termination of active intervention, and follow-up data may be gathered at a later date.

Perhaps the most crucial decision to be made in the design of such a study involves the selection of the patient population itself. The length of time that patients have experienced pain problems is a particularly important issue. It has already been noted that pain chronicity may be related to psychological status, and the treatment options available for acute and chronic pain patients are likely to differ significantly. Chronic pain is much more likely than acute pain to be potentiated by CNS factors, including psychological status, and acute pain due to tissue damage may bear little neurophysiological relationship to chronic pain (Crue, 1983). The negative effects of chronic pain are likely to be associated with iatrogenic factors, such as medication abuse and ineffective surgery, and with psychosocial factors, such as community and family changes (Chapman, 1977). Cox et al. (1978) found significant MMPI differences in patients experiencing acute pain associated with recovery from abdominal surgery and patients experiencing chronic pain of either known or unknown origin.

Whether to include patients with uniform or diverse pain loci is also an important decision. LBP patients have received the most research attention, but some studies have investigated pain with other loci. As will be noted later in this chapter, there is some variation in findings that may be attributable to pain locus, perhaps due to differing degrees of interference in life activities likely to be associated with differing types of pain. In fact, the conflicting findings of McGill et al. (1983) and Armentrout et al. (1982) regarding chronicity could be related to differences in pain loci. The former study included only LBP patients, while the latter involved multiple types of pain. It already has been noted that gender also may be an important variable, so it is desirable that data from male and female patients be analyzed separately whenever possible. At the very least, this caveat should be kept in mind in view of the gender-linked differences in interpretation of Scale 5 (*Mf*).

Studies investigating the relationship between physical findings and psychological status, commonly conceptualized as differences between functional and organic pain patients, are at particular risk for error when patients are assigned to groups based on the results of the physical examination. The liabilities of the functional vs. organic distinction will be discussed in detail below, but at a minimum the criteria on which this distinction was based should be clearly specified. If the investigators consider this distinction meaningful, the use of multiple raters will significantly strengthen the conclusions of the project. Multiple raters are particularly important if the study is descriptive in nature, since the validity of the study rests on the accuracy with which the functional vs. organic discrimination was made.

Descriptive studies not relying on a priori differentiation of the patient population, such as cluster analysis studies, must give careful thought to the decision rules underlying cluster selection. In an exploratory study, the sample should be divided into at least two subsets to ensure that the clusters selected are replicable. Studies attempting to replicate previously derived clusters are at an advantage, as the entire sample may be used in a single analysis. However, it is important that the sample be large enough to support a multivariate procedure such as cluster analysis. A 5:1 ratio between patients and variables is desirable for such procedures (Prokop & Bradley, 1981).

If treatment response is at issue, it is vitally important that the type of treatment used be specified. Reporting that a particular MMPI configuration is associated with treatment success or failure is of marginal value when it is not possible to determine whether the treatment included medical/surgical procedures, physical therapy, or psychological and behavioral interventions. It is also important to note whether psychological assessment data were used in treatment planning. In the typical clinical situation, divorcing the results of the psychological evaluation from treatment planning may be quite difficult, since a great many chronic pain patients exhibit psychological distress requiring treatment and since psychological status is likely to be an important consideration in medical treatment planning. The relationship between MMPI performance and responses to medical/surgical intervention will be discussed in more detail below, but the existence of these data clearly makes it difficult to maintain independence between psychological evaluation results and treatment planning. If the MMPI is used in treatment planning, this will alter the conclusions that may legitimately be drawn. For example, if patients identified as high risk due to MMPI findings receive surgery plus psychological intervention or psychotropic medication and patients not so identified receive surgery alone, this clearly affects the interpretation of treatment response data and the interpretation of how well the MMPI predicts treatment outcome. Therefore, it is very important that the type of treatment be clearly specified and the degree to which psychological status was considered in treatment planning be noted.

Finally, the nature of the outcome data that are collected is particularly important in the chronic pain population. The experience of pain is typically what motivates a patient for treatment, but that experience is also difficult to assess accurately because of its subjective nature. Employment and marital status, range of motion, and medication usage may be more observable, but may be relatively independent of pain level. Furthermore, activity levels assessed by means such as patient diaries may be of questionable reliability, so it is difficult to make fine discriminations in outcome measures or to determine the degree to which pain and illness perceptions are related to activity level (Fordyce et al., 1986). The outcome measures chosen to determine treatment effectiveness are likely to influence judgments as to the success or failure of an intervention program, and thus indirectly influence potential associations between the MMPI and treatment response. Whether the MMPI is viewed as a predictor of response to treatment in a particular study may very well depend on the outcome measure used.

STANDARD VALIDITY AND CLINICAL SCALES

DSM-III diagnostic categories have been used only infrequently in studies of MMPI profile characteristics of chronic pain patients. Instead, many studies have presented mean MMPI profiles for functional and organic pain patients or have investigated the ability of the MMPI to predict response to treatment. The following review will be organized into two sections, according to whether the study at issue was directed toward diagnostic or treatment concerns.

DIAGNOSTIC STUDIES

The results of investigations reporting MMPI characteristics of chronic pain patients have been remarkably consistent. Some studies have been purely descriptive, while others have searched for medical and psychological/behavioral correlates of MMPI performance. Due to the consistency of the results, relatively little space will be devoted to discussion of the studies; the reader may refer to Tables 2–1, 2–2, and 2–3 for details concerning the individual investigations. The text will summarize the main trends and critical issues in the research.

Studies presenting mean profiles of chronic pain patients have consistently reported elevations on Scales *1* (*Hs*) and *3* (*Hy*) (Beals & Hickman, 1972; Gentry et al., 1974; Maruta, Swanson, & Swenson, 1976; Naliboff, Cohen, & Yellen, 1982; Sternbach, Wolf, Murphy, & Akeson, 1973a; Sternbach, Wolf, Murphy,

TABLE 2–1. FREQUENCY OF ELEVATED MMPI CLINICAL SCALES IN PAIN PATIENTS BY GENDER AND CHRONICITY OF PAIN

MALES			Clinical scales	Methodologic issues								
Authors	*N*	Age	(≥ 70 *T*-points)	A	B	C	D	E	F	G	H	I
Beals & Hickman (1972)	110	42	*1–3–2*	+	+	–	+	–	+	+	+	
Gentry et al. (1974)	31	–	*1–3–2*	+	+	–	+			+		
Maruta et al. (1976)	12	41	*1–3–2*	+	+	–	+			+		
Naliboff et al. (1982) [M&F]	74	45	*1–3*	+	+	–	+			+		
Sternbach et al. (1973a) [M&F]	68	45	*1–3–2*	–	+	–	–			+		
Sternbach et al. (1973b)	57	40	*1–2*	+	+	–	+			+		
Swanson et al. (1976)	22	48	*1–3–2*	+	+	+	+	–	–	+	+	
Swanson et al. (1979)	82	45	*1–3*	+	+	+	+	–	+	+	+	
Timmermans & Sternbach (1974) [M&F]	119	46	*1–3–2*	–	+	–	+			+		
FEMALES:												
Authors												
Gentry et al. (1974)	25	–	*1–3*	+	+	–	+			+		
Maruta et al. (1976)	19	41	*1–3*	+	+	–	+			+		
Sternbach et al. (1973b)	60	44	*1–3*	+	+	–	+			+		
Swanson et al. (1976)	26	48	*1–3*	+	+	+	+	–	–	+	+	
Swanson et al. (1979)	113	45	*1–3*	+	+	+	+	–	+	+	+	
CHRONICITY OF PAIN:			Acute Pain	Chronic Pain								
Authors												
Beals & Hickman (1972)	–	42	*2*	*1–3*	+	+	–	+	–		+	+
Cox et al. (1978)	57	–	*WNL*	*1–3–2*	–	+	–	–	+	–	+	+
Sternbach et al. (1973b)	117	–	*WNL*	*1–3*	+	+	–	–	–	–	+	+

**TABLE 2–2.   FREQUENCY OF ELEVATED MMPI CLINICAL SCALES
IN PAIN PATIENTS BY CORRELATES**

Authors	N	Age	Correlates
Behavioral Correlates:			
Duckro et al. (1985)	34	46	Scales *2, 3, & 7* correlated with pain intensity
Fordyce et al. (1978)	100	45	Scales *2, 3, 4, & 6* correlated with walking time/week
McCreary & Colman (1984)	126	43	Narcotics + other medications > on Scales *1 & 3*
Naliboff et al. (1982)	74	45	Scales *1, 2, & 3* higher with greater functional limitation
Timmermans & Sternbach (1974)	119	46	MMPI loaded on factor separate from pain related behaviors
Psychological Correlates:			
Duckro et al. (1985)	34	46	Scale *7* correlated with State and Trait Anxiety
Kinder et al. (1986) [female]	35	41	Scales *1, 2, & 3* correlated with Trait Anxiety
Kinder et al. (1986) [male]	42	42	Scales *1, 2, & 3* correlated with Trait Anxiety
			Scales *1, 2, & 3* correlated negatively with Trait Anger
Leavitt (1982)	91	–	*1–3* codetype present in 34% of emotionally disturbed patients
Leavitt & Garron (1982)	148	–	Scales *1, 2, & 3* correlated with Rorschach F%

Note: All studies used both male and female patients except for Kinder et al. (1986).

TABLE 2–3.   COMPARISONS OF FUNCTIONAL AND ORGANIC PAIN

Authors	N	Age	Correlates
Calysn et al. (1976)	62	42	M > 0 on Scales *1, 2, 3, & 7*[*]
Cox et al. (1978)	33	–	No differences between chronic pain of known and unknown origin
Donham et al. (1984) [male]	40	44	F > 0 on Scales *F, 1, 6, 7, & 0*
Fordyce et al. (1978)	100	45	No differences between F & 0
Freeman et al. (1976) [male]	36	39	F & M > 0 on Scales *1, 3, 7, 8*; F > 0 on Scale *2*; M > 0 on Scale *F*[*]
Hanvik (1951)	60	–	F > 0 on Scales *1, 2, 3, 4, 7, & 8*
Kuperman et al. (1979)	104	41	F > 0 on Scale *F*; F < 0 on Scale *2*[**]
Leavitt (1985)	195	38	F > 0 on Scales *F, 1, 3, 4, 6, & 8*[**]
Louks et al. (1978)	64	42	*WNL* codetypes more frequent in 0 than F or M[*]
McCreary et al. (1977)	79	45	F > 0 on Scales *1, 3, 8, 9, & 0*; F < 0 on Scale *K*[**]
Rosen et al. (1980)	123	38	Scales *1* and *3* predicted F vs. 0 < base rate
Sternbach et al. (1973b)	117	42	F < 0 on Scale *9*

Note: F = Functional pain; M = Mixed pain; O = Organic pain. Patient samples were of mixed gender except where noted otherwise.
[*]Patients overlapped across the studies.
[**]The authors questioned the clinical utility of the statistically significant differences.

& Akeson, 1973b; Swanson, Maruta, & Swenson, 1979; Swanson, Swenson, Maruta, & McPhee, 1976; Timmermans & Sternbach, 1974). As seen in Tables 2–1 and 2–2, there has been a tendency for Scale 2 (D) to be elevated in male patients, while the pure 1-3 codetype is more common in female patients. Such studies are clearly useful for initial descriptive purposes, but more useful information may be gained from studying the correlates of specific scale elevations and codetypes.

The association between pain chronicity and the MMPI has been noted previously. Sternbach et al. (1973b) found that chronic LBP patients scored higher than acute patients on Scales 1, 2, and 3, and lower than acute patients on Scale 9 (Ma). Cox et al. (1978) found that chronic pain patients scored higher than patients experiencing acute pain associated with abdominal surgery on Scales 1, 2, and 3. Beals and Hickman (1972) conducted an unusual 2-year follow-up study of patients experiencing an acute back injury followed by chronic LBP. They reported that an elevation on Scale 2 only was characteristic of the acute phase, but elevations on Scales 1 and 3 were characteristic of the same patients' MMPI profiles after 2 years. Subclinical increases on Scales 7 (Pt) and 8 (Sc) also were noted. The relationship of depression to the chronicity of pain thus is somewhat unclear.

Other studies have investigated the association of other behavioral and pain-related characteristics with MMPI scale elevations and codetypes. Walking time per week has been associated with elevations on Scale 2 and the obvious items of Scales 2, 3, and 4 (Pd), and 6 (Pa) (Fordyce, Brena, Holcomb, De Lateur, & Loeser, 1978). Self-reported functional limitation has been reported to be correlated with elevations on Scales 1, 2, and 3 (Naliboff et al., 1982). Pain patients using narcotics in combination with other medications have been found to score higher on Scales 1 and 3 than those using single narcotics, aspirin-related drugs, or no medication (McCreary & Colman, 1984). The same authors reported that single-narcotic users scored higher than only aspirin users on Scale 4 (Pd).

The evidence concerning the relationship between pain intensity and tolerance and the MMPI is contradictory. Timmermans and Sternbach (1974) found that all scales of the MMPI loaded on factors separate from those involving pain intensity and endurance, but Duckro, Margolis, and Tait (1985) reported significant correlations between Likert-scale pain ratings and Scales 2, 3, and 7. Differences in the statistical analysis techniques of the two studies may account for this discrepancy. Scale 7 has been found to be related to the McGill Pain Questionnaire (Melzack, 1975) sensory dimension of pain, while Scale 2 has been found to be related to the affective dimension of pain (Duckro et al., 1985). Additional relationships between the MMPI and pain characteristics are discussed in the section on cluster analytic studies.

Psychological status as assessed by other objective personality techniques also has been studied in relationship to MMPI performance of chronic pain patients. As might be expected, depression and anxiety have received particular attention. T-scores >70 on Scale 2 have been found to identify 75 percent of pain patients experiencing major depression as diagnosed by DSM-III criteria (Turner & Romano, 1984), although the same authors reported that the Zung and Beck Depression Inventories (Beck, 1967; Zung, 1965) were more accurate than Scale 2. In a review of the evidence concerning the link between pain and depression, Romano and Turner (1985) argue that DSM-III or Research Diagnostic Criteria (Spitzer, Endicott, & Robins, 1978) provide better measures of depression than self-report measures.

State and trait anxiety as measured by the State-Trait Anxiety Inventory (Spielberger, Gorsuch, Lushene, Vagg, & Jacobs, 1983) also have been reported to be related to MMPI performance in chronic pain patients. Duckro et al. (1985) reported significant correlations between state and trait anxiety and Scale 7, but not Scale 3. However, Kinder, Curtiss, and Kalichman (1986) reported trait, but not state, anxiety to predict elevations on Scales 1, 2, and 3. Kinder et al. also suggested that a willingness to acknowledge anger may be associated with less elevated scores on the neurotic triad of the MMPI in male LBP patients.

The ability of the conversion "V" codetype to identify patients with psychological distress has been questioned. Leavitt (1985) reported that 64.5 percent of LBP patients with a conversion "V" codetype were judged to be psychologically disturbed by independent criteria, but 65.9 percent of the emotionally disturbed patients did not have a conversion "V" profile. The relevance of these findings to clinical practice is somewhat questionable, as few clinicians would view a conversion "V" as the only sign of disturbance in the MMPI profiles of chronic pain patients. However, it does illustrate the dangers of overreliance on this codetype. Leavitt and Garron (1982) questioned the hysterical interpretation of the conversion "V" in pain patients, reporting that increased F percent on the Rorschach, interpreted as indicating the presence of "tension and constraint, rather than the over-reactivity of hysteria" (p. 23), was associated with increased scores on Scales *1*, *2*, and *3*. The distinction here appears to be that the conversion "V" may be associated with conversion dynamics, which might be diagnosed as Psychogenic Pain or Conversion Disorder according to DSM-III, but not with a disorder such as Histrionic Personality Disorder. Thus, care should be taken in the way the term "hysteria" is used, and its Axis I somatic implications should be dissociated from its Axis II personality disorder implications.

The first study on the ability of the MMPI to differentiate between organic and functional pain patients was that of Hanvik (1951). Hanvik's investigation provided a prototype for many subsequent studies. The MMPI profiles of 30 male inpatient LBP patients with proven physical pathology were compared with the profiles of 30 matched male inpatient LBP patients without "clear-cut organic findings" and "essentially negative" physical and neurologic examinations. The mean profile of the functional patients differed significantly from that of the organic patients on Scales *1 (Hs)*, *2 (D)*, *3 (Hy)*, *4 (Pd)*, *7 (Pt)*, and *8 (Sc)*. The most commonly cited portion of these results concerns the presence of the conversion "V" profile in the functional but not the organic patients. The only clinical elevation in the functional mean profile was on Scale *1* ($T = 73$), although Scale *3* was marginally elevated ($T = 69$). In a second phase of the study, clinicians with MMPI experience were able to sort the profiles into functional and organic groups accurately, although there was some difference in accuracy among the judges. The judges accurately classified an average of 69 percent of the profiles.

Other studies comparing the MMPI codetypes of functional and organic pain patients are listed in Table 2–3. It is apparent that the conversion "V" codetype is characteristically found in functional pain patients. However, it is less reliably found that functional pain patients produce mean profiles significantly different from organic pain patients. Instead, organic pain patients also may present conversion "V" profiles. The degree of overlap between functional and organic pain patients raises questions about the validity and utility of the distinction and about the use of the conversion "V" codetype in making this differentiation (Leavitt, 1985).

There is some question as to the reliability with which the medical diagnosis of functional or organic pain may be made. Fordyce et al. (1978) reported that although the interjudge reliability with which this distinction could be made was significantly different from zero, there still was only "moderately better than chance agreement among the judges" (p. 298). Physicians made the judgments in the Fordyce et al. (1978) study by reviewing the diagnoses of other physicians rather than through patient contact. However, the reliability of the diagnosis may be questionable even with direct patient contact. For example, Donham, Mikhail, and Meyers (1984) compared physician and nurse ratings of the functional and organic components of a patient's pain complaints. This study was notable in that there was a considerable amount of training prior to the rating process so as to improve the reliability of the diagnoses. After training, there was disagreement between the physician and nurse raters on 32.5 percent of the LBP patients. In a retrospective study of normal clinical practice, Watson and Buranen (1979) reported a false-positive rate of 25 percent for hysteric diagnoses in a group of medical patients. That is, 25 percent of the patients diagnosed as experiencing conversion symptoms were later found to have medical disorders underlying their physical complaints. The MMPI profiles of the false-positive and true-positive hysterics were not significantly different, and both groups were characterized by conversion "V" codetypes. Studies reporting on how well the MMPI may be used to distinguish functional from organic pain patients are thus at risk for describing a technique for the imperfect replication of an unreliable criterion.

There is also a risk that the assignment of patients to functional, organic, or mixed diagnostic categories may be contaminated by judgments of the psychological status of a patient, and thus may not be based on data that are independent of the MMPI even if the classification is made without that knowledge. A review of the studies on organic and functional differences on the MMPI suggests that the less the classification was based on subjective judgments, such as inappropriate degrees of pain complaints and disability, and the more the classification was based on a review of the medical records or solely on physical diagnostic findings, the less likely it was that clinically useful MMPI differences were found. Studies by Calsyn, Freeman, and Louks (Calsyn, Louks, & Freeman, 1976; Freeman, Calsyn, & Louks, 1976; Louks, Freeman, & Calsyn, 1978) reported MMPI differences, but the assignment of patients to organic, mixed, and functional categories involved a judgment of whether the pathology was sufficient to account for pain complaints. It also should be noted that the patient pools of these three studies were not independent. McCreary, Turner, and Dawson (1977) and Leavitt (1985) reported MMPI differences between functional and organic patients, but the ratings were based on examining physicians' judgments of the degree of functional components in the patients' pain, and thus were likely to have been at least partially determined by the physicians' impressions of psychological status. In addition, the authors of both studies noted that the degree of differentiation was of questionable clinical utility. When the functional vs. organic assignment was based on physical findings alone or a review of the records (Cox et al., 1978; Fordyce et al., 1978; Sternbach et al., 1973b), there were no MMPI differences. Thus, there is the risk that the data on the use of the MMPI in differentiating functional and organic pain not only represent the prediction of an unreliable criterion, but also may be documenting little more than the ability of the MMPI to agree with physicians' judgments of psychological disturbance.

Although there are important clinical decisions to be made based on the etiology of pain complaints, the functional vs. organic question may be more profitably recast as a question on whether there is sufficient physical pathology to justify medical/surgical intervention. This is a question best answered by physical diagnostic techniques. In the absence of physical pathology, conservative and/or psychological treatments will be most appropriate. Psychological assessment may be useful in designing the treatment strategy in these cases. If pathology that may respond to medical/surgical intervention is present, psychological assessment may provide information useful in identifying patients likely to be at risk for poor recovery due to psychological involvement and thus in need of both medical and psychological treatment. Thus, the most important question for researchers and clinicians becomes the use of the MMPI for prediction of treatment response, not differentiation of functional and organic pain patients.

This line of argument does not deny the existence of functional pain or the usefulness of MMPI profiles of functional pain patients for gaining a theoretical understanding of psychogenic pain. Instead, it implies that the most useful approach to understanding the psychological aspects of pain is to study pain patients with and without sufficient physical pathology to justify medical/surgical intervention independently, rather than as contrasting groups. This type of research should be done with the understanding that some patients without physical findings may later be found to be suffering from pain with an undiagnosed physical etiology. It also should be remembered that pain with a clear physical pathology may nonetheless be affected by psychological factors or may serve a psychodynamic function. The results of such investigations may lead to a better theoretical understanding of the varieties of psychogenic pain, the likely psychological complications of pain not treatable by or responsive to traditional physiological methods, and the development of treatment strategies specific to varying pain complaints.

TREATMENT PREDICTION STUDIES

The MMPI has been used in a variety of studies seeking to determine predictors of response to medical and psychological interventions. These studies are summarized in Table 2–4. In one of the first of these projects, Wiltse and Rocchio (1975) reported that Scales *1* and *3* were

TABLE 2–4.   TREATMENT RESPONSE PREDICTORS

Authors	N	Age	Treatment	Outcome
Kuperman et al. (1979)	104	41	–	Scale *1* > in 0 with TMT–; Scale *K* < in F with TMT+[*]
Long (1981)	44	43	S	Scale *1* > with TMT–; *1–3* and *4* codetypes more frequent with TMT–; WNL codetypes more frequent with TMT+
McCreary et al. (1979)	76	–	C	Scale *1* > with TMT– for pain intensity and activity; Scale *2* > with TMT– for pain intensity
McCreary et al. (1980)	102	42	C	Somatic concern factor > for TMT–
Meilman et al. (1986)	71	43	C	MMPI elevations decreased with treatment
Meilman et al. (1986)	22	–	C	No MMPI scales predicted outcome
Pheasant et al. (1979)	103	40	S	Scales *1* & *3* > with TMT–[*]
Sternbach & Timmermans (1975)	113	–	S&C	Scales *3* & *9* > after C rather than C+S
Strassberg et al. (1981)	67	48	A	Scales *3* & *6* > with TMT–; Scale *5* > with TMT+
Strassberg et al. (1981)	48	48	P	Scale *K* > with TMT–; Scale *5* > with TMT+
Turner et al. (1986)	106	41	S	Scale *1* predicted outcome with 83% hit rate
Wilfling et al. (1973) [male]	26	54	S	Scales *1, 2,* & *3* > with TMT–
Wiltse & Rocchio (1975)	130	43	S	Scales *1* & *3* > with TMT–

Note: Treatment types: A = anesthesiologic; C = conservative; P = psychiatric; S = surgical; Treatment outcome: TMT+ = good or excellent; TMT– = fair or poor. F = functional pain; O = organic pain.
[*]The authors suggested caution in applying these results.

accurate predictors of LBP patients' responses to Chymopapain injection at 1 year posttreatment. Recovery ratings were based on surgeon's estimates, no patients had undergone prior surgery, and all patients had received conservative treatment prior to Chymopapain injection. When both Scales *1* and *3* were elevated above a *T*-score of 85, there was only a 10 percent chance of good to excellent functional recovery. The likelihood of a positive response increased as scores on these two scales decreased, to the point that if both scales were below a *T*-score of 54, there was a 90 percent chance of good to excellent recovery.

Similar results have been reported by other investigators, although the strength of the association between the MMPI and treatment response has not always been as strong as in the Wiltse and Rocchio (1975) study. Pheasant et al. (1979) reported a moderate relationship between elevations on Scales *1* and *3* and surgical outcome, but noted that the degree of overlap between the good, fair, and poor outcome groups suggested that the MMPI should not be relied on heavily in treatment choice decisions. However, they acknowledged that the MMPI may be useful in identifying patients requiring psychological treatment pre- or postoperatively. Long (1981) reported that patients who were surgical failures scored higher on only Scale *1*, although when profiles were sorted into configurational groupings, WNL codetypes were strongly related to success, and conversion "V" codetypes and Scale *4* elevations were strongly related to failure. As in the study by Pheasant et al. (1979), there was a large

degree of similarity between the mean profiles of the success and failure groups, leading Long to suggest that configurational analysis may provide better predictions than mean profiles. Both Long (1981) and Pheasant et al. (1979) included patients with a history of prior back surgery in their samples.

Other investigators have examined treatment response to nonsurgical interventions. Kuperman, Golden, and Blume (1979) reported that Scale *1* elevation was associated with poor pain relief in response to unspecified medical treatment in mixed pain patients with a confirmed physical etiology for their pain. However, elevations on Scale *K* correlated with negative outcomes in patients without confirmed etiology. Scale *1* has been reported to be directly related to high posttreatment pain intensity and a failure to return to normal activity levels, while Scale *2* has been found to be directly related only to posttreatment pain intensity (McCreary, Turner, & Dawson, 1979). These same investigators noted that "high-risk" profiles, including neurotic triad elevations and *1-8*, *3-8*, and *1-3-8* codetypes, were associated with poor outcomes, but these codetypes also were present in 61 percent of the patients with good outcomes. In a later study, McCreary, Turner, and Dawson (1980) found that 80 percent of chronic LBP patients scoring below average on a somatic concern factor that included Scales *1, 2, 3,* and *7* reported good outcomes as measured by subjective pain intensity at 1 year follow-up, while 60 percent of those scoring above average on this factor reported poor outcomes.

Noncompliance, as measured by a failure to return the follow-up form, was associated with elevation on an alienation and distrust factor.

A more comprehensive analysis of outcome was conducted by Strassberg, Reimherr, Ward, Russell, and Cole (1981). Outcome was assessed on both medical and subjective dimensions, and treatment was either medical/surgical or psychological depending on the recommendations of the referring physician. The MMPI did not significantly predict medical responses to medical/surgical treatment, but higher scores on Scales 3 and 6 and lower scores on Scale 5 were associated with poor subjective responses to medical treatment. Positive subjective response to psychological treatment was associated with higher Scale 5 scores, and positive objective response to psychological treatment was predicted by lower scores on Scales K and 1 and higher scores on Scale 5. Gender, pain chronicity, and the duration of treatment all were controlled for in this study.

Finally, changes in the MMPI with treatment have been reported. Sternbach and Timmermans (1975) studied chronic pain patients with pain attributable to somatic lesions. The authors statistically controlled for pretreatment MMPI elevations, and reported that patients who received surgery and rehabilitation showed clinically significant reductions on Scale 3 in comparison with those who underwent only rehabilitation. However, follow-up was an average of only 6 weeks posttreatment, and psychological status was involved in treatment planning decisions. Pretreatment scores were not statistically analyzed, but examination of the profiles suggests apparent differences on Scales 1, 3, and 8 in particular, with nonsurgery patients scoring higher. Meilman, Guck, Skutley, Robbins, and Jensen (1986) reported significant reductions on seven MMPI scales at the time of discharge from a 4-week inpatient comprehensive treatment program. No pretreatment MMPI predictors of success or failure were determined, where success was defined by decreases in T-scores on the clinical scales. However, only 11 patients were in the success and failure groups, and an investigation of the mean scores reported suggests that the lack of predictive ability may have been partially related to low statistical power.

In summary, research to date suggests that the MMPI is related to treatment outcome in the chronic pain population, although the nature of the relationship between the MMPI and outcome appears to vary with the patient and treatment charac-

teristics and the outcome measures at issue. Elevations on Scales 1 and 3 are reported most frequently to be predictors of poor outcome, although Scale 1 may be a more important predictor for patients with confirmed physical pathology or those receiving medical/surgical intervention. The use of configurational analysis rather than single scales appears advisable in treatment prediction. The degree of overlap between the MMPI scores of good and poor outcome groups suggests that the most appropriate use of the MMPI is to identify patients needing psychological intervention. Psychological treatment may then proceed either in tandem with or instead of medical/surgical treatment, depending on the physical status of the patient.

CLUSTER ANALYSIS STUDIES

Investigations reporting mean profiles (see Chapter 1) suffer from a potentially serious limitation in that they may foster an illusion of homogeneity. That is, only a relatively small number of patients within a sample may actually possess the characteristics of the reported mean profile. A potential solution to this difficulty is cluster analysis, in which relatively homogeneous subgroups of profiles are developed. A second benefit of such a procedure is that potentially invalid profiles become less of an analytic and interpretive problem, since such profiles are likely to be segregated into one subgroup.

Sternbach (1974) suggested the existence of subgroups of chronic pain patients and presented a tentative typology based on clinical impressions. He argued that MMPI profiles characteristic of hypochondriasis, reactive depression, somatization, and manipulative reaction could be identified, and he presented typical profiles and corresponding patient descriptors. He also predicted that hypochondriacal and manipulative patients might be poor treatment candidates, while somatization and reactive depression profiles might predict good treatment response.

The initial cluster analytic study of LBP MMPI profiles was conducted by Bradley, Prokop, Margolis, and Gentry (1978). The reliability of the subgroups was determined by searching for subgroup patterns that were replicated over cohorts composed of 3 consecutive years of LBP patients. Four replicable subgroups were found in the female sample, and three such subgroups were found in the male sample. Profiles representing the averages of the replicated subgroups are presented in Profiles 2–1

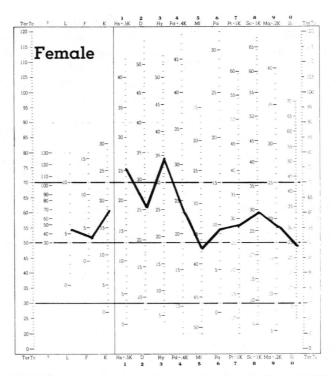

PROFILE 2–1. Cluster analysis derived profile. From Bradley et al., 1978.

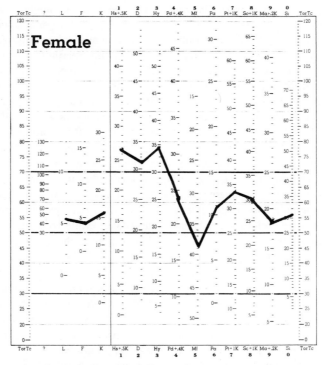

PROFILE 2–2. Cluster analysis derived profile. From Bradley et al., 1978.

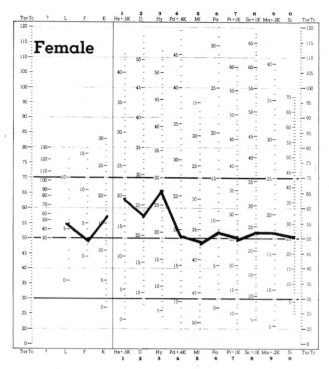

PROFILE 2–3. Cluster analysis derived profile. From Bradley et al., 1978.

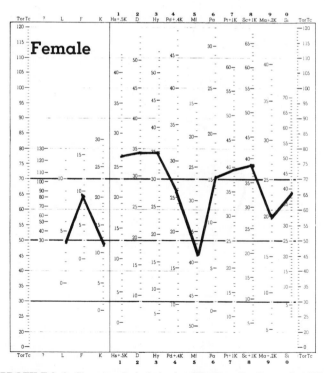

PROFILE 2–4. Cluster analysis derived profile. From Bradley et al., 1978.

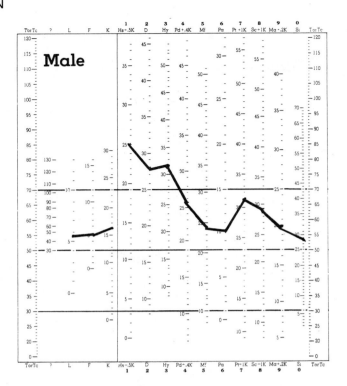

PROFILE 2–5. Cluster analysis derived profile. From Bradley et al., 1978.

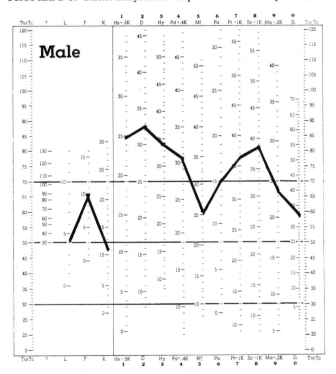

PROFILE 2–6. Cluster analysis derived profile. From Bradley et al., 1978.

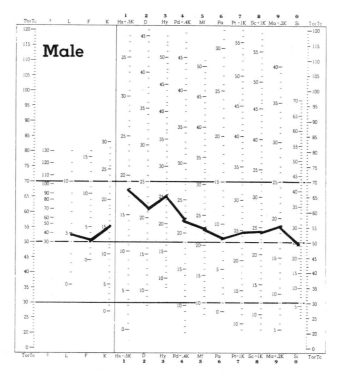

PROFILE 2–7. Cluster analysis derived profile. From Bradley et al., 1978.

through 2–7. Perhaps the most noteworthy finding of the Bradley et al. (1978) study was the relative infrequency of the classic conversion "V" codetype, which was found in only the female LBP sample and included only 24 percent of the sample. Other codetypes were found in both male and female samples, including a *WNL* codetype, a generally elevated codetype, and a codetype with elevations on Scales *1*, *3*, and *2*. The presence of substantially similar subgroups within the chronic pain population has since been replicated in several investigations (Armentrout et al., 1982; Bernstein & Garbin, 1983; Bradley & Van der Heide, 1984; Hart, 1984; McCreary, 1985; McGill et al., 1983; Prokop, Bradley, Margolis, & Gentry, 1980). These studies are summarized in Table 2–5.

Of course, the primary questions of interest involve the patient characteristics of these subgroups and their implications for treatment planning. Pain intensity and activity limitation have been reported to differ between subgroups (Armentrout et al., 1982; Bradley & Van der Heide, 1984; McCreary, 1985; McGill et al., 1983). In general, more elevated codetypes have been associated with greater levels of pain and functional limitation. Bradley and Van der Heide (1984) also suggested that elevations on the neurotic triad are associated with more disturbances in affect and activities of daily living, probably as a result of pain, while elevations on Scales *4* and *8*, in addition to the neurotic triad, are related to greater psychological disturbance and fewer pain-related sequelae, even though subjective pain intensity may be greater in the latter codetype. Findings for chronicity of pain have been less consistent; Armentrout et al. (1982) and McCreary (1985) reported no chronicity differences between subgroups, but McGill et al. (1983) reported that patients with *1-3* codetypes reported experiencing pain for a longer time than patients with *WNL* codetypes.

Mixed results also have been reported for treatment response differences between subgroups. All patients in the McGill et al. (1983) study were exposed to a 2-week inpatient conservative treatment program including biofeedback, behavior modification, psychotherapy, and physi-

TABLE 2–5. FREQUENCY OF CLUSTER TYPES IN PAIN PATIENTS BY GENDER

Authors	N	Age	1–3	1–2–3	Spike 2	WNL	Uncl
MALES:							
Adams et al.* (1986) [M&F]	72	50	34.0		14.0	30.0	22.0
Armentrout et al. (1982)	240	48		57.9		25.4	15.8
Bradley et al. (1978)	233	–		43.8		46.4	9.9
Bradley & Van der Heide (1984)	96	–				†	†
Hart (1984)	70	42	21.4	32.9		21.4	24.3
McCreary (1985)	401	–		†		†	†
McGill et al. (1983) [M&F]	92	–	43.5			27.2	29.3
Prokop et al. (1980)	123	–		37.0	19.8	37.0	6.2
Snyder & Power‡ (1981) [M&F]	141	40				100.0	
FEMALES:							
Bernstein & Garbin (1983)	77	–	13.0	32.4	32.4	15.6	6.5
Bradley et al. (1978)	315	–	34.4	23.5		39.4	12.7
Bradley & Van der Heide (1984)	218	–		†		†	†
McCreary (1985)	401	–	†	†		†	†
Prokop et al. (1980)	221	–	32.1	28.2		39.7	

Note: A dagger signifies that the cluster type was found but the percentage of patients within the cluster was not reported.
*Adams et al. (1986) based their clusters on clinical, not statistical sorting.
‡Snyder & Power (1981) analysed only *WNL* codetypes and found five clusters with history and interpretive differences.

cal and occupational therapy; response to treatment was assessed at the conclusion of the program. The only differences noted in treatment response involved pain intensity, with codetypes with multiple elevations associated with more pain than *WNL* or *1-3* codetypes. Differences in medication usage, hours out of bed, range of motion, self-rated goal attainment, and therapist-rated physical improvement were not found. Patients in the McCreary (1985) study were exposed to a treatment program emphasizing physical therapy and medication. Treatment response was measured at a 6–12-month follow-up. Marked differences in posttreatment pain intensity were reported. Subgroup membership predicted above or below average treatment response with 61 to 99 percent accuracy; *WNL* codetypes were associated with better response, and codetypes with multiple elevations or elevations on Scales *1* and *3* only were associated with poor treatment response. Interestingly, elevations on Scales *1*, *2*, and *3* were associated with good treatment response in females and poor response in males. Subgroup membership predicted treatment response more accurately for males than females, and more males reported greater psychological disturbance and poor treatment response.

Several factors are important to note when considering the implications of these studies for treatment response prediction. First, the results may be more similar than may appear at first glance; both studies reported differences associated with pain intensity. Second, although the *1-3* codetype was associated with poor treatment response in the McCreary (1985) study and good response in the McGill et al. (1983) study, McGill et al. did not analyze male and female treatment response data separately. However, they did report subgroup patterns for the two sexes combined and individually. While the *1-3* codetype was present in the combined male and female sample, it was found in only the male sample when the sexes were analyzed separately. The characteristics of the *1-3* codetypes in the two studies thus may have been markedly different. Third, treatment in the McGill et al. study was more multifaceted and focused much more on psychological issues than did treatment in the McCreary study. As McGill et al. noted, the multidimensional nature of the treatment may have masked treatment response differences. It would have been illuminating if the McCreary study would have included outcome measures other than pain relief. Finally, treatment response data were gathered immediately at the close of treatment in the McGill et al. study. As the authors noted, differences in outcome measures other than pain intensity may have appeared with longer follow-up.

Snyder and Power (1981) cluster-analyzed the MMPIs of chronic pain patients who had shown a lack of response to medical treatment, had physical findings insufficient to account for their pain and disability, and had also produced *WNL* codetypes. A subgroup characterized by a *WNL* codetype with Scales *1* and *3* as the most elevated scales, both of which were near a *T*-score of 50 (labeled a Type V codetype), was the least likely to possess characteristics suggesting a psychological component to their pain behavior. These characteristics included pain of relatively brief duration (an average of 21 months), pain with a specific locus in the body, relatively little change in work status, less previous surgery or psychiatric treatment, fewer family role models for pain behavior, and outpatient rather than inpatient treatment recommendations. No statistical analysis of the demographic and pain-related differences in the five *WNL* codetypes was provided, so the reliability of these findings is difficult to assess. It is noteworthy, however, that none of the Type V patients had received previous psychiatric treatment, while an average of 15 percent of the other four *WNL* codetypes had.

Relatively similar subgroups also have been derived from clinicians' sorting of the MMPIs of patients with chronic pain of obscure origin (Adams, Heilbronn, & Blumer, 1986). These authors reported that clinicians sorted the MMPIs into four groups: *WNL* with mild depression, somatization, substantial depression, and multiple neurotic symptoms. It was suggested that depression provided the best means of understanding the dimension underlying the subgroups, with the depression sometimes latent, as in the conversion "V" codetype, and sometimes expressed more directly.

In summary, cluster analytic studies of chronic pain patients have reliably determined the existence of replicable MMPI codetypes. Thus, it is crucial to avoid the assumption that chronic pain is consistently associated with a conversion "V" codetype or even with an elevated MMPI. These various codetypes appear to be associated with differences in the pain experience and behavior of the chronic pain patient, although additional research is needed to clarify these differences. The importance of these frequently encountered codetypes for treatment response is less certain. However, this issue has received attention only recently, and

it would seem unlikely that the codetype differences are unrelated to treatment response, particularly in view of the pretreatment differences that have been reported.

SPECIAL/RESEARCH SCALES

Two special scales have received the bulk of the research attention in the LBP population. Studies using these scales are noted in Table 2–6. The oldest and most frequently studied special scale developed for the chronic pain population is the Low Back (*Lb*) scale (Hanvik, 1949). The most common reference for the *Lb* scale is Hanvik's 1951 article. The reader searching for information concerning the item composition of the *Lb* scale should be aware that it is not mentioned in this article. Instead, the mean profile of the organic and functional patients and the ability of four clinicians to assign the codetypes to organic or functional groups are discussed. Item composition may be found in references such as Graham (1987) or Greene (1980). The *Lb* scale consists of 26 items that Hanvik selected by comparing MMPI protocols of 30 LBP patients diagnosed by surgery or spinogram findings as having an organic basis for their pain with the protocols of 30 matched LBP patients diagnosed as functional due to the absence of clear-cut organic findings on physical and neurologic examinations. Hanvik reported that if a cutting score of 11 was used, 70 percent of organic LBP patients were classified correctly (true positives), as were 90 percent of the functional patients (true negatives). This scale has been used in several other investigations, all attempting to differentiate between organic, functional, and/or mixed LBP patients.

The Dorsalles Functionales (*DOR*) scale is a 63-item scale developed in a French sample of functional dorsal and mid-back pain patients (Pichot et al., 1972). The comparison group for the development of this scale was a sample of healthy control subjects, rather than organic pain patients. Thus, this scale rests on a different logical base than the *Lb* scale and correlates weakly with the *Lb* scale (Freeman et al., 1976; Pichot et al., 1972). Pichot and his colleagues were able to identify 57 percent of their functional back pain patients with the *DOR* scale alone, while the *Lb* scale alone identified 43 percent of the pain patients. When a

TABLE 2–6. PERFORMANCE OF PAIN PATIENTS ON SPECIAL SCALES

Authors	N	Age	Correlates
Low Back Scale (Hanvik, 1949):			
Calsyn et al. (1976)	62	42	M > 0; 61–81% hit rate[*]
Dahlstrom (1954)	65	–	Correlated –.20 with surgical outcome
Freeman et al. (1976)	36	39	61–75% hit rate[*]
Leavitt (1982) [male]	91	–	37.4% hit rate for identifying emotional disturbance
Louks et al. (1978)	74	42	F & M > 0; lower in *WNL* codetypes[*]
McCreary et al. (1979)	76	–	Higher with poor response to treatment (pain relief and increased activity)
Rosen et al. (1980)	123	38	Did not predict organic status or disability
Sternbach et al. (1973b)	117	42	No differences between F and 0 patients
Towne & Tsushima (1978)	60	36	Not specific for LBP
Tsushima & Towne (1979)	40	36	No differences between F and 0 patients
Wilfling et al. (1973)	26	53	No differences between good, fair, and poor surgical outcome patients
Dorsalles Functionales Scale (Pichot et al., 1972):			
Calsyn et al. (1976)	62	42	M > 0; 52–81% hit rate[*]
Freeman et al. (1976)	36	39	F > M; 64–75% hit rate[*]
Louks et al. (1978)	74	42	F & M > 0; lower in *WNL* codetypes
Rosen et al. (1980)	123	38	Did not predict organic status or disability
Towne & Tsushima (1978)	60	36	Not specific for LBP
Other Special Scales:			
Prokop (1986) [female]	53	43	LBP > normals on *Hy2, Hy3,* & *Hy4*
Prokop (1986) [male]	40	34	LBP > normals on *Hy3* & *Hy4* LBP < normals on *Hy5*
Schmidt & Wallace (1982)	50	–	Factor I = Scale *2*, BP, & *Hy3* Factor II = Scales *4, 6,* & *8* Factor III = NBP, *Hy4, –K,* & *–Hy2*
Turner et al. (1986)	106	41	PAI < Scale 1 for predicting surgical outcome

Notes: F = functional pain; M = mixed pain; O = organic pain. BP = back pain; NBP = no back pain. *Hy2* = Harris & Lingoes' Need for affection; *Hy3* = Harris & Lingoes' Lassitude-malaise; *Hy4* = Harris & Lingoes' Somatic complaints; *Hy5* = Harris & Lingoes' Inhibition of aggression.
[*]Subject overlap across studies.

criterion of a *T*-score of 70 or higher on either scale was used, the authors were able to identify 80 percent of the pain patients correctly.

The first replication of the utility of the *Lb* scale's ability to predict organic or functional status was by Dahlstrom (1954). The scale was found to correlate negatively with the predictions based on the full MMPI and the Wechsler Bellevue and to correlate -.20 with 3-month treatment outcome. Patients with higher *Lb* scores recovered more slowly from surgery and were less likely to have a clear organic basis for their pain.

In two studies by Calsyn, Louks, and Freeman (Calsyn et al., 1976; Freeman et al., 1976), both the *Lb* and *DOR* scales were reported to be of little use in differentiating organic, functional, and mixed LBP patients if the scales were used independently. When used together, the two scales correctly predicted the diagnoses of about three quarters of the patients. In a third study by the same group (Louks et al., 1978), the two scales were reported to be significantly higher in functional and mixed diagnosis patients than in organic patients. Pathologic MMPIs were reported to be associated with higher scores on these two scales, although no specific codetype appeared associated with elevated scores on *Lb* and *DOR*. This series of studies initially appears to offer some support for the combined use of the two scales, even if their separate use is not supported. However, this conclusion is weakened by the fact that these were not completely independent replications, as many of the same patients were used in all three studies (Louks et al., 1978). Thus, additional supporting evidence seems necessary before the use of the scales may be recommended.

Six additional studies have investigated the utility of the *Lb* and *DOR* scales either alone or in combination. Scores on the *Lb* scale have been reported to be equivalent in organic and functional LBP patients (Sternbach et al., 1973b; Tsushima & Towne, 1979), and the two scales, both together and separately, have been reported to possess accuracy rates no better than chance in differentiating functional LBP patients from organic LBP patients, functional gastrointestinal patients, and/or neurotics (Rosen, Frymoyer, & Clements, 1980; Towne & Tsushima, 1978; Tsushima & Towne, 1979). The most common classification errors involved organic patients being labeled as functional. Rosen et al. (1980) also reported that the two scales were no better than chance in identifying patients rated as showing an inappropriately high level of disability. Leavitt (1982) reported that the accuracy rate of the *Lb* scale was only 37.4 percent in the identification of functional LBP patients rated as psychologically disturbed based on other findings, and Wilfling, Klonoff, and Kokan (1973) found that the *Lb* scale was unable to predict accurately which LBP patients would show poor, fair, or good responses to lumbar intervertebral fusion. The evidence accumulated to date thus strongly suggests that the two scales should be used with great caution, if at all, in clinical practice.

The Pain Assessment Index (PAI) is based on a weighted combination of Scales *1*, *2*, *3*, *7*, and *9*. Developed by Smith and Duerksen (1979) in a sample of 31 patients with diverse pain complaints and surgical treatments, it was reported to classify correctly 93.5 percent of patients with regard to the degree of pain relief postoperatively. It also has been related to pain relief and employment status 4 months postoperatively (Dhanens & Jarrett, 1984) in a sample of 53 industrial injury patients.

The most ambitious study of the PAI was conducted by Turner, Herron, and Weiner (1986); 106 LBP patients were reexamined and interviewed an average of 18 months after laminectomy and discectomy. Response was rated as good, fair, or poor based on pain relief, work status, medication use, and activity restriction. In this study, the preoperative PAI scores of the good and fair/poor outcome patients were found to differ significantly. Although 79 percent of the patients were classified correctly as to outcome, the sensitivity of the PAI (correctly identifying fair or poor responders) was only 33 percent. It was much more effective in its ability to identify good responders, with a specificity of 95 percent. However, Scale *1* used alone was a better predictor of outcome, with 83 percent correct classification (63 percent sensitivity and 90 percent specificity). The PAI fared somewhat better at predicting work status, with 87 percent correct classifications (47 percent sensitivity and 95 percent specificity). Scale *1* was more sensitive (63 percent), but less specific (85 percent) and less correct overall (81 percent). On balance, the authors noted that the PAI was poorest at identifying poor and fair responders, which is the question of most clinical interest. Scale *1* was more useful in this regard.

The Harris and Lingoes subscales of Scale *3* (described in Graham, 1987; Greene, 1980) also have been examined in the LBP population. Two of these subscales are related closely to reports of physical complaints (Lassitude-Malaise: *Hy3*, and Somatic Complaints: *Hy4*), while three reflect personality dynamics theoretically associated with hysteria (Denial of Social Anxiety: *Hy1*, Need for Affection: *Hy2*, and Inhibition of Aggression: *Hy5*). Schmidt and Wallace (1982) reported that *Hy3* loaded on the same factor as Scale *2* and Back Pain (*BP*), while *Hy4* loaded positively and *Hy2* loaded negatively on a factor including a negative loading by Scale *K* and a positive loading by Non-Back Pain (*NBP*). *BP* and *NBP*, scales developed specifically for this study, were composed of Scale *1* items rated by three judges as being direct effects of LBP (*BP* items) or not direct results of LBP (*NBP*). The authors suggested that *Hy3* elevations may thus be direct results of LBP, while elevations on *Hy4* and low scores on *Hy2* reflect a psychogenic component in the LBP experience. However, this interpretation contains the rather puzzling implication that defensiveness, at least as measured by Scale *K*, is associated negatively with psychogenic pain. This is contrary to the common interpretation of psychogenic pain as reflecting an unwillingness to acknowledge psychological distress. Two methodologic points may be important in interpreting this study. First, 50 functional LBP patients were analyzed in two factor analyses including 25 patients. Although the factors selected for interpretation were only those replicated in both analyses, the small sample size suggests an increased risk for unreliable findings. Second, there is substantial item overlap between the scales that loaded together, so the results may be reflecting item overlap as much as the existence of shared conceptual variance. For example, 5 of the 10 *BP* items also are scored on Scale *2*, and 10 Scale *2* items also are scored on the 15 item *Hy3* subscale.

Prokop (1986) investigated the Harris and Lingoes Scale *3* endorsement patterns of LBP patients and normal controls. The major contributions to the discrimination between the controls and the LBP patients were made by *Hy3* and *Hy4*. Minor gender differences were present, as female LBP patients also scored marginally but significantly higher than control patients on *Hy2*, while male LBP patients scored slightly lower than controls on *Hy5*. This endorsement pattern suggested that elevations on Scale *3* in LBP patients should not be interpreted as indicating a pattern of focusing on somatic symptoms to deny or avoid awareness of psychological conflict unless additional supporting evidence is available. Although not reported in the article, LBP patients with a conversion "V" were no more likely to elevate the personality dynamic oriented subscales (*Hy1*, *Hy2*, and *Hy5*) of Scale *3* than were LBP patients without a conversion "V." Consequently, Prokop (1986) suggested that the Harris and Lingoes subscales may provide a clue to the interpretation of a Scale *3* elevation in the LBP patient. When only *Hy3* and *Hy4* are elevated, it may be appropriate to infer an abnormal focus on physical symptomatology, but not the presence of conversion dynamics. Instead, the patient may be attempting to call attention to frightening or confusing symptomsm may be more correctly diagnosed as suffering from a nonconversion-based somatoform disorder, or may have been reinforced in the past for the report of physical distress. The correct interpretation of the Scale *3* elevation may thus convey significant information relevant to future psychological intervention plans.

SHORT FORM UTILITY

Several investigators have examined the utility of short forms of the MMPI in the chronic pain population. These studies are summarized in Table 2–7. At first glance, short forms may appear to hold out special promise in this patient group. Chronic pain patients may be resistant to the inference that psychological factors may be relevant to their condition, and a shorter instrument may meet with less resistance and be less likely to be only partially completed. Short forms also may be viewed as potentially useful because they are less time-consuming, which may be important if a battery of psychological tests is being administered.

Turner and McCreary (1978) investigated the degree to which the Faschingbauer abbreviated MMPI (FAM: Faschingbauer, 1974) and the Midi-Mult (Dean, 1972) agreed with the full MMPI for 176 back pain patients and predicted the presence of a physician-rated functional component in 64 of these patients. These ratings were made by a single physician after the patient's first visit to the clinic. Correlations of both short forms with the scale scores of the full MMPI were generally high (.69 to .93), although the FAM was more highly correlated with the full MMPI than was the Midi-Mult. Two-point codetype agreement was less impressive. When order was considered, 34 percent of the FAM codetypes and 22 percent of the Midi-Mult codetypes matched the full MMPI codetypes. When order was not considered, the respective agreement rates were 43 percent and 32 percent. As would be expected, three-point codetype agreement rates were lower for both instruments.

When functional and organic patients were compared, functional patients scored significantly higher on Scales *K*, *1*, *3*, *4*, *8*, and *0* of the full MMPI; Scales *1*, *2*, *3*, *7*, *8*, and *0* of the FAM; and Scales *1*, *2*, *3*, *4*, *6*, *7*, *8*, and *0* of the Midi-Mult. The authors interpreted these data as providing "tentative evidence" supporting the utility of these short forms, particularly the FAM, in the pain population. In view of the relatively low codetype agreement rates and the heterogeneity of the significant differences between the functional and organic groups, this evidence does appear to be tentative, at best. Beyond identifying a general dimension of somatization and distress, it seems unlikely that the short form data in this study would be of notable use in the individual pain patient.

Calsyn, Spengler, and Freeman (1977) investigated the applicability of the factors derived from the MMPI-168 (Overall, Hunter, & Butcher, 1973), consisting of the first 168 items of Form R

TABLE 2-7. SHORT FORMS

Study	Age	Sex	N	Results	Methodologic Issues							
					A	B	C	D	E	F	G	H
Calsyn et al. (1977)	42	M&F	58	M > 0 on MMPI-168 Somatization factor	+	-	-	+	+	+	+	+
	42	M	48	F & MP > 0 & MR on MMPI-168 Somatization and Depression factors	+	+	-	-	+	+	+	+
Griffin & Danahy (1982)		M&F	114	FAM & MMPI-168 made most errors in 65–74 T-score range on Scales 1 & 3	-	+	+	-	+	+	+	
Turner & McCreary (1978)	44	M&F	186	2-point code agreement with full MMPI: FAM: 34%; Midi-Mult: 22%	+	+	+	-	+	+	-	
		M&F	64	F > 0 on many FAM and Midi-Mult scales	+	-	+	-	-	+	-	-

Notes: FAM = Faschingbauer abbreviated MMPI; F = functional pain; M = mixed pain; MP = mixed with pain after treatment; MR = mixed with relief after treatment; O = organic pain.

of the MMPI, in two samples of back pain patients. The first sample was composed of the organic and mixed pain patients used in the Calsyn et al. (1976) study. A cutting score of 8 on the Somatization factor correctly classified 74.5 percent of the mixed patients. It is interesting to note that 20 of the 23 items comprising the Somatization factor are scored on Scales 1 and 3 of the MMPI. In a second sample, 48 patients were classified as organic, functional, or mixed, and the mixed group was divided into mixed-pain and mixed-relief groups according to their response to an unspecified treatment. Functional and mixed-pain patients differed significantly from organic and mixed-relief patients on the Somatization and Depression factors. A cutting score of 8 on the Somatization factor correctly identified 81 percent of the functional and mixed-pain patients and 85 percent of the organic and mixed-relief patients.

The most carefully conducted short-form study of LBP patients was by Griffin and Danahy (1982). These authors screened the full MMPI codetypes of 300 back pain patients for validity and the presence of mutual elevations on Scales 1 and 3. They retained 114 for further study. The valid codetypes were assigned to one of three groups based on the degree of elevation on Scales 1 and 3, and the FAM and MMPI-168 also were scored. Relatively strong correlations were reported once again between the three instruments with the FAM correlating slightly higher than the MMPI-168 with Scale 1 of the full MMPI ($r = .85$ and $.76$, respectively), and the two short forms correlating equally ($r = .92$) with the full MMPI on Scale 3. The short forms were equivalent in their ability to place the codetypes into groups based on elevations on Scales 1 and 3 of the full MMPI; both correctly placed 66

percent of the codetypes. However, the most error occurred in the group with elevations on Scales 1 and 3 between T-scores of 65 and 74. The FAM correctly classified only 21 percent of these codetypes, and the MMPI-168 correctly classified 36 percent. The authors noted that since the MMPI codetypes of many medical patients fall into this intermediate range, the use of the FAM and MMPI-168 with medical patients is contraindicated.

The studies discussed above provide little support for the use of short forms in the pain population. The study providing the most support for the use of short forms (Calsyn et al., 1977) suggests that the Somatization factor of the MMPI-168 may be useful in identifying functional patients or mixed patients who may not respond to treatment. However, the limitations of the functional/organic distinction have been discussed previously. In addition, the type of treatment was not specified and detailed hit rate information was not provided in the Calsyn et al. study.

The relatively small gain in time that the short form provides does not appear to be of sufficient value to justify the increased risk of error associated with short forms of the MMPI, particularly when the length of time that many chronic pain patients have experienced pain is considered. Administration of the MMPI is associated with minimal risks and discomfort, particularly when compared with many physical diagnostic techniques and the risks associated with unnecessary or unsuccessful medical/ surgical intervention. It is difficult to justify an increased risk of error in order to save no more than an hour or two when dealing with a pain problem that is likely to have been present for years and has not responded to treatment. Until it is demonstrated that a short form may lead to more useful diagnostic and treatment planning decisions than the full MMPI, the clinician should use short forms with extreme caution, if at all. If a short form must be used, the Somatization factor derived from the MMPI-168 may be most cost-effective and justifiable, although the *1-3* codetype from this same instrument appears less reliable.

SUMMARY

The use of the MMPI with chronic pain patients now has received more than 35 years of research attention. What conclusions may be drawn from this effort, and what issues remain for future investigations? The evidence to date supports the continued use of the MMPI in this population, but additional research is needed to delineate more explicitly the appropriate uses of the MMPI within subgroups of chronic pain patients.

The most consistent finding in the studies reviewed in this chapter is the presence of elevations on Scales *1* and *3* in chronic pain patients. These two scales are consistently the highest scales when mean codetypes are reported, although Scale *2* elevations are also common, especially in male patients. However, the presence of this pattern has lead to an overemphasis on the scales of the neurotic triad. Cluster analytic studies have demonstrated that replicable codetype subgroups exist, and there is some evidence that these subgroups are associated with reliable differences between patients. Although Scales *1* and *3* are the most common predictors of treatment response, the evidence suggests that other codetype configurations and individual scales also may contain useful information.

Many issues remain for future research. First, the possibility of important gender differences in the codetypes of chronic pain patients deserves further attention. Future investigators should analyze male and female codetypes separately whenever possible, not only because there may be reliable gender differences in the frequencies of codetypes subgroups, but because some evidence (McCreary, 1985) suggests that similar codetypes may be associated with different predictive value in males and females. Similar uncertainty exists regarding the effects of pain chronicity on the MMPI codetypes of pain patients. Pain of 6 months or more duration is the commonly accepted criterion for chronic pain; if future studies include both acute and chronic pain patients, separate reports concerning patients experiencing pain for greater and less than 6 months would be helpful in resolving this question.

Investigations of the ability of the MMPI to differentiate between functional and organic pain should be abandoned. Disregarding the question of the reliability of this distinction, the evidence suggests that the degree of overlap between the MMPIs of functional and organic patients is significant. Questions of both theoretical and clinical interest that have formerly been addressed through the functional vs. organic distinction may be more profitably approached by researching treatment response or examining patients with and without feasible medical/surgical intervention options. Note that none of these suggestions involves the ability of the MMPI to agree with inferences about the organic status of the pain patient. Many conservative treatment strategies are applicable to all chronic pain patients without regard to objective physical status. While MMPI codetypes may be relatively independent of physical findings, treatment response predictors may differ as a function of physical status and type of treatment. Similarly, different aspects of comprehensive treatment programs may be more or less important as a function of psychological status. The efficiency of treatment provision in the chronic pain population might be improved if such predictors were identified.

The MMPI has shown promise for identifying patients with documentable and treatable physical pathology who may be at risk for poor response to medical/surgical intervention. Although poor response is sometimes over-predicted (McCreary et al., 1979), this error is probably of less clinical consequence than under-identification of high-risk patients if the information from the MMPI is used to select patients needing special psychological attention and monitoring, rather than to deny medical treatment options. Future research might profitably focus on two groups of patients: those who would be identified as poor responders by current criteria, yet respond well, and those who would be identified as good responders, yet respond poorly. Snyder and Power's (1981) study of *WNL* codetypes who were nonresponders represents a beginning step in this direction.

As noted previously, the DSM-III diagnostic category of Psychogenic Pain Disorder may contain a heterogeneous group of patients. The ability of the MMPI to refine this diagnosis deserves study. For example, can the MMPI aid in the differentiation of patients whose pain is maintained largely by operant factors and those whose pain is more strongly controlled by dynamic or conversion factors? The ubiquity of the conversion "V" codetype in pain patients suggests that the answer to this question lies beyond the major scales of the neurotic triad, and instead is likely to involve other major scale elevations or subscale patterns. Fordyce (1976) presented suggestions for determining operant contributions to pain complaints. Future research might compare the MMPI performance of patients with large and small operant components. Beutler et al. (1986) suggested that constrained affect may be related to both pain and depression.

Research could be directed toward the uses of the MMPI in the identification of pain patients experiencing difficulties with the expression of intense affect. The evidence previously reported concerning the predictive power of the K scale (Kuperman et al., 1979; Strassberg et al., 1981) may be relevant to this question, and the Harris-Lingoes subscales of Scale 3 also might be useful in this regard (cf. Prokop, 1986).

Cluster analytic studies have demonstrated convincingly that replicable MMPI subgroups exist within the chronic pain population. The next question of interest involves the search for reliable correlates of these subgroups, if such exist. Studies to date have not satisfactorily answered this question. Henrichs (1987) has demonstrated that cluster analytic assignment of patients to subgroups leads to relatively heterogeneous subgroup composition and that patients more closely matching the subgroup codetype differ from those who match less well. This problem appears particularly acute in markedly elevated MMPIs. The search for correlates of subgroup membership might therefore benefit from assessing subgroup membership by measures such as Cronbach and Glaser's D (1953), as suggested by Sines (1964) and used by Henrichs (1987). Clinical judgments of codetype similarity on scales most important in interpretation also might be used. It is probably more important clinically how closely a codetype matches a subgroup template on one or more elevated scales than on several scales within a standard deviation of the mean. The investigation by Adams et al. (1986) suggests that such sorting may be both feasible and reliable.

Finally, most MMPI research has concentrated on psychological disturbance diagnosed on Axis I of DSM-III. Investigation of potential Axis II diagnoses in chronic pain patients might prove useful, particularly with regard to the identification of patients in need of psychotherapeutic intervention. MMPI improvement sometimes is seen after pain treatment, although deterioration also may be seen and mean profiles may still remain elevated (Meilman et al., 1986; Sternbach & Timmermans, 1975). If MMPI markers of personality disorder in chronic pain patients can be developed, these might aid in the identification of patients at risk for deterioration or continued psychological dysfunction.

REFERENCES

Adams, K. M., Heilbronn, M., & Blumer, D. P. (1986). A multimethod evaluation of the MMPI in a chronic pain sample. *Journal of Clinical Psychology, 42,* 878–886.

Armentrout, D. P., Moore, J. E., Parker, J. C., Hewett, J. E., & Feltz, C. (1982). Pain-patient MMPI subgroups: The psychological dimension of pain. *Journal of Behavioral Medicine, 5,* 201–212.

Beals, R. K., & Hickman, N. W. (1972). Industrial injuries of the back and extremities. *Journal of Bone and Joint Surgery, 54,* 1593–1611.

Beck, A. T. (1967). *Depression: Clinical, experimental, and theoretical aspects.* New York: Hoelber.

Bernstein, I. H., & Garbin, C. P. (1983). Hierarchical clustering of pain patient's MMPI profiles: A replication note. *Journal of Personality Assessment, 47,* 171–172.

Beutler, L. E., Engle, D., Oro'-Beutler, M. E., Daldrup, R., & Meredith, K. (1986). Inability to express intense affect: A common link between depression and pain? *Journal of Consulting and Clinical Psychology, 54,* 752–759.

Bradley, L. A., Prokop, C. K., Margolis, R. D., & Gentry, W. D. (1978). Multivariate analyses of the MMPI profiles of low back pain patients. *Journal of Behavioral Medicine, 1,* 253–272.

Bradley, L. A., & Van der Heide, L. H. (1984). Pain-related correlates of MMPI profile subgroups among back pain patients. *Health Psychology, 3,* 157–174.

Brena, S. F., Chapman, S. L., & Decker, R. (1981). Chronic pain as a learned experience. In L. K. Y. Ng (Ed.), *New approaches to treatment of chronic pain* (pp. 76–83). Washington, DC: U.S. Department of Health and Human Services.

Calsyn, D. A., Louks, J., & Freeman, C. W. (1976). The use of the MMPI with chronic low back pain patients with a mixed diagnosis. *Journal of Clinical Psychology, 32,* 532–536.

Calsyn, D. A., Spengler, D. M., & Freeman, C. W. (1977). Application of the somatization factor of the MMPI-168 with low back pain patients. *Journal of Clinical Psychology, 33,* 1017–1020.

Chapman, C. R. (1977). Psychological aspects of pain patient treatment. *Archives of Surgery, 112,* 767–772.

Cox, G. B., Chapman, C. R., & Black, R. G. (1978). The MMPI and chronic pain: The diagnosis of psychogenic pain. *Journal of Behavioral Medicine, 1,* 437–443.

Cronbach, L. J., & Glaser, G. (1953). Assessing similarity between profiles. *Psychological Bulletin, 50,* 456–473.

Crue, B. L., Jr. (1983). The neurophysiology and taxonomy of pain. In S. F. Brena & S. L. Chapman (Eds.), *Management of patients with chronic pain* (pp. 21–32). Jamaica, NY: Spectrum.

Dahlstrom, W. G. (1954). Prediction of adjustment after neurosurgery. *American Psychologist, 9,* 353–354.

Dean, E. F.(1972). A lengthened Mini: The Midi-Mult. *Journal of Clinical Psychology, 28,* 68–71.

Dhanens, T. P., & Jarrett, S. R. (1984). MMPI pain assessment index: Concurrent and predictive validity. *International Journal of Clinical Neuropsychology, 6,* 46–48.

Donham, G. W., Mikhail, S. F., & Meyers, R. (1984). Value of consensual ratings in differentiating organic and functional low back pain. *Journal of Clinical Psychology, 40,* 432–439.

Duckro, P. N., Margolis, R. B., & Tait, R. C. (1985). Psychological assessment in chronic pain. *Journal of Clinical Psychology, 41,* 499–504.

Faschingbauer, T. R. (1974). A 166-item short form of the group MMPI: The FAM. *Journal of Consulting and Clinical Psychology, 42,* 645–655.

Fordyce, W. E. (1976). *Behavioral methods for chronic pain and illness.* St. Louis: C. V. Mosby.

Fordyce, W. E., Brena, S. F., Holcomb, R. J., De Lateur, B. J., & Loeser, J. D. (1978). Relationship of patient semantic pain descriptions to physician diagnostic judgments, activity level measures and MMPI. *Pain, 5,* 293–303.

Fordyce, W. E., Brockway, J. A., Bergman, J. A., & Spengler, D. (1986). Acute back pain: A control-group comparison of behavioral vs. traditional management methods. *Journal of*

Behavioral Medicine, 9, 127–140.

Freeman, C., Calsyn, D., & Louks, J. (1976). The use of the MMPI with low back pain patients. *Journal of Clinical Psychology, 32,* 294–298.

Gentry, W. D., Shows, W. D., & Thomas, M. (1974). Chronic low back pain: A psychological profile. *Psychosomatics, 15,* 174–177.

Gottlieb, H., Strite, L. C., Koller, R., Madorsky, A., Hockersmith, V., Kleeman, M., & Wagner, B. A. (1977). Comprehensive rehabilitation of patients having chronic low back pain. *Archives of Physical Medicine and Rehabilitation, 58,* 101–108.

Graham, J. R. (1987). *The MMPI: A practical guide* (2nd ed.). New York: Oxford.

Greene, R. L. (1980). *The MMPI: An interpretive manual.* Philadelphia: Grune & Stratton.

Griffin, P. T., & Danahy, S. (1982). Short form MMPIs in medical consultation: Accuracy of the Hs-Hy dyad compared to the standard form. *Journal of Clinical Psychology, 38,* 134–136.

Hanvik, L. J. (1949). *Some psychological dimensions of low back pain.* Unpublished doctor's thesis, University of Minnesota, Minneapolis, MN.

Hanvik, L. J. (1951). MMPI profiles in patients with low back pain. *Journal of Consulting Psychology, 15,* 350–353.

Hart, R. R. (1984). Chronic pain: Replicated multivariate clustering of personality profiles. *Journal of Clinical Psychology, 40,* 129–133.

Henrichs, T. F. (1987). MMPI profiles of chronic pain patients: Some methodological considerations concerning clusters and descriptors. *Journal of Clinical Psychology, 43,* 650–660.

Hickling, E. J., Sison, G. F. P., & Holtz, J. L. (1985). Role of psychologists in multidisciplinary pain clinics: A national survey. *Professional Psychology: Research and Practice, 16,* 868–880.

Kinder, B. N., Curtiss, G., & Kalichman, S. (1986). Anxiety and anger as predictors of MMPI elevations in chronic pain patients. *Journal of Personality Assessment, 50,* 651–661.

Kuperman, S. K., Golden, C. J., & Blume, H. G. (1979). Predicting pain treatment results by personality variables in organic and functional patients. *Journal of Clinical Psychology, 35,* 832–837.

Leavitt, F. (1982). Comparison of three measures for detecting psychological disturbance in patients with low back pain. *Pain, 13,* 299–305.

Leavitt, F. (1985). The value of the MMPI conversion "V" in the assessment of psychogenic pain. *Journal of Psychosomatic Research, 29,* 125–131.

Leavitt, F., & Garron, D. C. (1982). Rorschach and pain characteristics of patients with low back pain and "Conversion V" MMPI profiles. *Journal of Personality Assessment, 46,* 18–25.

Linton, S. J. (1982). A critical review of behavioural treatments for chronic benign pain other than headache. *British Journal of Clinical Psychology, 21,* 321–337.

Loeser, J. D. (1980). Low back pain. In J. J. Bonica (Ed.), *Pain* (pp. 363–377). New York: Raven.

Long, C. J. (1981). The relationship between surgical outcome and MMPI profiles in chronic pain patients. *Journal of Clinical Psychology, 37,* 744–749.

Louks, J. L., Freeman, C. W., & Calsyn, D. A. (1978). Personality organization as an aspect of back pain in a medical setting. *Journal of Personality Assessment, 42,* 152–157.

Maruta, T., Swanson, D. W., & Swenson, W. M. (1976). Low back pain patients in a psychiatric population. *Mayo Clinic Proceedings, 51,* 57–61.

McCreary, C. (1985). Empirically derived MMPI profile clusters and characteristics of low back pain patients. *Journal of Consulting and Clinical Psychology, 53,* 558–560.

McCreary, C., & Colman, A. (1984). Medication usage, emotional disturbance, and pain behavior in chronic low back pain patients. *Journal of Clinical Psychology, 40,* 15–19.

McCreary, C., Turner, J., & Dawson, E. (1977). Differences between functional versus organic low back pain patients. *Pain, 4,* 73–78.

McCreary, C., Turner, J., & Dawson, E. (1979). The MMPI as a predictor of response to conservative treatment for low back pain. *Journal of Clinical Psychology, 35,* 278–284.

McCreary, C., Turner, J., & Dawson, E. (1980). Emotional disturbance and chronic low back pain. *Journal of Clinical Psychology, 36,* 709–715.

McGill, J. C., Lawlis, G. F., Selby, D., Mooney, V., & McCoy, C. E. (1983). The relationship of MMPI profile clusters to pain behaviors. *Journal of Behavioral Medicine, 6,* 77–92.

Meilman, P. W., Guck, T. P., Skutley, F. M., Robbins, D. E., & Jensen, K. (1986). Changes in psychopathology associated with multidisciplinary pain treatment. *Clinical Journal of Pain, 2,* 107–113.

Melzack, R. (1975). The McGill Pain Questionnaire: Major properties and scoring methods. *Pain, 1,* 277–299.

Naliboff, B. D., Cohen, M. J., & Yellen, A. N. (1982). Does the MMPI differentiate chronic illness from chronic pain? *Pain, 13,* 333–341.

National Institutes of Health (1979). *Report of the panel on pain to the National Advisory Neurological and Communicative Disorders and Stroke Council* (NIH Publication No. 79-1912). Washington, DC: Author.

Overall, J. E., Hunter, S., & Butcher, J. N. (1973). Factor structure of the MMPI-168 in a psychiatric population. *Journal of Consulting and Clinical Psychology, 41,* 284–286.

Pheasant, H. C., Gilbert, D., Goldfarb, J., & Herron, L. (1979). The MMPI as a predictor of outcome in low-back surgery. *Spine, 4,* 78–84.

Pichot, P., Perse, J., Lekeoux, M. O., Dureau, J. L., Perez, C. I., & Rychewaert, A. (1972). La personalite des sujets presentant des douleurs dorsales fonchonelles valeur de l'inventaire multiphasique de personalite de Minnesota. *Revue de Psychologie Appliquee, 22,* 145–172.

Prokop, C. K. (1986). Hysteria scale elevations in low back pain patients: A risk factor for misdiagnosis? *Journal of Consulting and Clinical Psychology, 54,* 558–562.

Prokop, C. K., & Bradley, L. A. (1981). Methodological issues in medical psychology research. In C. K. Prokop & L. A. Bradley (Eds.), *Medical psychology: Contributions to behavioral medicine* (pp. 485–496). San Diego: Academic Press.

Prokop, C. K., Bradley, L. A., Margolis, R. D., & Gentry, W. D. (1980). Multivariate analyses of the MMPI profiles of patients with multiple pain complaints. *Journal of Personality Assessment, 44,* 246–252.

Romano, J. M., & Turner, J. A. (1985). Chronic pain and depression: Does the evidence support a relationship? *Psychological Bulletin, 97,* 18–34.

Rosen, J. C., Frymoyer, J. W., & Clements, J. H. (1980). A further look at validity of the MMPI with low back pain patients. *Journal of Clinical Psychology, 36,* 994–1000.

Schmidt, J. P., & Wallace, R. W. (1982). Factorial analysis of the MMPI profiles of low back pain patients. *Journal of Personality Assessment, 46,* 366–369.

Sines, J. O. (1964). Actuarial methods as appropriate strategy for the validation of diagnostic tests. *Psychological Review, 71,* 517–523.

Smith, W. L., & Duerksen, D. L. (1979). Personality and the relief of chronic pain: Predicting surgical outcome. *Clinical*

Neuropsychology, 1(3), 35–38.

Snyder, D. K., & Power, D. G. (1981). Empirical descriptors of unelevated MMPI profiles among chronic pain patients: A typological approach. *Journal of Clinical Psychology, 37,* 602–607.

Spielberger, C. D., Gorsuch, R. L., Lushene, R., Vagg, P. R., & Jacobs, G. A. (1983). *Manual for the State-Trait anxiety inventory.* Palo Alto, CA: Consulting Psychologists Press.

Spitzer, R. L., Endicott, J., & Robins, E. (1978). Research diagnostic criteria: Rationale and reliability. *Archives of General Psychiatry, 35,* 773–782.

Sternbach, R. A. (1974). *Pain patients: Traits and treatment.* San Diego: Academic Press.

Sternbach, R. A., & Timmermans, G. (1975). Personality changes associated with reduction of pain. *Pain, 1,* 177–181.

Sternbach, R. A., Wolf, S. R., Murphy, R. W., & Akeson, W. H. (1973a). Aspects of chronic low back pain. *Psychosomatics, 14,* 52–56.

Sternbach, R. A., Wolf, S. R., Murphy, R. W., & Akeson, W. H. (1973b). Traits of pain patients: The low-back "loser." *Psychosomatics, 14,* 226–229.

Strassberg, D. S., Reimherr, F., Ward, M., Russell, S., & Cole, A. (1981). The MMPI and chronic pain. *Journal of Consulting and Clinical Psychology, 49,* 220–226.

Swanson, D. W., Maruta, T., & Swenson, W. M. (1979). Results of behavior modification in the treatment of chronic pain. *Psychosomatic Medicine, 41,* 55–61.

Swanson, D. W., Swenson, W. M., Maruta, T., & McPhee, M. C. (1976). Program for managing chronic pain. I. Program description and characteristics of patients. *Mayo Clinic Proceedings, 51,* 401–408.

Timmermans, G., & Sternbach, R. A. (1974). Factors of human chronic pain: An analysis of personality and pain reaction variables. *Science, 184,* 806–807.

Towne, W. S., & Tsushima, W. T. (1978). The use of the low back pain and the dorsal scales in the identification of functional low back patients. *Journal of Clinical Psychology, 34,* 88–91.

Tsushima, W. T., & Towne, W. S. (1979). Clinical limitations of the low back scale. *Journal of Clinical Psychology, 35,* 306–308.

Turner, J. A., Herron, L., & Weiner, P. (1986). Utility of the MMPI pain assessment index in predicting outcome after lumbar surgery. *Journal of Clinical Psychology, 42,* 764–769.

Turner, J., & McCreary, C. (1978). Short forms of the MMPI with back pain patients. *Journal of Consulting and Clinical Psychology, 46,* 354–355.

Turner, J. A., & Romano, J. M. (1984). Self-report screening measures for depression in chronic pain patients. *Journal of Clinical Psychology, 40,* 909–913.

Watson, C. G., & Buranen, C. (1979). The frequency and identification of false positive conversion reactions. *Journal of Nervous and Mental Diseases, 167,* 243–247.

Watson, C. G., & Tilleskjor, C. (1983). Interrelationships of conversion, psychogenic pain, and dissociative disorder symptoms. *Journal of Consulting and Clinical Psychology, 51,* 788–789.

Wilfling, F. J., Klonoff, H., & Kokan, P. (1973). Psychological, demographic, and orthopaedic factors associated with prediction of outcome of spinal fusion. *Clinical Orthopaedics and Related Research, 90,* 153–160.

Wiltse, L. L., & Rocchio, P. D. (1975). Preoperative psychological tests as predictors of success of chemonucleolysis in the treatment of the low-back syndrome. *Journal of Bone and Joint Surgery, 57-A,* 478–483.

Zung, W. W. K. (1965). A self-rating depression scale. *Archives of General Psychiatry, 12,* 63–70.

Chapter 3

Schizophrenia

GLENN D. WALTERS

OVERVIEW

Although we still need to learn a great deal more about schizophrenia, one thing we do know is that this disorder imposes a heavy toll on the patient, his or her family, and the community at large. While the direct cost of treating schizophrenia is estimated to be somewhere in the neighborhood of $17 billion a year, the indirect burden of schizophrenia on society through lost employment and an increased need for community support elevates this figure to somewhere around $40 billion (Strauss & Carpenter, 1981), and with approximately 100,000 new cases of schizophrenia diagnosed each year, the cost is sure to grow. In fact, nearly one-third of all schizophrenics released from inpatient psychiatric facilities are readmitted within 1 year, and half find themselves readmitted within 2 years (Neale & Oltmanns, 1980). These figures suggest that if schizophrenia is not currently a major health concern, then it should be.

The problems associated with adequately investigating the schizophrenic syndrome are well documented (see Neale & Oltmanns, 1980; Strauss & Carpenter, 1981). Thus, despite the moderately impressive amount of research published in this area, there are still many aspects of schizophrenia that remain elusive. The possibility of using psychological test data, such as that provided by the Minnesota Multiphasic Personality Inventory (MMPI: Dahlstrom, Welsh, & Dahlstrom, 1972), in order to gain a better understanding of schizophrenic patients is one area that requires further study. In an earlier review of the MMPI literature on schizophrenia, Walters (1983) found a large number of studies but a paucity of clinically meaningful results. This chapter reviews MMPI research on schizophrenia, with a focus on studies published since the earlier review (i.e., Walters, 1983), and also considers future research and clinical application of current MMPI-schizophrenia knowledge.

DIAGNOSTIC ISSUES AND MODERATOR VARIABLES

SCHIZOPHRENIC DIAGNOSIS

Kraepelin (1919) was the first theorist to consider a connection between hebephrenia, catatonia, and paranoia and is usually credited with identifying schizophrenia as a psychiatric syndrome. He viewed dementia praecox, his term for the disorder, as involving early and insidious onset with associated intellectual and emotional deterioration. Thus, the landmarks of schizophrenia, according to Kraepelin, were a gradually deteriorating course and poor prognosis.

The next major theorist in the area of schizophrenic diagnosis, Bleuler (1950), not only introduced the term *schizophrenia* into the psychiatric nomenclature but also delineated primary and secondary symptoms. Bleuler also believed strongly in the pathognomonic sign approach to diagnosis that postulates that a fixed set of signs or symptoms are specific to a particular diagnosis. As Table 3–1 clearly illustrates, Bleuler hypothesized that there were four pathognomonic

THE MMPI: USE WITH
SPECIFIC POPULATIONS

© 1988 by Grune & Stratton.

ISBN   0-8089-1913-X

TABLE 3–1. SIGNS AND SYMPTOMS OF FOUR SYSTEMS OF SCHIZOPHRENIC DIAGNOSIS

	Pathognomonic Approach (Bleuler, 1950)	First-Rank Symptoms (Schneider, 1959)	Symptom Clusters (Yusin et al., 1974)	Flexible System (Carpenter et al., 1973)
Common Symptoms	Ambivalence Flat or inappropriate affect Loose associations	Audible thoughts Voices arguing Voices commenting	Ambivalence Delusions Hallucinations Loose associations	Restricted affect Thoughts aloud Widespread delusions
Unique Symptoms	Autism	Delusional perception "Made" affect "Made" impulses "Made" volition Thought broadcasting Thought insertion Thought withdrawal Somatic passivity	Loss of ego boundaries Withdrawal	Bizarre delusions[a] Depressed facies (-) Elation (-) Incoherent speech Nihilistic delusions Poor insight Poor rapport Unreliable information Waking early (-)

Note: Common symptoms are signs or symptoms shared by two or more of these four diagnostic systems; unique symptoms are specific to that particular system.

[a](-) Signifies that the *absence* of this sign or symptom is thought to be diagnostic of schizophrenia.

signs or symptoms specific to schizophrenia. While this system has both theoretical and historical value, it is lacking in clinical usefulness due to the fact that it is so difficult to operationalize.

One of the more popular pathognomonic approaches to schizophrenic diagnosis is the one proposed by Schneider (1959). Schneider proposed a system of 11 pathognomonic signs, or First Rank Symptoms (FRS), that he felt were predictive of a schizophrenic diagnosis (see Table 3–1). While this system yields reasonably reliable diagnoses (Fenton, Mosher, & Matthews, 1981), it is generally ineffective in predicting patient outcome or response to treatment (cf. Abrams & Taylor, 1973; Bland & Orn, 1980; Carpenter & Strauss, 1973, 1974; Hawk, Carpenter, & Strauss, 1975; Silverstein & Harrow, 1981; Stephens, Astrup, Carpenter, Schaffer, & Goldberg, 1982).

Dissatisfied with the limitations inherent in using a pathognomonic approach to schizophrenic diagnosis, Yusin, Nihira, and Mortashed (1974) developed a symptom cluster approach to the problem (see Table 3–1). The basic premise behind this approach is that it is the number or configural relationship of symptoms, not the presence of pathognomonic signs, that defines schizophrenia. Yusin et al. delineated both major and minor symptoms that in various combinations are thought to be indicative of schizophrenia. Newmark, Raft, Toomey, Hunter,

and Mazzaglia (1975) found that a discriminant function equation (also known as the Newmark cluster approach to schizophrenic diagnosis) containing four of the primary symptoms of Yusin et al. (i.e., loose associations, loss of ego boundaries, autism, delusions) correctly classified 97 percent of the patients in their cross-validation sample as either schizophrenic or nonschizophrenic.

Probably the most researched symptom cluster approach is the 12-sign "Flexible System" developed by Carpenter, Strauss, and Bartko (1973) (see Table 3–1). Carpenter et al. (1973) found that a cutting score of 5 (presence of five or more symptoms being indicative of schizophrenia) successfully identified 81 percent of the schizophrenics and 78 percent of the nonschizophrenics in their cross-validation sample. One of the primary advantages of the Flexible System is the ability to modify the inclusiveness of the system through manipulation of the cutting score, although cutting scores of 5 or 6 have traditionally been employed with this system. Fenton et al. (1981) found the reliability of the Flexible System to be adequate, although studies investigating its validity have been mixed (Hawk et al., 1975; Kendell, Brockington, & Leff, 1979; Stephens et al., 1982).

Research has tended to support the superiority of the symptom cluster approach over the pathognomonic sign approach. For instance, Newmark, Falk, Johns, Boren, and Forehand

(1976) evaluated the relative performance of several symptom cluster and pathognomonic sign approaches in discriminating between 108 schizophrenics and 227 nonschizophrenics. They determined that the two cluster systems (Yusin, Newmark) significantly outperformed the pathognomonic models (Bleuler, Schneider). Furthermore, Pope and Lipinski (1978) report that putative pathognomonic signs and symptoms of schizophrenia such as delusions, hallucinations, and Schneiderian FRS have been found in a relatively large number of patients with bipolar disorder diagnoses (20 to 50 percent), thus questioning the pathognomonic status of these symptoms.

Even though symptom cluster approaches to schizophrenic diagnosis have received far more empirical support than pathognomonic approaches, Pope and Lipinski (1978) argue that mental health professionals in the United States have placed far too much emphasis on "schizophrenic" symptomatology. According to Pope and Lipinski, this approach has resulted in an overdiagnosis of schizophrenia and an underdiagnosis of bipolar affective disorder. They argue further that not only are "schizophrenic symptoms" ineffective in discriminating between schizophrenic and bipolar patients, but that they do an inadequate job of predicting future outcome. Such findings have led to a number of changes in the way researchers conceptualize schizophrenia.

Developed independently, the St. Louis criteria (Feighner, Robins, Guze, Woodruff, Winokur, & Munoz, 1972) and Research Diagnostic Criteria (RDC: Spitzer, Endicott, & Robins, 1975) ushered in a new approach to diagnosing schizophrenia by considering symptom, as well as nonsymptom, data and reviving Kraepelin's emphasis on poor prognosis and a deteriorating course in defining this disorder. DSM-III (American Psychiatric Association, 1980) provides criteria for schizophrenia that are similar to the criteria established by Feighner et al. (1972) and Spitzer et al. (1975); like the earlier approaches, DSM-III considers both symptom (e.g., delusions, hallucinations, seriously disorganized thought) and nonsymptom (e.g., duration of at least 6 months, onset prior to age 45; absence of primary affective disturbance) types of information. Like the RDC and St. Louis criteria, DSM-III is also much narrower in

its definition of schizophrenia than was its predecessor, DSM-II (American Psychiatric Association, 1968). Although the DSM-III criteria for schizophrenia have not been widely investigated, preliminary research on its reliability and validity has produced encouraging results (see Fenton et al., 1981; Stephens et al., 1982).

The characteristics of schizophrenic patients used in MMPI research on schizophrenia have tended to vary as a function of when the study was conducted. The present author examined published MMPI research on schizophrenia and found that studies conducted prior to 1980 (pre-DSM-III) contained mostly white, male inpatients who had been previously hospitalized. Researchers in these earlier studies typically employed a broad definition of schizophrenia and relied heavily on clinical diagnosis as a criterion against which the usefulness of the MMPI was assessed. The average patient in these studies was approximately 34 years old, reasonably well educated (mean educational level, 11 years), and of average to slightly-above-average intelligence.

Because DSM-III adheres to a much narrower definition of schizophrenia than its predecessors, studies published since 1980 have characteristically included more homogeneous groups of schizophrenic patients. Subjects in these later studies have also tended to be fairly well educated (mean educational level, 11.5 years) and of average intellectual ability. While the majority of subjects in these studies were white males, a larger number of females, blacks, and hispanics have been included in these studies than was the case in some of the earlier studies. Despite the rather restrictive nature of a DSM-III diagnosis of schizophrenia, post-DSM-III subjects have tended to be younger (mean age, 26 years) in comparison with their pre-DSM-III counterparts. This somewhat paradoxical finding may reflect a tendency on the part of post-DSM-III researchers to study schizophrenic patients originating from less chronic settings (e.g., acute psychiatric units) than those sampled by earlier researchers (i.e., state and VA inpatient facilities).

One issue that this review of "typical" patient characteristics points out is that the samples used have often not been representative of the vast majority of schizophrenic patients, particularly in terms of education and intelligence. MMPI researchers have tended to study schizophrenic patients possessing close to a high school education and average intellectual ability. While this is understandable given the fact that at least a sixth-grade education is required to obtain valid MMPI results, this level of education and ability is superior to that which is characteristic of most schizophrenic patients (cf. Neale & Oltmanns, 1980). This has tended to limit the generalizability of much of the research in this area.

Another issue important to consider when discussing diagnosis is that of base rates. Meehl and Rosen (1955) recommend that the performance of a particular measure, like an MMPI scale or index, be compared with the level of accuracy achieved simply through knowledge of the criterion diagnoses' prevalence in the population under study. For instance, if a T-score of 70 or higher on Scale 8 (Sc) of the MMPI accurately identifies 70 percent of the schizophrenics in a setting where only 25 percent of the patients are schizophrenic, then reliance on the base rate would yield more accurate results (hit rate, 75 percent) than use of Scale 8. The base rate becomes increasingly more difficult to "beat" the narrower the diagnostician's definition of schizophrenia becomes. Thus, while a DSM-II diagnosis of schizophrenia may yield a base rate (within a general psychiatric population) of from 25 to 40 percent schizophrenic, this base rate figure shrinks to somewhere between 15 and 25 percent when DSM-III criteria are used. If the MMPI, either in isolation or in combination with other measures, cannot improve on the simple base rate prediction that all patients will be non-schizophrenic (which will yield a hit rate of 75 percent), then its clinical utility in such situations is brought into serious question.

MODERATOR VARIABLES

Moderator variables are variables that could potentially modify the relationship between two or more variables, in this case, the MMPI and schizophrenia. The effect of five of these variables—age, sex, race, education, and marital status—on schizophrenic MMPIs will be reviewed.

Age

In one of the earliest MMPI studies conducted using schizophrenic patients, Wauck (1950) ob-

served a "leveling off" of MMPI scores with advancing age. Specifically, he noted a tendency on the part of older (40- to 53-year-old) schizophrenics to produce MMPI profiles that approached "normality." Davis (1972) observed a similar phenomenon when he contrasted young (18- to 28-year-old) and old (45- to 56-year-old) schizophrenics and nonschizophrenics. Davis reported that while young schizophrenics and nonschizophrenics produced significantly different scores on several MMPI scales, older schizophrenics and nonschizophrenics failed to differ on even one scale. He concluded that the MMPI loses its discriminative power as patients grow older and speculated that this is due to a greater commonality in the life experiences of older subjects, regardless of their diagnostic status.

Since the results of the Davis (1972) study may have been due to increased chronicity in the older group, Davis, Mozdzierz, and Macchitelli (1973) studied this question in an "acute" treatment setting. Like Davis (1972), they found significant MMPI differences between young (ages 18 to 29) schizophrenics and nonschizophrenics but not between older (ages 45 to 57) schizophrenics and nonschizophrenics. These results suggest that the leveling off of MMPI scores in schizophrenics of advancing age is probably not due to chronicity or long-term hospitalization. It should be noted, however, that the notion of schizophrenia developing after age 45 is incompatible with present day knowledge (see Strauss & Carpenter, 1981) and actually rules against a DSM-III diagnosis of schizophrenia. Several other researchers have also observed MMPI differences in schizophrenics as a function of age (Davis & Gustafson, 1971; Miller & Paciello, 1980).

Newmark, Gentry, Simpson, and Jones (1978) developed an MMPI decision index comprised of the following four rules: (1) T-score on Scale 8 (Sc) $\geq 80 \leq 100$; (2) T-score on Scale $F \geq 75 \leq 95$; (3) T-score on Scale 8 (Sc) $\geq$ Scale 7 (Pt); and (4) K items contribute no more than 35 percent to the Scale 8 (Sc) raw score. According to Newmark et al., a diagnosis of schizophrenia is indicated when all four rules or criteria are satisfied. They found that 72 percent of the male and 71 percent of the female schizophrenics in their sample achieved all four criteria, whereas only 5.5 percent of the nonschizophrenic controls did so. However, Newmark, Gentry, and Whitt (1983) determined that this index identified only 23 percent of a group of schizophrenic adolescents, ages 14 to 19, while Newmark and Hutchins (1980) noted that it accurately identified only 26 percent of a group of older schizophrenics (ages 44 to 54). Thus, while the usefulness of the Newmark et al. (1978) MMPI index has been demonstrated with young adults, ages 20 to 40 (Newmark, Jones, McKee, Simpson, Boren, & Prillaman, 1980), its utility appears to be quite seriously limited when applied to adolescents and older adults.

Gender

Only a few studies have investigated potential gender differences on the MMPIs of schizophrenic patients. While age differences have been noted on the Newmark et al. (1978) index, there is no evidence that male and female schizophrenics score differently on this measure (cf. Newmark et al., 1978; Newmark, Gentry, Warren, & Finch, 1981; Newmark, Gentry, & Whitt, 1983; Newmark & Hutchins, 1980). Wauck (1950) also failed to find significant MMPI differences between male and female schizophrenics. Gottesman and Shields (1972), on the other hand, assert that sexual identification—as measured by Scale 5 (*Mf*) of the MMPI—appears disturbed in male but not female schizophrenics. Additionally, Haier, Rosenthal, and Wender (1978) witnessed more highly elevated MMPI scores in a sample of schizophrenia spectrum males relative to a group of schizophrenia spectrum females. Finally, while Sillitti (1982) discovered that the MMPI was more effective in discriminating between female, as opposed to male, schizophrenic and organic patients, Watson and Thomas (1968) reported that a series of four MMPI rules successfully discriminated between schizophrenic and organic males but failed to differentiate between schizophrenic and organic females. Hence, whereas male-female differences have been noted on the MMPIs of schizophrenic patients, the actual impact of gender on the MMPI in these cases is uncertain. Nonetheless, Eichman (1959) felt these differences to be significant enough to develop a set of MMPI-schizophrenia rules for use with female psychiatric patients.

Ethnicity

Newmark et al. (1981) set out to investigate the differential impact of ethnicity and sex on the Newmark et al. (1978) MMPI index in a sample of 200 schizophrenic patients (50 white schizophrenic males, 50 black schizophrenic males, 50 white schizophrenic females, 50 black schizophrenic females). Criterion diagnoses were established through use of a structured diagnostic interview and the Newmark et al. (1975) cluster system. There were no statistically significant ethnic differences noted in terms of the number of patients correctly identified by this MMPI index, although black male schizophrenics tended to be misidentified more often than white male schizophrenics.

Clark and Miller (1971) examined the behavioral correlates of a sample of black VA patients achieving the *8-6* MMPI high-point profile. Although few differences were noted between these correlates and those derived by Gilberstadt and Duker (1965) in a sample of white VA patients (e.g., black patients reported more "odd" or "bizzare" experiences relative to white patients), the cardinal features of a paranoid schizophrenic process were present in both. Several other studies have found ethnic variations on the MMPIs of various groups of schizophrenics, but these effects often appear to be moderated by differences in education (see Davis, Beck, & Ryan, 1973). For a more comprehensive review of the effects of ethnicity on MMPI performance the reader is referred to Dahlstrom, Lachar, and Dahlstrom (1986) or Greene (1987).

Education

While the effect of education on the MMPI performance of schizophrenic patients has not been studied in isolation, it has received a fair amount of attention in terms of its impact on the relationship between ethnicity and MMPI performance. Davis and his colleagues (Davis, 1975; Davis, Beck, & Ryan, 1973; Davis & Jones, 1974) discovered that ethnic-related MMPI differences often disappear when a patient's educational level is taken into account. For instance, Davis and Jones (1974) considered the effects of ethnicity (black, white), education (≥ 12 years vs. < 12 years), and diagnosis (schizophrenic vs.

nonschizophrenic) on MMPI performance. They found that blacks with less education earned higher scores on Scales 6 (*Pa*) and 8 (*Sc*) relative to better educated blacks and whites at both levels of education. Thus, while there may be problems with ethnic bias on the MMPI when less-educated black patients are being considered, there is little evidence of bias in blacks possessing a high school education or better.

Cowan, Watkins, and Davis (1975) classified a series of MMPI profiles generated by black and white schizophrenic and nonschizophrenic patients of high (≥ 12 years) and low (< 12 years) education using two MMPI classification rules: (1) Scale 8 (*Sc*) T-score > 70; (2) Scale 8 (*Sc*) > Scale 7 (*Pt*). Patients satisfying both rules were classified as schizophrenic, while satisfaction of one or neither of these rules was considered indicative of nonschizophrenia. Cowan et al. found that all but the poorly educated black patients were classified at a level that significantly exceeded chance expectations. They speculated that these results reflect the fact that education may exert an enculturating effect on the MMPI responses of black patients.

Marital Status

Lacks, Rothenberg, and Unger (1970) examined the MMPI response patterns of single, married, and divorced schizophrenic inpatients. Married patients earned significantly higher Scale 9 (*Ma*) scores relative to single patients and significantly lower Scale 4 (*Pd*) scores in comparison with divorced patients. However, these were the only two statistically significant results out of the 30 separate *t*–tests calculated. Thus, there is a reasonably good possibility that these findings surfaced simply as a function of chance fluctuations in the data.

A relatively strong relationship has been noted between marital status and outcome in the literature on schizophrenia (cf. Klorman, Strauss, & Kokes, 1977). Newmark, Gentry, Whitt, McKee, and Wicker (1983) found that married schizophrenics displayed a much better ability to simulate "normal" MMPI profiles than unmarried schizophrenics and that such simulation was a good prognostic sign. These findings suggest that married schizophrenics are better able to assume a "nondeviant" perspective than are unmarried schizophrenics, which may eventually translate

into better outcome on the part of patients in the latter group.

METHODOLOGIC ISSUES

As a means of pointing out some of the methodologic issues associated with MMPI research on schizophrenia, a recent MMPI study will be reviewed and then referenced relative to some of these issues. Saccuzzo, Braff, Sprock, and Sudik (1984) set out to examine the relationship between visual masking, psychological test data, and schizophrenia spectrum diagnoses. Employing criterion diagnoses established through use of the RDC and DSM-III, Saccuzzo et al. contrasted 20 schizophrenia spectrum patients to 20 nonschizophrenia spectrum psychiatric patients matched on the basis of age, sex, and intelligence. All patients were administered the MMPI, Rorschach, and a visual backward masking task. Although schizophrenia spectrum patients performed significantly worse than the controls on the backward masking task, there were no significant MMPI differences and only one Rorschach difference (Deviant Verbalizations) between the two groups. A factor analysis was conducted on some of the test data and revealed a four-factor solution.

Saccuzzo et al. (1984) concluded that although there were no significant MMPI differences between their two groups, there was a relationship between Deviant Verbalizations on the Rorschach, performance on a visual backward masking task, and schizophrenia spectrum disorders. They add that the Rorschach Deviant Verbalization measure holds promise as an inexpensive aid in the diagnosis of schizophrenia spectrum disorders. Although this study does not shed much light on the MMPI characteristics of schizophrenic patients, it does serve to illustrate a number of methodologic points, issues, and concerns relevant to MMPI research on schizophrenia.

CRITERION DIAGNOSES

An important methodologic issue to consider when evaluating an MMPI study on schizophrenia is the criterion diagnoses utilized. Many of the studies in the past have used a rather loose approach to diagnosis and relied heavily on clinical judgment as a means of establishing criterion diagnoses. Such an approach, however, is no longer appropriate in that a wide array of more structured diagnostic measures are now available. For instance, in the Saccuzzo et al. (1984) study both the DSM-III and RDC criteria were employed by two mental health professionals working independently. While this procedure is reasonably sound, a structured diagnostic interview, like the Schedule for Affective Disorders and Schizophrenia (SADS: Endicott & Spitzer, 1978) or Psychiatric Diagnostic Interview (PDI: Othmer, Penick, & Powell, 1981), would provide a more standardized, reliable set of criterion diagnoses.

CRITERION CONTAMINATION

One common methodologic problem in MMPI research on schizophrenia has been a lack of independence between the criterion diagnoses and MMPI. For instance, physicians providing criterion diagnoses in the study conducted by Roy (1984) had access to a psychologist's interpretation of the MMPI profile prior to making their diagnoses, thus potentially contaminating the subsequent results. Saccuzzo et al. (1984), on the other hand, made certain that diagnosticians were unaware of the MMPI results of patients in their sample, thus assuring independence between predictor and criterion. While the actual impact of prior knowledge about MMPI results on the criterion diagnoses is unknown, it will most likely lead to a spuriously inflated estimate of that particular scale's predictive value.

Related to this issue of criterion contamination is the problem of shared method variance. As pointed out by Campbell and Fiske (1959) in their discussion of method variance, similar methods will produce similar results simply as a function of their shared variance. Neziroglou (1975) observed correlations in the neighborhood of .50 between a paper-and-pencil test designed to screen for the presence of schizophrenic thinking (i.e., the Hoffer-Osmond Diagnostic Test) and MMPI Scales 6 (*Pa*) and 8 (*Sc*) in a sample of schizophrenic patients. While this is a reasonably strong relationship, the correlation may have been inflated somewhat by the fact that both measures are paper-and-pencil tests and follow a true-false format. Needless to say,

researchers should strive to maintain independence between the predictor (MMPI) and criterion (diagnosis) and should avoid using measures that share significant amounts of method variance in common.

CONTROL GROUPS

A control or comparison group (or groups) is a necessary, although not sufficient, condition to achieve methodologic control over a set of research data. Some of the early work on schizophrenia and the MMPI simply evaluated the MMPI performance of schizophrenics without the aid of any sort of control or comparison group (e.g., Wauck, 1950). Other studies have used inadequate or inappropriate controls, such as normal individuals (e.g., Benarick, Guthrie, & Snyder, 1951). Still other researchers have employed control groups that differed significantly from the schizophrenic patients on important variables like the inclusiveness of the criterion diagnoses (see Aaronson and Welsh's [1950] criticisms of Rubin [1948]). Saccuzzo et al. (1984) contrasted schizophrenia spectrum inpatients to nonschizophrenia spectrum patients from the same setting. While this approach is adequate, investigators should make more of an effort to select control patients whose degree or severity of symptomatology is comparable with that experienced by the schizophrenic individuals in their studies. Such control groups might include schizophreniform patients, patients with bipolar affective difficulties, or those suffering signs of major depression (see Walters, 1984a; Winters, Newmark, Lumry, Leach, & Weintraub, 1985).

MODERATOR VARIABLES

The potential impact of moderator variables also must be considered in developing an optimal level of control over the research data. At a minimum, potential group differences on such variables as age, sex, education, and ethnicity need to be considered and, if present, controlled for in some manner. Thus, if initial group differences exist on certain moderator variables and such variables are found to correlate significantly with the MMPI results, then a researcher might choose to either match the groups on these variables, restrict the range of these variables, convert these moderator variables into independent variables, or statistically control for these initial group differences through a procedure like analysis of covariance or the partial correlation coefficient. Saccuzzo et al. (1984) considered a number of moderator variables in their study on the schizophrenia spectrum and attempted to match (as closely as they could) their non-schizophrenic controls to the 20 schizophrenic index cases on the basis of age, sex, and verbal intelligence (WAIS Vocabulary score). However, they did not consider race or ethnicity in their analysis.

SUBJECT TESTABILITY

A methodologic issue often overlooked by researchers working in the personality assessment field is that of patient testability. In regards to the MMPI, subjects need adequate reading skills if the researcher desires reasonably valid and reliable results (see Greene, 1980), although there are several additional aspects of patient testability that also need to be considered. For instance, Wilensky and Solomon (1960) studied a group of 36 paranoid schizophrenic patients and found that only 25 were testable on at least one of the three measures administered (i.e., portions of the Wechsler Adult Intelligence Scale [WAIS], a tapping test, and the Rorschach); one schizophrenic was untestable on the basis of confusion and ten refused to take part in the testing. Wilensky and Solomon concluded that test results, particularly those derived from samples of schizophrenic patients, represent a biased estimate of the overall population of patients. Although it is difficult, if not impossible, to obtain valid test results on all potential patients in a study, researchers should at least report on the number of patients who failed to take part in the testing due to poor reading skills, mental confusion, or lack of cooperation. Unfortunately, such information is reported only infrequently by investigators conducting research in this area, the Saccuzzo et al. (1984) study being a case in point.

Hospitalization may also exert a significant impact on MMPI performance. Mednick and McNeil (1968) suggest that there are at least two ways in which hospitalization potentially influences psychological test results: (1) through influencing the patient's attitudes, beliefs, or personality in such a manner as to produce changes in the test results, and (2) by leading the patient to bias his or her responses in a manner that satisfies a personal motive concerning future hospital status. Thus, one needs to control for both the type and length of hospitalization. As Zigler, Levine, and Zigler (1976) point out, disparate inpatient settings attract different types of patients and probably influence patients differentially. Saccuzzo et al. (1984) utilized schizophrenia spectrum and control subjects from the same inpatient facility, but like many of the researchers in this area, they failed to discuss whether there were group differences as to the length of hospitalization. Future researchers need to be mindful of the fact that the presence, length, and nature of psychiatric hospitalization can have a major impact on the MMPI results; such information needs to be reported routinely and, it is hoped, controlled.

ASSESSING THE VALIDITY OF AN MMPI PROTOCOL

There are several ways in which the veracity of an MMPI protocol can be evaluated. First, investigators should consider the number of items a respondent omits on the MMPI (Scale *?*) since this can have an important effect on the overall MMPI profile, i.e., by suppressing the different MMPI scale elevations (except for Scale *5* in females, which tends to be higher in protocols with a large number of omissions). Greene (1980) maintains that the number of omitted items should be less than 30 to have any degree of confidence in the MMPI results. Ruben (1948) made the mistake of including a large number of schizophrenics (21%) in his study who had omitted more than 100 items on the MMPI, thus leaving himself open to a number of legitimate criticisms (see Aaronson & Welsh, 1950).

Researchers also need to evaluate the consistency of a respondent's MMPI. The *T-R* Index (Greene, 1980) may be very useful in this regard since it provides the number of repeated MMPI items (out of a total of 16 items) answered inconsistently by the respondent (i.e., answering "true" to an item early in the test and then answering "false" when the item is repeated later in the test, or vice versa). Ideally, a patient's score on the *T-R* Index should be no greater than 4 (see Greene, 1980).

Third, elevations above a *T*-score of 70 or 80 on the standard MMPI validity scales can be taken as being indicative of an untruthful self-report. Elevations on Scale *F*, in particular, have been used to identify "invalid" MMPI profiles. However, Winters, Weintraub, and Neale's (1981) decision to exclude schizophrenic and affectively disordered patients from their study on the basis of an *F* score > 70 seems unduly conservative, particularly when one considers that Apfeldorf and Hunley (1975) have found that such a practice leads to a loss of important diagnostic information. Consequently, only extreme elevations on Scale *F* (i.e., ≥ *T*-score of 110) should ever be used to evaluate the veracity of an MMPI profile, particularly in schizophrenic samples where elevations on Scale *F* are quite common (Walters, 1983).

While researchers should avoid being overzealous in eliminating potential subjects from their studies on the basis of an "invalid" MMPI profile, certain criteria should be utilized (e.g., number of omitted items, *T-R* Index) and reported. Unfortunately, Saccuzzo et al. (1984) apparently failed to do either.

STATISTICAL PROCEDURES

Many of the researchers investigating the relationship between schizophrenia and the MMPI have used inappropriate statistical approaches in analyzing their data. For instance, Saccuzzo et al. (1984) compared schizophrenia spectrum and nonschizophrenia spectrum inmates on all 13 standard MMPI scales plus several Rorschach measures and then made several inferences about schizophrenia spectrum disorders based on the one Rorschach variable that achieved statistical significance. Since Saccuzzo et al. made no effort to control for the increase in the experiment-wise error rate that accompanies multiple comparisons, this one "significant" finding may have surfaced simply on the basis of chance. Rather than performing a large series of separate *t*-tests or chi-square analyses, researchers should consider using multivariate techniques like discriminant function analysis, multiple regression, factor analysis, and multivariate analysis of variance, or procedures like the Bonferroni technique that control for the inflation observed in the experiment-wise error rate when multiple comparisons are made.

Finally, in addition to evaluating the statistical significance of a set of research findings, the clinical significance of these findings also should be examined. All too often results are published that, while statistically significant, are of questionable clinical value. Researchers should establish the clinical significance of their data by examining the MMPI's ability to classify individual subjects.

STANDARD VALIDITY AND CLINICAL SCALES

SINGLE SCALE ELEVATIONS

Validity Scales

Schizophrenics have been found to score significantly higher on Scale *F* relative to general psychiatric patients (Braatz, 1970; Rosen, 1958), schizophreniform disorders (Walters, 1984a), patients with major affective diagnoses (Dahlstrom & Prange, 1960; Trifiletti, 1982; Walters, 1984a; Walters & Greene, 1988), and individuals with organic brain dysfunction (Golden, Sweet, & Osmon, 1979; Russell, 1977; Trifiletti, 1982). Although schizophrenics also tend to earn lower scores on Scales *L* and *K*, these differences are rarely statistically significant. Lewinsohn (1968) discovered that a group of hallucinating schizophrenics scored significantly higher on Scale *F* in comparison with a group of schizophrenic patients denying the presence of such hallucinations. Thus, schizophrenics, particularly those displaying symptoms suggestive of serious psychological decompensation (e.g., auditory hallucinations), report higher levels of psychological distress and discomfort on the MMPI validity scales relative to most other patient groups.

Studies comparing schizophrenic and borderline personality disorder patients have yielded results very different from those discussed above. It seems that borderline patients report even greater levels of confusion and psychological disorganization on the MMPI validity scales than do schizophrenic patients. For instance, using pre-DSM-III terminology, Harding, Holz, and Kawakami (1958) found that schizophrenic patients scored higher than a group of "acutely decompensated character disorders," many of whom could probably have been diagnosed Borderline Personality Disorder using DSM-III criteria, on Scales *L* and *K*. Edell (1987) and Evans, Ruff, Braff, and Ainsworth (1984) also have found significantly higher Scale *L* scores in schizophrenics when groups of DSM-III-defined schizophrenic and borderline patients are compared.

Clinical Scales

When schizophrenic and general psychiatric patients are compared on the MMPI, schizophrenics usually score higher on the majority of clinical scales. Dahlstrom and Prange (1960), for example, found that schizophrenic patients scored significantly higher than a group of depressed patients on 7 of the MMPI's 10 clinical scales, with Scales *5* (*Mf*), *7* (*Pt*), and *0* (*Si*) showing no difference. Rosen (1958) and Walters (1984a) also report that schizophrenics achieve significantly higher scores on the majority of clinical scales when they are viewed relative to general psychiatric patients. Again, the primary exception to this pattern occurs when schizophrenic and borderline patients are compared. Evans et al. (1984) found that a group of inpatient borderline personality disorders achieved significantly higher scores on Scales *2* (*D*), *3* (*Hy*), *4* (*Pd*), and *7* relative to a group of schizophrenic patients, with no group differences on any of the remaining clinical scales. Edell (1987) reports similar results; his borderline patients scored significantly higher on Scales *2*, *3*, *4*, and *0* in comparison with a group of "early schizophrenics."

Walters (1983) concluded on the basis of existing research data that while there are problems associated with using Scale *8* (*Sc*) as a diagnostic predictor, Scale *8* is a prominent point on many schizophrenic profiles and probably the single best MMPI correlate of schizophrenia currently available. More recently published research also tends to support this contention (cf. Page, 1982; Walters, 1984a; Walters & Greene, 1988). In addition, several studies exploring the MMPI's ability to discriminate between schizophrenic and organic patients have found Scale *8* to be as effective, if not more so, in making these determinations relative to a group of "special" MMPI scales constructed specifically for this purpose

(see Ayers, Templer, & Ruff, 1975; Golden et al., 1979; Sillitti, 1982).

Walters (1984b) used Scale *8* (*Sc*) to differentiate between 38 schizophrenic, 38 non-schizophrenic schizophrenia spectrum (schizophreniform and schizotypal personality disorder), and 38 general psychiatric control patients matched on the basis of age and gender. Schizophrenics achieved significantly higher scores on Scale *8* in comparison with patients in the other two groups, regardless of whether *K*- or non-*K*-corrected *T*-scores were employed. However, only the *K*-corrected scores yielded statistically significant results when individual patients were classified according to their scores on Scale *8* (i.e., if *8* $\geq$ *T*-score of 70, then diagnose schizophrenia; this rule yields an overall hit rate of 61 percent). These results suggest that *K*-corrected Scale *8* scores should probably be retained for use with psychiatric samples, particularly in light of the fact that the vast majority of research conducted on Scale *8* has employed *K*-corrected, rather than non-*K*-corrected, scores.

Understanding the internal characteristics or factor structure of a particular scale or measure is important in assessing its usefulness. Employing a large sample of subjects from five different clinical settings, Greene (1981) performed a factor analysis on Scale *8*. His results corroborated Comrey and Marggraff's (1958) earlier findings, conducted on a subsample of Scale *8* items. Major factors replicated across the two studies included: paranoia, poor concentration, poor physical health, psychotic tendencies, and sex concern. However, Greene (1981) found very little correspondence between his factors and those that Harris and Lingoes (1955) derived on the basis of item content.

Several authors have examined the construct validity of Scale *8* (*Sc*). Higgins, Mednick, and Philip (1965), for instance, found that Scale *8* correlated moderately well with a measure of life adjustment (i.e., higher Scale *8* scores being associated with poorer social and psychological adjustment) in a sample of schizophrenic inpatients. Fishkin, Lovello, and Pishkin (1977), on the other hand, determined that the Whitaker Index of Schizophrenic Thinking (WIST) correlated with Scale *8* in a group of "process," but not "reactive," schizophrenic inpatients. Cauthen, Sandman, Kilpatrick, and Deabler (1969) observed an even stronger relationship between

Scale *8* and the "bizarreness" or "immaturity" of human figure drawings. While the Cauthen et al. study took place in a VA hospital, the majority of subjects were nonschizophrenic. Finally, Keane and Gibbs (1980) explored the relationship between Scale *8* and a word association task in a group of 92 university students. They found that students generating high Scale *8* scores evidenced more pathologic associations relative to students whose scores on Scale *8* were within normal limits. Therefore, while high scores on Scale *8* do not always portend serious psychopathology (see Greene, 1980), used properly this scale may eventually be useful in denoting potential disturbances in the cognitive processing ability of psychiatric patients.

HIGH-POINT PAIRS

Table 3–2 outlines the studies providing information on the high-point correlates of schizophrenia and schizophreniform disorder. The modal high-point code in 8 of the 10 studies was the *6-8/8-6* pair. Although the mean frequency of the *6-8/8-6* combination in these 10 studies is only 16 percent, this exceeds its average frequency in nonschizophrenic samples (4.4 percent) by more than 11 percentage points. Thus, while the majority of schizophrenic patients do not achieve the *6-8/8-6* high-point pair, when observed, this combination is a fairly good indicator of a schizophrenic diagnosis (overall accuracy of 80 percent is achieved if the schizophrenic:nonschizophrenic ratio is even). Several investigators have found a diagnosis of schizophrenia to be two to three times more likely if Scale *8* (*Sc*) is elevated over Scale *6* (*Pa*), rather than the other way around, in patients achieving the *6-8/8-6* pattern (cf. Davies, Nichols, & Greene, 1985; Hathaway & Meehl, 1951).

Methodologically, the nine studies containing information on the MMPI high-point pair correlates of schizophrenia were reasonably successful in terms of providing basic subject/patient characteristics, specifying their diagnostic criteria, and analyzing their data using appropriate statistical procedures. These studies are largely inadequate, however, when it comes to considering the effects of moderator variables, assessing the "validity" of MMPI protocols, and employing sufficiently large sample sizes. These results reflect the general methodologic state of MMPI research on schizophrenia, which, unfortunately, is not as strong as it could be.

One thing the present author discovered while reviewing available research on the MMPI high-point correlates of schizophrenia was that there is a scarcity of information on this topic. In fact, it was necessary to communicate further with several of the original researchers whose work was reviewed here in order to complete Table 3–2 as fully as possible. Although, as Holland, Levi, and Watson (1981) point out, exclusive reliance on high-point data often results in a significant loss of diagnostic information, consideration of high-point pairs or triads can still prove useful. Investigators, as well as journal editors, need to be mindful of this and work to include high-point information, whenever possible, in future MMPI publications on schizophrenia.

CONFIGURAL PATTERNS

There have been several attempts made by researchers and clinicians to assess the configural pattern of MMPI scale relationships found with schizophrenic patients. For instance, some interpreters believe that a "saw-toothed" profile, whereby elevations are observed on Scales *2* (*D*), *4* (*Pd*), *6* (*Pa*), and *8* (*Sc*), suggest very serious psychological disturbance, perhaps even schizophrenia (see Greene, 1980). However, very little research has addressed this issue and the few investigations that have been conducted are not generally supportive of this position (see Graham, 1987; Greene, 1980).

The MMPI "floating" profile (see Newmark & Sines, 1972) is a second configural pattern that has characteristics thought to be potentially diagnostic of schizophrenia. The floating profile is said to exist when MMPI Scales *1* (*Hs*) through *9* (*Ma*) are all elevated (*T*-scores ≥ 70). Research on the diagnostic correlates of the floating profile, however, suggests that such profiles are more closely associated with personality disorder diagnoses, like the borderline personality disorder, than they are with schizophrenia (Edinger, Burnett, Hoffman, & Katranides, 1983; Newmark, Chassin, Evans, & Gentry, 1984). In fact, Newmark, Chassin, Gentry, and Evans (1983) found a noticeable absence of schizophrenic diagnoses in a group of psychiatric patients producing floating MMPI profiles. There has yet

TABLE 3–2. FREQUENCY OF MMPI CODETYPES IN SCHIZOPHRENIC PATIENTS

Authors	N	Age	Codetype			
			2-4/4-2	2-8/8-2	4-6/6-4	4-8/8-4
Dahlstrom & Prange (1960) [M&F]	50	36	8.0	5.0	10.6	4.0
Davies et al. (1985) [M&F]	99	30	2.0	12.1	8.1	10.1
Edell (1987) [M&F]	30	22	3.3	6.7	0.0	6.7
Gilberstadt (1975)	20	–	15.0	5.0	0.0	0.0
Hathaway & Meehl (1951) [M&F]	161	–		4.3		4.0
Holland et al. (1981)	150	42	8.7	12.0		6.7
Walters (1984a)	40	24	2.5	7.5	2.5	12.5
Walters (1984a)[a]	71	23	2.8	14.1	1.4	5.6
Walters (1986)	34	36		5.8	2.9	20.6
Winters et al. (1981) [M&F]	35	42		5.2	8.6	2.9
Winters et al. (1985) [M&F]	34	28		2.9	8.8	26.5
Weighted Totals			5.7	8.3	5.4	7.8

	Codetype				Methodological Issues								
	6-8/8-6	7-8/8-7	8-9/9-8	Total	A	B	C	D	E	F	G	H	I
Dahlstrom & Prange (1960) [M&F]	13.6	6.0	3.0	50.2	+	+	+	-	-	-	-	-	-
Davies et al. (1985) [M&F]	21.2	4.0	0.0	57.5	+	+	+	-	-	+	+	-	-
Edell (1987) [M&F]	16.7	6.7	6.7	46.8	+	+	-	-	+	-	+	-	-
Gilberstadt (1975)	5.0	15.0	5.0	45.0	-	-	-	-	-	-	+	-	-
Hathaway & Meehl (1951) [M&F]	12.2			20.5	-	-	-	-	-	+	-	-	-
Holland et al. (1981)	4.0	6.7	4.0	42.1	+	-	-	+	+	+	+	-	-
Walters (1984a)	27.5	7.5	15.0	75.0	+	+	+	+	+	-	+	-	-
Walters (1984a)[a]	12.7	7.0	12.7	56.3	+	+	+	+	+	-	+	-	-
Walters (1986)	20.6	5.8	5.8	61.5	+	+	+	-	-	-	+	-	-
Winters et al. (1981) [M&F]	14.3		5.7	36.7	+	+	+	-	+	-	+	-	-
Winters et al. (1985) [M&F]	29.4	5.9	14.7	88.2	+	+	-	+	+	-	+	-	-
Weighted Totals	14.0	6.4	6.1	58.2									

[a]This patient sample consisted of schizophreniform patients.

to be an MMPI configural pattern identified that has any reasonable degree of diagnostic relevance to schizophrenia.

SPECIAL/RESEARCH SCALES AND INDICES

Butcher and Tellegen (1978) report that there are now more MMPI scales than items. They add, dishearteningly, that the majority of these scales were inadequately derived and most have never been cross-validated. In an attempt to prevent these mistakes from being repeated in future research investigations, Butcher and Tellegen offer five recommendations to those researchers interested in adding to the already immense array of MMPI special scales presently available: (1) determine whether the MMPI item pool adequately covers the content area to be measured, in this case schizophrenia—since schizophrenia was one of the areas early developers of the MMPI were interested in measuring, most MMPI special scales and indices designed to assess schizophrenia would appear to satisfy this point; (2) determine whether their scale is conceptually interesting; (3) determine whether the derivation and cross-validation samples are adequate in terms of size and definition; (4) determine whether the internal consistency of the scale has been examined, through factor analysis, the alpha coefficient, or some other measure of internal consistency; and (5) determine whether the scale has any predictive value and whether it correlates with behaviorally mediated external criteria.

TABLE 3–3.   SPECIAL/RESEARCH SCALES FOR USE WITH SCHIZOPHRENIC POPULATIONS

Scale	Reference	Cross-Validational Research	Overall Accuracy		Butcher-Tellegen Criteria				
			Range	Md	1	2	3	4	5
Critical item *Sc*	Benarick et al. (1951)	Quay & Rowell (1955); Rubin (1954)	59–78	62	+	+	-	-	-
Pz; Pz + 1K	Rosen (1962)	Gottesman & Shields (1972); Davies et al. (1985)	54–79	66	+	+	+	-	-

Note: For Butcher-Tellegen criteria: *1* = construct appropriately sampled by MMPI; *2* = scale conceptually interesting; *3* = sample properly defined; *4* = internal consistency data; *5* = external validation and/or predictive value.

Several special scales and indices have been developed from the MMPI items and standard scale combinations, respectively, in an attempt to facilitate the clinician's ability to identify schizophrenia in various populations. The special/research scales relevant to schizophrenia are listed in Table 3–3 and the indices in Table 3–4. The degree of diagnostic accuracy achieved by each of these scales and indices, along with how each scale/index fares according to Butcher and Tellegen's five methodologic recommendations, can also be found in Tables 3–3 and 3–4. Methodologic point number *3* (internal consistency), however, will not be applied to the MMPI indices since these measures are composed of various scale combinations rather than items.

SPECIAL SCALES

Benarick et al. (1951) developed a "critical item *Sc*" scale by contrasting male psychotics to 30 "normal" college males matched on the basis of Scale *8* (*Sc*) scores. The 11 items that successfully discriminated between these two groups were organized into a special MMPI scale, the "critical item *Sc*." Besides the fact that Benarick et al. made the mistake of comparing hospitalized psychiatric patients with nonhospitalized college students, this scale has not received subsequent cross-validational support (see Quay & Rowell, 1955; Rubin, 1954). While Rosen's (1962) Paranoid Schizophrenia (*Pz*) scale was developed using a more appropriate control group (i.e., non-

TABLE 3–4.   MMPI INDICES FOR USE WITH SCHIZOPHRENIC POPULATIONS

Index	Reference	Cross-Validational Research	Overall Accuracy		Butcher-Tellegen Criteria			
			Range	Md	1	2	3	5
Peterson signs	Meehl (1946); Peterson (1954)	Affleck & Garfield (1960); Briggs (1958); Giannetti et al. (1978); Goldberg (1965); Goodson & King (1976); Grace (1964); Haier et al. (1978); Johnson et al. (1970); Taulbee & Sisson (1957); Walton et al. (1959); Winter & Stortroen (1963)	61–81	67	+	+	+	+
Taulbee-Sisson signs	Taulbee & Sisson (1957)	Garfield & Sineps (1959); Giannetti et al. (1978); Goldberg (1965); Taulbee (1958); Winter & Stortroen (1963)	54–88	66	+	+	-	-
Meehl-Dahlstrom Rules	Meehl & Dahlstrom (1960)	Giannetti et al. (1978); Goldberg (1965); Goodson & King (1976); Ritter (1974); Winter & Stortroen (1963)	53–90	61	+	+	+	-
L + Pa + Sc - Hy - Pt	Goldberg (1965)	Giannetti et al. (1978); Goodson & King (1976); Henrichs (1964); Holland & Watson (1978); Roy (1984)	55–75	66	+	+	-	+
Newmark index	Newmark et al. (1978)	Newmark et al. (1981); Newmark, Gentry, & Whitt (1983); Newmark & Hutchinsons (1980); Newmark et al. (1980)	22–72	46	+	+	+	-

Note: For Butcher-Tellegen criteria: *1* = construct appropriately sampled by MMPI; *2* = scale conceptually interesting; *3* = sample properly defined; *5* = external validation and/or predictive value.

schizophrenic psychiatric inpatients), it too has received very little empirical corroboration, not to mention a complete absence of data on the scale's internal consistency and predictive value.

Several special scales have been developed as a means of differentiating between schizophrenic and organic type disorders. Specially derived scales like the *Sc-0* (Watson, 1971) and *P-0* (Watson & Plemel, 1978) scales have received a fair amount of research support, discriminating between schizophrenic and organic patients at a rate of 65 to 75 percent (see Watson, 1984). However, these scales rarely outperform Scale *8* (*Sc*) (see Ayer et al., 1975; Golden et al., 1979; Sillitti, 1982). They also have been found inefficient in separating schizophrenics with and without positive neurologic signs (Holland, Lowenfeld, & Wadsworth, 1975). See Chapter 8 of this text for further discussion of this issue.

MMPI INDICES

Table 3–4 outlines the major MMPI indices that have been used to identify schizophrenia. Peterson (1954) examined Meehl's (1946) six MMPI signs and found that they successfully discriminated between "subclinical schizophrenics" and a group of nonschizophrenic psychiatric inpatients. The efficacy of these six signs has been demonstrated in a number of cross-validational studies and several investigations attempting to predict patient outcome (cf. Briggs, 1958; Grace, 1964; Johnson, Martin, & Vogler, 1970). The Peterson signs are probably the most replicable and potentially useful of the four configural approaches listed in Table 3–4 (i.e., Peterson, Taulbee-Sisson, Meehl-Dahlstrom, Newmark).

The Taulbee-Sisson (1957) signs have met with limited success, although some of the early findings (i.e., Taulbee, 1958; Garfield & Sineps, 1959) suggested a fairly strong relationship between these signs and schizophrenia. The Taulbee-Sisson (1957) signs are probably not a practical alternative to the Peterson signs, due to the fact that the derivation sample was inadequately defined and that very little data are available on its predictive validity. Meehl and Dahlstrom (1960) developed a neurotic-psychotic scale that seems to have some relevance to our discussion on schizophrenia.

However, in the only two studies focusing exclusively on schizophrenics, only 60 percent of the patients were accurately identified (cf. Ritter, 1974; Winter & Stortroen, 1963). As with the Taulbee-Sisson signs, there is no information on the external correlates or predictive value of the Meehl-Dahlstrom rules.

The Newmark et al. (1978) index is the newest in a line of several configural MMPI indices designed to assess schizophrenia. While the initial cross-validation of this index yielded encouraging results (cf. Newmark et al., 1978), subsequent research has produced much less positive results (cf. Newmark, Gentry, & Whitt, 1983; Newmark & Hutchins, 1980). It should be noted, however, that in many of the later studies this MMPI index was being used with groups of individuals who were very different from those used to derive the index (i.e., elderly and adolescent schizophrenics).

The one linear approach to be reviewed here, the Goldberg (1965) index ($L + Pa + Sc - Hy - Pt$), has received a fair amount of attention from researchers as well as several attempts at validating external correlates (cf. Holland & Watson, 1978; Roy, 1984). The major limitation of the Goldberg index is that the samples on which it was based were not well defined and in several cases left unspecified altogether. The primary advantage of the Goldberg index is that, like most linear approaches to profile interpretation, it is just as effective, if not superior to, the more complex and cumbersome configural approaches (see Goldberg, 1965; Meehl, 1959; Walters, White, & Greene, 1988; Watson & Thomas, 1968).

In deciding whether a special scale, like the *Pz* scale, or an index, like the Goldberg, warrants consideration in a clinical decision-making situation, it should be compared with the standard MMPI profile, in this case Scale *8* (*Sc*). It already has been noted that special schizophrenic-organic scales characteristically fail to add significantly to the information provided by Scale *8*. It is much the same case when special MMPI scales and indices are considered against Scale *8* in making general schizophrenic-nonschizophrenic decisions. For instance, Davies et al. (1985) failed to observe a difference in the diagnostic accuracy of Scale *8* and Rosen's *Pz* scale. Gottesman and Shields (1972), on the other hand, found that Scale *8* (*Sc* + 1*K*) produced results superior to those provided by the Pz scale ($Pz + 1K$). Winter and Stortroen (1963) discovered that Scale 8 was more effective than either the Taulbee-Sisson signs or Meehl-Dahlstrom rules and just as effective as the Peterson signs in differentiating between schizophrenic and "normal" individuals.

In conclusion, there appears to be very little support for the clinical utility of special MMPI scales and indices in identifying schizophrenia since most fail to generate any more information than that routinely provided by the standard MMPI scales. This point is particularly difficult to overlook when considering the amount of data on the internal consistency, external correlative/predictive ability, and construct validity of Scale 8 relative to that which is available on the special MMPI scales and indices reviewed above.

CURRENT RESEARCH TOPICS

Although much of the MMPI research on schizophrenia has centered around improving diagnostic accuracy, several more integrated research trends have been noted. Two of the more frequently investigated topics in MMPI research on schizophrenia will be reviewed here. The first topic, schizotaxia, has a strong theoretical emphasis, whereas the second topic, predicting patient outcome, is more clinically oriented.

Schizotaxia

Meehl (1962) is typically credited with directing our attention toward the possibility that an underlying personality characteristic, schizotypy, predisposes one to the development of clinically diagnosable schizophrenia. Meehl proposes that a neuro-integrative deficit, schizotaxia, is inherited by these individuals and that certain social learning experiences then interact with the deficit to form a schizotypic character structure. Since this personality configuration is at increased risk for the development of a formal thought disorder, these individuals tend to decompensate into a schizophrenic-type disturbance if sufficiently stressed. Several researchers have attempted to derive more accurate diagnoses of schizotaxia,

also known as the schizoid taxon, and schizotypy through examination of various MMPI scales and scores. These attempts have, at times, involved developing special MMPI scales, considering certain MMPI high-point combinations, and reviewing the MMPI responses of individuals who are hypothetically vulnerable to schizophrenia but have never been actively psychotic.

Golden and Meehl (1979) compared schizophrenic and normal individuals on the MMPI and after several complex statistical manipulations, identified seven MMPI items that they felt were predictive of schizotaxia. Reasoning that actively schizophrenic patients also should be members of the schizoid taxon, Miller, Streiner, and Kahgee (1982) compared inpatient schizophrenics with groups of acutely depressed and remitted depressive patients on the seven-item Golden-Meehl Schizoidia scale. A cutting score of four on this scale identified only slightly more than 50 percent of the schizophrenics, while misclassifying 71 percent of the acutely depressed patients as "taxon" members. The stability of this scale also was assessed by Miller et al. (1982) and found to be wanting, with only 33.3 percent of the schizophrenics falling into Golden and Meehl's schizoid taxon group when the MMPI was administered on two separate occasions. On the other hand, 37.8 percent of the schizophrenic group were consistently rated as nonmembers of the schizoid taxon across the two testings. Nichols and Jones (1985) found similar results in a more recent examination of this issue. They reported that less than 40 percent of the schizophrenics in their sample achieved a score of four or more on the Golden-Meehl scale, whereas 42 percent of the affectively disturbed and 55 percent of the general psychiatric (nonpsychotic) patients earned scores of four or higher on this putative measure of schizotaxia.

A major limitation of the Miller et al. (1982) and Nichols and Jones (1985) studies, however, is that they used actively schizophrenic individuals as subjects. Therefore, these results may not be generalizable to compensated schizotypes who are vulnerable to the disorder but have not yet displayed active schizophrenic symptomatology. Chapman, Chapman, and Miller (1982), on the other hand, studied compensated schizotypy using a large sample of college students. They discovered that while the Schizoidia scale correlated with a number of other measures of schizotypy, it fared poorly in terms of its test-retest reliability and internal consistency (alpha coefficient). In summary, Golden and Meehl's Schizoidia scale has not been found useful in identifying individuals thought to possess schizotaxia or a schizotypic personality organization.

Another trend in MMPI research on schizotaxia has involved the 2-7-8 codetype. Gilberstadt and Duker (1965) characterized this codetype as indicative of a pseudoneurotic or chronic form of schizophrenia, while Marks, Seeman, and Haller (1984) viewed it as an obsessive, overideational schizophrenic reaction. Fine (1973) compared 17 college students producing the 2-7-8 codetype with 16 "normal" college controls and 20 schizophrenic inpatients. The 2-7-8 group was found to be much more similar to the schizophrenic group than it was to the "normal" group on such characteristics as anhedonia and the presence of a formal thought disorder. Fujioka and Chapman (1984) compared college students earning the 2-7-8 codetype with students elevating Chapman's Perceptual Aberration-Magical Ideation (Per-Mag) scale on symptoms thought to be associated with "schizotypal" experience. While both groups reported problematic behaviors and symptoms (e.g., depersonalization experiences, aberrant beliefs, bizarre perceptions), including RDC schizotypal features, the Per-Mag group showed significantly more deviance (relative to college student norms) than did the 2-7-8 group.

Research has suggested that there is a deficit in the information-processing ability of schizophrenics (see Neale & Oltmanns, 1980). Koh and Peterson (1974) attempted to extend this finding to schizotypal individuals through use of the 2-7-8 codetype. They compared 23 undergraduate students earning the 2-7-8 codetype with 23 undergraduates obtaining unelevated profiles (i.e., all scales < T-score of 70) on a delayed paired-comparison task, the object of which was to compare the relative magnitude (numerousness) of two dot patterns presented one after the other. Koh and Peterson found moderate support for their hypothesis that 2-7-8 subjects would experience greater difficulty with this task. As part of his dissertation research, Schulman (1976) presented letter pairs (half of

the pairs being uppercase-uppercase [AA] and half of the pairs being uppercase-lowercase [Aa]) to subjects with and without "elevated" MMPIs (i.e., the 2-7-8 codetype), asking them to judge whether the pairs were the same or different. He found longer reaction times in the 2-7-8 group and interpreted this to mean that there was an impairment in these subjects' ability to access information from long-term memory.

Steronko and Woods (1978) also studied the information-processing ability of college students acheiving the 2-7-8 codetype. They compared 2-7-8 students with two control groups, one of which contained no MMPI elevations ("inflation-free") and the other one of which contained elevations on any two MMPI scales except Scale 8 ("other inflation"). Using the critical interstimulus interval (ISI) on a backward visual masking task as the dependent variable, they discovered that the 2-7-8 group required significantly longer periods of exposure for successful performance compared with the "inflation-free" group, but that differences between the 2-7-8 and "other inflation" groups failed to achieve statistical significance. Merritt and Balogh (1984) investigated this issue further and found a significant information-processing deficit in college students achieving the 2-7-8 and 8-9 codetypes relative to students in the "inflation-free" and "other inflation" groups. Several other studies have confirmed this deficit in a series of "Type A" masking function tasks (the masking stimulus is decreased monotonically as the delay in presentation is increased) administered to college students displaying the 2-7-8 codetype (cf. Merritt & Balogh, 1985; Nakano & Saccuzzo, 1985). Merritt, Balogh, and Leventhal (1986) attempted to extend these findings to "Type B" masking functions, where the "mask" energy is no greater than that of the target, resulting in a nonmonotonic "U"-shaped function. Merritt et al. (1986) found that 2-7-8 students required more time to identify target stimuli in this "Type B" backward masking task compared with students in three different control groups (i.e., a 4-9 group, an 8-9 group, and an "inflation-free" group).

While there do appear to be information-processing deficits in college students producing the 2-7-8 codetype, this does not necessarily qualify this MMPI configuration as diagnostic of either schizotaxia or schizotypy. As Greene (1980) asserts, there are a number of ways in which a 2-7-8 pattern can arise, particularly when college students are studied, and in only a few of these configurations—typically when Scale 8 (Sc) is elevated above Scales 2 (D) and 7 (Pt)—is schizotypal personality development suggested. A second problem with research in this area has been that the control groups are often not fully comparable with the 2-7-8 group in terms of overall profile elevation since even the "other inflation" groups are frequently not as highly elevated as the 2-7-8 group. Thus, these studies may actually be investigating the information-processing ability of college students achieving highly elevated MMPI profiles rather than the 2-7-8 codetype per se. Finally, investigators are encouraged to include other putative measures of schizotypy, such as Chapman's Physical Anhedonia and Perceptual Aberration-Magical Ideation scales, when examining the 2-7-8 codetype relative to schizotaxia.

A third trend in MMPI research on schizotaxia is to assess the performance and characteristics of individuals presumed to be at risk for the development of schizophrenic symptomatology due to a genetic association with a diagnosed schizophrenic patient. Haier et al. (1978) compared 64 adopted-away offspring of schizophrenics with 64 matched controls and found that a combination of interview-based diagnoses and MMPI criteria significantly differentiated between these two groups (22 vs. 6 percent of the adopted-away and control subjects, respectively, fell into the schizophrenia spectrum). Although male index cases recorded higher scores on all 10 MMPI clinical scales, only 1 of the univariate differences achieved statistical significance (i.e., Scale 8), and the multivariate results failed to reveal an overall difference between the mean index and control profiles. Index cases also scored higher on the three special MMPI indices examined—Peterson signs, Eichman rules, and Disturbance Index (DI: Cooke, 1967)—but only the difference on the DI achieved statistical significance.

Gottesman and Shields (1972) explored the MMPI response patterns of monozygotic (MZ) and dizygotic (DZ) twins of consensus schizophrenics with the knowledge that MZ twins have more in common with each other genetically than do DZ twins. They observed significantly

higher scores on MMPI scales 6 (Pa), 7 (Pt), and 8 (Sc) in the MZ co-twins compared with the DZ co-twins. However, these differences became nonsignificant when diagnosed cases of schizophrenia were removed from the two co-twin groups. Therefore, while the MMPI provides some interesting information for theoretical speculation, it appears to be generally ill-equipped to handle the job of identifying compensated schizotypes.

PREDICTING PATIENT OUTCOME

Since Kraepelin (1911) first identified schizophrenia as a psychiatric syndrome, there has been an emphasis on long-term outcome in defining and assessing schizophrenia. As such, it seems appropriate that the MMPI be studied as a possible aid in such an endeavor. Strauss and Carpenter (1972) have argued that a multivariable approach should be used in assessing the long-term outcome of schizophrenic patients. Specifically, they recommend that outcome be evaluated along several dimensions—length of hospitalization, severity of symptomatology, social contacts, employment—and they also recommend use of a total or composite score based on an all four dimensions considered as a group. MMPI research studies attempting to predict outcome in schizophrenic patients have examined each of these dimensions, although they rarely consider more than one dimension at a time.

Several researchers have attempted to predict length of hospitalization in schizophrenic patients using the MMPI. McKeever, May, and Tuma (1965) examined the relationship between the MMPI and subsequent length of hospitalization in a group of 100 state hospital patients diagnosed schizophrenic. They uncovered just two statistically significant findings: lower Scale 6 (Pa) scores predicted better outcome, in the form of shorter hospital stays, in male schizophrenics, while lower Scale 5 (Mf) scores were associated with better outcome in female schizophrenics. Watson (1968) also failed to find many clinically significant MMPI correlates of eventual length of psychiatric hospitalization. In a more recent study, Glosz and Grant (1981) studied the MMPI's ability to predict length of hospitalization in 41 schizophrenics housed in a VA inpatient facility. They report that Scales 2

(*D*), 5 (*Mf*), and 8 (*Sc*) correlated significantly with length of hospitalization: Scale 8 scores were directly related to the criterion and Scale 2 scores were inversely related. According to these results, moderate levels of depression and lesser degrees of cognitive disorganization may be predictive of shorter hospital stays in schizophrenic inpatients.

Rehospitalization after release also has been used as a criterion measure in MMPI research on outcome. For instance, Johnston and McNeal (1965) administered the MMPI to a group of 160 psychiatric inpatients (approximately 80 percent of whom were diagnosed schizophrenic) on admission and again just prior to release. A group of psychologists then "blindly" compared these two profiles and selected one as "healthier." Subsequent data analyses revealed that patients viewed as leaving the hospital with a healthier profile than that with which they entered remained out of the hospital significantly longer than patients leaving the hospital with more "disturbed" profiles (23.3 months vs. 16.8 months). Johnson and his colleagues, on the other hand, failed to find a relationship between rehospitalization and the standard MMPI scales, Harris-Lingoes subscales (Johnson, Fox, Schaefer, & Ishikawa, 1971), or Peterson signs (Johnson et al., 1970). Briggs (1958) found a somewhat paradoxical relationship in which bizarreness of symptomatology, as measured by the Peterson signs, predicted better outcome or a lower likelihood of readmission to a psychiatric hospital.

Severity of subsequent symptomatology was employed as the criterion for outcome in a study conducted by Marks, Stauffacher, and Lyle (1963) on a sample of 115 hospitalized schizophrenic males. The MMPI was administered prior to a patient being released from the hospital and patients were followed-up for 1 year post-release. Marks et al. noted that of 111 predictive measures, three of the strongest were MMPI Scales *F*, 6 (*Pa*), and 8 (*Sc*), with MMPI-criterion correlations ranging between -.50 and -.69. However, demographic variables were found to predict outcome better than psychological test results. Newmark, Gentry, Whitt, McKee, and Wicker (1983) took a somewhat different approach to predicting outcome by means of the MMPI. They examined the ability of schizophrenic patients to simulate a "normal" MMPI

profile and found that successful simulation was associated with better outcome in the form of lower ratings on several measures of "schizophrenic" thinking. Young, Gould, Glick, and Hargreaves (1980), on the other hand, were unable to find a relationship between symptom outcome, as measured by the Health-Sickness Rating Scale and Psychiatric Evaluation Form, and the MMPI in 86 schizophrenic patients.

Gross (1959) considered both symptom outcome and social adjustment in a study probing the predictive value of the three MMPI validity scales, *L*, *F*, and *K*. Greater behavioral disturbance and relatively poor social adjustment were found to be associated with a "caret"-shaped validity profile (*F* higher than *L* and *K*), while less behavioral disturbance and better social adjustment were found in schizophrenics achieving the "V"-shaped validity profile (*L* and *K* higher than *F*). In the only identified MMPI study on schizophrenia considering successful employment as a demarcation of outcome, Grace (1964) compared schizophrenics who were and were not promoted to advanced rehabilitative (vocational training) standing; in this study the Peterson signs were found to be negatively associated with good work performance as measured by promotion to advanced rehabilitative status.

Research attempting to predict outcome from performance on the MMPI has met with limited success, although elevations on Scales *F*, 6 (*Pa*), and 8 (*Sc*) appear to predict poor outcome while moderate elevations on Scales *L*, *K*, and 2 (*D*) appear to augur a reasonably good prognosis. This latter finding suggests that the presence of significant emotional features in an individual displaying signs of schizophrenic psychopathology may be prognostic of relatively good outcome, a finding that has already been noted by Pope and Lipinski (1978). Future research will have greater practical utility if larger sample sizes, multivariate statistical analyses, multivariable outcome measures, and diagnostic criteria more compatible with DSM-III are used.

SUMMARY

Despite all the MMPI research that has been conducted on schizophrenia, our knowledge is still very limited. Carpenter, Gunderson, and Strauss (1977) assert that psychological test data may provide us with an approach to validating specific classes of psychopathology. Unfortunately, this has not been successfully accomplished in the case of MMPI research on schizophrenia. Although a diagnosis of schizophrenia is strengthened by the presence of an elevated score on Scale 8 (Sc), simultaneous elevations (i.e., high-point pair) on Scales 6 (Pa) and 8, or scores in the psychotic/schizophrenic direction on certain MMPI indices (i.e., Goldberg index, Peterson signs), a brief interview will usually provide one with more information about a possible diagnosis of schizophrenia than will the MMPI. The potential for greater clinical application of current MMPI knowledge to patients suffering from schizophrenia and other serious forms of psychopathology still exists, however.

Johnson, Klingler, and Giannetti (1980) found that the MMPI correlated better with 13 specific or "molecular" diagnoses than it did with four global or "molar" diagnoses, suggesting that the MMPI may be more applicable to narrow-band (as opposed to wide-band) diagnostic systems. Such a finding takes on added significance when we consider that DSM-III holds to a very narrow definition of schizophrenia. This is certainly an area worthy of continued research effort.

One area in which the MMPI might be practically useful is in predicting outcome. Although very few clinically meaningful findings have surfaced when the MMPI has been used to predict outcome in various groups of schizophrenic patients, the samples studied have often been so heterogeneous as to deem the findings almost uninterpretable. The use of narrow, homogeneous schizophrenic samples, possibly modeled after the RDC or DSM-III criteria, may prove more fruitful. In fact, the only study in this area of research adopting a DSM-III-like definition of schizophrenia (i.e., Newmark, Gentry, Whitt, McKee, & Wicker, 1983) produced results that appear to be clinically significant. The Newmark et al. (1983) study also points to another possible application of the MMPI in this area, namely, use of the MMPI for examining the personal resources and strengths of schizophrenic individuals rather than focusing exclusively on pathology.

Since the MMPI changes over time, it might be useful in assessing the changes that normally take place in schizophrenic patients with the passage of time. Walters (1984a) found that MMPIs administered several weeks post-diagnosis were much more highly elevated in schizophrenics relative to a group of schizophreniform patients. He speculated that these MMPI results may reflect the more rapid recompensation of patients with schizophreniform diagnoses. This hypothesis could be tested by administering the MMPI to schizophrenic and schizophreniform patients at several different times (e.g., at intake, 2 weeks later, 8 weeks later, 6 months later) and then making the appropriate statistical comparisons.

The use of the MMPI to ferret out the degree of variance contributed by temporary "states" vs. characterologic "traits" also may be helpful (see Dahlstrom, 1972).

Garb (1984) offers several recommendations pertaining to use of personality assessment procedures that may have relevance to MMPI research on schizophrenia. One possible avenue of future research endeavor discussed by Garb is to inspect the incremental validity of diagnostic judgments as the MMPI is coupled with demographic information and/or other psychological test data (e.g., Rorschach). Garb also asserts that we need to investigate the process of clinical decision-making in an effort to isolate and refine cost-effective decision-making strategies. Such an approach may yield clinically useful material in our search for practical application of the MMPI in schizophrenic populations.

As previously discussed by Walters (1983), the MMPI research on schizophrenia lacks a coherent, integrated theoretical framework. Research using the 2-7-8 codetype to identify schizotypy in college students probably comes closest to providing us with a coherent theoretical framework. That is, the series of investigations instituted by Koh and his colleagues (cf. Koh & Peterson, 1974) and the more recent work of Merritt and Balogh (Merritt & Balogh, 1984, 1985; Merritt, Balogh, & Leventhal, 1986) considering the relationship between the 2-7-8 codetype and inadequate information-processing have all the hallmarks of a well-intergrated program of research. The problem is, however, that while these researchers appear to have found the right forest, they seem to be barking up the wrong tree. There are a multitude of problems associated with using the 2-7-8 codetype as a "marker" of potential schizotypy in college students, not the least of which is that the correlates of the 2-7-8 codetype change depending on which of the three scales is the most highly elevated (see Greene, 1980). A generally elevated MMPI profile may be a more appropriate measure of schizotaxia or schizotypy (cf. Haier, Rieder, Khouri, & Buchsbaum, 1979), although attempts also should be made to integrate MMPI data with other measures, such as Chapman's schizotypal scales (see Fujioka & Chapman, 1984).

In summary, there has been very limited change in the status of MMPI research on schizophrenia since the earlier review of Walters (1983). That is, there is an even larger reservoir of studies now but still a poverty of meaningful information concerning the MMPI correlates of schizophrenia. Undoubtedly, the greater use of multivariate statistics and criterion diagnoses that adhere to a much narrower definition of schizophrenia (i.e., DSM-III, RDC, St. Louis criteria) has made these recent studies more useful from a clinical, as well as research, standpoint. However, there is still a fundamental need for greater theoretical/conceptual organization, research-clinical integration, long-term follow-up, and empirical fervor seasoned with creativity if this area of research endeavor is ever going to contribute significantly to the assessment, treatment, and management of schizophrenic individuals.

REFERENCES

Aaronson, B. A., & Welsh, G. S. (1950). The MMPI as a diagnostic differentiator: A reply to Rubin. *Journal of Consulting Psychology, 14*, 324–326.

Abrams, R., & Taylor, M. (1973). First-rank symptoms, severity of illness, and treatment response in schizophrenia. *Comprehensive Psychiatry, 14*, 353–355.

Affleck, D. C., & Garfield, S. L. (1960). The prediction of psychosis with the MMPI. *Journal of Clinical Psychology, 16*, 24–26.

American Psychiatric Association. (1968). *DSM-II: Diagnostic and statistical manual of mental disorders* (2nd ed.). Washington, DC: Author.

American Psychiatric Association. (1980). *DSM-III: Diagnostic and statistical manual of mental disorders* (3rd ed.). Washington, DC: Author.

Apfeldorf, M., & Hunley, P. J. (1976). Exclusion of subjects with *F* scores at or above 16 in MMPI research on alcoholism. *Journal of Clinical Psychology, 32*, 498–500.

Ayers, J., Templer, D. I., & Ruff, C. F. (1975). The MMPI in the differential diagnosis of organicity vs. schizophrenia: Empirical findings and a somewhat different perspective. *Journal of Clinical Psychology, 31*, 685–686.

Benarick, S. J., Guthrie, G. M., & Snyder, W. U. (1951). An interpretive aid for the *Sc* scale of the MMPI. *Journal of Consulting Psychology, 15*, 142–144.

Bland, R. C., & Orn, H. (1980). Schizophrenia: Schneider's first-rank symptoms and outcome. *British Journal of Psychiatry, 137*, 63–68.

Bleuler, E. (1950). *Dementia praecox; or The group of schizophrenias.* New York: International Universities Press.

Braatz, G. A. (1970). Preference intrasivity as an indicator of cognitive slippage in schizophrenia. *Journal of Abnormal Psychology, 75*, 1–6.

Briggs, P. F. (1958). Prediction of rehospitalization using the MMPI. *Journal of Clinical Psychology, 14*, 83–84.

Butcher, J. N., & Tellegen, A. (1978). Common methodological problems in MMPI research. *Journal of Consulting and Clinical Psychology, 46*, 620–628.

Campbell, D. T., & Fiske, D. W. (1959). Convergent and discriminant validation by the multitrait-multimethod matrix. *Psychological Bulletin, 56*, 81–105.

Carpenter, W. T., Gunderson, J. G., & Strauss, J. S. (1977). Consideration of the borderline syndrome: A longitudinal comparative study of borderline and schizophrenic patients. In P. Hartocollis (Ed.), *Borderline personality disorders: The concept, the syndrome, the patient* (pp. 231–253). New York: International Universities Press.

Carpenter, W. T., & Strauss, J. S. (1973). Are there pathognomonic symptoms in schizophrenia? An empirical investigation of Schneider's first-rank symptoms. *Archives of General Psychiatry, 28*, 847–852.

Carpenter, W. T., & Strauss, J. S. (1974). Cross-cultural evaluation of Schneider's first-rank symptoms of schizophrenia: A report from the International Pilot Study of Schizophrenia. *American Journal of Psychiatry, 131*, 682–687.

Carpenter, W. T., Strauss, J. S., & Bartko, J. J. (1973). Flexible system for the diagnosis of schizophrenia: Report from the WHO International Pilot Study of Schizophrenia. *Science, 182*, 1275–1277.

Cauthen, N. R., Sandman, C. A., Kilpatrick, D. G., & Deabler, H. L. (1969). DAP correlates of *Sc* scores on the MMPI. *Journal of Personality Assessment, 33*, 262–264.

Chapman, L. J., Chapman, J. P., & Miller, E. N. (1982). Reliabilities and intercorrelations of eight measures of proneness to psychosis. *Journal of Consulting and Clinical Psychology, 50*, 187–195.

Clark, C. G., & Miller, H. L. (1971). Validation of Gilberstadt and Duker's *8-6* profile type on a black sample. *Psychological Reports, 29*, 259–264.

Comrey, A. L., & Marggraff, W. M. (1958). A factor analysis of items on the MMPI schizophrenia scale. *Educational and Psychological Measurement, 18*, 301–311.

Cooke, J. K. (1967). Clinicians decisions as a basis for deriving actuarial formulae. *Journal of Clinical Psychology, 23*, 232–233.

Cowan, M. A., Watkins, B. A., & Davis, W. E. (1975). Level of education, diagnosis and race-related differences in MMPI performance. *Journal of Clinical Psychology, 31*, 442–444.

Dahlstrom, W. G. (1972). Whither the MMPI? In J. N. Butcher (Ed.), *Objective personality assessment: Changing perspectives* (pp. 85–115). San Diego: Academic Press.

Dahlstrom, W. G., Lachar, D., & Dahlstrom, L. E. (1986). *MMPI patterns of American minorities.* Minneapolis: University of Minnesota Press.

Dahlstrom, W. G., & Prange, A. J. (1960). Characteristics of depressive and paranoid schizophrenic reactions on the MMPI. *Journal of Nervous and Mental Disease, 131*, 513–522.

Dahlstrom, W. G., Welsh, G. S., & Dahlstrom, L. E. (1972). *An MMPI handbook: Vol. I* (rev. ed.). Minneapolis: University of Minnesota Press.

Davies, J. W., Nichols, D. S., & Greene, R. L. (1985, March). *A new schizophrenia scale for the MMPI.* Paper presented at the 20th Annual Symposium on Recent Advances in the Use of the MMPI, Honolulu.

Davis, W. E. (1972). Age and the discriminative "power" of the MMPI with schizophrenic and nonschizophrenic patients. *Journal of Consulting and Clinical Psychology, 38*, 151.

Davis, W. E. (1975). Race and the differential "power" of the MMPI. *Journal of Personality Assessment, 39*, 138–140.

Davis, W. E., Beck, S. J., & Ryan, T. A. (1973). Race-related and educationally-related MMPI profile differences among hospitalized schizophrenics. *Journal of Clinical Psychology, 29*, 478–479.

Davis, W. E., & Gustafson, R. C. (1971, April). *The generation gap in psychiatric patients: Differences in clinical picture of three age groups.* Paper presented at annual meeting of the Western Psychological Association, San Francisco.

Davis, W. E., & Jones, M. H. (1974). Negro versus Caucasian psychological test performance revisited. *Journal of Consulting and Clinical Psychology, 42*, 675–679.

Davis, W. E., Mozdzierz, G. J., & Macchitelli, F. J. (1973).

Loss of discriminative "power" of the MMPI with older psychiatric patients. *Journal of Personality Assessment, 37,* 555–558.

Edell, W. S. (1987). Relationship of borderline syndrome disorders to early schizophrenia on the MMPI. *Journal of Clinical Psychology, 43,* 163–176.

Edinger, J. D., Burnette, E., Hoffman, J., & Katranides, M. (1983). Validity of invalid MMPI profiles: Floating profiles revisited. *Psychological Reports, 53,* 907–914.

Eichman, W. J. (1959). Discrimination of female schizophrenics with configural analysis of the MMPI profile. *Journal of Consulting Psychology, 23,* 442–449.

Endicott, J., & Spitzer, R. L. (1978). A diagnostic interview: The Schedule for Affective Disorders and Schizophrenia. *Archives of General Psychiatry, 35,* 837–844.

Evans, R. W., Ruff, R. M., Braff, D. L., & Ainsworth, T. L. (1984). MMPI characteristics of borderline personality inpatients. *Journal of Nervous and Mental Disease, 172,* 742–748.

Feighner, J. P., Robins, E., Guze, S. B., Woodruff, R. A., Winokur, G., & Munoz, R. (1972). Diagnostic criteria for use in psychiatric research. *Archives of General Psychiatry, 26,* 57–63.

Fenton, W. W., Mosher, L. R., & Matthews, S. M. (1981). Diagnosis of schizophrenia: A critical review of current diagnostic systems. *Schizophrenia Bulletin, 7,* 452–476.

Fine, H. K. (1973). Studying schizophrenia outside the psychiatric setting. *Journal of Youth and Adolescence, 2,* 291–301.

Fishkin, S. M., Lovallo, W. R., & Pishkin, V. (1977). Relationship between schizophrenic thinking and MMPI for process and reactive patients. *Journal of Clinical Psychology, 33,* 116–119.

Fujioka, T. A. T., & Chapman, L. J. (1984). Comparison of the *2-7-8* MMPI profile and the Perceptual Aberration-Magical Ideation scale in identifying hypothetically psychosis-prone college students. *Journal of Consulting and Clinical Psychology, 52,* 458–467.

Garb, H. N. (1984). The incremental validity of information used in personality assessment. *Clinical Psychology Review, 4,* 641–655.

Garfield, S. L., & Sineps, J. (1959). An appraisal of Taulbee and Sisson's "configural analysis of MMPI profiles of psychiatric groups." *Journal of Consulting Psychology, 23,* 333–335.

Giannetti, R. A., Johnson, J. H., Klinger, D. E., & Williams, T. A. (1978). Comparison of linear and configural MMPI diagnostic methods with an uncontaminated criterion. *Journal of Consulting and Clinical Psychology, 46,* 1046–1052.

Gilberstadt, H. (1975). *Comprehensive MMPI code book for males.* Minneapolis: Veterans Administration.

Gilberstadt, H., & Duker, J. (1965). *A handbook for clinical and actuarial MMPI interpretation.* Philadelphia: W. B. Saunders.

Glosz, J. T., & Grant, I. (1981). Prognostic validity of the MMPI. *Journal of Clinical Psychology, 37,* 147–151.

Goldberg, L. R. (1965). Diagnosticians vs. diagnostic signs: The diagnosis of psychosis vs. neurosis from the MMPI. *Psychological Monographs, 79* (9, Whole No. 602).

Golden, C. J., Sweet, J. J., & Osmon, D. C. (1979). The diagnosis of brain-damage by the MMPI: A comprehensive evaluation. *Journal of Personality Assessment, 43,* 138–142.

Golden, R. R., & Meehl, P. E. (1979). Detection of the schizoid taxon with MMPI indicators. *Journal of Abnormal Psychology, 88,* 217–233.

Goodson, J. H., & King, G. D. (1976). A clinical and actuarial study on the validity of the Goldberg index for the MMPI. *Journal of Clinical Psychology, 32,* 328–335.

Gottesman, I. I., & Shields, J. (1972). *Schizophrenia and genetics: A twin study vantage point.* San Diego: Academic Press.

Grace, D. P. (1964). Predicting progress of schizophrenics in a work-oriented rehabilitation programs. *Journal of Consulting Psychology, 28,* 560.

Graham, J. R. (1987). *The MMPI: A practical guide.* (2nd. ed.) New York: Oxford University Press.

Greene, R. L. (1980). *The MMPI: An interpretive manual.* Philadelphia: Grune & Stratton.

Greene, R. L. (1981, April). *A factor analysis of items on Scale 8 (Schizophrenia) of the MMPI.* Paper presented at the annual meeting of the Southwestern Psychological Association, Houston.

Greene, R. L. (1987). Ethnicity and the MMPI: A review. *Journal of Consulting and Clinical Psychology, 55,* 497–512.

Gross, L. R. (1959). MMPI *L-F-K* relationships with criteria of behavioral disturbance and social adjustment in a schizophrenic population. *Journal of Consulting Psychology, 23,* 319–323.

Haier, R. J., Rieder, R. O., Khouri, P. J., & Buchsbaum, M. S. (1979). Extreme MMPI scores and the Research Diagnostic Criteria: Screening college men for psychopathology. *Archives of General Psychiatry, 36,* 528–534.

Haier, R. J., Rosenthal, D., & Wender, P. H. (1978). MMPI assessment of psychopathology in adopted-away offspring of schizophrenics. *Archives of General Psychiatry, 35,* 171–175.

Harding, G. F., Holz, W. C., & Kawakami, D. (1958). The differentiation of schizophrenic and superficially similar reactions. *Journal of Clinical Pychology, 14,* 147–149.

Harris, R. E., & Lingoes, J. C. (1955). *Subscales for the MMPI: An aid to profile interpretation.* Unpublished manuscript, University of California, Berkeley.

Hathaway, S. R., & Meehl, P. E. (1951). *An atlas for the clinical use of the MMPI.* Minneapolis: University of Minnesota Press.

Hawk, A. B., Carpenter, W. T., & Strauss, J. S. (1975). Diagnostic criteria and five-year outcome in schizophrenia. *Archives of General Psychiatry, 32,* 343–347.

Henrichs, T. (1964). Objective configural rules for discriminating MMPI profiles in a psychiatric population. *Journal of Clinical Psychology, 20,* 157–159.

Higgins, J., Mednick, S. A., & Philip, F. J. (1965). The Schizophrenia scale of the MMPI and life adjustment in schizophrenics. *Psychology, 2,* 26–27.

Holland, T. R., Levi, M., & Watson, C. G. (1981). MMPI basic scales vs. two-point codes in the discrimination of psychopathological groups. *Journal of Clinical Psychology, 37,* 394–396.

Holland, T. R., Lowenfeld, J., & Wadsworth, H. M. (1975). MMPI indices in the discrimination of brain-damaged and schizophrenic groups. *Journal of Consulting and Clinical*

Psychology, 43, 426.

Holland, T. R., & Watson, C. G. (1978). Utilization of the Goldberg MMPI profile classification rules for the assessment of psychopathology in different clinical populations. *Journal of Clinical Psychology, 34,* 893–901.

Johnson, G., Fox, J., Schaefer, H. H., & Ishikawa, W. (1971). Predicting rehospitalization from community placement. *Psychological Reports, 29,* 475–478.

Johnson, G. R., Martin, P. L., & Vogler, R. E. (1970). Prediction of rehospitalization of family-care patients using the MMPI. *Psychological Reports, 26,* 273–274.

Johnson, J. H., Klingler, D. E., & Giannetti, R. A. (1980). Band width in diagnostic classification using the MMPI as a predictor. *Journal of Consulting and Clinical Psychology, 48,* 340–349.

Johnston, R., & McNeal, B. F. (1965). Residual psychopathology in released psychiatric patients and its relation to readmission. *Journal of Abnormal Psychology, 70,* 337–342.

Keane, S. P., & Gibbs, M. (1980). Construct validation of the *Sc* scale of the MMPI. *Journal of Clinical Psychology, 36,* 152–158.

Kendell, R. E., Brockington, I. F., & Leff, J. P. (1979). Prognostic implications of six alternative definitions of schizophrenia. *Archives of General Psychiatry, 36,* 25–31.

Klorman, R., Strauss, J. S., & Kokes, R. F. (1977). The relationship of demographic and diagnostic factors to premorbid adjustment. *Schizophrenia Bulletin, 3,* 186–213.

Koh, S. D., & Peterson, R. A. (1974). Perceptual memory for numerousness in "nonpsychotic schizophrenics." *Journal of Abnormal Psychology, 83,* 215–226.

Kraepelin, E. (1919). *Dementia praecox and paraphrenia.* Edinburgh, NY: Churchill Livingstone.

Lacks, P. B., Rothenberg, P. J., & Unger, B. L. (1970). MMPI scores and marital status in male schizophrenics. *Journal of Clinical Psychology, 26,* 221–222.

Lewinsohn, P. M. (1968). Characteristics of patients with hallucinations. *Journal of Clinical Psychology, 24,* 423.

Marks, J., Stauffacher, J. C., & Lyle, C. (1963). Predicting outcome in schizophrenia. *Journal of Abnormal and Social Psychology, 66,* 117–127.

Marks, P. A., Seeman, W., & Haller, D. L. (1974). *The actuarial use of the MMPI with adolescents and adults.* Baltimore: Williams & Wilkins.

McKeever, W. F., May, P. R. A., & Tuma, A. H. (1965). Prognosis in schizophrenia: Prediction of length of hospitalizaiton from psychological test variables. *Journal of Clinical Psychology, 21,* 214–221.

Mednick, S. A., & McNeil, T. F. (1968). Current methodology in research on the etiology of schizophrenia: Serious difficulties which suggest the use of the high-risk-group method. *Psychological Bulletin, 70,* 681–693.

Meehl, P. E. (1946). Profile analysis of the MMPI in differential diagnosis. *Journal of Applied Psychology, 30,* 517–524.

Meehl, P. E. (1959). A comparison of clinicians with five statistical methods of identifying psychotic MMPI profiles. *Journal of Counseling Psychology, 6,* 102–109.

Meehl, P. E. (1962). Schizotaxia, schizotypy, and schizophrenia. *American Psychologist, 17,* 827–838.

Meehl, P. E., & Dahlstrom, W. G. (1960). Objective configural rules for discriminating psychotic from neurotic MMPI profiles. *Journal of Consulting Psychology, 24,* 375–387.

Meehl, P. E., & Rosen, A. (1955). Antecedent probability and the efficiency of psychometric signs, patterns, or cutting scores. *Psychological Bulletin, 52,* 194–216.

Merritt, R. D., & Balogh, D. W. (1984). The use of a backward masking paradigm to assess information processing deficits among schizotypics: A re-evaluation of Steronko and Woods. *Journal of Nervous and Mental Disease, 172,* 216–224.

Merritt, R. D., & Balogh, D. W. (1985). Critical stimulus duration: Schizophrenic trait or state. *Schizophrenia Bulletin, 11,* 341–343.

Merritt, R. D., Balogh, D. W., & Leventhal, D. B. (1986). Use of a metacontrast and a paracontrast procedure to assess visual information processing of hypothetically schizotypic college students. *Journal of Abnormal Psychology, 95,* 74–80.

Miller, H. R., Streiner, D. L., & Kahgee, S. L. (1982). Use of the Golden-Meehl indicators in the detection of schizoid-taxon membership. *Journal of Abnormal Psychology, 91,* 55–60.

Miller, T. W., & Paciello, R. A. (1980). Discriminative dimension of the MMPI as a function of age and psychopathology. *Journal of Clinical Psychology, 36,* 758–759.

Nakano, K., & Saccuzzo, D. P. (1985). Schizotaxia, information processing, and the MMPI *2-7-8* code type. *British Journal of Clinical Psychology, 24,* 217–218.

Neale, J. M. & Oltmanns, T. F. (1980). *Schizophrenia.* New York: John Wiley and Sons.

Newmark, C. S., Chassin, P., Evans, D. L., & Gentry, L. (1984). "Floating" MMPI profiles revisited. *Journal of Clinical Psychology, 40,* 199–201.

Newmark, C. S., Chassin, P., Gentry, L., & Evans, D. L. (1983). "Floating" MMPI profiles and DSM-III diagnoses. *Psychological Reports, 53,* 1119–1122.

Newmark, C. S., Falk, R., Johns, N., Boren, R., & Forehand, R. (1976). Comparing traditional clinical procedures with four systems to diagnose schizophrenia. *Journal of Abnormal Psychology, 85,* 66–72.

Newmark, C. S., Gentry, L., Simpson, M., & Jones, T. (1978). MMPI criteria for diagnosing schizophrenia. *Journal of Personality Assessment, 42,* 366–373.

Newmark, C. S., Gentry, L., Warren, N., & Finch, A. J. (1981). Racial bias in an MMPI index of schizophrenia. *British Journal of Clinical Psychology, 20,* 215–216.

Newmark, C. S., Gentry, L., & Whitt, J. K. (1983). Utility of MMPI indices of schizophrenia with adolescents. *Journal of Clinical Psychology, 39,* 170–172.

Newmark, C. S., Gentry, L., Whitt, J. K., McKee, D. C., & Wicker, C. (1983). Simulating normal MMPI profiles as a favourable prognostic sign in schizophrenia. *Australian Journal of Psychology, 35,* 433–444.

Newmark, C. S., & Hutchins, T. C. (1980). Age and MMPI indices of schizophrenia. *Journal of Clinical Psychology, 36,* 768–769.

Newmark, C. S., Jones, M. T., McKee, D. C., Simpson, M., Boren, R. B., & Prillaman, K. (1980). Using discriminant function analysis with clinical, demographic, and historical variables to diagnose schizophrenia. *British Journal of Medical Psychology, 53,* 365–374.

Newmark, C. S., Raft, D., Toomey, T., Hunter, W., & Mazzaglia, J. (1975). Diagnosis of schizophrenia: Pathognomonic signs or symptom clusters. *Comprehensive Psychiatry, 16*, 155–163.

Newmark, C. S., & Sines, L. K. (1972). Characteristics of hospitalized patients who produce the "floating" MMPI profile. *Journal of Clinical Psychology, 28*, 74–76.

Neziroglu, F. (1975). The relationships among the Hoffer-Osmond Diagnostic Test, the MMPI and independent clinical diagnosis. *Journal of Clinical Psychology, 31*, 430–433.

Nichols, D. S., & Jones, R. E. (1985). Identifying schizoid-taxon membership with the Golden-Meehl MMPI items. *Journal of Abnormal Psychology, 94*, 191–194.

Othmer, E., Penick, E. C., & Powell, B. J. (1981). *Psychiatric Diagnostic Interview (PDI) manual.* Los Angeles: Western Psychological Services.

Page, S. (1982). Psychologist and physician diagnoses of hospitalized patients with similar MMPI symptomatology. *Canadian Journal of Psychiatry, 27*, 471–473.

Peterson, D. R. (1954). The diagnosis of subclinical schizophrenia. *Journal of Consulting Psychology, 18*, 198–200.

Pope, H. G., & Lipinski, J. F. (1978). Diagnosis in schizophrenia and manic-depressive illness. *Archives of General Psychiatry, 35*, 811–828.

Quay, H., & Rowell, J. T. (1955). The validity of a schizophrenic screening scale of the MMPI. *Journal of Clinical Psychology, 11*, 92–93.

Ritter, D. R. (1974). Concurrence of psychiatric diagnosis and psychological diagnosis based on the MMPI. *Journal of Personality Assessment, 38*, 52–54.

Rosen, A. (1958). Differentiation of diagnostic groups by individual MMPI scales. *Journal of Consulting Psychology, 22*, 453–457.

Rosen, A. (1962). Development of MMPI scales based on a reference group of pychiatric patients. *Psychological Monographs, 76* (8, Whole No. 527).

Roy, R. E. (1984). The Goldberg neurotic-psychotic rule and MMPI 2-7-8 patients. *Journal of Personality Assessment, 48*, 398–402.

Rubin, H. (1948). The Minnesota Multiphasic Personality Inventory as a diagnostic aid in a veterans hospital. *Journal of Consulting Psychology, 12*, 251–254.

Rubin, H. (1954). Validity of a critical-item scale for schizophrenia on the MMPI. *Journal of Consulting Psychology, 18*, 219–220.

Russell, E. W. (1977). MMPI profiles of brain-damaged and schizophrenic subjects. *Journal of Clinical Psychology, 33*, 190–193.

Saccuzzo, D. P., Braff, D. L., Sprock, J., & Sudik, N. (1984). The schizophrenia spectrum: A study of the relationship among the Rorschach, MMPI and visual backward masking. *Journal of Clinical Psychology, 40*, 1288–1294.

Schneider, K. (1959). *Clinical Psychopathology.* Philadelphia: Grune & Stratton.

Schulman, S. M. (1976). Cognitive deficit in students identified by the elevated *2-7-8* code of the MMPI. *Dissertation Abstracts International, 37*, 3096B. (University Microfilms No. 76-28,305)

Sillitti, J. (1982). MMPI-derived indicators of organic brain dysfunction. *Journal of Clinical Psychology, 38*, 601–605.

Silverstein, M. L., & Harrow, M. (1981). Schneiderian first-rank symptoms in schizophrenia. *Archives of General Psychiatry, 38*, 288–293.

Spitzer, R. L., Endicott, J., & Robins, E. (1975). *Research Diagnostic Criteria.* New York: Biometrics Research.

Stephens, J. H., Astrup, C., Carpenter, W. T., Schaffer, J. W., & Goldberg, J. (1982). A comparison of nine systems to diagnose schizophrenia. *Psychiatry Research, 6*, 127–143.

Steronko, R. J., & Woods, D. J. (1978). Impairment in early stages of visual information processing in nonpsychotic schizotypic individuals. *Journal of Abnormal Psychology, 87*, 481–490.

Strauss, J. S., & Carpenter, W. T., Jr. (1972). The prediction of outcome in schizophrenia: I. Characteristics of outcome. *Archives of General Psychiatry, 27*, 739–746.

Strauss, J. S., & Carpenter, W. T., Jr. (1981). *Schizophrenia.* New York: Plenum.

Taulbee, E. S. (1958). A validation of MMPI scale pairs in psychiatric diagnosis. *Journal of Clinical Psychology, 14*, 316.

Taulbee, E. S., & Sisson, B. D. (1957). Configurational analysis of MMPI profiles of psychiatric groups. *Journal of Consulting Psychology, 21*, 413–417.

Trifiletti, R. J. (1982). Differentiating brain damage from schizophrenia: A further test of Russell's MMPI key. *Journal of Clinical Psychology, 38*, 39–44.

Walters, G. D. (1983). The MMPI and schizophrenia: A review. *Schizophrenia Bulletin, 9*, 226–246.

Walters, G. D. (1984a). Empirically derived characteristics of psychiatric inpatients with DSM-III diagnoses of schizophreniform disorder. *Journal of Abnormal Psychology, 93*, 71–79.

Walters, G. D. (1984b). Identifying schizophrenia by means of Scale 8 (*Sc*) of the MMPI. *Journal of Personality Assessment, 48*, 390–391.

Walters, G. D. (1986). [MMPI high-point codes of incarcerated offenders satisfying Psychiatric Diagnostic Interview (PDI) criteria for schizophrenia]. Unpublished raw data.

Walters, G. D., & Greene, R. L. (1988). Differentiating between schizophrenic and manic inpatients by means of the MMPI. *Journal of Personality Assessment, 52*, 91–95.

Walters, G. D., White, T. W., & Greene, R. L. (1988). Use of the MMPI to identify malingering and exaggeration of psychiatric symptomatology in male prison inmates. *Journal of Consulting and Clinical Psychology, 56*, 111–117.

Walton, D., Mather, M., & Black, D. A. (1959). The validity of the Meehl MMPI psychotic scale in the diagnosis of schizophrenia. *Journal of Mental Science, 105*, 869–871.

Watson, C. G. (1968). Prediction of length of hospital stay from MMPI scales. *Journal of Clinical Psychology, 24*, 444–447.

Watson, C. G. (1971). An MMPI scale to separate brain-damaged from schizophrenic men. *Journal of Consulting and Clinical Psychology, 36*, 121–125.

Watson, C. G. (1984). The Schizophrenia-Organic (*Sc-O*) and Psychiatric-Organic (*P-O*) MMPI scales: A review. *Journal of Clinical Psychology, 40*, 1008–1023.

Watson, C. G., & Plemel, D. (1978). An MMPI scale to separate brain-damaged from functional psychiatric patients in neuropsychiatric settings. *Journal of Consulting and Clinical Psychology, 46*, 1127–1132.

Watson, C. G., & Thomas, R. W. (1968). MMPI profiles of brain-damaged and schizophrenic patients. *Perceptual and Motor Skills, 27*, 567–573.

Wauck, L. A. (1950). Schizophrenia and the MMPI. *Journal of Clinical Psychology, 6,* 279–284.

Wilensky, H., & Solomon, L. (1960). Characteristics of untestable chronic schizophrenics. *Journal of Abnormal and Social Psychology, 61,* 155–158.

Winter, W. D., & Stortroen, M. (1963). A comparison of several MMPI indices to differentiate psychotics from normals. *Journal of Clinical Psychology, 19,* 220–223.

Winters, K. C., Newmark, C. S., Lumry, A. E., Leach, K., & Weintraub, S. (1985). MMPI codetypes characteristic of DSM-III schizophrenics, depressives, and bipolars. *Journal of Clinical Psychology, 41,* 382–386.

Winters, K. C., Weintraub, S., & Neale, J. M. (1981). Validity of MMPI code types in identifying DSM-III schizo-phrenics, unipolars, and bipolars. *Journal of Consulting and Clinical Psychology, 49,* 486–487.

Young, R. C., Gould, E., Glick, I. D., & Hargreaves, W. (1980). Personality inventory correlates of outcome in a follow-up study of psychiatric hospitalization. *Psychological Reports, 46,* 903–906.

Yusin, A., Nihira, K., & Mortashed, C. (1974). Major and minor criteria in schizophrenia. *Archives of General Psychiatry, 131,* 688–692.

Zigler, E., Levine, J., & Zigler, B. (1976). The relation between premorbid competence and paranoid-nonparanoid status in schizophrenia: A methodological and theoretical critique. *Psychological Bulletin, 83,* 303–313.

Chapter 4

Mood Disorders

DAVID S. NICHOLS

OVERVIEW

The concept of disordered mood is as old as antiquity. In the fourth century B.C., Hippocrates described a syndrome already known for several centuries that was caused by an accumulation of black bile and led to a "darkening of the spirit." He called this syndrome *melancholia* (melan-black; cholia-bile). Hippocratic writings also contain reference to *mania*, a term roughly equivalent to madness, which applied to more acute, non-delirious, nonfebrile mental disorders, including cases of what might now be called schizophrenia. The connection between melancholia and mania dates to the first century A.D. when Aretaeus described these states in alternation, antedating the descriptions of Kahlbaum (cyclothymia) and Kraepelin in the modern era. In fact, the term *manic-depressive* (maniaco-melancholicus) predates the Kraepelinian usage by at least 300 years. The distinction between major and minor depression is similarly ancient. The Apostle Paul in his second letter to the Corinthians compares the sorrow "from God" with that "of the world." With subsequent theological refinement this contrast became one of a "'disturbed, irrational' type of depression with the beneficient 'temperate and rational'" kind (Altschule, 1976, p. 158). Despite or because of the long history of disordered mood, there is still great interest in understanding these disorders. This chapter reviews research findings on the use of the MMPI with mood disordered patient groups.

This chapter substantially updates an earlier treatment of the appraisal of symptomatic excitement and depression given by Dahlstrom and Welsh in the first edition of the *MMPI Handbook* (1960). That volume appeared only 4 years after Meehl (1956) placed his famous want ad in the *American Psychologist*, reporting the feasibility of a "good cookbook." The latter would apply actuarial methods to develop codetype recipes, each consisting of a group of rules setting the requirements for membership in a given class of profiles and a set of correlated items descriptive of the case history, symptoms, mental status, and diagnostic characteristics for cases meeting the membership rules for that class. Each item would be associated with its profile type at a known level of probability that could then be compared with the item's base rate and its probability of occurrence in other types of profiles. Within 10 years after Meehl's petition, no fewer than three MMPI cookbooks were in print, and despite their occasionally misleading culinary attributes as shown below, codetypes had become the *lingua franca* of MMPI discourse among clinicians. Although they did not ignore code patterns, Dahlstrom and Welsh placed relatively greater emphasis on single scales in assessing depression and mania. In the more than 25 years since their *Handbook* appeared, much has been learned about the profile patterns typical of groups of affectively disordered patients, and these will be given correspondingly greater emphasis here.

MOOD DISORDERS

MAJOR SYMPTOMS OF DEPRESSION

Depressive symptomatology is so variable in the intensity and patterning of its manifestations

THE MMPI: USE WITH
SPECIFIC POPULATIONS

© 1988 by Grune & Stratton.

ISBN 0-8089-1913-X

that patients with depressive disorders may come to the attention of psychologists and psychiatrists from innumerable directions. Physicians of all specialties, ministers of all faiths, and counselors of all persuasions have frequently encountered people with depressive symptoms and complaints.

The most common symptoms of depression include: feeling sad, blue, unhappy, or depressed; a loss of interest in sex, work, hobbies, friends, and family; and problems in concentration and attention. These symptoms can be categorized into four areas: affective, cognitive, behavioral, and vegetative.

Affective symptoms may include not only a predominantly dysphoric mood but flat affect as well, even to the extent of denial of any feelings at all. Feelings of listlessness, fatigue, and weakness are common, although these may coexist with a sense of inner restiveness. In most patients there are feelings of tension and anxiety. The patient experiences apprehension and foreboding, an inability to relax, and possibly irritability. At the extreme, there may be anxious or anguished restlessness or agitation, and the patient may suffer outbursts of temper or crying that are poorly related to their antecedents. Exaggerated feelings of guilt or blameworthiness over past misdeeds, real or imagined, may lead to a conviction of the need for punishment. Indeed, the patient may feel guilty about bringing on the depression itself. It should be noted that depressive mood is not itself a necessary condition for a diagnosis of depression. In major depressions, especially those of unipolar type, emotional expression may become virtually immobilized in a fashion reminiscent of the affective flattening or emotional blunting of schizophrenia. The patient may feel "dead," "empty," "beyond tears," and be unable to cry, find the normal response to humor inaccessible, and consider the depression not merely an exaggeration of previously felt misery or unhappiness but a qualitative change to a new and alien state of being.

Cognitive symptoms may include convictions of helplessness, hopelessness, worthlessness, and sinfulness. The cognitive life narrows to a degree that allows only a brooding, morbid focus. The patient may deny the value of past successes and achievements, no matter how substantial these may be, seeing them as pointless or even as failures. Attitudes toward the future are equally distorted and pessimistic; the patient's outlook is gloomy and bleak regarding any prospect for future success or even recovery. Suicidal ideation, intent, and germinal plans may arise from the regrets of the past or the pessimistic and painful anticipations of the future, or both. Constant preoccupation with worry, fluctuating attention, and the inability to sustain concentration without great fatigue may give rise to forgetfulness and indecision. The patient may lose track of intentions, thoughts, and ideas, what is said to him or her, or even attending to physical needs. The stream of thought may be halting, confused, and retarded. There is usually some preservation of insight into the fact of illness, but the patient may be unable to apply it to his or her own advantage. There is always some risk that suicide will supervene before assistance is sought. In the more severe depressions, judgment typically is impaired by an overwhelmingly negative bias to the patient's outlook. In a sizeable minority of cases, hallucinations, delusions, and symptoms of formal thought disorder (e.g., thought insertion, withdrawal, broadcasting, etc.) are present. These are typically, *but not necessarily*, congruent with depressive themes of death, disease, guilt, inadequacy, nihilism, and sinfulness. Also relatively common are hypochondriacal preoccupations. These are usually mild and include symptoms such as back or abdominal pain; headache; digestive complaints including nausea, vomiting, diarrhea, and constipation; cardiac complaints; apnea; and so on. In cases of so-called "masked depression," these and related symptoms are reported by patients who do not recognize feelings of depression even though other signs of depression are present. In the more severe depressions, however, these preoccupations may take on a quasi-delusional character with the patient maintaining a conviction that he or she has cancer, heart disease, or some other dread illness and remaining impervious to evidence or reassurance to the contrary.

Behavioral symptoms represent an extension of cognitive and affective symptoms to the motor sphere. Motor retardation, postural immobility, a softening of voice and monotony of pitch, immobile facies, and slowed speech with extended latencies or even mutism may be present. Any movement may be anergic, effortful, and conservative. Alternatively, or even coexisting with motor retardation, movement may be agitated with tense pacing back and forth, picking at skin or hair, handwringing, fidgeting with fingers or small objects, monotonous grooming gestures, and chainsmoking. Vocalization may be limited to wailing and moaning, and repetitious statements of self-condemnation or pleas for forgiveness or punishment. The patient may be unable to sit still, stand, lie down, or maintain any other position without a flood of anxiety and discomfort. There is a withdrawal from interpersonal contact as the patient feels burdened and unable to carry his or her own weight in interaction, and is likely to view conversation as a burdensome imposition on others as well. Responses to questions tend to be relevant, but brief, perfunctory, and impotent.

Vegetative symptoms include loss of appetite and sexual desire, and sleep disturbance. The cognitive and behavioral slowing noted previously has a physiologic counterpart in the increased latency between intake and elimination in the major depressions. The loss of appetite and consequent weight loss may be accelerated by a loss of gustatory pleasure and feelings of unworthiness to take nourishment. The patient may feel full, therefore having no need for food, or empty, having nothing to nourish. Or, he or she may feel that to consume food is to deprive another who is more deserving of its value. Ejaculatory and erectile failure in men and intolerance of sexual intercourse in women are common. Sleep disturbance is usually manifested in initial insomnia as the patient lies awake and worries. When sleep is finally achieved, it may be fitful and punctuated with unpleasant dreams. In the more severe depressions, the patient may have little trouble going to sleep, but awakens in the early morning and is unable to go back to sleep. The patient may complain that sleep provides neither rest nor respite from depression. In some patients, sleep disturbance takes the form of hypersomnia as the patient uses sleep to withdraw or escape, and this may complicate nocturnal sleep difficulties.

MAJOR SYMPTOMS OF MANIA

The symptoms of mania are less protean than those of depression, and some unwarranted comfort has been taken in the alleged ease with which manic symptoms may be elicited and identified. Unfortunately, manic symptoms often coincide with those of other major psychiatric and personality disorders, especially schizophrenia, as discussed later. The cardinal features of mania include elevated mood, flight of ideas, and hyperactivity.

Affect is characteristically elated, euphoric, enthusiastic, expansive, triumphant, and disinhibited.

The patient may present as playful, jocular, quick-witted, and high spirited, free of all normal cares and concerns, in tip-top shape, and ready for action. This picture is unstable, however, and may change suddenly into one of anger and hostility if the patient is blocked in the pursuit of some goal, has his or her self-esteem challenged, experiences rebuff, or in some other way feels thwarted. The patient often feels highly vulnerable to real or implied personal criticism even though he or she may be quite imperturbable regarding other matters. For a large minority of patients the dominant mood is one of irritability rather than elation, and affect may even be somewhat dysphoric. The patient may seem cantankerous and constantly in transit between flare-ups of litigiousness, contentiousness, and antagonism. Fear may emerge in some cases, usually relatively late in the manic episode, and may be related to reverses, rejections, and alienation, secondary to the reactions of friends, family, or staff to the patient's obnoxiousness. Major lapses in judgment, including sexual or financial indiscretions occurring earlier in the episode, which become clear to the patient, may also stimulate a fearful response. Finally, fear may be a reaction to the realization that the manic flight will soon expire and be supplanted by depression. Not uncommonly, such fears may reach delusional proportions and involve themes of retribution or of being poisoned (by medication, i.e., being slowed down to the point that depression may catch up).

Cognitive symptoms include an inflated, if not grandiose, and fragile self-esteem, boundless self-confidence, and an accelerated stream of thought. The patient may speak of mental "soaring," experiencing a sense of brilliance and exhiliration at the pell mell rush of ideas and the feeling of freedom from worldly constraints, obstacles, and resistances. When thought is not too disrupted, the patient may have grandiose and far-fetched plans for inventions, new businesses, and so on, may discover important "secrets" of science, philosophy, or religion that he or she must work out in detail, or may hit on ingenious schemes for making money, winning at horses, and so on. But usually the patient is too distractable for such plans to be developed more than a few steps, and they are quickly abandoned in favor of some new possibility that will soon share the same fate. In some cases the patient's preoccupation with keeping up with his or her own stream of thought can be so extensive as to mask speech and motor symptoms of mania. Movement may even appear retarded, and speech may be in the minimal, halting style of depression. Judgment is typically impaired and often severely so. Unlike depression, in mania insight usually is completely lacking. The patient may claim to have "never felt better," feels the present state to be an improvement over his or her normal state, and recognizes no abnormality of behavior or attitude even when these are of manifest concern to family and other close associates. Psychotic symptoms such as hallucinations and delusions, once thought to be relatively rare in mania, are now recognized as common if not typical. Likewise, symptoms of formal thought disorder have been found to be at least as frequent in mania as in schizophrenia (e.g., Harrow, Grossman, Silverstein, & Meltzer, 1982). Hallucinations are usually auditory but visual hallucinations are not uncommon. Both types of hallucinations often have a sharp, vivid sensory quality. Delusions of persecution are most frequent, but delusions of grandeur are also quite common, and the two are usually connected. Sexual and religious themes are often prominent in delusional material. In some cases with prominent paranoid symptoms, thought processes often are well preserved and the patient may manifest tense hyperrationality, especially in defense of delusional ideas.

Behavior is proud, energized, impulsive, and overactive. The patient is overtalkative and speech may be loud, pressured, and colored by punning, rhyming, singing, chanting, and distant associations. Shifts in topic are often abrupt, arbitrary, or irrelevantly digressive. At the extreme, speech may become completely disorganized and incoherent. The patient may be in constant motion and able to go for several days without sleep. Aggressive sociability (social hunger) is characteristic, and sexual interest and availability are high. Others often are attracted by the patient's disinhibition, outgoingness, ready sense of humor, and freedom from anxiety. However, they may be repelled just as quickly as the patient shows a callous disregard for their feelings and sensibilities by interrupting, embarrassing, rejecting, or degrading them without qualm. Moral and financial obligations may be slighted or disregarded as the patient consumes relationships, borrows with scant intent of repayment, makes ill-considered if not foolish investments, and goes on spending sprees. Dress and grooming may be neglected as the patient rushes around attending to "more important matters." Alternatively, dress and grooming may be ostentatious, flamboyant, or bizarre, with outlandish costumes, odd combinations of apparel, make-up applied excessively or idiosyncratically, stripping, or streaking. The presence of psychotic symptoms increases the patient's intolerance of frustration and the risk of verbal attack, or assault, when crossed. Such symptoms also may serve to mask hyperactivity. In particular, patients with prominent paranoid symptoms often do not show evidence of gross hyperactivity; rather they appear tense, overtalkative (though not necessarily pressured), and may reveal a great deal of delusional material under patient questioning.

PREVALENCE AND INCIDENCE

Epidemiologic data on the prevalence, incidence, and lifetime risk of affective disturbance show considerable variation as a consequence of differences in case-finding and case-definition. Nevertheless, a crude breakdown into depressive symptoms, nonbipolar depression, and bipolar disorder has been offered by Weissman and Boyd (1983). They report that at any given time, from 13 to 20 percent of the population have depressive symptoms, and approximately 1 in 6 men and 5 in 12 women have a diagnosable major or minor depressive disorder. New cases of unipolar depression are found at rates of 82 to 201 per 100,000 men and 247 to 598 per 100,000 women each year. Comparable figures for bipolar disorder are 9 to 15.2 per 100,000 men and 7.4 to 32 per 100,000 women. In conservative round numbers, these figures translate into a million new cases of diagnosable depression and 50,000 new cases of bipolar disorder each year within the United States.

A recent survey of the lifetime prevalence of major psychiatric disorders in New Haven, Baltimore, and St. Louis, which were identified on the basis of Diagnostic Interview Schedule (DIS: Robins, Helzer, Croughan, & Ratcliff, 1981) criteria, found rates of 0.9, 5.2, and 3.0 percent for manic episode, major depressive episode, and dysthymia, respectively (Robins et al., 1984). These figures may not reflect lifetime prevalence for these disorders nationwide, however. Major depression, at least, may be as much as twice as common in urban as in rural areas (Blazer et al., 1985).

TYPICAL PATIENTS

The typical unipolar depressive is a 35- to 65-year-old woman of any race or social class with a personal or family history of depression or alcoholism. As a child she may have lived in hostile, disruptive, or otherwise unfavorable home conditions and may have suffered a recent loss such as a job or a boyfriend or have undergone a marital separation or divorce. Her premorbid personality may have been described as insecure, guilty, dependent, unassertive, worried, shy, and lacking in social skills.

The typical bipolar depressive is a 25- to 35-year-old middle or higher social class male or female of any race with above average educational and occupational achievement. He or she may have had one or more previous manic or depressive episodes and may well have a positive family history for mania, depression, suicide, or possibly alcoholism. Premorbid personality was probably well within normal limits, but may have been notable for extraversion, independence, and achievement motivation. The typical bipolar manic is similar but perhaps younger: 20 to 30 years old.

Since Dysthymic Disorder is relatively new and its DSM-II predecessor, Depressive Neurosis, often was employed as a wastebasket category for virtually any relatively mild, nonpsychotic condition without prominent vegetative features, little reliable information exists concerning these disorders. The diagnosis of Depressive Neurosis in DSM-II was apparently also quite unstable. Akiskal, Bitar, Puzantian, Rosenthal, and Walker (1978) found that 40 percent of neurotic depressives met the criteria for unipolar or bipolar illness on follow-up, while Winokur and Pitts (1964) found no differences in family history between neurotic and psychotic depressives. Results such as these suggest that Depressive Neurosis, at least, may be merely a subclinical form of major affective illness. The following description is therefore quite tentative. The typical dysthymic is a 25- to 50-year-old woman of any race or social class. She has a history of similar episodes but no clear age of onset, may be separated or divorced, and demonstrate past or current passivity and dependency, self-disparaging attitudes and low self-esteem, guilt, shyness or lack of social skills, and self-defeating behavior.

DIFFERENTIAL DIAGNOSIS

The classification of affective disorders within the United States has changed little since the American Psychiatric Association's Official Classification of Mental Disorders, which was approved in 1934, became incorporated in the second edition of the *Standard Classified Nomenclature of Disease* (SCND) of 1935. The Standard Veterans Administration classification (SVA) of 1951 added a new category, Psychotic Depressive Reaction, which had been in semi-formal use for some time. A year later, the first edition of the American Psychiatric Association's *Diagnostic and Statistical Manual of Mental Disorders* (DSM-I) added Schizophrenic Reaction, Schizoaffective Type, the schizoaffective concept having been introduced 20 years earlier by Kasanin (1933). As can be seen in Table 4–1, subsequent developments in standardized nosology have been largely confined to recasting or subdividing earlier categories. For example, DSM-II distinguished excited and depressed subcategories of schizoaffective schizophrenia; DSM-III recollapsed these and demoted this disorder from a subtype of schizophrenia to a category, Schizoaffective Disorder, among neither the affective nor schizophrenic disorders. The most significant changes in the nosology of the affective disorders with the advent of DSM-III is the elimination of Depressive Neurosis and its substitution with Dysthymic Disorder (discussed later), and the division of major depressions into unipolar and bipolar types. This distinction was proposed by Leonhard (1979) and represented a shift away from the endogenous-reactive continuum that previously had guided the subdivision of the affective disorders. The unipolar-bipolar distinction became rapidly assimilated into American psychiatry and was accepted by the DSM-III committee. The earlier editions of DSM did not require episodes of both depression and mania for a diagnosis of Manic-depressive illness, and DSM-II *proscribed* periods of mania and depression for the depressed and manic types of this disorder, respectively. With the adoption of the unipolar-bipolar terminology in DSM-III, Involutional Melancholia and Psychotic Depressive Reaction were abandoned.

While the general, if not the specific, criteria for the affective disorders have been fairly constant for the last half-century, the frequency with which many of these disorders have been diagnosed in recent years has significantly increased from earlier rates. This increase may be largely due to a narrowing in the concept of schizophrenia. A large body of research in the decade and a half following

TABLE 4–1.   COMPARATIVE SYSTEMS FOR THE CLASSIFICATION OF AFFECTIVE DISORDERS

System	SCND (1935)	SVA (1951)	DSM-I (1952)	DSM-II (1968)	DSM-III (1980)	DSM-III-R (1987)
Major affective disorders	Involutional melancholia	Involutional melancholia	20 Involutional psychotic reaction	296.00 Involutional melancholia	296.23 Major depression, single episode with melancholia, or 296.24 with psychotic features	296.2x Major depression, single episode, melancholic type, or 296.3x Recurrent, melancholic type, or code 296.24 or 296.34 if with psychotic features
	Manic depressive psychosis, manic	Manic depressive reaction, manic	21.0 Manic depressive reaction, manic type	296.10 Manic depressive illness, manic type	296.4x Bipolar disorder, manic	296.4x Bipolar disorder, manic
	Manic depressive psychosis, depressed	Manic depressive reaction, depressive	21.1 Manic depressive reaction, depressed type	296.20 Manic depressive illness, depressed type (incl. "endogenous depression")	296.2x Major depression, single episode, or 296.3x recurrent	296.2x Major depression, single episode, or 296.3x recurrent
	Manic depressive psychosis, circular	Manic depressive reaction, circular		296.33 Manic depressive illness, circular type, manic, or 296.34 depressed	296.4x Bipolar disorder, manic, 296.5x depressed, or 296.6x mixed	296.4x Bipolar disorder, manic, 296.5x depressed, or 296.6x mixed
	Manic depressive psychosis, mixed	Manic depressive reaction, mixed	21.2 Manic depressive reaction, other	296.80 Other major affective disorder		
		Psychotic depressive reaction	21.3 Psychotic depressive reaction	298.00 Psychotic depressive reaction	296.24 Major depression, single episode, with psychotic features	296.24 Major depression, single episode, with psychotic features
Schizo-affective disorders			22.6 Schizophrenic reaction, schizo-affective type	295.73 Schizophrenia, schizoaffective type, excited, or 295.74 depressed	295.70 Schizoaffective disorder	295.70 Schizoaffective, disorder, specify bipolar or depressive type
"Minor" affective disorders	Reactive depression	Depressive reaction	40.5 Depressive reaction	300.40 Depressive neurosis	300.40 Dysthymic disorder, or 296.22 Major depression, without melancholia, single episode, or 296.23 recurrent	300.40 Dysthymia, or 296.21 Major depression without melancholia, single episode, or 296.31 recurrent

DSM-II suggested that schizophrenia was over-diagnosed in the United States, especially in relation to the major affective disorders. Several studies found that the impressionistic criteria for schizophrenia in DSM-II, earlier diagnostic systems, and basic authoritative sources (e.g., Bleuler, 1950) performed poorly in discriminating schizophrenia from certain affective disorders, especially mania. In particular, such criteria lacked specificity. Even some systems based on fixed criteria such as Bleuler's "four As" (autism, associations, affect, and ambivalence) or that of Schneider (1959) were found to lack specificity. For example, in their comprehensive review of the diagnosis of schizophrenia and manic-depressive illness, Pope and Lipinski (1978) found that Schneider's First Rank Symptoms of schizophrenia were "reported in 20% to 50% of well validated cases of manic-depressive illness" (p. 826). In DSM-III, the use of operational criteria for schizophrenia and the major affective disorders became institutionalized. These criteria were based on the earlier efforts of Feighner et al. (1972) and Spitzer, Endicott, and Robins (1975) to enhance diagnostic reliability by recourse to fixed-rule systems. While these efforts realized the goal of increased interdiagnostician agreement, the latter was accompanied by reductions in the numbers of patients meeting criteria for schizophrenia and sharp increases in the numbers of patients meeting criteria for most of the affective disorders.

This result perhaps was anticipated in the conclusion of Pope and Lipinski (1978) that "rigorously speaking, every study of 'schizophrenia' in the literature that does not make reference to prognostic, family history, or treatment-response criteria must be considered, *until shown otherwise*, to be contaminated with up to 40% cases of manic-depressive illness" (p. 826).

But if previously constituted groups of schizophrenics were contaminated with a large minority of affectively disordered patients—and presumably this would include the criterion samples used by Hathaway (1980) in developing Scale *8* of the MMPI—it can be argued that corresponding groups of affectively disordered patients have the virtue of few false positives, since cases deviating from textbook pictures of pure mood disorder were at risk of misclassification as schizophrenics. Cases manifesting thought disorder, hallucinations, delusions, or even excitement may have been called schizophrenic at a time when such symptoms often were considered virtually pathognomonic and the diagnosis of mood disorder was made on the basis of excluding a diagnosis of schizophrenia. In fact, McKinley and Hathaway give some suggestion of the process in their discussion of the development of Scale *9*. They note that in the selection of the manic patients, "care was exercised to exclude individuals with delirium, confusional states, or with excitements associated with other psychoses such as schizophrenia" (1980, p. 52). Thus, the counterpart of a bias toward overinclusion in the diagnosis of schizophrenia was a tendency to underdiagnose major affective illnesses. As a predictable result, contemporary groups of these latter disorders were biased toward unusually high homogeneity, even though they may have lacked representativeness. With references to Scale *9* then, the criterion group of manics assembled by McKinley and Hathaway may well have included few or no false positives. While these cases may have lacked the features of thought disorder, hallucinations, and delusions found among more recently constituted manic samples, the bias toward specificity would have rendered Scale *9* an unusually valid measure of the core features of the manic syndrome.

The primary differential diagnosis for mania, then, is schizophrenia. Data from interview, mental status examination, and personal and family history may all contribute to the successful differentiation of these disorders. Thought disorder in mania is especially characterized by flight-of-ideas, pressured, distractible, and excessive speech, and circumstantiality. Derailment or associative looseness has a overinclusive character, and ideas tend to be combined in opportunistic, dramatic, or playful ways, no matter how incoherent. Schizophrenic thought disorder emphasizes improverished speech and content (Andreasen, 1979) and associative loosening that is absurd, confused, or fragmented. Strikingly idiosyncratic verbalizations, though not especially common, appear specific to schizophrenia (e.g., "Every time I light up a cigarette, Blam!, a wave of communism just seems to go all over everything"). Andreasen, Hoffman, and Grove (1985) found that the characteristics of manic thought disorder were more discriminating than those of schizophrenic thought disorder, hence it is the *absence* of manic symptoms rather than the presence of schizophrenic symptoms that contributes most to the correct classification of schizophrenia. Grandiose and religious content are less common in schizophrenia than in mania. Manic affect typically is elated, euphoric, and expansive or irritable, although euphoria and irritability may coexist or alternate within brief periods (emotional lability). Schizophrenic affect typically is emotionally blunted, flattened, or impassive and is manifested by apathetic mood, a limited range of affect, and deanimated facies, leading to a characteristically "deadened" rapport in interview. Affect is virtually never genuinely warm or friendly, although it may be ingratiating. Motor behavior in mania is typically hyperactive, e.g., hypermobility, rapid speech, overtalkativeness, and impulsiveness. Motor behavior in schizophrenia is of normal tempo if not anergic and undermotivated. Social behavior in mania is oriented toward approach and is typically confident, eager, and aggressively outgoing, whereas in schizophrenia it is oriented toward withdrawal/avoidance and is typically detached and isolative, awkward and inept, and indifferent or apprehensive.

Paranoid types of mania and schizophrenia can be especially difficult to discriminate because the former are less euphoric and hyperactive than manics in general, while the latter are less thought-disordered than schizophrenics in general. Both may be equally paranoid and delusional, but compared with paranoid schizophrenics, paranoid manics are more tense, hostile, irritable, labile, excitable, and overreactive. However, they are less likely to be depressed, apathetic, aloof, and uninterested.

Personal history characteristics that favor a diagnosis of mania over that of schizophrenia include social, educational, and vocational achievement such as several close friends, extracurricular participation in secondary education, completion of college, extensive dating and marriage, and occupational stability with promotion or progressive increases in responsibility. If present, prior psychiatric history reveals affective symptoms such as hyperactivity, flight-of-ideas, and euphoria, or depression, and reflects a periodic course with complete or near-complete recovery between episodes of illness. A family history of mental disorder, especially affective disorder, or suicide strongly favors a diagnosis of mania over schizophrenia. The reverse is not true, however. While a family history of schizophrenia may support such a diagnosis for the patient, diagnoses of schizophrenia for mentally ill relatives should not be taken at face value. The overdiagnosis of schizophrenia and underdiagnosis of affective disorder within the United States until recently casts suspicion on diagnoses of schizophrenia made prior to 1980, and especially those made prior to the early 1970s. Suspicion is enhanced when more than one or two "schizophrenics" are found among the patient's first or second degree relatives because of the greater heritability of affective disorders, particularly bipolar disorder.

Additional differential diagnoses for mania include physical and neurologic diseases and cyclothymia. A variety of medical conditions caused by infectious, endocrine, neurologic, or other conditions may mimic mania, including thyrotoxicosis, stroke, multiple sclerosis, systemic lupus erythematosus, and certain kinds of encephalitis and brain tumors. Manic symptoms may also occur secondary to the intoxicating effects of psychostimulants (e.g., amphetamines, cocaine, methylphenidate) or as side effects of antidepressants, steroids, levodopa, and other drugs. The DSM-III criteria for Organic Affective Syndrome requires an etiologically significant organic factor that is judged to be related to the affective disturbance and that, in turn, rules out a manic episode. DSM-III Cyclothymic Disorder represents an attenuated form of bipolar disorder in which affec-

tive symptoms are not of sufficient duration or do not reach the socially incapacitating levels of severity typical of mania and in which psychotic symptoms are absent.

Differentiating among the depressive affective disorders and Uncomplicated Bereavement and between these and several other psychopathologic and medical disorders can be difficult. Depression occurs as a presenting symptom in a great number of infectious diseases (e.g., hepatitis, influenza, mononucleosis, pneumonia, tertiary syphilis, tuberculosis), endocrine disorders (e.g., Cushing's and Addison's diseases, hypothyroidism), neurologic disorders (e.g., Parkinson's disease, multiple sclerosis, stroke, tumor), rheumatoid arthritis, cerebral arteriosclerosis, and dementia. Toxic reactions or side effects that present with depression as a major symptom are seen with alpha-methyldopa, reserpine, steroids, antihypertensives, sedative-hypnotics, alcohol, and benzodiazepines. Withdrawal from psychostimulants also is associated with depression. In psychiatric settings, depression may present as dementia (pseudodementia), particularly among the elderly. The differentiation usually rests on the mental status or neuropsychologic assessment of memory, orientation, and intelligence. Similarly, true dementia may occasion a secondary depression that needs to be discriminated from the major affective disorders.

Anxiety disorders ordinarily may be distinguished from depressive conditions by an earlier age of onset, panic or phobic symptoms, a relatively greater "weight" of anxiety symptoms, and the absence of suicidal ideation, anorexia, or even genuinely depressed mood. The order in which symptoms appeared can also be important: symptoms of depression preceding anxiety symptoms suggest a depressive rather than an anxiety condition.

Schizophrenia is distinguished from depression by its chronic course, poorer premorbid adjustment, lower level of reconstitution during periods of remission, and the absence of a family history of affective illness. Andreasen et al. (1985) found less overall thought disorder for depressives than for schizophrenics. In particular, the depressives were less likely to show poverty of content, derailment, illogicality, and perseveration, but were more likely to manifest circumstantiality.

Depression may be concealed or obscured by somatic symptoms ("masked depression"). Somatization Disorder, Hypochondriasis, and Psychogenic Pain Disorder may all coexist with depressive conditions. When a dual diagnosis of a depressive and a somatoform disorder is unjustified, the depression usually post-dates and is secondary to the somatoform disorder.

The presence of psychotic symptoms like hallucinations and delusions rules out a single diagnosis of Dysthymic Disorder, but a superimposed Major Depressive Episode may be consistent with such symptoms and both may be diagnosed if the criteria are met. The major differential diagnoses for Dysthymic Disorder are the personality disorders, especially Histrionic, Borderline, Dependent, and Passive-aggressive. However, DSM-III encourages diagnoses on both Axes I and II so that it is unnecessary to determine causal priority between Dysthymic Disorder and these Axis II conditions.

Uncomplicated Bereavement may be associated with all of the positive criteria for a Major Depressive Episode, but is not considered a mental disorder. However, if grief persists longer than 1 year, or if the symptoms are unusually severe or include fears of losing one's mind and thoughts of self-harm, a major depression diagnosis may be justified (Goodwin & Guze, 1979).

STATE DEPENDENCY

The issue of state dependency is of particular significance in many of the affective disorders. Indeed, for many of these, the instability of mood is a cardinal feature contributing to the very definition of the affective disorders, particularly bipolar disorder. The investigation of samples of bipolar patients without regard to the position of each patient in his or her own mood cycle is likely to obscure if not distort the characterization of the sample in a mean profile and even in a distribution of codetypes.

A dramatic illustration of changes in mood is afforded in the following series of four MMPI profiles produced by a female bipolar patient who was 53 years old at the time of her first admission to Dammasch Hospital. She initially presented with depression. For the previous 6 months she had experienced insomnia, anergy, anorexia, weight loss, loss of interest, hopelessness, and death wishes. While able to maintain employment as a sales clerk, she spent most of her discretionary time in bed. Except for a single hospitalization for the successful treatment of her alcoholism 3 years earlier,

the patient had no psychiatric history. Family history was positive for alcoholism in the patient's father and a brother. She was admitted to the ward in tears and immediately started on Elavil, 150 mg/d, but was seen to have improved by the next day. Nursing notes describe her as cooperative, friendly, and eager to help the staff make beds, clean the ward, and put other patients to bed, and indicated that she "is a hard worker who likes to keep busy." Concerned about the meaning of her improvement before her medication could have had any effect, she was referred to Psychology and tested 26 days after admission. Her profile is illustrated in Profile 4–1a. In the following week she was noted to become increasingly hyperactive, began to show euphoria and poor judgment, and was therefore re-referred for a second MMPI, completed 8 days after the first. The second profile, illustrated in Profile 4–1b, was thought to be consistent with lithium response, and the patient was accordingly started on this medication, responded well, and was discharged 31 days later.

The patient was readmitted 9 months later, presenting with low mood, anergy, and self-deprecatory ideas. Interim history revealed that she had discontinued medication shortly after her previous discharge and had resumed drinking. She was initially treated without medication and observed for symptoms of alcohol withdrawal. The day following admission the patient confided to staff that she wished to be more active, had her hair done, and completed the MMPI, illustrated in Profile 4–2a. In the following week the patient was noted to spend time hiding in bed and to have to push herself into activity. In the next week she was seen to "brighten" and express relief at not having to push herself. One staff member wrote, "I see this patient as slowly coming out of her depression." The patient appeared to stabilize at a mild hypomanic level for the next month until she became loud, overtalkative, and hyperactive, rapidly making and changing her plans for the future. She was retested in this state and produced the profile illustrated in Profile 4–2b.

This series of profiles reflects a succession of mood states, each of which provides an inadequate basis for a reliable personality description based on the MMPI. The first two profiles show Scale 4 as the highest or second highest point in the profile. The interpretation of either profile might well emphasize characterologic features like acting out, impulsivity, authority problems, rebelliousness, and

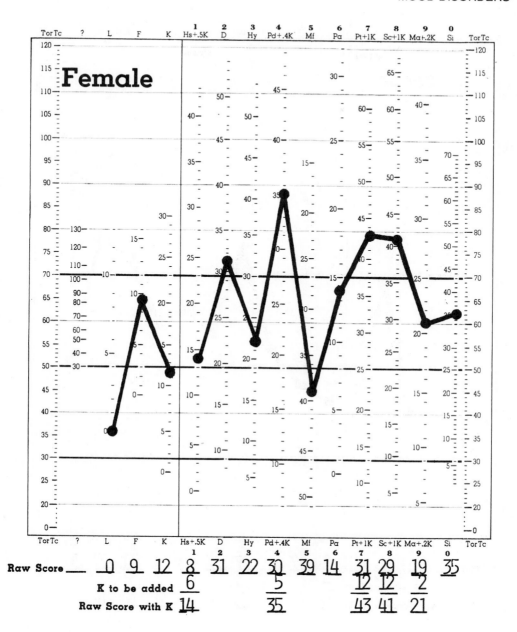

Female

	?	L	F	K	Hs+.5K 1	D 2	Hy 3	Pd+.4K 4	Mf 5	Pa 6	Pt+1K 7	Sc+1K 8	Ma+.2K 9	Si 0
Raw Score	0	9	12	8	31	22	30	39	14	31	29	19	35
K to be added					6			5			12	12	2	
Raw Score with K					14			35			43	41	21	

PROFILE 4–1A.

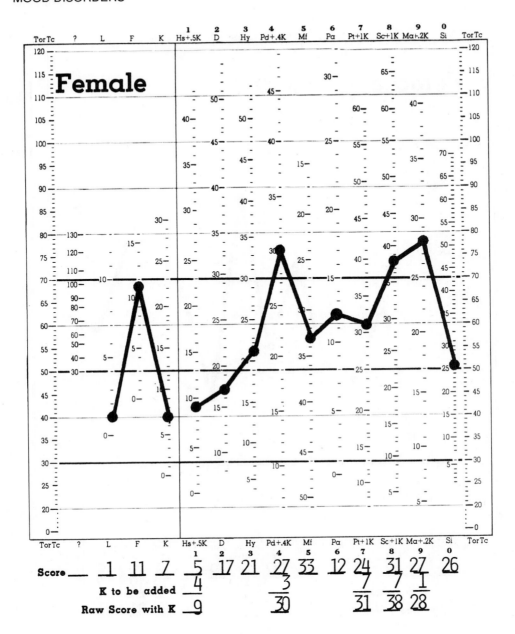

					1	2	3	4	5	6	7	8	9	0	
TorTc	?	L	F	K	Hs+.5K	D	Hy	Pd+.4K	Mf	Pa	Pt+1K	Sc+1K	Ma+.2K	Si	TorTc

Score __ 1 11 7 5 17 21 27 33 12 24 31 27 26

K to be added __4 3 7 7 1

Raw Score with K __9 30 31 38 28

PROFILE 4–1B.

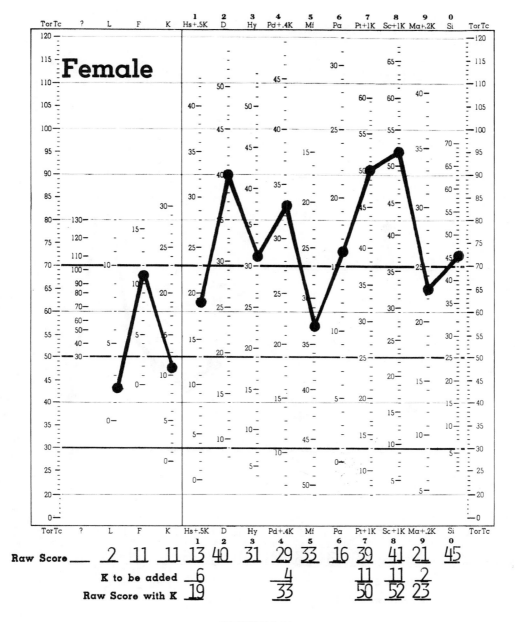

| | | | | | 1 | 2 | 3 | 4 | 5 | 6 | 7 | 8 | 9 | 0 | |
| TorTc | ? | L | F | K | Hs+.5K | D | Hy | Pd+.4K | Mf | Pa | Pt+1K | Sc+1K | Ma+.2K | Si | TorTc |

Female

PROFILE 4–2A.

					1	2	3	4	5	6	7	8	9	0	
TorTc	?	L	F	K	Hs+.5K	D	Hy	Pd+.4K	Mf	Pa	Pt+1K	Sc+1K	Ma+.2K	Si	TorTc

Raw Score ___ 2 11 11 13 40 31 29 33 16 39 41 21 45

K to be added ___ 6   4   11 11 2

Raw Score with K ___ 19   33   50 52 23

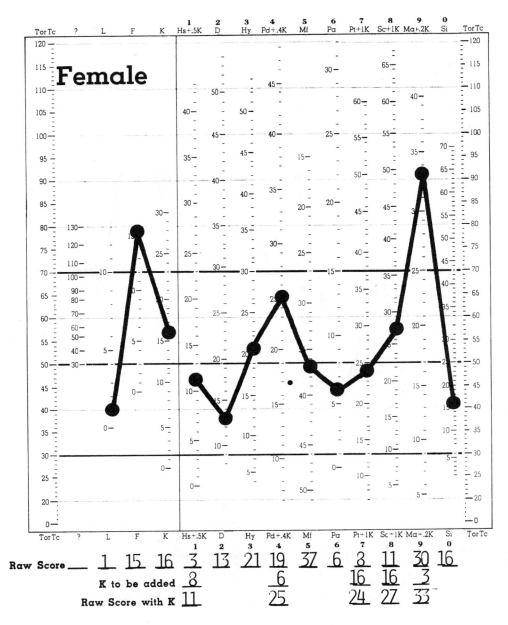

PROFILE 4–2B.

	?	L	F	K	1 Hs+.5K	2 D	3 Hy	4 Pd+.4K	5 Mf	6 Pa	7 Pt+1K	8 Sc+1K	9 Ma+.2K	0 Si
Raw Score		1	15	16	3	13	21	19	37	6	8	11	30	16
K to be added					8			6			16	16	3	
Raw Score with K					11			25			24	27	33	

so forth. Unless seen in relation to each other, the possibility of a major mood disorder might be missed. Seen together, however, these profiles strongly suggest a transition in mood states. From the first (Profile 4–1a) to the second (Profile 4–1b) profile, Scale 2 dropped 27 *T*-points, Scale 7 dropped 19, and Scale 9 increased by 18. The third profile (Profile 4–2a) is of a type associated with depressed mood, but in the context of a wide variety of diagnoses, including unipolar and bipolar depressions, and schizophrenia. It is the final profile (Profile 4–2b) that allows a clear choice to be made from among these possibilities.

Lumry, Gottesman, and Tuason (1982) illustrated this same point in a study of 22 carefully diagnosed bipolar patients tested at various points during their mood cycles. The mean profiles of the bipolars during their euthymic phase (Welsh code: *4-38627 591/0: K-F/L:*) and their siblings (Welsh code: *364782 951/0: KF/L:*) were well within normal limits and virtually indistinguishable. The bipolar patients tested during a depressive phase produced a *2-7-3-4* codetype (Welsh code: *2"734'8 601-95/ F-K/L:*), while the patients tested during a (hypo-) maniac phase produced a *9* codetype (Welsh code: *9'486-5731/02: FK/L:*). The individual codetypes within both the depressive and manic groups showed considerable variability: depressives, *2-3* (3), *2-4* (2), *2-7* (2), *2-0* (1), *3-4* (1), *7-8* (1); and manics, *4-3* (1), *4-9* (1), *6-9* (2), *8-6* (1), *9-1* (1), *9-4* (4), *9-5* (1), *9-6* (1). This same variability in MMPI performance also occurred within the same patient at different phases of the illness. One such patient, a 40-year-old female, produced a *2-8-3* codetype (Welsh code: *2**83"4170'695/ F-K/L:*) toward the end of a depressive episode. Less than a month later as she entered a manic phase, a *9-4* codetype was obtained (Welsh code: *94'8-671/25:0# K'L/F:*). This pattern was repeated just over 2 years later when a depressive *2-7-8-3* codetype (Welsh code: *2**783"40'16-59/ F-K/L:*) was followed a month later by a *3-1-9* codetype (Welsh code: *3"19'468-725/:0# KL/F:*) as a manic state ensued.

These illustrations emphasize the importance of knowing the phase of the patient's mood cycle for an appropriate evaluation of MMPI findings. Failure to take state dependency into account in the clinical interpretation of the MMPI results of affectively disordered patients may lead to gross distortions in trait attributions and personality description. Similar problems attend the evalua-

tion of the results of research with affective samples. Both intragroup and intraindividual variability in mood state may sharply degrade the signal-to-noise ratio in the results of research with these conditions, even when such results are presented at the relatively molecular level of codetypes and items.

PROTOTYPIC STUDY

In the context of diagnosis, the prototypic MMPI investigation of the affective disorders is one in which a comparison is made between the profiles (or other MMPI variables) of (1) a given affectively disordered group that has been subdivided on some variable of interest such as childhood bereavement (Wilson, Alltop, & Buffaloe, 1967) or lithium response (Donnelly, Goodwin, Waldman, & Murphy, 1978); and (2) another affectively disordered group (e.g., Donnelly & Murphy, 1973); or (3) a nonaffective diagnostic group (e.g., Dahlstrom & Prange, 1960). Differences in mean profiles, scale scores, codetype frequencies, or item endorsement rates generally are interpreted as the result of treatment or diagnostic group differences. This conclusion may or may not be warranted, however. Greene (1988) has listed a number of methodologic issues that may affect the degree to which confidence in the diagnostic implications group differences is justified. The reader is referred to Chapter 1 for an overview of these issues.

The prototypic study discussed here, Walters' "Empirically Derived Characteristics of Psychiatric Inpatients with DSM-III Diagnoses of Schizophreniform Disorder" (1984), illustrates several strengths of design, execution, and interpretation to which future investigations of MMPI performance among the affective disorders should aspire.

Walters (1984) sought to compare the demographic, behavioral, and psychometric characteristics among 165 active duty servicemen hospitalized in the psychiatry service of an army medical center. Diagnoses were independent of the MMPI and made by psychiatric residents using DSM-III criteria. Walters took advantage of the fact that nearly three-fourths of these patients had received diagnoses from 3 days to 3 weeks earlier at local military station hospitals, prior to transfer to the medical center, by calculating coefficients of agreement (Kappa) between station and center diagnoses. He noted, however, that these diagnoses were not independent: The center psychiatrists typically were aware of the station diagnoses. Patients were screened for inclusion in the study, and those who were outside an age range of 18 to 50, were admitted before 1980 or after 1982, had evidence of alcoholism, drug abuse, or organic brain syndrome, had an estimated IQ of < 75, omitted 30 or more MMPI items, or produced random profiles were excluded. Four groups were compared: 71 schizophreniform disorders (SFM), 40 schizophrenics (SCH), 25 bipolar manics (BPM), and 29 unipolar (major) depressions (UPD). Kappa values ranged from .54 (schizophreniform disorder) to .80 (unipolar depression).

Demographic information obtained from structured chart review included age, education, ethnic status (white, nonwhite), marital status, military rank, previous psychiatric hospitalization, and family psychiatric history (first- and second-degree relatives). Behavioral correlates having non-extreme base rates also were gathered via structured chart reviews, and a reliability check using a random subsample was conducted. The author adequately described the time span during which these data and the MMPI protocols were collected.

Data analysis relied on phi coefficients for computations on the nominal variables and on multivariate and univariate analyses of variance and covariance for computations involving continuous variables. Appropriate procedures were instituted to control for experiment-wise error. MMPI analyses used non-K-corrected raw scores. Tables present demographic and behavioral correlates, MMPI raw score means and standard deviations, and frequencies of the six most common codetypes for each diagnostic group.

When compared with patients with schizophreniform disorder, Walters found his manics to be older, more educated, of higher military rank, and more often hyperactive, but no significant group differences on MMPI scales or codetypes were found. SFM-UPD comparisons found the depressives older, of higher military rank, less often single, displaying less disturbed thought, and more frequently exhibiting depression and suicidal ideation. Scales L and K were higher and all clinical scales except 9 were lower among the SFM than among the UPD patients. If the raw scores for these two groups were converted to K-corrected T-scores, 10 of these 11 scales would show differences of 5 or more T-scores between groups. SFM-SCH comparisons found no differentiating demographic or behavioral correlates, although when age was controlled for, the SCH group showed higher scores on Scales F, 6, 7, 8, and 0.

The report leaves unclear whether thorough statistical comparisons were made between the BPM and UPD groups, but inspection of the tabular material suggests that they were not. Review of the data Walters presented may support the conclusions that, relative to the depressives, the manics had fewer somatic complaints, were less likely to be rated as depressed, withdrawn, physically aggressive, and as having suicidal ideation, and were more likely to be described as agitated and hyperactive. Again, compared with UPD patients, the manics appeared to have lower scores on Scales 2, 7, 8, and 0. The frequency with which each group obtained particular codetypes also is suggestive of important differences between these two groups: only 4 percent of the manics obtained 2-8/8-2 or 7-8/8-7 codetypes, compared with almost a fourth of the depressives. None of the depressives showed the normal K+ profile, but it was the second most frequent profile (24 percent) among manics. The most frequent profile for manics was the 8-9/9-8 codetype at 28 percent, as contrasted to a frequency of 17.2 percent among depressives. It should be emphasized that these comparisons result from a review of Walters' article and not on any rigorous analysis of the data on which it is based. They should, therefore, be considered speculative and in need of confirmation.

It is an unflattering commentary that the prototypic study chosen for this chapter was not one that addressed directly the MMPI performance of groups of affectively disordered patients. The author was simply unable to find a more germane report of comparable quality. The Walters' investigation still can be criticized at a number of points. Walters discussed weaknesses in the way patients were assigned to diagnostic conditions, recognizing that diagnoses arrived at on the basis of independent evaluations using standardized interview schedules might have assured greater homogeneity among his groups, but even groups composed in this fashion may be "atypical." Although the author is not explicit, the diagnoses used to establish his groups appear to be those arrived at on patients' *admission* to the medical center. In general, discharge diagnoses are to be preferred over those established on admission, since the latter are best considered provisional. It is not at all uncommon for an initial diagnostic impression to change over time as additional observations and data from sources unavailable on admission are brought to bear to resolve diagnostic uncertainty.

Such diagnostic uncertainty is especially common among patients admitted for the first time and those presenting with acute symptoms. Both schizophrenia and the affective disorders can present mixed and confusing clinical pictures, combining features of thought, mood, and behavioral disturbances that only weeks or even months of treatment and observation may clarify. When group membership is based on admission diagnoses, the numbers of patients with changes in diagnosis over the course of hospitalization need to be specified, along with the nature of those changes. Walters also was unclear as to the precise criteria used to establish the validity of the MMPI data for the study. A simple affirmation that random profiles were excluded is not sufficient. A final criticism that might be made concerns Walters' choice of limiting his test variables to the standard MMPI validity and clinical scales. There is nothing in his conception or design that requires this restriction, and reliance on the multidimensional clinical scales may leave obscure differences in the way each group responds to various areas of content within the item pool. The addition of content-homogeneous scales such as those of Wiggins (1966) or some of the item-factor scales (Johnson, Butcher, Null, & Johnson, 1984) might have afforded a clearer picture of the MMPI performance of Walters' diagnostic groups.

STANDARD VALIDITY AND CLINICAL SCALES

The MMPI performance of several categories of mood disordered patients will be summarized in this section under three general categories: Minor Depression, Major Depression, and Mania. Research involving the MMPI among the affective disorders remains too limited to warrant a highly systematic treatment using finer subdivisions among these broader headings. The evolving character of diagnostic nomenclature render each narrow category of disorder something of a moving target as DSM-II has been supplanted by DSM-III. But this problem is only the beginning. Regional differences in diagnostic attitudes have always existed, and these too tend to shift over time as fashions change. The influence of psychodynamic ideas following Freud's visit to the United States in

1909 eventually grew to overshadow the more conservative descriptive-phenomenologic approach that had previously held sway. In some areas of the country, psychoanalytic credentials became necessary to assume important positions such as department chairmanships in psychiatry and hospital superintendencies. The past two decades have seen a dramatic reversal of this trend, a reversal no doubt stimulated by the discovery of effective antipsychotic and antidepressant drugs in the mid and late 1950s. The trend away from the idiographic psychodynamic study and understanding of individual patients and toward a greater emphasis on a quantitative-descriptive approach to the psychiatric disorders from which they suffer was accelerated by the publication of the Research Diagnostic Criteria in 1972 (Feighner et al.), which in turn was the major stimulus to the third edition of the *Diagnostic and Statistical Manual*.

Consequently, one group of neurotic depressives, for example, may differ from another. Such differences may be traceable as much to fundamental attitudes toward diagnosis in different regions, settings, and times, as to differences in the nominal criteria for diagnoses, patient demographics, symptoms, history, and other specific factors. In this light, the failure of virtually all of the research reports summarized in this chapter that were published prior to 1975 to specify adequately the basis for diagnostic assignments suggests not so much a shocking lack of methodologic rigor as a feature of a zeitgeist in which the technology of diagnosis was more limited than it is at the present time. That zeitgeist was, of course, the same one in which the labors of Hathaway and McKinley brought forth the MMPI.

Most of the literature involving the MMPI performance of groups of affectively disordered patients is summarized in Tables 4–2 through 4–7. These tables have been subdivided into three major categories of affective illness as follows: Minor Depression, including samples variously labeled depressive reaction, reactive depression, depressive neurosis, or dysthymic disorder; Major Depression, including involutional melancholia, psychotic depression or psychotic depresive reaction, unipolar depression, major depression, manic-depressive illness, depressed type or circular type depressed, or bipolar depression; and Mania, including manic-depressive reaction, manic type, manic-depressive illness, manic type or circular type manic, manic episode, or bipolar mania. The various terms within each major category generally follow the sequence of editions of the *Diagnostic and Statistical Manual* and the diagnostic designations given in the cited research reports. Studies inadequately specifying the diagnostic composition of affective samples (e.g., "affective disorders": Silver & Sines, 1961) have been excluded from consideration.

Studies featuring minor depressive conditions typically report elevations on Scale 2 that are higher than those for other psychopathologic conditions with the exception of more severe (i.e., psychotic) depressions (Johnson, Klingler, & Gianetti, 1980; Overall, Higgins, & De Schweinitz, 1976; Rosen, 1958). Rosen's (1958) neurotic depressives obtained significantly higher Scale 2 scores than four comparison groups: paranoid schizophrenics, anxiety reactions, somatization, and conversion disorders.

The mean codetypes[1] reported in Table 4–2 show strong consistency in terms of the peak scale, but the succeeding scales are more variable. While Scales 1 and 3 are well represented, Scales having more malignant implications, 4 and 8, also appear. Some idea of the variety of frequent codetypes found within samples of depressed patients can be gathered from Table 4–3. Fifteen codetypes contain at least 5 percent of the patients within at least one sample. Of these, 13 occur in 2 or more samples.

Lachar (1968) found 3 of his 13 codetype groups showed reactive depression as the modal diagnosis: *1-2/2-1*, *2-3/3-2*, and *2-7/7-2*. Of these, the *2-7/7-2* and *2-3/3-2* are the most common codetypes among the neurotic depressives in Hathaway and Meehl's *Atlas* (1951), accounting for 40 percent of the total. No other codetypes accounted for as much as 10 percent of the sample. Scale 2 was the peak score in fully half of the cases. These results are similar to those found in Gilberstadt's *Atlas* (1975), in which the *2-7/7-2* and *2-3/3-2* codetypes again accounted for approximately 40 percent of the depressive neurotics. Scale 2 was the highest scale in the majority of cases. When the profiles of this sample were classified on the basis of the Gilberstadt and Duker (1965) codetype to which each was most similar using the D^2 measure of generalized distance (Cronbach & Gleser, 1953), 59 percent were assigned to the *2-7-1 (3)* codetype. Another 12, 9, and 9 percent were assigned to one of the *1-2*, *1-3*, or the *8-2-4* codetypes, respectively. The Marks and Seeman (1963) atlas of codetypes illustrates a similar association between the *2-7/7-2* and *2-3/3-2* codetypes and neurotic depression. Of the 34 depressive neurotics in their sample, 23.5 percent fell into each of their *2-3-1/2-1-3* and *2-7* groups. Another 14.7 percent fall into the *2-7-4/2-4-7/4-7-2* group, and between 5 and 10 percent of the remaining cases appear in each of the following groups:

TABLE 4–2.   FREQUENCY OF ELEVATED MMPI CLINICAL SCALES IN MINOR DEPRESSIONS

Authors	N	Age	Clinical Scales (≥ 70 *T*-points)
Depressive Reaction:			
Gilberstadt (1975) [male]	62	–	–
Hathaway & Meehl (1951)	82	–	–
Lachar (1968)	88	50	*2-1-3-7-4-8*
Lachar (1968)	140	43	*2-3-1-7*
Lachar (1968)	167	42	*2-7-8-3-4*
Marks & Seeman (1963)	–	–	–
Rosen (1958)	36	–	*2-7-1-3*
Depressive Neurosis:			
Hedlund & Won Cho (1979)	776	–	*2-8-4*
Johnson et al. (1980) [male]	32	–	*2-4-8-7*
Overall et al. (1976) [female]	–	–	*4-2-8*
Overall et al. (1976) [male]	–	–	*2-4-8*
Dysthymic Disorder:			
Silver et al. (1981)	24	–	*2-7-8-4*

Note: All studies combined men and women unless indicated otherwise.

---

[1]Unless otherwise indicated by Welsh elevation symbols, the mean profile code includes only scales equal to or exceeding a *T*-score of 70. It should be noted that in many cases throughout this chapter, MMPI scales scores have had to be estimated visually from published figures.

TABLE 4–3. FREQUENCY OF MMPI CODETYPES IN DEPRESSED PATIENTS

Authors	N	Age	Codetypes				
			1-3/3-1	2-3/3-2	2-4/4-2	2-7/7-2	2-8/8-2
Minor Depression:							
Gilberstadt(1975)	62	–	6.0	11.0	6.0	31.0	8.0
Hathaway & Meehl (1951)[a]	110	–	7.5	9.1	4.5	30.3	9.1
Hedlund & Won Cho (1979)	746	36		5.0	8.0	9.0	7.0
Weighted Totals			6.8	5.7	7.6	12.2	7.2

Authors	Codetypes			Total	Methodologic Issues								
	3-4/4-3	4-8/8-4	6-8/8-6		A	B	C	D	E	F	G	H	I
Minor Depression:													
Gilberstadt (1975)				62.0	-	-	-	-	-	-	-	-	-
Hathaway & Meehl (1951)[a]	3.0	1.5	4.5	69.5	+	+	-	-	-	-	-	-	-
Hedlund & Won Cho (1979)	5.0	6.0	6.0	46.0	+	+	+	-	-	+	+	-	-
Weighted Totals	4.8	5.6	5.9	48.9									

Authors	N	Age	Codetypes				
			1-2/2-1	1-3/3-1	2-4/4-2	2-7/7-2	2-8/8-2
Major Depression:							
Psychotic Depression:							
Dahlstrom & Prange (1960)	50	47	15.0	5.0	10.0	25.0	14.0
Hedlund & Won Cho (1979)	72	41			7.0	6.0	8.0
Involutional Melancholia:							
Hathaway & Meehl (1951)[a]	32	–	9.4		3.1	25.0	28.1
Hedlund & Won Cho (1979)	82	52	9.0			9.0	13.0
Unipolar Depression:							
Walters (1984)	29	–					10.0
Manic-Depressive, Depressed:							
Hathaway & Meehl (1951)[a]	63	–	6.3	3.2	1.6	41.2	7.9
Hedlund & Won Cho (1979)	136	40				10.0	9.0
Weighted Totals			9.6	4.0	5.5	16.5	11.3

	Codetypes				
	3-4/4-3	4-6/6-4	4-8/8-4	4-9/9-4	6-8/8-6
Major Depression:					
Psychotic Depression:					
Dahlstrom & Prange (1960)					
Hedlund & Won Cho (1979)	6.0		10.0	8.0	6.0
Involutional Melancholia:					
Hathaway & Meehl (1951)[a]		3.1			
Hedlund & Won Cho (1979)	6.0			6.0	
Unipolar Depression:					
Walters (1984)			7.0		7.0
Manic-Depression, Depressed:					
Hathaway & Meehl (1951)[a]			1.6	1.6	3.2
Hedlund & Won Cho (1979)		6.0		7.0	13.0
Weighted Totals	6.0	5.4	6.2	6.0	8.7

	Codetypes		Total	Methodologic Issues								
	7-8/8-7	8-9/9-8		A	B	C	D	E	F	G	H	I
Major Depression:												
Psychotic Depression:												
Dahlstrom & Prange (1960)			69.0	+	+	-	-	+	-	-	-	-
Hedlund & Won Cho (1979)			51.0	+	+	+	-	-	+	+	-	-
Involutional Melancholia:												
Hathaway & Meehl (1951)[a]			68.7	+	+	-	-	-	-	-	-	-
Hedlund & Won Cho (1979)			43.0	+	+	+	-	-	+	+	-	-
Unipolar Depression:												
Walters (1984)	14.0	17.0	55.0	+	-	-	-	+	-	+	+	+
Manic-Depressive, Depressed:												
Hathaway & Meehl (1951)	6.3		72.9	+	+	-	-	-	-	-	-	-
Hedlund & Won Cho (1979)	9.0		54.0	+	+	+	-	-	+	+	-	-
Weighted Totals	8.9	17.0	56.8									

[a]These percentages are based on the codetype for the main diagnosis from the Diagnosis Index (pp. 785–793).

TABLE 4–4.   FREQUENCY OF ELEVATED MMPI CLINICAL SCALES IN MAJOR DEPRESSIONS

Authors	N	Age	Clinical Scales (≥ 70 *T*-points)
Psychotic Depressive Reaction:			
Dahlstrom & Prange (1960) [F]	33	45	*2-3-1-7*
Dahlstrom & Prange (1960) [M]	17	50	*2-1-3-7*
Hedlund & Won Cho (1979)	72	–	*8-4-2*
Johnson et al. (1980)	36	39	*2-8-7-4*
Lachar (1968)	158	40	*2-8-7-4-6-0*
Overall et al. (1976) [F]	–	–	*8-4-2-6*
Overall et al. (1976) [M]	–	–	*2-1-8-4*
Primary Depression:			
Wilson et al. (1967) [bereaved]	28	–	*8-2-7-3-1*
Wilson et al. (1967) [non-bereaved]	64	–	*2-3-7*
Wilson et al. (1967) [father loss]	14	–	*8-2-3-6-7-1-4*
Wilson et al. (1967) [mother loss]	10	–	*8-7-2-1-6-3-4*
Involutional Melancholia:			
Hathaway & Meehl (1951)	38	–	–
Hedlund & Won Cho (1979)	82	–	*2-8-7*
Marks & Seeman (1963)	30	–	–
Unipolar Depression:			
Donnelly & Murphy (1973)	20	48	*2-7-8*
Donnelly, Murphy, Waldman & Reynolds (1976)	34	–	*2-7-8-3-4*
Donnelly, Murphy, & Goodwin (1976)	17	–	
Admission			*2-7-8*
Remission			*2-4*
Faravelli et al. (1986)			
Relapsed	50	53	*8-7-2*
Nonrelapsed	51	55	*2-3-1*
Silver et al. (1981)	24	–	*2-4-7-8*
Walters (1984)	29	26	*8-2-7-6-4-1*
Winters et al. (1985)	63	–	–
Manic-Depressive, Depressed Type:			
Hathaway & Meehl (1951)	67	–	—
Hedlund & Won Cho (1979)	136	–	*8-2-4-7*
Manic-Depressive, Circular Type, Depressed:			
Hedlund & Won Cho (1979)	19	–	*8-2-7-4-6-3*
Bipolar Depressed:			
Donnelly & Murphy (1973)	19	44	*4-8-2*
Donnelly, Murphy, Waldman & Reynolds (1976)	34	–	*2-4-7-8*
Donnelly, Murphy, & Goodwin (1976)	17	–	
Admission			*4-6-8-9*
Remission			*4-9-2-6*
Winters et al. (1985)	35	–	–

TABLE 4–5. MEAN CLINICAL AND CONTENT SCALE PROFILES OF MISSOURI DSM-II AFFECTIVE DISORDERS

Variable	Depressive State Categories						Manic State Categories		
	295.74 (N=84)	296.00 (N=82)	296.20 (N=136)	296.34 (N=19)	298.00 (N=72)	300.40 (N=776)	295.73 (N=64)	296.10 (N=151)	296.33 (N=38)
Age	33.9	52.1	39.8	40.7	40.8	36.4	36.0	39.3	38.5
Sex M/F	43/41	10/72	64/72	15/4	29/43	274/502	18/46	87/64	16/22
L	51.4	55.6	50.9	52.9	52.4	51.8	53.7	51.3	53.4
F	69.4	62.6	67.0	69.8	63.8	64.2	70.4	66.5	64.1
K	50.8	52.7	49.1	51.1	52.2	49.4	51.5	51.4	52.1
Hs	63.4	65.9	62.5	68.1	63.0	63.7	59.9	57.2	57.9
D	73.7	74.9	73.8	78.3	69.6	73.1	58.5	57.0	56.7
Hy	63.5	68.1	64.8	70.7	63.2	66.2	58.8	57.2	57.8
Pd	73.0	65.3	70.8	73.4	69.9	71.5	70.2	69.4	67.0
Mf	57.4	51.7	56.0	52.0	54.3	53.8	55.7	58.5	56.4
Pa	69.3	66.5	68.3	71.7	66.2	67.1	70.5	66.5	64.1
Pt	73.7	69.9	70.4	76.2	67.4	69.8	64.0	61.6	58.4
Sc	79.3	71.8	74.0	79.9	70.1	71.7	74.5	69.8	68.4
Ma	63.9	54.1	61.8	60.1	58.2	60.1	70.4	71.8	70.1
Si	62.9	64.3	62.3	65.4	60.1	62.5	55.1	51.3	50.7
HEA	60.0	61.9	60.1	64.1	59.0	60.7	59.4	56.4	58.4
DEP	64.5	61.0	64.6	67.2	60.0	64.4	56.3	55.2	52.2
ORG	62.4	64.1	62.5	65.9	59.4	62.7	59.1	57.3	56.5
FAM	62.7	55.1	63.2	66.1	59.9	63.1	64.2	63.8	64.3
AUT	50.9	46.0	53.7	46.8	51.5	51.3	54.0	55.4	54.3
FEM	50.9	49.3	52.8	50.6	51.4	50.5	54.0	57.2	54.3
REL	53.4	52.1	50.6	53.1	49.8	50.6	55.7	55.0	53.5
HOS	52.5	48.6	53.5	50.8	51.1	52.8	55.2	55.0	55.3
MOR	61.3	58.3	61.4	62.0	58.1	61.1	55.6	53.8	50.5
PHO	58.7	55.8	59.3	62.3	56.7	57.5	54.9	53.9	52.6
PSY	64.3	58.5	62.6	61.9	60.0	59.4	71.7	64.4	63.8
HYP	53.8	48.4	53.3	52.4	51.9	53.5	56.0	58.5	57.0
SOC	60.5	57.7	58.1	59.3	55.2	57.5	50.5	47.4	47.4

Note: 295.74 = schizophrenia, schizoaffective type, depressed; 296.00 = involutional melancholia; 296.20 = manic-depressive illness, depressed type; 296.34 = manic-depressive illness, circular type, depressed; 298.00 = psychotic depressive reaction; 300.40 = depressive neurosis; 295.73 = schizophrenia, schizoaffective type, excited; 296.10 = manic-depressive illness, manic type; 296.33 = manic-depressive illness, circular type, manic. HEA = poor health; DEP = depression; ORG = organic symptoms; FAM = family problems; AUT = authority conflict; FEM = feminine interests; REL = religious fundamentalism; HOS = manifest hostility; MOR = poor morale; PHO = phobias; PSY = psychoticism; HYP = hypomania; SOC = social maladjustment.

TABLE 4–6. FREQUENCY OF ELEVATED MMPI CLINICAL SCALES IN MANIC DISORDERS

Authors	N	Age	Clinical Scales (≥ 70 *T*-points)
Manic-Depressive Reaction, Manic Type:			
Gilberstadt & Duker (1965)	–	–	–
Guthrie (1950)	8	–	Spike *9*
Hathaway & Meehl (1951)	–	–	–
Marks & Seeman (1963)	12	–	–
Manic-Depressive Illness, Manic Type:			
Hedlund & Won Cho (1979)	151	39	Spike *9*
Overall et al. (1976)	8	–	*4–2*
Post et al. (1986)	64	34	*9–8*
Manic-Depressive Illness, Circular Type, Manic:			
Hedlund & Won Cho (1979)	38	–	Spike *9*
Bipolar Disorder, Manic:			
Davies et al. (1985)	101	–	*9-8-4*
Walters (1984)	25	27	*8-9*
Winters et al. (1985)	35	–	–

TABLE 4–7.   FREQUENCY OF MMPI CODETYPES IN MANIC PATIENTS

Authors	N	Age	Codetypes			
			4-6/6-4	4-8/8-4	4-9/9-4	6-8/8-6
Manic-Depressive Reaction, Manic Type:						
Hathaway & Meehl (1951)[a]	32	–			12.5	12.5
Manic-Depressive Illness, Manic Type:						
Hedlund & Won Cho (1979)	151	39			19.0	7.0
Post et al. (1986)	64	34				
Manic-Depressive Illness, Circular Type, Manic:						
Hedlund & Won Cho (1979)	38	39		11.0	11.0	11.0
Bipolar Disorder, Manic:						
Davies et al. (1985)	101	–	8.0	6.0	16.0	7.0
Walters (1984)	25	27				8.0
Weighted Totals			8.0	7.4	16.5	8.0

	Codetypes			Methodologic Issues								
	6-9/9-6	8-9/9-8	Totals	A	B	C	D	E	F	G	H	I
Manic-Depressive Reaction, Manic Type:												
Hathaway & Meehl (1951)[a]		9.4	34.4[b]	+	+	-	-	-	-	-	-	-
Manic-Depressive Illness, Manic Type:												
Hedlund & Won Cho (1979)	7.0	15.0	48.0	+	+	+	-	-	+	+	-	-
Post et al. (1986)	19.0	30.0	49.0									
Manic-Depressive Illness, Circular Type, Manic:												
Hedlund & Won Cho (1979)		16.0	49.0	+	+	+	-	-	+	+	-	-
Bipolar Disorder, Manic:												
Davies et al. (1985)	12.0	19.0	68.0	+	+	+	-	+	-	+	-	-
Walters (1984)		28.0	32.0	+	-	-	-	+	-	+	+	+
Weighted Totals	11.0	18.8	51.1									

[a]These percentages are based on the codetype for the main diagnosis from the Diagnosis Index (pp. 785–793).

[b]46.8% of these patients had Spike 9 codetypes which were not included in this table.

2-7-8/8-7-2, 3-2-1, 4-6-2/6-4-2, 8-3/3-8, and 8-9/9-8.

The concordance among these *Atlas* cases, in which 40 percent of each of two samples of depressive neurosis are encompassed by only two codetypes, proves hard to sustain when compared with 776 neurotic depressives from a statewide Missouri psychiatric sample (Hedlund & Won Cho, 1979). No codetype accounted for as much as 10 percent of these cases. Scale 2 was the highest or second highest scale in only 42 percent of the total, with Scales 4 and 8 not far behind at 36 and 30 percent of the neurotic depressives, respectively. The discrepancy between the *Atlas* and the Missouri cases might be attributable to regional differences (both the Hathaway and Meehl and the Gilberstadt *Atlas* samples were from Minnesota). It is also possible that Depressive Neurosis may have been employed to some extent as a wastebasket category in Missouri. The failure of any codetype(s) to predominate and the relative frequency of the 6-8/8-6 codetype (vs. the

2-3/3-2 pair) in the Hedlund and Won Cho sample would seem to argue for the latter explanation.

The prominence of Scales 4 and 8 in recent samples may reflect a shift in the conception of minor depressions. The DSM-III criteria for Dysthymic Disorder, for example, represent a major change in emphasis from the Depressive Neurosis of DSM-II. The earlier manual stresses "internal conflict" or "an identifiable event" as the antecedents of an "excessive *reaction* of depression" (emphasis added). The DSM-III emphasis on a chronic course (2 years) suggests a disorder that represents less a reaction than an *adjustment*. Silver, Isaacs, and Mansky (1981) examined the MMPI performance of a group of 24 chronic intermittent depressives, a diagnosis equivalent to DSM-III Dysthymic Disorder, who were independently diagnosed using the Research Diagnostic Criteria (RDC: Spitzer et al., 1975). The mean profile of this group was slightly higher in elevation but highly similar in configuration to a group of 24 unipolar depressives. Both groups show peaks on Scales *2*, *7*, *8*, and *4*. The authors speculate that chronicity rather than severity is the major difference between these two groups.

The frequency with which Scale *2* emerges as the highest or second highest scale in the minor depressions is impressive evidence for the construct validity of this scale. Changes in the conception of these conditions and the diagnostic criteria used to identify the minor depressions have had no discernible effect on the sensitivity of Scale *2*. Regional differences in diagnostic practice, however, may reveal large differences in the sensitivity and specificity of this scale. The different descriptions of these disorders in DSM-II and DSM-III may be associated with a shift toward a greater prominence of Scales *4* and *8*, and their corresponding characterologic features, in the profiles of patients diagnosed Dysthymic Disorder and a relative decline in Scales *1*, *3*, and *7*, elevations on which were often typical in cases of DSM-II Depressive Neurosis. It may be that these cases would now be subsumed under the DSM-III somatoform or anxiety disorders, with any associated depressions being considered a secondary reaction to one or the other of these disorders. Certainly, further study is needed, both to clarify the fate of patients obtaining profiles with peaks on Scale *2* and secondary elevations on Scales *7*, *3*, and *1*, in terms of current DSM-III categories, and to illuminate the position of Dysthymic Disorder in relation to both the remaining affective disorders and the personality disorders.

The major depressions are associated with more variation in the mean codetypes than minor depressive conditions, as seen in Table 4–4. Lachar (1968) found only one of his profile groups, *2-8/8-2*, was associated with Psychotic Depressive Reaction as the modal diagnosis. The mean of this group is virtually identical ($D^2 = 420$) with that reported for another group of Psychotic Depressive Reaction patients (Johnson et al., 1980). However, the mean codetype of Dahlstrom and Prange's (1960) earlier group of psychotic depressives is quite similar to that of Lachar's (1968) *1-2/2-1* profile group. Dahlstrom and Prange found Scale *2* to be the peak score for 54 percent of their sample. Five codetypes occurred with a frequency of > 10 percent each: *2-7/7-2*, *1-2/2-1*, *2-3/3-2*, *2-8/8-2*, and *2-4/4-2* (10 percent). None of these exceeded a frequency of 10 percent among a comparison sample of paranoid schizophrenics. In contrast, there was no frequently oc-

curring codetype among the Hedlund and Won Cho (1979) Psychotic Depressives, and only 39 percent of these cases had Scale *2* highest or second highest.

Almost half of the Hathaway and Meehl *Atlas* (1951) cases of Involutional Melancholia had *2-7/7-2* or *2-8/8-2* codetypes. Scale *2* was the highest or second highest point in > 80 percent of the cases. In the Marks and Seeman (1963) atlas, however, the 30 Involutional Melancholia cases are distributed across half of their codetypes. These patients were most common in the *2-7* (16.7 percent) and the *2-3-1/2-1-3*, *2-7-8*, and *3-2-1* groups (13.3 percent). From 5 to 10 percent of the remaining involutionals were found in each of the *2-8/8-2*, *8-6/6-8*, *1-3/3-1*, and K+ groups. Hedlund and Won Cho's Involutional Melancholia cases showed a similarly wide distribution across codetypes with only the *2-8/8-2* accounting for more than a tenth of the cases. Only 50 percent of these patients had Scale *2* the first or second highest scale.

More than 80 percent of Manic-Depressive-Depressed *Atlas* (Hathaway & Meehl, 1951) cases had Scale *2* as the peak or second highest scale. The *2-7/7-2* codetype was most common, with all other pairs accounting for < 10 percent each of the remaining cases. The distribution of the depressed Missouri Manic-Depressives (Hedlund & Won Cho, 1979) is much more variable. Only 37 percent had Scale *2* highest or second highest, and only one codetype accounted for > 10 percent of the cases, *6-8/8-6* (13 percent). In a much smaller sample of 19 Missouri patients diagnosed Manic-Depressive, Circular Type-Depressed (Hedlund & Won Cho, 1979), 58 percent had Scale *2* highest or second highest, and only three codetypes contained more than one patient each: *2-8/8-2*, *2-4/4-2*, and *4-8/8-4*. The seven Marks and Seeman (1963) atlas patients diagnosed Manic-Depressive-Depressed were distributed across five of their codetypes, with two patients each in the *2-3-1/2-1-3* and *4-8-2/8-4-2/8-2-4* groups, and one each in the *2-7*, *2-8/8-2*, and *4-6/6-4* groups.

The distribution of Unipolar Depression cases within codetypes reported by Walters (1984) was incomplete since he listed only codetypes that achieved a frequency of > 5 percent in his combined samples of schizophreniform, schizophrenic, bipolar-manic, and unipolar-depressed patients. It is notable, however, that the most frequent codetype reported for the unipolar depressives was the

8-9/9-8. In none of the other depressive samples summarized in Table 4–3 did this codetype account for > 5 percent of the cases. Nor did it contain any of the depressives in another recent study.

Winters, Newmark, Lumry, Leach, and Weintraub (1985) examined the association between four groups of patients (schizophrenics, *n* = 34; unipolar depressives, *n* = 63; bipolar depressives, *n* = 35; and bipolar manics, *n* = 37) and 21 codetypes, 11 of which were taken from the Marks, Seeman, and Haller codebook (M-S-H: 1974). Of the eight codetypes for which schizophrenia was the M-S-H modal diagnosis (*2-7-8/8-7-2, 2-8/8-2, 4-6/6-4, 4-8-2/8-4-2/8-2-4, 8-6/6-8, 8-9/9-8, 9-6/6-9,* and *K+*), only the *8-6/6-8* code contained more schizophrenic than affectively disordered patients among the Winters et al. samples. In contrast, the three M-S-H codes for which depression had been the modal diagnosis, *2-3-1/2-1-3, 2-7,* and *2-7-4/4-7-2,* contained none of the Winters et al. schizophrenics. These findings confirm an earlier report by Winters, Weintraub, and Neale (1981) indicating a greater association between the *2-7-8/8-7-2, 2-8/8-2, 4-8-2/8-4-2/8-2-4, 8-9/9-8,* and *9-6/6-9* M-S-H codetypes and DSM-III affective disorders than between these codetypes and DSM-III schizophrenia. In both studies, the three M-S-H "depression" codetypes were able to predict DSM-III depression.

Donnelly and his colleagues have published a series of reports (Donnelly & Murphy, 1973; Donnelly, Murphy, & Goodwin, 1976; Donnelly, Murphy, Waldman, & Reynolds, 1976) contrasting the MMPI performance of unipolar and bipolar depressives of comparable age, race, education, intelligence, number of prior hospitalizations, and Bunney-Hamburg (1963) rated depression. They found that the profiles of unipolars, when compared with the bipolars, were more elevated, had higher scores on Scales *2* and *7,* and declined significantly over the course of treatment. They also tended to have lower scores on Scales *K* and *9.* The mean profiles for all of the unipolar groups had clear configurations, with Scales *2, 7,* and *8* highest. The mean profiles of the bipolar depressive groups had all scales below *T*-scores of 70 and were configurally much less distinct. In examining the performance of these two groups on

several subscales and research scales, Donnelly, Murphy, and Waldman (1980) found that compared with the unipolars, the bipolars achieved significantly higher scores on scales related to denial, ego-strength, and somatization. The relative lack of overt and covert anxiety among bipolars suggested in these results has been confirmed by these investigators in two non-MMPI studies, using both objective (Donnelly, Murphy, & Goodwin, 1978) and projective (Donnelly, Murphy, & Scott, 1975) measures.

Despite the consistency of the findings regarding the unipolar-bipolar differences reported by Donnelly and his colleagues, there are several reasons to doubt their generalizability. First, the extent of psychopathology among their bipolars may have been concealed by limiting raw scores on the *F* scale to 16. Second, the excessive control of variables such as age, education, and the number of prior hospitalizations may have rendered their groups unrepresentative. For example, bipolar illness traditionally has been considered to have a greater tendency toward recurrence than unipolar depression, so that equating unipolar and bipolar groups for prior hospitalizations may make either or both groups atypical. Third, the trends noted for the Donnelly et al. samples have not always been confirmed in other samples. For example, Winters et al. (1985) found that the proportions of unipolar and bipolar depressives within each of five common codetypes, *2-7-8/8-7-2, 2-8/8-2, 8-6/6-8, 8-9/9-8, 9-8-4/9-4-8/4-8-9,* were not significantly different. Among the major depression groups in the Missouri sample (Hedlund & Won Cho, 1979), the unipolars (i.e., Psychotic Depressive Reaction, Involutional Melancholia) obtained somewhat *lower* profiles on the average than bipolar depressives (i.e., Manic-Depressive-Depressed, Manic-Depressive, Circular Type-Depressed; see Table[2] 4–5). They also, on the average, had lower scores on scales related to denial/ego-strength (*K*), and higher scores on scales related to anxiety (Scale *7, PHO*).

While elevations on Scale *2* are most characteristic of the major depressions, Scale *8* also is typically elevated over a *T*-score of 70, reflecting the presence of signs and symptoms of psychosis. Of the eight studies reporting codetype frequen-

---

[2]The author wishes to thank Dr. James L. Hedlund and the Missouri Institute of Psychiatry for providing the MMPI protocols referred to here and elsewhere in this chapter. The mean profiles for the various diagnostic groups listed are presented only for the purpose of illustrating various points made in the text. They should not necessarily be assumed to be typical of specific diagnostic groups, either in Missouri or elsewhere, and should not be used for diagnostic decision making.

cies, only the *2-8/8-2* codetype occurred with a frequency of 5 percent or more in all of them. The dependability of this codetype as a characteristic of affective samples is enhanced by the findings of an investigation in which a cohort of college males was screened using the MMPI and the Research Diagnostic Criteria (RDC: Haier, Rieder, Khouri, & Buchsbaum, 1979). Of 12 subjects who produced *2-8/8-2* or *2-7-8/8-7-2* codetypes, 5 met RDC criteria for major affective disorder and 6 for minor affective disorder, respectively. None of these subjects met the RDC criteria for schizophrenia. The persistence of Scale *8* in the profiles of patients tested during asymptomatic phases may reflect incomplete recovery from a depressive episode and the potential for relapse. Faravelli, Ambonetti, Pallanti, and Pazzagli (1986) administered the MMPI to 101 unipolar depressive patients who had been symptom-free for 2 months following a depressive episode. Those who relapsed within the year following discharge had significantly higher scores on Scale *8* (and *F*, *6*, *7*, and *9*) than the nonrelapsed patients.

The differences between unipolar and bipolar depressions, and between each of these and dysthymic disorder, remain unclear, even though one group of investigators has reported replicated differences between the first two of these two groups. Additional research therefore is needed to determine what differences in MMPI performance may characterize these disorders. As seen in Table 4–5, however, the mean profiles of psychotically depressed groups, a group of neurotic depressives, and a group of patients diagnosed schizophrenia, schizo-affective type, depressed, are all highly similar on both standard and content scale scores, despite minor differences in two- or three-point codetypes. Many of the other major (and minor) depressive samples reviewed here also have similar mean profiles, at least to judge from their codetypes. Even given the assumption that the Missouri diagnoses and many others are frequently of questionable validity, the lack of clearly discriminating features between groups widely thought to differ in important respects (e.g., neurotic vs. psychotic depressives) may blunt any optimism that merely tightening diagnostic practices will produce strong and consistent scale or profile differences between such groups in the future. It may be that MMPI differences for these groups, if any, are to be found only at the subscale, special scale, or item level, rather than in terms of the standard validity and clinical scales.

In general, research studies on manic samples are fewer in number but more recent than those reporting results for depressives. Scale *9* tends to be the peak or second highest scale when mean codetypes are reported (Table 4–6). Among samples for which frequencies are available, Scale *9* is the highpoint in one third of the cases, and among the two highest scales in at least half. Manic samples also are more consistent in terms of the numbers of codetypes that characterize them (Table 4–7). Only seven codetypes are needed to contain cases that occur with a frequency of at least 5 percent in any sample, and only four of these occur in four or more samples: *4-9/9-4*, *6-8/8-6*, *6-9/9-6*, and *8-9/9-8*. For example, more than half of the 37 Winters et al. (1985) bipolar manics were contained in three of the M-S-H codetypes: *8-6/6-8* (5.4 percent), *8-9/9-8* (32.4 percent), and *9-6/6-9* (16.2 percent). Another 40.5 percent of their manics fell into a *9-8-4/9-4-8/4-8-9* code type. There is considerable contrast between these results and those reported in the original Marks and Seeman *Atlas* (1963). More than half of the *Atlas* patients in each of the *8-6/6-8*, *8-9/9-8*, and *9-6/6-9* code groups carried a diagnosis of schizophrenia, but Winters et al. (1985) found significant proportions of their schizophrenics in only the *8-6/6-8* (29.4 percent) and *8-9/9-8* (14.7 percent) groups. Their *9-6/6-9* and *9-8-4/9-4-8/4-8-9* code groups contained no DSM-III schizophrenics. These results are also consistent with the findings of Post et al. (1986). These investigators reported that the *8-9/9-8* and *6-9/9-6* codetypes accounted for almost half of their DSM-II manics, whereas < 10 percent of their schizophrenics obtained either of these codetypes, a proportion not significantly different from that of a comparison sample of patients diagnosed neither manic nor schizophrenic.

The 12 manic patients in the Marks and Seeman sample were distributed across eight of their codetypes: *8-3/3-8* (25 percent), *2-7* and *9-6/6-9* (16.7 percent each), and *2-7-4/2-4-7/4-7-2*, *2-7-8/8-7-2*, *3-2-1*, *8-9/9-8*, and *K+* (8.3 percent each). The disparity between the Marks and Seeman (1963) findings and those of Winters et al. (1985) and Post et al. (1986) may not be due solely to changes in diagnostic criteria or fashion. The former authors suggest that *interest* may have been lacking in the diagnostic enterprise at the time their data were gathered (1963; p. 60).

In summary, Scale *9* figures prominently in the codetypes of most of the manic samples reviewed here. Elevations on Scales *4*, *6*, *8*, however, also are relatively frequent. Notably absent in manic sample codetypes are the "neurotic" scales: *1*, *2*, *3*, and *7*. The importance of the *9-8-4/9-4-8/4-8-9* codetype in the study by Winters et al. (1985) and the frequency with which elevations on *4*, *6*, and *8* generally occur in manic samples may recommend reporting the third highest scale when the codetypes within manic samples are listed, a practice of proven value in other contexts (cf. Gilberstadt & Duker, 1960).

In a variety of samples referenced in this section, elevations on Scale *2* are seen to coincide with clinical diagnoses of depression, while Scale *9* elevations are most characteristic in diagnoses of mania. In both older and more recent samples, these scales appear to be operating much as their authors intended. In general, they seem to have retained construct validity as the evolution of diagnostic systems has continued. Associations between specific categories of depressive disorder and particular codetypes are less certain. While the *2-8/8-2* codetype appears much more consistently associated with major depressions than minor ones, the *2-3/3-2* and *2-7/7-2* codetypes have been found with about equal frequency in both (Table 4–3). Furthermore, a wide variety of codetypes have been found in both major and minor depressive samples. Finally, the samples themselves show considerable variation, in terms both of which codetypes are most frequent and of the number and kinds of codetypes needed to characterize a significant proportion of the cases within each sample.

In contrast, manic samples require fewer codetypes to describe them, and at least three, *4-9/9-4*, *6-9/9-6*, and *8-9/9-8*, occur in sufficient proportions across enough samples to contribute something to the diagnosis of mania. These codetypes occur only rarely in most of the depressive samples reviewed.

SPECIAL/RESEARCH SCALES

Several scales have been proposed to discriminate affective states or conditions from other disorders or normals, or to discriminate between affective disorders of different types. Both internal consistency and contrasted groups approaches have been used in these scale development efforts, and these will be examined in turn.

The original Depression scale of the MMPI was developed to distinguish between clinically depressed patients and normal subjects. But the contrasted groups method used for selecting the final Scale *2* items may have made this scale poorly suited to detecting differences in the extent of depressive symptomatology within patients previously identified as depressed or non-depressed. Using a procedure (contextual scaling) to eliminate items poorly related to the major dimension of Scale *2* as revealed in his male and female normal and psychiatric samples, Dempsey (1964) developed a 30-item version of Scale *2* to facilitate distinctions *within* abnormal and normal groups. Despite being only half the length of the standard scale, the new version, *D30*, showed larger split-half reliabilities in the four normative and four cross validation samples than Scale *2*. The increment in the reliability of *D30* over Scale *2* was especially striking among the normal groups. Dempsey further found that while correlated from .78 to .92 with Scale *2* among his eight samples, *D30* was essentially uncorrelated with the 30 items from Scale *2* not appearing on *D30*. In a comparison of three MMPI scales among 60 pairs of normal monozygotic and 32 pairs of normal dizygotic twins, Wierzbicki (1986) reported heritability coefficients of .43, .41, and .28 for *D30*, *Dr* (Rosen, 1962; see below), and Scale *2*, respectively. Thus, the *D30* scale appears to be a satisfactory internally consistent analogue of Scale *2*. As such, it may have some utility in reducing false positives for depression on the basis of Scale *2* elevations. This increase in specificity may be achieved, however, at some loss in sensitivity for *D30*. Furthermore, since the content of *D30* is obvious, this scale may be more vulnerable to dissimulation than Scale *2*. These questions clearly warrant further empirical study, as do other questions regarding its range of application, interpretive significance, and possible value in configuration with other measures of depression. In any case, it is doubtful that *D30* has compelling unique properties. For example, 28 (93 percent) of the *D30* items overlap with the 40-item D-0 scale (Wiener, 1948). Dempsey himself mentions the extensive overlap between *D30* and one of Comrey's (1957) Scale *2* factors. But does *D30* discriminate between major and minor depressions better than Scale *2*? In a comparison between a mixed sample of 309 DSM-II psychotic depressives and 776 neurotic depressives from Missouri

(Hedlund & Won Cho, 1979), neither Scale *2* nor *D30* discriminated between these groups at a significant level. The neurotic depressives, in fact, showed a somewhat higher mean score on *D30* than the psychotics.

Starting from the 26 initial item content categories of Hathaway and McKinley, Wiggins (1966) developed 13 internally consistent scales intended to reflect the major substantive dimensions of the full MMPI item pool. One measure of the success of Wiggins' effort is the close correspondence between his content scales and the factors identified in a large-scale item factor analysis of the MMPI in a psychiatric population (Johnson et al., 1984). Research into the concurrent (Wiggins, Goldberg, & Appelbaum, 1971; Payne & Wiggins, 1972; Taylor, Ptacek, Carithers, Griffin, & Coyne, 1972) and construct validity (Mezzich, Damarin, & Erickson, 1974; Boerger, 1975; Lachar & Alexander, 1978) and their generalizability to new populations (Mezzich et al., 1974; Jarnecke & Chambers, 1977) has consistently supported the value of these scales. Three of these scales, Depression (*DEP*), Poor Morale (*MOR*), and Hypomania (*HYP*), suggest constructs closely related to affective conditions. Mezzich et al. (1974) compared the discriminative efficiency of the standard and content scales in a sample of 118 patients with various depressive diagnoses and a comparison sample of 105 patients with other diagnoses. They found scale vs. criterion correlations of .357 for Scale *2*, -.352 for *HYP*, and -.317 for Scale *9*. Correlations between the diagnostic criterion and the *DEP* and *MOR* scales were substantially lower at .178 and .181, respectively, although still significant at the .01 level. Nichols (1986, 1987) suggested that *DEP*, which has only eight items in common with Scale *2*, shows a greater emphasis on characterologic and attitudinal features found not only in depressive but in other syndromes as well, while in Scale *2*, the more discriminating emotional and vegetative features of clinical depression are represented. He further suggests that Scale *2* and *DEP* can be used configurally to evaluate the characterologic complications that may attend depressive phenomena, and to predict response to treatment. To date, no one has evaluated these hypotheses.

Two scales have been proposed to address more specific diagnostic questions. Both have employed the contrasted group method to construct scales discriminating reactive depressions from a variety of other psychiatric conditions (*Dr*: Rosen, 1962) or to separate endogenous from reactively depressed patients (*TTDS*: Wilson, Carson, Rabon, & Alltop, 1970).

Using Minneapolis VA males, Rosen (1962) selected a sample of 24 cases of neurotic depression and compared their item responses with those of 155 general psychiatric patients with diagnoses other than neurotic depression. In a subsequent cross-validation sample, the 42-item Depressive Reaction Scale (*Dr*) correctly identified 44 percent of the reactive depressions and 83 percent of the patients with diagnoses other than depressive reaction when the cutting score was set equivalent to a T-score ≥ 60. Most of the *Dr* items deny somatic complaints and socially undesirable or undercontrolled behavior; a few affirm depression and religiousness.

There are several grounds on which to question the validity of Rosen's scale. *Dr* is correlated negatively with all of the standard scales except *L* and *K*. Rosen reported a correlation between *Dr* and Scale *2* of -.10 in a large general VA male psychiatric sample, but Seitz (1970) found a correlation of .38 between these two scales in a sample of 30 male neurotic depressive VA inpatients. Unlike Scale *2*, however, which produced satisfactory correlations with the Beck Depression Inventory and the Zung Depression Scale, Seitz found *Dr* to be unrelated if not negatively related to these scales. One explanation for these findings is that the *Dr* items are subtle. Rosen reported that 71 percent of *Dr* consists of zero items. Not surprisingly, the mean of Rosen's general abnormal sample (23.04) is not appreciably higher than that of the Minnesota normal males (22.88) or the Missouri (Hedlund & Won Cho, 1979) neurotic (22.37) or psychotic depressives (22.98). The mean profile of Rosen's depressed sample was a *2-7-1-3* codetype, similar to Gilberstadt and Duker's (1965) *2-7 (3)* code (*2-7-3-1*). Gilberstadt later developed a purified *2-7-3* scale, *P-3*, by contrasting the item responses of *2-7-3* cases with those of a representative sample of Minneapolis VA cases (1970). Despite the identical setting within which these two scales were developed, the similarity of the mean profiles of the criterion groups, and of the scale development strategies used, *Dr* and *P-3* have only one item in common (264F).

The Two-type Depression Scale (*TTDS*) was developed to assist in the identification of endogenous vs. reactively depressed patients. Wilson et al. (1970) selected 100 consecutive hospital admissions for depression and rated each patient on an endogenous-reactive rating scale (Wilson, Vernon, Guin, & Sandifer, 1963). Endogenous and reactive groups were determined by dividing the total sample at the point of rarity for ratings scores. An item analysis identified 24 highly significant items, which were selected for the *TTDS*. The scale was cross-validated on a second sample of 84 depressives who produced the same point of rarity as the standardization sample. The new sample was dichotomized, and the difference between the mean scores for endogenous (*M*: 15.30; *SD* = 4.8) and reactive (*M*: 10.11; *SD* = 4.3) was found to be highly significant. It may be notable that the item Rosen found to be the most discriminating for neurotic depression, 414T, is keyed for *endogenous* depression on the *TTDS*. Item 379F also has opposite implications for the two scales. Perhaps because the *TTDS* remains unpubished, no reports of attempts at cross-validation could be found. However, the results of a comparison between the Missouri (Hedlund & Won Cho, 1979) neurotic and psychotic depressives are not encouraging. With the same patients referred to above, *TTDS* scores were not only significantly different, the mean score of the neurotics was somewhat higher (*M*: 12.26; *SD* = 3.45) than that of the psychotic depressives (*M*: 11.84; *SD* = 3.66).

Mezzich et al. (1974) used stepwise multiple regression in a replication design to devise a formula to discriminate depressive from other psychiatric conditions. The *raw* score formula, (10 x *D*) - (5 x *Pd*) + (4 x *Pa*) - (4 x *Sc*) + (2 x *Si*) = 190, yielded a multiple correlation of .529 with the criterion, which compared favorably with the highest biserial correlation between a single scale and the criterion of .357, for Scale *2*, and hit rates of 77 and 73 percent for the original and replication samples, respectively. Post and Lobitz (1980) cross-validated the Mezzich et al. formula on a sample of 74 depressed and 88 nondepressed psychiatric inpatients and found correct classification rates of 71 and 65 percent for the formula and Scale *2*, respectively. They noted that the primary advantage of the Mezzich formula over Scale *2* in their sample was in eliminating false positives. Data from a different sample are not entirely reassuring on this point, however. Of 189 Missouri manics (Hedlund & Won Cho, 1979), more than one-fifth exceeded the Mezzich formula cutting

score. But since these patients may have been tested at different phases of illness, this finding may be less damaging than it appears.

In both of the Mezzich et al. samples, neurotic depressives outnumbered major depressives in a ratio exceeding 3:1, raising the question of whether their formula may perform better in identifying minor depressions than major ones. In the Missouri sample of 309 psychotic and 776 neurotic depressives, however, cases failing to reach the formula cutting score amounted to 36 and 39 percent, respectively. This suggests that the disproportionate numbers of neurotic depressives in Mezzich et al.'s initial and replication samples did not adversely affect the sensitivity of their formula to psychotic depressives.

Only two research scales could be found that may have some application to the diagnosis of manic conditions: Wiggins (1966) *HYP* and Gilberstadt's (1970) *P-6*. As noted above, Mezzich et al. (1974) found moderate *HYP* and Scale *2* correlations with diagnoses of clinical depression. These were about equal in magnitude but opposite in direction, suggesting that high *HYP* scores may be common in manic conditions. This expectation was not borne out among the Missouri manics (Hedlund & Won Cho, 1979), however. For both manic groups, scores on *HYP* averaged less than a *T*-score of 60, not appreciably higher than the mean scores for the depressive groups (Table 4–5). *HYP* may contain too much extraneous variance to perform well as an indicator of mania. Several data sources suggest that *HYP* is more related to general maladjustment-subjective distress (i.e., the first factor of the MMPI) than is Scale *9*. Nearly one-third of the *HYP* items appear on the first Johnson et al. (1984) item factor, Neuroticism—General Anxiety and Worry; none appear on any of the other item factors. Among normal college students, Scale *9* correlates with Scale *7*, a marker for the first factor, at .16 (Duckworth & Anderson, 1986), while *HYP* does so at over .50 (Graham, 1977). The implication may be that while *HYP* might be as sensitive to any uncomfortable and ego-alien state of drivenness as to mania per se, Scale *9*, perhaps because of its multidimensionality, is sensitive to manic arousal regardless of whether this is accompanied by distress or euphoria.

P-6 was developed by contrasting the item responses of patients with the Gilberstadt and Duker (1965) Spike *9* profile type, with those of a representative sample of VA males. Gilberstadt

(1975) states that *P-6* measures "hypomania, denial of depression, social outgoingness, undercontrol of impulses and emotions, under-repression and lack of 'neurotic' defenses, [and] denial of social or psychological maladjustment" (p. 4). In a sample of 150 VA males, Rybolt (1976) found moderate but highly significant correlations between *P-6* and several of the standard scales: *L* (-.39), *1* (-.37), *2* (-.59), *3* (-.48), *7* (-.34), *9* (.61), and *0* (-.48). These correlations accord well with Gilberstadt's description. Swenson, Pearson, and Osborne (1973) reported correlations between Scale *9* and the other six scales above as follows: *L*(-.22), *1* (.13), *2* (-.03), *3* (.03), *7* (.32), and *0* (-.14). A comparison of these two sets of correlations suggests that, relative to Scale *9*, *P-6* may be more sensitive to the euphoric, grandiose, excited features of the manic syndrome and may be of some value in identifying Scale *9* false negatives. Another reason for this suspicion is that the *P-6* items, on the average, are more subtle (Christian, Burkhart, & Gynther, 1978) than those of Scale *9* (2.28 vs. 2.86). Further research is needed to establish this possibility and to support any other use of this scale.

Davies et al. (1985) evaluated Nichols' (personal communication) Schizophrenia-mania index, a linear combination of *T*-scores—[(Sc - Hy) - (Ma - D)]—on state hospital samples of 82 DSM-II and DSM-III manics and 65 DSM-III schizophrenics. The index differentiated the groups at a highly significant level, with the schizophrenics obtaining a mean score of 25.1 as compared with a mean of -8.7 for the manics. Replication with new manic and schizophrenic samples and an evaluation of classification rates must be undertaken before this index can be recommended for either clinical or research purposes.

None of the scales or indices reviewed in this section appear likely to supplant more familiar MMPI scales, codetypes, and rules of thumb for assisting diagnosis. None of the research depression scales reviewed here are clearly superior to Scale *2* and, with the possible exception of *DEP* and *MOR*, none appear to have features that are both interesting and unique. The Mezzich et al. (1974) formula seems to warrant further research. It may have a special use in purifying large samples when a relatively high proportion of false negatives can be tolerated, but its clinical use is not yet justified. Both of the mania scales, *HYP* and *P-6*, may have some value in evaluating hyperactivity, tension, and euphoria in manic and related syndromes. *P-6*, in particular, should be evaluated for its potential for detecting mania in patients who do not elevate Scale *9*.

PSYCHIATRIC DRUG RESPONSE

The approval of lithium for the treatment of mania by the Food and Drug Administration in 1970 was an important stimulus for the revival of interest in psychiatric diagnosis that occurred shortly thereafter. Prior to that year, the differential diagnosis of mania and schizophrenia had been largely a matter of academic interest since the standard treatment for both consisted of antipsychotic drugs. With the availability of differential treatments, a demand was created for more specific diagnostic ascertainments in these disorders.

The first attempt to identify lithium responders was made by Steinbook and Chapman (1970). Twenty-nine newly admitted inpatients of mixed diagnoses (mostly manic-depressive, manic schizoaffective, and schizophrenic) were selected for lithium therapy by "a resident and his staff supervisor" because of failure to respond adequately to milieu or moderate doses of phenothiazines. Improvement was evaluated by summary ratings of 17 target symptoms after a 1-month trial during which a minimum blood lithium level of .9 mEq/L was maintained. Several MMPI scales showed significant zero-order correlations with lithium response, including Scale *9* (.56), *K* (-.56), F (.47), *R* (-.44), and *2* (-.35). The largest correlation, .59, was found with Shaffer's (1963) measure of acquiescence independent of social desirability, *Ac*. When these scales were regressed against improvement ratings, only *Ac* was found to contribute a statistically significant increment to R^2.

In a retrospective study of variously diagnosed inpatients and outpatients, Steinberg (1979) used psychiatric record data to assign 15 patients to each of three groups: lithium responders, nonresponders, and a comparison ("Psychotropic") group of patients tried on medications other than lithium. All MMPIs were given prior to drug trials. When compared with the nonresponders, the lithium responders showed significantly higher scores on Scale *9* and lower scores on Scales *2*, *7*, and *0*. The responder group showed a *4-9* mean profile; the mean profiles of the nonresponders and psychotropic groups were coded *7-2-8* and *2-8*, respectively, but were quite similar in overall configuration.

House and Martin (1975) administered the MMPI to 26 unipolar and bipolar depressive inpatients during the first week of admission and prior to the initiation of chemotherapy. The sample was subdivided into patients with Scales *2* and *7* exceeding a *T*-score of 70 (*n* = 21) and those with these scales below *T*-scores of 70 (*n* = 5). All 5 patients in the low *2-7* group failed to respond to a 12-day trial of lithium as judged by depression ratings, while 17 of the 21 patients in the high *2-7* group did show a therapeutic response over the same time period.

Ananth, Engelsmann, and Kiriakos (1980) compared the MMPI scores of 28 lithium-responsive and 10 nonresponsive bipolars, all of whom had been treated with lithium for at least 2 years and completed the MMPI during the course of treatment. No significant scale differences were found.

An item-analytic approach to the prediction of an antidepressant response to lithium was taken by Donnelly et al. (1978) in an unusually well-designed study. Fifty-three major depressive inpatients were given the MMPI in the first 2 weeks of admission, during which time they were drug-free. A double-blind placebo-control design was used, with patients, raters, and personnel administering medication blind regarding whether patients were receiving lithium or placebo. Rated changes from the 5-day pretreatment placebo to the final 5 days of the 28-day lithium trial period served as the basis for designating patients as responders or nonresponders. Patients were then assigned to a standardization group consisting of 15 responders (10 women, 5 men) and 12 nonresponders (8 women, 4 men). Item analyses resulted in completely nonoverlapping nine-item scales for men and women, designated *LRS-M* and *LRS-F*, respectively. When turned back on the standardization group, these scales identified all of the responders and 10 of the 12 nonresponders, for an overall correct decision rate of 93 percent. The scales then were applied in a cross-validation group of 14 responders (10 women, 4 men) and 12 nonresponders (8 women, 4 men), identifying these patients with 100 percent accuracy. Internal consistency values for these scales were not reported.

The results of the study by Donnelly et al. (1978) were sufficiently encouraging to stimulate an unusually large number of studies trying to replicate their findings (Burdick & Holmes, 1980; Garvey, Johnson, Valentine, & Schuster, 1983; Campbell & Kimball, 1984). Unfortunately, these efforts have unanimously failed to support the validity of *LRS-M* and *LRS-F*.

In a study of virtually identical design to that of Donnelly et al. (1978), Donnelly, Murphy, Waldman, and Goodwin (1979) attempted to develop a scale predictive of response to the antidepressant drug imipramine. Forty-five major depressive inpatients were assigned to a standardization group including 12 responders (7 women, 5 men) and 11 nonresponders (8 women, 3 men), and a cross-validation group of 12 responders (7 women, 5 men) and 10 nonresponders (7 women, 3 men). As in their earlier study, separate nine-item scales were devised for men and women, *IRS-M* and *IRS-F*; no estimates of internal consistency were reported. These scales discriminated responders from nonresponders with 96 percent accuracy in the standardization group, and 95 percent in the cross-validation group. An attempt to cross-validate the *IRS-M*, however, failed to achieve better than chance separation between imipramine responsive and nonresponsive groups (Ramsey, Strand, Stern, & Mendels, 1981).

Stein, Downing, and Rickels (1979) evaluated the response to randomly assigned antianxiety or antidepressant treatment among a mixed group of chronic neurotic outpatients, of whom 54 were prescribed antianxiety agents and 43 were given antidepressants. Diagnoses were limited to anxiety neurosis, depressive neurosis, and mixed anxiety-depression and appear to have been assigned rather casually; patients with evidence of psychosis were excluded, as were patients with *6-8/8-6, 8-9/9-8, 8',* or *9'* profiles, regardless of whether they appeared psychotic. The MMPI was administered prior to the initiation of treatment, and response was evaluated 4 weeks later by rating scales that were completed by both physicians and patients. Discriminant function analysis revealed significantly higher elevations on Scale *4* among the 29 unimproved (Welsh code: *28"47'30619- F'KL:*) patients than for the 68 patients that were rated as improved (Welsh code: *278'341609-F-KL:*). This difference appeared to be stronger among the antidepressant- than the antianxiety-treated patients, at least in terms of the patient ratings.

The value of reliable predictors of response to psychiatric medication can hardly be overestimated. This is especially true of depressive conditions, since a trial of antidepressant treatment may require 3 to 4 weeks before response can be evaluated. Unfortunately, flawed research designs, small samples, and heterogeneous subject groupings have limited progress in finding response indicators. Research on the prediction of lithium response among manics has fared somewhat better than investigations of drug response among depressives, but the work to date does not indicate the superiority of any scales or indices over prediction based on the clinical judgment of profiles. The prediction of lithium response in mania seems to come down to whether the profile "looks" manic or not.

AN UPDATE ON SUICIDE

In a review of 15 MMPI studies of suicide through 1972, Clopton (1974) concluded that "neither standard MMPI scales, MMPI profile analysis, nor specially developed MMPI suicide scales have been found to be reliable in predicting suicide at useful levels" (p. 129). Research into the MMPI correlates of suicidal behavior in the years since Clopton's review have not outdated his conclusion. The present update is highly selective because of space limitations, but does include the most important of the MMPI-suicide studies since Clopton's review.

Leonard (1977) compared the MMPI performance of 20 male and 16 female psychiatric patients who completed suicide within a median of 112 days after completing the MMPI, with age- and sex-matched groups of suicidal and nonsuicidal psychiatric controls. Discriminant analysis differentiated the female suicides from their suicidal and nonsuicidal controls, and the male suicides from the nonsuicidal (but not suicidal) controls. Effect sizes were small, however. For the men, scores across the three groups were within 10 T-scores for 12 of the 13 standard scales; for the female groups, 11 of the 13 scales were within 10 T-scores. The possibility of differentiating items was not explored.

After reviewing eight studies in which at least one MMPI scale appeared related to suicidal behavior, Watson, Klett, Walters, and Laughlin (1983) hypothesized that suicidality might be more a state than a trait factor, and that the MMPI scales might have more success in predicting a suicidal episode than an eventual suicide. They compared 25 VA patients who showed an average elapsed time between taking the MMPI and suicide of one month with 75 patients who committed suicide at least 3 months after testing. Only Scale 6 showed a statistical difference between the recent and remote suicides, but the effect size was too small to be use-

ful. It might be noted that Scale 6 did not figure into Leonard's (1977) discriminant functions for either her males or females.

An omnibus investigation by Watson, Klett, Walters, and Vassar (1984) compared 84 male VA patients and former patients who had committed suicide within an average of 9 months from the test date with a matched control group of patients of roughly the same age and date of testing. The authors analyzed their results with respect to MMPI scales, profile patterns, items, and sets of items developed in previous MMPI-suicide research, but found generally nonsignificant differences and valueless effect sizes when significant differences did emerge.

The relationship between MMPI variables and suicidal behavior can hardly be described as a neglected area of research, yet the many studies done over the last 30 years have produced few, if any, valid correlates and nothing of clinical value. With respect to suicidal ideation, attempts, and threats, the base-rates appear not to be so extreme as to preclude the possibility of useful levels of prediction. In the Marks and Seeman (1963) sample, these behaviors occurred at rates of 23, 17, and 5 percent, respectively. The prediction of actual suicide, however, is likely to prove refractory. At this point, it seems likely that future research in this area, if it is to be productive, will require collaborative efforts to amass adequately sized samples of subjects who have completed suicide within a very short time, say 1 week, after having completed the MMPI. Since suicide may more closely approximate the final common pathway of a concatenation of demographic, situational, and personologic variables than a unitary trait disposition, the constitution of suicidal and appropriate comparison groups may require the institution of more extensive and sophisticated inclusion criteria and controls than those found tolerable in previous studies. The use of hierarchical clustering procedures to allow item-level comparisons between suicidal and nonsuicidal groups having similar cluster characteristics is one possible strategy. The simple control of major factorial dimensions of the MMPI prior to item analyses represents a more general approach to control that remains untried. There is no special reason to suppose that the suicides of patients who score high on scales reflecting general distress and maladjustment but low on scales reflecting general impulsiveness and undercontrol are going to be comparable to the suicides of patients showing the opposite scale patterns, either psychologically or psychometrically. Such efforts would represent an abandonment of the search for general MMPI suicide predictors, but one which, given the pattern of research results to date, may be long overdue. Yet even efforts along these lines may well fail to produce profile, scale, or item findings of clinical utility. A recently proposed Rorschach index of suicidality showed an impressive sensitivity of .75 (Exner & Wylie, 1977), which is probably better than any known pattern, scale, or index based on the MMPI. Assuming a similar level of specificity and a base rate for suicide 20 times that in the general population, this unreplicated index would result in approximately 165 false positives for every correctly predicted suicide. The point is that the clinical payoff for even valid and reliable MMPI correlates of suicide, assuming that such might eventually be found, is most unlikely to compensate the research efforts necessary to develop them. Such correlates may nevertheless contribute something of value to the classification and theory of suicidal behavior.

For the time being, the clinician is largely limited to standard sources of MMPI interpretation, clinical lore, and personal experience for test-based judgments about suicidal behavior. Some evidence (Clopton & Baucom, 1979) would suggest that these sources are limited indeed. However, the MMPI item pool contains a dozen or so items that appear to implicate at least the depressive forms of suicidal motivation (e.g., TRUE: 104, 106, 139, 202, 209, 252, 339, 413, 517, 526, 565; FALSE: 88). As face-valid indicators of such motivation, these may serve a useful alerting function, and as a springboard to inquiries within the interview. It is most doubtful that they may be used to identify genuine suicide potential or to assign levels of risk for suicidal behavior.

SUMMARY

Despite a respectable and increasing amount of MMPI research into the mood disorders over the last 40 years, the number of findings that can serve as reliable guides for clinical practice remains meager. Past research has clearly tended to support the construct validity of the basic scales most closely associated with mood disorders, *2* and *9*, even though major changes in the "official" definitions of these disorders have made the latter moving targets. If anything, more recent research has supported the construct validity of Scale *9* to

an extent scarcely envisioned by McKinley and Hathaway, and far greater than standard MMPI texts have tended to acknowledge. The strengths of both scales appear weighted toward their sensitivities to mood conditions. Their specificities, however, leave much to be desired. For example, Scale *2* appears as the highest or second highest scale in a large number of nonmood samples described elsewhere in this volume. But efforts to modify this scale to increase its specificity might only result in reducing its sensitivity to secondary depression and syndromes in which depression is an accessory symptom.

The codetype literature that has provided the primary focus of this review is far more problematic. The number of codetypes needed to describe depressive samples is unwieldy, and there are few, if any, compelling differences between neurotic or dysthymic and major depressive groups, at least at the scale or profile level. It is unclear whether this excessive variety represents limitations within the MMPI item pool, failures to control adequately for associated symptomatic, characterologic, or cyclic mood state features of depressed subjects, diagnostic error, or some combination of these and other factors. With respect to mania, the situation is somewhat better. The number of codetypes necessary to describe manic samples is manageable and within expectations. The most commonly appearing codetypes have often been reported in the past to be characteristic of schizophrenic rather than manic conditions (e.g., Marks & Seeman, 1963). The more recent data, however, recommend caution before accepting the guidelines of the codebooks and the interpretive material based on these that appears in introductory MMPI texts, as least so far as their diagnostic conclusions are concerned.

The sheer volume of research dealing with one or another aspect of the mood disorders, of which the references cited herein are only a small portion, contrasts sharply with what can be said to be known at this point about the MMPI correlates of depression and mania. The methodologic shortcomings of MMPI research in the mood disorders reflect those of MMPI research in general. Some of these problems are identified in Tables 4–2, 4–4, and 4–6. But these are not and are not intended to be exhaustive. Data are seldom analyzed and reported thoroughly. Analyses rarely go beyond the initial research question (which is often too narrowly drawn anyway) to uncover new and potentially fruitful directions for the future. Discussions rarely penetrate into adjacent areas of research that stand to enrich the context for considering the reported findings. Perhaps most importantly, studies in this area tend to reflect a lack of ambition and appear motivated by convenience rather than by any sustained interest in either the MMPI or the mood disorders. These and related failings are obstacles to the establishment of sustainable lines of inquiry, impede theory development, and leave the field looking scattered and undirected. If research in this area is to acquire the cumulative character of research in the more mature areas of psychological measurement, a great deal more commitment and sophistication on the part of investigators will be required.

The DSM-III emphasis on "most recent episode" highlights the caution that may be required to constitute adequately homogeneous samples of affectively disordered patients for study or comparison with other psychiatric groups. That is, unless sample sizes are unusually large, diagnosis alone is likely to prove an inadequate basis for selecting patients for study *no matter how painstaking the procedures used to guarantee diagnostic accuracy*. Important supplemental bases for subject selection include ratings of mood state, subdivision into phenomenologic (Grinker, Miller, Sabshin, Nunn, & Nunnally, 1961; Leonhard, 1979; Overall, 1962), family history (Van Valkenburg & Winokur, 1979; Winokur, 1979), or informal (e.g., hypochondriacal, agitated, paranoid) categories, or categories based on course and chronicity, or biochemical test or marker outcomes, depending on the investigator's purposes.

Some of the most recent research manifests an appropriate level of concern for homogeneous subject samples that was largely lacking in earlier studies. This improvement owes much to the availability of a variety of research criteria, often embedded in semistructured interview schedules, or their modifications as in the DSM-III. At this point, MMPI studies of mood disorders have by no means adequately capitalized on the availability of such criteria, and their use should be accepted as a minimal condition for the formation of diagnostic groups in future work. Nevertheless, the value of such criteria, especially if they form the sole basis for group composition, can easily be overstated, as indicated above. The signs and symptoms of depression and mania can issue from a variety of etiologies, and even when the more exhaustive interview schedules are used and diagnostic evaluations in other respects are more rigorous than usual, only a few of such competing etiologies may be adequately ruled out. Futhermore, interview schedules and psychiatric examinations are vulnerable to the same problems of response bias well known to MMPI clinicians. Symptoms may be falsely elicited (false positives) and/or fail to be elicited (false negatives), just as inventory items may be overendorsed or underendorsed. Since many of these disorders have a strong genetic predisposition, one way of circumventing the problem of the etiologic heterogeneity of symptoms is to require that subjects have a history of similar disorders among first- and second-degree relatives. Such a requirement would add considerably to the labors of subject selection and data collection and might negatively impact sample sizes to the point of impracticability. But the incorporation of this requirement in collaborative investigations involving multiple sites or even in independently conducted research in settings with large and complete record archives seems entirely feasible.

Buchsbaum and Haier (1978) have recommended the strategy of forming groups on the basis of biologic as opposed to symptomatic variables as another way around the problem of multiple symptom etiologies. The few available exploratory studies suggest that the MMPI is sensitive to a number of biochemical variables, including blood serotonin (Halevy, Moos, & Solomon, 1965), platelet monoamine oxidase (MAO: Donnelly, Murphy, Waldman, Buchsbaum, & Coursey, 1979; Haier, Murphy, & Buchsbaum, 1979), CSF dopamine beta-hydroxylase (Major et al., 1980), and dexamethasone suppression (Norman, Keitner, & Miller, 1985). Some of these and other psychometrically uninvestigated metabolites of central indoleamines and catecholamines appear to warrant careful study. Conceivable investigations might include not only comparisons between subjects above and below normal on one or another metabolite of interest, but also comparisons between subjects with a frequently occurring abnormal *profile* of biochemical values and those with a different abnormal profile, or subjects having normal values on all variables. Similarly, potentially worthwhile studies might focus on response to pharmacologic treatment. For example, the MMPI performance of subjects who have failed to respond to adequate trials of noradrenergic antidepressants but who subsequently responded well to serotonergic antidepressants might be compared with subjects with an opposite response pattern, or with subjects having histories of satisfactory response to both types of drugs.

Another potentially fruitful research avenue involves reversing the usual relationship between independent and dependent variables, which is another way of avoiding the problem of symptom heterogeneity within diagnostic categories. The rationale for treating the MMPI as the source of independent variables has been well discussed by Sines (1966). The feasibility of identifying frequently occurring profile groups using cluster analytic procedures has been demonstrated in a variety of populations discussed elsewhere in this volume, although efforts to develop empirical correlates of profile clusters have tended to lag. Yet Davis and Sines (1971) have demonstrated that the correlates of cluster analytically-derived groups can be woven into surprising, complete, and well-textured personality descriptions.

The examination of MMPI profiles collected in the course of research projects should include consideration of how best to reflect their variability. The arguments against the use of mean profiles to represent entire samples are well known, but the same arguments apply, if less forcefully, to any procrustean format, including two-point code distributions. The latter may or may not represent

MMPI patterns with sufficient accuracy and completeness. If three- or four-point codes can better reflect areas of density in profile data, these should be used instead of or in combination with two-point codes. When justified, more complex codes may also contribute to the convergent validation of cluster analytically-derived groups.

The MMPI literature continues to manifest an excessive emphasis on the standard validity and clinical scales, an emphasis (understandably) more evident in the psychiatric than the psychological literature. These scales are often chosen when investigation of the topic of interest would be far better served by using content-homogenous scales such as the content scales of Wiggins (1966) or the item factor scales of Johnson et al. (1984) or by adopting designs that allow for group comparisons at the item level. Since virtually all of the standard scales are multidimensional, they may conceal group differences almost as often as they reveal them. Or, they may do both. Haier, Murphy, and Buchsbaum (1979) found significant correlations between platelet MAO and Scale 6 in several nonschizophrenic pathologic samples. But the meaning of this finding is left obscure. Since Scale 6 includes groups of items indicating persecutory ideas, resentment, oversensitivity, and obtuse trustfulness, one, some, or all of these may have contributed to the obtained correlation. Butcher and Tellegen (1978) have been justly critical of scale development efforts that are inadequately informed by familiarity with the item pool and the hundreds of scales already available. As these authors note, such efforts have been responsible for a proliferation of redundant scales that demonstrate low internal consistency, have unknown factor structure and relations with better-known MMPI scales, and have never been cross-validated. Yet item analysis need not imply a scale development goal. A study reporting significant differences, between say, major and minor depressive groups on Scales 2, 4, 7, and 8, is unlikely to contribute much to clinical practice (apart from the obvious conclusion that one group is apparently "sicker" than the other) because of the extent of intercorrelation and item overlap among these scales. But a knowledge of the items that most contribute to significant scale differences may provide valuable insight into the psychopathology of these depressive conditions as well as potentially advancing their differential diagnosis.

When a new scale is the aim of group comparisons, correlations between the new scale and existing scales that may illuminate the nature of the construct embodied in it, including marker variables such as the factor scales of Welsh (1956) or Block (1965), should be computed and reported, along with a comparison between the scale variances for the index group and those of appropriate comparison samples, including normal groups. Replication efforts on behalf of a new scale should pit it against the performance of theoretically related existing scales to determine the incremental value of the new scale in achieving separations between relevant groups and improved rates of correct classification.

Whatever the conceptual and methodologic shortcomings of past research, it is clear that the MMPI is sensitive to a wide variety of factors that contribute to an understanding of the mood disorders. Several MMPI scales, patterns, and indices have been shown to reflect important nontest behaviors and attitudes of importance to diagnostic decision-making. Others show at least limited promise in this regard. On the whole, the available evidence suggests that the MMPI may have substantial value in the diagnosis of mania and in the differential diagnosis of mania and schizophrenia. Its value in the diagnosis and differential diagnosis of the depressions is less well established. If its value in the diagnosis of the mood disorders falls short of the hopes of its developers, a firm foundation for new research efforts now exists to support better conceived studies to explore the potential and limits of the MMPI for this purpose. Meehl's (1972) conviction that much blood remains in "the MMPI psychometric turnip" remains justified. But its extraction will require levels of imagination, rigor, and persistence greater than have been typical to date.

ACKNOWLEDGMENTS

The author wishes to express his gratitude to Roger L. Greene and Cathy Shehorn for their substantial assistance in the preparation of this chapter. Dr. Greene provided general encouragement, statistical analyses, and helpful comments on an earlier draft of the manuscript. Cathy Shehorn provided support in the form of extensive library research, as well as editorial suggestions on an earlier version of the manuscript.

REFERENCES

Akiskal, H.S., Bitar, A.H., Puzantian, V.R., Rosenthal, T.L., & Walker, P.W. (1978). The nosological status of neurotic depression: A prospective three-to-four year examination in light of the primary-secondary and unipolar-bipolar dichotomies. *Archives of General Psychiatry, 35,* 756–766.

Altschule, M.D., (1976). *The development of traditional psychopathology.* New York: Halsted Press.

Ananth, J., Engelsmann, F., & Kiriakos, R. (1980). Evaluation of lithium response: Psychometric findings. *Canadian Journal of Psychiatry, 25,* 151–154.

Andreasen, N.C. (1979). Thought, language, and communication disorders: II. Diagnostic significance. *Archives of General Psychiatry, 36,* 1325–1330.

Andreasen, N.C., Hoffman, R.E., & Grove, W.M. (1985). Mapping abnormalities in language and cognition. In M.

Alpert (Ed.), *Controversies in schizophrenia: Changes and constancies* (pp. 199–227). New York: Guilford Press.

Blazer, D., George, L.K., Landerman, R., Pennybacker, M., Melville, M.L., Woodbury, M., Manton, K.G., Jordan, K., & Locke, B. (1985). Psychiatric disorders: A rural/urban comparison. *Archives of General Psychiatry, 42*, 651–656.

Bleuler, E. (1950). *Dementia praecox; or The group of schizophrenias*. New York: International Universities Press.

Block, J. (1965). *The challenge of response sets: Unconfounding meaning, acquiescence and social desirability in the MMPI*. New York: Appleton-Century-Crofts.

Boerger, A.R. (1975). *The utility of some alternative approaches to MMPI scale construction*. Unpublished doctoral dissertation, Kent State University, Kent, OH.

Buchsbaum, M.S., & Haier, R.J. (1978). Biological homogeniety, symptomatic heterogeniety, and the diagnosis of schizophrenia. *Schizophrenia Bulletin, 4*, 473–475.

Bunney, W.E., & Hamburg, D.A. (1963). Methods for reliable longitudinal observation of behavior. *Archives of General Psychiatry, 9*, 280–294.

Burdick, B.M., & Holmes, C.B. (1980). Use of the lithium response scale with an outpatient psychiatric sample. *Psychological Reports, 47*, 69–70.

Butcher, J.N., & Tellegen, A. (1978). Common methodological problems in MMPI research. *Journal of Consulting and Clinical Psychology, 46*, 620–628.

Campbell, D.R., & Kimball, R.R. (1984). Replication of "Prediction of antidepressant response to lithium": Problems in generalizing to a clinical setting. *American Journal of Psychiatry, 141*, 706–707.

Christian, W.L., Burkhart, B.R., & Gynther, M.D. (1978). Subtle-obvious ratings of MMPI items: New interest in an old concept. *Journal of Consulting and Clinical Psychology, 46*, 1178–1186.

Clopton, J.R. (1974). Suicide risk assessment via the Minnesota Multiphasic Personality Inventory (MMPI). In C. Neuringer (Ed.), *Psychological assessment of suicidal risk* (pp. 118–133). Springfield, IL: Charles C. Thomas.

Clopton, J.R., & Baucom, D.H. (1979). MMPI ratings of suicide risk. *Journal of Personality Assessment, 43*, 293–296.

Comrey, A.L. (1957). A factor analysis of the items on the MMPI Depression scale. *Educational and Psychological Measurement, 17*, 578–585.

Cronbach, L.J., & Gleser, G.C. (1953). Assessing similarity between profiles. *Psychological Bulletin, 50*, 456–473.

Dahlstrom, W.G. & Prange, A.J. (1960). Characteristics of depressive and paranoid reactions on the Minnesota Multiphasic Personality Inventory. *Journal of Nervous and Mental Disease, 131*, 513–522.

Dahlstrom, W.G., & Welsh, G.S. (1960). *An MMPI handbook*. Minneapolis: University of Minnesota Press.

Davies, J.W., Nichols, D.S., & Greene, R.L. (1985, March). *A new schizophrenia scale for the MMPI*. Paper presented at the 20th Annual Symposium on Recent Advances in the Clinical Use of the MMPI, Honolulu.

Davis, K.R., & Sines, J.O. (1971). An antisocial behavior pattern associated with a specific MMPI profile. *Journal of Consulting and Clinical Psychology, 36*, 229–234.

Dempsey, P. (1964). A unidimensional depression scale for the MMPI. *Journal of Consulting Psychology, 4*, 364–370.

Donnelly, E.F., Goodwin, F.K., Waldman, I.N., & Murphy, D.L. (1978). Prediction of antidepressant responses to lithium. *American Journal of Psychiatry, 135*, 552–556.

Donnelly, E.F., & Murphy, D.L. (1973). Primary affective disorder: MMPI differences between unipolar and bipolar depressed subjects. *Journal of Clinical Psychology, 29*, 303–306.

Donnelly, E.F., Murphy, D.L., & Goodwin, F.K. (1976). Cross-sectional and longitudinal comparisons of bipolar and unipolar depressed groups on the MMPI. *Journal of Consulting and Clinical Psychology, 44*, 233–237.

Donnelly, E.F., Murphy, D.L., & Goodwin, F.K. (1978). Primary affective disorder: Anxiety in unipolar and bipolar depressed groups. *Journal of Clinical Psychology, 34*, 621–623.

Donnelly, E.F., Murphy, D.L., & Scott, W.H. (1975). Perception and cognition in patients with bipolar and unipolar depressed disorders: A study in Rorschach responding. *Archives of General Psychiatry, 32*, 1128–1131.

Donnelly, E.F., Murphy, D.L., & Waldman, I.N. (1980). Denial and somatization as characteristics of bipolar depressed groups. *Journal of Clinical Psychology, 36*, 159–162.

Donnelly, E.F., Murphy, D.L., Waldman, I.N., Buchsbaum, M.S., & Coursey, R.D. (1979). Psychological characteristics corresponding to low versus high platelet monoamine oxidase activity. *Biological Psychiatry, 14*, 375–383.

Donnelly, E.F., Murphy, D.L., Waldman, I.N., & Goodwin, F.K. (1979). Prediction of antidepressant responses to imipramine. *Neuropsychobiology, 5*, 94–101.

Donnelly, E.F., Murphy, D.L., Waldman, I.N., & Reynolds, T.D. (1976). MMPI differences between unipolar and bipolar depressed subjects: A replication. *Journal of Clinical Psychology, 32*, 610–612.

Duckworth, J.C., & Anderson, W. P. (1986). *MMPI interpretation manual for counselors and clinicians* (3rd ed.). Muncie, IN: Accelerated Development.

Exner, J.E., Jr. & Wylie, J. (1977). Some Rorschach data concerning suicide. *Journal of Personality Assessment, 41*, 339–348.

Faravelli, C., Ambonetti, A., Pallanti, S., & Pazzagli, A. (1986). Depressive relapses and incomplete recovery from index episode. *American Journal of Psychiatry, 143*, 888–891.

Feighner, J.P., Robins, E., Guze, S.B., Woodruff, R.A., Winokur, G., & Munoz, R. (1972). Diagnostic criteria for use in psychiatric research. *Archives of General Psychiatry, 26*, 57–63.

Garvey, M.J., Johnson, R.A., Valentine, R.H., & Schuster, V. (1983). Use of an MMPI scale to predict antidepressant response to lithium. *Psychiatry Research, 10*, 17–20.

Gilberstadt, H. (1970). *Comprehensive MMPI codebook for males*. Minneapolis: VAH MMPI Research Laboratory.

Gilberstadt, H. (1975). *An atlas for the P-code system of MMPI interpretation*. Minneapolis: VAH MMPI Research Laboratory.

Gilberstadt, H., & Duker, J. (1960). Case history correlates of three MMPI profile types. *Journal of Consulting Psychology, 24*, 361–367.

Gilberstadt, H., & Duker, J. (1965). *A handbook for clinical and actuarial MMPI interpretation*. Philadelphia: W.B. Saunders.

Goodwin, D.W., & Guze, S.B. (1979). *Psychiatric diagnosis* (2nd ed.). New York: Oxford.

Graham, J.R. (1987). *The MMPI: A practical guide* (2nd ed.). New York: Oxford.

Greene, R.L. (1988). Introduction. In R. Greene (Ed.), *The MMPI: Use with specific populations*. Philadelphia: Grune & Stratton. (pp. 1–21).

Grinker, R.R., Miller, J., Sabshin, M., Nunn, R., & Nunnally, J. (1961). *The phenomena of depressions*. New York: Hoeber.

Guthrie, G.M. (1950). Six MMPI diagnostic patterns. *Journal of Psychology, 30*, 317–323.

Haier, R.J., Murphy, D.L., & Buchsbaum, M.S. (1979). Paranoia and platelet MAO in normals and non-schizophrenic psychiatric groups. *American Journal of Psychiatry, 136*, 306–310.

Haier, R.J., Rieder, R.O., Khouri, P.J., & Buchsbaum, M.S. (1979). Extreme MMPI scores and the Research Diagnostic

Criteria: Screening college men for psychopathology. *Archives of General Psychiatry, 36,* 528–534.

Halevy, A., Moos, R.H., & Solomon, G.F. (1965). A relationship between blood serotonin concentrations and behavior in psychiatric patients. *Journal of Psychiatric Research, 3,* 1–10.

Harrow, M., Grossman, L.S., Silverstein, M.L., & Meltzer, H.Y. (1982). Thought pathology in manic and schizophrenic patients. *Archives of General Psychiatry, 39,* 665–671.

Hathaway, S.R. (1980). Scales 5 (masculinity-feminity), 6 (paranoia), and 8 (schizophrenia). In W.G. Dahlstrom & L.E. Dahlstrom (Eds.), *Basic readings on the MMPI: A new selection on personality measurement* (pp. 65–75). Minneapolis: University of Minnesota Press.

Hathaway, S.R., & Meehl, P.E. (1951). *An atlas for the clinical use of the MMPI.* Minneapolis: University of Minnesota Press.

Hedlund, J., & Won Cho, D. (1979). *[MMPI data research tape for Missouri Department of Mental Health patients.]* Unpublished raw data.

House, K.M., & Martin, R.L. (1975). MMPI delineation of a subgroup of depressed patients refractory to lithium carbonate therapy. *American Journal of Psychiatry, 132,* 644–646.

Jarnecke, R.W., & Chambers, E.D. (1977). MMPI content scales: Dimensional structure, construct validity and interpretive norms in a psychiatric population. *Journal of Consulting and Clinical Psychology, 45,* 1126–1131.

Johnson, J.H., Butcher, J.N., Null, C., & Johnson, K.N. (1984). Replicated item level factor analysis of the full MMPI. *Journal of Personality and Social Psychology, 47,* 105–114.

Johnson, J.H., Klingler, D.E. & Giannetti, R.A. (1980). Band width in diagnostic classification using the MMPI as a predictor. *Journal of Consulting and Clinical Psychology, 48,* 340–349.

Kasanin, J.S. (1933). The acute schizoaffective psychoses. *American Journal of Psychiatry, 13,* 97–126.

Lacher, D. (1968). MMPI two-point code-type correlates in a state hospital population. *Journal of Clinical Psychology, 24,* 424–427.

Lachar, D., & Alexander, R.S. (1978). Veridicality of self-report: Replicated correlates of the Wiggins MMPI content scales. *Journal of Consulting and Clinical Psychology, 46,* 1349–1356.

Leonard, C.V. (1977). The MMPI as a suicide predictor. *Journal of Consulting and Clinical Psychology, 45,* 367–377.

Leonhard, K. (1979). *The classification of the endogenous psychoses.* New York: Irvington.

Lumry, A.E., Gottesman, I.I., & Tuason, V.B. (1982). MMPI state dependency during the course of bipolar psychosis. *Psychiatry Research, 7,* 59–67.

Major, L.F., Lerner, P., Goodwin, F.K., Ballenger, J.C., Brown, G.L., & Lovenberg, W. (1980). Dopamine beta-hydroxylase in CSF: Relationship to personality measures. *Archives of General Psychiatry, 37,* 308–310.

Marks, P.A., & Seeman, W. (1963). *The actuarial description of abnormal personality: An atlas for use with the MMPI.* Baltimore: Williams & Wilkins.

Marks, P.A., Seeman, W., & Haller, D.L. (1974). *The actuarial use of the MMPI with adolescents and adults.* New York: Oxford.

McKinley, J.C., & Hathaway, S.R. (1980). Scales 3 (hysteria), 9 (hypomania), and 4 (psychopathic deviate). In W.G. Dahlstrom & L.E. Dahlstrom (Eds.), *Basic readings on the MMPI: A new selection on personality measurement* (pp. 40–64). Minneapolis: University of Minnesota Press.

Meehl, P.E. (1956). Wanted—a good cookbook. *American Psychologist, 11,* 263–272.

Meehl, P.E. (1972). Reactions, reflections, projections. In J.N. Butcher (Ed.), *Objective personality assessment* (pp. 131–189). San Diego: Academic Press.

Mezzich, J.E., Damarin, F.L., & Erickson, J.R. (1974). Comparative validity of strategies and indices for differential diagnosis of depressive states from other psychiatric conditions using the MMPI. *Journal of Consulting and Clinical Psychology, 42,* 691–698.

Nichols, D.S. (1986). The use of the MMPI content scales. *Critical Items, 2,* 2–3.

Nichols, D.S. (1987). *Interpreting the Wiggins MMPI content scales.* (Clinical Notes on the MMPI, no. 10). Minneapolis: National Computer Systems.

Norman, W.H., Keitner, G.I., & Miller, I.W. (1985). MMPI, personality dysfunction and the dexamethasone suppression test in major depression. *Journal of Affective Disorders, 9,* 97–101.

Overall. J.E. (1962). Dimensions of manifest depression. *Journal of Psychiatric Research, 1,* 239–245.

Overall, J.E., Higgins, W., & De Schweinitz, A. (1976). Comparison of differential diagnostic discrimination for abbreviated and standard MMPI. *Journal of Clinical Psychology, 32,* 237–245.

Payne, F.D., & Wiggins, J.S. (1972). MMPI profile types and the self-report of psychiatric patients. *Journal of Abnormal Psychology, 79,* 1–8.

Pope, H.G., & Lipinski, J.F. (1978). Diagnosis in schizophrenia and manic-depressive illness: A reassessment of the specificity of 'schizophrenic' symptoms in the light of current research. *Archives of General Psychiatry, 35,* 811–828.

Post, R.D., Clopton, J.R., Keefer, G., Rosenberg, D., Blyth, L.S., & Stein, M. (1986). MMPI predictors of mania among psychiatric inpatients. *Journal of Personality Assessment, 50,* 248–256.

Post, R.D., & Lobitz, W.C. (1980). The utility of Mezzich's MMPI regression formula as a diagnostic criterion in depression research. *Journal of Consulting and Clinical Psychology, 48,* 673–674.

Ramsey, T.A., Strand, S., Stern, S., & Mendels, J. (1981). MMPI prediction of imipramine response: A replication study. *Neuropsychobiology, 7,* 94–98.

Robins, L.N., Helzer, J.E., Croughan, J., & Ratcliff, K.S. (1981). The NIMH Diagnostic Interview Schedule: Its history, characteristics, and validity. *Archives of General Psychiatry, 38,* 381–389.

Robins, L.N., Helzer, J.E., Weissman, M.M., Orvaschel, H., Gruenberg, E., Burke, J.D., & Regier, D.A. (1984). Lifetime prevalence of specific psychiatric disorders in three sites. *Archives of General Psychiatry, 41,* 949–958.

Rosen, A. (1958). Differentiation of diagnostic groups by individual MMPI scales. *Journal of Consulting Psychology, 22,* 453–457.

Rosen, A. (1962). Development of MMPI scales based on a reference group of psychiatric patients. *Psychological Monographs, 76* (8, Whole No. 527).

Rybolt, G.A. (1976). The P scales for the MMPI: An attempt at validation. *VA Newsletter for Research in Mental Health and Behavioral Sciences, 18,* 25–29.

Schneider, K. (1959). *Clinical psychopathology.* Philadelphia: Grune & Stratton.

Seitz, F.C. (1970). Five psychological measures of neurotic depression: A correlation study. *Journal of Clinical Psychology, 26,* 504–505.

Shaffer, J.W. (1963). A new acquiescence scale for the MMPI. *Journal of Clinical Psychology, 19,* 412–415.

Silver, R.J., Isaacs, K., & Mansky, P. (1981). MMPI correlates of affective disorders. *Journal of Clinical Psychology, 37,* 836–839.

Silver, R.J. & Sines, L.K. (1961). MMPI characteristics of a state hospital population. *Journal of Clinical Psychology, 17*, 142–146.

Sines, J.O. (1966). Actuarial methods in personality assessment. In B.A. Maher (Ed.), *Progress in Experimental Personality Research* (pp. 133–193). San Diego: Academic Press.

Spitzer, R.L., Endicott, J., & Robins, E. (1975). *Research diagnostic criteria (RDC) for a selected group of functional disorders* (2nd ed.). New York: Biometrics Research, New York State Psychiatric Institute.

Stein, M.K., Downing, R.W., & Rickels, K. (1979). The Minnesota Multiphasic Personality Inventory in predicting response to pharmacotherapy of neurotic outpatients. *Journal of Nervous and Mental Disease, 167*, 542–547.

Steinberg, F.A. (1979). The delineation of an MMPI symptom pattern unique to lithium responders. *American Journal of Psychiatry, 136*, 567–569.

Steinbook, R.M., & Chapman, A.B. (1970). Lithium responders: An evaluation of psychological test characteristics. *Comprehensive Psychiatry, 11*, 524–530.

Swenson, W.M., Pearson, J.S., & Osborne, D. (1973). *An MMPI source book*. Minneapolis: University of Minnesota Press.

Taylor, J.B., Ptacek, M., Carithers, M., Griffin, C., & Coyne, L. (1972). Rating scales as measures of clinical judgment: III. Judgments of the self on personality inventory scales and direct ratings. *Educational and Psychological Measurement, 32*, 543–557.

Van Valkenburg, C., & Winokur, L. (1979). Depressive spectrum disease. *The Psychiatry Cinics of North America, 2*, 469–482.

Walters, G.D. (1984). Empirically derived characteristics of psychiatric inpatients with DSM-III diagnoses of schizophreniform disorder. *Journal of Abnormal Psychology, 93*, 71–79.

Watson, C.G., Klett, W.G., Walters, C., & Laughlin, P.R. (1983). Identification of suicidal episodes with the MMPI. *Psychological Reports, 53*, 919–922.

Watson, C.G., Klett, W.G., Walters, C., & Vassar, P. (1984). Suicide and the MMPI: A cross-validation of predictors. *Journal of Clinical Psychology, 40*, 115–119.

Weissman, M.M., & Boyd, J.H. (1983). The epidemiology of affective disorders: Rates and risk factors. In L. Grinspoon (Ed.); *Psychiatry update Vol. II* (pp. 406–428). Washington: American Psychiatric Press.

Welsh, G.S. (1956). Factor dimensions A and R. In G.S. Welsh & W.G. Dahlstrom (Eds.), *Basic readings on the MMPI in psychology and medicine* (pp. 264–281). Minneapolis: University of Minnesota Press.

Wiener, D.N. (1948). Subtle and obvious keys for the MMPI. *Journal of Consulting Psychology, 12*, 164–170.

Wierzbicki, M. (1986). Similarity of monozygotic and dizygotic twins in level and lability of subclinically depressed mood. *Journal of Clinical Psychology, 42*, 577–585.

Wiggins, J.S. (1966). Substantive dimensions of self-report in the MMPI item pool. *Psychological Monographs, 80* (22, Whole No. 630).

Wiggins, J.S., Goldberg, L.R., & Appelbaum, M. (1971). MMPI content scales: Interpretive norms and correlations with other scales. *Journal of Consulting and Clinical Psychology, 37*, 403–410.

Wilson, I.C., Alltop, L.B., & Buffaloe, W.J. (1967). Parental bereavement in childhood: MMPI profiles in a depressed population. *British Journal of Psychiatry, 113*, 761–764.

Wilson, I.C., Carson, R.G., Rabon, A.M., & Alltop, L.B. (1970). *An MMPI two-type depressive scale*. Unpublished paper, North Carolina Department of Mental Health, Raleigh.

Wilson, I.C., Vernon, J.T., Guin, T., & Sandifer, M.G. (1963). A controlled study of the treatments of depression. *Journal of Neuropsychiatry, 4*, 331–337.

Winokur, G. (1979). Unipolar depression: Is it divisible into autonomous subtypes? *Archives of General Psychiatry, 36*, 47–52.

Winokur, G., & Pitts, F.N. (1964). Affective disorder: Is reactive depression an entity? *Journal of Nervous and Mental Disease, 138*, 541–547.

Winters, K.C., Newmark, C.S., Lumry, A.E., Leach, K., & Weintraub, S. (1985). MMPI codetypes characteristic of DSM-III schizophrenics, depressives, and bipolars. *Journal of Clinical Psychology, 41*, 382–386.

Winters, K.C., Weintraub, S., & Neale, J.M. (1981). Validity of MMPI codetypes in identifying DSM-III schizophrenics, unipolars, and bipolars. *Journal of Consulting and Clinical Psychology, 49*, 486–487.

Chapter 5

Personality Disorders

LESLIE C. MOREY and MARCIA R. SMITH

OVERVIEW

The diagnosis of personality disorder represents a particular challenge to the mental health researcher and clinician. In part, this difficulty stems from the puzzling and inconsistent behavior of individuals bearing this diagnosis, but it also reflects the vague and ill-defined nature of the very concept of personality disorder. As a further complication, the definition of personality disorder has undergone substantial changes in recent years. Thus, it is not surprising to find that, in comparison to many of the other conditions outlined in this volume, diagnostic research in the personality disorders area is at a relatively primitive level.

Perhaps one of the most important developments in the history of the concept of personality disorders came with the introduction of the third edition of the *Diagnostic and Statistical Manual of Mental Disorder* (DSM-III: American Psychiatric Association, 1980). This classification system attempted to make explicit the qualitative differences between peronality disorders (coded on Axis II in DSM-III) and traditional psychiatric diagnoses such as schizophrenia (an Axis I condition in DSM-III). In particular, the personality disorders were seen as *trait* disturbances; that is, according to DSM-III, a personality disorder reflects a long-standing trait (or traits) that came to be inflexible, maladaptive, and causally related to subjective distress or impairment in functioning.

The personality disorders are important differential diagnoses for a number of reasons. First, personality disorders are thought to represent the largest diagnostic group presenting for treatment in outpatient settings (Auchincloss & Michels, 1983). In addition, they are important considerations in diagnosing Axis I clinical syndromes such as depression or anxiety disorder, since a concomitant personality disorder can affect the presentation of these conditions (Widiger & Frances, 1985). Despite their importance, personality disorders are the least reliable diagnostic categories in DSM-III (Mellsop, Varghese, Joshua, & Hicks, 1982; Spitzer, Forman, & Nee, 1979) and they are certainly among the most controversial (Frances, 1980).

Part of the difficulty in diagnosing personality disorder stems from the nature of this construct. In general, most personality disorders involve constructs that are not typically measurable through overt behavior (Widiger & Kelso, 1983), and as such, observational and structured interview types of assessment approaches may have limited utility in this area. Given the strong personality assessment tradition in psychology, many researchers have turned to psychological tests in the hope of establishing reliable and valid methods of diagnosing personality disorder, and foremost among these tests has been the MMPI. This chapter seeks to provide an overview of research utilizing the MMPI in the diagnosis of personality disorder.

This chapter consists of two major sections. The first section reviews the MMPI research conducted with each of the 11 DSM-III personality disorder diagnoses. Because of the substantial changes in

THE MMPI: USE WITH
SPECIFIC POPULATIONS
ISBN 0-8089-1913-X

the conceptualization of personality disorder with the advent of DSM-III, most relevant research has been conducted since its introduction in 1980. Prior to that time, the majority of these diagnostic categories either did not exist (e.g., Avoidant Personality Disorder) or existed in a form substantially different from the current DSM-III definition. Because of these recent developments, much of the research conducted has been at a fairly preliminary stage, typically seeking to establish a mean profile or codetype corresponding to a particular personality disorder.

The chapter concludes with a discussion of a new set of MMPI research scales, recently developed by Morey, Waugh, and Blashfield (1985), which were designed for the specific purpose of assessing the DSM-III personality disorder diagnoses. Although the research on these scales is at an early stage, they may be particularly useful in assessing the personality disorder domain.

In examining the evidence presented in the following pages, certain crucial methodologic issues should be kept in mind. First, how do these studies define their criterion groups? In the personality disorders area, this issue is particularly important since there are no well-validated markers for these concepts. In addition, the diagnosis of "Mixed Personality Disorder" is fairly common (Koenigsberg, Kaplan, Gilmore, & Cooper, 1985); consequently, it is typical to find patients presenting with features of a number of different personality disorders. Thus, identifying a relatively pure "criterion group" in this area becomes exceedingly difficult.

A second question to consider involves the effects of moderator variables. Again, the consideration of such variables is particularly salient for the personality disorder area. For example, the relationship between gender and personality disorder has been a controversial one, with some authors claiming that certain personality categories reflect sex role stereotypes that should have differential implications for males and females (Kaplan, 1983). In fact, as discussed in the following pages, some studies have provided evidence suggesting that the diagnosis of personality disorders is strongly affected by sex role biases. Such issues are critical in the evaluation of diagnostic studies.

Finally, in reviewing these studies one must consider how the data are analyzed and interpreted. The multivariate nature of the MMPI generally calls for multivariate analyses, but these techniques are complex and often misused. In addition, separate multivariate methods are based on different assumptions. As a result, when two different methods are used to address the same problem (e.g., cluster analysis vs. factor analysis in deriving MMPI "subtypes"), the researcher can obtain drastically different answers. Issues such as these influence the results a researcher obtains; they are examined for particular studies in this chapter.

In these subsequent sections, the DSM-III format is followed since it is currently the standard nomenclature in mental health. However, the reader should be warned against a reification of these DSM-III concepts, since the research in this area is at a very preliminary basis. Indeed, the studies outlined in this chapter have undertaken a difficult task; they have sought to determine the utility of the MMPI in diagnosing conditions that are ill-defined and unreliably identified. As such, negative results are difficult to interpret: Is the MMPI not useful for diagnosing DSM-III defined personality disorder constructs, or are the constructs themselves not useful? Despite the difficulties inherent in this area, a number of studies have indicated that the MMPI may indeed have promise in resolving these diagnostic dilemmas. These studies are examined in the following pages.

THE MMPI WITH SPECIFIC PERSONALITY DISORDERS

BORDERLINE PERSONALITY DISORDER

The inclusion of Borderline Personality Disorder in DSM-III is official recognition of the popularity of the term in the current literature. Despite this popularity, considerable confusion as well as debate exists as to the meaning, relevance, and validity of this category as a diagnostic entity. The heterogeneity of the borderline concept was illustrated by the work of Perry and Klerman (1978) who compared four sets of criteria extracted from articles that were thought to be outstanding examples of clinical description. They demonstrated a significant lack of agreement between accounts; a comparison of the work of Kernberg (1975), Grinker, Werble, and Drye (1968), Knight (1953), and Gunderson and Singer (1975) resulted in only one criterion, "superficially appropriate social behavior," that appeared in all descriptions. Part of the current confusion over the borderline concept may stem from the fact that the DSM-III category is an amalgamation of the work of several influential authors, and as such the internal consistency of the category may have been compromised. Futhermore, although DSM-III was intended to be atheoretical with respect to etiology, the majority of the literature on Borderline Personality Disorder relies heavily on theoretical personality structures. Until recently, few empirical studies existed that examined this construct.

The term *borderline* has had several usages in the literature. Borderline often has been used in reference to schizophrenia spectrum disorders that alternatively have been described as latent schizophrenia, ambulatory schizophrenia, or pre-schizophrenia. This usage is exemplified by the work of Kety et al. (1971). These authors used the term *borderline schizophrenia* to characterize the first-degree relatives of schizophrenics who appeared to have abnormalities of thought and behavior that were not of sufficient magnitude to be identified as schizophrenia. In DSM-III, this pattern has been separated from the borderline concept and is termed Schizotypal Personality Disorder, as described in a later section.

The second class of referents to borderline does not emphasize the relationship to psychosis, but rather denotes a particular form of highly disturbed personality functioning. This use of the term has been traced to Deutsch's (1942) concept of the "as-if" personality, in which superficial social appropriateness masked highly disturbed personal relationships. To an extent, the existing borderline category in DSM-III is derivative of some of these notions since it is designed to identify a stable configuration of behaviors characterized by intense and problematic interpersonal relationships.

Each of the viewpoints described above present the concept of borderline as a category of psychopathology. An alternative viewpoint, taken by Kernberg (1975) and Millon (1981a), is that borderline refers to a severely dysfunctional *level* of personality organization. This viewpoint represents a dimensional model with borderline located in the more severe range of an overall continuum of personality pathology. Adopting a dimensional conceptualization of borderline may be useful in explaining the apparent heterogeneity of clinical accounts of Borderline Personality.

The DSM-III itself provides what might be considered a "prototypic" model for the classification of personality disorders, which implies that personality disorders exist in distinct though not necessarily mutually exclusive categories. Polythetic criteria are provided for Borderline Personality Disorder (see Chapter 1); thus, individuals within a given diagnostic class need not be entirely homogeneous. For example, the diagnosis of Borderline Personality Disorder requires the presence of any five of eight diagnostic criteria. As a result, there are 93 combinations of symptoms that can constitute Borderline Personality Disorder. In addition, the individual criteria them-selves also allow for considerable variance; for example, "self-destructive behavior" can include substance abuse, sex, spending, overeating, or physically self-damaging acts. A group of individuals identified as homogeneous for the diagnosis of Borderline Personality Disorder may in fact be quite heterogeneous with respect to presenting symptoms. Obviously, this situation presents a challenge to any diagnostic instrument seeking to identify such individuals with any consistency.

Another complicating factor in diagnostic research stems from the fact that many of the criteria for the various personality disorders appear in more than one category. For example, interpersonal hypersensitivity is a criterion for Paranoid, Schizotypal, Narcissistic, and Avoidant Personality Disorder. Although some overlap may be desirable in order to facilitate coverage of important phenomena, excessive amounts of overlap may limit the utility of the system because individual diagnostic categories will lack specificity. For example, research on Borderline Personality Disorder suggests that it is an exception when a patient from this category fails to meet the criteria for another personality disorder (Widiger, Sanderson, & Warner, 1986). Such factors make the identification of this and other personality disorders very difficult and should be kept in mind as the reader reviews the research presented in this and subsequent sections.

CLINICAL FEATURES

The cardinal features of Borderline Personality Disorder, according to the DSM-III conceptualization, include unstable and intense interpersonal relationships, affective instability, and self-destructive behavior. The most prominent affect may be anger. Self-destructive behavior often takes the form of suicide attempts or gestures. Other features include identity disturbance and chronic feelings of emptiness or boredom. Individuals with Borderline Personality Disorder are thought to be predisposed to negative treatment response and may require modification of standard therapeutic approaches (Stone, 1980). Specifically, techniques that offer little structure and ego support such as traditional psychoanalysis are thought to be contraindicated because of the borderline patient's tendency to regress under low structure. Because of the proclivity for impulsive behavior, particularly suicide attempts, early identification of this disorder may allow the clinician to take measures that could avert more serious consequences.

Some individuals may experience brief psychotic episodes, which often remit quickly with hospitalization. Despite this observation, the current clinical literature does not favor a close relationship between borderline personality and schizophrenia. Instead, this condition has recently been linked conceptually to the affective disorders by some authors. The affective instability of these patients, which often includes angry and dysphoric mood states, is thought to be related to the dysregulation of mood seen in depression and bipolar disorder (Stone, 1980).

According to DSM-III, Borderline Personality Disorder is thought to be a common personality configuration in psychiatric patients. While community-based prevalence rates have not been clearly established, the existing empirical literature is consistent with this conclusion. For example, Koenigsberg et al. (1985) studied the records of 2,462 medical center patients who had received psychiatric diagnoses. The patients were obtained from a variety of settings: inpatient units, walk-in clinics, and outpatient departments. Diagnoses were made by psychiatric residents who had received special training in the use of the DSM-III. The data entry format allowed for only one diagnosis per Axis. These authors reported that 36 percent of the sample received a personality disorder diagnosis. Of the individuals with personality disorders, 43 percent were diagnosed as Borderline Personality Disorder (15.5 percent of the entire sample).

Another estimate of the prevalence of this condition can be made from a study by Pfohl, Coryell, Zimmerman, and Stangl (1986). These authors administered a structured interview designed for the DSM-III personality disorders to a cohort of 131 nonpsychotic patients obtained primarily from inpatient settings. For these authors, 51 percent of the sample was identified as having a personality disorder, and of this group, 43 percent were diagnosed as Borderline Personality Disorder (22 percent of the entire sample). Thus, this study confirmed that Borderline Personality Disorder is by far the most commonly assigned DSM-III Axis II diagnosis.

A third study that offers an estimate of the prevalence of borderline personality disorder was conducted by Morey, Blashfield, Webb, and Jewell (1988). This sample resulted from an exhaustive search for patients at two university inpatient psychiatric units who had (1) a DSM-III personality disorder diagnosis, and (2) a complete and valid MMPI. Patients with organic or schizophrenic diagnoses were excluded from this sample, resulting in 108 patients. Morey et al. (1988) found that Borderline Personality Disorder also was the most frequent diagnosis; 27 percent of these personality-disordered inpatients received a diagnosis of Borderline Personality Disorder.

Another consideration in the diagnosis of Borderline Personality Disorder involves the frequent role of concomitant Axis I clinical syndrome diagnoses. Koenigsberg et al. (1985) reported that Borderline Personality Disorder was distributed among many Axis I disorders with a high percentage having concomitant substance abuse disorders. Affective disorders, in particular dysthymic disorder and major depression, were also associated with Borderline Personality Disorder in their sample. It is possible that certain Axis I disorders such as alcohol abuse may complicate the presentation of borderline symptomatology (Nace, Saxon, & Shore, 1983; Smith, 1986). Furthermore, the presence of an Axis I syndrome may obscure the features of a personality disorder diagnosis, which may not be identified until the patient has been in treatment for some time.

It has been hypothesized that the label of Borderline Personality Disorder may be subject to cultural or clinical biases. For example, Borderline Personality Disorder is diagnosed more frequently in women than in men (American Psychiatric Association, 1980). Henry and Cohen (1983) have suggested that Borderline Personality Disorder may appear to be more prevalent in women because borderline characteristics are more consonant with the male role and thus are seen as less pathologic in males. It is possible that Borderline Personality Disorder has different manifestations in men and women and may simply be more discernible in women, but this has yet to be demonstrated. Borderline Personality Disorder also has a negative and potentially pejorative meaning. Borderline patients are notoriously difficult to work with, and their intense anger and manipulative behavior may cause the clinician to experience considerable negative countertransference. Clinicians may hesitate to use this diagnosis to avoid having the staff take a negative view of the patient. Finally, some clinicians are skeptical of the view that Borderline Personality Disorder is a valid diagnostic entity and refuse to use it (Spitzer, Endicott, & Gibbon, 1979).

Since the introduction of DSM-III, the Borderline Personality Disorder has received more attention from MMPI researchers than any of the other 10 personality disorder categories. As a result, some preliminary findings regarding the performance of such individuals on the MMPI are becoming established, and there is cause for some optimism for the use of the MMPI with this diagnostic category. However, certain methodologic issues limit the generality of this research and many important questions have yet to be addressed. The following section examines in detail a study by Widiger et al. (1986), which illustrates many of the questions that must be answered in future MMPI research, not only with Borderline Personality Disorder but with each of the personality disorders described in this chapter.

A PROTOTYPIC STUDY

As mentioned above, considerable overlap exists between Borderline Personality Disorder and the other personality disorders. Given the difficulties that such overlap presents for assessment instruments, characterization of the overlap of Borderline Personality Disorder and other personality disorders is an important research issue. Widiger et al. (1986) address this issue in their recent article, which will be discussed in detail in this section.

The characteristics of samples utilized in this research area are particularly important considerations, since the effects of many sample variables are not known. Often, it is advantageous to identify samples that are as homogeneous as possible within the personality disorder category being examined. For example, in Borderline Personality Disorder an inpatient group may not be comparable with an outpatient group because of the larger proportion of individuals with psychotic features in the hospitalized group. The sample utilized by Widiger et al. consisted of 71 inpatients at a state hospital. All patients were short term and from both locked and unlocked wards. Patients who were actively psychotic or who met the criteria for major affective disorder, schizophrenia, or organic brain syndrome were excluded. Thus, several potential moderator variables (setting, concomitant Axis I symptoms, chronicity) were held constant.

These authors identified their patients on the basis of chart review and/or unstructured interview. They then confirmed the diagnosis with a semi-structured interview of their own design administered by a layperson. Although the diagnostic validity of this approach has not been established, this procedure represents a more ambitious approach to defining the criterion group than is typical of most research in this area.

This study also differs from many in the current literature because it reports symptom frequencies. Such frequencies are important because specific combinations of symptoms may result in different MMPI profiles. In the Widiger study, the sample size was too small to permit individual symptoms being examined. However, it was found that profile characteristics were significantly different depending on the total number of symptoms of Borderline Personality Disorder present. Patients who had only five symptoms (as compared with six or more) had profiles that were more similar to nonborderline patients than to other borderline patients.

A central variable in the Widiger study involved the effect of overlap between Borderline Personality Disorder and other personality disorders. Overlap with other personality disorders is the rule rather than the exception in Borderline Personality Disorder, and such overlap can result in a considerable amount of variance in MMPI profiles. Only 7 percent of the sample in the Widiger study did not meet the criteria for a second personality disorder and 81 percent met the criteria for three or more. Consistent with previous accounts (Frances, Clarkin, Gilmore, Hurt, & Brown, 1984; Pope, Jonas, Hudson, Cohen, & Gunderson,

1983), primary overlap was with Schizotypal (50 percent), and Antisocial (48 percent) Personality Disorders. These authors made a number of comparisons between Borderline Personality Disorder with and without these three overlapping diagnoses and found significant differences on a numer of the MMPI clinical scales.

These authors also examined both the specificity (rate of identification of true positives) and sensitivity (rate of identification of true negatives) of the *8-2-4* codetype, which had been reported as the mean codetype for Borderline Personality Disorder in previous studies (Snyder, Pitts, Goodpaster, Sajadi, & Gustin, 1982; Kroll et al., 1981). They demonstrated that classification hit rates based on the *8-2-4* were dependent on overlap with other personality diagnoses. The sensitivity of this codetype varied from 57 percent for the entire group to 81 percent for Borderline Personality Disorder when overlapped with Antisocial Personality Disorder. Specificity varied between 54 percent for Borderline Personality Disorder without overlap with Antisocial Personality Disorder to 85 percent for the entire group. Despite such variation, the *8-2-4* codetype was the most frequent codetype in this sample, with 41 percent of the profiles classified as an *8-2-4*.

The conclusion drawn by these authors was that although the *8-2-4* codetype was the most useful codetype, classification hit rates were dependent to a large extent on overlap with Antisocial Personality Disorder, and to a lesser extent with Histrionic and Schizotypal Personality Disorder. This study supports others in the current literature, which demonstrate that a single codetype that is specific to Borderline Personality Disorder (as it is

conceptualized in DSM-III) is unlikely to be identified. These results underscore the complexity of research in the personality disorders area and illustrate a few of the many factors that can affect the utility of particular MMPI configurations. The reader should keep such issues in mind while examining the results of studies presented in later sections, since few authors examine the effect of sample composition in such detail.

MMPI SCALES

Borderline Personality Disorder has received the most attention in the recent literature of all personality disorders reviewed in the chapter, including those studies that used the MMPI. The following review is based primarily on these studies, which are summarized by mean scale scores in Table 5–1.

One major trend that is observable in Borderline Personality Disorder is the consistent elevation of the *F* scale. These elevations are often such that the clinician might be led to question the validity of the profile. According to conventional clinical practice, a *T*-score on Scale *F* that is > 70 represents a marked elevation, indicating that other indices of validity should be checked. Profiles in this range are often interpretable, though reflecting a severe degree of distress and psychopathology. A *T*-score > 90 is considered an extreme elevation. Elevations of Scale *F* in this range suggest that the profile is likely to be invalid (Greene, 1980). Several of the mean sample profiles in Table 5–1 approach this threshold. One

TABLE 5–1. FREQUENCY OF ELEVATED MMPI CLINICAL SCALES IN BORDERLINE PERSONALITY DISORDERS

Authors	N	Age	Clinical Scales (≥ 70 *T*-points)
Archer et al. (1985)	28	14.6	*8-1-2-4-6*
Evans et al. (1984)	45	27.0	*8-4-2-7-6-3*
Gustin et al. (1983)	29	–	*8-7-2-4-6-1-3-9*
Hurt et al. (1985)	21	23.0	*8-2-4-7-6-3*
Hurt et al. (1985) [outpatients]	21	31.7	*8-2-4-7-6-9*
Kroll et al. (1981)	21	27.0	*8-4-2-6-7-1-3*
Lloyd et al. (1983)[a]	27	–	*4-7-2-3-1-9*
Morey et al. (1988)	28	26.9	*8-4-6-2-7-3*
Patrick (1984)	27	–	*8-4-2-6*
Resnick et al. (1983) [outpatients]	12	–	*4-8-2-7-6*
Snyder et al. (1982)	26	–	*8-7-2-4-6-1-9*
Widiger et al. (1986)	71	28.3	*8-4-2-6-7-1*

Note: All samples are inpatients unless noted otherwise.
[a]Lloyd et al. (1983) administered the MMPI-168 short form of the MMPI.

possible explanation for the elevation of Scale *F* could be due to the inclusion of invalid profiles in the sample. Of the studies included in Table 5–1, only Gustin et al. (1983) used extreme elevations of Scale *F* (a *T*-score of ≥ 100) as a criterion for exclusion. Since Gustin et al. report a mean profile that is among the most elevated, this suggests that MMPI profiles for Borderline Personality Disorder reported in the literature are elevated for reasons other than the inclusion of invalid profiles in research samples.

Gustin et al. (1983) suggest that Borderline Personality Disorder patients may exaggerate their symptoms as a plea for help since many of these individuals seem overwhelmed by their problems. These authors report that withholding ward privileges until the MMPI is repeated did not significantly change the profiles of borderline patients. An alternative hypothesis provided by these authors is that the invalid profile is indicative of a resistive response style in which little meaningful information is disclosed; the acknowledgment of too many symptoms obscures the true picture just as too few responses would. This resistance was hypothesized to be unconscious, serving to protect the fragile ego of the borderline patient.

A second global characteristic of MMPI borderline profiles is a high degree of overall profile elevation. Many of the studies reviewed for this section reported profiles that were elevated relative to other diagnostic groups. These comparison groups included dysthymic disorder (Snyder, Sajidi, Pitts, & Goodpaster, 1982), other mixed personality disorders (Gustin et al., 1983), chronic and acute psychotic disorders (Evans, Ruff, Braff, & Ainsworth, 1984), and mixed psychiatric patients (Hurt, Clarkin, Frances, Abrams, & Hunt, 1985; Lloyd, Overall, Kimsey, & Click, 1983b; Kroll et al., 1981). Several authors note the similarity between Borderline Personality Disorder profiles and the "floating" profile described by Newmark and Sines (1972). A floating profile is one in which all scores of Scales *1* through *9* exceed a *T*-score of 70, usually accompanied by high elevations on Scale *F*. Newmark, Chassin, Evans, and Gentry (1984) recently replicated their original work on 69 patients who obtained a floating profile. The premorbid behavior of the floating profile patients was characterized by sexual confusion, serious difficulties in empathy and communication, a history of impulsivity, unpredictability, and self-damaging acts, and limited stress

tolerance and low self-esteem. On admission they manifested multiple psychiatric symptoms with the majority being considered serious suicide risks. Typical response to hospitalization was varied or minimal. Approximately 30 percent of the floating profile patients met the criteria for Borderline Personality Disorder.

It is plausible that high overall profile elevation may be a more reliable clinical indicator of Borderline Personality Disorder than information contained in individual scales. Hurt et al. (1985) examined the discriminant validity of MMPI in relationship to Borderline Personality Disorder. An analysis of variance yielded significant differences between Borderline Personality Disorders and controls on all three validity scales as well as Scales *1*, *6*, *7*, and *8*. However, in descriptive discriminant analysis only one variable, *F*, entered the equation. Therefore, they concluded that the MMPI was not sensitive to Borderline Personality Disorder specifically but rather tapped more general features of severe psychopathology.

An examination of other instruments for diagnosing Borderline Personality Disorder provides further support for the relationship between this construct and global profile elevation. For example, the Millon Clinical Multiaxial Inventory (MCMI: Millon, 1982) contains 11 scales that purportedly correspond to DSM-III personality disorder concepts (Millon, 1985). However, conclusions drawn from the MCMI in this and following sections must be tentative, because the MCMI is somewhat controversial as to whether it adequately reflects DSM-III conceptualizations as opposed to the particular theory of personality advanced by Millon (Widiger, Williams, Spitzer, & Frances, 1986). The intercorrelations between the Borderline-Cycloid (C) scale of the MCMI and the MMPI scales are approximately .5 or greater for both *F* and *K* and Scales *1*, *2*, *3*, *7*, and *8*. Similar results were reported by Edell (1984), who utilized the Borderline Syndrome Index, a 52-item self-report questionnaire designed to tap DSM-III borderline criteria. Significant correlations were found between this index and all but two clinical scales of the MMPI. These correlations were interpreted as evidence that the Borderline Syndrome Index is tapping a generalized dimension of inadequacy, chronicity, and self-degradation rather than specific symptom complexes, which would have been evidenced by high correlations on fewer scales. From the results described above, a similar conclusion can be drawn about the Borderline scale of the MCMI.

Aside from these two general characteristics, a specific codetype has not been consistently identified in the literature. Examination of Tables 5–1 and 5–2 confirms that Scales *2, 4, 7,* and *8* are generally elevated above a *T*-score of 70, and Scale *6* also is elevated in nearly all samples. Although no single codetype appears to represent Borderline Personality Disorder, there is some consistency between studies with respect to codetypes. Frequently observed codetypes from various MMPI studies of Borderline Personality Disorder are presented in Table 5–2. These codetypes generally included combinations of Scales *2, 4, 7,* and *8*; a few studies also included Scale *6*.

A comparison of Tables 5–2 and 5–1 demonstrates that codetypes are not necessarily representative of individual Borderline Personality Disorder patients because of substantial heterogeneity within samples. For example, Gustin et al. (1983) reported a mean codetype of *8-7-2,* yet no individual in their sample had this codetype, although two similar codetypes (*2-7-8* and *7-8*) were represented in 34.5 and 10.3 percent of the sample, respectively. In contrast, for Morey et al. (1988) the mean codetype was *8-4-6,* also the

most frequently observed codetype, noted in 17.9 percent of the sample. However, the Gustin et al. (1983) sample appears to have considerably less overall variance. Their sample of 29 male veteran inpatients could be represented by 7 codetypes, while the Morey et al. data from 28 medical center inpatients were composed of 14 different codetypes.

Similar findings were reported by Patrick (1984), who investigated the utility of the *8-4-2* codetype as a marker for Borderline Personality Disorder. He reported the MMPI codetype of 27 (8 male, 19 female) psychiatric inpatients, whose diagnoses were determined on the basis of a clinical interview. In this study, none of the sample had this codetype, although it was the mean codetype. Furthermore, it was concluded that although certain Scales such as *8, 4, 2,* and *7* tend to be elevated, no individual codetype appeared to be representative of the entire sample.

These findings make it apparent that the mean profiles do not necessarily reflect the distribution of codetypes within a particular sample. This observation has been made in research on other diagnostic categories as well, but it has particular relevance for the study of personality disorder since few researchers in this area include codetype distributions in reporting their research. In fact,

TABLE 5–2. FREQUENCY OF MMPI CODETYPES IN BORDERLINE PERSONALITY DISORDER PATIENTS

Authors	N	Age	Codetype			
			2-7/7-2	*2-8/8-2*	*4-8/8-4*	*6-8/8-6*
Gustin et al. (1983)	29	–	34.5	20.1		20.1
Hurt et al. (1985)	21	23.0		9.5	19.0	9.5
Hurt et al. (1985) [outpatients]	21	31.7		23.8	19.0	23.8
Morey et al. (1988)	28	26.9		10.7	17.9	21.4
Widiger et al. (1986)	71	28.3	21.1	40.8		12.7
Weighted Totals			25.0	26.3	18.6	16.4

	Codetype		Methodologic Issues								
	7-8/8-7	Totals	A	B	C	D	E	F	G	H	I
	10.3	85.0	–	+	+	+	+	–	+	+	+
		38.0	+	+	–	–	+	–	–	+	+
		66.6	+	+	–	–	+	–	–	+	+
		50.0	+	+	+	–	+	+	+	+	+
		74.6	+	+	–	–	+	+	+	+	+
Gustin et al. (1983)	10.3	66.8									
Hurt et al. (1985)											
Hurt et al. (1985) [outpatients]											
Morey et al. (1988)											
Widiger et al. (1986)											
Weighted Totals											

Note: All samples are inpatients unless noted otherwise.

with the exception of Borderline Personality Disorder, no published research that presented such distributions for the DSM-III personality disorders could be located. Thus, in following sections where mean profiles are presented, it should be remembered that these profiles do not indicate that a similar codetype is necessarily most representative of the diagnostic category in question.

In summary, MMPI users should be cautious about interpreting any particular codetypes as a specific indicator of Borderline Personality Disorder. However, the overall characteristics of extreme elevation, particularly with high points on Scales *2*, *4*, *7*, and *8* in the context of Scale *F* elevated, are suggestive of Borderline Personality Disorder. Despite the lack of specific codetypes for this disorder, subtle differences from other diagnostic groups such as schizophrenia or affective disorders can be discerned. Consequently, the MMPI may be useful in discriminating Borderline Personality Disorder from other groups of psychiatric patients. In the following section, individual studies that address differential diagnosis will be reviewed.

DIFFERENTIAL DIAGNOSIS: RESEARCH FINDINGS

BORDERLINE VS. SCHIZOPHRENIA

Evans et al. (1984) compared inpatient borderlines with both chronic and acute psychotic patients. This comparison is of particular interest because of the tendency of Borderline Personality Disorder to present with psychotic symptoms, particularly in inpatient settings. Patients were identified via clinical interviews conducted by two of the authors. A total of 113 patients were studied with the borderline group consisting of 29 females and 16 males. Overall profile shape was similar among three groups. When compared with the chronic schizophrenic cohort, the borderline group had significantly higher elevations on Scales *2*, *3*, *4*, and *7*. Evans et al. (1984) reported that the most striking dissimilarity between borderline personality and chronic schizophrenic groups is an elevated Scale *4*. Together, elevations on Scales *4* and *8* suggest irritability, hostility, and resentfulness consistent with the intense anger often noted in borderline patients. Even when Scale *4* is not a high-point but still elevated, it tends to be

indicative of psychological disturbance of a chronic, characterologic nature rather than psychosis.

The Goldberg Index (1969) may be another source of information from the MMPI when a differential diagnosis from psychosis is required. The Goldberg Index, which is a composite of MMPI scale scores, offers a measure of probability of psychotic disturbance. Using MMPI T-scores, Goldberg (1969) calculated this index as:

$$\text{Goldberg Index} = (L + 6 + 8) - (3 + 7)$$

Goldberg Index scores of < 40 indicate neurotic profiles, while scores of > 50 suggest psychotic profiles. To determine the utility of this cutting score for borderline personality diagnosis, this index was calculated for the mean profiles in Table 5–1. Values obtained range from 51 for the Hurt et al. (1985) inpatient sample to 76 for the Kroll et al. (1981) sample, with a median value of 67. Apparently, a different interpretation of the Goldberg Index may be necessary when dealing with Borderline Personality Disorder. Since Borderline Personality Disorder is a recent addition to the psychiatric nomenclature, a revised interpretation of the expected ranges of the Goldberg Index may be required, given the transient psychotic episodes thought to be characteristic of this personality disorder.

BORDERLINE VS. AFFECTIVE DISORDER

Snyder et al. (1981) compared the MMPI profiles of 26 male inpatients with Borderline Personality Disorder, using a clinical interview and the more strict cutpoint of six rather than five DSM-III symptoms, with 19 patients with dysthymic disorder. Paired *t*-tests found significant differences on Scales *L*, *F*, *4*, *5*, *6*, and *8* with all but *L* being elevated in borderline group relative to the comparison group. Snyder, Sajadi, Pitts, and Goodpaster (1982) further examined the relationship between depression and Borderline Personality Disorder. The intercorrelations between Scale *2* and three well-known scales for depression were examined in both Borderline Personality and Dysthymic Disorder. These authors concluded that although there is considerable overlap in the depressive symptomatology of the two groups, specific features may set Borderline Personality Disorder with depression apart from Dysthymic Disorder. Features characteristic of Borderline Personality Disorder that are not usually seen in major depression, such as intense anger, may be present. In addition, these authors speculated that depression in Borderline Personality Disorder may be qualitatively different with features such as loneliness and emptiness being more prominent.

BORDERLINE VS. OTHER
PERSONALITY DISORDERS

Gustin et al. (1983) compared male veteran inpatients with Borderline Personality Disorder to inpatients with other personality disorders. These authors utilized a routine clinical interview, but used the more strict inclusion criteria of six rather than five symptoms to qualify for the diagnosis of Borderline Personality Disorder. These authors found no differences in profile shape or dispersion, but the overall profile was elevated in the borderline group. Borderline patients scored significantly higher on Scales *F*, *3*, *4*, *5*, *6*, and *8*. Hurt et al. (1985) also compared Borderline patients with patients with other personality disorders, using an outpatient sample and the Diagnostic Interview for Borderlines (DIB: Gunderson, Kolb, & Austin, 1981) as a criterion. These authors also found the profile shape to be quite similar between groups, although significant differences were noted on Scales *L*, *F*, *K*, *3*, *4*, *6*, *7*, *8*, and *9*; Borderline patients were higher on all Scales but *L* and *K*.

Comparison with a heterogeneous group of personality disorders represents a first step in addressing whether Borderline Personality Disorder is a unique constellation within the domain of personality disorders. A second and more ambitious step would be to compare Borderline patients with other specific personality disordered patients, particularly those with high conceptual overlap such as Antisocial, Narcissistic, and Schizotypal disorders. This area has just begun to be investigated. To date, two studies have addressed this issue: Widiger et al. (1986), which was discussed previously, and Resnick, Schulz, Schulz, Hamer, Friedel, and Goldberg (1983). This latter study examined the MMPI profiles of 20 subjects diagnosed as Borderline and/or Schizotypal Personality Disorder (as mentioned earlier, Schizotypal frequently overlaps with Borderline). The sample consisted of 9 men and 11

women. Ten out of the total of 11 Borderline patients also met the criteria for Schizotypal. The Borderline group was compared with nine Schizotypal patients, none of which met the criteria for Borderline Personality Disorder. Diagnoses were assigned on the basis of the Schedule for Interviewing Borderlines (SIB: Baron & Gruen, 1980), a semistructured interview that has 21 dimensions and characterizes pathology pertaining to both Borderline and Schizotypal Personality Disorders. The MMPI profiles for the Borderline group were elevated relative to the Schizotypal group, although no statistical comparisons were made because of small sample sizes. The Borderline group had *T*-scores on Scales *6*, *8*, and *9* that were at least 10 points higher than the Schizotypal group. On the basis of these observations, Resnick et al. (1983) concluded that the MMPI could be used as a coarse initial screening instrument for Borderline Personality Disorder.

Pitts, Gustin, Mitchell, and Snyder (1985) attempted to differentiate Borderline Personality Disorder from other personality disorders on the basis of a critical item list. The subjects were male VA inpatients, with 40 having a Borderline diagnosis and 35 having other personality disorders. In this study, concomitant Axis I diagnosis was not controlled for. Thus, 30 percent of the Borderline group had Dysthymic Disorder, 30 percent had alcohol abuse, and 35 percent were polydrug users. Diagnosis was made on the basis of the consensus of the staff. These authors did not report mean profile types or individual scale elevations, concentrating instead on the content of 111 critical items described by Lachar and Wrobel (1979). These items are divided into nine content areas. Five of these content areas were significantly different between the groups: depression and worry, substance abuse, antisocial attitudes, problematic anger, and somatic symptoms. A predictive discriminant function based on these content areas correctly identified 85 percent of the Borderline group. Although the implications of this study are limited due to the nature of the sample, the results suggest that scales could be constructed from MMPI items to identify patients with Borderline Personality Disorder. Such scales for this and other personality disorders have been developed by Morey, Waugh, and Blashfield (1985) and will be described in a subsequent section.

BORDERLINE PERSONALITY DISORDER IN ADOLESCENTS

Archer, Ball, and Hunter (1985) compared the MMPI profiles of 28 male and female adolescent inpatients with Borderline Personality Disorder with comparable groups with primary diagnoses of Conduct Disorder (n = 21), Dysthymic Disorder (n = 50), other personality disorders (n = 17), and other psychiatric diagnoses (n = 30). This study addresses an important issue, because although DSM-III discourages personality disorder diagnosis in individuals under 18 years of age, Borderline Personality Disorder is frequently attributed to adolescents. Comparison of the MMPI profiles supports the contention that Borderline Personality Disorder is a meaningful diagnosis in this age group. Consistent with adult populations, adolescents obtained markedly elevated clinical profiles and an elevated Scale *F*. Scales *1*, *2*, and *8* were significantly different from the other diagnostic groups. Scales *3*, *4*, *6*, and *7* also were elevated relative to other diagnostic groups, but this difference was not statistically significant. Archer et al. were optimistic about the discriminating power of the MMPI in the diagnostic groups highlighted in their study. In view of the elevations obtained by this adolescent sample on Scales *6* and *8*, however, they were skeptical as to whether the MMPI could distinguish adolescents with Borderline Personality Disorder from those with Schizotypal Personality Disorder or schizophrenia. To date, this hypothesis remains to be tested.

SCREENING WITH THE MMPI-168

The MMPI-168 is an abbreviated version of the MMPI, in which only the first 168 items are administered and then converted to estimates of full-scale scores (Overall, Higgins, & de Schweinitz, 1976). This application can be viewed as primarily a screening device. Lloyd, Overall, Kimsey, and Click (1983) compared the MMPI-168 of borderline outpatients with three groups of outpatients: a group with affective disorders, a group with other personality disorders, and a residual group of adjustment, marital, and anxiety disorders. Consistent with the results using the full MMPI, the overall profile is elevated. These authors found significant differences on Scales *F*, *K*, *4*, and *8* when the Borderline group was compared with all others. In addition, they also divided the groups into males and females and repeated the analyses for each sex. They found that Borderline women were elevated on Scales *F*, *K*, *4*, *6*, and *8* relative to the comparison groups. In males, only Scale *K* was significantly elevated, although Lloyd et al. suggested that the small sample of males may not be representative. Lloyd, Overall, and Click (1983) also demonstrated the use of the MMPI-168 to identify Borderline Personality Disorder in a population of normal individuals. In this study, criterion subjects were identified in a voluntary population at an outpatient clinic via a clinical interview. Not surprisingly, they found that 8 of the 10 clinical scales and Scale *F* were above the 90th percentile for the normal college population. Thus, if the purpose of testing is to screen patients, to be followed up by a more extensive interview or testing, the MMPI-168 may suffice. However, if the purpose of administering the MMPI is an in-depth assessment, a full MMPI supplemented with research scales is preferable.

BORDERLINE WITH SPECIFIC SYMPTOMS

The relationship of specific symptoms to Borderline Personality Disorder has not been adequately addressed. Abramowitz, Carroll, and Schaffer (1984) compared a group of 13 Borderline patients with 7 other psychiatric patients. The Borderline group was selected on the basis of the Diagnostic Interview for Borderlines (DIB: Gunderson, Kolb, & Austin, 1981), and contained 11 women and 2 men. Both outpatients and inpatients were used. While the comparison with such a small and heterogeneous group of other psychiatric patients limits the generality of this study, the fact that 12 of the 13 Borderline patients were identified as self-mutilators makes this study interesting. The Borderline patients were elevated relative to the control group and significantly different on Scales *1*, *2*, and *3*. This pattern is quite different from most studies and may be specific to the symptom of self-mutilation. These authors also investigated whether subtle as opposed to obvious items on the individual scales were better at identifying Borderline Personality Disorder and found no difference between item types.

SPECIAL/RESEARCH SCALES

The information contained in the standard MMPI scales may not be specific enough to Borderline Personality Disorder to confirm the diagnosis. It is plausible that some of the special research scales may be useful in this regard. Unfortunately, most of the studies reviewed for this section restricted themselves to the standard MMPI clinical scales. In view of the heterogeneity of findings reported above, research scales may be an important supplement to the MMPI. Research scales may add specificity to the MMPI by characterizing relevant areas of functioning not specifically tapped by the standard clinical scales.

The few reported findings suggest that some research scales may be associated with Borderline Personality Disorder. For example, Millon (1982) has shown substantial correlations between the MCMI Borderline scale and several special scales: positive correlations with the Wiggins' (1966) Poor Morale, Phobias, and Psychoticism scales, and negative associations with Barron's (1953) Ego Strength (*Es*) scale. The latter observation is interesting, because *Es* was developed to predict improvement in psychotherapy. More specifically, *Es* was thought to assess the latent ego strength of an individual that would be an important determinant in psychotherapy outcome. The negative correlation of Millon's scale with *Es* is consistent with the clinical observation that Borderline patients often do poorly in treatment.

Gustin et al. (1983) ambitiously reported a total of 85 MMPI variables including clinical and special scales in their study of Borderline Personality Disorder. A total of 28 significantly comparisons were found. Although the number of independent *t*-tests is sufficiently large so that some positive findings would be expected by chance, these results suggest that reliable differences can be identified for special scales in this population. Significant differences were reported for Wiggins' (1966) Depression, Poor Morale, and Poor Health scale, Welsh's (1965) Anxiety scale, and Rosen's (1962) Paranoid Schizophrenia and Conversion Reaction scales.

Further research is necessary before a characteristic pattern on special and research scales can be established. Other special scales that may have promise but have yet to be investigated in this population include Wiggins' Manifest Hostility (*HOS*) scale, which measures problems with unmodulated anger, various suicide scales, and indices of schizophrenia.

SUPPLEMENTING THE MMPI WITH OTHER INSTRUMENTS

Since the standard scales of the MMPI were developed considerably before the advent of the DSM-III, certain aspects of Axis II personality disorders may not be adequately characterized by the MMPI. One method of improving diagnostic precision with the MMPI is to supplement it with other assessment instruments. A discussion of the potential supplements to the MMPI is certainly beyond the scope of this volume; nonetheless, in consideration of the current popularity of the Borderline concept, brief mention of this literature must be made.

Many authors discuss the assessment of Borderline Personality Disorder using various psychological tests (e.g., Meyer, 1983). Purportedly, a classic indicator of Borderline Personality Disorder involves good performance on structured tasks such as the Wechsler Adult Intelligence Scale and poor performance on unstructured tasks such as the Rorschach (Carr, Goldstein, Hunt, & Kernberg, 1979). However, some authors question the validity of this notion (Widiger, 1982), probably with some justification. For example, the MMPI can be more aptly characterized as a structured task, but Borderline individuals tend to achieve higher scale elevations than almost any comparison group. Thus, clinicians and researchers should be cautious in using this cross-task comparison as a diagnostic indicator.

Recently, several articles have appeared that demonstrate how MMPI codetypes can be refined by the addition of the MCMI (Antoni, Tischer, Levine, Green, & Millon, 1985a,b; Levine, Tischer, Antoni, Green, & Millon, 1985). For example, Antoni et al. (1985a) have shown how an *8-2/2-8* codetype can be clarified by adding the MCMI, and the *8-2* codetype is frequently observed in Borderline Personality Disorder. These authors suggest that the combination of these tests might be useful in identifying specific variants of particular MMPI codetypes, although the accuracy of this combination in identifying DSM-III diagnosis remains to be demonstrated.

Many efforts have been made to increase the diagnostic reliability of Borderline Personality Disorder. As an example, structured interviews such as the DIB have been developed. Widiger and Frances (1987), in reviewing the literature on the measurement of personality disorders, suggest that the supplementing of inventory scores with interview material is probably the most effective strategy for assessment in this area, and this recommendation is a sound one.

CONCLUSION

The MMPI has received considerable attention as a potential diagnostic tool in Borderline Personality Disorder. At present, conclusions that can be drawn are limited by several features of the current literature. These include the lack of attention to special and research scales, small and loosely defined samples, and inattention to the issue of diagnostic overlap, particularly with respect to other personality disorders. Despite these limitations, several MMPI profile commonalities can be identified across studies. These include high overall profile elevations in the context of an elevated Scale *F* and particular codetypes that often include Scale *8*. In addition, the construct of Borderline Personality Disorder is still being developed in the theoretical literature and must be validated with research using the DSM-III and its future revisions.

HISTRIONIC PERSONALITY DISORDER

The concept of histrionic personality is relatively new, although its origins lie in *hystera*, which can be traced back to classical Greece. In classical times, hysteria was thought to be a condition in which a "wandering womb" (*hystera* being Greek for uterus) floated to different areas of the body, causing dysfunction in those areas. Because of this supposed etiology, the disorder could be diagnosed in only women. The concept underwent an evolution over the centuries (Veith, 1963), although the idea of physical dysfunction without overt organic causes continued to be the central feature of the disorder. Janet, the French physician, proposed that a psychological *dissociation* was at the core of this disorder, with different conscious processes being dissociated from each other. Freud felt that this dissociation was the result of repressed traumatic material, which also resulted in certain typical personality features being present in these patients (Freud, 1905a). Thus, the recent conceptualization of hysteria

subsumed three central features: (1) physical dysfunction without organic basis, (2) dissociative experience, and (3) histrionic personality features.

The DSM-III classification separated these three components of hysteria into separate syndromes: Somatization Disorder, Dissociative Disorders (including fugue states, psychogenic amnesias, etc.), and Histrionic Personality Disorder. In doing so, the DSM-III committee removed the concept of hysteria from its nosology. This conceptual organization followed certain distinctions drawn by Chodoff and Lyons (1958), in which the character features (i.e., hysterical personality) were separated from the somatic symptom manifestations (i.e., conversion reaction). Perhaps because of the general acceptance of the importance of this distinction, these two diagnoses were separated in the DSM-II classification, and the DSM-III further elaborated this distinction.

However, the utility of distinguishing between these two concepts remains controversial to this day. For example, Kimble, Williams, and Agras (1975) identified a sample of 10 females with Hysterical Personality Disorder diagnosed according to DSM-II) and found that 9 met criteria for Briquet's syndrome (i.e., somatization reaction). As a result, these authors argued that the distinction between these two concepts was not a useful one. In addition, Lilienfeld, VanValkenberg, Larntz, and Akiskal (1986) report high degrees of overlap between DSM-III populations of Histrionic Personality Disorder and Somatization Disorder. However, other studies have shown that the concepts are not synonymous. For example, both of the self-report personality scales developed by Millon (1982) and Morey et al. (1985) to measure DSM-III Histrionic Personality Disorder correlated *negatively* with the MMPI Scale *3* (Morey, 1986), which was developed utilizing the concept of conversion hysteria. Thus, the exact nature of the relationship between the character features of hysteria and conversion/somatization symptoms remains to be established.

CLINICAL POPULATION

According to the DSM-III, the core feature of the Histrionic Personality Disorder is behavior that is overly dramatic, reactive, and intensely expressed. Perhaps as a result of this behavior, these individuals tend to have characteristic disturbances in interpersonal relationships, such that they are perceived by others as superficial, vain, and demanding. It is thought that the presenting complaints in this population often involve somatic features, marital or sexual difficulties, depression, or anxiety. Such features are thought to occur typically in response to interpersonal conflict or loss (Tupin, 1981).

The DSM-III provides no evidence of the base rate of Histrionic Personality Disorder beyond stating that it is "apparently common." In part because of the lack of reliable diagnostic tools in this area, it has been difficult to establish an estimate of the prevalence of this disorder. Koenigsberg et al. (1985), in reviewing the charts and DSM-III diagnoses of 2,462 psychiatric patients from a wide array of clinical settings, found that 2.8 percent of these patients received a diagnosis of Histrionic Personality Disorder, which constituted 7.8 percent of all patients receiving any personality disorder diagnosis. Morey et al. (1986), also using clinical diagnosis as a criterion, found a 16.7 percent prevalence rate among their personality-disordered inpatient sample. In contrast, Pfohl et al. (1986) utilized a structured interview and found that 22.9 percent of their entire sample (44.8 percent of their personality-disordered patients) met DSM-III criteria for this diagnosis, implying that this diagnosis may be underassigned in routine clinical practice. In fact, in the study by Pfohl et al., Histrionic Personality Disorder was the most frequently observed personality disorder. In a study of male psychiatric patients, Luisada, Peele, and Pittard (1974) found that 1 in 1,000 patients met criteria for Hysterical Personality Disorder, as derived from the DSM-II definition of this condition.

The gender ratio for this diagnostic category is a very controversial issue, and those figures that are given vary widely. For example, estimates of the ratio of females to males meeting this diagnosis range from 19:1 to 2:1 (Vaillant & Perry, 1980; 1985). A study utilizing a Swedish hospital sample (Lindberg & Lindgard, 1963) reports a 3:2 female to male ratio. The DSM-III states only that the disorder is diagnosed "far more frequently" in females. One of the primary difficulties hampering research in this area is the likelihood that a gender bias in diagnosing this condition is operating (Winstead, 1984). For example, Warner (1978) conducted a study in which a hypothetical case study was diagnosed by 175 mental health professionals. The case, which included both histrionic and antisocial manifestations, was randomly described as being either male or female to different professionals. When the patient was female, 76 percent of the clinicians identified the patient as "Hysterical Personality," while 22 percent diagnosed "Antisocial Personality." However, when the same patient was described as male, these rates changed to 49 and 41 percent, respectively. It is interesting to note that the research of Lilienfeld et al. (1986) suggests that there is a great deal of overlap between these two diagnoses. It is likely that certain sex role expectations influence the assignment of a Histrionic Personality Disorder diagnosis.

MMPI SCALES

Very little research has been conducted examining the diagnosis of Histrionic Personality Disorder using the MMPI. Much of the classic MMPI research, including the original derivation sample of Scale *3* (*Hy*) itself, utilized samples comprised primarily of conversion hysterics. For example, Fricke's (1956) and Hovey's (1949) early studies addressed strictly conversion reactions, and as discussed above, the relationship between this concept and Histrionic Personality Disorder is uncertain.

One study that did make a separate examination of the MMPI characteristics associated with hysterical personality (as opposed to conversion and/or dissociative hysteria) was performed by Slavney and McHugh (1975). These authors utilized 29 inpatients (90 percent female; mean age, 28 years) who had received a DSM-II (American Psychiatric Association, 1968) discharge diagnosis of hysterical personality. Although the DSM-II diagnosis differs from the DSM-III in that no definitional criteria are provided, the two diagnostic constructs are similar and each reflects the distinction between the symptomatic and personologic features of hysteria drawn by Chodoff and Lyons (1958). However, the absence of criteria in DSM-II makes it likely that the reliability of the diagnoses of the criterion group was suspect.

The mean profile obtained in Slavney and McHugh's (1975) criterion group (presented in Table 5–3) was a *4-8* codetype with T-scores of 70 or higher also noted on Scales *2, 7,* and *3*. MMPI profiles of two control groups, one composed of

TABLE 5–3. FREQUENCY OF ELEVATED MMPI CLINICAL SCALES IN HISTRIONIC PERSONALITY DISORDERS AND RELATED CONDITIONS

Authors	N	Age	Clinical Scales (≥ 70 *T*-points)
Hovey (1949) [Dissociative-conversion]	34	–	*3-1*
Hovey (1949) [Somatization]	105	–	Spike *1*
Fricke (1956) [Conversion hysterics]	63	–	*WNL*
Liskow et al. (1977) [Briquet's Syndrome]	21	38.4	*8-1-2-4-3-7-6*
Morey et al. (1988) [Histrionic Personality Disorder]	16	34.8	*2-4-8-7-6-3*
Slavney & McHugh (1975) [Hysterical personality]	29	27.9	*4-8-2-7-3*

paranoid schizophrenics and the other a mixed inpatient group, also were examined and contrasted with the hysterical personality criterion group. The criterion group scored significantly higher than the paranoid schizophrenic group on Scales *1*, *2*, *3*, and *7*. No significant differences between the criterion and mixed control group were noted, although trends were similar to the findings obtained in the paranoid schizophrenic comparison, particularly on Scales *1* and *3*. The criterion group was more likely to have at least one markedly elevated scale than either control group.

Although Slavney and McHugh (1976) did not provide frequency distributions for high-point pairs, they did give information regarding the distribution of single highest scale scores. For the hysterical personality criterion group, the largest portion of the sample obtained Scale *4* highpoints (32 percent), followed by Scales *2* and *8* (each 17 percent) and Scales *3* and *9* (each 14 percent). However, Scale *4* was also the most common high point in each of the control groups.

Liskow, Clayton, Woodruff, Guze, and Cloninger (1977) utilized the MMPI to examine the distinction between the symptomatic and personologic manifestations of hysteria as discussed above. These authors reported on 21 outpatients (100 percent female; mean age, 38 years) with a diagnosis of "Briquet's syndrome," a conceptualization of hysteria restricted to patients with multiple somatic complaints with no organic basis (similar to DSM-III Somatization Disorder). Liskow et al. (1977) compared the MMPIs from this group with those obtained on hysterical personalities by Slavney and McHugh (1975) and only found significant differences on Scales *L* and

1 (Briquet's patients scoring higher in each instance). As a result, these authors felt that these results supported the contention of Kimble et al. (1975) that the two conditions might be indistinguishable. However, the mean profile for the Liskow et al. sample was an *8-1* codetype with clinical elevations also noted on Scales *2*, *3*, *4*, *6*, and *7*. Thus, the configuration was somewhat different from that reported for the hysterical personality with Scale *1* playing a more prominent role as might be expected in a sample manifesting multiple somatic complaints.

In the Morey et al. (1988) sample of 108 inpatients described earlier, 16 (15 percent) received a discharge diagnosis of Histrionic Personality Disorder. The mean profile for these patients, as presented in Table 5–3, was a *2-4-8* configuration with elevations also noted on Scales *3*, *6*, and *7*. Thus, this mean profile appears somewhat similar in configuration to that noted by Slavney and McHugh (1975). However, as noted earlier, mean profiles can be misleading as they may not represent any of the actual profiles contained within the sample. This was particularly true with the Histrionic Personality Disorder sample, as the distribution of codetypes was widely scattered. Only the *2-3/3-2* codetype was observed in more than one instance, with 36 percent of these cases manifesting this codetype. Only one patient demonstrated a configuration similar to the *2-4-8* codetype. Thus, although in this sample the general trends suggest elevations on Scales *4* and *8*, these scales were rarely seen as a codetype among these MMPI protocols.

In summary, the little available evidence suggests that hysterical personalities most typically obtain elevations on Scales *4*, *8*, and the neurotic triad. However, this pattern has had limited success in distinguishing this condition from Axis I disorders such as somatization disorder or paranoid schizophrenia. As such, this pattern may be suggestive of Histrionic Personality Disorder, but it is unlikely that the pattern has specificity with respect to this disorder.

The MMPI research scales have seen little use in identifying Histrionic Personality Disorder, although certain scales may hold some promise in this regard. For example, Rosen's (1952) Conversion Reaction (*Cr*) research scale, which was developed primarily to distinguish conversion reactions from other syndromes, may have some utility in identifying Histrionic Personality Disorder. Certain Wiggins' (1966) content scales (particularly high Family Problems, high Hypomania, and low Social Maladjustment) may also have utility in this area, since the content tapped by these items bears some similarity to DSM-III criteria for this category. In partial support of these hypotheses, Millon (1982) found that the MCMI Histrionic scale correlated -.72 with Wiggins' Social Maladjustment scale in a sample of psychiatric patients.

NARCISSISTIC PERSONALITY DISORDER

The incorporation of Narcissistic Personality Disorder in the DSM-III reflected a growing interest within the psychodynamic school in the phenomenon of pathologic narcissism. Although Freud described this concept in detail in his 1914 paper, "On Narcissism: An Introduction," interest in this area developed relatively slowly. In recent years, however, the development of this concept has been given impetus through the works of Kernberg (1975) and Kohut (1966). Each of these authors discuss the narcissistic personality, which both agree tends to present with chronic problems characterized by grandiosity and impaired capacity for empathy. However, the descriptions of Kernberg and Kohut diverge in many respects. For example, Kernberg focuses on characteristic failures in interpersonal relationships (Phillips, 1981). These relationships tend to fall at the extremes of idealization and devaluation, with certain individuals being idealized because of some perceived potential to gratify the narcissism of the

patient (Kernberg, 1967). According to Kernberg, most of the relationships these individuals have are thought to be exploitative and parasitic. Kohut, on the other hand, concentrates much more on the intrapsychic manifestations of this condition. From this perspective, a pervasive sense of emptiness, fragile self-esteem, and tendencies towards hypochondriasis are among the more frequent manifestations in this population (Forman, 1976). However, it is important to keep in mind that Kohut is describing a developmental theory of the self that is thought to parallel the traditional psychoanalytic model of development; he did not seek to describe a particular psychiatric syndrome. As such, many have speculated that Kernberg and Kohut are discussing different concepts that may reflect different groups of patients (Pulver, 1970).

The DSM-III, in attempting to operationalize the concept of narcissism, selected criteria derived to a certain extent from the work of both Kernberg and Kohut. However, the task of putting complex psychodynamic concepts into a form that can be used reliably by clinicians who may not have had any psychodynamic training is a difficult one, and the extent to which DSM-III succeeded has been questioned (Frances, 1980). Nonetheless, this concept has been increasing in popularity recently, and it may be expected that this diagnosis will be assigned with increasing frequency in the coming years.

CLINICAL POPULATION

The central features of the DSM-III definition of Narcissistic Personality are a sense of grandiose self-importance, a need for attention and admiration, a lack of empathy, and an exploitative attitude in interpersonal relationships. In addition, these individuals often have a fragile sense of self-esteem with marked emotional reactions to criticism or disappointment. Interpersonal relationships are thought to vacillate between an over-idealization and a devaluation of others, often called "splitting."

According to DSM-III, depression is a frequent clinical syndrome diagnosis observed in conjunction with Narcissistic Personality Disorder. In addition, a focus on somatic symptoms may be present, and observation consistent with Kohut's (1966) writings. Often, histrionic, borderline, and antisocial features are thought to be observed in these individuals as well, and this overlap has been documented in some studies (Pfohl et al., 1986).

The DSM-III makes no estimate of the prevalence of Narcissistic Personality Disorder. It does mention that the disorder seems to be more common in recent years, but speculates that this increase is likely a function of greater professional interest in the concept. Koenigsberg et al. (1985) reported that 0.9 percent of their psychiatric patients received this diagnosis. When Morey et al. (1986) examined the clinical diagnoses in two university inpatient units, they found only 1.8 percent of personality disorder patients receiving this diagnosis, somewhat lower than the Koenigsberg et al. figure of 2.6 percent of personality disordered patients. Pfohl et al. (1986) identified 3.8 percent of their nonpsychotic sample as meeting DSM-III criteria for Narcissistic Personality Disorder (7.5 percent of personality-disordered patients). This latter estimate is slightly higher than either figure obtained in studies of clinical diagnosis, suggesting that this condition may be somewhat under-diagnosed in routine clinical practice. Nevertheless, this initial prevalence data suggests that Narcissistic Personality Disorder may not among the more prevalent personality disorders.

MMPI SCALES

A number of volumes have been written about pathologic narcissism from a psychodynamic perspective. Because of the relatively recent interest in this diagnostic concept, very little empirical work has been directed at Narcissistic Personality Disorder. As a result, the little data that are available must be interpreted with caution.

The only MMPI study that examined a criterion group of Narcissistic Personality Disorders was one reported by Ashby, Lee, and Duke (1979). These authors proposed an MMPI research scale, consisting of 19 items, designed to identify individuals manifesting this disorder. They found that a criterion sample of 20 patients, diagnosed by psychotherapists who were trained in treating Narcissistic Personality Disorder, could be differentiated from a sample of 20 carefully screened normal. The authors found that the scale had good internal consistency (Kuder-Richardson, .81). On cross-validation, the scale had an 86 percent hit rate in a sample of 76 patients, where the base rate of diagnosis was 54 percent (Solomon, 1982).

Solomon (1982) reported a study examining the validity of the Ashby et al. (1979) scale. Solomon used a sample of 100 undergraduate students, most of whom were female. The focus of the study was the relationship of the Ashby et al. Narcissism scale with the Tennessee Self-concept scale (used to distinguish between individuals with healthy as opposed to pathologic self-esteem), and a questionnaire designed to tap the quality of love relationships (among other constructs). High and low narcissism groups, as defined by the MMPI scale, could be differentiated with respect to self-esteem (high narcissism associated with low self-esteem) and successful love relationships (high narcissism associated with lack of success). In addition, narcissism was positively associated with incidence of nightmares. Solomon concluded that the Ashby et al. scale had promise as a valid measure of Narcissistic Personality Disorder. Along similar lines, Gerson (1984) found that the Ashby et al. Narcissism scale correlated significantly with a questionnaire designed to tap the defense mechanism of splitting, which theoretically is expected to be prominent in the defensive repertoire of narcissistic personalities. Thus, although such evidence is preliminary, it does seem that the Ashby et al. (1979) scale has promise for identifying Narcissistic Personality Disorder.

Unfortunately, most of the remaining information on the use of MMPI with Narcissistic Personality Disorder is based on inference and indirect evidence. The MCMI Narcissistic scale does correlate significantly with a number of MMPI scales. The highest association involved a strong negative correlation (-.72) with Scale θ. This finding is consistent with the observation of Meyer (1983) and Lachar (1974) that very low scores on Scale θ are consistent with the superficial interpersonal relationships typical of narcissistic characters. Other strong negative associations were noted with MMPI Scales 7 (-.52) and 2 (-.52), representing a general lack of reported discomfort that might not be found in a treatment sample. The largest positive correlation between this MCMI scale and MMPI clinical scales was observed with Scale 9 (.32). It is surprising that Scale 4 did not covary more directly with the MCMI scale, given the exploitative nature of these individuals as described in DSM-III and other sources.

Millon (1982) also provides correlational data comparing his Narcissism scale with certain MMPI research scales. A number of sizable correlations were obtained with the Wiggins' (1966) content scales, and again most of these correlations were negative. Among these were Social Maladjustment (-.72), Depression (-.57), and Poor Morale (-.55) scales, consistent with the pattern of superficial social success and high self-esteem noted on the clinical scales. The single highest positive correlation was with the *Es* research scale (+.40). However, it is probably unlikely that high elevations on *Es* would be noted in Narcissistic Personality Disorder tested in treatment settings, as in this situation the fragile nature of their self-esteem would likely be manifest.

It is apparent that a great deal of further research is needed in describing the MMPI performance of individuals with Narcissistic Personality Disorder. Because of the vagueness of the diagnostic criteria for this condition, it is very difficult to identify criterion groups with this diagnosis and consequently few researchers have even made an attempt to study it empirically. This state of affairs has led some authors to suggest dropping the category from the nomenclature (Vaillant & Perry, 1980). However, given the increased theoretical interest in this concept, it will likely be represented in future personality classification schemes.

ANTISOCIAL PERSONALITY DISORDER

The condition known today as Antisocial Personality was perhaps the first personality disorder to be isolated from traditional clinical syndromes. Because of this relatively lengthy history, this concept has gone through many changes since it was first introduced, and its DSM-III definition reflects yet another substantial alteration in its meaning. Nonetheless, it is expected that Antisocial Personality Disorder will continue to be one of the personality disorders that is most frequently diagnosed.

The origins of the concept of Antisocial Personality Disorder are generally traced back to Phillippe Pinel's notion of *manie sans delire* (madness without delirium), which he described at the turn of the nineteenth century. This concept was one of the first in which a mental disorder was described that did not include a defect in reasoning, and as such some have described Pinel's concept as the forerunner of all modern personality disorders (Mack, 1975). The patients to which Pinel was referring were impulsive and often self-damaging, but were fully aware of the irrational nature of their behavior. Pinel's notion was adapted by the British physician Prichard, who described the condition as *moral insanity*. However, Prichard's concept was specific to individuals whose "moral or active principles of the mind are strangely perverted or deranged. . ." (1837, p. 85), and as such he added a moralistic element to the concept that Pinel had not emphasized (Millon, 1981a).

Prichard's description of this concept became a popular one, and consistent with the general interest in genetics during the mid to late nineteenth century, it eventually evolved into a notion resembling one of the "born criminal." Koch (1891) selected the term *psychopathic inferiority* for this condition to emphasize the purported constitutional basis for this condition. Koch's description of this diagnosis was comparable in scope with Pinel's in that each included much of what today would be considered a personality disorder (as well as many neurotic conditions). However, once again the moral element introduced by Prichard crept back into the meaning of the term, and the term *psychopath* gradually came to be used for a variety of descriptive purposes.

During the first half of the 20th century, a term related to psychopathy came into common use, that of sociopathy. The original intent of this concept seemed directed at removing the constitutional connotations of the former term, instead emphasizing that this disorder had primarily social manifestations. The term *sociopathic personality* was eventually incorporated into DSM-I (American Psychiatric Association, 1952), but there it was used to connote a broad class of conditions such as sexual deviations and addictions, as well as antisocial behavior.

Perhaps the most influential development in the evolution of this concept was the publication of *The Mask of Sanity* by Cleckley (1941). This book made explicit the personologic features that set the psychopathic personality apart from criminality. Among the features that Cleckley stressed as pathognomonic of this personality constellation were a lack of guilt, a general absence of anxiety or depression, and a seeming inability to learn from experience. Cleckley's work was influential in the conceptualization of the *Antisocial Personality*, as the term was used within DSM-II.

The DSM-III conceptualization of Antisocial Personality Disorder, as previously mentioned, represented a substantial departure from its DSM-II predecessor. The DSM-III definition is based extensively on a history of delinquent or antisocial behavior in contrast to the personality elements described by Cleckley and others. To a large extent, the DSM-III criteria were derived from a well-known study by Robins (1966), which attempted to establish the adolescent antecedents of antisocial behavior in adults. However, as will be seen below, these criteria seem to tap a somewhat different population than did the older "psychopathic personality" concept. As a result, the reference group of interest must be kept in mind in attempting to use the MMPI with "antisocial personality."

CLINICAL POPULATION

The central feature of the DSM-III definition of Antisocial Personality Disorder is a history of continous antisocial behavior, invariably beginning before the age of 15. Thus, this definition relies on behavioral rather than personologic manifestations. These behaviors include criminality, fighting, and promiscuity during adulthood, which are thought to follow a childhood characterized by truancy, stealing, and lying. As mentioned above, the personologic elements traditionally associated with the antisocial concept (such as absence of guilt or anticipatory anxiety, limited capacity for loyalty, and inability to learn from experience) are not represented in the DSM-III definition. This exclusion has been criticized by many (Frances, 1980), and the extent to which the DSM-III concept resembles older conceptualizations of this disorder remains ambiguous. However, one potential advantage of this increased focus on behavioral rather than personologic definition is an increase in diagnostic reliability. In fact, reliability of the Antisocial Personality Disorder diagnosis is the best of any of the DSM-III personality disorders (Mellsop et al., 1982).

The alteration of the definitional features of this concept has probably influenced the prevalence of the disorder. Traditionally, prevalence estimates for Antisocial Personality have varied widely, with figures ranging between 0.05 and 15 percent (Rosenthal, 1970). However, the revisions presented in DSM-III may well have altered these figures. For example, research using diagnostic criteria similar to DSM-III reveals that approximately 80 percent of prison inmates may be diagnosed as manifesting an Antisocial Personality, while researchers using criteria similar to those offered by Cleckley found that this percentage was much smaller, roughly 20 to 30 percent (Guze, Goodwin, & Crane, 1969). Thus, prevalence rates obtained in earlier studies may have limited utility under the new diagnostic guidelines.

The DSM-III lists the prevalence of Antisocial Personality Disorder at approximately 3 percent American men, and < 1 percent for American women. These estimates were probably based on the work of Cloninger, Reich, and Guze (1975). Blazer et al. (1985), reporting data from a large (n = 3,798) community sample, examined the base rate of Antisocial Personality Disorder as assigned by the Diagnostic Interview Schedule (DIS: Robins, Helzer, Crough, & Ratcliff, 1981), which was designed to yield certain DSM-III diagnoses. The Blazer et al. study found a 6-month prevalence of 0.93 percent for Antisocial Personality Disorder. Koenigsberg et al. (1985) reported that only 2 percent of their psychiatric patients received this diagnosis. When Morey et al. (1988) examined the clinical diagnoses in two university inpatient units, they found that 13 percent of personality disorder patients received this diagnosis, substantially higher than the Koenigsberg et al. figure of 5.4 percent of personality disordered patients. Pfohl et al.'s (1986) study identified 3.8 percent of their nonpsychotic sample as meeting DSM-III criteria for Antisocial Personality Disorder (7.5 percent of personality disordered patients). Given the changes in the definition of this concept in DSM-III, the percentage of patients meeting this diagnosis may drop somewhat compared with DSM-II, while the percentage of criminals meeting the diagnosis seems to have increased substantially, as evidenced by the research described above.

According to DSM-III, Antisocial Personality Disorder is thought to be much more common in men than in women. Much of the research described above seems to support this contention. However, the Warner (1978) study described in the Histrionic Personality section suggests that this may partially reflect gender bias on the part of diagnosticians. In that study, clinicians were generally reluctant to assign an Antisocial Personality diagnosis to a case described as female, although they did assign this diagnosis much more frequently when the same case was described as a male.

Another potential source of bias in this diagnosis could involve social class. For example, Frances (1980) points out that the nature of the DSM-III criteria for Antisocial Personality Disorder might be such that they are too easily met by individuals from rough and deprived areas. The epidemiologic study reported by Blazer et al. (1985) is somewhat contrary to this hypothesis, as no differences were found in the prevalence of this disorder in urban vs. rural areas. Nonetheless, there are a myriad of other factors that might influence the assignment of this diagnostic label that remain to be investigated.

MMPI SCALES

Perhaps the most obvious expectation of the MMPI characteristics of the Antisocial Personality Disorder would involve elevations on Scale 4 (*Pd*). The "Psychopathic Deviate" scale of the MMPI was developed in an attempt to identify the asocial and amoral variants of the psychopathic personality. In fact, the symptomatic features of the criterion group utilized by McKinley and Hathaway in deriving this scale were similar to those listed in DSM-III: for example, "stealing, lying, truancy, sexual promiscuity, alcoholic over-indulgence, forgery, and similar delinquencies" (1956, p. 98). Thus, findings that elevations on Scale 4 are often associated with antisocial acts and criminal offenses (Graham, 1987; Greene, 1980; Elion, 1975) are not surprising.

The utility of Scale 4 elevations as an indicator of Antisocial Personality Disorder remains open to question, however. For example, it has been observed frequently that Scale 4 is often elevated in college student samples, generally in the absence of a documentable antisocial personality (King & Kelley, 1977; Murray, Munley, & Gilbart, 1965). In addition, a perusal of profile types for other personality disorders described in this chapter reveals that Scale 4 elevations are commonly observed in nearly every personality disorder group. Despite this lack of specificity, in certain populations elevations on this scale can be suggestive of Antisocial Personality Disorder. For example, Walters (1985) examined the utility of Scale 4 for identifying Antisocial Personality Disorder in a prison in-

mate sample of 225 male military criminal offenders. Criterion diagnoses of Antisocial Personality Disorder were assigned using the Psychiatric Diagnostic Interview (PDI: Othmer, Penick, & Powell, 1981), a structured interview designed to yield certain DSM-III diagnoses. The reliability of the criterion diagnoses, as calculated using inter-diagnostician agreement, was 80.8 percent.

The Walters (1985) study found that both *K*-corrected and non-*K*-corrected scores on Scale 4 could successfully identify the antisocial inmates at levels above chance expectancies. For the *K*-corrected *T*-scores, Walters found that a cutting score of 70 resulted in a hit rate of 60.4 percent and a cutting score of 75 yielded a 63.1 percent hit rate. Both hit rates were above chance levels, although not impressively so. One interesting aspect of the Walters study was an examination of the impact of certain moderator variables (such as education, age, IQ, race, and confining offense) on Scale 4 elevations. Only the type of criminal offense demonstrated a significant interaction with diagnosis, with nonperson offenders (e.g., burglary) achieving higher Scale 4 values than person offenders (e.g., assault, murder). This latter finding supports the DSM-III contention that the criminal activity of these individuals is more likely to involve minor crimes.

Because of the relative lack of specificity of Scale 4 elevation as an indicator for Antisocial Personality Disorder, the investigation of codetype configurations for this diagnostic category is particularly salient. Traditional clinical wisdom holds that the prototypic MMPI codetype for the antisocial character is a *4-9* codetype (Dahlstrom, Welsh, & Dahlstrom, 1972; Gilberstadt & Duker, 1965; Marks, Seeman, & Haller, 1974). For example, Marks et al. (1974), reporting codetype distributions on 16 sociopathic personalities, found that 45 percent of these individuals displayed the *4-9* codetype, with the second most frequent codetype being the *4-6* (10 percent). A number of authors have found, however, that the *4-9* codetype is not specific to antisocial personality, and in fact has few specific correlates with respect to psychiatric symptomatology (Gynther, Altman, & Warbin, 1973; Lewandowski & Graham, 1972; King & Kelley, 1977). In summary, it is important to note that the *4-9* profile, although certainly suggestive of Antisocial Personality Disorder, should in no way be mistaken as a pathognomonic indicator of this diagnosis.

A number of other two-point codetypes have also been frequently noted in association with antisocial personality. For example, Hathaway and Meehl (1951) reported data gathered on 94 psychopathic personalities and found that the *4-8* codetype was the most frequently (16.5 percent) observed in this sample. Other common codetypes included the *4-9* (12.8 percent), *4-2* (7.4 percent), and *4-6* (6.4 percent) patterns. Although the criterion group examined by Hathaway and Meehl reflected diagnoses made under a different system, more recent research has yielded comparable results. For example, Haier, Rieder, Khouri, and Buchsbaum (1979) reported that the majority of their antisocial personality group (as defined using the Research Diagnostic Criteria, which are very similar to DSM-III) displayed a *4-8/8-4* codetype, while none had the *4-9* profile often assumed to characterize this group. The inpatient sample investigated by Morey et al. (1988) yielded a *4-8* mean profile (see Table 5–4), but this was not among the more common codetypes observed in that sample. Rather, the *4-9*, *4-6*, and *2-8* codetypes were the most commonly noted. There are a number of profile types, aside from the *4-9*, that involve Scale *4* elevations that have potential in the identification of Antisocial Personality Disorder. The *4-8* codetype also is observed commonly, particularly in inpatient samples. However, as seen in previous sections of this chapter, this codetype is found in a variety of other personality disorders (e.g., Borderline and Histrionic), and as such no single codetype should be regarded as a specific marker for Antisocial Personality Disorder.

Table 5–4 presents mean profiles that various authors have identified in samples of antisocial personalities. Hare (1970) presented data on penitentiary inmates that sought to distinguish psychopathic from nonpsychopathic inmates; no mention was made of any specific criteria used to identify his criterion group. Sutker and Allain (1983) presented data that are an interesting contrast to the typical samples of criminal inmates utilized in this area. These authors sought to identify a sample of "adaptive sociopaths"; in other words, individuals with psychopathic features who were experiencing no impairment in functioning. They selected their sample from students entering medical school. Unfortunately, the MMPI was part of the criteria by which these individuals were identified, and as such the mean profile presented in Table 5–4 reflects contamination between MMPI profile and the criterion. Nonetheless, the differences between this and other mean antisocial profiles (particularly the lack of elevation on Scales *8* and *9*) may give some indication of differences between successful and unsuccessful variants of this personality style. Another interesting aspect of the Sutker and Allain study involved a comparison between the "adaptive sociopath" group and normal controls on each of the DSM-III criteria for Antisocial Personality Disorder. They found that although there were significant differences between the two groups with respect to childhood and adolescent acting out, no differences were observed on the criteria that tap adulthood behavior. In other words, the antisocial aspects of these "adaptive sociopaths" seemed to diminish when they reached young adulthood.

Perhaps the most thorough examination of the utility of the MMPI in identifying the DSM-III concept of antisocial personality was conducted by Hare (1985). Hare compared the performance of

TABLE 5–4.   FREQUENCY OF ELEVATED MMPI CLINICAL SCALES IN ANTISOCIAL PERSONALITY DISORDERS AND RELATED CONDITIONS

Authors	N	Age	Clinical Scales (≥ 70 *T*-points)
Hare (1970) [Psychopathic criminals]	30	–	*4-9*
Hare (1985) [Antisocial Personality Disorders]	43	29.8	Spike *4*
Hare (1985) [High psychopathy]	40	29.8	Spike *4*
Morey et al. (1988) [Antisocial Personality Disorders]	14	23.6	*4-8-9-6-7*
Sutker & Allain (1983) [Adaptive sociopaths]	16	26.8	Spike *4*

several behavioral and self-report measures of psychopathy in a sample of 274 male prison inmates. Among the measures that he examined were ratings made according to both DSM-III (kappa reliability estimate, .79) and Cleckley (interrater reliability, .90) criteria for antisocial personality. Thus, Hare's study was exemplary in that he established reliable criterion diagnoses, using two important constructs as criterion measures. These two measures correlated .57, which points out the imperfect convergence between these two perspectives on the concept of antisocial personality.

Hare (1985) investigated the correlation and the convergence of various classification rules with these diagnostic decisions. For the MMPI, he examined four measures: Scale 4 T-scores, Scale 9 T-scores, the sum of T-scores from Scales 4 and 9, and Scale 4 T-score minus a T-score obtained from the Socialization (So) scale of the California Personality Inventory (CPI: Gough, 1957). Hare found that of these four measures, the 4-So composite score yielded the highest correlation with both DSM-III diagnosis (.44) and with the Cleckley ratings (.36). The sum of T-scores on Scales 4 and 9 and Scale 4 in isolation also correlated significantly with DSM-III diagnosis (.33 and .29, respectively), although neither correlated significantly with the Cleckley ratings. MMPI Scale 9 scores did not correlate significantly with either of these psychopathy measures.

Hare (1985) also investigated the convergence between diagnosis and various decision rules using these measures. Again, he found that the greatest convergence with DSM-III diagnosis was obtained using the 4-So decision rule (a score of 37 or above indicated high psychopathy). Of the three rules derived strictly from the MMPI, the sum of T-scores on Scales 4 and 9 (above 145 for high psychopathy) and Scale 4 alone (above 78 for high psychopathy) yielded the best results, with comparable convergence with DSM-III diagnosis. However, none of these four rules demonstrated a great deal of convergence with DSM-III diagnosis, with agreements being in the weak-to-moderate range. Hare suggests that caution be used in assuming that high 4 or 4-9 codetypes are necessarily reflective of Antisocial Personality Disorder.

The Antisocial-Aggressive scale from the MCMI (Millon, 1982) yields a pattern of correlations with MMPI clinical scales that is somewhat unexpected, given many of the trends noted above. For example, the MCMI Antisocial scale does *not* correlate to any extent (correlation, .17) with MMPI Scale 4, nor does it correlate with Wiggins' (1966) Authority Conflict (*AUT*) scale. The highest correspondences with this MCMI scale are found for the MacAndrew (MacAndrew, 1965) Alcoholism scale (.38), Scale 9 (.36), and Wiggins' Hostility (.36) scale. Given the results discussed above, these findings suggest that this MCMI scale differs somewhat from the DSM-III conceptualization for Antisocial Personality Disorder. However, one might expect that these latter MMPI scales would be of some utility in identifying antisocial characters.

DEPENDENT PERSONALITY DISORDER

The history of Dependent Personality Disorder can be traced to psychoanalytic discussions of the oral character (Freud, 1905). Individuals with this personality configuration are said to manifest an attitude of eternal optimism, particularly that some kind person will always take care of them. In DSM-I, this construct appeared as passive-dependent and was considered a subtype of passive-aggressive personality. The similarity of the two disorders may not be readily apparent, but both are thought to arise from hostile dependency and latent aggression (Manilow, 1981). The passive-dependent personality diagnosis was dropped from DSM-II, with the closest approximation being inadequate personality. In DSM-III, Dependent Personality Disorder reappears as a separate syndrome. Because dependency appears to be a dimension in almost all psychiatric patients, some authors question the validity of Dependent Personality Disorder as a unique constellation of behaviors (Vaillant & Perry, 1985).

CLINICAL POPULATION

The cardinal features of Dependent Personality Disorder are passively allowing others to assume responsibility for major areas of life, subordination of needs to those persons on whom one depends, and a lack of self-confidence. According to DSM-III the disorder is identified more frequently in women. This bias is not surprising in view of the fact that Dependent Personality Disorder is in some respects an exaggerated form of the traditional feminine role (Kaplan, 1983). Associated features may include other personality disorders, anxiety disorders, and depression. Some authors note a link between Dependent Personality Disorder and phobic disorders, in particular agoraphobia (Millon, 1981a). In this personality style, many symptoms can be viewed as attempts at secondary gain via soliciting concern from others and decreased responsibility.

Few studies have reported the base rate of this disorder in psychiatric patients. Koenigsberg et al. (1985) reported that 7.9 percent of patients with Axis II diagnoses had Dependent Personality Disorders. Pfohl et al. (1986) identified 12 percent of their sample of patients with Axis II diagnoses as having Dependent Personality Disorder only; a total of 25 percent of their sample had Dependent Personality Disorder in addition to another personality disorder diagnosis. In the Morey et al. (1988) study, 22 percent of a sample of inpatients with personality disorders received this diagnosis. These results are consistent with DSM-III, which reports the disorder to be common.

MMPI SCALES

In view of the apparent prevalence of Dependent Personality Disorder, there has been remarkably little empirical research, including the use of the MMPI. Morey et al. (1988) identified a total of 24 patients with MMPI data who also received a diagnosis of Dependent Personality Disorder. Consistent with DSM-III estimates, the majority of the sample (85 percent) was female. The most frequent codetype was *2-8-7/2-7-8*, found in 14.3 percent of the sample. Only two other codetypes, *1-2-3/2-1-3* and *2-8* were found in more than one patient. Both of these codetypes were observed in 9.5 percent of the sample. Overall, the sample was extremely heterogeneous, with 16 different codetypes obtained from the sample of 21 patients.

The codetype for the mean profile obtained with this sample would be *2-8*. Since 8 of the 10 clinical scales are elevated above a T-score of 70, the standard interpretation of this two-point codetype may not be applicable; acutally, this mean profile type resembles the floating profile described by Newmark and Sines (1972), often seen in Borderline Personality Disorder as discussed earlier. Nonetheless, in general the *2-8* codetype can be conceptualized as a severe depression with associated anxiety, frequently resulting in fear of loss of control (Greene, 1980). The elevations on Scales *4* and *6* modify this interpretation by introducing elements of anger, frustration, and hostility into the clinical picture. One might speculate that Scales *4* and *6* are elevated in response to events that precipitated hospitalization, such as the loss of a significant other. Given the fact that this sample is predominantly female, a somewhat lower mean on Scale *5* might have been predicted, reflecting passivity and adherence to a stereotypical feminine role. As it is, Scale *5* is substantially lower than Scales *4* and *6*, giving the profile the look of the "Scarlett O'Hara V" (Greene, 1980) thought to be characteristic of demanding and dependent women.

Many interpretive manuals include dependency as a descriptor for various codetypes, but whether such codetypes will ultimately prove to be covariates of Dependent Personality Disorder remains to be seen. Both Marks et al. (1974) and Meyer (1983) identify the *2-7* codetype as potentially associated with Dependent Personality Disorder, although the most essential features of this codetype are anxiety and depression, not interpersonal dependency. Marks et al. (1974) reported that 5 percent of their sample of *1-3/3-1* codetype patients were diagnosed as dependent personality, although the majority were conversion and psychophysiologic diagnoses. Greene (1980) also identifies dependent features in both *1-3/3-1* and *2-3/3-2* codetypes. In addition, the relatively infrequent three-point triad of *2-7-3/7-3-2* can be interpreted as a passive individual who is comfortable in very dependent interpersonal relations. Gilberstadt and Duker (1965) also described a *1-2-3-7* codetype as "psychophysiological reaction in a passive-dependent personality." Interestingly, when dependency is considered as a symptom across codetypes, it has been found most frequently in *4-9* (66.6 percent), *8-3* (65 percent), and *4-6* (44.4 percent) configurations (Marks et al., 1974).

Several special scales may be useful in this population. Both the Dependency Scale (*Dy*: Navran, 1954) and the Dominance Scale (*Do*: Gough, McClosky, & Meehl, 1951) tap behaviors relevant to Dependent Personality Disorder. The *Do* scale is designed to measure social dominance, although low scores which that presumably indicate submissiveness have not been investigated adequately. The *Dy* scale is designed to identify dependent, submissive, and passive individuals, but systematic research using this scale has been limited as well (Greene, 1980). The *Dy* scale is constructed from items that were judged to be indicative of a "hypothetical dependent person who was responding frankly" (Navran, 1954). The item pool was derived from the responses of a heterogeneous group of psychiatric patients. These psychiatric patients scored significantly higher than 200 normals from the original MMPI normative sample, as well as 265 graduate students. Presumably, the items reflect a type of pathologic dependency seen across a variety of psychiatric patients. Given the current conceptualization of Dependent Personality Disorder as a syndrome in DSM-III, the *Dy* scale needs to be reexamined using a group of patients carrying this diagnosis before it can be accepted as an adequate measure of the current category.

The MCMI may again be used as a source of hypotheses with respect to the effect of Dependent Personality Disorder on MMPI scales. Millon (1982) reports correlations between the MCMI Dependent-Submissive scale and MMPI scales. Scales *7* and *0* are positively correlated and Scale *9* is negatively correlated. Also positively correlated are the Wiggins' (1966) content scales tapping Poor Morale and Depression. Compared with other MCMI scales, there are fewer large correlations between this Dependent scale and the MMPI clinical and research scales.

In conclusion, there has been insufficient research directed at identifying specific MMPI features of Dependent Personality Disorder. From preliminary data, it appears that the MMPI of an individual with Dependent Personality Disorder during inpatient treatment may have many scales elevated above a *T*-score of 70. Little research has been conducted with special or research scales, but both the *Do* and *Dy* scales may have potential based on their intended focus. Given the frequency of dependent features in psychiatric patients, this issue clearly needs further investigation.

COMPULSIVE PERSONALITY DISORDER

The constellation of behaviors that constitutes Compulsive Personality Disorder has been described consistently for many years. Freud and his followers gave detailed descriptions of the "anal personality," which is characterized by orderliness, stubbornness, and perfectionism (Abraham, 1923). Obsessive-compulsive personality disturbances also appeared in DSM-I and DSM-II. The current DSM-III category of Compulsive Personality Disorder is sometimes confused with Obsessive-Compulsive Disorder, which is an Axis I condition and considered to be an anxiety disorder. Perhaps some of the confusion comes from the similarity in theories of etiology. In the psychodynamic literature, obsessions and compulsions as well as the presumably milder manifestations of compulsive personality traits are thought to arise in response to anxiety over unconscious impulses. However, such responses in Compulsive Personality Disorders are experienced as part of the self and are ego-syntonic as opposed to true obsessions and compulsions, which are experienced as alien to the self, or ego-dystonic.

CLINICAL POPULATION

Compulsive Personality Disorder is characterized by emotional constriction, orderliness, stubbornness, and indecisiveness. According to DSM-III, the disorder is apparently common and diagnosed more frequently in males. The actual prevalence of the disorder is difficult to estimate, because many elements of the syndrome may be occupationally adapative. Unlike Avoidant and Paranoid Presonality Disorders, individuals with Compulsive Personality Disorder do seek treatment when the behavior pattern causes sufficient discomfort (Vaillant & Perry, 1980). Although considered separate disorders in the current nomenclature, individuals with Compulsive Personality Disorder can develop a superimposed Obsessive-Compulsive Disorder. For example, one study found that 72 percent of obsessional patients had a premorbid compulsive personality (Kringlen, 1965). Depression and dysthymic disorder also can develop as complications, being particularly common at midlife (Marmar, 1984).

Few studies have examined the base rate of Compulsive Personality Disorder. Koenigsberg et al. (1985) report that 2.4 percent of their large sample of medical center patients with Axis II diagnoses had Compulsive Personality Disorder. In the total sample of patients both with and without Axis II diagnoses, 1 percent carried a diagnosis of Compulsive Personality Disorder.

Pfohl et al. (1986) found 3 percent of their sample of 67 personality-disordered patients had Compulsive Personality Disorder as a single diagnosis, and 10 percent met the criteria for this diagnosis in addition to another Axis II diagnosis. In the sample gathered by Morey et al. (1988), 5.6 percent of these personality-disordered patients received a diagnosis of Compulsive Personality Disorder. A possible explanation for the low base rates for Compulsive Personality Disorder reported in these studies is that few features of this diagnostic category are markedly deviant from normal social and occupational behavior. As such, this syndrome may be rarely identified in diagnostic workups unless severe impairment is present.

MMPI SCALES

Although compulsive personality has received considerable attention within the psychodynamic literature, little research using the MMPI has been attempted. However, a number of hypotheses can be generated from the existing interpretive literature. Two codetypes have been identified that may be observed in Compulsive Personality Disorder. The *2-7* codetype is described as frequently exhibiting compulsive, meticulous, and perfectionistic trends (Marks et al., 1974). However, the *2-7* codetype is common in clinical samples and is probably not specific to Compulsive Personality Disorder. The second, which is relatively uncommon because of overlap between Scale *7* and other clinical scales, is a Spike *7* codetype. Individuals with this codetype are seen as tense, anxious, and rigid, usually exhibiting obsessive-compulsive defenses that are no longer effective (Greene, 1980).

In compulsive personality one might also predict extremely low Scale *4*, reflecting conventional and conforming attitudes and a tendency to be moralistic (Lachar, 1974). Meyer (1983) states that compulsives seldom obtain highly elevated profiles because they are not inclined toward self-disclosure. In addition, Scale *9* may be relatively elevated, reflecting the dominant and autocratic approach toward interpersonal relationships. Compulsive Personality Disorder may be best inferred from a detailed examination of MMPI data rather than from a specific codetype.

Millon (1982) reports negative correlations between the Compulsive-Conforming Scale of the MCMI and MMPI Scales *4* and *8*. Therefore, extreme elevations of these two scales would not be expected in Compulsive Personality Disorder. Correlations between the MCMI and a number of special scales are consistent with clinical descriptions of Compulsive Personality Disorder as well. For example, there is a positive correlation with the Wiggins' (1966) Religious Fundamentalism scale that may reflect the tendency of Compulsive Personalities to be overly moralistic and judgmental. Consistent with the purported emotional constriction, a negative correlation is reported between the MCMI Compulsive scale and the Wiggins' Hostility scale. Conformist tendencies are reflected in negative correlations with the Wiggins' Authority Conflict scale. Interestingly, although the DSM-III identifies depression as an associated feature, both Wiggins' Depression and Poor Morale scales are negatively correlated with the MCMI Compulsive-Conforming scale.

Special scales have not been adequately investigated in Compulsive Personality Disorder. The content of some of these scales is consistent with clinical descriptions and may provide useful diagnostic information. For example, the Dominance Scale (Gough et al., 1951) could tap the compulsive patients' tendency to be domineering and insistent on getting his or her own way.

Clearly, considerable research is needed before a characteristic MMPI performance for Compulsive Personality Disorder can be described. The best sources of information about features of this disorder may eventually be found to involve special and research scales and also perhaps isolated elevations of Scale *7*.

AVOIDANT PERSONALITY DISORDER

This is a new diagnostic category that was introduced in DSM-III. Millon (1981b) traces the history of this syndrome to Kretschmer (1926), who made a distinction between "anaesthetic" and "hyperaesthetic" constitutions. Although both types were characterized by difficulties in interpersonal adjustment, Kretschmer identified the former personality style as indifferent, cold and emotionally empty, while the latter type was seen as abnormally sensitive, tense, and easily wounded. This distinction is similar to the one drawn in DSM-III between the Schizoid and Avoidant Personality Disorders, respectively.

CLINICAL POPULATION

The predominant clinical characteristic of the Avoidant Personality Disorder is an avoidance of close interpersonal relationships due to an intense fear of rejection. Unlike other withdrawn personality styles, this type desires such relationships but cannot master the anxiety associated with them. Perhaps as a result of this anxiety, these individuals tend to have low self-esteem, be socially isolated, and want very strong guarantees of acceptance before entering into relationships. The DSM-III mentions that depression or self-directed anger may be correlates of this disorder.

Little is known about the base rate of Avoidant Personality Disorder. The DSM-III states that Avoidant Personality Disorder is "apparently common," but few studies demonstrate that it is diagnosed commonly. The Koenigsberg et al. (1985) study described earlier only found 1 percent of their total sample of psychiatric patients receiving this diagnosis. The examination of clinical diagnoses by Morey et al. (1988) found only 3.7 percent of personality-disordered patients receiving this diagnosis, comparable with the Koenigsberg et al. figure of 2.9 percent of personality-disordered patients. However, in their structured interview study, Pfohl et al. (1986) identified 11 percent of their nonpsychotic sample as meeting DSM-III criteria for Avoidant Personality Disorder (22 percent of personality-disordered patients), suggesting that this condition may be underdiagnosed in routine clinical practice. Given the rather liberal (i.e., unrestrictive) definition of Avoidant Personality Disorder in DSM-III, the percentage of patients meeting this diagnosis is probably fairly high. No information is available on the gender distribution of this condition.

MMPI SCALES

Because of the relatively recent development of the diagnostic concept of Avoidant Personality Disorder and the apparent rarity with which it is diagnosed, very little research of any sort has been conducted. As a result, the little data that are available may only be applied indirectly. The work of Millon (1982) with the MCMI may be par-

ticularly informative, since Millon's writings (e.g., 1969) were influential in the emergence of this concept. The MCMI Avoidant scale correlates significantly with a number of MMPI scales. As might be expected, the highest correlation obtained with the MMPI clinical scales was Scale 0 (.62), followed by Scales 8 (.59), 2 (.56), and 7 (.45). Interestingly, none of the 10 MMPI clinical scales correlated negatively with Millon's Avoidant scale. Consistent with Millon's findings, Meyer (1983) notes that a 2-7 codetype is commonly obtained with these individuals, although he does not cite any data in support of this conclusion.

Millon (1982) also provides correlational data comparing his Avoidant scale with certain MMPI research scales. A number of sizable correlations were obtained with the Wiggins' (1966) content scales. As might be expected, the Social Maladjustment scale was highly correlated (.74), suggesting that it may be a promising marker for Avoidant Personality. In addition, Wiggins scales of Depression (.69), Poor Morale (.61), Psychoticism (.54), and Phobias (.52) yielded sizable correlations, consistent with the DSM-III description of these individuals as dysphoric, isolated, and fearful. Finally, Millon observed a -.51 correlation between his scale and Barron's (1953) Es scale.

It is apparent that a great deal of additional research is needed in describing the MMPI performance of individuals with Avoidant Personality Disorder. A single study could not be identified that used a criterion group composed of such individuals; as such, much of what is presented above is at best indirect evidence. However, certain promising clues such as a 2-7-0 codetype and elevations on Wiggins' Social Maladjustment scale are worth further investigation in future research.

PASSIVE-AGGRESSIVE PERSONALITY DISORDER

Passive-aggressive personality first appeared as part of the nomenclature developed by the Veterans Administration following World War II (Whitman, Trosman, & Koenig, 1954). Passive-aggressive personality has since appeared in all three editions of DSM, although the term has undergone considerable evolution since its inception. In the theoretical literature two psychoanalytic character types, the oral-sadistic and masochistic, bear certain relationships to the present day conceptualization. Passive-aggressive personality rivals borderline and dependent features as a common descriptor of psychiatric patients. In previous editions of the DSM, Passive-Aggressive and Passive-Dependent were linked conceptually due to similar etiologic explanations that centered on pathologic dependency.

CLINICAL POPULATION

Passive-aggressive behavior entails the expression of aggression through indirect means. Millon (1981a) describes such a personality pattern as negativistic and characterizes such individuals as interpersonally ambivalent, erratically moody, and tending to use unpredictable and sulking behaviors to provoke discomfort in others. In contrast, the DSM-III definition emphasizes a much narrower aspect of passive-aggressive behavior, focusing on a tendency to resist indirectly adequate performance in response to social and occupational demands. This pervasive resistance invariably leads to occupational and social ineffectiveness.

Although Passive-Aggressive Personality has appeared in all three editions of DSM, there has been little descriptive research on this disorder. A frequently cited study by Small, Small, Alig, and Moore (1970) provided prospective data on 100 passive-aggressive patients followed up for 7 to 15 years. In these patients, alcoholism, depression, and somatic complaints were frequent concomitants of the passive-aggressive personality style. Small et al. (1970) also noted that those patients who received supportive psychotherapy had the best outcomes. However, it must be noted that these patients were diagnosed under DSM-II, and the resemblance to the current DSM-III Passive-Aggressive Personality Disorder is not strong. The behaviors that they describe for this cohort could easily be descriptive of Borderline or Histrionic Personality Disorders: suicidal gestures, verbal (not physical) aggressiveness, emotional storms, impulsivity, and manipulative behavior.

The DSM-III states that there is no information on the base rate of Passive-Aggressive Personality. Leighton et al. (1963) reported a prevalence of 0.9 percent for passive-aggressive (including passive-dependent) personality in a community study. Of the three studies used in this chapter to estimate prevalence, the frequencies within the domain of personality disorders are 12 percent (Morey et al., 1988), 4.5 percent (Pfohl et al., 1986), and 3 percent (Koenigsberg et al., 1985). The higher frequency in the first study may be due to the fact that more than one personality disorder diagnosis per patient was allowed, while the latter study recorded the primary Axis II diagnosis only. Thus, the disorder as it is described in DSM-III may be diagnosed relatively infrequently, particularly as a primary diagnosis.

MMPI SCALES

No characteristic codetypes have been established for DSM-III Passive-Aggressive Personality Disorder, although a number of codetypes have been described under previous editions of DSM. Morey et al. (1988) found a mean codetype for a sample of 13 patients with Passive-Aggressive Personality Disorder as a *4-2*. Only two codetypes were observed in more than one patient. The 4-2 codetype was obtained by three patients (23 percent), and a *2-8-7* was obtained by two (15 percent) patients. Both patients with the *2-8-7* profiles carried both Passive-Aggressive and Dependent Personality Disorder Diagnoses. In addition, 75 percent of the patients had codetypes in which Scale *4* was high-point. This latter observation is consistent with the clinical assumption that aggression is central in the dynamics of this disorder. Similar to the mean codetypes of some other personality disorders presented in this chapter, the overall elevation of this profile indicates a relatively severe degree of pathology. It is unlikely that an outpatient sample would yield profiles of comparable elevation, however.

Consistent with these results, Marks et al. (1974) reported Passive-Aggressive Personality Disorder to be descriptive of 33 percent of their sample of *2-7-4/2-4-7/4-7-2* profiles. These authors also identified Passive-Aggressive Personality as being associated with both the *3-2-1* and *4-6-2/6-4-2* codetype, with 17 and 66 percent of these respective codetypes showing this personality trait. Interestingly, the descriptors of the *4-6-2* codetype, which had the largest proportion of Passive-Aggressive Personality Disorder in the sample, include "self-dramatizing and histrionic" and emphasize poor impulse control. Strongly conflicted dependency needs are also discussed, but passive resistance to external demands was not included. These features probably reflect the broader conceptualization of Passive-Aggressive Personality Disorder that was in effect under DSM-II.

Another codetype that has appeared as a potential finding in Passive-Aggressive Personality is *4-3/3-4* (Graham, 1987; Greene, 1980; Meyer, 1983). Depending on which scale is elevated, different interpretations are indicated. Individuals with a *3-4* codetype have a tendency to discharge hostility in an indirect fashion, which is consistent with the current DSM-III conceptualization of Passive-Aggressive Personality Disorder. Individuals with a *4-3* codetype have also been described as passive-aggressive (Lachar, 1974), but closer examination of the data reveals that the actual interpretation is passive-aggressive, aggressive type. Thus, poorly controlled anger and violent acts are often observed with this codetype, and such behaviors would fall more appropriately in the realm of Antisocial or Borderline Personality Disorder in the current nomenclature.

Lachar (1974) also describes a *4-6* codetype in combination with an extremely low (a *T*-score of ≤ 35) Scale *5* in females, which is often termed the "passive-aggressive V" or "Scarlett O'Hara V" (Greene, 1980). Women with this codetype are very passive and dependent and identified with the traditional feminine role. However, their dependency is usually of a hostile type. In this codetype Scale *6* does not represent paranoid thinking but rather resentment, bitterness, and a tendency to project blame. Such individuals may be diagnosed as having a Passive-Aggressive or Dependent Personality Disorder.

Kelley and King (1977) reported finding Passive-Aggressive Personality Disorder to be associated with a Spike *9* codetype in male outpatients. They also reported that a second group of Spike *9* males was observed whose behavior was indicative of primary antisocial personality. Considering the fact these findings were based on a total of 12 Spike *9* profiles, any generalizations from these data are tentative at best.

Correlations reported by Millon (1982) for the Passive-Aggressive scale of the MCMI include MMPI Scales *2* (.55), *4* (.42), *7* (.54), *8* (.53), *F* (.58), and *K* (-.53). Thus, the most likely codetype associated with high scores on the MCMI Passive-Aggressive scale would be some combination of *2*, *4*, *7*, and *8*, possibly with a relatively large *F-K* index. In addition, the Wiggins' (1966) content scales for Depression (.74), Poor Morale (.69), and Hostility (.56), as well as Barron's *Es* (-.47) also were found to be correlates of this MCMI scale. These results are consistent with the observation that depression is frequently associated with Passive-Aggressive Personality Disorder. In addition, the negative correlation with the *Es* scale suggests that such individuals would be relatively poor candidates for psychotherapy. Interestingly, the correlation reported between the MacAndrew Alcoholism scale (MacAndrew, 1965) and the MCMI Passive-Aggressive scale (.35) is among the highest for any of the MCMI personality scales. While the strength of the association is not extreme, this provides some support for the statement that alcoholism may be associated with Passive-Aggressive Personality Disorder.

Little data are available on the use of special scales with Passive-Aggressive Personality Disorder. One might speculate that if dependency is an important dynamic issue in this personality configuration, the special scales *Dy* (Navran, 1954) and *Do* (Gough et al., 1951) might reflect this. Wiggins' (1966) Manifest Hostility is certainly face-valid for Passive-Aggressive Personality Disorder. The content of the Manifest Hostility scale includes the characteristics of: (1) harboring intense hostile and aggressive impulses; (2) usually expressing negative impulses in a passive way; (3) resentfulness of demands of other people; (4) resentfulness of being taken advantage of; and (5) retaliatory behavior in interpersonal relationships (Graham, 1987). The content of the Tryon, Stein, and Chu's (Stein, 1968) cluster scale *R*, Resentment also is consistent with Passive-Aggressive Personality Disorder, although it does not appear to be as specific as the content of the Manifest Hostility scale.

Since the definition of Passive-Aggressive Personality Disorder has undergone considerable evolution to its current relatively restricted definition in DSM-III, interpretive statements published prior to this nomenclature need to be applied with caution. New data are needed on the MMPI profiles of individuals with this disorder as it is currently defined. Those special scales that tap resentment and hostility may be particularly informative in making this diagnosis, although many of these scales have very little validation research behind them.

PARANOID PERSONALITY DISORDER

The term *paranoia* has had a long and varied history in the psychiatric literature. Originally used by Hippocrates to designate serious forms of mental disturbance, paranoia currently applies to psychiatric disturbances ranging from a suspicious and mistrustful cognitive style to the highly systematized delusional system characteristic of a paranoid schizophrenic. Some authors have attributed the notion of a paranoid character style, in contrast to a paranoid psychosis, to Adolph Meyer (Muncie, 1939). Paranoid Personality Disorder has appeared in all three editions of DSM and represents the mildest form of paranoid disorder. It is often considered severe relative to other personality disorders, because of the apparently limited nature of the coping strategies used by such individuals (Millon, 1981a).

CLINICAL FEATURES

Paranoid Personality Disorder is characterized by pervasive and unwarranted suspiciousness, hypersensitivity, and restricted affective expression. Such individuals are often hypervigilant, continually scanning the environment for signs of threat. Other potential characteristics include guardedness, avoidance of accepting blame when warranted, frequently questioning the loyalty of others, a tendency to be easily slighted, pathologic jealousy, and lack of a sense of humor. Actual empirical data on these individuals are sparse, because they rarely seek treatment. Many clinicians assume that this disorder is related to other paranoid disorders such as paranoid schizophrenia and delusional disorder, although this has not been conclusively demonstrated (Weintraub, 1981).

Estimating the base rate of the disorder is difficult, but it appears to be rare in clinical populations. Estimates of prevalence in personality-disordered samples are given as 1.2 percent (Koenigsberg et al., 1985), 1.4 percent (Pfohl et al., 1986), and 0.9 percent (Morey et al., 1988), consistently demonstrating the rarity with which it is diagnosed. According to DSM-III, the disorder is diagnosed more frequently in men, although obviously there is a lack of reliable data to support this conclusion.

MMPI SCALES

Not surprisingly, there is little research on Paranoid Personality Disorder that uses the MMPI. To the casual observer, it would seem that the MMPI would be an excellent instrument to use with this population because of the Paranoid scale (6). However, it has not been conclusively demonstrated that increasing elevations of Scale 6 are associated with Paranoid Personality Disorder. In part, this lack of a relationship between Paranoid Personality Disorder and elevations on Scale 6 may be due to the characteristics of Scale 6. The criterion group used to develop Scale 6 included patients judged to have paranoid symptoms, including ideas of reference, feelings of persecution, and a grandiose self-concept (Hathaway, 1956). The patients in this derivation group were generally diagnosed as paranoid state, paranoid condition, or paranoid schizophrenia; the relationship of these diagnoses to paranoid personality is uncertain. A number of the items on Scale 6 appear to be characteristic of the fixed paranoid delusions seen in paranoid schizophrenia.

Hovanitz, Gynther, and Marks (1983) examined the relationship between MMPI items and paranoid characteristics in a population of male college students. Paranoia was identified by several self-report questionnaires designed to tap multiple aspects of the construct, including lack of interpersonal trust, rigidity, interpersonal sensitivity ("poignancy"), and morality. While this sample is a nonpsychiatric population, one might speculate that high scorers would meet the criteria for Paranoid Personality Disorder. This study compared both obvious (face-valid) and subtle items from Scale 6 (Weiner, 1948); each were found to have significant correlations with a number of the criterion measures. The distinction between obvious and subtle items could be expected to be particularly relevant in this population, because individuals with Paranoid Personality Disorder may not respond to obvious items because of guardedness. However, the results reported by Hovanitz et al. (1983) suggest that Scale 6 may have some utility in identifying a paranoid criterion group, even if the items do not directly reflect the core feature of suspiciousness and mistrust.

The standard interpretation of codetypes that include Scale 6 most often is paranoid schizophrenia, not Paranoid Personality Disorder. Marks et al. (1974) identify only one codetype as potentially indicative of Paranoid Personality Disorder, and even in this case the modal diagnosis was paranoid schizophrenia: 36 percent of their sample of 6-8/8-6 codetype were diagnosed as being paranoid schizophrenic and only 13 percent as paranoid personality. All other codetypes described by these authors that include Scale 6 are attributed to other personality or psychotic disorders. Another codetype that may be diagnostic of Paranoid Personality Disorder is a Spike 6 codetype, which is extremely rare. In this instance, paranoid symptomatology is usually evident (Greene, 1980). However, whether individuals with Spike 6 codetypes would present with symptoms that qualify them for a more severe paranoid diagnosis has yet to be determined.

Marks et al. (1974) also describe a $K+$ profile that may be a possible correlate of Paranoid Personality Disorder. In this codetype all of the clinical scales are below a T-score of 70, with six or more scales below a T-score of 60. The highest scale in the codetype is Scale K. This codetype may often represent a test miss, because it appears quite normal. When observed in psychiatric populations, individuals who obtain this codetype are described as "genotypically paranoid," which includes suspiciousness, fearfulness, and sensitivity. The metaphor of "genotype" suggests that the underlying personality configuration is paranoid. However, the "phenotypic" manifestations present in these authors' sample were primarily psychotic (33 percent), with three DSM-II personality disorders, cyclothymic (4.8 percent), unstable (4.8 percent), and sociopathic (4.8 percent) present in small numbers. Because so few individuals with Paranoid Personality Disorder present in psychiatric settings for treatment, actuarial data such as these may be misleading. Paranoid Personality Disorder may be a reasonable diagnostic hypothesis for a $K+$ codetype, given the guardedness and unwillingness to admit to psychiatric difficulties that are often associated with this personality style.

Tarter and Perley (1975) administered the MMPI to 12 patients who were diagnosed as paranoid on the basis of two independent psychiatric interviews. These authors defined a paranoid patient as one who shows evidence of a thought disorder in which delusions of persecution or grandiosity were most evident. An absence of hallucinations, affective impoverishment, or inappropriate behavior also were required for this diagnosis. While such a symptom profile would qualify for a Paranoid Delusional Disorder under DSM-III, these results may be similar to what would be observed in a severe Paranoid Personality Disorder. Interestingly, the mean codetype for this group was a 2-4-8. Overall, the elevation of this codetype was lower than a comparison group of 20 paranoid schizophrenics, who obtained a 2-6-8. In addition, Scales L and K were elevated in the personality disorder group relative to the comparison group of schizophrenics, which was interpreted as guardedness. In fact, these authors reported that the MMPI of the paranoid group was relatively normal, and they suggested that paranoid disorders may difficult to diagnose with the MMPI.

Millon reports a fairly respectable correlation (.49) between the MCMI Paranoid scale and Scale 6. This correlation may in part reflect Millon's conceptualization of Paranoid Personality Disorder, which is seen as severe personality pathology. The MCMI Paranoid scale also correlates with the Wiggins' (1966) Psychoticism scale (.41), suggesting that the MCMI may tap an aspect of paranoia more closely allied with schizophrenic spectrum disorders. However, the MCMI Paranoid scale is positively correlated with Wiggins' Manifest Hostility (.42) and Authority Conflict (.29) scales and negatively correlated with MMPI Scale 0 (-.42), which are not consistent with a schizophrenic disorder. These latter correlations suggest an element of resentment and anger in the Paranoid Personality Disorder, perhaps also leading to an elevation on Scale 4.

Not surprisingly, little information has been published on special scales for Paranoid Personality Disorder, and some of these scales may prove useful in this population. Since the current consensus regarding Paranoid Personality Disorder is that the essential feature is suspiciousness and mistrust, scales that measure this factor will be useful. Tryon, Stein, and Chu (Stein, 1968) have developed a cluster scale that purportedly measures the dimension of suspicion and mistrust. This scale has a low correlation with Scale 6 (.16), but has a high negative correlation with Scale K (-.73). Graham (1987) provides an interpretation of high scores on this scale. Unfortunately, from

Graham's comments the Suspicion and Mistrust cluster scale appears to capture not only the core features of paranoid personality, but psychotic symptoms such as hallucinations, mannerisms, and delusions when applied in psychiatric patients.

Some special scales have content that identify peripheral aspects of Paranoid Personality Disorder such as anger and need for social dominance. Wiggins' Authority Conflict and Manifest Hostility scales and the *Do* scale (Gough et al., 1951) may prove to be good measures of some of these aspects, but this remains to be determined.

In summary, little research using the MMPI in Paranoid Personality Disorder has been reported. Furthermore, the few available results are somewhat confusing due to a lack of agreement as to the composition of criterion groups in previous studies. DSM-III represents the first effort to explicitly define criteria for diagnosing Paranoid Personality Disorder that separate this condition from delusional psychosis. This development, coupled with the fact that individuals with paranoid characteristics in the personality disorder range rarely present for treatment, combine to ensure that few data have been collected on such individuals. Scale 6, which bears the label of Paranoia, could be misleading because it may not be elevated in Paranoid Personality Disorder. However, some special scales derived from the MMPI appear to have potential for identifying this elusive disorder in future research.

SCHIZOID PERSONALITY DISORDER

The nature of the term *schizoid* is yet another example of how the meaning of diagnostic concepts can evolve over time. At various points in its history, this term included much of what DSM-III now describes as *avoidant* or *schizotypal*. In its earliest incarnations, *schizoid character* was a term used by the German and Swiss psychiatrists of the early twentieth century to describe various peculiar features often observed in nonpsychotic relatives of schizophrenics (Siever, 1981). Among these features were social isolation, communication eccentricities, suspiciousness, and vague grandiosity. The hypothesized constitutional underpinnings of this character style were thought to be in some way related to schizophrenia; thus, the term *schizoid* as used by authors such as Kahn and

Eugen Bleuler bears a greater similarity of meaning to the DSM-III *schizotypal* concept than to its present definition. As mentioned in the section describing Avoidant Personality Disorder, Kretschmer (1926) described a variant of schizoid personality, the *anaesthetic* character style, which was seen as indifferent, cold, and emotionally empty. This latter, narrower concept is generally recognized as the forerunner of the present DSM-III conceptualization of Schizoid Personality Disorder (Millon, 1981a).

CLINICAL POPULATION

The central feature of the DSM-III definition of the Schizoid Personality Disorder involves a defect in the motivation and capacity for emotional involvement in interpersonal relationships. These deficits are manifest in the social withdrawal exhibited by such individuals. Additional diagnostic features specified by DSM-III include an indifference to praise or criticism, as well as an indifference to the feelings of others. One relatively unique aspect of this disorder is that it is hierarchically beneath another personality disorder; if the eccentricities characteristic of Schizotypal Personality Disorder are present, Schizoid Personality Disorder is not to be diagnosed.

The prevalence of Schizoid Personality Disorder is not clear, given the increasingly narrow breadth of the concept. Rosenthal et al. (1975) estimated that the "schizoid disorders" may include 7.5 percent of the general population, but their estimate included phenomena that would not be considered Schizoid Personality Disorder in DSM-III. The DSM-III itself makes no estimate of the prevalence of this disorder, only stating that it may be common in certain job contexts where social interaction is minimal. Koenigsberg et al. (1985) did not have *any* of their 2,462 patients receive this diagnosis. Morey et al. (1988) found 3.7 percent of personality-disordered inpatients receiving this diagnosis. Pfohl et al.'s (1986) structured interview study identified 0.8 percent of their nonpsychotic sample as meeting DSM-III criteria (1.5 percent of personality-disordered patients). In each case, this condition was among the least prevalent of all personality disorders, suggesting that the DSM-III definition has indeed served to narrow this concept.

DSM-III yields no information with respect to the gender distribution of schizoid personality.

Some researchers have suggested that the disorder is more commonly observed in males (Cadoret, 1978), but the extremely small samples yielded in recent investigations using DSM-III criteria make such conclusions unreliable.

MMPI SCALES

Little information is available about the MMPI performance of individuals with Schizoid Personality Disorder. A fair body of research exists that has attempted to document MMPI performance in preschizophrenic individuals and in "schizoid" relatives of schizophrenics (e.g., Golden & Meehl, 1979), but this research is more directed at the DSM-III concept of Schizotypal Personality Disorder and is discussed under that heading. The apparent rarity of this diagnosis under DSM-III guidelines makes the establishment of criterion groups exceedingly difficult. Marks et al. (1974), reporting codetype distributions on seven schizoid personalities using a pre-DSM-III conceptualization, found that the most common codetypes were the *4-6* and *8-3* patterns. Lachar (1974) and Meyer (1983) speculate that Scale *0* would be the only scale that would be expected to be consistently elevated in this population, but provide no empirical support for this observation.

Other indirect evidence may provide a better understanding of the MMPI in Schizoid Personality Disorder. Again, an examination of Millon's (1982) MCMI Schizoid scale may be informative. This MCMI scale correlates significantly with a number of MMPI scales, and as might be expected the pattern of correlations is quite similar to that observed with Avoidant and Schizotypal Personality Disorders. The highest correlation obtained with the MMPI clinical scales was Scale *0* (.64), followed by Scales *8* (.47), *2* (.39), and also Scale *F* (.37). The sole MMPI clinical scale that correlated negatively with Millon's Schizoid Scale was Scale *9* (-.17).

The MCMI Schizoid scale also correlated significantly with many MMPI research scales, and again the pattern was nearly identical to that described for the MCMI Avoidant and Schizotypal scales. The Schizoid scale was highly correlated with the Wiggins' (1966) Social Maladjustment scale (.73). In addition, Wiggins' scales of Depression (.61), Poor Morale (.57), Organic Symptoms (.49), Poor Health (.42), Psychoticism (.40), and

Phobias (.40) yielded sizable correlations, consistent with the DSM-III description of these individuals. However, the similarity of these correlations with those observed for Millon's Avoidant and Schizotypal Personality scales suggests that elevations on the scales described here are unlikely to be of much assistance in distinguishing among these three conditions.

Thus, it should be noted once more that no single codetype is likely to be specific to a particular personality disorder; it is plausible that the diagnostician may need to examine subscales or research scales to make some of the diagnostic distinctions required for DSM-III definitions of these conditions.

SCHIZOTYPAL PERSONALITY DISORDER

Schizotypal Personality Disorder is a new category in DSM-III, but the concept it encompasses has a lengthy history. As early as the turn of the twentieth century, it was recognized that certain peculiarities characterized the behavior of nonpsychotic relatives of schizophrenic patients (Siever, 1981). The actual term *schizotype* was coined by Rado (1960) as a contraction of *schizophrenic phenotype*. The current meanings of the term can be derived from writings such as Zilboorg (1941), Rapaport, Gill, and Schafer (1946), and Meehl (1962). Zilboorg described "ambulatory schizophrenia," which is essentially an early stage of schizophrenia in which flagrant symptoms of psychosis were not obvious, but some dysfunctional behavior is observed. Rapaport et al. (1946) also described a prepsychotic form of schizophrenia in their psychodiagnostic studies, which they termed "preschizophrenic." Meehl (1962) speculated that an inherited defect, which he called "schizotaxia," evolved into the "schizotype" personality. In the DSM-II, many of these individuals would have been diagnosed as "schizophrenia, latent type," as the manual considered this condition to be a symptomatic manifestation rather than a personality style.

Within the DSM-III Axis II nomenclature, there are two major points of potential conceptual confusion. The first is the distinction between Schizoid and Schizotypal Personality Disorders. In the past, clinicians have often used the term *schizoid* to refer to a personality disorder thought to be related to schizophrenic disorders. In DSM-III, however, Schizoid Personality Disorder denotes a constellation of interpersonal behavior characterized by poor motivation and capacity for emotional involvement (Spitzer, Williams, & Skodol, 1980). Psychotic symptoms and less marked symptoms such as eccentric behavior or peculiar speech patterns are cause for exclusion from the category of Schizoid Personality Disorder. Such symptoms are now classified as elements of Schizotypal Personality Disorder.

The second point of potential confusion is between Schizotypal Personality Disorder and Borderline Personality Disorder in DSM-III. This potential confusion stems from the fact that the Schizotypal Personality Disorder was derived from work on family studies of schizophrenia. This work is exemplified by Kety, Rosenthal, Wender, and colleagues (Kety et al., 1971; Rosenthal et al., 1971) who found that the first-degree relatives of schizophrenics often showed behavioral abnormalities that were not of sufficient magnitude to constitute schizophrenia. These individuals were called "borderline schizophrenics" to denote their position on the border of a schizophrenic disorder. The second main usage of the term *borderline*, which has been discussed in detail in a previous section, refers to enduring personality features of affective and behavioral instability. Two categories were created in DSM-III based on the work of Spitzer et al. (1979), who concluded on the basis of their research that Borderline and Schizotypal Personality Disorders represented two separate dimensions of the borderline construct. Unfortunately, although the two may be relatively independent conceptually, they occur simultaneously in a fair number of patients, complicating diagnostic research.

CLINICAL FEATURES

Schizotypal Personality Disorder is characterized by unusual patterns of thought, perception, speech, and behavior that are not of sufficient magnitude to warrant a diagnosis of schizophrenia. These features include magical thinking, ideas of reference, recurrent illusions, odd speech, and suspiciousness. In addition, Schizotypal shares with Avoidant and Schizoid Personality Disorders the criteria of social isolation and undue social anxiety or hypersensitivity. Frequently associated features

include mood disturbance, concomitant Borderline Personality Disorder, and transient psychotic symptoms. Schizotypal Personality Disorder is thought to be more prevalent in families with a history of chronic schizophrenia (American Psychiatric Association, 1980).

Because this is a new diagnostic category, studies reporting base rates of this disorder are rare. Rosenthal et al. (1975) estimated that 7.5 percent of the general population may have disorders within the "schizophrenia spectrum"; the largest part of these individuals would be considered Schizotypal Personality Disorder under the DSM-III nomenclature. Koenigsberg et al. (1985) reported that 5.4 percent of patients receiving an Axis II diagnosis in their sample had Schizotypal Personality Disorder as a primary diagnosis. These patients represented 1.9 percent of the total sample of patients, both with and without Axis II diagnoses. Pfohl et al. (1986) reported that 17.9 percent of their sample with personality disorder diagnoses met criteria for Schizotypal Personality Disorder, although nearly all of these patients had an additional Axis II diagnosis. In their study, the greatest overlap was with Borderline and Avoidant Personality Disorders. Morey et al. (1988) found that 2.8 percent of their personality-disordered sample received a schizotypal diagnosis.

MMPI SCALES

Given the recent introduction of the schizotypal concept, it is necessary to look for studies using other descriptors such as "latent schizophrenia" (a related concept used in DSM-II) to identify the criterion group. Gilberstadt and Duker (1965) provide decision rules for identifying a *2-7-8* profile that has Scales *2*, *7*, and *8* above a *T*-score of 70, Scale *6* less than a *T*-score of 80, and Scale *9* less than a *T*-score of 70. The most descriptive diagnosis of this codetype is said to be pseudoneurotic or chronic undifferentiated schizophrenia. Lachar (1974) also identifies the *2-7-8* profile as probable pseudoneurotic schizophrenia or severe obsessive-compulsive reaction. Kelley and King (1979) have reported that male college students at a university mental health center with a *2-7-8* profile received a diagnosis of latent schizophrenia. Females with the same codetype were more likely to be diagnosed neurotic.

Greene (1980) provides interpretive information on the *2-7-8* codetype that is consistent with

Schizotypal Personality Disorder. Individuals with this codetype present with multiple neurotic symptoms such as depression and anxiety, which may mask an underlying thought disorder. Difficulty in concentration and thinking are common, and suicidal ruminations are fairly frequently observed. Social withdrawal and introversion are often present in individuals with this codetype, which may exacerbate obsessive and ruminative behaviors.

Unfortunately, the 2-7-8 codetype is frequent in psychiatric populations (Lachar, 1974) and may not be particularly specific to Schizotypal Personality Disorder. For example, Marks et al. (1974) report that 58 percent of their sample that had this codetype were diagnosed schizophrenic, 33 percent were diagnosed as having anxiety disorder, and only 4 percent were diagnosed as having schizoid personality disorder. The latter diagnosis in DSM-II identifies a similar criterion group to Schizotypal Personality Disorder in DSM-III.

Fujioka and Chapman (1984) examined a group of college students with 2-7-8 codetypes for signs of psychotic-like experiences and schizotypy. The 2-7-8 codetype has been used to identify individuals who are at risk for schizophrenia in a number of studies. The rarity of this codetype in nonpsychiatric populations is evident in this study: of 2,584 undergraduates, only 3.9 percent of the sample had this codetype. They then administered the Schedule for Affective Disorders and Schizophrenia-Lifetime Version (SADS-L: Endicott & Spitzer, 1978). Both symptoms of thought disorder such as auditory and visual hallucinations and more subtle schizotypal experiences such as derealization, depersonalization, out-of-body experiences, and loss of emotions were tapped by the interview procedure. In a comparison with normal college students, both males and females with 2-7-8 codetypes scored significantly higher on psychotic symptoms, but not on schizotypal ex-

periences. These latter individuals also had a significantly higher incidence of previous major or minor depressive episodes.

Resnick et al. (1983) have reported MMPI data on a sample of patients with Borderline and Schizotypal Personality Disorders. In their sample, 10 of their 11 Borderline patients also met the criteria for Schizotypal Personality Disorder. Mean codetypes reported by these authors appear in Table 5–5.

A comparison between these two mean codetypes is important diagnostically because of the strong overlap between these two Axis II disorders. The "pure" Schizotypal codetype is Spike 2 while that of the Borderline/Schizotypal group is 4-8-2. In addition, the overall profile elevation for the pure Schizotypal group was lower, with only one Scale (2) elevated above a T-score of 70. The mean schizotypal personality codetype is not as distinctive as that of the borderline group; many psychiatric patients in an inpatient setting might obtain such a codetype. As a result, Resnick et al. were more optimistic about the MMPI as a screening device for Borderline Personality than for Schizotypal Personality Disorder.

Various scales have been suggested as potential markers for schizotypy. Peterson (1954) noted that 33 outpatients who were later diagnosed as having schizophrenia obtained a mean codetype of 8-7-2, with Scale 8 being particularly elevated. Mosher, Pollin, and Stabenau (1971) obtained MMPIs on discordant identical twins of a schizophrenic cohort and found that Barron's Es was significantly lower in these individuals than for a matched control group. Haier, Rosenthal, and Wender (1978) administered the MMPI to the adopted-away offspring of schizophrenic parents. The mean codetype for both males and females was a 3-2-1, but the profile shape was not significantly different from matched controls. The MMPI research on the detection of schizotypy has been reviewed by Grove (1982). The conclusion drawn by Grove was that the standard MMPI scales are

TABLE 5–5. FREQUENCY OF ELEVATED MMPI CLINICAL SCALES IN SCHIZOTYPAL PERSONALITY DISORDERS

Authors	N	Age	Clinical Scales (≥ 70 T-points)
Resnick et al. (1983) [Schizotypal Personality Disorders]	9	–	Spike 2
Resnick et al. (1983) [Schizotypal and Borderline Personality Disorders]	10	–	4-8-2-7-6

not very sensitive to this construct. Thus, an alternative approach that may have more promise is to construct special scales from MMPI items that are more specific to Schizotypal Personality Disorder.

Along these lines, Golden and Meehl (1979) designed a scale for schizotypy that consists of only seven MMPI items. The derivation of this scale was based on Meehl's (1973) maximum covariance model for the identification of "loose genetic syndromes." Meehl's model contains many assumptions that differ substantially from classical test theory; his approach is analogous to the latent-trait model, which has recently become popular in psychometric theory (Lord & Novick, 1968). Golden and Meehl (1979) demonstrated that the scale was effective in identifying members of what Meehl terms the schizoid-taxon, which is a conceptually similar construct to the DSM-III Schizotypal Personality Disorder. Using these seven items these authors then backtracked to identify an MMPI profile of the criterion group. The codetype described by these authors was an 8-7-2.

Unfortunately, the Golden and Meehl (1979) scale has not held up well in validation studies. Both Miller, Streiner, and Kahgee (1982) and Nichols and Jones (1985) report that the Golden and Meehl items do not perform adequately. Miller et al. (1982) found that the items underclassified the criterion group and overclassified a comparison group of depressives. Nichols and Jones (1985) reported findings consistent with those described by Miller and colleagues. Nichols and Jones suggested that future efforts at scale building should use carefully selected criterion groups, the most optimal being known relatives of schizophrenics.

A second strategy that has not been investigated in this diagnostic group is the performance of various measures of psychoticism derived from the MMPI. For example, Wiggins' (1966) Psychoticism Scale, the Tyron, Stein, and Chu (Stein, 1968) cluster scale of Autism and Disruptive Thought vs. Absence of Such Disturbance, and the Goldberg Index (Goldberg, 1969) may prove to be useful in diagnosis of Schizotypal Personality Disorder.

The Schizotypal-Schizoid Scale of the MCMI identifies a group of patients with both behavioral eccentricities and social withdrawal. Millon (1982) reports high correlations between the MCMI Schizotypal-Schizoid scale and Wiggins'

(1966) Poor Morale (.60), Social Maladjustment (.72), Depression (.64), and Psychoticism (.42) scales. Consistent with other reports linking the 2-7-8 codetype with this diagnostic group, the largest correlations between the MCMI and MMPI scales are 2 (.56), 7 (.50), 8 (.65), and 0 (.66).

Since Schizotypal Personality Disorder is such a new addition to the nomenclature, research on the use of the MMPI with this diagnostic group is sparse. However, MMPI studies on the relatives of schizophrenics as well as those that use conceptually related criterion groups such as pseudoneurotic schizophrenia yield some additional information. The 2-7-8 codetype has been linked to Schizotypal Personality Disorder, but the clinician must be careful not to overgeneralize this finding because this codetype is common in psychiatric populations and is obtained from a wide variety of diagnostic groups. Special scales that measure aspects of psychoticism may eventually prove to be more useful in the diagnosis of this disorder.

MMPI SCALES FOR DSM-III PERSONALITY DISORDERS

Recently, a set of MMPI scales were derived that were specifically designed to assist in the assessment of the DSM-III personality disorders (Morey et al., 1985). Given the recency of their introduction, the validation evidence on these scales is preliminary. Nonetheless, these scales have the advantage of being directly focused on this particular diagnostic area, and as such the scales have the potential to refine the use of the MMPI with the personality disorders. The following sections describe the derivation, structure, and validity of these scales.

SCALE DERIVATION

The strategy used to derive the Personality Disorder Scales was analogous to that utilized by Wiggins (1966) in the derivation of the content scales. In this case, however, items were selected whose content represented the DSM-III criteria for the particular personality disorders. Thus, unlike most of the MMPI clinical scales, these scales were not derived empirically; no criterion groups were utilized in the derivation of the scales.

The actual derivation of the Personality Disorder scales proceeded in two stages. The first stage involved a rational selection of MMPI items that reflected the DSM-III criteria, while the second stage was an iterative item-analytic refinement of the scales obtained following the first stage. For the initial stage, four experienced clinicians examined each of the 550 MMPI items to determine if the item reflected the criteria given in DSM-III for any of the 11 personality disorders. For example, all four clinicians agreed that item 170, "What others think of me does not bother me," reflected the criteria for Avoidant Personality Disorder if answered false. Given the extent of overlap in DSM-III criteria for the different personality disorders (Widiger, Sanderson, & Warner, 1986), the clinicians were allowed to designate items as reflecting more than one personality disorder. On the basis of these assignments, preliminary scales (1 for each of the 11 DSM-III personality disorders) were developed by including those items on which at least two of the four clinicians agreed reflected the DSM-III criteria.

The second stage was designed to refine these preliminary scales using item analysis. Here, items were examined to determine if they could discriminate successfully between high scorers and low scorers on the scale in which the item was included. For example, items on the Paranoid Scale were tested to see if high scorers on the Paranoid Scale tended to answer these items differently than did low scorers on this scale. Each item that failed to discriminate in this manner was then dropped from the scale, and the analyses were repeated in an iterative fashion until item composition of the scales was stable. Overall, relatively few items (median, 3) were dropped from the scales on the basis of these analyses. The item length of the final versions of the complete Personality Disorder Scales were as follows: Histrionic (*HST*), 20 items; Narcissistic (*NAR*), 31 items; Borderline (*BDL*), 22 items; Antisocial (*ANT*), 25 items; Dependent (*DEP*), 20 items; Compulsive (*CPS*), 15 items; Passive-Aggressive (*PAG*), 14 items; Paranoid (*PAR*), 22 items; Schizotypal (*STY*), 36 items; Avoidant (*AVD*), 38 items; and Schizoid (*SZD*), 22 items.

As might be expected on the basis of the criterion overlap described above, many items contained in the final versions of the scales were common to more than one scale. Although this overlap is consistent with the DSM-III definitions of the personality disorders, it can be problematic in studies examining relationships between scales

(Welsh, 1952). To address this problem, a set of scales without item overlap also was created by assigning overlapping items to the one scale with which these items demonstrated the maximum biserial correlation. As a result, the complete set and the nonoverlapping set of scales contained the same total number of items (164), but in the latter set each item was assigned to only one personality disorder scale. Morey et al. reported that the correspondence between the complete and the nonoverlapping versions of scales was quite high (median correlation, .95).

INTERNAL SCALE PROPERTIES

Morey et al. (1985) reported internal consistency estimates for the both the complete and nonoverlapping versions of their Personality Disorder Scales. These KR-20 values ranged from .675 for *CPS* to .859 for *AVD* for the complete scales (median internal consistency, .761), and from .619 for *HST* to .791 for *STY* for the nonoverlapping scales (median, .684). These internal consistency estimates are fairly high, in some cases higher than comparable estimates that have been derived for the DSM-III criteria themselves (Morey, 1985). However, given the iterative item-analysis procedure described above it is not surprising to find satisfactory internal consistency, as inconsistent items were by definition removed from the final versions of the Scales.

Some representative normative values for performance on these Personality Disorder scales are presented in Tables 5–6 and 5–7. Means and standard deviations are presented for both complete and nonoverlapping versions of the Scales, as collected on three different samples. The first sample, "General Psychiatric," consisted of 475 patients selected from a larger sample collected by Hedlund, Sletten, Evenson, Altman, and Cho (1977). This sample included a mixture of inpatients and outpatients who had received a wide variety of DSM-II diagnoses. This group of patients served as the derivation sample for scale development. The second sample, "Personality Disorders," was a group of 108 inpatients who had received any DSM-III personality diagnosis and was gathered by Morey et al. (1988), as described earlier in this chapter. The third sample, "Mayo Clinic Normals," consisted of 640 normal individuals (335 men, 305 women) utilized in the Mayo Clinic renorming study described by Colligan, Osborne,

TABLE 5–6.   NORMATIVE PERFORMANCE ON COMPLETE PERSONALITY DISORDER SCALES

	Scale										
Sample	**HST**	**NAR**	**BDL**	**ANT**	**DEP**	**CPS**	**PAG**	**PAR**	**STY**	**AVD**	**SZD**
General psychiatric											
Total sample, n = 475											
Scale mean	11.3	15.1	9.7	9.2	8.0	8.6	6.2	8.6	14.1	17.6	7.6
Standard deviation	3.8	5.0	3.9	4.6	3.6	3.0	3.0	4.4	6.3	7.4	3.7
Males, n = 266											
Scale mean	—	15.8	—	10.7	—	—	—	—	—	—	8.0
Standard deviation	—	4.8	—	4.4	—	—	—	—	—	—	3.8
Females, n = 209											
Scale mean	—	14.1	—	7.2	—	—	—	—	—	—	7.2
Standard deviation	—	5.1	—	4.0	—	—	—	—	—	—	3.5
Personality disorder											
Total sample, n = 108											
Scale mean	10.0	12.8	12.6	10.3	10.9	9.8	7.8	9.1	16.9	23.1	9.0
Standard deviation	3.7	4.6	3.7	4.2	4.0	2.3	2.6	3.6	6.3	7.9	4.1
Mayo Clinic normals											
Total sample, n = 640											
Scale mean	11.8	15.6	7.9	6.4	6.5	7.6	4.8	5.1	9.0	13.9	6.6
Standard deviation	3.4	4.0	3.5	3.5	3.3	2.8	2.7	2.9	5.0	7.8	3.4
Males, n = 305											
Scale mean	—	16.2	—	7.5	5.8	—	5.3	—	—	13.2	7.2
Standard deviation	—	3.9	—	4.0	3.1	—	2.8	—	—	7.1	3.5
Females, n = 335											
Scale mean	—	15.0	—	5.4	7.2	—	4.3	—	—	14.4	6.1
Standard deviation	—	4.1	—	3.1	3.5	—	2.6	—	—	7.5	3.4

TABLE 5–7.   NORMATIVE PERFORMANCE ON NON-OVERLAPPING PERSONALITY DISORDER SCALES

	Scale										
Sample	**HST**	**NAR**	**BDL**	**ANT**	**DEP**	**CPS**	**PAG**	**PAR**	**STY**	**AVD**	**SZD**
General psychiatric											
Total sample, n = 475											
Scale mean	7.2	6.8	7.0	7.3	6.6	8.0	6.2	5.5	6.0	6.6	4.5
Standard deviation	2.6	3.0	3.6	3.9	2.9	2.6	3.0	3.1	3.2	2.8	2.5
Males, n = 266											
Scale mean	—	—	—	8.6	—	—	—	—	—	—	4.8
Standard deviation	—	—	—	3.6	—	—	—	—	—	—	2.7
Females, n = 209											
Scale mean	—	—	—	4.9	—	—	—	—	—	—	3.9
Standard deviation	—	—	—	3.1	—	—	—	—	—	—	2.1
Personality disorder											
Total sample, n = 108											
Scale mean	6.9	5.3	10.1	8.1	8.6	8.7	7.8	5.4	6.4	8.9	5.5
Standard deviation	2.3	2.6	3.0	3.5	3.2	2.0	2.6	2.6	3.1	2.9	2.7
Mayo Clinic normals											
Total sample, n = 640											
Scale mean	7.3	6.0	5.7	4.7	5.3	6.8	4.8	2.6	2.8	5.3	3.5
Standard deviation	2.3	2.3	2.8	3.0	2.8	2.4	2.7	1.9	2.0	2.9	2.3
Males, n = 305											
Scale mean	—	6.3	5.2	5.6	4.7	—	5.3	—	—	5.0	3.8
Standard deviation	—	2.4	2.9	3.3	2.7	—	2.8	—	—	2.8	2.4
Females, n = 335											
Scale mean	—	5.7	6.0	3.9	5.8	—	4.3	—	—	5.7	3.3
Standard deviation	—	2.3	2.8	2.6	3.0	—	2.6	—	—	2.9	2.3

Swenson, and Offord (1983). This latter sample can be used as an estimate of scale characteristics in the normal population, and T-scores reported in subsequent sections are standardized with reference to this group. In two of the samples, separate norms are presented for males and females if a statistically significant difference between genders was found.

VALIDATION STUDIES

There are a number of steps involved in establishing the verisimilitude of these Personality Disorder scales with respect to the DSM-III diagnoses from which they were derived. Basically, three strategies have been followed thus far. First, the relationship between these Scales and the traditional MMPI scales has been examined, as certain associations and trends would be expected from the results described in preceding sections. Second, the pattern of interrelationships between the Personality Disorder scales has been examined to see if it conforms to the hypothetical structure of personality disorders proposed by the DSM-III authors. Finally, the investigation of the relationship between these scales and other diagnostic indicators for personality disorder has begun. The following sections briefly summarize the research conducted in these three areas.

MMPI CLINICAL SCALE COMPARISONS

Morey et al. (1985) reported the correlations between their Personality Disorder scales and the standard clinical scales of the MMPI. Many of these correlations were of the direction and magnitude that would be expected, on the basis of the research described above as well as the conceptual basis from which the Personality Disorder scales were derived.

The HST scale was related to gregariousness (correlation with Scale 0: -.73), denial of dysphoria (2: -.47), and a generally energetic presentation (9: .30). Interestingly, this scale was inversely related to the MMPI Hysteria scale (Scale 3: -.20); Millon obtained the same inverse relationship between Scale 3 and the MCMI Histrionic Personality scale. There are two likely reasons for this finding. First, as discussed in a previous section, the DSM-III concept of Histrionic Personality is not synony-

mous with the older concept of Hysteria, as the latter included somatic features that were not a part of the DSM-III concept. A second reason may involve the nature of the samples used by Morey et al. (1985) and Millon (1982); each was a sample composed primarily of psychiatric inpatients. In such samples, *relative* elevations on HST would be an indicator of relative mental health, since they would indicate adequate social interaction and lack of depression; it is unlikely that Histrionic Personality Disorder in isolation would lead to hospitalization. The relationship between MMPI Scale 3 and HST might well be different if tested in the general population.

The pattern of intercorrelations with the NAR scale were fairly similar to those described with HST above, as the two scales themselves were highly correlated. Although not as highly correlated with a social orientation as HST (0: -.62), NAR involves an even greater denial of intrapsychic discomfort. Again, relative elevations on NAR in an inpatient setting could be considered an indication of better adjustment, since this concept involves a relatively positive self-concept.

The BDL scale seems to accurately portray the borderline psychotic experience (8: .53; 7: .58; 6: .37) as well as the anger and "acting out" behavior (4: .39; 9: .57) outlined in the DSM-III definition of this disorder. This pattern of correlations is consistent also with the frequently noted scale elevations described in the earlier section on Borderline Personality Disorder.

As might be expected, the ANT scale was highly associated with both Scales 4 (.52) and 9 (.57). In addition, ANT was significantly correlated with 8 (.48). Again, this pattern is consistent with the results obtained from MMPI studies of antisocial personality, as 4-9 and 4-8 profiles are identified frequently in this population as noted earlier.

The most prominent relationships observed with the DEP scale were anxiety (7: .60) and discomfort in social situations (0: .54). Also noteworthy were feelings of dysphoria (2: .47) and alienation (8: .44). The CPS scale also was most strongly related to Scale 7, although CPS scores were probably more related to the obsessionality items from Scale 7.

Scale PAG, which had a similar pattern of relationships to DEP and CPS, tended to have stronger relationships with many scales, suggesting that PAG may reflect a generally more severe level of pathology. In addition, the greater relationship between PAG and 4 (.38) and 6 (.45) gives evidence for the suppressed anger and resentment thought to characterize passive-aggressive individuals.

The *PAR* scale, as might be expected, was related to the "psychotic" MMPI scales (*6*: .68; *7*: .62; *8*: .75). Also, to a lesser extent, relationships to character-disordered organization were noted (*4*: .48; *9*: .66).

Character pathology was less represented in the *STY* scale; rather, prominent correlations were observed between *STY* and Scales *8* (.80), *7* (.75), *0* (.70), and *6* (.69). This pattern of eccentricity, anxiety, social withdrawal, and suspiciousness closely approximates the DSM-III description of the schizotypal individual.

The *AVD* scale was highly associated with discomfort in social situations (*0*: .89), anxiety (*7*: .71), and depression (*2*: .63). This pattern closely corresponds to the *2-7-0* codetype thought to characterize Avoidant Personality Disorder.

The *SZD* scale demonstrated a similar pattern of correlations, although the relationship with Scale *7* (.30) was not as pronounced. This latter finding may reflect the relative disinterest and hence lack of anxiety in social interaction, which, according to DSM-III, is the primary difference between schizoid and avoidant personalities.

These results demonstrate that the pattern of correlations between the Personality Disorder scales and the MMPI clinical scales are consistent with expectations formed from previous research using the MMPI with personality disorders. However, this demonstration is clearly only a first step in establishing the construct validity of the scales.

SCALE CORRELATIONAL STRUCTURE

Another step in evaluating the MMPI Personality Disorder scales involves an examination of the relationships between the scales themselves. According to DSM-III, the 11 personality disorders can be grouped into three conceptual clusters. One cluster (including schizoid, paranoid, and schizotypal) involves "odd" or "eccentric" personalities; a second (histrionic, narcissistic, antisocial, borderline) includes "dramatic" or "erratic" personalities; and the third (dependent, passive-aggressive, compulsive, avoidant) consist of "anxious" or "fearful" personalities. If this conceptual grouping is accurate, then the personality disorder scale intercorrelations should reflect this structure, and a factor analysis of this matrix should yield results comparable with the three groups.

Morey et al. (1985) reported the results of a factor analysis that roughly corresponded to this conceptual grouping. This factor analysis, which utilized a varimax rotation, yielded a large factor that ordered these variables in a manner consistent with the disorder groups. The ordering of the Personality Disorder scales in Tables 5–6 and 5–7 reflect the results obtained from that analysis, with the erratic personalities found on the left side of the tables and the odd disorders on the right. From that ordering, one can see that the only "misplaced" scale is *AVD*, which the factor analysis placed with the odd disorders as opposed to the anxious, as was hypothesized in DSM-III.

A more specific examination of the correspondence between these scales and the DSM-III conceptual grouping was reported by Morey (1986). Morey used a data analysis technique proposed by Skinner (1978), whereby a component weighting matrix derived from a principal components analysis was transformed, using a procrustes procedure, with a hypothesis matrix derived from the DSM-III. This hypothesis matrix had three factors, representing the odd, erratic, and anxious disorder groupings. The resulting factor solution was quite consistent with the DSM-III grouping: Tucker coefficients of congruence were .833 for the odd factor, .760 for the erratic factor, and .809 for the anxious factor. In each case, the Tucker coefficients were higher for the MMPI Personality Disorder scales than for comparable figures calculated for the MCMI, using the correlation matrix reported by Millon (1982). These results suggest that the pattern of relationships among the MMPI Personality Disorder scales are similar to the patterns among the DSM-III disorders, providing further evidence of the verisimilitude of the scales.

CRITERION VALIDATION STUDIES

Ultimately, the most important question to be answered regarding the Personality Disorder scales is whether these scales accurately identify individuals with DSM-III personality disorders. This section will examine two studies that sought to investigate this hypothesis.

The first study was performed by Morey et al. (1988), which has been mentioned earlier. These investigators conducted an exhaustive search for subjects at two university inpatient psychiatric units who had received (1) a DSM-III personality disorder clinical diagnosis, and (2) a complete and valid MMPI. Subjects with organic or schizophrenic disorders were excluded from this sample, resulting in 108 subjects. The largest diagnostic group consisted of Borderlines (27 percent), followed by Dependent (26 percent), Histrionic (17 percent), Passive-Aggressive (15 percent), and Antisocial (13 percent). No other diagnosis represented over 10 percent of the sample.

The specific hypothesis investigated in the Morey et al. (1988) study was that patients receiving a clinical diagnosis of a particular personality disorder should score higher on the corresponding scale than individuals not receiving the diagnosis. For this comparison, three sample groups were examined: those receiving a criterion personality disorder (CPD) diagnosis, i.e., the diagnosis in question; those receiving some other personality disorder diagnosis (OPD); and a normal control group (NC), which was the Mayo Clinic sample described earlier. For the overall analyses, the results were collapsed across the different diagnostic categories because of the rarity of patients in some of the personality disorder categories. Thus, the composition of the CPD group varied; if the criterion diagnosis in question was Borderline Personality Disorder, then a patient diagnosed as Borderline would be in the CPD group for Borderline Personality Disorder, but in the OPD group for Avoidant Personality Disorder.

The results of their analysis supported this hypothesis. If a patient received a particular personality disorder diagnosis (i.e., was a *CPD* patient), the patient (on average) had a *T*-score of 65.4 on the corresponding Personality Disorder scale. If the patient had some other personality disorder diagnosis (i.e., was an *OPD* patient), the average *T*-score was 57.7. By definition, the normal group obtained a mean of 50 on the Personality Disorder scales. All differences between these three *T*-scores were statistically significant. Thus, at a global level the scales could differentiate those receiving a particular diagnosis from those who did not.

A more specific examination of the performance of each scale was difficult, as the base rate of many of the individual diagnoses was quite low. In general, if the sample size in the criterion group was large enough to perform a statistical comparison (i.e., more than 14 patients), the criterion group scored significantly higher than either the OPD or NC groups. This relationship was true for the *BDL*, *ANT*, and *DEP* scales. The exceptions to this trend were noted on *HST*, in which NC and CPD were not significantly different; and *PAG*, where the difference between CPD and OPD was not significant. In the latter case, this difference just missed reaching significance. The results for *HST* may reaffirm the hypothesis, advanced earlier, that moderate elevations on this scale in an inpatient sample may be an indicator of relative health, rather than of Histrionic Personality Disorder.

The second set of studies in this area was performed by Dubro, Wetzler, and Kahn (in press; 1987). These authors examined the diagnostic accuracy of three different self-report instruments: the MMPI Personality Disorder scales, the MCMI scales, and the Personality Diagnostic Questionnaire (PDQ: Hyler, Reider, Spitzer, & Williams, 1983), a 150-item questionnaire designed to specifically tap DSM-III criteria. Dubro et al. (in press) sought to determine the convergence between diagnoses assigned by these instruments and criterion diagnoses, as determined through the administration of the Structured Interview for DSM-III Personality Disorder (SIDP: Stangl et al., 1985). Thus, this study improved on the Morey et al. (1988) study in that the criterion diagnoses were assigned in a more reliable fashion.

Dubro et al. (in press; 1987) examined two patient samples. One sample (n = 37) consisted of hospitalized psychiatric patients, the other (utilized as a control) involved nonpsychiatric patients from various medical services (n = 20). A total of 62 percent of the psychiatric patients met criteria for one or more DSM-III personality disorders as determined by the SIDP; only 5 percent of the medical patients could be diagnosed as such.

Dubro et al. separated their sample into three groups: those meeting DSM-III criteria for one or more personality disorders (PD group, n = 23); those having personality disorder traits but not meeting criteria for any disorder (PD traits, n = 13); and nondisordered controls (No PD, n = 12). As a first test, these authors sought to determine if the different instruments could differentiate between these three broad patient groups. For the MMPI Personality Disorder scales, significant differences were obtained on all scales except *HST* and *SZD*; thus, a total of 9 of 11 scales yielded significant differences. These figures were comparable or superior to those obtained with the MCMI (7 of 11) and the PDQ (9 of 11), each of which were developed in the years since the introduction of the DSM-III. These results are consistent with those of Morey et al. (1988) in suggesting that at a global level, the MMPI Personality Disorder scales are useful in identifying pathologic personality conditions.

The Dubro et al. (in press) study also sought to investigate the accuracy of personality disorder diagnosis at a more specific level. First, they sought to determine the accuracy of the assessment techniques in dividing patients into the three broad clusters of DSM-III personality disorders (odd, erratic, and anxious, as discussed earlier). Each of the three instruments performed this task well, with resulting assignments being fairly specific and sensitive. When it came to assigning specific diagnoses in four particular personality categories, however, none of the instruments performed very well. Also, it seemed that the MMPI Personality Disorder scales did not do as well as the other two instruments, with low sensitivity/high specificity being the typical result. In other words, the scales rarely misidentified individuals as having a personality disorder when they did not (high specificity), but in several cases the scales failed to identify patients who did have a disorder (low sensitivity). In a further investigation of these data, Dubro et al. (1987) found that including elevations on Scale F (T-score ≥ 80) to reflect the DSM-III criterion of subjective distress increased the performance of the MMPI Personality Disorder scales to levels comparable with those obtained with the MCMI and PDQ.

As a final examination of the convergence of these three instruments, Dubro et al. (1987) calculated the correlations between the MMPI Personality Disorder scales and the corresponding MCMI and PDQ scales. In general, the association between the MMPI and PDQ scales was fairly high; the median correlation between corresponding scales was .64, ranging from .05 for Narcissistic to .81 for Dependent. However, correlations with the MCMI were appreciably lower, with the median correlation between corresponding scales being .37, ranging from -.35 for Compulsive to .51 for Avoidant Personality. Given that both the MMPI and PDQ scale were specifically derived to measure the DSM-III constructs and the MCMI was not, it is understandable why

there would be greater correspondence between the two former instruments.

However, there are certain limitations to the Durbo et al. study that must be considered in interpreting their results. First, the MMPI Personality Disorder scale cutoff scores in this study were developed from their medical control sample, and such cutoff scores may not be optimal in other settings. In addition, the small number of patients in these four specific criterion diagnostic groups (between 8 and 10) severely limit the generalizability of the findings. As such, this evidence must be regarded as preliminary and future research with larger criterion groups is essential.

In conclusion, the preliminary validation evidence for the MMPI Personality Disorder scales developed by Morey et al. (1985) is promising. However, it is apparent that much research remains to be done in investigating the utility of these scales; in particular, cutoff points for making categorical decisions for specific diagnoses need to be established. However, the scales certainly seem to be useful as a screening measure for the exploration of possible DSM-III personality disorder conditions.

A SAMPLE CASE HISTORY

To obtain a better idea of the applicability of the data yielded by the Personality Disorder scales, a particular profile configuration will be examined and the case history and pertinent data also will be reviewed. The following information details an actual case, although certain points have been changed to protect the anonymity of the patient.

The patient was a 20-year-old woman who was hospitalized following a suicide attempt in which she consumed approximately 30 aspirin. This episode occurred following a period of approximately 3 or 4 months in which she felt increasingly anxious, pressured, and ineffective. The immediate precipitant to the suicidal gesture seemed to involve a period of approximately 1 month during which her judgment deteriorated markedly. During this time she went on several spending sprees, which severely depleted the financial resources of the family. She described these sprees as almost dissociative in nature; it was as if she "blacked out" and spent a great deal of money without remembering it. Not surprisingly, this behavior led to serious arguments with her husband of 2 years. She reported a great deal of resentment toward her husband for his inability to understand her problems, although she was very afraid that her recent behavior might cause him to leave her. The diagnostic impression of the clinician involved a Major Depressive Episode with an accompanying Dependent Personality Disorder.

With respect to the onset of her difficulties, she reported feeling increasingly pressured, both at work and at home. She worked in a clerical position that involved both some bookkeeping duties as well as contact with the public, and over the past few months her workload had apparently increased significantly. At home, she reported that the birth of her first child 1 year previously had added to the demands placed on her. Her functioning during adolescence had apparently been good. She completed high school near the top of her class and had done well in technical training classes taken at a local junior college. She had married shortly out of high school and

had moved from her parents' home directly into an apartment that she and her husband rented following their marriage.

At the time of testing, her performance on the WAIS-R placed her in the average to low-average range of intellectual functioning with little intertest scatter. From cognitive screening, there were no data to suggest that her "blackout" experiences might have had a neuropsychological basis. Projective testing was performed, including the Rorschach, TAT, and a sentence completion blank. The results from these tests indicated a fair amount of anxiety and distress, issues of anger and hostility, morbid preoccupations, and impaired judgment and reality testing; however, no signs of formal thought disorder were observed.

The patient received both an MMPI and an MCMI, allowing a chance to compare the results of these different approaches with personality disorder assessment. The profile obtained from the MMPI clinical and research scales is presented in Figure 5–1, while the MCMI profile is seen in Figure 5–2.

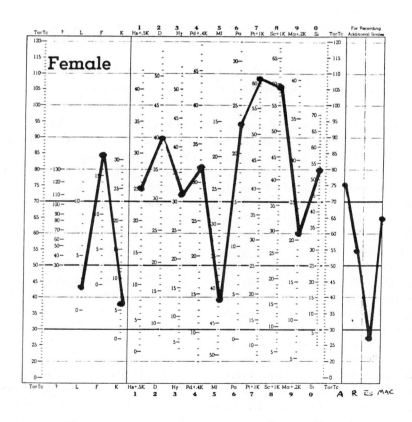

FIGURE 5–1. MMPI profile for a 20-year-old female inpatient.

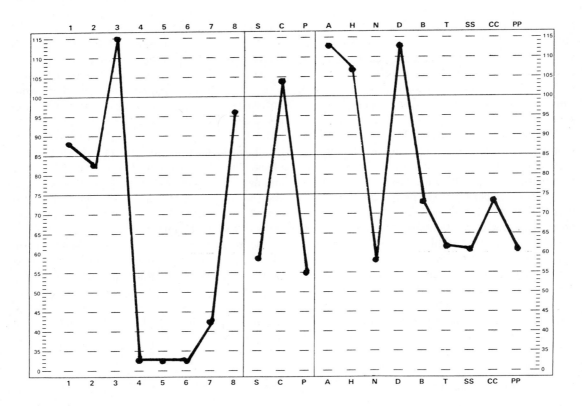

FIGURE 5–2. MCMI profile for a 20-year-old female inpatient.

Perhaps the most striking elements resulting from an initial perusal of the MMPI involve the high overall elevation of the profile and the high F–K index. As described in a previous section, this is a finding frequently observed with Borderline Personality Disorder. The configuration itself also has many of the elevations consistently noted in this diagnostic group, most notably Scales *4* and *6*. MMPI cookbooks such as Gilberstadt and Duker (1965) or Lachar (1974), which describe the *7-8* codetype, generally raise the possibility of a severe obsessive-compulsive reaction, although schizoid or borderline personality as well as schizophrenia are diagnostic groups in whom this profile pattern is frequently observed. Thus, although the MMPI is somewhat suggestive of Borderline Personality Disorder, the lack of specificity of the findings in this research area (as discussed previously) make any conclusions in this line very preliminary.

The patient's performance on the MCMI (Figure 5–2) yields additional data regarding the possibility of a diagnosis of personality disorder. MCMI scales are reported as *base rate* (BR) scores, which were designed to yield scores indicating the likelihood that a person is a member of a particular diagnostic category. These scores range from 0 to 115, with BR cutoff of 75 (for traits) and 85 (for diagnosis) being regarded as optimal (Millon, 1982). This patient had a number of elevations on the scales corresponding to DSM-III personality disorder. Using DSM-III diagnostic label names, significant elevations were noted on Dependent (BR 115), Borderline (BR 104), Passive-Aggressive (BR 96), Schizoid (BR 88), and Avoidant (BR 82) scales. Thus, the MCMI personality scale that was most elevated was the Dependency scale, which was consistent with the clinician's interpretation of the case. However, the Borderline scale was also markedly elevated, perhaps confirming the tentative observations formed from the MMPI clinical scales.

The profile that this patient obtained on the MMPI Personality Disorder scales proposed by Morey et al. (1985) is presented in Figure 5–3. This pattern is consistent with much of the material already described. As was the case with the MCMI, the single highest scale score was noted on Dependent, with significant elevations also noted on Paranoid, Schizotypal, Borderline, and Avoidant scales. The primary discrepancy between the MCMI and MMPI Personality Disorder scales involves the characterization of the resentment and interpersonal anger experienced by this woman; the MCMI labels this as passive-aggresiveness, while the Personality Disorder scales reflect a more paranoid content. Nonetheless, there is a great deal of correspondence between the MMPI, MCMI, and other clinical material. In particular, a consensus for three marked personologic trends emerged: (1) strong dependency needs, as manifest in all self-report data and the description given by the clinician; (2) borderline personality organization, as demonstrated by the MMPI and

MCMI data, the manipulative suicidal gesture, the dysphoric mood, and the ambivalence and anger directed toward the husband; and (3) a general discomfort and anxiety in interpersonal relations, variously labeled avoidant, schizoid, or social introversion by the different diagnostic instruments. This interpersonal discomfort was likely interacting in some way with her dependency, as she may have depended heavily on the few people with whom she felt comfortable. The dependency features probably had been fairly long-standing, as witnessed by her history, while the borderline characteristics may have been exacerbated as a function of recent stress.

It is apparent in this example that many of the conclusions reached from the combination of the MMPI Personality Disorder scales and the clinical scales were fairly accurate and could be verified from other sources of data. It is felt that these scales can supplement the valuable data that are obtained from the MMPI; this information can be particularly useful in making contemporary diagnostic decisions.

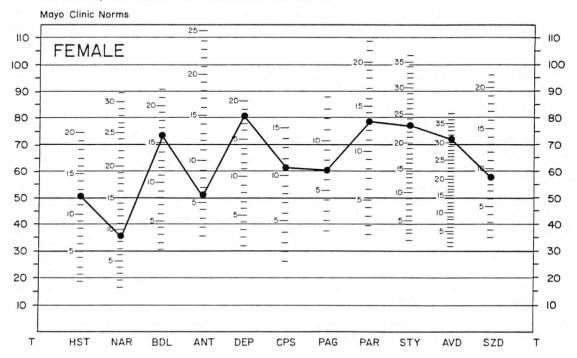

FIGURE 5–3. MMPI personality disorder scale profile for a 20-year-old inpatient.

SUMMARY

From the research literature described in this chapter, it is apparent that the MMPI can be very useful for establishing contemporary personality disorder diagnoses. However, the reader should not be left with a sense that there are relatively simple rules that can be applied in making such diagnoses. Despite Meehl's (1956) call for a "good cookbook," made over 30 years ago, no such cookbook exists for the personality disorders. Certain codetypes do occur with frequency, but identical codetypes often are noted for different personality disorders, while different codetypes are proposed as markers for the same personality disorder. Widiger and Frances (1987), in reviewing the literature on the measurement of personality disorder, make the following comment: "We recommend that any clinician or researcher employ both an interview schedule and a self-report inventory. The employment of multiple methods of measurement should be the norm in any assessment of personality disorder" (p. 70). This observation is astute and should be heeded. The assessment of personality is a complex task in any case, and the great divergence among different theories of personality as to what variables are salient greatly adds to this complexity. The MMPI is but one diagnostic device available to the clinician and researcher, albeit a powerful one. Nonetheless, as research on the MMPI with personality disorders progresses, it may be expected that this venerable instrument will continue to be a most valuable asset to scientists and professionals interested in these conditions.

ACKNOWLEDGMENTS

The assistance of Drs. David Osborne and Robert Colligan of the Mayo Clinic in providing us with their normative data is gratefully acknowledged.

Many thanks to Pamela Auble, Ph.D., for providing us with much interesting data for use as case studies.

REFERENCES

Abraham, K. (1923). Contributions to the theory of the anal character. *International Journal of Psychonanalysis, 4,* 400–418.

Abramowitz, S., Carroll, J., & Schaffer, C. (1984). Borderline personality disorder and the MMPI. *Journal of Clinical Psychology, 40,* 410–413.

American Psychiatric Association. (1952). *Diagnostic and Statistical Manual of Mental Disorder.* Washington, DC: Author.

Americn Psychiatric Association. (1968). *Diagnostic and Statistical Manual of Mental Disorder* (2nd ed.). Washington, DC: Author.

American Psychiatric Association. (1980). *Diagnostic and Statistical Manual of Mental Disorders* (3rd ed.). Washington, DC: Author.

Antoni, M., Tischer, P., Levine, J., Green, C., & Millon, T. (1985a). Refining personality assessment by combining MCMI high point profiles with MCMI codes, Part I: MMPI code 28/82. *Journal of Personality Assessment, 49,* 392–398.

Antoni, M., Tischer, P., Levine, J., Green, C., & Millon, T. (1985b). Refining personality assessments by combining MCMI high point profiles and MCMI codes, Part III. MMPI code 24/42. *Journal of Personality Assessment, 49,* 508–515.

Archer, R.P., Ball, J.P., & Hunter, J.A. (1985). MMPI characteristics of borderline psychopathology in adolescent inpatients. *Journal of Personality Assessment, 49,* 47–55.

Ashby, H.V., Lee, R.R., & Duke, E.H. (August 1979). *A narcissistic personality disorder MMPI scale.* Paper presented at the annual meeting of the American Psychological Association, New York.

Auchincloss, E., & Michels, R. (1983). Psychoanalytic theory of character. In J. Frosch (Ed.), *Current perspectives on personality disorders.* Washington: American Psychiatric Press.

Baron, M., & Gruen, R. (1980). *Schedule for interviewing borderlines.* New York: New York State Psychiatric Institute.

Barron, F. (1953). An ego-strength scale which predicts response to psychotherapy. *Journal of Consulting and Clinical Psychology, 17,* 327–333.

Blazer, D., George, L.K., Landerman, R., Pennybacker, M., Melville, M., Woodbury, M., Manton, K.G., Jordan, K., & Locke, B. (1985). Psychiatric disorders: A rural/urban comparison. *Archives of General Psychiatry, 42,* 651–656.

Cadoret, R.J. (1978). Psychopathology in adopted-away offspring of biologic parents with antisocial behavior. *Archives of General Psychiatry, 35,* 176–184.

Carr, A., Goldstein, E., Hunt, H., & Kernberg, O. (1979). Psychological tests and borderline patients. *Journal of Personality Assessment, 43,* 582–590.

Chodoff, P., & Lyons, H. (1958). Hysteria, the hysterical personality and "hysterical" conversion. *American Journal of Psychiatry, 114,* 734–740.

Cleckley, H. (1941). *The mask of sanity.* St Louis: Mosby.

Cloninger, C.R., Reich, T., & Guze, S.B. (1975). The multifactorial model of disease transmission: II. Sex differences in the familial transmission of sociopathy (antisocial personality). *British Journal of Psychiatry, 127,* 11–22.

Colligan, R.C., Osborne, D., Swenson, W.M., & Offord, K.P. (1983). *The MMPI: A contemporary normative study.* New York: Praeger.

Deutch, H. (1942). Some forms of emotional disturbance and their relationship to schizophrenia. *Psychoanalytic Quarterly, 11,* 301–321.

Dahlstrom, W.G., Welsh, G.S., & Dahlstrom, L.E. (1972). *An MMPI handbook. Volume I: Clinical Interpretation.* Minneapolis: University of Minnesota Press.

Dubro, A.F., Wetzler, S., & Kahn, M.W. (in press). A comparison of three self-report inventories for the diagnosis of DSM-III personality disorders. *Journal of Personality Disorders.*

Dubro, A.F., Wetzler, S., & Kahn, M.W. (1987). *Psychometric properties of the MMPI personality disorder scales.* Paper presented at the annual meeting of The American Psychological Association, August, New York.

Edell, W.S. (1984). The Borderline Syndrome Index: Clinical validity and utility. *Journal of Nervous and Mental Disease, 172,* 254–263.

Elion, V.H. (1975). The validity of the MMPI as a discriminator of social deviance among black men. *FCI Research Reports, 6,* 1–18.

Endicott, J., & Spitzer, R.L. (1978). A diagnostic interview: The Schedule for Affective Disorders and Schizophrenia. *Archives of General Psychiatry, 35*, 837–844.

Evans, R.W., Ruff, R.M., Braff, D. L., & Ainsworth, T.L. (1984). MMPI characteristics of borderline personality inpatients. *Journal of Nervous and Mental Disease, 172*, 742–748.

Forman, M. (1976). Narcissistic personality disorders and the oedipal fixations. *Annual of Psychoanalysis, 4*, 65–92.

Frances, A. (1980). The DSM-III personality disorders section: A commentary. *American Journal of Psychiatry, 137*, 1050–1054.

Frances, A., Clarkin, J.F., Gilmore, M., Hurt, S.W., & Brown, R. (1984). Reliability of criteria for borderline personality disorder: A comparison of DSM-III and the Diagnostic Interview for Borderline patients. *American Journal of Psychiatry, 141*, 1080–1084.

Freud, S. (1905a). A case of hysteria. In J. Strachey (Ed.), *The standard edition of the complete psychological works of Sigmund Freud* (Vol. 1, pp. 24–42). London: Hogarth Press.

Freud, S. (1905b). Three essays of the theory of sexuality. In J. Strachey (Ed.), *The standard edition of the complete psychological works of Sigmund Freud* (Vol. 7, pp. 130–243). London: Hogarth Press.

Fricke, B.G. (1956). Conversion hysterics and the MMPI. *Journal of Clinical Psychology, 12*, 322–326.

Fujioka, T.A., & Chapman, L.J. (1984). Comparison of the 2-7-8 MMPI profile and the perceptual aberration-magical ideation scale in identifying hypothetically psychosis prone college students. *Journal of Consulting and Clinical Psychology, 52*, 458–467.

Gerson, M.J. (1984). Splitting: The development of a measure. *Journal of Clinical Psychology, 40*, 157–162.

Gilberstadt, H., & Duker, J. (1965). *A handbook for clinical and actuarial MMPI interpretation*. Philidelphia: W.B. Saunders.

Goldberg, L.R. (1969). The search for configural relationships in personality assessment: The diagnosis of psychosis vs. neurosis from the MMPI. *Multivariate Behavior Research, 4*, 523–536.

Golden, R.R., & Meehl, P.E. (1979). Detection of the schizoid taxon with MMPI indicators. *Journal of Abnormal Psychology, 88*, 217–233.

Gough, H.G. (1957). *California Psychological Inventory manual*. Palo Alto: Consulting Psychologists Press.

Gough, H.G., McClosky, H., & Meehl, P.E. (1951). A personality scale for dominance. *Journal of Abnormal and Social Psychology, 46*, 360–366.

Graham, J.R. (1987). *The MMPI: A practical guide* (2nd ed.). New York: Oxford University Press.

Greene, R.L. (1980). *The MMPI: An interpretive manual*. Philadelphia: Grune & Stratton.

Grinker, R.R., Werble, B., & Drye, R.C. (1968). *The borderline syndrome*. New York: Basic Books.

Grove, W. (1982). Psychometric detection of schizotypy. *Psychological Bulletin, 92*, 27–38.

Gunderson, J., Kolb, J., & Austin, V. (1981). The diagnostic interview for borderline patients. *American Journal of Psychiatry, 138*, 896–903.

Gunderson, J., & Singer, M. (1975). Defining borderline patients: An overview. *American Journal of Psychiatry, 132*, 1–10.

Gustin, Q., Goodpaster, W., Sajadi, C., Pitts, W., LaBasse, D., & Snyder, S. (1983). MMPI characteristics of the DSM-III Borderline Personality Disorder. *Journal of Personality Assessment, 47*, 50–59.

Guze, S., Goodwin, D., & Crane, J. (1969). Criminality and psychiatric disorders. *Archives of General Psychiatry, 20*, 583–591.

Gynther, M.D., Altman, H., & Warbin, R.W. (1973). Behavioral correlates for the MMPI 4-9/9-4 code types: A case of the emperor's new clothes? *Journal of Consulting and Clinical Psychology, 40*, 259–263.

Haier, R.J., Rosenthal, D., & Wender, P.H. (1978). MMPI assessment of psychopathology in the adopted-away offspring of schizophrenics. *Archives of General Psychiatry, 35*, 171–175.

Haier, R., Rieder, R., Khouri, P., & Buchsbaum, M. (1979). Extreme MMPI scores and the research diagnostic criteria. *Archives of General Psychiatry, 36*, 528–534.

Hare, R.D. (1970). *Psychopathy: Theory and research*. New York: John Wiley and Sons.

Hare, R.D. (1985). Comparison of procedures for the assessment of psychopathy. *Journal of Consulting and Clinical Psychology, 53*, 7–16.

Hathaway, S.R. (1956). Scales 5 (masculinity-femininity), 6 (paranoia) and 8 (schizophrenia). In G.S. Welsh & W.G. Dahlstrom (Eds.), *Basic readings on the MMPI in psychology and medicine* (pp. 104–111). Minneapolis: University of Minnesota Press.

Hathaway, S.R., & Meehl, P.E. (1951). *An atlas for the clinical use of the MMPI*. Minneapolis: University of Minnesota Press.

Hedlund, J.L., Sletten, I., Evenson, R., Altman, H., & Won Cho, D. (1977). Automated psychiatric information systems: A critical review of Missouri's Standard System of Psychiatry (SSOP). *Journal of Operational Psychiatry, 8*, 5–26.

Henry, K.A., & Cohen, C.I. (1983). The role of labeling processes in diagnosing borderline personality disorder. *American Journal of Psychiatry, 140*, 1527–1529.

Hovanitz, C.A., Gynther, M.D., & Marks, P.A. (1983). The prediction of paranoid behavior: Comparative validities of obvious versus subtle MMPI paranoia (Pa) items. *Journal of Clinical Psychology, 39*, 407–411.

Hovey, H.B. (1949). Somatization and other neurotic reactions and MMPI profiles. *Journal of Clinical Psychology, 5*, 153–157.

Hurt, S., Clarkin, J., Frances, A., Abrams, R., & Hunt, H. (1985). Discriminant validity of the MMPI for borderline personality disorder. *Journal of Personality Assessment, 49*, 56–61.

Hyler, S.E., Reider, R., Spitzer, R.L., & Williams, J.B.W. (1983). *Personality Disorder Questionnaire (PDQ)*. New York: State Psychiatric Institute.

Kaplan, M. (1983). A woman's view of DSM-III. *American Psychologist, 38*, 786–792.

Kelley, C.K., & King, G.D. (1979). Behavioral correlates of the 2-7-8 MMPI profile type in students at a university mental health center. *Journal of Consulting and Clinical Psychology, 47*, 679–685.

Kernberg, O.F. (1967). Borderline personality organization. *Journal of the American Psychoanalytic Association, 15*, 641–685.

Kernberg, O.F. (1975). *Borderline conditions and pathological narcissism*. New York: Jason Aronson.

Kety, S.S., Rosenthal, D., Wender, P.H., & Schulsinger, F. (1971). Mental illness in the biological and adoptive families of adopted schizophrenics. *American Journal of Psychiatry, 128*, 302–306.

Kimble, R., Williams, J., & Agras, S. (1975). A comparison of two methods of diagnosing hysteria. *American Journal of Psychiatry, 132*, 1197–1199.

King, G.D., & Kelley, C.K. (1977). Behavioral correlates for spike-4, spike-9, and 4-9/9-4 MMPI profile in students at a university mental health center. *Journal of Clinical Psychology, 33*, 718–724.

Knight, R. (1953). Borderline states. *Bulletin of the Menninger Clinic, 17*, 1–12.

Koch, J.L. (1891). *Die psychopathischen minderwertigkeiten.* Ravensburg: Maier.

Koenigsberg, H.W., Kaplan, R.D., Gilmore, M.M., & Cooper, A.M. (1985). The relationship between syndrome and personality disorder in DSM-III: Experience with 2,462 patients. *American Journal of Psychiatry, 142*, 207–212.

Kohut, H. (1966). Forms and transformations of narcissism. *Journal of the American Psychoanalytic Association, 14*, 243–272.

Kretschmer, E. (1926). *Hysteria* (English translation). New York: Nervous and Mental Disease Publishers.

Kringlen, E. (1965). Obsessional neurotics. *British Journal of Psychiatry, 111*, 709–722.

Kroll, J., Sines, L., Martin, K., Lari, L., Pyle, R., & Zander, J. (1981). Borderline personality disorder: Construct validity of the concept. *Archives of General Psychiatry, 38*, 1021–1026.

Lachar, D. (1974). *The MMPI: Clinical and automated interpretation.* Los Angeles: Western Psychological Services.

Lachar, D., & Wrobel, T.A. (1979). Validating clinicians' hunches: Construction of a new MMPI critical item set. *Journal of Consulting and Clinical Psychology, 47*, 277–284.

Leighton, D.C., Harding, J.S., Macklin, D.B., Hughes, C.C., & Leighton, A.H. (1963). Psychiatric findings of the Stirling County study. *American Journal of Psychiatry, 119*, 1021–1032.

Levine, J., Tischer, P., Antoni, M., Green, C., & Millon, T. (1985). Refining personality assessments by combining MCMI highpoint profiles and MMPI codes, Part II: MMPI code 27/72. *Journal of Personality Assessment, 49*, 501–507.

Lewandowski, D., & Graham, J.R. (1972). Empirical correlates of frequently occurring two-point MMPI code types: A replicated study. *Journal of Consulting and Clinical Psychology, 39*, 467–472.

Lilienfeld, S.O., VanValkenburg, C., Larntz, K., & Akiskal, H.S. (1986). The relationship of histrionic personality disorder to antisocial personality and somatization disorders. *American Journal of Psychiatry, 143*, 718–722.

Lindberg, B.J., & Lindgard, B. (1963). Studies of the hysteroid personality attitude. *Acta Psychiatrica Scandinavia, 39*, 170–180.

Liskow, B.I., Clayton, P., Woodruff, R., Guze, S., & Cloninger, R. (1977). Briquet's syndrome, hysterical personality, and the MMPI. *American Journal of Psychiatry, 134*, 1137–1139.

Lloyd, C., Overall, J.E., & Click, M. (1983a). Screening for borderline personality disorders with the MMPI-168. *Journal of Clinical Psychology, 39*, 722–726.

Lloyd, C., Overall, J.E., Kimsey, L.R., & Click, M. (1983b). A comparison of the MMPI-168 profiles of borderline and nonborderline outpatients. *Journal of Nervous and Mental Disease, 171*, 207–215.

Lord, F.M., & Novick, M.R. (1968). *Statistical theories of mental test scores.* Menlo Park, CA: Addison-Wesley.

Luisada, P.V., Peele, R., & Pittard, E.A. (1974). The hysterical personality in men. *American Journal of Psychiatry, 131*, 518–522.

MacAndrew, C. (1965). The differentiation of male alcoholic outpatients from nonalcoholic psychiatric outpatients by means of the MMPI. *Quarterly Journal of Studies on Alcohol, 26*, 238–246.

Mack, J.E. (1975). Borderline states: An historical perspective. In J.E. Mack (Ed.), *Borderline states in psychiatry* (pp. 1–27). Philadelphia: Grune & Stratton.

Manilow, K.L. (1981). Dependent personality. In J.R. Lion (Ed.), *Personality Disorders: Diagnosis and Management* (2nd ed., pp. 97–102). Baltimore: Williams and Wilkins.

Marks, P.A., Seeman, W., & Haller, D.L. (1974). *The actuarial use of the MMPI with adolescents and adults.* Baltimore: Williams & Wilkins.

Marmar, C.R. (1984). Personality disorders. In H.R. Goldman (Ed.), *Review of general psychiatry* (pp. 413–435). Los Altos, CA: Lange Medical.

McKinley, J.C., & Hathaway, S.R. (1956). Scales 3 (hysteria), 9 (hypomania) and 4 (psychopathic deviate). In G. S. Welsh & W. G. Dahlstrom (Eds.), *Basic readings on the MMPI in psychology and medicine* (pp. 87–103). Minneapolis: University of Minnesota Press.

Meehl, P.E. (1956). Wanted—A good cookbook. *American Psychologist, 11*, 263–272.

Meehl, P.E. (1962). Schizotaxia, schizotypy, schizophrenia. *American Psychologist, 17*, 827–838.

Meehl, P.E. (1973). MAXCOV-HITMAX: A taxonomic search method for loose genetic syndromes. In P. E. Meehl (Ed.), *Psychodiagnosis: Selected papers* (pp. 200–224). New York: Norton.

Mellsop, G., Varghese, F., Joshua, S., & Hicks, A. (1982). The reliability of Axis II of DSM-III. *American Journal of Psychiatry, 139*, 1360–1361.

Meyer, R.G. (1983). *The clinician's handbook.* Boston: Allyn & Bacon.

Miller, H.R., Streiner, D.L., & Kahgee, S.L. (1982). Use of the Golden-Meehl indicators in the detection of schizoid-taxon membership. *Journal of Abnormal Psychology, 91*, 55–60.

Millon, T. (1969). *Modern psychopathology.* Philadelphia: W. B. Saunders.

Millon, T. (1981a). *Disorders of personality: DSM-III Axis II.* New York: John Wiley and Sons.

Millon, T. (1981b). The avoidant personality. In J.R. Lion (Ed.), *Personality disorders: Diagnosis and management* (2nd ed., pp. 103–120). Baltimore: Williams & Wilkins.

Millon, T. (1982). *Millon Clinical Multiaxial Inventory manual.* Minneapolis: National Computer Systems.

Millon, T. (1985). The MCMI provides a good assessment of DSM-III disorders: The MCMI-II will prove even better. *Journal of Personality Assessment, 49*, 379–391.

Morey, L.C. (1985). A psychometric analysis of five DSM-III categories. *Personality and Individual Differences, 6*, 323–329.

Morey, L.C. (1986). A comparison of three personality disorder assessment approaches. *Journal of Psychopathology and Behavior Assessment, 8*, 25–30.

Morey, L.C., Blashfield, R.K., Webb, W.W., & Jewell, J. (1988). MMPI scales for DSM-III personality disorders: A preliminary validation study. *Journals of Clinical Psychology, 44*, 47–50.

Morey, L.C., Waugh, M.H., & Blashfield, R.K. (1985). MMPI scales for DSM-III personality disorders: Their derivation and correlates. *Journal of Personality Assessment, 49*, 245–251.

Mosher, L.R., Pollin, W., & Stabenau, J.R. (1971). Families with identical twins discordant for schizophrenia: Some relationships between identification, thinking styles, psychopathology, and dominance-submissiveness. *British Journal of Psychiatry, 118*, 29–42.

Muncie, W. (1939). *Psychobiology and psychiatry.* St. Louis: Mosby.

Murray, J.B., Munley, M.J., & Gilbart, T.E. (1965). The Pd scale of the MMPI for college students. *Journal of Clinical Psychology, 21*, 48–51.

Nace, E., Saxon, J., & Shore, N. (1983). A comparison of borderline and nonborderline alcoholic patients. *Archives of General Psychiatry, 40*, 54–56.

Navran, L. (1954). A rationally derived MMPI scale to measure dependence. *Journal of Consulting Psychology, 18*, 192.

Newmark, C.S., & Sines, L.K. (1972). Characteristics of

hospitalized patients who produce the "floating" MMPI profiles. *Journal of Clinical Psychology, 28*, 74–76.

Newmark, C.S., Chassin, P., Evans, D.L., & Gentry, L. (1984). Floating MMPI profiles revisited. *Journal of Clinical Psychology, 40*, 199–201.

Nichols, D.S., & Jones, R.E. (1985). Identifying schizoid-taxon membership with the Golden-Meehl MMPI items. *Journal of Abnormal Psychology, 94*, 191–194.

Othmer, E., Penick, E.C., & Powell, B.J. (1981). *Psychiatric Diagnostic Interview (PDI) manual.* Los Angeles: Western Psychological Services.

Overall, J.E., Higgins, W., & de Schweinitz, A. (1976). Comparison of differential diagnostic discrimination for abbreviated and standard MMPI. *Journal of Clinical Psychology, 32*, 237–245.

Patrick, J. (1984). Characteristics of DSM-III borderline MMPI profiles. *Journal of Clinical Psychology, 40*, 655–658.

Perry, J.C., & Klerman, G.L. (1978). The borderline patient: A comparative analysis of four sets of diagnostic criteria. *Archives of General Psychiatry, 35*, 141–150.

Peterson, D.R. (1954). The diagnosis of subclinical schizophrenia. *Journal of Consulting Psychology, 18*, 198–200.

Pfohl, B., Coryell, W., Zimmerman, M., & Stangl, D. (1986). DSM-III personality disorders: Diagnostic overlap and internal consistency of individual DSM-III criteria. *Comprehensive Psychiatry, 27*, 21–34.

Phillips, J.A. (1981). Narcissistic personality. In J.R. Lion (Ed.), *Personality disorders: Diagnosis and management* (2nd ed., pp. 65–73). Baltimore: Williams & Wilkins.

Pitts, W., Gustin, Q., Mitchell, C., & Snyder, S. (1985). MMPI critical item characteristics of the DSM-III borderline personality disorder. *Journal of Nervous and Mental Disease, 173*, 628–631.

Pope, H.G., Jonas, J.M., Hudson, J.I., Cohen, B.M., & Gunderson, J.G. (1983). The validity of DSM-III borderline personality disorder: A phenomenologic, family history, treatment response, and long-term follow-up study. *Archives of General Psychiatry, 40*, 23–30.

Prichard, J.C. (1837). *A treatise on insanity and other disorders affecting the mind.* Philadelphia: Haswell, Barrington, & Haswell.

Pulver, S. (1970). Narcissism: The term and the concept. *Journal of the American Psychoanalytic Association, 18*, 319–341.

Rado, S. (1960). Theory and therapy: The theory of schizotypal organization and its application to the treatment of decompensated schizotypal behavior. In S. C. Scher, & H. R. Davis (Eds.), *The out-patient treatment of schizophrenia* (pp. 87–101). Philadelphia: Grune & Stratton.

Rapaport, D., Gill, M., & Schafer, R. (1946). *Diagnostic psychological testing* (Vol. 1). Chicago: Year Book Publishers.

Resnick, R.J., Schulz, P., Schulz, C., Hamer, R., Friedel, R., & Goldberg, S. (1983). Borderline personality disorder: Symptomology and MMPI characteristics. *Journal of Clinical Psychiatry, 44*, 289–291.

Robins, L. N. (1966). *Deviant children grown up: A sociological and psychiatric study of sociopathic personality.* Baltimore: Williams & Wilkins.

Robins, L.N., Helzer, J.E., Crough, J., & Ratcliff, R.S. (1981). National Institute of Mental Health diagnostic interview schedule. *Archives of General Psychiatry, 38*, 381–389.

Rosen, A. (1952). *Development of some new MMPI scales for differentiation of psychiatric syndromes within an abnormal population.* Unpublished doctoral dissertation, University of Minnesota.

Rosen, A. (1962). Development of MMPI scales based on a reference group of psychiatric patients. *Psychological Monographs, 76* (8, Whole No. 527).

Rosenthal, D. (1970). *Genetic theory and abnormal behavior.* New York: McGraw-Hill.

Rosenthal, D., Wender, P.H., Kety, S.S., Welner, J., & Schulsinger, F. (1971). The adopted-away offspring of schizophrenics. *American Journal of Psychiatry, 128*, 307–311.

Rosenthal, D., Wender, P.H., Kety, S.S., Schulsinger, F., Weiner, T., & Reider, R.O. (1975). Parent-child relationships and psychopathological disorder in the child. *Archives of General Psychiatry, 32*, 466–476.

Siever, L.J. (1981). Schizoid and schizotypal personality disorders. In J.R. Lion (Ed.), *Personality disorders: Diagnosis and management* (2nd ed., pp. 32–64). Baltimore: Williams & Wilkins.

Skinner, H.A. (1978). The art of exploring predictor-criterion relationships. *Psychological Bulletin, 85*, 327–337.

Slavney, P. R., & McHugh, P.R. (1975). The hysterical personality-an attempt at validation with the MMPI. *Archives of General Psychiatry, 32*, 186–190.

Small, I.F., Small, J. G., Alig, V.B., & Moore, D.F. (1970). Passive-aggressive personality disorder: A search for a syndrome. *American Journal of Psychiatry, 126*, 973–983.

Smith, M.R. (1986). *Clinical correlates of borderline personality in alcohol abuse.* Unpublished master's thesis, Vanderbilt University.

Snyder, S., Pitts, W., Goodpaster, W., Sajadi, C., & Gustin, Q. (1982). MMPI profile of DSM-III borderline personality disorder. *American Journal of Psychiatry, 139*, 1046–1048.

Snyder, S., Sajadi, C., Pitts, W., & Goodpaster, W. (1982). Identifying the depressive border of the borderline personality disorder. *American Journal of Psychiatry, 139*, 814–817.

Solomon, R.S. (1982). Validity of the MMPI narcissistic personality disorder scale. *Psychological Reports, 50*, 463–466.

Spitzer, R.L., Endicott, J., & Gibbon, M. (1979). Crossing the border into borderline personality and borderline schizophrenia: The development of criteria. *Archives of General Psychiatry, 36*, 17–24.

Spitzer, R.L., Forman, J.B., & Nee, J. (1979). DSM-III field trials: I. Initial interrater diagnostic reliability. *American Journal of Psychiatry, 136*, 815–817.

Spitzer, R.L., Williams, J.B., & Skodol, A.G. (1980). DSM-III: The major achievements and an overview. *American Journal of Psychiatry, 137*, 151–164.

Stangl, D., Pfohl, B., Zimmerman, M., Bowers, W., & Corenthal, C. (1985). A structured interview for the DSM-III personality disorders. *Archives of General Psychiatry, 42*, 591–596.

Stein, K.B. (1968). The TSC scales: The outcome of a cluster analysis of the 550 MMPI items. In P. McReynolds (Ed.), *Advances in Psychological Assessment* (Vol. 1). Palo Alto, CA: Science & Behavior Books.

Stone, M.H. (1980). *The borderline syndrome.* New York: McGraw-Hill.

Sutker, P.B., & Allain, A.N. (1983). Behavior and personality assessment in men labeled adaptive sociopaths. *Journal of Behavior Assessment, 5*, 65–79.

Tarter, R.E., & Perley, R.N. (1975). Clinical and perceptual characteristics of paranoids and paranoid schizophrenics. *Journal of Clinical Psychology, 31*, 42–44.

Tubin, J.P. (1981). Historic personality. In J. R. Lion (Ed.), *Personality disorders: Diagnosis and management* (2nd ed., pp. 85–96). Baltimore: Williams & Wilkins.

Vaillant, G.E., & Perry, J.C. (1980). Personality disorders. In H. I. Kaplan, A. M. Freedman, & B. J. Sadock (Eds.), *Comprehensive textbook of psychiatry* (3rd ed., pp. 1562–1590). Baltimore: Williams & Wilkins.

Vaillant, G.E., & Perry, J.C. (1985). Personality disorders. In H. I. Kaplan & B. J. Sadock (Eds.), *Comprehensive textbook of psychiatry* (4th ed., pp. 958–986). Baltimore: Williams & Wilkins.

Veith, I. (1963). *Hysteria: History of a disease*. Chicago: University of Chicago Press.

Walters, G.D. (1985). Scale *4 (Pd)* of the MMPI and the diagnosis antisocial personality. *Journal of Personality Assessment, 49,* 474–476.

Warner, R. (1978). The diagnosis of antisocial and hysterical personality disorders: An example of sex bias. *Journal of Nervous and Mental Disease, 166,* 839–845.

Welsh, G.S. (1952). A factor study of the MMPI using scales with item overlap eliminated. *American Psychologist, 7,* 341–342.

Welsh, G.S. (1965). MMPI profiles and factor scales A and R. *Journal of Clinical Psychology, 21,* 43–47.

Weiner, D.N. (1948). Subtle and obvious keys for the MMPI. *Journal of Consulting Psychology, 1,* 164–170.

Weintraub, W. (1981). Compulsive and paranoid personalities. In J. R. Lion (Ed.), *Personality disorders: Diagnosis and management* (2nd ed., pp. 163–181). Baltimore: Williams & Wilkins.

Whiteman, R., Trosman, H., & Koenig, R. (1954). Clinical assessment of passive-aggressive personality. *Archives of Neurology and Psychiatry, 72,* 540–549.

Widiger, T.A. (1982). Psychological tests and the borderline diagnosis. *Journal of Personality Assessment, 46,* 227–238.

Widiger, T.A., & Frances, A. (1985). The DSM-III personality disorders: Perspectives from psychology. *Archives of General Psychiatry, 42,* 615–623.

Widiger, T.A., & Frances, A. (1987). Instruments and inventories for the measurement of personality disorders. *Clinical Psychology Review, 7,* 49–76.

Widiger, T.A., & Kelso, K. (1983). Psychodiagnosis of Axis II. *Clinical Psychology Review, 3,* 491–510.

Widiger, T.A., Sanderson, C., & Warner, L. (1986). The MMPI, prototypal typology, and borderline personality disorder. *Journal of Personality Assessment, 50,* 540–553.

Widiger, T.A., Williams, J.B., Spitzer, R., & Frances, A. (1986). The MCMI and DSM-III: A brief rejoinder to Millon (1985). *Journal of Personality Assessment, 50,* 198–204.

Wiggins, J.S. (1966). Subtantive dimensions of self-report in the MMPI item pool. *Psychological Monographs, 80* (22, Whole No. 630).

Winstead, B.A., (1984). Hysteria. In C. S. Widom (Ed.), *Sex roles and psychopathology* (pp. 73–100). New York: Plenum.

Zilboorg, G. (1941). Ambulatory schizophrenias. *Psychiatry, 4,* 149–155.

Chapter 6

Substance Abuse/Dependence

ROGER L. GREENE and
ROBERT D. GARVIN

OVERVIEW

This chapter reviews MMPI performance in persons who misuse alcohol and other types of substances. Although alcohol is a drug that is misused much like the other drugs covered in this chapter, research in this area tends to consider the misuse of alcohol as a separate process from the misuse of other substances. The term *misuse* is used throughout this chapter as a generic term to encompass both substance abuse or substance dependence. The latter two terms are only used when required by and appropriate to the context.

ALCOHOL ABUSE/DEPENDENCE

The misuse of alcohol has been recognized for a number of years as one of the most serious medical problems in the United States, although it has only begun to receive widespread publicity in the popular press in the last few years because of the deaths of a number of prominent athletes (cf. Emmons, Gomez, & Barnes, 1987). The statistics on alcoholism are staggering. Alcohol misuse costs for 1982 have been estimated at $50 billion for health care costs, accidents, violence, and loss of productivity (Health and Public Policy, 1985).

Approximately 5 to 10 percent of the adult American population (18 years of age and older) and 15 to 20 percent of adolescents (14 to 17 years old) are problem drinkers (Public Health Service, 1983). The normal life expectancy of an individual with untreated alcoholism is reduced by about 12 years (West, 1984), and 10 percent of all deaths in the United States are alcohol-related. Cirrhosis, which is attributable largely to alcohol consumption, ranks among the 10 leading causes of death. Alcoholism is involved in at least 50 percent of all automobile fatalities, 67 percent of drownings, 70 to 80 percent of deaths in fires, 67 percent of murders, 35 percent of suicides, and 85 percent of the annual deaths from liver disease, making alcohol misuse the leading cause of death for persons aged 15 to 45 (Public Health Service, 1983).

Nearly 90 percent of the individuals who misuse alcohol are seen by primary care, nonpsychiatric physicians in a year, yet only 10 percent are questioned about their alcohol misuse (Kamerown, Pincus, & Macdonald, 1986). Physicians tend to focus on the complications or symptoms of alcohol misuse such as cirrhosis and pancreatitis, rather than the disease itself. At least 10 percent of all adults seen by a physician annually have an alcohol-related problem, but few of these patients are recognized as misusing alcohol and even fewer are referred for treatment; for ex-

THE MMPI: USE WITH
SPECIFIC POPULATIONS

© 1988 by Grune & Stratton.

ample, < 9 percent of the patients in alcohol treatment have been referred by physicians (Mendelson, Miller, Mello, Pratt, & Schmitz, 1982). Consequently, alcohol-related problems will be identified and referred for treatment by a variety of individuals other than physicians.

The "typical" alcoholic patient is a white male who is 40 years of age with a high school education. He has abused alcohol for 10 to 20 years and has been in alcohol treatment previously. Although consideration of the parameters of the drinking behavior (cf. Horn, Wanberg, & Adams, 1974; Schuckit, Morrison, & Gold, 1984) are recommended frequently, most often such variables are ignored or at least not reported. The diagnosis of alcoholism generally is made on the basis of the patient's presence in the treatment facility with little consideration as to how the patient entered the facility (i.e., voluntary admission, court referral, employee assistance program referral, etc.). Rarely are attempts made to confirm this diagnosis or even more importantly to exclude other psychiatric diagnoses.

A number of moderator variables are of utmost importance in examining the MMPI performance of alcoholics. The influence of variables such as age, gender, education/intelligence, and socioeconomic class are so common in psychological research that it should be unnecessary to point out the need to monitor their effects in alcoholism. However, clinicians frequently report data on a group of alcoholics without providing even these basic demographics on their sample. The potential effects of these variables may be less explicit when the clinician compares the sample of alcoholics with the original MMPI normative group without considering whether such variables may be as important for the obtained results as the presence of alcoholism. Since the original normative group for the MMPI consisted of persons in their mid-30s who lived in rural Minnesota and who had approximately 10 years of education (cf. Dahlstrom, Welsh, & Dahlstrom, 1972, pp. 7–8), the MMPI results of a sample of alcoholic patients that differs on any of these variables cannot be assumed to be solely a function of alcoholism. Even when the clinician compares alcoholics with other samples within the same facility, the potential bias of these variables cannot be overlooked since they may interact with diagnosis in some way; for example, alcoholics may be older and better educated than schizophrenic patients.

A number of moderator variables are specific to persons who misuse substances, so they must be given explicit consideration in this research. First, the parameters of the person's misuse of substances needs to be reported explicitly. These data can be as simple as whether the person misuses substances constantly, only on weekends, or during binges. The type of substance(s) misused also may be important, at least as to generic class—for example, sedative-hypnotics, stimulants, and so on—as well as whether the person misuses only one substance or multiple substances. The work of Skinner and his colleagues (cf. Morey & Skinner, 1986; Morey, Skinner, & Blashfield, 1984; Skinner, Jackson, & Hoffmann, 1974) may be very useful in this area in terms of identifying patterns of misuse that then can be compared with MMPI performance. Second, the social/interpersonal aspects of the misuse should be identified. The person may misuse substances only by himself or herself, may withdraw and isolate himself or herself as the result of the misuse of substances, may misuse in only social contexts, or some combination of these behaviors. Third, the factors that have led the person to receive treatment for the misuse of substance(s) need to be identified. Although patients enter treatment as a result of "hitting bottom," the factors that lead to that point are very different. Patients may be entering treatment because of the "encouragement" of the legal system, employers, spouses, and so on. Fourth, the time at which the data are collected is very important. If the data are collected too early in treatment the patients may be too toxic to report accurately. It appears that data should not be collected before a week or 10 days after admission if the person is being detoxified (Libb & Taulbee, 1971). How the patients respond after they entered treatment also must be considered, particularly in any study that is evaluating treatment effectiveness or outcome. Some patients will continue to deny or minimize their misuse of substance(s) throughout treatment, and/or leave treatment prematurely. Clinicians who collect their data early in treatment and do not consider that some patients may leave before completing treatment will have different results than those who collect data later or toward the end of treatment. Finally, the basis on which the diagnosis of misuse of substance(s) is made must be given careful consideration. All too often the only criterion for the diagnosis is the person's presence in a treatment facility with little regard for whether the diagnosis is appropriate or whether other psychiatric diagnoses are present. The assumption appears to be that false-positive diagnoses do not occur in these facilities, which may be fairly safe given the denial and minimization that are characteristic of the misuse of substance(s). However, it is important to be aware of the variety of social, interpersonal, and legal factors that resulted in this person being identified as needing treatment. These issues/factors may be less important within a given facility since patients may be referred for similar reasons, but they clearly are important when patients are compared across a variety of facilities. Individuals who misuse substance(s) and receive treatment in a state or VA hospital may differ in a number of important ways from individuals in a private hospital or who are maintained in an outpatient setting (cf. English & Curtin, 1975; Krauthamer, 1979; Pattison, Coe, & Doerr, 1973).

DIFFERENTIAL DIAGNOSIS

DSM-III (American Psychiatric Association, 1980) defines two categories of alcohol misuse: alcohol abuse and alcohol dependence. Alcohol abuse is defined as nonpathologic recreational use of alcohol or episodes of intoxication without a pattern of pathologic use, impairment in social or occupational functioning, and duration of disturbance for a period of at least 1 month. Alcohol dependence is defined by either (1) a pattern of pathologic use or (2) an impairment in social or occupational functioning due to alcohol use and either tolerance or withdrawal. There are a number of ambiguities in operationalizing these definitions that make reliable diagnosis difficult: need for daily use of alcohol for adequate functioning, inability to cut down or stop drinking, and restriction of drinking to certain times of day. Although alcohol dependence is intended to be a subset of alcohol abuse in DSM-III, the criteria are actually less restrictive for the diagnosis of alcohol dependence since either of the first two criteria may be present. A number of other definitions of alcoholism are used frequently, and there is only limited agreement among these various definitions about which or how many problems or how much drinking is excessive (Boyd, Weissman, Thompson, & Myers, 1983). Since the definition of alcohol misuse will influence whether a person is referred for treatment, different definitions may result in the comparisons of very hetergeneous samples.

DSM-III-R (American Psychiatric Association, 1987) has changed the criteria for alcohol misuse somewhat in that the same diagnositic criteria are used to define abuse and dependence regardless of the substance. The diagnosis of substance dependence requires that the person exhibit at least three of nine different criteria for at least 1 month (pp. 167–168). The diagnosis of substance abuse is indicated by the existence of one of the following two criteria for at least 1 month:

> continued use despite knowledge of having a persistent or recurrent social, occupational, psychological, or physical problem that is caused by or exacerbated by use of the psychoactive substance; or recurrent use in situations in which use is physically hazardous (e.g., driving while intoxicated) (p. 169).

It is too early to ascertain the implications of these changes in diagnostic criteria.

PROTOTYPIC STUDY

A study by Rosen (1960) will be used as a prototypic example of how researchers have used the MMPI in comparing alcoholics with nonalcoholics. Rosen was interested particularly in determining whether moderator variables such as socioeconomic class, history of drinking, age, and so on may have been responsible for earlier findings of differences between alcoholics and nonalcoholic psychiatric patients (e.g., Brown, 1950) rather than any real differences in personality structure. Although Rosen compared six different groups of patients (alcohol clinic males, psychiatric outpatient males, skid row male alcoholics, hospitalized male alcoholics, alcohol clinic females, and psychiatric outpatient females), only data from the alcohol clinic males ($n = 78$) and the psychiatric outpatient males ($n = 35$) will be reviewed here. Rosen compared these two samples of male patients because they were drawn from similar geographic and socioeconomic areas. They also were similar in education and intelligence and nearly the same age (alcoholics—39 mean years of age; psychiatric outpatients—32 mean years of age). Rosen then compared the mean profiles for these two groups of patients. The alcoholics had a *2-7-4-8* codetype while the psychiatric outpatients had a *2-7* codetype. In general the two profiles were very similar with the outpatients scoring from 3 to 5 *T*-points lower on Scales *4*, *7*, and *8*, and nearly identical on the other scales. Rosen concluded that "alcoholism is not a primary disorder, that alcoholics do not form a homogeneous group and that they are not so different from other psychiatric patients as to require a unique diagnostic designation" (p. 263).

Rosen can be commended for a number of positive attributes of his study: (1) he adequately described his samples and he controlled for the effects of a number of moderator variables, (2) he indicated that *K*-corrections were used in constructing profiles, and (3) he provided the raw data so that his results could be compared with other studies. However, there also are a number of shortcomings that limit the generalizations that can be made from his study: (1) he did not indicate whether any validity criteria were used in selecting patients, (2) he reported a mean profile that would conceal the existence of any subgroups within the sample despite his interest in determining whether alcoholics formed a homogeneous group, (3) he did not describe nor define how alcoholism was diagnosed, and (4) he conducted a multitude of *t*-tests between his various samples without controlling for experiment-wise error rate.

Some of the problems that are inherent in Rosen's (1960) study continue to plague current research in this area. The two most prevalent problems are the failure to provide any definition of alcoholism other than presence in some identified group or facility and the reporting of mean profiles that obscure any differences that may exist within the samples.

STANDARD VALIDITY AND CLINICAL SCALES

The initial research on the MMPI with alcoholics focused on the identification of an alcoholic "personality," and to that end a sample of alcoholics would be evaluated and a composite profile plotted. These initial studies usually involved a comparison of alcoholics with normal groups, generally the original Minnesota normative group, and they demonstrated that groups of alcoholics were experiencing significant emotional distress (see Table 6–1). Even a cursory review of

Table 6–1 will reveal that Scales *2* (*D*) and *4* (*Pd*) are more likely to be elevated in samples of alcoholic patients than the other clinical scales, and these types of data provided the basis for the statement that *2-4/4-2* codetypes are frequently seen in alcoholics (cf. Clopton, 1978; Hodo & Fowler, 1976). Slightly over one-third (36.8 percent) of the samples reported in Table 6–1 had *2-4/4-2* codetypes, and if Spike *2* and *4* profiles are included within this codetype, 65.8 percent of the samples would be included. However, nine (11.8 percent) studies of white male alcoholics cited in Table 6–1 obtained *WNL* codetypes (Button, 1956; Curlee, 1970; Dietvorst, Swenson, Niven, & Morse, 1979; Hewitt, 1943; Hill, Haertzen, & Davis, 1962; McGinnis & Ryan, 1965; Page & Bozlee, 1982; Templer, Ruff, Barthlow, Halcomb, & Ayers, 1978). Consequently, even based on group data it is somewhat precarious to state that *2-4/4-2* codetypes are characteristic of alcoholic patients, although it is a frequent codetype. Several investigators (McGinnis & Ryan, 1965; Penk, Charles, Patterson, Roberts, Dolan, & Brown, 1982) have reported that older alcoholics have fewer clinical scales elevated above a *T*-score of 70 and are more likely to elevate Scales *1* and *2* rather than Scales *4* and *9*. Age may be an important moderator variable affecting which clinical scales will be elevated in groups of alcoholics.

When groups of white female alcoholics are studied, any conclusion about frequently occurring codetypes must be more tentative because there are fewer studies on which to base trends. No study actually found a *2-4/4-2* codetype in these groups of white female alcoholics, although Scale *4* elevations occurred frequently. No study has examined whether age is a moderator variable affecting clinical scale elevations in women alcoholics as noted in men alcoholics above.

The fallacies inherent in the use of mean profiles to describe any diagnostic group were discussed in Chapter 1; the possibility of gender differences in alcoholic patients, which are suggested by the data in Table 6–1, will be considered later in this chapter. When it became clear that these mean or group profiles tended to vary among settings, researchers began to question the search for a "unitary" alcoholic personality.

The next flurry of research examined whether alcoholic patients could be classified into various diagnostic categories based on their MMPI

TABLE 6–1.   FREQUENCY OF ELEVATED MMPI CLINICAL SCALES
IN ALCOHOLIC SAMPLES BY GENDER

Authors	N	Age	Clinical Scales (≥ 70 T-points)
White males			
Abbott (1982) [Group S]	14	46.6	Spike 2
Abbott (1982) [Group D]	14	36.4	4-8-7-9-2
Brown (1950) [neurotic]	34	35.0	Spike 2
Brown (1950) [psychopathic]	33	30.3	Spike 4
Button (1956)	64	—	WNL
Chang et al. (1973)	407	—	Spike 4
Curlee (1970)	100	47.7	WNL
Davis et al. (1979) [androg.]	21	42.4	4-2
Davis et al. (1979) [nonandrog.]	21	42.5	2-4-8-7
Dietvorst et al. (1979)	17	51.2	WNL
Donovan & O'Leary (1976)	21	46.4	Spike 4
Donovan & O'Leary (1976) [hi dis]	21	46.4	2-1-4-7-8
English & Curtin (1975) [VA]	25	43.0	2-7-4-8
English & Curtin (1975) [Halfway]	25	47.2	Spike 4
English & Curtin (1975) [State Hosp]	24	39.1	Spike 2
Faulstich et al. (1985)	20	25.0	9-4-8-2-1
Faulstich et al. (1985)	24	35.0	2-8-7
Faulstich et al. (1985)	26	45.0	2-4
Faulstich et al. (1985)	21	57.5	Spike 2
Frankel & Murphy (1974)	214	45.0	2-4-7
Goss & Morosko (1969)	100	43.2	4-2
Goss & Morosko (1969) [cross-valid]	100	44.2	4-2
Hewett & Martin (1980)	53	38.0	Spike 4
Hewitt (1943)	37	44.0	WNL
Hill et al. (1962)	184	44.2	WNL
Hodo & Fowler (1976)	1009	43.4	4-2
Hoffmann & Nelson (1971)	148	43.0	4-2
Holcomb & Adams (1985)	41	—	8-4-2-7
Holland (1977)	45	26.5	Spike 4
Holland & Watson (1980)	91	41.6	2-4-8
Huber & Danahy (1975) [comp]	67	46.5	Spike 4
Huber & Danahy (1975) [non-comp]	37	46.5	4-2
Jansen & Hoffmann (1973)	975	43.2	Spike 4
Kammeier et al. (1973)	38	33.5	Spike 4
Lowe & Thomas (1976)	128	44.9	2-4
MacAndrew & Geertsma (1963)	200	40.8	4-2-7
McGinnis & Ryan (1965)	33	37.5	Spike 4
McGinnis & Ryan (1965)	63	44.8	WNL
McGinnis & Ryan (1965)	24	53.3	WNL
McWilliams & Brown (1977) [grp 1]	49	42.5	2-8-4-7
McWilliams & Brown (1977) [grp 2]	27	42.5	8-4-7-2-9
McWilliams & Brown (1977) [grp 3]	35	42.5	4-8-2
O'Leary et al. (1976)	68	46.2	2-4
O'Neil et al. (1983)	194	44.0	2-1-4-8-7
Page & Bozlee (1982)	11	41.1	WNL
Paredes et al. (1974)	21	38.1	4-2-8
Paredes et al. (1974) [non-drk]	21	41.7	2-4
Passini et al. (1977)	25	45.6	Spike 4
Passini et al. (1977) [biofeed]	25	42.0	4-2
Pattison et al. (1973) [Hospital]	30	50.3	Spike 2
Pattison et al. (1973) [Clinic]	26	42.2	2-4-7-8-3
Pattison et al. (1973) [Halfway]	31	42.2	4-2-9
Pattison et al. (1973) [Work Center]	34	46.5	4-2
Penk et al. (1982)	81	25.0	4-8-2-9-7
Penk et al. (1982)	152	35.0	4-8-2-7

(Continues.)

TABLE 6–1. *(Continued.)*

Authors	N	Age	Clinical Scales (≥ 70 T-points)
Penk et al. (1982)	165	45.0	*2-4-1-8-3*
Penk et al. (1982)	186	55.0	*2-1-4*
Penk et al. (1982)	45	65.0	*2-1*
Pettinati et al. (1982)	133	43.9	Spike *2*
Pfost et al. (1984)	38	45.9	Spike *2*
Rardin et al. (1974)	20	25.9	*4-2*
Rohan (1972)	40	43.3	*2-4*
Rohan et al. (1969)	58	46.1	*2-4*
Rosen (1960) [clinic]	78	39.0	*2-7-4-8*
Rosen (1960) [skid row]	17	—	*2-4-8-7*
Schroeder & Piercy (1979)	920	45.4	*2-4*
Soskin (1970) [Lysergide]	41	46.0	*4-2*
Soskin (1970) [HRTL]	41	45.6	*4-2*
Templer et al. (1978) [felons]	101	29.6	*WNL*
Watson & Vassar (1983) [left]	72	37.7	Spike *4*
Watson & Vassar (1983) [right]	687	41.1	Spike *4*
Wilkinson et al. (1971)	132	44.0	*2-4-1*
Zelen et al. (1966)	20	39.8	*7-4-8-1*
Zelen et al. (1966) [clinic]	20	39.9	*7-8-4-1-2-9*
Ziegler et al. (1978)	79	41.0	Spike *4*
Zielinski (1979)	100	44.1	Spike *2*
White females			
Curlee (1970)	100	46.8	*WNL*
Hoffmann & Wehler (1978) [abst. 2 yr]	33	42.0	*WNL*
Jansen & Hoffmann (1973)	404	42.5	Spike *4*
Jones et al. (1980)	21	44.1	*WNL*
Jones et al. (1980) [menstr.]	10	44.1	*9-8-4*
Krauthamer (1979)	30	—	*WNL*
MacAndrew (1978)	195	40.8	Spike *4*
Rosen (1960)	25	—	Spike *4*
Zelen et al. (1966)	20	41.4	*4-7-8*
Zelen et al. (1966) [clinic]	20	40.4	*7-8-4-1-2-9*
Zielinski (1979)	23	47.9	Spike *2*
Hispanic males			
Page & Bozlee (1982)	11	50.6	*2*
American Indian males			
Page & Bozlee (1982)	11	42.1	*WNL*

codetypes. The usual procedure for these studies was to identify general categories of diagnostic groups based on MMPI codetypes and then to determine how many patients fell within each diagnostic group (see Table 6–2). For example, *4-9/9-4* codetypes were generally classified as being psychopathic, combinations of Scales *1, 2, 3,* and *7* as being neurotic, combinations of Scales *6, 7, 8,* and *9* as being psychotic, and so on. There are a number of general problems with these studies. First, there was no general consensus as to which codetypes should be placed within a specific diagnostic group. The same combination of clinical scales could be placed into different diagnostic groups depending on how the researcher cate-

gorized them. Second, the actual rules whereby a specific profile was placed within a given diagnostic category frequently were not stated. Third, some researchers would categorize an individual profile regardless of its elevation, while others required that the scale be equal to or greater than a *T*-score of 60 or 70. Fourth, researchers did not report Spike *2* or Spike *4* codetypes, although the data presented in Table 6–1 would suggest that they might occur frequently. It is possible that some of these researchers used the high-point pair to determine the codetype regardless of scale elevation, which would eliminate any spike codetypes. Finally, most studies found that a large percentage of the profiles could not be classified

TABLE 6–2.   FREQUENCY OF GROUP DIAGNOSES IN ALCOHOLIC SAMPLES BY GENDER

Authors	N	Age	Neurotic 1-2-3-7	Classic 2-4-7	Psychopathic 4-9	Psychotic 6-7-8-9	WNL	Unclassified
White males								
Conley (1981)	317	42.0	9.8	15.5	11.7	12.9	—	50.1
Conley & Prioleau (1983)	633	43.0	7.7	10.0	9.3	13.6	11.7	47.7
Conley & Prioleau (1983) [cross-val]	837	43.0	7.2	16.0	9.6	14.6	9.3	43.3
Lachar et al. (1979b)	130	41.0	34.0	—	29.0	23.0	12.0	2.5
Mogar et al. (1970)	101	45.0	15.0	29.0	32.0	25.0	—	—
Robyak et al. (1984)	201	47.0	17.4	—	44.3	22.4	15.4	—
Swain-Holcomb & Thorne (1984)	126	—	19.0	22.0	15.0	15.0	—	29.0
Weighted totals	2345	43.2	11.0	15.1	15.1	15.7	11.0	42.2
White females								
Conley & Prioleau (1983)	355	45.0	7.3	9.8	7.9	18.3	11.3	45.4
Conley & Prioleau (1983) [cross-val]	338	45.0	6.2	9.2	9.8	16.3	10.3	48.2
Mogar et al. (1970)	100	41.0	13.0	40.0	47.0	—	—	—
Swain-Holcomb & Thorne (1984)	44	—	11.0	23.0	20.0	16.0	—	30.0
Weighted totals	837	44.5	7.7	13.9	14.0	17.2	10.8	45.8

into any of these frequently occurring diagnostic groups, which suggests that there is an amazing degree of heterogeneity of codetypes in alcoholic patients (see Table 6–2).

Given all these caveats about the inherent difficulties of associating codetypes with specific diagnostic groups, some information can still be gleaned from the studies summarized in Table 6–2. Psychopathic (4-9/9-4) codetypes were identified in 15.1 percent of the males (range, 9.3 to 44.3 percent) and 14.0 percent of the females (range, 7.9 to 47.0 percent), while "classic alcoholic" (2-4-7) codetypes were identified in 15.1 percent of the males (range, 10.0 to 29.0 percent) and 13.9 percent of the females (range, 9.2 to 40.0 percent). Despite the impression created by the mean profiles reported in Table 6–1 that 2-4/4-2 codetypes would be the most common, it appears that all five group diagnoses (neurotic, classic, psychopathic, psychotic, and WNL) occurred with about the same frequency in both male and female alcoholics. Psychotic codetypes (6-7-8-9) were slightly more frequent than these two former codetypes occurring in 15.7 percent of the males (range, 12.9 to 25 percent) and 17.2 percent of the females (range, 16.0 to 18.3 percent), which is not apparent from the data presented by the mean profiles. A sizeable percentage (9.3 to 15.4 percent, males; 10.3 to 11.3 percent, females) of these patients had WNL codetypes. These data, summarized in Table 6–2, would suggest that there

should be several common codetypes in alcoholic patients. The gender differences that appeared in the mean profiles summarized in Table 6–1 are not evident when these alcoholic patients are grouped in diagnostic categories. It also appears that there is significantly more heterogeneity in alcoholic patients than originally expected since a large number (2.5 to 50.1 percent, males; 30.0 to 48.2 percent, females) of the patients did not fall into any of these four diagnostic categories.

Another line of research utilized empirically based classification procedures on the MMPI clinical scales to identify commonly occurring groups of alcoholic patients (see Table 6–3). This line of research is more consistent with the development of the MMPI in that empirical procedures identified the groups of alcoholic patients rather than researchers trying to decide what codetypes should be associated with specific diagnostic groups as described above. A number of reviews of this line of research exist (cf. Morey & Blashfield, 1981; Morey & Skinner, 1986; Nerviano & Gross, 1983; Skinner, 1982), which should be consulted by the interested reader. In addition to the general critiques of the studies cited above on group diagnoses, a number of issues also can be raised with these studies. First, researchers rarely provided the basic information on their multivariate procedures so that they could be replicated (cf. Blashfield, 1980). A number of these studies used cluster analytic techniques

TABLE 6–3. FREQUENCY OF CLUSTER TYPES IN ALCOHOLIC PATIENTS BY GENDER

Authors	N	Age	1-2-3-4	2-4	2-7-8-4	Spike 4	4-9	WNL	Uncl
White males									
Bean & Karasievich (1975)	80	47	40.0	—	18.0	36.0	—	—	—
Button (1956)	24	—	—	—	—	50.0	—	50.0	—
Donovan et al. (1978)	102	46	—	37.3	55.9	—	—	—	—
Eshbaugh et al. (1978)	208	49	5.3	13.5	4.8	—	6.3	8.7	51.4
Filstead et al. (1983)	150	—	—	47.1	18.1	—	12.9	—	—
Glen et al. (1973)	145	—	—	—	*	*	—	—	—
Goldstein & Linden (1969)	239	—	—	—	16.3	19.2	1.7	10.5	54.6
Goldstein & Linden (1969) [replication]	251	—	—	—	17.5	16.0	—	8.8	57.8
Hill et al. (1962)	184	44	—	—	*	*	*	*	—
Kline & Snyder (1985)	94	40	—	—	21.3	—	37.2	41.5	—
Kline & Snyder (1985) [replication]	94	40	—	39.4	31.9	—	—	28.7	—
Loberg (1981)	109	40	—	30.3	35.8	—	—	—	—
Mulligan et al. (1978) [DWI – 68% black]	100	42	—	—	4.0	—	—	96.0	—
Nerviano et al. (1980)	206	45	11.0	6.0	47.0	—	12.0	—	23.0
Price & Curlee-Salsibury (1975)	51	44	39.2	—	17.7	—	23.5	—	19.6
Sutker et al. (1980) [DUI Offenders]	500	36	—	—	—	—	—	82.2	17.8
Svanum & Dallas (1981)	175	42	24.2	—	18.4	—	—	38.2	19.3
Whitelock et al. (1971)	136	41	—	*	—	*	—	—	—
Weighted Totals		41.8	17.8	25.2	22.7	21.4	11.4	42.6	34.5
N	2848	2039	720	869	1859	594	948	1685	1630
White females									
Eshbaugh et al. (1980)	183	47	7.7	6.7	7.7	13.1	—	23.5	54.6
Kline & Snyder (1985)	56	41	33.9	—	26.8	—	39.3	—	—
Kline & Snyder (1985) [replication]	56	41	—	—	30.4	69.6	—	—	—
Weighted totals		44.7	13.8		15.6	26.3			
N	295	295	239	183	295	239	56	183	183

Note: An asterisk signifies that the cluster type was found but the percentage of patients within the cluster was not reported. The weighted totals are based on the percentages in studies that found the specific cluster type, since the absence of data on a cluster may mean that it was not reported rather than it was not found. Consequently, the percentages in the row of weighted totals sum to a total > 100 percent.

without indicating the type of clustering procedure, the measure of profile similarity, or the statistical system, any of which can produce different outcomes. Second, researchers assume that mean profiles for empirically derived clusters of alcoholic patients actually represent the individual profiles within the cluster, even though the same critique can be made of mean cluster profiles that has been made repeatedly about mean group profiles. Again, it is relatively uncommon for a large percentage of the individual profiles to be actually similar to the mean cluster profile, and none of these researchers reported this information. An example of this potential problem will be provided in Table 6–5 later in this chapter. Third, there is little agreement about whether all of the profiles should be clustered, which forces some individual profiles to be classified into the most similar cluster with the resulting distortion of its inherent integrity, or whether there should be some stopping point for adding profiles used to exclude outliers (statistically discrepant profiles) and to increase profile homogeneity within clusters. Fourth, there is limited agreement on the rules to define a stopping point that should be used to identify the number of clusters within a given sample. A researcher who decides that three clusters are appropriate for describing the MMPI data will have a different set of codetypes than a researcher who determines that six clusters are present. Finally, researchers have not compared those clusters identified in alcoholic patients with those found in psychiatric patients to assess whether they are specific to alcoholism (Morey, Roberts, & Penk, 1987) or more generally to psychopathology. The limited research in this area (Hoffmann & Nelson, 1971) suggests that these clusters may be more likely to reflect psychopathology per se than alcoholism. It also is possible that these common clusters reflect some artefact of the clustering procedure or the psychometric flavor of the MMPI scales.

Table 6–3 illustrates that several codetypes are found very frequently when the MMPIs of alcoholics are cluster analyzed. The most frequent codetypes appear to be *2-7-8- 4*, occurring in 22.7 percent of the males (range, 4.0 to 55.9 percent) and 15.6 percent of the females (range, 7.7 to 30.4 percent). This finding has led Morey et al. (1987) to posit that the *2-7-8-4* codetype may be characteristic of alcohol dependence with higher elevations reflecting more severe degrees of dependency. Potential fallacies in this hypothesis will be discussed below. Most of the codetypes that were identified occurred with approximately the same frequency in male and female alcoholics. Codetypes *4-9* were identified in 11.4 percent of the males (range, 1.7 to 37.2 percent), and *1-2-3-4* ("neurotic") codetypes were found in 17.8 percent of the males (range, 11.0 to 40.0 percent) and 13.8 percent of the females (range, 7.7 to 33.9 percent). Again it appears that several codetypes are identified commonly (i.e., *2-7-8-4*, *4-9*, and *1-2-3-4*) and occur with about the same frequency. More "psychotic" codetypes (e.g., *6-8*) were not found in these studies in contrast to both the studies of mean profiles (see Table 6–1) and diagnostic groupings (see Table 6–2) reported earlier. *WNL* codetypes were actually the most frequent of any of the codetypes, that were identified, occurring in 42.6 percent of the males. A sizeable proportion of both male and female alcoholics were not classified into any of these codetypes, which again documents the heterogeneity that is characteristic of alcoholic patients.

The results of a cluster analysis of the MMPI data of a sample of 188 male alcoholics (all male patients who completed valid MMPIs during calendar years 1984, 1985, and 1986) in an alcohol treatment program in a private hospital will be used to illustrate the problems that are encountered in this line of research (Greene & Nichols, 1987). The raw scores without *K*-corrections for the standard validity and clinical scales masking Scale *5* were subjected to two methods of hierarchical cluster analysis using CLUSTAN (Wishart, 1978). The two methods of cluster analysis used most frequently with MMPI data were compared: Ward's method using Euclidian distance as the measure of similarity, and Complete Linkage (Furthest Neighbor) using product-moment correlation as the measure of similarity. Mojena's rule was used as a stopping criterion to determine the number of clusters within Ward's method, and then the same number of clusters were extracted within Complete Linkage. Table 6–4 summarizes the results of these two cluster analyses and Table 6–5 illustrates two of the cluster profiles and a sample of the variety of codetypes that were found within this group of alcoholic patients. The profiles for Clusters 2 and 3 are similar for the two methods, while the other two clusters for each method match less well. Cluster 1 for Ward's Method, which was *WNL*, was a subclinical *4-9* codetype with Scale *4* at a *T*-score of 68 and Scale *9* at a *T*-score of 65 and was somewhat like Cluster 4 for Complete Linkage. When the number of individuals who are found within similar clusters are determined for the two methods of clustering, 68.6 percent (24/35) overlap in Cluster 2 and 56.1 percent (23/41) overlap in Cluster 3. It appears that despite similar cluster profiles, there is only a moderate level of overlap of individuals. Table 6–5 illustrates how a variety of codetypes are found within Clusters 2 and 3 for

TABLE 6–4. CODETYPE CLUSTERS FROM TWO METHODS OF CLUSTER ANALYSIS IN MALE ALCOHOLICS

Ward's Method (Euclidean Distance)			Complete Linkage (Product-Moment Correlation)		
Cluster	Codetype	N	Cluster	Codetype	N
1	*WNL*	106	1	*2*	76
2	*4-8-9-7-6-2*	35	2	*9-4-7-8*	36
3	*2-7-1-3*	41	3	*2-7-8-4-3-1*	41
4	*8-2-7-1-3-4-6-5*	6	4	*9-4*	35

Greene, R.L. & Nichols, D.S. (1987). *Replicability and validity of the **2-8-7-4** codetype: A comment and some data*. Manuscript submitted for publication.

Note: Codetypes are based on clinical scales greater than or equal to a *T*-score of 70.

TABLE 6–5.   FREQUENCIES OF SPECIFIC CODETYPES WITHIN
TWO CLUSTERS FOR TWO METHODS OF CLUSTER ANALYSIS
IN MALE ALCOHOLICS

Ward's Method (Euclidean Distance)				Complete Linkage (Product-Moment Correlation)			
Codetype	N	Codetype	N	Codetype	N	Codetype	N
Codetypes within Cluster 2							
7-8/8-7	7	6-9	1	4-9/9-4	6	4-6	1
4-9/9-4	6	6-0	1	7-8/8-7	5	6-9	1
2-4/4-2	5	7-4	1	4-8	4	7	1
2-7/7-2	3	7-9	1	WNL	4	7-4	1
4-8	3	8-9	1	2	2	7-9	1
4-6	2	9	1	2-7	2	7-0	1
6-8/8-6	2	WNL	1	8-6	2	8	1
				9	2	8-9	1
				4	1		
Codetypes within Cluster 3							
2-7/7-2	11	2-8/8-2	3	2-4/4-2	10	WNL	2
1-2/2-1	8	1-6/6-1	2	2-7/7-2	6	1-7	1
2-4/4-2	6	1-7	1	2-8/8-2	4	4-7	1
1-3	4	2-3	1	7-8/8-7	4	4-9	1
2	4	7-8	1	1-2	2	6-8	1
				1-3	2	6-0	1
				2	2	7-3	1
				4-6/6-4	2	8-1	1

Greene, R.L., & Nichols, D.S. (1987). *Replicability and validity of the* **2-8-7-4** *codetype: A comment and some data*. Manuscript submitted for publication.
Note: Hierarchical cluster analyses were performed using CLUSTAN (Wishart, 1978) with the method and similarity index indicated on the raw scores without *K*-corrections for the standard validity and clinical scales masking Scale *5*.

these two methods of cluster analysis. From 10 to 16 different codetypes are found within these clusters, and the most frequent codetype (*2-7/7-2* in Cluster 3 for Ward's Method) occurs in only 26.8 percent (11/41) of the patients. It remains to be determined whether the results of the cluster analysis or the more traditional codetype analysis provides better description of these alcoholic patients. In any event, clinicians should be cautious in applying the results of cluster analysis to groups of patients until data are available on these issues.

The MMPIs of alcoholic patients also can be classified by codetype to identify any commonly occurring groups of profiles. Table 6–6 categorizes the various codetypes found in alcoholic patients by gender and ethnic group. Table 6–6 also provides the frequencies of these codetypes in psychiatric patients so that it can be determined whether the observed codetypes are specific to alcoholics or are seen in psychiatric samples more generally. A *2-4/4-2* codetype was the most frequent in white, male alcoholics, occurring in 15.3 percent of the cases (range, 7.7 to 20.8 percent). A *2-4/4-2* codetype also was the most frequent in

psychiatric patients at 7.7 percent of the cases. The next three most frequent codetypes (*2-7/7-2*, *4-9/9-4*, and *1-2/2-1*) occurred in 8.1, 8.5, and 6.5 percent of the cases, respectively. No other codetype occurred in over 4.0 percent of the alcoholics. A total of 57.5 percent of the white, male alcoholics could be classified in the 12 codetypes represented in Table 6–6, while 63.9 percent of the psychiatric patients were so classified. There appears to be little difference in the overall percentage of patients classified between these two samples, although some specific codetypes occur more or less frequently among alcoholics. Codetypes *2-4/4-2* and *2-7/7-2* are almost twice as frequent in the alcoholic samples as the psychiatric samples, while *4-8/8-4* codetypes are twice and *6-8/8-6* codetypes are six times as frequent in psychiatric samples.

It is more difficult to make any definitive statement about the codetypes seen in female alcoholics because of the limited number of studies (see Table 6–6). Again, it seems that *2-4/4-2* codetypes are the most frequent in white, female alcoholics, occurring in 14.8 percent of the cases (range, 10.4 to 15.4 percent). As was seen in

TABLE 6–6.   FREQUENCY OF MMPI CODETYPES IN ALCOHOLIC SAMPLES BY GENDER AND ETHNIC GROUP

Authors	N	Age	1-2/2-1	1-3/3-1	2-4/4-2	2-7/7-2	2-8/8-2	3-4/4-3	4-6/6-4	4-8/8-4	4-9/9-4	6-8/8-6	7-8/8-7	8-9/9-8	Total	A	B	C	D	E	F	G	H
White males																							
Colligan et al. (1985)	168	—	3.0	—	7.7	3.0	—	4.2	3.0	—	4.8	—	—	—	25.7	+	-	-	-	+	-	+	-
Evans (1984)	772	38.1	5.6	—	13.6	3.9	2.1	1.8	2.2	4.7	6.0	—	3.2	3.5	56.2	+	-	-	-	+	+	+	-
Hightower (1984)	72	23.3	—	—	—	2.8	6.9	—	—	6.9	11.1	6.9	5.6	12.5	65.2	+	-	+	+	-	+	-	
Hodo & Fowler (1976)	1009	43.4	—	—	20.8	9.1	3.9	—	—	4.3	11.2	0.6	3.0	1.7	54.5	+	-	+	+	-	+	-	
Hoffmann (1973) [1959]	393	44.8	4.0	2.3	15.8	2.8	2.6	4.3	4.0	3.3	13.7	2.3	1.0	0.5	56.5	+	-	-	-	-	+	+	-
Hoffmann (1973) [1971]	279	44.7	4.3	1.4	16.5	5.4	2.1	6.5	3.3	2.2	10.1	2.1	2.5	1.1	57.5	+	-	-	-	-	+	+	-
Holland et al. (1981)	79	42.0	2.5	5.1	16.5	5.1	7.6	2.5	—	2.5	6.3	2.5	8.9	3.8	60.8	+	-	-	-	-	+	-	
McLachlan (1975)	1681	45.6	6.7	3.1	12.2	12.3	4.7	2.0	1.2	3.4	7.1	0.8	2.8	3.1	56.3	+	-	-	-	+	+	-	-
Paige & Zappella (1969)	323	43.0	4.3	3.7	20.1	5.9	2.5	9.0	3.4	3.7	9.3	1.6	4.3	0.6	68.4	+	-	-	-	+	+	+	-
Schroeder & Piercy (1979)	920	45.4	10.2	2.8	15.3	8.4	4.6	3.9	2.2	3.7	7.7	1.5	3.6	1.7	65.6	+	-	+	-	+	+	-	-
Weighted totals	5528	43.5	6.5	2.9	15.3	8.1	3.8	3.4	2.1	3.8	8.5	1.3	3.1	2.4	57.5								
Indian males																							
Kline et al. (1973)	33	32.5	6.1	—	9.1	9.1	—	—	—	21.2	15.2	15.2	—	—	75.9	+	-	+	-	+	-	-	-
Male psychiatric patients																							
Hedlund & Won Cho (1979)	6154		4.9	2.3	7.7	4.8	5.5	1.4	3.1	7.3	6.4	7.2	5.6	3.6	63.9								
White females																							
Colligan et al. (1985)	77	—	—	6.5	10.4	7.8	—	20.8	6.5	10.4	6.5	—	—	—	68.9	+	-	-	-	+	-	+	-
McLachlan (1975)	519	45.6	2.9	2.1	15.4	9.6	5.2	5.6	5.2	6.4	6.2	1.5	2.3	2.7	63.0	+	-	-	-	+	+	-	-
Weighted totals	—	45.6	—	—	14.8	9.4	—	7.6	5.4	6.9	6.2	—	—	—	63.8								
Female psychiatric patients																							
Hedlund & Won Cho (1979)	2574		1.9	3.8	5.2	3.8	4.7	3.1	6.5	8.8	5.1	9.6	4.2	3.5	60.2								

males, the next most frequent codetypes (*2-7/7-2, 3-4/4-3, 4-8/8-4, 4-9/9-4,* and *4-6/6-4*) occurred in 9.4, 7.6, 6.9, 6.2, and 5.4 percent of the cases, respectively. No other codetype was even reported in the alcoholic and psychiatric samples summarized in Table 6–6. A total of 63.8 percent of the white, female alcoholics could be classified in the 12 codetypes represented in Table 6–6, while 60.2 percent of the female psychiatric patients were so classified. Again, there is little difference in the total number of patients classified in these codetypes, although several codetypes (*2-4/4-2, 2-7/7-2,* and *3-4/4-3*) were two to three times as frequent among the alcoholic patients compared with the psychiatric patients.

Table 6–6 also provides the ratings on the eight methodologic variables that are used to evaluate studies throughout this text. No study was evaluated positively on all eight variables with most studies only providing basic descriptions of their subjects (A), using appropriate statistical analyses (E), having adequate sample sizes (F), and reporting what scores were analyzed (G). It should be noted that none of these studies verified their diagnosis of substance misuse (B) other than to state that the patient was in some treatment program. The ratings on these eight methodologic variables provide a good indication of the state of the research on substance misuse and the issues that need to be considered in the future.

SUMMARY

A number of conclusions can be drawn from the performance of alcoholic patients on the standard MMPI validity and clinical scales. First, it is clear that there is not a unitary alcoholic personality. Instead, there seems to be a number of smaller, more discrete subgroups of alcoholics, although the composition of these subgroups depends on the method used to identify them. The codetype research suggests several subgroups (*2-4/4-2, 2-7/7-2,* and *4-9/9-4*) in both male and female alcoholics, and additional codetypes that are specific to males (*1-2/2-1*) and females (*3-4/4-3, 4-6/6-4,* and *4-8/8-4*). Empirical methods such as cluster analysis also identify subgroups of alcoholic patients (*2-7-8-4, 4-9,* and *1-2-3-4*) that have some degree of overlap with those identified by codetype research. These subgroups, however, account for only 25 to 35 percent of the alcoholic patients. Second, research into treatment outcomes/processes and/or drinking histories among the various subgroups of alcoholics has been limited. It would be interesting to know whether specific subgroups of alcoholic patients are more successful in par-

ticular types of treatment or whether they have particular histories of substance misuse. The influence of the multitude of moderator variables described earlier on these subgroups of alcoholics must be considered in any research in this area. Finally, more research is needed on groups other than the typical white, male alcoholic. As can be seen in Tables 6–1 to 6–6, there is almost no research on other groups of alcoholics. Again, it must be emphasized that the influence of moderator variables becomes more important as the MMPI performance of these other groups of alcoholic patients are studied.

SPECIAL/RESEARCH SCALES

A number of scales have been developed to identify individuals who have misused or have the potential to misuse alcohol: Hampton's (1951) *Al* Scale; Holmes' (1953) *Am* Scale; Hoyt and Sedlacek's (1958) *Ah* Scale; MacAndrew's (1965) *MAC* Scale; Linden's (1969) *ALX* Scale; Rosenberg's (1972) Composite Alcoholism Key (*Cak*); and Atsaides, Neuringer, and Davis' (1977) Institutionalized Chronic Alcoholism Scale (*ICAS*). MacAndrew (1986) developed the Substance Abuse Proclivity Scale (*SAP*) to identify substance misuse in adolescents. Two other scales have been developed to identify individuals who abuse drugs: Cavior, Kurtzberg, and Lipton's (1967) Heroin Addiction (*He*) Scale and Panton and Brisson's (1971) Drug Abuse (*DaS*) Scale. These latter two scales are reviewed in the next section of this chapter, and the items that comprise each of these scales can be found in Dahlstrom, Welsh, and Dahlstrom (1975). Sinnett (1986) has clarified the item composition of the *MAC*.

These first three alcoholism scales (*Al, Am,* and *Ah*) were developed by contrasting the item responses of alcoholics with normal individuals. Subsequent research has shown that these scales have difficulty separating alcoholics from other forms of psychopathology (Holmes, Dungan, & McLaughlin, 1982; MacAndrew & Geertsma, 1964; Rotman & Vestre, 1964). Since this diagnostic problem is generally of primary interest to the clinician, these three scales will not be reviewed here. The *ICAS* (Atsaides et al., 1977) was designed to separate alcoholics from neurotic psychiatric patients, which also has limited its usefulness in general psychiatric settings. Subsequent research (Rhodes & Chang, 1978) has confirmed this limitation of the *ICAS*. The *SAP* scale is too new to have any published research, so it will not be reviewed either. Consequently, most research with special scales in alcoholics has focused on the *MAC*.

It is informative to examine the specific items that are found on these five alcoholism scales (*Ah, Al, Am, ALX, Cak,* and *MAC*). Only three items (215, 294, and 460) are found on all six of these scales, and two of these items (215 and 460) are excluded by MacAndrew (1965) because they have direct reference to alcoholism. An additional 10 items (61, 95, 127, 140, 251, 365, 378, 387, 446, and 477) are found on any four of these six scales. Five of these 13 items are found among the 7 items (46, 61, 156, 215, 251, 378, and 460) that discriminated male and female alcoholics from both normal individuals and psychiatric patients (Conley & Kammeier, 1980a, 1980b), and the five items have substantial face validity. Davis, Colligan, Morse, and Offord (1987) also found that item 215 provided a higher hit rate than any of the alcoholism scales they studied in medical patients. The variability in the items on specific alcoholism scales and the question on whether face-valid items should be included on these scales are two issues that need to be kept in mind when reviewing the data below.

All of these alcoholism scales are based on a unitary concept of alcoholism. The inherent difficulties with such an approach were described previously and will not be repeated here. MacAndrew's (1981b) conceptualization of the *MAC* as a bipolar measure of sensitivity to reward and punishment, with neurotics who drink too much earning low scores, is one attempt to go beyond this unitary concept of alcoholism. This issue will be explored further once the general characteristics of the *MAC* have been described.

MacAndrew (1965) developed the *MAC* to separate male alcoholic outpatients from male nonalcoholic psychiatric outpatients. He also suggested that a cutting score of 24 was optimal in this setting for identifying the alcoholic patients. MacAndrew excluded any patient whose raw score on Scale *F* was > 16, although he later decided that the Scale *F* criterion should be abandoned in favor of excluding patients whose Scale *L* was > 9 (MacAndrew, 1979). The alcoholic patients were older (41.8 years of age) than the psychiatric patients (34.7 years of age). The potential effects of gender, age, and profile validity (Apfeldorf & Hunley, 1976) on classification accuracy must be

kept in mind when these data are generalized to other settings. MacAndrew created a base rate of alcoholism of 50 percent in his study by including equal numbers of alcoholic outpatients and nonalcoholic psychiatric outpatients. A cutting score of 24 or greater on the *MAC* correctly classified 162 alcoholic patients (true positives) and incorrectly classified 38 (false negatives). This cutting score also correctly classified 165 psychiatric patients (true negatives) and incorrectly classified 35 (false positives) for an overall hit rate or classification rate of 81.75 percent. The sensitivity rating, the number of alcoholic patients who were classified correctly, was 82.23 percent, and the specificity rating, the number of psychiatric patients who were classified correctly, was 81.28 percent, which indicates that this cutting score of 24 or greater was not biased toward over- or under-classification of either group in this study. This same point can be made by noting the relationship between the percentage of false negatives (9.5 percent) and false positives (8.75 percent). The *MAC* did an excellent job of improving on the classification rate of the alcoholics in this study since it produced an overall classification rate of 81.75 percent in comparison with the base rate of 50 percent. MacAndrew appropriately cross-validated his scale and found that classification accuracy only shrank to 81.5 percent, which is phenomenally small shrinkage. MacAndrew's success in identifying alcoholics in this study was followed by a deluge of research investigating various aspects of the *MAC*.

Probably no single special scale on the MMPI has generated the amount of research as the *MAC*. Even a cursory review of Tables 6–7 to 6–11 will show that the *MAC* has been investigated widely in a variety of settings with a number of different samples. In order to facilitate the interpretation of these data, these tables have been divided by sample (normals, Table 6–8; psychiatric patients, Table 6–9; medical patients, Table 6–10; and alcoholics, Table 6–11), and within each table, the data have been subdivided by age (adults and adolescents), gender, and ethnicity (white, black, Hispanic, and American Indian). Before trying to draw any conclusions based on the data in Tables 6–8 to 6–10, several comments must be made about the types of studies that are available to review. Table 6–7 summarizes the research that has been conducted on the *MAC* by sample, age, gender, and ethnic group. Several conclusions are readily apparent. First, almost two-thirds (60.2

**TABLE 6–7.   FREQUENCY OF RESEARCH ON THE MACANDREW
SCALE (*MAC*) BY SAMPLE, ETHNIC GROUP,
GENDER, AND AGE**

Ethnic Group	Sample				
	Normal	Psychiatric	Alcoholic	Polydrug	Total
White					
Adult					
Female	9	6	12	2	29
Male	17	35	68	10	130
Adolescent					
Female	3	7	2	0	12
Male	8	7	9	0	24
Black					
Adult					
Female	0	0	1	0	1
Male	1	4	8	7	20
Adolescent					
Female	0	0	0	0	0
Male	0	0	0	0	0
Totals	38	59	100	19	216

percent) of the studies are on white males. There are essentially no data reported on nonwhite ethnic groups other than blacks and surprising little data on blacks compared with the amount of data on whites. Second, there is a fair amount of data (13.4 percent of the studies) on white adult females, and virtually no data on any other nonwhite female groups. Over 70 percent of these samples have been drawn from white adults. Third, there are no data on adolescent samples in any minority group and relatively few studies of white adolescent alcoholics. It is somewhat surprising with the recent emphasis on substance use and misuse in adolescents that there are so few studies reported. Table 6–7 also highlights the areas in which research is needed to address the issues raised throughout this chapter.

Table 6–8 provides the descriptive data for the *MAC* by gender, age, and ethnic group in normal samples. The weighted mean score for white, adult males was 23.13 (SD, 4.31), which is only slightly below MacAndrew's traditional cutting score of 24. There are notable variations in scores among these white, adult male samples with means ranging from 16.82 (Saunders & Schuckit, 1981) to 27.40 (Vega, 1971), and standard deviations ranging from 2.79 (Ollendick, 1984) to 6.90 (Rich & Davis, 1969). These mean scores also are significantly discrepant from the original Minnesota normative group, in which males had a mean score on the *MAC* of 19.52 (SD, 3.58). This large difference in mean scores on the *MAC* between males in the original normative group and the scores reported in Table 6–8 indicates that *T*-score conversions based on the original normative group should be used cautiously. For example, a raw score of 24 is equivalent to a *T*-score of 63.

One explanation of these variations in mean *MAC* scores in normal, white, adult males would be that older samples have higher mean scores on the *MAC* (the correlation between age and mean *MAC* score in Table 6–8 is 0.656; this correlation decreases to 0.52 if white adolescent males are included). However, Colligan and Offord (1987) reported that *MAC* scores in their sample of normal, white, adult males hardly varied with age (ages 20 to 29, 22.71; ages 30 to 39, 22.27; ages 40 to 49, 22.43; ages 50 to 59, 22.50; ages 60 to 69, 22.40; ages 70+, 22.49), which limits the appropriateness of such an explanation. There also are few differences in mean scores on the *MAC* between white, male adults (M, 23.13; SD, 4.31) and adolescents (M, 22.65; SD, 3.72) summarized in Table 6–8, which further limits any explanation based on age effects. No doubt a number of moderator variables are affecting performance on the *MAC* in these normal, white, adult male samples.

Gender differences in these normal, white, adult and adolescent samples are very consistent, with women scoring approximately two raw-score points lower than men. The weighted mean score for white, adult females was 20.33 (SD, 3.82), while the weighted mean score for men was 23.13 (SD, 4.31). Again, there are limited differences between normal adult and adolescent (M, 20.86; SD,

TABLE 6–8.   PERFORMANCE ON THE MACANDREW ALCOHOLISM SCALE *(MAC)* IN NORMAL SAMPLES AS A FUNCTION OF AGE, GENDER, AND ETHNICITY

Authors	N	Age	MAC M	MAC SD	Cutting Score	False Positives	Hit Rate	Base Rate
White males								
Adults								
Apfeldorf & Hunley (1975)	118	64.50	24.98	4.71	27	30.0	62.0	79
Apfeldorf & Hunley (1981)	151	63.00	26.99	5.57	—	—	—	—
Colligan & Offord (1987)	646	47.50	22.46	4.19	24	38.0	—	—
Hightower (1984)	37	22.05	20.30	3.87	—	—	—	—
Hoffmann et al. (1974)	148	20.50	23.99	3.79	26	28.0	72.0	—
Hoffmann et al. (1984)	1403	26.00	—	—	26	21.0	78.0	86
Leon et al. (1979)	44	35.53	24.86	3.85	—	—	—	—
Leon et al. (1979)	37	31.83	21.96	3.66	—	—	—	—
MacAndrew (1979)	79	19.10	20.22	3.88	—	—	—	—
Newlin (1985) [fam hist +]	11	—	25.80	—	—	—	—	—
Newlin (1985) [fam hist -]	74	—	23.30	—	—	—	—	—
Ollendick (1984)								
[non-custody]	38	—	22.89	3.50	—	—	—	—
Ollendick (1984) [custody]	38	—	20.11	2.79	—	—	—	—
Rich & Davis (1969)	60	—	24.60	6.90	—	—	74.0	67
Saunders & Schuckit (1981)								
[fam +]	30	23.00	18.86	4.08	—	—	—	—
Saunders & Schuckit (1981)								
[fam -]	30	23.00	16.82	3.24	—	—	—	—
Vega (1971)	31	40.20	27.40	3.90	26	19.0	71.0	55
Weighted totals		34.50	23.13	4.31		26.5	76.2	
N	2975	2754	1572	1487		2346	1760	—
Adolescents								
Klinge (1983) [minimal users]	—	11.17	14.81	[12.08]	—	—	—	—
Moore (1984) [rare]	40	17.70	21.20	3.21	25	8.0	83.0	67
Moore (1984) [occasional]	40	17.70	23.60	3.68	25	50.0	69.0	67
Moore (1985) [rare]	50	18.10	21.60	3.11	—	8.0	84.0	67
Moore (1985) [occasional]	50	18.10	23.60	3.68	—	30.0	77.0	67
Wisniewski et al. (1985)	89	16.26	—	—	26	10.0	83.0	50
Wolfson & Erbaugh (1984)	59	16.12	21.95	4.15	26	20.0	68.0	54
Yescalis (1984)	24	15.50	25.36	4.92	—	—	—	—
Weighted totals		17.03	22.65	3.72		19.2	77.8	
N	352	352	263	263		328	328	
White females								
Adults								
Colligan & Offord (1987)	762	46.10	20.55	3.48	24	21.0	—	—
Friedrich & Loftsgard (1978b)	36	34.70	22.00	5.20	24	29.0	—	—
Hoffmann et al. (1984)	323	30.00	—	—	26	13.0	81.0	81
Leon et al. (1979)	73	44.94	20.36	3.42	—	—	—	—
Leon et al. (1979)	81	36.25	19.62	3.33	—	—	—	—
Leon et al. (1979)	56	39.96	20.30	4.65	—	—	—	—
Navarro (1979)	20	34.00	[7.78]	5.72	—	—	—	—
Rich & Davis (1969)	60	—	22.00	5.50	—	—	77.0	67
Tarter et al. (1977)	49	32.30	20.00	5.80	—	—	—	—
Weighted totals		40.56	20.33	3.82		19.0	80.4	
N	1460	1400	1137	1137		1121	383	
Adolescents								
Wisniewski et al. (1985)	113	15.87	—	—	26	3.0	95.0	50
Wolfson & Erbaugh (1984)	76	15.84	20.47	3.80	24	14.0	74.0	60
Yescalis (1984)	24	15.50	22.09	4.66	—	—	—	—
Weighted totals		15.82	20.86	4.01		7.4	86.6	
N	213	213	100	100		189	189	
Black males								
Adults								
Hightower (1984)	19	23.26	21.30	3.29	24	—	—	—

4.01) samples of women. There is less variation in the *MAC* scores of these adult women as compared with adult men with means ranging from 19.62 (Leon et al., 1979) to 22.00 (Friedrich & Loftsgard, 1978b; Rich & Davis, 1969) and standard deviations ranging from 3.33 (Leon et al., 1979) to 5.80 (Tarter, McBride, Buonpane, & Schneider, 1977). Colligan and Offord (1987) also found that the *MAC* scores in their sample of normal, white, adult females were two raw-score points lower than their male counterparts (ages 20 to 29, 19.80; ages 30 to 39, 20.29; ages 40 to 49, 20.54; ages 50 to 59, 20.76; ages 60 to 69, 20.28; ages 70+, 21.58). These mean scores again are significantly discrepant from the original Minnesota normative group, in which females had a mean score on the *MAC* of 17.43 (SD, 3.50). However, the discrepancy of two raw-score points between males (M, 19.52; SD, 3.58) and females is still found in the original Minnesota normative group. It appears that consistent gender differences are found on the *MAC*, with women scoring approximately two raw-score points lower than their male cohorts.

In the only study of normal, black, adult males, the weighted score (M, 21.30; SD, 3.29) on the *MAC* was only slightly higher than in white samples (M, 23.13; SD, 4.31). These limited data suggest that the *MAC* should be used cautiously in black samples, which has been noted by several authors (cf. Graham & Mayo, 1985; Walters, Greene, Jeffrey, Kruzich, & Haskin, 1983). The absence of data on other nonwhite ethnic groups prevents any generalizations about performance on the *MAC* in these groups. In addition, normative data is sorely needed on female and adolescent samples in all nonwhite ethnic groups.

Few of the studies summarized in Table 6–8 have provided any information on the percentage of false positives and/or hit rates. The percentage of false positives in white, male adults ranged from 19 to 38 percent and averaged 26.5 percent. White male adolescents and white females averaged nearly 19 percent false positives, while the white, female adolescents only averaged 7.4 percent. Hit rates across all four groups were fairly comparable, ranging from 76.2 to 86.6 percent. One pattern that is apparent in Table 6–8 is the tendency of the percentage of false positives to increase and the hit rate to decrease as the number of studies increases. Thus, white, adult males have been studied the most extensively (17 samples, N

= 2975) and have the highest percentage of false positives and lowest hit rate, while the few studies of white, female adolescents (3 samples, N = 213), have demonstrated the lowest percentage of false positives and the highest hit rate among these normal individuals.

Table 6–9 provides the descriptive data for the *MAC* by gender, age, and ethnic group in psychiatric samples. Both white, adult male (M, 23.30; SD, 4.60) and female (M, 21.74; SD, 4.78) psychiatric samples score slightly higher (approximately one raw-score point) than their normal counterparts (male: M, 23.13; SD, 4.31; female: M, 20.33; SD, 3.82). Again, males score approximately two raw-score points higher than females. Both male and female psychiatric patients appear to be more variable in their performance on the *MAC* with slightly larger standard deviations. This increase in variability of *MAC* scores implies that hit rates or classification accuracy will decline when alcoholic patients are contrasted to psychiatric patients instead of normal individuals, which will be reviewed below. In contrast to the adult samples, both male and female adolescent psychiatric patients have lower mean scores on the *MAC* than their normal counterparts. This difference is most apparent in the male adolescents whose scores are almost three points lower in the psychiatric samples. The adolescent samples also are extremely variable in their performance with standard deviations, which are almost twice as large as found in their normal colleagues.

Black, male psychiatric patients have a weighted mean score of 26.32 (SD, 4.86) on the *MAC*, which is significantly higher than MacAndrew's (1965) recommended cutting score of 24. These black patients have a mean score that is approximately one raw-score point higher than their normal colleagues. There is no increase in the variability of their performance as was noted in the white samples of psychiatric patients. The limited number of studies on black psychiatric patients precludes making any definitive statements about their performance on the *MAC*. However, the caution previously noted about the use of the *MAC* in nonwhite ethnic groups clearly can be reiterated on the basis of these data. The total absence of data on psychiatric patients in other nonwhite ethnic groups or with any female nonwhite ethnic group is an area of research that needs prompt attention.

TABLE 6–9. PERFORMANCE ON THE MACANDREW ALCOHOLISM SCALE *(MAC)*
IN PSYCHIATRIC SAMPLES AS A FUNCTION OF AGE, GENDER, AND ETHNICITY

Authors	N	Age	MAC		Cutting Score	False Positives	Hit Rate	Base Rate
			M	SD				
White males								
Adults								
Apfeldorf & Hunley (1981) [drinking]	15	51.50	24.00	4.55	—	—	—	—
Apfeldorf & Hunley (1981)	71	51.90	23.94	5.32	—	—	—	—
Atsaides et al. (1977)	70	41.30	—	—	28	31.0	—	—
Bruder (1982)	60	40.50	—	—	24	70.0	55.0	50
Burke & Marcus (1977)	45	37.00	23.00	5.20	24	33.0	—	—
Burke & Marcus (1977)	27	34.20	21.20	4.10	24	22.0	—	—
Clopton et al. (1980) [original]	56	—	26.70	—	27	41.0	68.0	50
Clopton et al. (1980) [cross-valid]	56	—	26.70	—	27	50.0	66.0	50
Davis et al. (1987)	92	37.50	—	—	24	46.0	—	—
de Groot & Adamson (1973)	98	44.00	22.90	5.23	24	27.0	69.0	60
Graham & Mayo (1985)	150	35.15	24.94	—	28	25.0	68.0	50
Hightower (1984)	22	22.15	22.36	4.29	24	34.0	69.0	42
Holmes et al. (1982)	60	—	—	—	24	53.0	64.0	67
Kranitz (1972)	50	—	22.54	4.22	—	—	—	—
Lachar et al. (1976)	101	42.40	22.85	4.95	24	44.0	68.0	39
MacAndrew (1965) [original]	200	34.70	19.56	4.58	24	10.0	82.0	50
MacAndrew (1965) [cross-valid]	100	34.70	20.30	4.10	24	10.0	82.0	50
MacAndrew (1982)	48	19.20	19.52	3.98	—	—	—	—
Preng & Clopton (1986a) [neurotic]	28	42.43	26.07	4.72	29	—	65.0	33
Preng & Clopton (1986a) [pers. dis.]	28	36.00	27.14	4.03	29	—	65.0	33
Rhodes (1969)	200	36.05	20.89	4.51	24	28.0	76.0	50
Rhodes & Chang (1978)	50	43.80	—	—	24	—	81.0	60
Rich & Davis (1969)	60	—	24.40	5.30	—	—	73.0	67
Rosenberg (1972)	56	38.80	25.20	4.00	—	—	—	—
Ruff et al. (1975)	33	34.37	25.97	—	—	—	—	—
Schwartz & Graham (1979) [antisoc]	57	—	27.10	3.90	—	—	—	—
Schwartz & Graham (1979) [general]	60	—	26.30	5.40	—	—	—	—
Svanum et al. (1982)	95	27.00	21.47	5.10	25	24.0	83.0	50
Uecker (1970)	56	38.70	25.18	4.01	24	61.0	70.0	66
Vega (1971)	27	39.70	23.20	4.60	26	19.0	71.0	55
Walters et al. (1983)	46	26.26	24.48	4.53	24	50.0	66.0	50
Whisler & Cantor (1966)	67	43.90	25.67	4.36	28	21.0	62.0	52
Williams et al. (1971)	50	47.40	25.50	—	—	—	—	—
Williams et al. (1971) [hvy drk]	12	47.40	27.70	—	—	—	—	—
Zager & Megargee (1981) [prisoners]	39	22.60	25.70	3.90	—	—	—	—
Weighted totals		37.21	23.30	4.60		31.4	72.3	
N	2285	1886	1953	1596		1628	1560	
Adolescents								
Watson et al. (1983)	31	13.5	17.94	6.49	—	—	—	—
Watson et al. (1983)	56	15.0	18.45	8.04	—	—	—	—
Watson et al. (1983)	117	16.0	18.09	8.02	—	—	—	—
Watson et al. (1983)	172	17.0	20.12	8.36	—	—	—	—
Watson et al. (1983)	288	18.0	19.57	8.15	—	—	—	—

(Continues.)

TABLE 6–9.   *(Continued.)*

Authors	N	Age	MAC M	MAC SD	Cutting Score	False Positives	Hit Rate	Base Rate
Adolelscents *(continued)*								
Wolfson & Erbaugh (1984) [inpts.]	47	14.68	24.91	5.08	26	53.0	68.0	52
Wolfson & Erbaugh (1984) [outpts.]	38	15.13	22.87	5.15	26	29.0	68.0	57
Weighted totals		16.69	19.82	7.76		42.3	68.0	
N	749	749	749			85	85	
White females								
Adults								
Davis et al. (1987)	122	41.80	—	—	24	24.0	—	—
Navarro (1979)	20	35.00	[10.45]	3.50	—	—	—	—
Rich & Davis (1969)	60	—	21.90	4.60	—	—	75.0	67
Schwartz & Graham (1979) [antisoc]	73	—	23.80	4.50	28	21.0	76.0	91
Schwartz & Graham (1979) [general]	135	—	23.50	5.20	28	21.0	76.0	91
Svanum et al. (1982)	75	29.00	19.45	4.77	23	20.0	83.0	50
Weighted totals		36.75	21.74	4.78		21.7	77.4	
N	485	217	363	363		405	343	
Adolescents								
Watson et al. (1983)	18	13.5	20.00	7.20	—	—	—	—
Watson et al. (1983)	40	15.0	17.83	6.23	—	—	—	—
Watson et al. (1983)	79	16.0	21.16	8.05	—	—	—	—
Watson et al. (1983)	109	17.0	20.15	7.93	—	—	—	—
Watson et al. (1983)	112	18.0	20.07	7.06	—	—	—	—
Wolfson & Erbaugh (1984) [inpts.]	43	15.23	22.33	4.64	24	44.0	74.0	54
Wolfson & Erbaugh (1984) [outpts.]	43	15.42	21.02	4.18	24	30.0	74.0	54
Weighted totals		16.43	20.39	6.87		37.0	74.0	
N	444	444	444	444		86	86	
Black males								
Adults								
Graham & Mayo (1985)	40	—	27.18	—	26	63.0	58.0	50
Hightower (1984)	21	23.70	22.58	5.02	24	34.0	69.0	42
Walters et al. (1983)	27	24.41	27.37	4.53	25	74.0	56.0	50
Zager & Megargee (1981)	40	22.30	26.70	5.00	—	—	—	—
Weighted totals		23.28	26.32	4.86		59.5	60.0	
N	128	88	128	88		88	88	

It is slightly more common for percentages of false positives and hit rates to be reported for psychiatric patients than was seen in the normal individuals described above. The percentage of false positives in white, male adults ranged from 10 to 70 percent and averaged 31.4 percent. White, male adolescents averaged 42.3 percent false positives (range, 29 to 53 percent) and white, female adolescents averaged 37.0 percent (range, 30 to 44 percent); these findings must be tempered by the fact that both are based on only two samples.

White females averaged 21.7 percent false positives (range, 20 to 24 percent). The percentage of false positives was significantly higher in black, adult males, where it averaged 59.5 percent and ranged from 34 to 74 percent. All of these percentages of false positives are higher than in the comparable group of normal individuals. This increased rate of false positives is part of the basis for the more limited success with the *MAC* in separating alcoholic patients from psychiatric patients (cf. Apfeldorf & Hunley, 1981; Preng & Clopton, 1986b).

Hit rates across these groups of psychiatric patients varied substantially. While hit rates in the groups of normal individuals averaged from 76.2 to 86.6 percent, hit rates in the psychiatric patients averaged from 60.0 to 77.4 percent. Of course, this decrease in hit rate is a function of the increase in false positives already noted. White, adult males had an average hit rate of 72.3 percent (range, 55 to 83 percent), and white, adult females averaged 77.4 percent (range, 75 to 83 percent). Black, adult males had an average hit rate of only 60.0 percent (range, 56 to 69 percent). This latter finding is the basis for the caution about using the *MAC* with members of ethnic minorities (cf. Graham & Mayo, 1985; Walters et al., 1983). The question of whether these results in black, adult male psychiatric patients also would be found in females and members of other ethnic groups has not been examined. Until such data are available, use of the *MAC* with any ethnic minority must be considered carefully.

Table 6–10 provides the limited amount of descriptive data that are available for the *MAC* by gender in medical samples. The virtual lack of data on medical patients is somewhat surprising since it was noted earlier that nearly 90 percent of the individuals who misuse alcohol are seen by their physician in a year (Kamerown et al., 1986). Davis et al. (1987) reported that their white, adult, male medical patients had an average of 37.3 percent false positives, and their female medical patients averaged 20.3 percent. These percentages of false positives in medical patients are fairly comparable with those reported in psychiatric patients, so it would be expected that hit rates also would be comparable. The need for research on this population should be evident, particularly with other age groups and ethnic minorities.

Table 6–11 provides the descriptive data for the *MAC* by gender, age, and ethnic group in alcoholic

samples. Even a cursory examination of Table 6–11 will reveal the multitude of studies on the *MAC* in alcoholics. White, adult, male alcoholics scored significantly higher (M, 28.41; SD, 5.45) than their female counterparts (M, 25.33; SD, 4.28). The pattern already noted in normal individuals and psychiatric patients for males to score about two raw-score points higher than females also is apparent, and even larger in alcoholic samples. These samples of alcoholic patients demonstrated significant variability in their *MAC* scores with mean scores in white, adult males ranging from 23.30 (Tarter et al., 1977) to 30.83 (Faulstich, Carey, Delatte, & Delatte, 1985), and in white, adult females from 25.10 (McKenna & Pickens, 1983) to 28.60 (Schwartz & Graham, 1979). Male and female, white adolescents have weighted mean scores intermediate to those for adults. Male adolescents (M, 27.09) score a little over one raw-score point lower than adult males (M, 28.41), and female adolescents (M, 26.20) score almost one raw-score point higher than adult females (M, 25.33). There is little difference in the weighted mean score between male and female adolescents in contrast to the rather standard two-point raw-score difference seen in all of adult groups. There is a pronounced difference in the mean scores between adolescent alcoholics and their psychiatric and normal counterparts. These substantial differences between adolescent alcoholics and other adolescent groups will produce very large increments in hit rates compared with adult groups.

Black, male alcoholics have a weighted mean score of 27.40 (SD, 4.67) that is only one raw-score point higher than their psychiatric colleagues. These small differences in mean scores between black alcoholics and psychiatric patients make it nearly impossible for the *MAC* to discriminate between these groups, which is another basis for the caution about using the *MAC* with

TABLE 6–10.   PERFORMANCE ON THE MACANDREW ALCOHOLISM SCALE *(MAC)* **IN MEDICAL SAMPLES AS A FUNCTION OF AGE AND GENDER**

Authors	N	Age	MAC		Cutting Score	False Positives	Hit Rate	Base Rate
			M	SD				
White male adults								
Davis et al. (1987) [unselected]	2500	50.5	—	—	24	33.0	—	—
Davis et al. (1987) [contemporary]	2853	47.6	—	—	24	41.0	—	—
Weighted totals	5353	49.0				37.3		
White female adults								
Davis et al. (1987) [unselected]	2500	49.7	—	—	24	19.0	—	—
Davis et al. (1987) [contemporary]	4237	48.3	—	—	24	21.0	—	—
Weighted totals	6737	48.8				20.3		

TABLE 6–11. PERFORMANCE ON THE MACANDREW ALCOHOLISM SCALE (MAC) IN ALCOHOLIC SAMPLES AS A FUNCTION OF AGE, GENDER, AND ETHNICITY

Authors	N	Age	MAC M	MAC SD	Cutting Score	False Negatives	Hit Rate	Base Rate
White males								
Adults								
Apfeldorf & Hunley (1975)	31	58.90	28.10	4.58	27	7.0	62.0	79
Apfeldorf & Hunley (1975) [prbm drk]	94	60.80	27.72	4.08	27	16.0	63.0	56
Apfeldorf & Hunley (1981)	15	56.30	30.80	4.20	—	—	—	—
Apfeldorf & Hunley (1981) [excess]	28	55.10	30.32	4.24	—	—	—	—
Apfeldorf & Hunley (1981) [drinking]	29	57.10	29.28	6.01	—	—	—	—
Atsaides et al. (1977)	70	42.00	—	—	28	34.0	67.0	50
Bruder (1982)	60	41.70	—	—	24	20.0	55.0	50
Burke & Marcus (1977)	73	37.80	27.10	4.40	24	—	85.0	—
Chang et al. (1973)	407	—	—	—	24	17.0	—	—
Clopton et al. (1980) [original]	56	—	29.20	—	27	23.0	68.0	50
Clopton et al. (1980) [cross-valid]	56	—	29.20	—	27	18.0	66.0	50
Davis et al. (1987)	525	46.00	—	—	24	29.0	—	—
de Groot & Adamson (1973)	64	43.00	28.90	4.45	24	4.0	69.0	60
Faulstich et al. (1985)	20	25.00	29.10	—	—	—	—	—
Faulstich et al. (1985)	24	35.00	30.83	—	—	—	—	—
Faulstich et al. (1985)	26	45.00	29.15	—	—	—	—	—
Faulstich et al. (1985)	21	57.50	26.47	—	—	—	—	—
Friedrich & Loftsgard (1978a)	100	35.00	25.40	4.20	24	29.0	—	—
Friedrich & Loftsgard (1978b)	36	37.90	25.50	4.40	24	21.0	—	—
Gellens et al. (1976)	80	—	29.50	—	—	—	—	—
Graham & Mayo (1985)	150	39.71	28.67	—	28	39.0	68.0	50
Hightower (1984)	46	22.76	25.98	4.37	24	28.0	69.0	42
Hoffmann et al. (1974)	25	20.50	26.60	5.09	26	28.0	72.0	50
Hoffmann et al. (1974) [retest]	25	33.50	27.72	3.36	26	28.0	72.0	50
Hoffmann et al. (1984)	228	35.00	—	—	26	24.0	85.0	14
Holmes et al. (1982) [court com.]	60	—	—	—	24	35.0	64.0	67
Holmes et al. (1982) [voluntary]	60	—	—	—	—	25.0	64.0	67
Kranitz (1972)	50	—	26.94	5.01	—	—	—	—
Lachar et al. (1976)	65	42.40	28.30	4.30	24	12.0	79.0	50
MacAndrew (1965) [original]	200	41.80	28.00	4.48	24	9.0	82.0	50
MacAndrew (1965) [cross-valid]	100	41.80	27.34	4.33	24	9.0	82.0	50
MacAndrew (1979)	53	46.80	28.49	3.94	24	11.0	—	—
MacAndrew (1979) [DWI]	49	43.24	25.86	4.72	—	—	—	—
McKenna & Pickens (1983) [fm his-]	1115	40.60	28.20	—	—	—	—	—
McKenna & Pickens (1983) [1 al par]	249	40.60	28.40	—	—	—	—	—
McKenna & Pickens (1983) [2 al par]	47	40.60	29.00	—	—	—	—	—
O'Neil et al. (1983)	194	44.00	29.80	4.37	24	10.0	—	—
Pfost et al. (1984)	38	45.90	27.90	4.90	24	18.0	—	—
Preng & Clopton (1986a)	28	48.36	30.32	3.66	26	—	64.0	60
Preng & Clopton (1986a) [neurotic]	28	43.29	26.75	4.42	26	—	64.0	60
Preng & Clopton (1986a) [pers. dis.]	28	38.57	30.43	4.02	26	—	64.0	60

Rhodes (1969)	200	40.30	30.06	[9.34]	24	20.0	76.0	50
Rhodes & Chang (1978)	75	48.17	—	—	24	8.0	81.0	60
Rich & Davis (1969)	60	—	30.50	4.40	—	—	73.0	67
Rohan (1972)	40	43.30	28.10	3.28	—	15.0	—	—
Rohan et al. (1969)	58	46.10	28.24	4.53	24	14.0	—	—
Rosenburg (1972)	111	43.60	28.00	4.20	—	—	—	—
Ruff et al. (1975)	27	33.61	26.44	—	—	—	—	—
Schwartz & Graham (1979)	44	—	26.90	3.90	—	—	—	—
Sher & McCrady (1984)	19	38.00	27.30	4.50	—	—	—	—
Sher & McCrady (1984)	42	38.00	29.40	4.20	—	—	—	—
Snyder et al. (1985)	43	33.50	29.40	4.00	—	—	—	—
Sutker et al. (1979)	175	44.00	30.65	—	—	34.0	—	—
Svanum et al. (1982)	95	27.00	29.99	3.65	25	9.0	73.0	50
Tarter et al. (1977)	28	48.00	23.30	3.10	—	—	—	—
Tarter et al. (1977)	38	38.90	28.50	3.70	—	—	—	—
Thornton et al. (1979)	25	40.00	30.20	4.11	—	—	—	—
Uecker (1970)	111	43.60	28.05	4.24	24	15.0	70.0	66
Uecker et al. (1980)	40	41.60	26.80	4.38	24	20.0	83.0	100
Vega (1971)	38	44.20	30.80	5.30	26	10.0	71.0	55
Vega (1971) [replication]	40	42.00	30.30	5.70	26	10.0	71.0	55
Walters et al. (1983)	46	34.89	27.63	3.80	24	17.0	66.0	50
Whisler & Cantor (1966)	73	46.80	28.06	4.99	28	18.0	62.0	52
Williams et al. (1971)	53	43.20	28.70	—	—	—	—	—
Willis et al. (1979)	122	37.20	29.08	—	—	—	—	—
Willis et al. (1979) [nonsmokers]	19	37.20	26.79	—	—	—	—	—
Zager & Megargee (1981) [heavy]	55	23.60	28.00	4.30	—	—	—	—
Zager & Megargee (1981) [moderate]	182	22.40	27.40	4.30	—	—	—	—
Weighted totals		40.82	28.41	5.45		20.4	73.1	
N	6512	5639	5027	2787		3734	2325	
Adolescents								
Klinge (1983) [moderate users]	—	11-17	20.40	[10.12]	—	—	—	—
Klinge (1983) [heavy users]	—	11-17	25.16	[9.70]	—	—	—	—
MacAndrew (1982)	91	18.90	27.46	4.42	—	—	—	—
Moore (1984) [weekly]	40	17.70	26.20	3.61	25	18.0	73.0	33
Moore (1984) [biweekly]	40	17.70	27.60	3.91	25	25.0	75.0	33
Moore (1985) [weekly]	50	18.10	26.30	3.92	—	24.0	79.0	33
Moore (1985) [biweekly]	50	18.10	27.30	3.71	—	16.0	82.0	33
Wisniewski et al. (1985) [prb drk]	88	16.26	—	—	27	7.0	83.0	50
Wolfson & Erbaugh (1984)	50	16.06	27.32	4.24	26	30.0	68.0	54
Weighted totals		17.55	27.09	4.04		18.4	77.6	
N	409	409	321	321		318	318	
White females								
Adults								
Davis et al. (1987)	211	46.00	—	—	24	62.0	—	—
Hoffmann et al. (1984)	76	38.00	—	—	26	44.0	81.0	19
Jones et al. (1980)	21	44.10	28.29	3.86	—	—	—	—
Jones et al. (1980) [menstr.]	10	44.10	28.30	5.29	—	—	—	—

(Continues.)

TABLE 6–11.   *(Continued.)*

Authors	N	Age	MAC M	MAC SD	Cutting Score	False Negatives	Hit Rate	Base Rate
White females								
Adults *(continued.)*								
McKenna & Pickens (1983) [fam his-]	376	41.00	25.10	—	—	—	—	—
McKenna & Pickens (1983) [1 al par]	107	41.00	25.30	—	—	—	—	—
McKenna & Pickens (1983) [2 al par]	35	41.00	26.10	—	—	—	—	—
Navarro (1979)	20	35.00	[9.53]	4.98	—	—	75.0	67
Rich & Davis (1969)	60	—	26.60	4.10	—	—	76.0	91
Schwartz & Graham (1979)	20	—	28.60	5.00	28	3.0	76.0	91
Snyder et al. (1985)	34	38.00	26.60	4.70	—	—	—	—
Svanum et al. (1982)	75	29.00	26.72	3.84	23	17.0	73.0	50
Weighted totals		40.79	25.33	4.28		46.5	76.4	
N	1045	965	758	240		382	231	
Adolescents								
Wisniewski et al. (1985) [prb drk]	113	15.87	—	—	26	6.0	94.0	50
Wolfson & Erbaugh (1984)	50	15.66	26.20	4.57	24	24.0	74.0	60
Weighted totals	163	15.81	26.20	4.57	—	11.5	87.9	—
Black males								
Adults								
Graham & Mayo (1985)	40	37.42	28.22	—	26	22.0	58.0	50
Hightower (1984)	26	24.19	25.04	3.73	24	28.0	69.0	42
Smith et al. (1979) [tremor dcr]	9	38.92	28.91	—	—	—	—	—
Smith et al. (1979) [tremor incr]	12	41.11	32.78	—	—	—	—	—
Snyder et al. (1985)	69	33.10	29.30	4.90	—	—	—	—
Walters et al. (1983)	27	33.41	26.92	3.76	25	15.0	56.0	50
Zager & Megargee (1981) [heavy]	15	22.30	27.40	4.70	—	—	—	—
Zager & Megargee (1981) [moderate]	99	22.30	25.70	5.00	—	—	—	—
Weighted totals		29.28	27.40	4.67		21.6	60.5	
N	297	297	297	236		93	93	
Black females								
Adults								
Snyder et al. (1985)	25	38.10	28.00	4.00	—	—	—	—
American Indian males								
Adults								
Uecker et al (1980)	40	41.62	27.10	2.75	24	15.0	83.0	100

ethnic minorities. Black, male alcoholics also tend to be almost 10 years younger than white, male alcoholics. The potential influence of age when comparing black and white alcoholics should be considered even though the existing data suggest that age does not affect the *MAC*. The one study (Snyder, Kline, & Podany, 1985) on black, female alcoholics suggests that they score in the same range as black males. Since there are no data on

black, female psychiatric patients it is not known whether they also elevate the *MAC*.

The percentages of false negatives and hit rates are more likely to be reported for alcoholics. The percentage of false negatives in male samples were very comparable: white adults averaged 20.4 percent (range, 4 to 39 percent), white adolescents averaged 18.4 percent (range, 7 to 30 percent), and black adults averaged 21.6 percent (range, 15 to

28 percent). The percentages of false negatives in female samples tended to be much more variable, particularly in adults. White, female adolescents averaged 11.5 percent (range, 6 to 24 percent); a finding that must be tempered by the fact that is based on only two samples. White females averaged 46.5 percent false negatives (range, 3 to 62 percent). This result is partially a function of the large percentage of false negatives (62 percent) reported by Davis et al. (1987). If this study is excluded, the percentage of false negatives in female alcoholics averaged 27.4 percent (range, 3 to 44 percent), which is still higher than that found in male samples.

Hit rates across these groups of alcoholic patients varied substantially and were very similar to the hit rates in psychiatric patients. White, adult males had an average hit rate of 73.1 percent (range, 55 to 85 percent), and white, adult females averaged 76.4 percent (range, 73 to 81 percent). White, adolescent males had an average hit rate of 77.6 percent (range, 68 to 83 percent), which is nearly identical to the hit rate seen in white adults, both male and female. Black, adult males had an average hit rate of only 60.5 percent (range, 56 to 69 percent), again largely as a function of the comparisons being made with psychiatric patients who produced similar scores on the *MAC*.

Table 6–12 provides a quick summary of the scores on the *MAC* that have been presented in Tables 6–8 to 6–11. Table 6–12 must be considered

TABLE 6–12.   SUMMARY TABLE OF THE PERFORMANCE ON THE MACANDREW ALCOHOLISM SCALE *(MAC)* AS A FUNCTION OF AGE, GENDER, AND ETHNICITY

Sample	N	Age	*MAC* M	*MAC* SD	False Positives	Hit Rate
Normal individuals						
White						
Male adults	2975	34.50	23.13	4.31	26.5	76.2
Male adolescents	352	17.03	22.65	3.72	19.2	77.8
Female adults	1460	40.56	20.33	3.82	19.0	80.4
Female adolescents	213	15.82	20.86	4.01	7.4	86.6
Black						
Male adults	19	23.26	21.30	3.29	—	—
Psychiatric patients						
White						
Male adults	2285	37.21	23.30	4.60	31.4	72.3
Male adolescents	749	16.69	19.82	7.76	42.3	68.0
Female adults	485	36.75	21.74	4.78	21.7	77.4
Female adolescents	444	16.43	20.39	6.87	37.0	74.0
Black						
Male adults	128	23.28	26.32	4.86	59.5	60.0
Medical patients						
White						
Male adults	5353	49.00	—	—	37.3	—
Female adults	6737	48.80	—	—	20.3	—

Sample	N	Age	*(MAC)* M	*(MAC)* SD	False Negatives	Hit Rate
Alcoholics						
White						
Male adults	6512	40.82	28.41	5.45	20.4	73.1
Male adolescents	409	17.55	27.09	4.04	18.4	77.6
Female adults	1045	40.79	25.33	4.28	46.5	76.4
Female adolescents	163	15.81	26.20	4.57	11.5	87.9
Black						
Male adults	297	29.28	27.40	4.67	21.6	60.5
Polydrug patients						
White						
Male adults	952	26.86	27.67	4.12	37.6	—
Female adults	127	41.48	—	—	72.5	—
Black						
Male adults	607	27.89	27.95	5.82	20.8	—

in its entirety to avoid misleading conclusions. For example, if the reader examined only the mean scores on the *MAC* in alcoholics, it could be concluded that the *MAC* is equally effective in all ethnic groups. Only when the mean scores and/or hit rates in black psychiatric patients are considered, do the potential problems with the *MAC* in minority groups become evident.

Having reviewed the performance of different patients groups on the *MAC*, the few studies that have reported or verified any of the correlates will now be reviewed. The *MAC* is stable across treatment for alcoholism (Chang, Caldwell, & Moss, 1973; Huber & Danahy, 1975; Rohan, 1972; Rohan et al., 1969; Vega, 1971) as well as in longitudinal studies (Hoffmann, Loper, & Kammeier, 1974; Kammeier, Hoffmann, & Loper, 1973), which suggests that the *MAC* is sensitive to some enduring aspect of personality rather than short-term consequences of substance misuse. Since scores on the *MAC* are not related to age (Colligan & Offord, 1987; Uecker, Boutilier, & Richardson, 1980), it also appears that the *MAC* is not tapping the long-term consequences of prolonged substance misuse either. When these findings are combined with the fact that the *MAC* is elevated by most, if not all, types of substance abuse, which are described below, it seems even clearer that the *MAC* is measuring some stable aspect of personality. MacAndrew (1981) conjectured that the *MAC* taps a fundamental bipolar dimension of character with high scorers (raw scores of 24 or higher) being described as "moving (with 'boldness') into the world, albeit in a sometimes rancorous and ill-considered fashion, with little regard for future consequences" (p. 618), while low scorers (raw scores of 23 or lower) "give every appearance of being 'neurotics-who-also-happen-to-drink-too-much'" (p. 620). MacAndrew suggested that high scorers could be labeled primary alcoholics while low scorers are reactive or secondary alcoholics. MacAndrew's formulation of two types of alcoholics is consistent with the data suggesting that there is not a unitary alcoholic personality. The data reviewed above, however, indicate that such a bipolar classification may not do justice to the variety of subgroups of alcoholics that can be identified. No research has tested MacAndrew's hypothesis directly.

Several studies have outlined the personality characteristics of high-scoring *males* on the *MAC*.

These men have been described as rebellious, resentful of authorities, maladjusted in school, impulsive, risk-takers, prone to acting out, sociable people who mix well with others, self-confident, religious, morally indignant, more likely to drink earlier and heavier, having previous alcohol treatment, and having a history of employment disruptions, marital conflict, and legal difficulties (Finney, Smith, Skeeters, & Auvenshine, 1971; Lachar, Berman, Grisell, & Schooff, 1976; MacAndrew, 1967, 1981; O'Neil, Giacinto, Waid, Roitzsch, Miller, & Kilpatrick, 1983; Schwartz & Graham, 1979). There is some debate about whether these correlates reflect general antisocial tendencies with advocates both pro (Apfeldorf & Hunley, 1975; Ruff, Ayers, & Templer, 1975; Williams, McCourt, & Schneider, 1971) and con (Schwartz & Graham, 1979). Some studies have reported that high scorers demonstrate cognitive impairment (Schwartz & Graham, 1979), while others find that high scorers are less likely to complain of difficulties in concentration (MacAndrew, 1967).

No study has reported the correlates of the *MAC* for samples of women or men from any minority group. Clinicians should be cautious in generalizing the above correlates from white, male alcoholics to other groups. It might be noted that MacAndrew (1965, 1981) designed and discussed the use of the *MAC* only with men.

SUMMARY

It appears that the *MAC* has a viable future in the understanding of persons who misuse substances, since the voluminous research that has been summarized in this chapter generally supports its widespread popularity. Rather than summarize all of the points made, only a few major issues will be reiterated. First, the *MAC* identifies white males who have a propensity to misuse substances with 70 to 75 percent hit rates and percentages of false negatives around 20 percent. Data on adolescents and white females who misuse substances are less reliable because of the limited research. Second, when white males who misuse substances must be discriminated from other psychiatric patients, hit rates decrease and the percentage of false positives increases. When patients have dual disorders (a substance abuse/-dependence diagnosis and some other DSM-III-R Axis I or II diagnosis), these discriminations become even more difficult. Finally, the *MAC* should be used very cautiously with black males because of the extremely low hit rates and high percentages of false positives in psychiatric patients. It is unclear whether similar problems occur in other ethnic groups and with black females because there is no research on which to make any conclusions.

It may be somewhat redundant to describe the directions for future research on the *MAC*. Basic descriptive data are needed on virtually all groups other than white males, and particularly all minority groups. In addition, these studies should obtain and verify the correlates of the *MAC*. This research must consider the potential effects of moderator variables such as gender, education, socioeconomic class, profile validity, and ethnicity in order to provide a clearer picture of the results. Despite the multitude of studies on the *MAC*, there is still plenty of opportunity for well-designed research to address very basic issues.

POLYDRUG ABUSE/DEPENDENCE

STANDARD VALIDITY AND CLINICAL SCALES

The research on the MMPI with polydrug patients has been very similar to the research on alcoholics, except that it has received limited attention until the last few years. All of the methodologic issues that have been raised in the previous sections will be germane with polydrug patients as well. However, these issues will not be reiterated. One of the first questions examined was whether there was a polydrug "personality," and whether polydrug patients differed from alcoholics; i.e., did some personality types have a specific drug of choice? These initial studies usually involved a comparison of polydrug patients with alcoholics, and they demonstrated that groups of polydrug patients were experiencing more emotional distress than alcoholic patients (see Table 6–13 in contrast to Table 6–1). Even a cursory review of Table 6–13 will reveal that a number of clinical scales are likely to be elevated in polydrug patients. Scales from the psychotic tetrad (Scales 6, 7, 8, and 9) are more likely to be elevated in polydrug patients along with Scales 2 and 4. Only 4 of the 65 samples (6.2 percent) of white males reported in Table 6–13 found 2-4/4-2 codetypes. Consequently, it is apparent that 2-4/4-2 codetypes are *not* characteristic of polydrug patients, even though slightly over one-third (36.8 percent) of the alcoholic samples had this codetype (see Table 6–1). Several codetypes were seen frequently in these 65 samples of white male polydrug patients: 14 samples (21.5 percent) had

Spike *4* codetypes; 36 samples (55.4 percent) produced some combination of Scales *2, 4,* and *8* (Spike codetypes and high-point pairs and triads), and 47 samples (72.3 percent) produced some combination of Scales *4, 8,* and *9*. (The percentages for these codetypes exceed 100 percent since they are not mutually exclusive; e.g., Spike *4* codetypes also have been included in the latter two categories.) In contrast to the alcoholics where 10.5 percent of the samples had *WNL* codetypes, only 2 of the 65 samples (3.1 percent) of white male polydrug patients had *WNL* codetypes. Again, similar to alcoholics, it appears that older polydrug patients have fewer clinical scales elevated at or above a *T*-score of 70 and are more likely to elevate Scales *2* and *3*. However, this conclusion must be made with some reservation since only two studies (Dietvorst et al., 1979; Dorr, 1981) have examined this issue and both patient samples were physicians.

Groups of white, male, adolescent polydrug patients have been studied rather extensively (see Table 6–13), and similar to their adult counterparts, codetypes involving some combination of Scales *4, 8,* and *9* were found in 10 of 12 samples (83.3 percent). Black, adult, male polydrug patients have been studied less extensively. However, the few studies available have consistently found *4-9* codetypes.

When groups of white, female polydrug patients are studied, any conclusion about frequently occurring codetypes must be very tentative since only 69 adults in a total of four samples and 150 adolescents in three samples have been reported. However, it is tempting to conjecture that combinations of Scales *4, 8,* and *9* will be seen regardless of age, since these codetypes were found in six of these seven samples (see Table 6–13).

Two conclusions seem readily apparent based on the data that are summarized in Table 6–13. First, polydrug patients will elevate a greater number of the clinical scales than alcoholic patients. Codetypes in polydrug patients frequently involved some combination of Scales *8* and *9*, in conjunction with Scales *2* and *4*, while alcoholics were more likely to elevate Scales *2* and *4*. Second, there appear to be limited age and gender differences in polydrug patients.

Another line of research examined whether polydrug patients could be classified into various diagnostic categories based on their MMPI codetypes: neurotic, psychopathic, psychotic, and

**TABLE 6–13.   FREQUENCY OF ELEVATED MMPI CLINICAL SCALES
IN POLYDRUG ABUSE SAMPLES BY GENDER AND ETHNICITY**

Authors	N	Age	Clinical Scales (≥ 70 T-points)
White males			
Adults			
Berzins et al. (1971) [NARA]	200	30.0	4-8-2
Berzins et al. (1971) [VOLS]	204	30.0	4-2-8
Berzins et al. (1971) [PROB]	210	30.0	4-2-8
Berzins et al. (1971) [PRIS]	213	30.0	Spike 4
Carlin et al. (1978)	11	25.3	8-2-7-9-4-1-3
Carrol & Zuckerman (1977)	80	22.4	4-8-2-9-7
Dietvorst et al. (1979)	15	51.2	2
Dietvorst et al. (1979) [alc & drug]	11	51.2	2-3
Dorr (1981)	14	43.5	Spike 2
Gilbert & Lombardi (1967)	45	22.7	4-2-7-8
Gilbertson (1984) [high]	22	24.5	4-9
Gilbertson (1984) [low]	20	24.5	4-8-7-2
Graf et al. (1977) [stimulant]	15	25.8	8-4-9-6-7
Graf et al. (1977) [sedative]	14	23.6	8-4-7-2-6
Graf et al. (1977) [barbiturate]	17	24.4	4-8-2-1-3-7-6-9
Graf et al. (1977) [polydrug]	20	22.9	8-4-7-6-2-9-3-1
Haertzen & Hooks (1969)	10	—	Spike 4
Hewett & Martin (1980) [prisoners]	11	35.0	4-8
Hill et al. (1962)	200	37.4	Spike 4
Holland (1977)	61	26.5	Spike 4
Holland (1978) [cannabis]	50	—	WNL
Holland (1978) [opiate]	24	—	Spike 4
Holland (1978) [polydrug]	62	—	Spike 4
Kamback et al. (1977)	8	—	Spike 4
Keller & Redfering (1973) [LSD]	60	21.1	8-9
Ottomanelli (1976)	26	20.5	4-9
Ottomanelli (1977) [employed]	36	—	Spike 4
Ottomanelli (1977) [unemployed]	42	—	Spike 4
Ottomanelli (1977) [unempl.; arrested]	12	—	4-8-2
Ottomanelli (1977) [discharged]	15	—	4-8
Ottomanelli et al. (1978) [success]	7	27.1	Spike 4
Ottomanelli et al. (1978) [in tmt]	33	27.1	4-2
Ottomanelli et al. (1978) [unsuccess]	53	27.1	4-9
Penk & Robinowitz (1976) [heroin-vol]	34	21.9	8-4-9-2-7-1-6
Penk & Robinowitz (1976) [poly-vol]	34	21.7	8-4-9-2
Penk & Robinowitz (1976) [heroin-nonvol]	34	20.2	Spike 9
Penk & Robinowitz (1976) [poly-nonvol]	34	20.0	4-9
Penk et al. (1978)	87	28.0	4-8-2-7-9
Penk et al. (1979) [heroin]	65	23.0	WNL
Penk et al. (1979) [amphetamine]	45	23.0	4-8-7
Penk et al. (1979) [barbiturate]	34	23.0	Spike 8
Rardin et al. (1974) [opiate]	20	20.2	4-8-2-9-1
Rardin et al. (1974) [amphetamine]	20	21.7	8-2-4-9-3
Savage & Marchington (1977)	34	21.0	Spike 4
Sheppard et al. (1969)	23	30.0	4-2
Sheppard et al. (1969) [elev.]	38	28.0	4-8-2-7-9
Spotts & Shontz (1983) [cocaine]	9	28.0	4-9
Spotts & Shontz (1983) [amphetamine]	9	28.0	4-9
Spotts & Shontz (1983) [opiate]	9	27.0	9-4-8
Spotts & Shontz (1983) [barbiturate]	9	29.0	4-9-8-2
Stein & Rozynko (1974)	201	25.5	4-2-8-9

(Continues.)

TABLE 6–13.   *(Continued.)*

Authors	N	Age	Clinical Scales (≥ 70 *T*-points)
Sutker (1971)	40	27.1	*4-2*
Sutker et al. (1976) [failures]	26	26.2	*4-2-7-8-9-1-6*
Sutker et al. (1976) [successes]	36	29.9	*4-2*
Sutker et al. (1978) [low SSS]	14	24.3	Spike *4*
Sutker et al. (1978) [middle SSS]	57	24.3	*4-9*
Sutker et al. (1978) [high SSS]	13	24.3	*4-9-8*
Sutker et al. (1979) [opiate]	125	25.0	Spike *4*
Sutker et al. (1981)	121	24.0	Spike *4*
Toomey (1974)	20	22.8	*8-4-7-2-9-3-1*
Trevithick & Hosch (1978)	65	26.8	*4-8-2-7*
Zuckerman et al. (1975) [soft-stay]	27	19.6	*4-8-2-7*
Zuckerman et al. (1975) [soft-quit]	32	19.4	*8-4-7-2-6-9*
Zuckerman et al. (1975) [hard-stay]	28	22.4	*4-8-9-2*
Zuckerman et al (1975) [hard-quit]	30	23.8	*4-8-9-6-2*
Adolescents			
Brook et al. (1974) [amphetamine]	60	18.5	*7-1-4-8-2*
Burke & Eichberg (1972) [YDSU]	53	19.7	*8-4-7-2-6-5-9-3*
Burke & Eichberg (1972) [DAWN]	34	17.2	*8-4-5-7-9*
Cox & Smart (1972) [casual]	15	18.0	*8-4-9*
Cox & Smart (1972) [moderate]	27	18.0	*8-4-9-2-7-1-6-3*
Cox & Smart (1972) [heavy]	30	19.0	*8-9-4-7-1-6*
McGuire & Megargee (1974) [heavy users]	24	—	Spike *4*
McGuire & Megargee (1974) [users]	48	—	*WNL*
Patalano (1980a) [50% black]	80	21.1	*4-8-9*
Silver (1977)	27	20.8	*8-4-7-2*
Smart & Jones (1970) [LSD]	100	19.0	*8-9-4*
Toomey (1974)	14	16.5	*8-4-7-2-6-9-3*
Black males			
Adults			
Craig (1983) [during detox]	90	31.0	*4-9-8-2*
Craig (1983) [after detox]	100	31.0	*4-8-9-2*
Edinger et al. (1975)	25	23.5	Spike *4*
Foureman et al. (1981)	200	25.9	*4-9*
Penk et al. (1978)	136	28.0	Spike *4*
White females			
Adults			
Kamback et al. (1977)	8	—	*4-9*
Sutker et al. (1981)	33	24.0	*4-9*
Zuckerman et al. (1975) [stay]	14	20.1	*4-8-9-6-2*
Zuckerman et al. (1975) [quit]	14	17.7	*8-6-4-9-7-1-2-3*
Adolescents			
Burke & Eichberg (1972) [YDSU]	34	18.7	*8-4-6-2-7-9*
Burke & Eichberg (1972) [DAWN]	36	17.0	*8-4-9*
Patalano (1980a) [50% black]	80	20.2	*4-8-9*

WNL (see Table 6–14). As can be seen in Table 6–14, data are available only on white males. Psychopathic (*4-9/9-4*) codetypes occurred most frequently (38.4 percent) in these groups of polydrug patients, followed closely by psychotic (*6-7-8-9*) codetypes (27.5 percent). Neurotic (*1-2-3-7*) codetypes were found in 19.9 percent of these patients, and *WNL* codetypes in 10.1 percent. There are several differences in the percentage of polydrug patients found in these diagnostic categories as compared with alcoholic patients (see Table 6–2). First, there is the total lack of *2-4-7* codetypes reported in the polydrug patients that were found in 15.1 percent of the men and 13.9 percent of the women alcoholics. Second, psychotic and neurotic codetypes were more frequent in the polydrug patients, while these four diagnostic

TABLE 6–14.   FREQUENCY OF GROUP DIAGNOSES IN POLYDRUG ABUSE PATIENTS BY GENDER

Authors	N	Age	Neurotic 1-2-3-7	Psychopathic 4-9	Psychotic 6-7-8-9	WNL	Unclassified
White males							
Foureman et al. (1981) [82% black]	200	26	7.5	54.5	23.0	12.0	3.0
Herl (1976)	24	32	46.0	33.0	13.0	8.0	—
Herl (1976) [Hispanic]	31	32	52.0	26.0	22.0	0.0	—
Lachar et al. (1979b)	104	25	12.5	33.0	38.5	11.0	5.0
Lachar et al. (1979b) [heroin]	96	25	12.5	30.0	40.0	12.0	5.5
Monroe et al. (1971)	202	—	31.2	31.2	29.2	8.4	—
Monroe et al. (1971) [voluntary]	209	—	36.4	39.2	17.7	6.7	—
Pugliese (1975)	65	—	3.0	27.0	10.0	12.0	48.0
Sutker et al. (1981)	154	24	5.2	43.1	39.6	12.1	—
Weighted totals		25.7	19.9	38.4	27.5	10.1	10.3
N	1085	609	1085	1085	1085	1054	465
White females							
Herl (1976)	15	30	33.0	54.0	13.0	0.0	

groupings (neurotic, classic, psychopathic, and psychotic) were about equally represented in both male and female alcoholic samples. Finally, fewer (10.3 percent) white, male, polydrug patients remained unclassified within these four diagnostic categories, while 42.2 percent of the alcoholics were unclassified.

Few studies have utilized empirically based classification procedures on the MMPI clinical scales to identify commonly occurring groups of polydrug patients (see Table 6–15). Table 6–15 illustrates that few codetypes are found frequently when the MMPIs of polydrug patients are cluster analyzed. No single codetype was identified more than twice in the five studies summarized in Table 6–15. The 2-7-8-4 codetype, which was one of the most frequent in alcoholics (see Table 6–3), was found in only one study (Berzins, Ross, English, & Haley, 1974) of polydrug patients. Only Spike 4 and 4-9 codetypes were found in both alcoholic and polydrug patients.

The MMPIs of polydrug patients also can be classified by codetype to identify any commonly occurring groups of profiles. Table 6–16 categorizes the various codetypes found in polydrug patients by gender and ethnic group and provides the frequencies with which these codetypes are seen in psychiatric patients so that it can be determined whether the observed codetypes are specific to polydrug or are seen in psychiatric samples more generally. Table 6–16 can be contrasted with Table 6–6 to compare and contrast polydrug and alcoholic patients. A 4-9/9-4 codetype was the most frequent in white, male polydrug patients, occurring in 16.8 percent of the cases; the frequency of this codetype in individual studies varied from 6.6 to 21.7 percent. By comparison, a 4-9/9-4 codetype occurred in 6.4 percent of the psychiatric patients and 8.5 percent of the alcoholic patients (see Table 6–6). A 4-9/9-4 codetype is over twice as common in polydrug patients as in

TABLE 6–15.   FREQUENCY OF CLUSTER TYPES IN POLYDRUG ABUSE PATIENTS BY GENDER

Authors	N	Age	2-4-7-8	Spike 4	4-9	Spike 9	4-2-7	8-4	9-8	1-2-8	Uncl.
White males											
Berzins et al. (1974)	—	—	28.8	8.9	—	—	—	—	—	—	62.3
Collins et al. (1976)	56	—	—	—	26.8	—	—	21.4	16.1	—	35.7
Herrera et al. (1986)	99	25	—	—	47.0	25.0	—	25.0	—	—	3.0
Herrera et al. (1986)	97	25	—	—	—	—	23.0	—	48.0	—	6.0
Rothaizer (1980)	67	20	—	17.9	—	—	—	—	—	26.9	55.2
Weighted totals		23.7			39.7			23.7	36.3		20.6
N	319				155			155	153		319
White Females			4-8-2	Spike 4	4-9	4-6	4-2	4-8-9-7	WNL		Uncl.
Berzins et al. (1974)	—	—	37.9	5.5	—	8.4	—	—	—		56.7
Eshbaugh et al. (1982)	178	26	7.9	13.5	7.9	—	9.6	12.9	9.6		30.2

Note: The weighted totals are based on the percentages in studies that found the specific cluster type, since the absence of data on a cluster may mean that it was not reported rather than it was not found. Consequently, the percentages in the row of weighted totals sum to a total > 100 percent.

TABLE 6–16.   FREQUENCY OF MMPI CODETYPES IN POLYDRUG ABUSE SAMPLES BY GENDER AND ETHNIC GROUP

Authors	N	Age	Codetype					
			1-2/2-1	1-3/3-1	2-4/4-2	2-7/7-2	2-8/8-2	3-4/4-3
White males								
Brook et al. (1974) [adol.]	60	18.5	—	—	—	—	12.0	—
Collins et al. (1977)	91	25.0	—	—	11.0	—	5.5	4.4
Patalano (1980b)	40	20.7	—	—	15.0	—	7.5	5.0
Smart & Jones (1970)	100	20.5	—	—	—	—	4.0	4.0
Zuckerman et al. (1975) [stay]	69	20.8	—	—	14.5	5.8	8.7	4.3
Zuckerman et al. (1975) [quit]	76	20.8	—	—	13.2	5.3	9.2	—
Weighted totals		21.3	—	—	13.1	5.5	7.4	4.3
N	436	436			276	145	436	300
Psychiatric patients								
Hedlund & Won Cho (1979)			4.9	2.3	7.7	4.8	5.5	1.4

	Codetype					
	4-6/6-4	4-8/8-4	4-9/9-4	6-8/8-6	7-8/8-7	8-9/9-8	Total
White males							
Brook et al. (1974) [adol.]	—	25.0	—	—	20.0	10.0	67.0
Collins et al. (1977)	4.4	5.5	20.9	—	5.5	5.5	62.7
Patalano (1980b)	5.0	17.5	15.0	—	17.5	10.0	92.5
Smart & Jones (1970)	6.0	9.0	18.0	—	8.0	27.0	76.0
Zuckerman et al. (1975) [stay]	5.8	7.2	21.7	5.8	7.2	—	81.0
Zuckerman et al. (1975) [quit]	3.9	7.9	6.6	15.8	5.3	14.5	81.7
Weighted totals	5.1	10.8	16.8	11.0	9.4	14.5	75.3
N	376	436	376	145	436	145	
Psychiatric patients							
Hedlund & Won Cho (1979)	3.1	7.3	6.4	7.2	5.6	3.6	63.9

	N	Age	Codetype						
			1-2/2-1	1-3/3-1	2-4/4-2	2-7/7-2	2-8/8-2	3-4/4-3	4-6/6-4
Black Males									
Craig (1980) [79% black]	36	29.6	—	—	16.0	—	—	—	—
Craig (1984a) [90% black]	442	30.0	5.0	1.6	14.2	2.3	4.5	0.7	3.2
Patalano (1980b)	40	20.7	—	—	10.0	—	12.5	2.5	5.0
Weissman (1970)	39	37.0	—	—	17.0	—	—	—	—
Weighted totals		29.8	5.0	1.6	14.2	2.3	5.2	0.8	3.3
N	557	557	442	442	557	442	482	482	482
Psychiatric patients									
Hedlund & Won Cho (1979)	6154		4.9	2.3	7.7	4.8	5.5	1.4	3.1

	Codetype						Methodologic Variables	
	4-8/8-4	4-9/9-4	6-8/8-6	7-8/8-7	8-9/9-8	Total	A B C D E F G H	
Black males								
Craig (1980) [79% black]	41.0	40.0	—	—	—	97.0	+ - + - + + - -	
Craig (1984a)	9.0	21.3	4.7	3.6	6.1	76.2	+ - + - + + - -	
Patalano (1980b)	15.0	25.0	—	2.5	15.0	87.5	+ + - - + - - -	
Weissman (1970)	—	20.0	—	—	—	39.0	- - - - + - - -	
Weighted totals	11.7	22.7	4.7	3.5	6.8	75.8		
N	518	557	442	482	482			
Psychiatric patients								
Hedlund & Won Cho (1979)	7.3	6.4	7.2	5.6	3.6	63.9		

(Continues.)

TABLE 6–16.   *(Continued.)*

	N	Age	1-2/2-1	1-3/3-1	2-4/4-2	2-7/7-2	2-8/8-2	3-4/4-3	4-6/6-4
					Codetype				
White females									
Patalano (1980b) [white]	40	20.7	—	—	10.0	—	—	—	10.0
Patalano (1980b) [black]	40	20.7	—	—	7.5	—	2.5	—	5.0
Weighted totals		20.7	—	—	8.8	—	2.5	—	7.5
N	80	80			80		40		80
Psychiatric patients									
Hedlund & Won Cho (1979)	2574		1.9	3.8	5.2	3.8	4.7	3.1	6.5

	4-8/8-4	4-9/9-4	6-8/8-6	7-8/8-7	8-9/9-8	Total	A B C D E F G H
		Codetype					**Methodologic Variables**
White females							
Patalano (1980b) [white]	32.5	12.5	5.0	2.5	7.5	80.0	+ + - - + - - -
Patalano (1980b) [black]	20.0	32.5	10.0	2.5	5.0	85.0	+ + - - + - - -
Weighted totals	26.3	22.5	7.5	2.5	6.3	82.5	
N	80	80	80	80	80		
Psychiatric patients							
Hedlund & Won Cho (1979)	8.8	5.1	9.6	4.2	3.5	60.2	

alcoholic and psychiatric patients. Five other codetypes (*8-9/9-8*, *2-4/4-2*, *6-8/8-6*, *4-8/8-4*, and *7-8/8-7*) were encountered frequently, 14.5, 13.1, 11.0, 10.8, and 9.4 percent, respectively. Codetypes *8-9/9-8* are over five times more frequent in polydrug patients compared with alcoholic and psychiatric patients. No other codetype occurred in over 8.0 percent of the polydrug patients, and *1-2/2-1* and *1-3/3-1* codetypes are notable by their total absence in polydrug patients. A total of 75.3 percent of the white, male polydrug patients could be classified in the 12 codetypes represented in Table 6–16, while 57.5 percent of the alcoholic patients and 63.9 percent of the psychiatric patients were so classified (see Table 6–6). The polydrug patients are much more likely to be classified into these 12 codetypes, and those codetypes that involve Scales *6*, *7*, *8*, and *9* are more likely to be seen, which is consistent with the data summarized in Table 6–13 on the most frequently elevated clinical scales.

Black, male polydrug patients had approximately the same frequency of occurrence of the 12 codetypes summarized in Table 6–16 as the white, male polydrug patients except for the psychotic codetypes. Black, male polydrug patients had half as many *6-8/8-6*, *7-8/8-7*, and *8-9/9-8* codetypes as their white counterparts. These data suggest that the black polydrug patients were less emotionally disturbed than whites, which has been reported frequently (cf. Greene, 1987; Penk, Woodward, Robinowitz, & Hess, 1978).

There has been only a single study (Patalano, 1980b) of the codetypes that are seen in female polydrug patients (see Table 6–16). Almost 50 percent of these women patients had *4-8/8-4* or *4-9/9-4* codetypes, which are more frequent than in either the black or white, male polydrug patients. The small sample sizes and the singularity of the study, however, limit any conclusions that can be drawn.

In summary, a number of conclusions can be drawn from the MMPI performance of polydrug patients. First, it is clear that there is not a unitary polydrug personality, just as there is not a unitary alcoholic personality. Instead, there seems to be a number of smaller, more discrete subgroups of polydrug patients, although the composition of these subgroups differs from those seen in alcoholic patients. The codetype research suggests several subgroups (*4-8/8-4* and *4-9/9-4*) are seen frequently in both male and female, white polydrug patients, and additional codetypes that are specific to white males (*6-8/8-6*, *7-8/8-7*, and *8-9/9-8*). Second, black, male polydrug patients appear to be less emotionally disturbed than white males. Third, and again similar to the alcoholic patients, there has been virtually no work on possible differences in treatment outcomes and/or histories of drug misuse among the various subgroups of polydrug patients. It would be interesting to know whether specific subgroups of polydrug patients are more successful in a particular type of treatment or whether they have a particular history of substance misuse. The influence of the multitude of moderator variables described above on these subgroups of polydrug patients must be considered in any research in this area. Finally, more research is needed on groups other than the typical white and black, male polydrug patients. As can be seen in Tables 6–13 to 6–16, there is almost no research on other groups of polydrug patients. Again, it must be emphasized that the influence of moderator variables becomes more important as the MMPI performance of these other groups of polydrug patients are studied.

SPECIAL/RESEARCH SCALES

Two special scales have been developed to identify individuals who abuse drugs: Cavior et al.'s (1967) Heroin Addiction (*He*) Scale and Panton and Brisson's (1971) Drug Abuse (*DaS*) Scale. Subsequent research on the *He* has found that it did not discriminate between heroin addicts and psychiatric patients (Lachar, Berman, Grisell, & Schooff, 1979a), polydrug patients (Craig, 1980; Parr, Woodward, Robinowitz, & Penk, 1981) or alcoholics (Burke & Marcus, 1977). At best the *He* is a general measure of the propensity to misuse substances (Zager & Megargee, 1981), and consequently, it has given way to the use of the *MAC*. There has only been limited research on the *DaS*, primarily in correctional settings (cf. Zager & Megargee, 1981). The *DaS* appears to be a viable measure of the propensity to abuse drugs, which needs further investigation. Research on the *MAC* also revealed quickly that it was sensitive to any type of substance abuse, not simply alcohol abuse. Thus, most of the special scale research in polydrug patients has involved the *MAC*.

The *MAC* has been investigated widely in a variety of settings with a number of different samples of polydrug patients. The only data that will be reviewed here will be the performance of polydrug patients on the MAC since all other samples, such as normal individuals (see Table 6–8), psychiatric patients (see Table 6–9), and alcoholic patients (see Table 6–11), were summarized previously. The reader will need to consult these tables to see the data that are the bases for the comparisons that are being made in the following section.

Table 6–17 provides the descriptive data for the *MAC* by gender, age, and ethnic group in polydrug patients. The weighted mean score for white, adult males was 27.67 (SD, 4.12), which is almost three-quarters of a standard deviation above MacAndrew's traditional cutting score of 24. There is surprisingly limited variation in scores among these white, adult male polydrug patients samples with means ranging from 25.50 (Burke & Marcus, 1977) to 29.30 (Lachar, Berman, Grisell, & Schooff, 1976), and standard deviations ranging from 3.50 (Burke & Marcus, 1977) to 4.50 (Zager & Megargee, 1981). The fact that these polydrug patients average only 26.86 years of age while white, male alcoholic patients average 40.82 must be kept in mind as a potential confounded moderator variable when comparing the performance of these two ethnic groups on the *MAC*, even though the data in normals suggest that there are no age effects on the *MAC*.

The weighted mean score for black, adult, male polydrug patients on the *MAC* was 27.95 (SD, 5.82). These patients also tended to have very consistent scores on the *MAC* with means ranging from 25.13 (Craig, 1983) to 30.04 (Craig, 1984b), and standard deviations ranging from 4.23 (Craig, 1984b) to 5.00 (Zager & Megargee, 1981). Although these mean scores are elevated significantly above MacAndrew's (1965) recommended cutting score of 24, it must be recalled that black, adult, male psychiatric patients had mean scores on the *MAC* of 26.32 (SD, 4.86). The virtual absence of any data on false positives, false negatives, and hit rates precludes any conclusions. It would be instructive to compare a group of black polydrug patients with a group of black psychiatric patients, who have been screened carefully to eliminate patients with any history of substance misuse, to determine the actual effectiveness of the *MAC*. Until such data are available, clinicians again need to be cautioned about using the *MAC* with any minority group.

The research on the *MAC* with polydrug patients clearly is less complete than with alcoholic patients. Several conclusions still can be drawn and a number of recommendations can be made for future research in this area. First, the elevated scores on the *MAC* in polydrug patients indicate that the

TABLE 6–17.   PERFORMANCE ON THE MACANDREW ALCOHOLISM SCALE *(MAC)*
IN POLYDRUG ABUSE SAMPLES AS A FUNCTION OF AGE, GENDER,
AND ETHNICITY

Authors	N	Age	MAC M	MAC SD	Cutting Score	False Negatives	Hit Rate	Base Rate
White male adults								
Burke (1983)	19	—	—	—	25	21.0	—	—
Burke & Marcus (1977)	13	27.60	25.50	3.60	24	31.0	—	—
Burke & Marcus (1977) [drug & alc]	33	26.20	27.50	3.50	24	6.0	—	—
Davis et al. (1987)	71	39.40	—	—	24	70.0	—	—
Davis et al. (1987) [drug & alc]	143	34.00	—	—	24	29.0	—	—
Kranitz (1972)	100	30.00	27.76	3.88	—	—	—	—
Lachar et al. (1976)	52	25.20	29.30	4.20	24	15.0	65	34
Sutker et al. (1979)	125	25.00	28.89	—	—	50.0	—	—
Zager & Megargee (1981) [heavy]	351	22.10	27.20	4.20	—	—	—	—
Zager & Megargee (1981) [moderate]	45	21.80	26.60	4.50	—	—	—	—
Weighted totals		26.86	27.67	4.12		37.6	—	
N	952	933	719	594		456		
White female adults								
Davis et al. (1987)	70	43.10	—	—	24	77.0	—	—
Davis et al. (1987) [drug & alc]	57	39.50	—	—	24	67.0	—	—
Weighted totals	127	41.48				72.5	—	
Black male adults								
Craig (1983) [during detox]	90	31.00	25.13	[13.34]	—	—	—	—
Craig (1983) [after detox]	110	31.00	29.44	4.48	—	—	—	—
Craig (1984b) [with alcoholism]	93	33.00	30.04	4.23	25	11.0	—	—
Craig (1984b) [without alcoholism]	49	33.00	27.51	4.39	27	45.0	—	—
Lachar et al. (1976) [heroin]	48	25.10	28.60	4.60	24	15.0	66	32
Zager & Megargee (1981) [heavy]	192	22.30	27.40	4.60	—	—	—	—
Zager & Megargee (1981) [moderate]	25	22.30	27.50	5.00	—	—	—	—
Weighted totals		27.89	27.95	5.82		20.8	—	
N	607	607	607	607		190		

MAC is sensitive to the misuse of all types of substances including alcohol. The *MAC* could be called more appropriately a "substance abuse" scale rather than an "alcoholism" scale. The "substances" that are misused do not have to be "street" drugs either, since legally prescribed medications are equally prone to misuse. Second, there do not appear to be any ethnic differences between black and white male polydrug patients in terms of their mean performance on the *MAC*. Yet the finding that black, male, psychiatric patients score nearly in the same range as black polydrug and alcoholic patients suggests that the *MAC* is probably less effective with members of minority groups. Finally, data are needed on the performance on the *MAC* in other samples of polydrug patients such as women and adolescents. Until such information is available, the *MAC* should be used cautiously in these groups, too.

SUMMARY AND DIRECTIONS FOR FUTURE RESEARCH

Future research in this area needs to focus on several areas and to consider the potential role of a number of moderator variables. There is a real need for basic data on the MMPI performance of all groups who misuse substances beside white, adult males. Data collected on these groups also should consider including psychiatric and normal reference groups in order to better understand the actual role of substance misuse. Any comparisons made between polydrug and alcoholic patients must consider the potential effects of age, since polydrug patients average 15 to 20 years younger than alcoholics. The influence of socioeconomic class and education, which have significant effects on MMPI performance, also must be considered. The general failure to even consider the role of such moderator variables, which is so characteristic of research in this area, must be corrected if meaningful data are to be obtained. The most significant needs in this entire area, however, are treatment process and outcome issues, i.e., whether subgroups of patients who misuse specific substances respond better to one type of treatment and whether they have differential recovery rates. The time is long past when delineating whether alcohol or polydrug misusers are a unitary group is a viable question; the data are clear that substance misusers are very heterogeneous. The data summarized in this chapter indicate some of the subgroups that are frequently encountered and it is time to start investigating them more closely. Research questions need to be more sharply focused. For example, do alcoholics with a *2-4/4-2* codetype with an elevated score on the *MAC* have better recovery rates in a confrontational-based AA program? Or, are attrition rates across the course of treatment within this codetype higher or lower than in a *4-9/9-4* codetype, and if so, how can this problem be addressed? It also would be informative to determine whether patients within these specific subgroups have different histories of personal and familial substance misuse. Consequently, it is mandatory that researchers do more than simply report that the patients who are misusing substances are in some unspecified treatment program. Detailed data bases that encompass both the individual's personal and his or her familial history of substance misuse as well as social and environmental factors that may be involved must be reported as well as the patient's MMPI performance. Substance misuse is a complex process; it is time that researchers start to appreciate this complexity and to report data that give some insight into the multitude of factors involved.

REFERENCES

Abbott, W. L. (1982). Dropouts from an inpatient treatment program for alcoholics. *International Journal of the Addictions, 17*, 199–204.

American Psychiatric Association (1987). *Diagnostic and statistical manual—3rd, revised.* Washington, D.C.: Author.

Apfeldorf, M., & Hunley, P. J. (1975). Application of MMPI alcoholism scales to older alcoholics and problem drinkers. *Journal of Studies on Alcohol, 36*, 645–653.

Apfeldorf, M., & Hunley, P. J. (1976). Exclusion of subjects with *F* scores at or above 16 in MMPI research on alcoholism. *Journal of Clinical Psychology, 32*, 498–500.

Apfeldorf, M., & Hunley, P. J. (1981). The MacAndrew Scale: A measure of the diagnosis of alcoholism. *Journal of Studies on Alcohol, 42*, 80–86.

Atsaides, J. P., Neuringer, C., & Davis, K. L. (1977). Development of an institutionalized chronic alcoholic scale. *Journal of Consulting and Clinical Psychology, 45*, 609–611.

Bean, K. L., & Karasievich, G. O. (1975). Psychological test results at three stages of inpatient alcoholism treatment. *Journal of Studies on Alcohol, 36*, 838–852.

Berzins, J. I., Ross, W. F., English, G. E., & Haley, J. V. (1974). Subgroups among opiate addicts: A typological investigation. *Journal of Abnormal Psychology, 83*, 65–73.

Berzins, J. I., Ross, W. F., & Monroe, J. J. (1971). A multivariate study of the personality characteristics of hospitalized narcotic addicts on the MMPI. *Journal of Clinical Psychology, 27*, 174–181.

Blashfield, R. K. (1980). Propositions regarding the use of cluster analysis in clinical research. *Journal of Consulting and Clinical Psychology, 48*, 456–459.

Boyd, J. H., Weissman, M. M., Thompson, W. D., & Myers, J. K. (1983). Different definitions of alcoholism: I. Impact of seven definitions on prevalence rates in a community survey. *American Journal of Psychiatry, 140*, 1309–1317.

Brook, R., Kaplun, J., & Whitehead, P. C. (1974). Personality characteristics of adolescent amphetamine users as measured by the MMPI. *British Journal of Addictions, 69*, 61–66.

Brown, M. A. (1950). Alcoholic profiles on the MMPI. *Journal of Clinical Psychology, 6*, 266–269.

Bruder, C. I. (1982). A multivariate approach to the classification of alcoholics in an inpatient clinical population. *Journal of Studies on Alcohol, 43*, 843–850.

Burke, E. L., & Eichberg, R. H. (1972). Personality characteristics of adolescent users of dangerous drugs as indicated by the MMPI. *Journal of Nervous and Mental Disease, 154*, 291–298.

Burke, H. R. (1983). "Markers" for the MacAndrew and the Cavior Heroin Addiction MMPI scales. *Journal of Studies on Alcohol, 44*, 558–563.

Burke, H. R., & Marcus, R. (1977). MacAndrew MMPI alcoholism scale: Alcoholism and drug addictiveness. *Journal of Psychology, 96*, 141–148.

Button, A. D. (1956). A study of alcoholics with the MMPI. *Quarterly Journal of Studies on Alcohol, 17*, 263–281.

Carlin, A. S., Detzer, E., & Stauss, F. F. (1978). Psychopathology and nonmedical drug use: A comparison of patient and nonpatient drug users. *International Journal of the Addictions, 13*, 337–348.

Carrol, E. N., & Zuckerman, M. (1977). Psychopathology and sensation seeking in "Downers," "Speeders," and "Trippers": A study of the relationship between personality and drug choice. *International Journal of the Addictions, 12*, 591–601.

Cavior, N., Kurtzberg, R. L., & Lipton, D. S. (1967). The development and validation of a heroin addiction scale with the MMPI. *International Journal of the Addictions, 2*, 129–137.

Chang, A. F., Caldwell, A. B., & Moss, T. (1973). Stability of personality traits in alcoholics during and after treatment as measured by the MMPI: A one-year follow-up study. *Proceedings of the American Psychological Association, 8*, 387–388.

Clopton, J. R. (1978). Alcoholism and the MMPI: A review. *Journal of Studies on Alcohol, 39*, 1540–1558.

Clopton, J. R., Weiner, R. H., & Davis, H. G. (1980). Use of the MMPI in identification of alcoholic psychiatric patients. *Journal of Consulting and Clinical Psychology, 48*, 416–417.

Colligan, R. C., & Offord, K. P. (1987). The MacAndrew alcoholism scale applied to a contemporary normative sample. *Journal of Clinical Psychology, 43*, 291–293.

Colligan, R. C., Osborne, D., Swenson, W. M., & Offord, K. P. (1985). Using the 1983 norms for the MMPI: Code type frequencies in four clinical samples. *Journal of Clinical Psychology, 41*, 629–633.

Collins, H. A., Burger, G. K., & Taylor, G. A. (1976). An empirical typology of heroin abusers. *Journal of Clinical Psychology*, *32*, 473–476.

Collins, H. A., Burger, G. K., & Taylor, G. A. (1977). Personality patterns of drug abusers as shown by MMPI profiles. *Journal of Clinical Psychology*, *33*, 897–900.

Conley, J. J. (1981). An MMPI typology of male alcoholics: Admission, discharge and outcome comparisons. *Journal of Personality Assessment*, *45*, 33–39.

Conley, J. J., & Kammeier, M. L. (1980a). Alcoholism-related content in the MMPI: Item analysis of alcoholics vs. normal and general psychiatric populations. In M. Galanter (Ed.), *Currents in alcoholism*, Vol. 7 (pp. 253–259). Philadelphia: Grune & Stratton.

Conley, J. J., & Kammeier, M. L. (1980b). MMPI item responses of alcoholics in treatment: Comparisons with normals and psychiatric patients. *Journal of Consulting and Clinical Psychology*, *48*, 668–669.

Conley, J. J., & Prioleau, L. A. (1983). Personality typology of men and women alcoholics in relation to etiology and prognosis. *Journal of Studies on Alcohol*, *44*, 996–1010.

Cox, C., & Smart, R. G. (1972). Social and psychological aspects of speed use: A study of types of speed users in Toronto. *International Journal of the Addictions*, *7*, 201–217.

Craig, R. J. (1980). Characteristics of inner city heroin addicts applying for treatment in a Veteran Administration Hospital drug program (Chicago). *International Journal of the Addictions*, *15*, 409–418.

Craig, R. J. (1983). Effects of opiate withdrawal on MMPI profile scores. *International Journal of the Addictions*, *18*, 1187–1193.

Craig, R. J. (1984a). A comparison of MMPI profiles of heroin addicts based on multiple methods of classification. *Journal of Personality Assessment*, *48*, 115–120.

Craig, R. J. (1984b). MMPI substance abuse scales on drug addicts with and without concurrent alcoholism. *Journal of Personality Assessment*, *48*, 495–499.

Curlee, J. (1970). A comparison of male and female patients at an alcoholism treatment center. *Journal of Psychology*, *74*, 239–247.

Dahlstrom, W. G., Welsh, G. S., & Dahlstrom, L. E. (1972). *An MMPI handbook*, Vol. 1: *Clinical interpretation*. Minneapolis: University of Minnesota Press.

Dahlstrom, W. G., Welsh, G. S., & Dahlstrom, L. E. (1975). *An MMPI handbook*, Vol. 2: *Research applications*. Minneapolis: University of Minnesota Press.

Davis, L. J., Colligan, R. C., Morse, R. M., & Offord, K. P. (in press). The validity of the MacAndrew Scale in a general medical population. *Journal of Studies on Alcohol*.

Davis, W. E., Pursell, S. A., & Burnham, R. A. (1979). Alcoholism, sex-role orientation and psychological distress. *Journal of Clinical Psychology*, *35*, 209–212.

de Groot, G. W., & Adamson, J. D. (1973). Responses of psychiatric inpatients to the MacAndrew alcoholism scale. *Quarterly Journal of Studies on Alcohol*, *34*, 1133–1139.

Dietvorst, T. F., Swenson, W. M., Niven, R. G., & Morse, R. M. (1979). Analysis of the MMPI profiles of physicians in treatment for drug dependency. *Journal of Studies on Alcohol*, *40*, 1023–1029.

Donovan, D. M., Chaney, E. F., & O'Leary, M. R. (1978). Alcoholic MMPI subtypes: Relationship to drinking styles, benefits, and consequences. *Journal of Nervous and Mental Disease*, *166*, 553–561.

Donovan, D. M., & O'Leary, M. R. (1976). Relationship between distortions in self-perception of depression and psychopathology. *Journal of Clinical Psychology*, *32*, 16–19.

Dorr, D. (1981). MMPI profiles of emotionally impaired physicians. *Journal of Clinical Psychology*, *37*, 451–455.

Edinger, J. D., Bogan, J. B., Harrigan, P. H., & Ellis, M. F. (1975). Altitude quotient-IQ discrepancy as an index of personality disorganization among drug offenders. *Journal of Clinical Psychology*, *31*, 575–578.

Emmons, K., Gomez, L. & Barnes, E. (1987). 9 Days in June. *Life*, *10*, 83–85.

English, G. E., & Curtin, M. E. (1975). Personality differences in patients at three alcoholism treatment agencies. *Journal of Studies on Alcohol*, *36*, 52–61.

Eshbaugh, D. M., Dick, K. V., & Tosi, D. J. (1982). Typological analysis of MMPI personality patterns of drug dependent females. *Journal of Personality Assessment*, 1982, *46*, 488–494.

Eshbaugh, D. M., Tosi, D. J., & Hoyt, C. (1978). Some personality patterns and dimensions of male alcoholics: A multivariate description. *Journal of Personality Assessment*, *42*, 409–417.

Eshbaugh, D. M., Tosi, D. J., & Hoyt, C. N. (1980). Women alcoholics: A typological description using the MMPI. *Journal of Studies on Alcohol*, *41*, 310–317.

Evans, R. G. (1984). Utility of the MMPI-168 with men inpatient alcoholics. *Journal of Studies on Alcohol*, *45*, 371–373.

Faulstich, M. E., Carey, M. P., Delatte, J. G., Jr., & Delatte, G. M. (1985). Age differences on alcoholic MMPI scales: A discriminant analysis approach. *Journal of Clinical Psychology*, *41*, 433–439.

Filstead, W. J., Drachman, D. A., Rossi, J. J., & Getsinger, S. H. (1983). The relationship of MMPI subtype membership to demographic variables and treatment outcome among substance misusers. *Journal of Studies on Alcohol*, *44*, 917–922.

Finney, J. C., Smith, D. F., Skeeters, D. E., & Auvenshine, C. D. (1971). MMPI alcoholism scales: Factor structure and content analysis. *Quarterly Journal of Studies on Alcohol*, *32*, 1055–1060.

Foureman, W. C., Parks, R., & Gardin, T. H. (1981). The MMPI as a predictor of retention in a therapeutic community for heroin addicts. *International Journal of the Addictions*, *16*, 893–903.

Frankel, A., & Murphy, J. (1974). Physical fitness and personality in alcoholism: Canonical analysis of measures before and after treatment. *Quarterly Journal of Studies on Alcohol*, *35*, 1272–1278.

Friedrich, W. N., & Loftsgard, S. O. (1978a). A comparison of the MacAndrew alcoholism scale and the Michigan alcoholism screening test in a sample of problem drinkers. *Journal of Studies on Alcohol*, *39*, 1940–1944.

Friedrich, W. N., & Loftsgard, S. O. (1978b). Comparison of two alcoholism scales with alcoholics and their wives. *Journal of Clinical Psychology*, *34*, 784–786.

Gellens, H. K., Gottheil, E., & Alterman, A. I. (1976). Drinking outcome of specific alcoholic subgroups. *Journal of Studies on Alcohol*, *37*, 986–989.

Gilbert, J. G., & Lombardi, D. N. (1967). Personality characteristics of young male narcotic addicts. *Journal of Consulting Psychology*, *31*, 536–538.

Gilbertson, A. D. (1984). Perceptual differentiation among drug addicts: Correlations with intelligence and MMPI scores. *Journal of Clinical Psychology*, *40*, 334–339.

Glen, A., Royer, F. L., & Custer, R. (1973). A study of MMPI-profile types of hospitalized alcoholic veterans. *Newsletter for Research in Psychology*, *15*, 53–56.

Goldstein, S. G., & Linden, J. D. (1969). Multivariate classification of alcoholics by means of the MMPI. *Journal of Abnormal Psychology*, *74*, 661–669.

Goss, A., & Morosko, T. E. (1969). Alcoholism and clinical symptoms. *Journal of Abnormal Psychology*, *74*, 682–684.

Graf, K., Baer, P. E., & Comstock, B. S. (1977). MMPI changes in briefly hospitalized non-narcotic drug users. *Journal of Nervous and Mental Disease, 165,* 126–133.

Graham, J. R., & Mayo, M. A. (1985, March). *A comparison of MMPI strategies for identifying black and white male alcoholics.* Paper presented at the 20th Annual Symposium on Recent Developments in the Use of the MMPI, Honolulu.

Greene, R. L. (1987). The MMPI and ethnicity: A review. *Journal of Consulting and Clinical Psychology, 55,* 497–512.

Greene, R. L., & Nichols, D. S. (1987). *Replicability and validity of the 2-8-7-4 codetype: A comment and some data.* Manuscript submitted for publication.

Haertzen, C., & Hooks, N. T., Jr. (1969). Changes in personality and subjective experience associated with the chronic administration and withdrawal of opiates. *Journal of Nervous and Mental Disease, 148,* 606–614.

Hampton, P. J. (1951). A psychometric study of drinkers. *Journal of Consulting Psychology, 15,* 501–504.

Health and Public Policy Committee (1985). Chemical dependence. *Annals of Internal Medicine, 102,* 405–408.

Hedlund, J. H., & Won Cho, D. (1979). [MMPI data research tape for Missouri Department of Mental Health patients.] Unpublished raw data.

Herl, D. (1976). Personality characteristics in a sample of heroin addict methadone maintenance applicants. *British Journal of Addictions, 71,* 253–259.

Herrera, J. M., Okonek, A., Parent, M., & Roy, S. (1986, August). *MMPI subtypes for chronic phencyclidine (PCP) abusers.* Paper presented at the annual meeting of the American Psychological Association, Washington, D.C.

Hewett, B. B., & Martin, W. R. (1980). Psychometric comparisons of sociopathic and psychopathological behaviors of alcoholics and drug abusers versus a low drug use control population. *International Journal of the Addictions, 15,* 77–105.

Hewitt, C. C. (1943). A personality study of alcohol addiction. *Quarterly Journal of Studies on Alcohol, 4,* 368–386.

Hightower, N. (1984). *Validity of the MacAndrew alcoholism scale: Racial variations and effects of offender status.* Unpublished doctoral dissertation, Texas Tech University, Lubbock.

Hill, H. E., Haertzen, C. A., & Davis, H. (1962). An MMPI factor analytic study of alcoholics, narcotic addicts and criminals. *Quarterly Journal of Studies on Alcohol, 23,* 411–431.

Hodo, G. L., & Fowler, R. D. (1976). Frequency of MMPI two-point codes in a large alcoholic sample. *Journal of Clinical Psychology, 32,* 487–489.

Hoffmann, H. (1973). MMPI changes for a male alcoholic state hospital population—1959 to 1971. *Psychological Reports, 33,* 139–142.

Hoffmann, H., Loper, R. G., & Kammeier, M. L. (1974). Identifying future alcoholics with MMPI alcoholism scales. *Quarterly Journal of Studies on Alcohol, 35,* 490–498.

Hoffmann, H., & Nelson, P. C. (1971). Personality characteristics of alcoholics in relation to age and intelligence. *Psychological Reports, 29,* 143–146.

Hoffmann, H., & Wehler, R. (1978). Pre- and posttraining MMPI scores of women alcoholism counselors. *Journal of Studies on Alcohol, 39,* 1952–1955.

Hoffman, N.G., Lumry, A.E., Hamson, P.A., & Lessard, R.J. (1984). Brief MMPI scales to screen for substance abuse. *Drug and Alcohol Dependence, 14,* 209–214.

Holcomb, W. R., & Adams, N. A. (1985). Personality mechanisms of alcohol-related violence. *Journal of Clinical Psychology, 41,* 714–722.

Holland, T. R. (1977). Multivariate analysis of personality correlates of alcohol and drug abuse in a prison population. *Journal of Abnormal Psychology, 86,* 644–650.

Holland, T. R. (1978). Dimensions, patterns, and personality correlates of drug abuse in an offender population. *Journal of Consulting and Clinical Psychology, 46,* 577–578.

Holland, T. R., Levi, M., & Watson, C. G. (1981). MMPI basic scales vs. two-point codes in the discrimination of psychopathological groups. *Journal of Clinical Psychology, 37,* 394–396.

Holland, T. R., & Watson, C. G. (1980). Multivariate analysis of WAIS-MMPI relationships among brain-damaged, schizophrenic, neurotic, and alcoholic patients. *Journal of Clinical Psychology, 36,* 352–359.

Holmes, W. O. (1953). *The development of an empirical MMPI scale for addiction.* Unpublished manuscript, San Jose (CA) State College.

Holmes, C. B., Dungan, D. S., & McLaughlin, T. P. (1982). Validity of five MMPI alcoholism scales. *Journal of Clinical Psychology, 38,* 661–664.

Horn, J. L., Wanberg, K. W., & Adams, G. (1974). Diagnosis of alcoholism: Factors of drinking, background, and current conditions in alcoholics. *Quarterly Journal of Studies on Alcohol, 35,* 147–175.

Hoyt, D. P., & Sedlacek, G. M. (1958). Differentiating alcoholics from normals and abnormals with the MMPI. *Journal of Clinical Psychology, 14,* 69–74.

Huber, N. A., & Danahy, S. (1975). Use of the MMPI in predicting completion and evaluating changes in a long-term alcoholism treatment program. *Journal of Studies on Alcohol, 36,* 1230–1237.

Jansen, D. G., & Hoffmann, H. (1973). Demographic and MMPI characteristics of male and female state hospital alcoholic patients. *Psychological Reports, 33,* 561–562.

Jones, B. M., Jones, M. K., & Hatcher, E. M. (1980). Cognitive deficits in women alcoholics as a function of gynecological status. *Journal of Studies on Alcohol, 41,* 140–146.

Kamback, M. C., Bosma, W. G. A., & D'Lugoff, B. C. (1977). Family surrogates? The drug culture or the methadone maintenance program. *British Journal of Addiction, 72,* 171–176.

Kamerown, D, B., Pincus, H. A., & Macdonald, D. I. (1986). Alcohol abuse, other drug abuse, and mental disorders in medical practice. *Journal of the American Medical Association, 255,* 2054–2057.

Kammeier, M. L., Hoffmann, H., & Loper, R. G. (1973). Personality characteristics of alcoholics as college freshmen and at time of treatment. *Quarterly Journal of Studies on Alcohol, 34,* 390–399.

Keller, J., & Redfering, D. L. (1973). Comparison between the personalities of LSD users and nonusers as measured by the MMPI. *Journal of Nervous and Mental Disease, 156,* 271–277.

Kline, J. A., Rozynko, V. V., Flint, G., & Roberts, A. C. (1973). Personality characteristics of male Native American alcoholic patients. *International Journal of the Addictions, 8,* 729–732.

Kline, R. B., & Snyder, D. K. (1985). Replicated MMPI subtypes for alcoholic men and women: Relationship to self-reported drinking behaviors. *Journal of Consulting and Clinical Psychology, 53,* 70–79.

Klinge, V. (1983). A comparison of parental and adolescent MMPIs as related to substance use. *International Journal of the Addictions, 18,* 1179–1185.

Kranitz, L. (1972). Alcoholics, heroin addicts and nonaddicts; Comparisons on the MacAndrew alcoholism scale of the MMPI. *Quarterly Journal of Studies on Alcohol, 33,* 807–809.

Krauthamer, C. (1979). The personality of alcoholic middle-class women: A comparative study with the MMPI. *Journal of Clinical Psychology, 35,* 442–448.

Lachar, D., Berman, W., Grisell, J. L., & Schooff, K. (1976). The MacAndrew alcoholism scale as a general measure of substance abuse. *Journal of Studies on Alcohol, 37,* 1609–1615.

Lachar, D., Berman, W., Grisell, J. L., & Schooff, K. (1979a). A heroin addiction scale for the MMPI: Effectiveness in differential diagnosis in a psychiatric setting. *International Journal of the Addictions, 14,* 135–142.

Lachar, D., Gdowski, C. L., & Keegan, J. F. (1979b). MMPI profiles of men alcoholics, drug addicts and psychiatric patients. *Journal of Studies on Alcohol, 40,* 45–56.

Leon, G. R., Kolotkin, R., & Korgeski, G. (1979). MacAndrew addiction scale and other MMPI characteristics associated with obesity, anorexia and smoking behavior. *Addictive Behaviors, 4,* 401–407.

Libb, J. W., & Taulbee, E. S. (1971). Psychotic-appearing MMPI profiles among alcoholics. *Journal of Clinical Psychology, 27,* 101–102.

Linden, J. D. (1969). *The differential utility of a scale to identify alcoholics.* Paper presented at the annual meeting of the Midwestern Psychological Association.

Loberg, T. (1981). MMPI-based personality subtypes of alcoholics: Relationships to drinking history, psychometrics and neuropsychological deficits. *Journal of Studies on Alcohol, 42,* 766–782.

Loper, R. G., Kammeier, M. L., & Hoffmann, H. (1973). MMPI characteristics of college freshman males who later became alcoholics. *Journal of Abnormal Psychology, 82,* 159–161.

Lowe, W. C., & Thomas, S. D. (1976). Assessing alcoholism treatment effectiveness: A comparison of three evaluative measures. *Journal of Studies on Alcohol, 37,* 883–889.

MacAndrew, C. (1965). The differentiation of male alcoholic outpatients from nonalcoholic psychiatric outpatients by means of the MMPI. *Quarterly Journal of Studies on Alcohol, 26,* 238–246.

MacAndrew, C. (1967). Self-reports of male alcoholics: A dimensional analysis of certain differences from nonalcoholic male psychiatric outpatients. *Quarterly Journal of Studies on Alcohol, 28,* 43–51.

MacAndrew, C. (1978). Women alcoholics' responses to Scale 4 of the MMPI. *Journal of Studies on Alcohol, 39,* 1841–1854.

MacAndrew, C. (1979). MAC scale scores of three samples of men under conditions of conventional versus independent scale administration. *Journal of Studies on Alcohol, 40,* 138–141.

MacAndrew, C. (1981a). Similarities in the self-depictions of men alcoholics and psychiatric outpatients. *Journal of Studies on Alcohol, 42,* 421–431.

MacAndrew, C. (1981b). What the *MAC* scale tells us about men alcoholics: An interpretive review. *Journal of Studies on Alcohol, 42,* 604–625.

MacAndrew, C. (1982). An examination of the relevance of the individual differences (A-trait) formulation of the tension-reduction theory to the etiology of alcohol abuse in young males. *Addictive Behaviors, 7,* 39–45.

MacAndrew, C. (1986). Toward the psychometric detection of substance misuse in young men: The SAP scale. *Journal of Studies on Alcohol, 47,* 161–166.

MacAndrew, C., & Geertsma, R. H. (1963). An analysis of responses of alcoholics to Scale 4 of the MMPI. *Quarterly Journal of Studies on Alcohol, 24,* 23–38.

MacAndrew, C., & Geertsma, R. H. (1964). A critique of alcoholism scales derived from the MMPI. *Quarterly Journal of Studies on Alcohol, 25,* 68–76.

McGinnis, C. A., & Ryan, C. W. (1965). The influence of age on MMPI scores of chronic alcoholics. *Journal of Clinical Psychology, 21,* 271–272.

McGuire, J. S., & Megargee, E. I. (1974). Personality correlates of marijuana use among youthful offenders. *Journal of Consulting and Clinical Psychology, 42,* 124–133.

McKenna, T., & Pickens, R. (1983). Personality characteristics of alcoholic children of alcoholics. *Journal of Studies on Alcohol, 44,* 688–700.

McLachlan, J. F. C. (1975). Classification of alcoholics by an MMPI actuarial system. *Journal of Clinical Psychology, 31,* 145–147.

McWilliams, J., & Brown, C. C. (1977). Treatment termination variables, MMPI scores and frequencies of relapse in alcoholics. *Journal of Studies on Alcohol, 38,* 477–486.

Mendelson, J. H., Miller, K. D., Mello, N. K., Pratt, H., & Schmitz, R. (1982). Hospital treatment of alcoholism: A profile of middle income Americans. *Alcoholism (NY), 83,* 377–383.

Mogar, R. E., Wilson, W. M., & Helm, S. T. (1970). Personality subtypes of male and female alcoholic patients. *International Journal of the Addictions, 5,* 99–113.

Monroe, J. J., Ross, W. F., & Berzins, J. I. (1971). The decline of the addict as "psychopath": Implications for community care. *International Journal of the Addictions, 6,* 601–608.

Moore, R. H. (1984). The concurrent and construct validity of the MacAndrew alcoholism scale among at-risk adolescent males. *Journal of Clinical Psychology, 40,* 1264–1269.

Moore, R. H. (1985). Construct validity of the MacAndrew scale: Secondary psychopathic and dysthymic-neurotic character orientations among adolescent male misdemeanor offenders. *Journal of Studies on Alcohol, 46,* 128–131.

Morey, L. C., & Blashfield, R. K. (1981). Empirical classifications of alcoholism: A review. *Journal of Studies on Alcohol, 42,* 925–937.

Morey, L. C., Roberts, W. R., & Penk, W. (1987). MMPI alcoholic subtypes: Replicability and validity of the 2-8-7-4 subtype. *Journal of Abnormal Psychology, 96,* 164–166.

Morey, L. C., & Skinner, H. A. (1986). Empirically derived classifications of alcohol-related problems. In M. Galanter (Ed.), *Recent developments in alcoholism,* Vol. 4 (pp. 145–168). New York: Plenum Press.

Morey, L. C., Skinner, H. A., & Blashfield, R. K. (1984). A typology of alcohol abusers: Correlates and implications. *Journal of Abnormal Psychology, 93,* 408–417.

Mulligan, M. J., Steer, R. A., & Fine, E. W. (1978). Psychiatric disturbance in drunk driving offenders referred for treatment of alcoholism. *Alcoholism: Clinical and Experimental Research, 2,* 107–111.

Navarro, D. J. (1979). Women A.A. members and nonalcoholics; Scores on the Holmes and MacAndrew scales of the MMPI. *Journal of Studies on Alcohol, 40,* 496–498.

Nerviano, V. J., & Gross, H. W. (1983). Personality types of alcoholics on objective inventories. *Journal of Studies on Alcohol, 44,* 837–851.

Nerviano, V. J., McCarty, D., & McCarty, S. M. (1980). MMPI profile patterns of men alcoholics in two contrasting settings. *Journal of Studies on Alcohol, 41,* 1143–1152.

Newlin, D. B. (1985). Offspring of alcoholics have enhanced antagonistic placebo response. *Journal of Studies on Alcohol, 46,* 490–494.

O'Leary, M. R., Donovan, D. M., Freeman, C. W., & Chaney, E. F. (1976). Relationship between psychopathology, experienced control and perceived locus of control: In search of alcohol subtypes. *Journal of Clinical Psychology, 32,* 899–904.

Ollendick, D. G. (1984). Scores on three MMPI alcohol scales of parents who receive child custody. *Psychological Reports, 55,* 337–338.

O'Neil, P. M., Giacinto, J. P., Waid, L. R., Roitzsch, J. C., Miller, W. C., & Kilpatrick, D. G. (1983). Behavioral, psychological, and historical correlates of MacAndrew scale scores among male alcoholics. *Journal of Behavioral Assessment, 5,* 261–273.

Ottomanelli, G. A. (1976). Follow-up of a token economy applied to civilly committed narcotic addicts. *International Journal of the Addictions, 11,* 793–806.

Ottomanelli, G. A. (1977). MMPI and Pyp prediction compared to base rate prediction of six-month behavioral outcome for methadone patients. *British Journal of Addiction, 72,* 177–186.

Ottomanelli, G., Wilson, P., & Whyte, R. (1978). MMPI evaluation of 5-year methadone treatment status. *Journal of Consulting and Clinical Psychology, 46,* 579–581.

Page, R. D., & Bozlee, S. (1982). A cross-cultural MMPI comparison of alcoholics. *Psychological Reports, 50,* 639–646.

Paige, P. E., & Zappella, D. G. (1969). The incidence of MMPI code high combinations and extreme scores of a select group of male alcoholic patients. *Psychology, 6,* 13–21.

Panton, J. H., & Brisson, R. C. (1971). Characteristics associated with drug abuse within a state prison population. *Corrective Psychiatry and Journal of Social Therapy, 17,* 3–33.

Paredes, A., Gregory, D., & Jones, B. M. (1974). Induced drinking and social adjustment in alcoholics: Development of a therapeutic model. *Quarterly Journal of Studies on Alcohol, 35,* 1279–1293.

Parr, W. C., Woodward, W. A., Robinowitz, R., & Penk, W. E. (1981). Cross-validation of a heroin addiction (*He*) scale in a treatment setting. *International Journal of the Addictions, 16,* 549–553.

Passini, F. T., Watson, C. G., Dehnel, L., Herder, J., & Watkins, B. (1977). Alpha wave biofeedback training therapy in alcoholics. *Journal of Clinical Psychology, 33,* 292–299.

Patalano, F. (1980a). Comparison of MMPI scores of drug abusers and Mayo Clinic normative groups. *Journal of Clinical Psychology, 36,* 576–579.

Patalano, F. (1980b). MMPI two-point code-type frequencies of drug abusers in a therapeutic community. *Psychological Reports, 46,* 1019–1022.

Pattison, E. M., Coe, R., & Doerr, H. O. (1973). Population variation among alcoholism treatment facilities. *International Journal of the Addictions, 8,* 199–229.

Penk, W. E., Charles, H. L., Patterson, E. T., Roberts, W. R., Dolan, M. P., & Brown, A. S. (1982). Chronological age differences in MMPI scores of male chronic alcoholics seeking treatment. *Journal of Consulting and Clinical Psychology, 50,* 322–324.

Penk, W. E., Fudge, J. W., Robinowitz, R., & Neman, R. S. (1979). Personality characteristics of compulsive heroin, amphetamine, and barbiturate users. *Journal of Consulting and Clinical Psychology, 47,* 583–585.

Penk, W. E., & Robinowitz, R. (1976). Personality differences of volunteer and nonvolunteer heroin and nonheroin drug users. *Journal of Abnormal Psychology, 85,* 91–100.

Penk, W. E., Woodward, W. A., Robinowitz, R., & Hess, J. L. (1978). Differences in MMPI scores of black and white compulsive heroin users. *Journal of Abnormal Psychology, 87,* 505–513.

Pettinati, H. M., Sugerman, A. A., & Maurer, H. S. (1982). Four year MMPI changes in abstinent and drinking alcoholics. *Alcoholism: Clinical and Experimental Research, 6,* 487–494.

Pfost, K. S., Kunce, J. T., Stevens, M. J. (1984). The relationship of MacAndrew alcoholism scale scores to MMPI profile type and degree of elevation. *Journal of Clinical Psychology, 40,* 852–855.

Preng, K. W., & Clopton, J. R. (1986a). Application of the MacAndrew alcoholism scale to alcoholics with psychiatric diagnoses. *Journal of Personality Assessment, 50,* 113–122.

Preng, K. W., & Clopton, J. R. (1986b). The MacAndrew Scale: Clinical application and theoretical issues. *Journal of Studies on Alcohol, 47,* 228–236.

Price, R. H., & Curlee-Salisbury, J. (1975). Patient-treatment interactions among alcoholics. *Journal of Studies on Alcohol, 36,* 659–669.

Public Health Service (September-October, 1983). Alcohol and drug misuse prevention: Summary of the problem. *Public Health Reports Supplement,* 116–117.

Pugliese, A. C. (1975). A study of methadone maintenance patients with the MMPI. *British Journal of the Addictions, 70,* 198–204.

Rardin, D. R., Lawson, T. R., & Kruzich, D. J. (1974). Opiates, amphetamines, alcohol: A comparative study of American soldiers. *International Journal of the Addictions, 9,* 891–898.

Rhodes, R. J. (1969). The MacAndrew alcoholism scale: A replication. *Journal of Clinical Psychology, 25,* 189–191.

Rhodes, R. J., & Chang, A.F. (1978). A further look at the Institutionalized Chronic Alcoholic Scale. *Journal of Clinical Psychology, 34,* 779–780.

Rich, C. C., & Davis, H. G. (1969). Concurrent validity of MMPI alcoholism scales. *Journal of Clinical Psychology, 25,* 425–426.

Robyak, J. E., Donham, G. W., Roy, R., & Ludenia, K. (1984). Differential patterns of alcohol abuse among normal, neurotic, psychotic, and characterological types. *Journal of Personality Assessment, 48,* 132–136.

Rohan, W. P. (1972). MMPI changes in hospitalized alcoholics: A second study. *Quarterly Journal of Studies on Alcohol, 33,* 65–76.

Rohan, W. P., Tatro, R. L., & Rotman, S. R. (1969). MMPI changes in alcoholics during hospitalization. *Quarterly Journal of Studies on Alcohol, 30,* 389–400.

Rosen, A. C. (1960). A comparative study of alcoholic and psychiatric patients with the MMPI. *Quarterly Journal of Studies on Alcohol, 21,* 253–266.

Rosenberg, N. (1972). MMPI alcoholism scales. *Journal of Clinical Psychology, 28,* 515–522.

Rothaizer, J. M. (1980). A typological study of substance abusers using the MMPI. *Journal of Clinical Psychology, 36,* 1019–1021.

Rotman, S. R., & Vestre, N. D. (1964). The use of the MMPI in identifying problem drinkers among psychiatric hospital admissions. *Journal of Clinical Psychology, 20,* 526–530.

Ruff, C. F., Ayers, J., & Templer, D. I. (1975). Alcoholics' and criminals' similarity of scores on the MacAndrew alcoholism scale. *Psychological Reports, 36,* 921–922.

Saunders, G. R., & Schuckit, M. A. (1981). MMPI scores in young men with alcoholic relatives and controls. *Journal of Nervous and Mental Disease, 169,* 456–458.

Savage, P. P. E., & Marchington, T. D. (1977). Common personality characteristics of male drug abusers in New Zealand. *British Journal of Addiction, 72,* 349–356.

Schroeder, D. J., & Piercy, D. C. (1979). A comparison of MMPI two-point codes in four alcoholism treatment facilities. *Journal of Clinical Psychology, 35,* 656–663.

Schuckit, M. A., Morrison, C. R., & Gold, E. O. (1984). A pragmatic alcoholism treatment outcome scale. *American Journal of Alcohol Abuse, 10,* 125–131.

Schwartz, M. F., & Graham, J. R. (1979). Construct validity of the MacAndrew alcoholism scale. *Journal of Consulting and Clinical Psychology, 47,* 1090–1095.

Sheppard, C., Fiorentino, D., Collins, L., & Merlis, S. (1969). Comparison of emotion profiles as defined by two additional MMPI profile types in male narcotic addicts. *Journal of Clinical Psychology, 25,* 186–188.

Sher, K. J., & McCrady, B. S. (1984). The MacAndrew alcoholism scale: Severity of alcohol abuse and parental alcoholism. *Addictive Behaviors, 9,* 99–102.

Silver, A. M. (1977). Some personality characteristics of groups of young drug misusers and delinquents. *British Journal of Addictions*, 72, 143–150.

Sinnett, E. R. (1985). What art thou MacAndrew scale? Confusion and errata in high places. *Psychological Reports*, 56, 384–386.

Skinner, H. A. (1982). Statistical approaches to the classification of alcohol and drug addiction. *British Journal of Addiction*, 77, 259–273.

Skinner, H. A., Jackson, D. N., & Hoffmann, H. (1974). Alcoholic personality types: Identification and correlates. *Journal of Abnormal Psychology*, 83, 658–666.

Smart, R. G., & Jones, D. (1970). Illicit LSD users: Their personality characteristics and psychopathology. *Journal of Abnormal Psychology*, 75, 286–292.

Smith, R. B., Burgess, A. E., Guinee, V. J., & Reifsnider, L. C. (1979). A curvilinear relationship between alcoholic withdrawal tremor and personality. *Journal of Clinical Psychology*, 35, 199–203.

Snyder, D. K., Kline, R. B., & Podany, E. C. (1985). Comparison of external correlates of MMPI substance abuse scales across sex and race. *Journal of Consulting and Clinical Psychology*, 53, 520–525.

Soskin, R. A. (1970). Personality and attitude change after two alcoholism treatment programs: Comparative contributions of Lysergide and human relations training. *Quarterly Journal of Studies on Alcohol*, 31, 920–931.

Spotts, J. V., & Shontz, F. C. (1983). Psychopathology and chronic drug use: A methodological paradigm. *International Journal of the Addictions*, 18, 633–680.

Stein, K. B., & Rozynko, V. (1974). Psychological and social variables and personality patterns of drug abusers. *International Journal of the Addictions*, 9, 431–446.

Sutker, P. B. (1971). Personality differences and sociopathy in heroin addicts and nonaddict prisoners. *Journal of Abnormal Psychology*, 78, 247–251.

Sutker, P. B., Archer, R. P., & Allain, A. N. (1978). Drug abuse patterns, personality characteristics, and relationships with sex, race, and sensation seeking. *Journal of Consulting and Clinical Psychology*, 46, 1374–1378.

Sutker, P. B., Archer, R. P., Brantley, P. J., & Kilpatrick, D. G. (1979). Alcoholics and opiate addicts: Comparison of personality characteristics. *Journal of Studies on Alcohol*, 40, 635–644.

Sutker, P. B., Brantley, P. J., & Allain, A. N. (1980). MMPI response patterns and alcohol consumption in DUI offenders. *Journal of Consulting and Clinical Psychology*, 48, 350–355.

Sutker, P. B., Cohen, G. H., & Allain, A. N. (1976). Prediction of successful response to multimodality treatment among heroin addicts. *International Journal of the Addictions*, 11, 861–879.

Sutker, P. B., Patsiokas, A. T., & Allain, A. N. (1981). Chronic illicit drug abusers: Gender comparisons. *Psychological Reports*, 49, 383–390.

Svanum, S., & Dallas, C. L. (1981). Alcoholic MMPI types and their relationship to patient characteristics, polydrug abuse, and abstinence following treatment. *Journal of Personality Assessment*, 45, 278–287.

Svanum, S., Levitt, E. E., & McAdoo, W. G. (1982). Differentiating male and female alcoholics from psychiatric outpatients: The MacAndrew and Rosenberg alcoholism scales. *Journal of Personality Assessment*, 46, 81–84.

Swain-Holcomb, B., & Thorne, B. M. (1984). A comparison of male and female alcoholics with an MMPI classification system. *Journal of Personality Assessment*, 48, 392–397.

Tarter, R. E., McBride, H., Buonpane, N., & Schneider, D. U. (1977). Differentiation of alcoholics: Childhood history of minimal brain dysfunction, family history, and drinking

pattern. *Archives of General Psychiatry*, 34, 761–768.

Templer, D. I., Ruff, C. F., Barthlow, V. L., Halcomb, P. H., & Ayers, J. L. (1978). Psychometric assessment of alcoholism in convicted felons. *Journal of Studies on Alcohol*, 39, 1948–1951.

Thornton, C. C., Gellens, H. K., Alterman, A. I., & Gottheil, E. (1979). Developmental level and prognosis in alcoholics. *Alcoholism: Clinical and Experimental Research*, 3, 70–77.

Toomey, T. C. (1974). Personality and demographic characteristics of two sub-types of drug abusers. *British Journal of the Addictions*, 69, 155–158.

Trevithick, L., & Hosch, H. M. (1978). MMPI correlates of drug addiction based on drug of choice. *Journal of Consulting and Clinical Psychology*, 46, 180.

Uecker, A. E. (1970). Differentiating male alcoholic from other psychiatric inpatients: Validity of the MacAndrew scale. *Quarterly Journal of Studies on Alcohol*, 31, 379–383.

Uecker, A. E., Boutilier, L. R., & Richardson, E. H. (1980). "Indianism" and MMPI scores of men alcoholics. *Journal of Studies on Alcohol*, 41, 357–362.

Vega, A. (1971). Cross-validation of four MMPI scales for alcoholism. *Quarterly Journal of Studies on Alcohol*, 32, 791–797.

Walters, G. D., Greene, R. L., Jeffrey, T. B., Kruzich, D. J., & Haskin, J. J. (1983). Racial variations on the MacAndrew alcoholism scale of the MMPI. *Journal of Consulting and Clinical Psychology*, 51, 947–948.

Watson, C. G., & Vassar, P. (1983). The MMPIs of left- and right-handed subjects. *Perceptual and Motor Skills*, 57, 487–490.

Watson, N., Harris, W. G., Johnson, J. H., & LaBeck, L. (1983). MMPI clinical and content norms for a mixed psychiatric adolescent population. *Journal of Clinical Psychology*, 39, 696–709.

Weissman, S. (1970). The significance of diagnosis in the treatment of narcotics addicts. *International Journal of the Addictions*, 5, 717–730.

West, L. J. (1984). Alcoholism. *Annals of Internal Medicine*, 100, 405–416.

Whisler, R. H., & Cantor, J. M., (1966). The MacAndrew alcoholism scale: A cross-validation in a domiciliary setting. *Journal of Clinical Psychology*, 22, 311–312.

Whitelock, P. R., Overall, J. E., & Patrick, J. H. (1971). Personality patterns and alcohol abuse in a state hospital population. *Journal of Abnormal Psychology*, 78, 9–16.

Wilkinson, A. E., Prado, W. M., Williams, W. O., & Schnadt, F. W. (1971). Psychological test characteristics and length of stay in alcoholism treatment. *Quarterly Journal of Studies on Alcohol*, 32, 60–65.

Williams, A. F., McCourt, W. F., & Schneider, L. (1971). Personality self-descriptions of alcoholics and heavy drinkers. *Quarterly Journal of Studies on Alcohol*, 32, 310–317.

Willis, K. A., Wehler, R., & Rush, W. A. (1979). MacAndrew scale scores of smoking and nonsmoking alcoholics. *Journal of Studies on Alcohol*, 40, 906–907.

Wishart, D. (1978). *CLUSTAN user manual*. St. Andrews, Scotland, Computing Laboratory, University of St. Andrews.

Wisniewski, N. M., Glenwick, D. S., & Graham, J. R. (1985). MacAndrew scale and sociodemographic correlates of adolescent alcohol and drug use. *Addictive Behaviors*, 10, 55–67.

Wolfson, K. P., & Erbaugh, S. E. (1984). Adolescent responses to the MacAndrew alcoholism scale. *Journal of Consulting and Clinical Psychology*, 52, 625–630.

Yescalis, W. (1984). [MacAndrew alcoholism scale scores in normal high school students.] Unpublished raw data.

Zager, L. D., & Megargee, E. I. (1981). Seven MMPI alcohol and drug abuse scales: An empirical investigation of their interrelationships, convergent and discriminant validity, and degree of racial bias. *Journal of Personality and Social Psychology, 40,* 532–544.

Zelen, S. L., Fox, J., Gould, E., & Olson, R. W. (1966). Sex-contingent differences between male and female alcoholics. *Journal of Clinical Psychology, 22,* 160–165.

Ziegler, R., Kohutek, K., & Owen, P. (1978). A multimodal treatment approach for incarcerated alcoholics. *Journal of Clinical Psychology, 34,* 1005–1009.

Zielinski, J. J. (1979). Psychological test data of depressed, nondepressed and relapsed alcoholics receiving pharmacological aversion. *British Journal of Addiction, 74,* 175–182.

Zuckerman, M., Sola, S., Masterson, J., & Angelone, J.V. (1975). MMPI patterns in drug abusers before and after treatment in therapeutic communities. *Journal of Consulting and Clinical Psychology, 48,* 286–296.

Chapter 7

Post-traumatic Stress Disorder

WALTER PENK, TERENCE KEANE,
RALPH ROBINOWITZ, D. ROBERT FOWLER,
WILLIAM E. BELL, and ALLAN FINKELSTEIN

OVERVIEW

MMPI clinical studies of patients with Post-traumatic Stress Disorder (PTSD) are still rare, compared with the thousands of studies that have been conducted with other diagnostic categories. So little research has been published on PTSD and the MMPI that this chapter, in contrast to those on other clinical groups preceding it, must begin with the following precautions. First, descriptive criteria for diagnosing PTSD were formulated only recently. PTSD criteria were not introduced until 1980 with the publication of the Third Edition of the *Diagnostic and Statistical Manual of the American Psychiatric Association* (DSM-III: American Psychiatric Association, 1980). Although stress-like disorders were described previously in the Gray Manual (DSM-I: American Psychiatric Association, 1952), categories like traumatic war neuroses and adult situational disorder were conceptualized as *temporary* disturbances; as such, diagnosticians were advised to note the symptoms and to wait to see if they disappeared or turned into something more substantial.

Since the formulation of PTSD as a persisting disorder is a comparatively recent development, it is not surprising that MMPI research on PTSD is not well-advanced methodologically or substantively. Neither prevalence nor incidence of PTSD have been established; no treatment outcome studies have been published. Clinical research on PTSD is comparatively more descriptive than clinical research on other disorders; PTSD research still focuses on empirically establishing dimensions comprising the syndrome rather than addressing more complex questions such as the longitudinal course of the disorder or treatment effects (Figley, 1978; 1985; 1986).

Second, descriptive criteria for diagnosing PTSD are not firmly fixed; indeed, they have been revised (see Table 7–1 below for the 1987 version of criteria DSM-III-Revised). The evolutions in the criteria for PTSD indicate that, when comparing MMPI studies of PTSD, similarities of PTSD criteria may exist, but not equivalence. Moreover, revisions of PTSD criteria are likely to continue, but for the best of reasons; more and more is being learned about the structure and function of PTSD.

Third, techniques for diagnosing PTSD are still being developed. The study of PTSD, being a comparatively new diagnostic category, has been conducted through the medium of newly developed instruments (e.g., the survivors of the Beverly Hills Supper club fire were evaluated by the recently developed Diagnostic Interview Schedule [Green, Grace, & Gleser, 1985]). Descriptive PTSD criteria have not been fully operationalized; empirical measures are still being constructed and measurement strategies are still being devised. Keane, Wolfe, and Taylor

THE MMPI: USE WITH
SPECIFIC POPULATIONS

© 1988 by Grune & Stratton.

ISBN 0-8089-1913-X

**TABLE 7–1. DSM-III-REVISED CRITERIA FOR
309.89 POST-TRAUMATIC STRESS DISORDER (PTSD)**

A. The person has experienced an event that is outside the range of usual human experience and that would be markedly distressing to almost anyone, e.g., serious threat to one's life or physical integrity; serious threat or harm to one's children, spouse, or other close relatives and friends; sudden destruction of one's home or community; or seeing another person who has recently been, or is being, seriously injured or killed as the result of an accident or physical violence.

B. The traumatic event is persistently reexperienced in at least one of the following ways:
   (1) recurrent and intrusive distressing recollections of the event (in young children, repetitive play in which themes or aspects of the trauma are expressed)
   (2) recurrent distressing dreams of the event
   (3) sudden acting or feeling as if the traumatic event were recurring (includes a sense of reliving the experience, illusions, hallucinations, and dissociative [flashback] episodes, even those that occur upon awakening or when intoxicated)
   (4) intense psychological distress at exposure to events that symbolize or resemble an aspect of the traumatic event, including anniversaries of the trauma

C. Persistent avoidance of stimuli associated with the trauma or numbing of general responsiveness (not present before the trauma), as indicated by at least three of the following:
   (1) efforts to avoid thoughts or feelings associated with the trauma
   (2) efforts to avoid activities or situations that arouse recollections of the trauma
   (3) inability to recall an important aspect of the trauma (psychogenic amnesia)
   (4) markedly diminished interest in significant activities (in young children, loss of recently acquired developmental skills such as toilet training or language skills)
   (5) feeling of detachment or estrangement from others
   (6) restricted range of affect, e.g., unable to have loving feelings
   (7) sense of a foreshortened future, e.g., does not expect to have a career, marriage, or children, or a long life

D. Persistent symptoms of increased arousal (not present before the trauma), as indicated by at least two of the following:
   (1) difficulty falling or staying asleep
   (2) irritability or outbursts of anger
   (3) difficulty concentrating
   (4) hypervigilance
   (5) exaggerated startle response
   (6) physiologic reactivity upon exposure to events that symbolize or resemble an aspect of the traumatic event (e.g., a woman who was raped in an elevator breaks out in a sweat when entering any elevator)

E. Duration of the disturbance (symptoms in B, C, and D) of at least one month.
   Specify delayed onset if the onset of symptoms was at least 6 months after the trauma.

Note: From *Diagnostic and statistical manual of mental disorders* (3rd ed., revised) by American Psychiatric Association, 1987. Washington, D.C.: Author. Reprinted with permission.

(1987) have provided an assessment of progress and recommendations for multimethod, multimeasure approaches in diagnostic strategies and tactics for studying PTSD. Measures of dimensions comprising PTSD await completion of reliability and validity studies with both cross-sectional and longitudinal forms of analyses.

Fourth, the MMPI was not designed to formulate diagnoses or to perform differential diagnosis. The MMPI is a multifactorial instrument for measuring adjustment and problem specification (Hathaway & Meehl, 1951). PTSD-classified patients were not included in the process of selecting items for either scale construction or subsequent psychometric development. Although the MMPI is saturated with items about somatic and/or psychophysiological arousal and reactivity, item content is minimal in areas of memories about surviving life-threatening events, active avoidance of stimuli reminiscent of trauma, or re-

experiencing traumatic events (e.g., "flashback" was not as popular a term in the 1930s as it is in the 1980s). Even the current revision of the MMPI (Dahlstrom & Butcher, 1987) does not increase MMPI item content for PTSD criteria.

But this lack of PTSD content in MMPI items may not be a deficiency, since empirically derived scales do not require that item content be totally relevant to the construct of interest. For example, hit rates in the 80 to 90 percent range for a recently developed MMPI PTSD scale (i.e., Keane, Malloy, & Fairbank, 1984) suggest that empirically derived scales using contrasted group techniques hold considerable promise for using the MMPI to classify PTSD (see review by Denny, Robinowitz, & Penk, 1987).

Fifth, the methods for diagnosing PTSD have been, and are, changing. Clinical methods specific to the study of PTSD with any measure (the MMPI included) are still under development. On the whole, MMPI research on PTSD is more likely to be conceptualized and conducted as single-cause, single-measure, single-effect, cross-sectional research, rather than the preferred multicasual, multimeasured, multieffect, longitudinal designs (see Schwartz, 1982). Literature reviews about the MMPI and PTSD and trauma, however, reveal a satisfying progression in research methods from the overly general to the welcome specific, from the vague to the precise, and from the static to stochastic research designs.

Sixth, PTSD is not like other disorders. PTSD is one of a few DSM-III disorders that require the clinician to assess the impact of an environmental event. Unlike diagnosing other disorders, the clinician is obligated to collect objective information that a trauma occurred, making PTSD one of only a few disorders for which an environmental event must be established in some way. Thus, diagnosing PTSD means that the clinician must measure both the trauma and the person's phenomenology of trauma. It also is preferable *not* to rely solely on the person "traumatized," i.e., the symptom-reporter, to describe the trauma and to be the only source for verifying that a trauma was experienced.

Moreover, a broader range of people may be at risk for developing PTSD than for other disorders. Anyone may be susceptible to PTSD symptoms, as anyone who has had a nightmare about death the evening after a near-miss accident on the morning's drive to work will attest. To be classified as PTSD, however, a complex of symptoms must persist for at least a month. Considering that many people may be at risk for PTSD, even people without a history of traditional psychopathogenic childhood indicators, clinicans are obligated to canvass clients' and patients' histories routinely for traumatic experiences.

Research has not answered, as yet, the critical question of causality in PTSD. *Cur alii, prae aliis?* Why some and not others? Metaphorically, how can the same fire that melts the butter harden the egg?

PTSD can happen to nearly anyone, even children, as recent additions to the previously adult-centered list of PTSD criteria suggests (e.g., symptoms of repetitive play, regression to earlier levels of maturation, expectations of a foreshortened future, etc.). Lyons (in press) has reviewed PTSD studies about children. And just as there are varying manifestations of PTSD as a

function of differences in the "host," so there are differences in the kinds of trauma and/or stressors producing PTSD. To establish PTSD, clinicians must differentiate between events that are within and beyond "the range of usual human experience. . . ." The first criterion for PTSD in DSM-III requires that the person has sustained a life-threatening experiences. PTSD is not like other disorders: both sides of the equation in diagnosing the person-by-environmental interaction must be specified (Keane, Scott, Chavoya, Lamparski, & Fairbanks, 1985).

Seventh, untreated or unsuccessfully treated PTSD may lead to complications and possibly other forms of psychological maladjustment. One major aspect of PTSD symptomatology is that the person traumatized frequently avoids reminders of the trauma. One practical implication of such avoidance is that the person may delay seeking treatment in hopes the symptoms will subside, may delay and struggle against symptoms until new stressors and/or traumas mount and overwhelm means of coping and defending against original PTSD symptoms, or may delay until susceptibility to a new disorder develops. PTSD may have been called a delayed stress syndrome because so many traumatized persons coped by avoiding or postponing treatment. As a consequence, a clinician may not see a traumatized person, or a person with PTSD, until a secondary set of symptoms has developed. For example, many substance abusers are treated for their addiction rather than an underlying traumatogenic event for which the heavy use of alcohol and/or drugs is a defense (cf. Penk, Peck, Robinowitz, Bell, & Little, 1987; Rounsaville, Weissman, Wilbur, & Kleber, 1982).

Any disorder that may be characterized in part by coping through avoidance runs the risk of leading to complications through either not treating the disorder or not successfully treating the disorder. Consequently, it is not surprising that the debates on the existence of PTSD as an independent disorder continue. It is possible that a clinician may unwittingly reinforce positively the traumatized person's coping by denial and avoidance because of the therapist's difficulties in dealing with his or her own aggressive impulses and horror of being aggressed against. The first victim in war, Oliver Stone says in *Platoon*, is innocence. Those who have not been traumatized do not like to lose their innocence, which might have to occur in order to acknowledge and to deal directly with the life-threatening horror of trauma in another. It is easier to permit the traumatized to avoid dealing with the horror of a trauma than to encourage the traumatized to cope by confronting, by engaging, by persisting, and by achieving a solution that resolves the unsettling memories of a trauma. Consequently, many forms of PTSD are not seen in their "pure" state, free of secondary complications that, on the surface, appear falsely as the primary cause of difficulty. Such interactions suggest that the MMPI not only assesses PTSD signs and symptoms but also evaluates any pretrauma problems. The MMPI has not been calibrated, yet, to distinguish between PTSD and non-PTSD symptoms.

Finally, most MMPI studies of PTSD have focused on and are limited to Vietnam combat veterans. As yet, little is known about MMPI responses among PTSD clinical samples associated with noncombat forms of trauma. Most MMPI PTSD research is gender-specific: little is known about trauma in women and nothing—from the perspective of the MMPI—is known about the 8,000 or so women nurses who served in the Vietnam combat zones (Schnaier, 1986). Whereas PTSD research conducted among Vietnam combat verterans may serve as a model for planning non-combat trauma PTSD studies, it is very likely that each form of trauma may require its own unique form of clinical research. For example, some PTSD measures are so specific to events of the Vietnam War that they do not even generalize to veterans of other wars, much less to those who have not experienced combat. More subtle differences relate to issues of personal control, duration, preparation, and self-blame about not being careful in risk areas. Moreover, there is limited research on PTSD for noncombat trauma (e.g., rape, incest, natural disasters, catastrophic events). Hopefully, the study of PTSD using the MMPI will expand from male combat veterans to other persons who have experienced other forms of trauma.

At present, then, clinicians are encouraged to approach the use of the MMPI in the study of PTSD with caution, noting both the limitations in the scope of what has been empirically demonstrated as well as the rich tradition of the MMPI that consistently has yielded a solid body of scientific findings.

Stating these numerous precautions about research on PTSD at the outset does not imply the situation is hopeless. Rather, it means that the use of the MMPI with PTSD clinical groups must be approached very carefully, since new clinical endeavors are developing quickly and old formulations are giving way to new discoveries. It is highly likely that this current summary soon will be rendered obsolete by research presently underway in many quarters. Studies such as the National Institutes of Health (NIH) Environmental Catchment Area research (Robins et al., 1981) and the National Vietnam Veterans Readjustment Study (Kulka & Schlenger, 1986) undoubtly will change the way in which MMPI studies of PTSD are planned and executed as well as increase the understanding of the causes and course of PTSD.

Although the field of clinical research on PTSD is quickly advancing and rapidly changing, considerable progress has been achieved within the span of only a few years. PTSD criteria have been reformulated and refined on the basis of empirical investigations published within the last 6 years, a comparatively brief period in which to compile evidence substantiating the cogency and relevance of any clinical disorder. So then, what is the nature of this disorder, which clinicians have set out to describe with shifting criteria, obviously inadequate methods of measurement, and, as yet, limited tactics and strategies in clinical research?

DSM-III-R PTSD CRITERIA

Publication of PTSD criteria in 1980 occurred amid unresolved disagreements not only about the dimensions of the syndrome but even whether PTSD had any basis in reality (e.g., Figley, 1978). Even when challenges to the reality of PTSD were not voiced directly, questions persisted about the validity of the diagnosis based on evidence that PTSD symptoms can be "faked" (Fairbank, McCaffrey, & Keane, 1985) or that many who meet PTSD criteria also meet criteria for Axis II diagnoses (Keane, Wolfe, & Taylor, 1987). The clinical utility of PTSD cannot be judged on the basis of the personality features of those who develop the disorder or the existence of false positives. These are issues of classification, not proofs of invalidity.

The changes made in PTSD criteria in revising DSM-III were derived from empirical research and not from resistances to applying the criteria. Moreover, these changes included the systematic way in which the criteria were organized rather than altering any of the criteria. Three fundamental dimensions now are postulated for DSM-III-Revised PTSD criteria: (1) signs of re-experiencing traumatic, life-threatening events; (2) deficiencies in coping with traumatic memories by avoidance and emotional numbing; and (3) psychophysiological reactivity to traumatic memories. These three dimensions are more theory-driven than in the 1980 version, drawing on a consensus among dynamic theories of PTSD (e.g., Freud et al., 1921; Brett & Ostroff, 1985; Lifton, 1979), cognitive theories (e.g., Horowitz, 1976). learning theories (e.g., Dollard & Miller, 1950; Foy, Carroll, & Donohue, 1987; Keane, Zimering, & Caddell, 1985; Mowrer, 1960) and biologic theories or mechanisms (e.g., Kardiner & Spiegel, 1947; Kolb, 1984; van der Kolk et al., 1984).

PTSD criteria for children were added in 1987, although it was originally thought that the 1980 criteria could apply to children. Amnesia for the traumatic event (or events) is less likely to be noted in children, whose more characteristic response is reluctance to discuss the trauma or repetitive play containing themes or aspects of the trauma (cf. Brett, Spitzer, & Williams, in press).

The question about whether PTSD was to be classified as an anxiety disorder or a dissociative disorder was debated at some length by the Task Force on PTSD for DSM-III-R. Until empirical evidence indicates to the contrary, PTSD remains classified under the anxiety disorders.

The 1987 revised PTSD criteria were presented earlier in Table 7–1. PTSD may begin at any age, including childhood. No MMPI studies have been reported for adolescents, despite the fact that child abuse may reach traumatic proportions and that PTSD is thought to be more severe and longer lasting when the trauma is of human design (e.g., Spitzer, 1986). PTSD symptoms usually begin soon after the trauma, although symptoms may develop after a latency period of several months or several years (e.g., Figley, 1978). Social support networks are noted to interact in both presence/absence and severity of PTSD following exposure to trauma (e.g., Keane, Scott, Chavoya, Lamparski, & Fairbank, 1985).

Impairment associated with PTSD ranges from mild to severe, depending on a variety of interacting pre- and posttrauma factors. Pre-existing psychopathology apparently predisposes to PTSD development, but empirical research has demonstrated that, in the case of Vietnam combat-related PTSD, combat stressors, not premilitary adjustment, account for postwar PTSD symptoms (cf. Card, 1987, for one of the few prospective, longitudinal studies completed to date). Substance Use Disorders are a common complication. Associated features of PTSD include depression and anxiety, although research has shown that clinicians can clearly differentiate PTSD from Major Mood Disorders and Generalized Anxiety Disorders (e.g., Keane, Taylor, & Penk, 1987). In PTSD, impulsive behaviors (e.g., sudden trips, unexpected absences, etc.) and dissociative reactions may occur.

No published information is available at present regarding the incidence of PTSD, although the range is commonly thought to be from 10 percent (Kulka & Schlenger, 1987) to 19 percent (Card, 1987). No information is available for prevalence, gender ratio, or familial patterns. There are no base rates, no "typical patient," no modal MMPI profile by which to define PTSD, given the possibility of a variety of demographic and moderator variables that are just beginning to be demonstrated as influencing the clinical onset of PTSD, the development of PTSD severity, and the occurrence of complications.

Presented with incomplete information about PTSD as a diagnostic category, the clinician is encouraged (1) to consider each case of PTSD on an individual basis by reference to indices of maladjustment/adjustment in general and (2) *not* to expect to find a "typical" patient. MMPI evidence presented in the following sections empirically argues against the notion of a typical patient and argues for the possibility that many different sorts of personalities are vulnerable to the development of PTSD symptomatology subsequent to the experience of a life-threatening event (Table 7–2). That is, when classifying MMPI profiles of Vietnam combat veterans meeting PTSD and Substance Use Disorder criteria, using the Gilberstadt and Duker form of codetype classification, 17 of 20 codetypes were represented, no one category accounting for more than 15 percent of the classifications. This empirically demonstrated finding argues conclusively against the notion of a prototypic PTSD MMPI profile, particularly when considering the homogeneity of this clinical group, which consisted of substance abusers seeking treatment (Penk, Robinowitz, Cannon, Fowler, Bell, & Roberts, 1983).

TABLE 7–2. FREQUENCY OF MMPI CODETYPES IN PTSD AND NON-PTSD SUBSTANCE ABUSERS

Codetype	Substance Abuse Patients PTSD (N = 248)	Non-PTSD (N = 186)
1-2/2-1	3.4%	4.3%
1-3/3-1	6.5	6.5
2-7/7-2	15.3	12.9
2-8/8-2	18.6	15.6
Spike 4	9.7	6.5
3-4/4-3	5.2	1.6
4-9/9-4	3.6	2.7
6-8/8-6	12.9	12.9
7-8/8-7	3.6	7.0
8-9/9-8	11.7	13.4
Spike 9	2.4	2.7
WNL	6.9	8.1
Other	—	5.9

PROTOTYPIC STUDY

The prototypic, and best, study conducted to date using the MMPI was commissioned by the United States Congress (Public Law 98-160) and is in the process of being carried out by the combined forces of the Center for Social Policy Studies of the Research Triangle Institute (Richard Kulka and William Schlenger, Co-Principal Investigators) and Louis Harris and Associates. This study is designed to establish the current incidence and retrospective prevalence of PTSD among Vietnam combat veterans. An MMPI study was included during the first phase of the epidemiologic survey designed to test comparative effectiveness and efficiency of several measures in diagnosing PTSD. This study—a validation pretest of instruments to be used in the larger epidemiologic survey—was distinguished by the large sample (i.e., over 240 subjects in a field thus far charaterized by small clinical sample research) and by collecting samples from several points across the nation (i.e., Boston; San Francisco; Jackson, MS; Portland).

As originally designed, equal numbers of subjects were to be collected for a 2 (PTSD/no PTSD) X 2 (Other Axis I disorder/No Other Axis I disorder) factorial design. Results are presented at the beginning of Table 7–3, a comprehensive table summarizing many of the MMPI studies of the first PTSD criterion (i.e., presence of life-threatening, traumatic events) or of the full complement of PTSD criteria (see Table 7–3, separating MMPI studies into studies of trauma vs. studies of PTSD

symptoms). As Kulka and Schlenger (1987) found, cases of "pure" PTSD were difficult to locate, where "pure" PTSD refers to subjects who meet criteria for only PTSD and no other Axis I criteria. PTSD diagnoses were based on concordance between two expert clinicians interviewing volunteer subjects/patients for diagnostic classification, using the Structured Clinical Interview for DSM-III (SCID: Spitzer & Williams, 1986) with a specially developed Vietnam combat-related PTSD section. All interviewers for this study had been trained by Spitzer and Williams to ensure uniformity in clinical interviewing and scoring.

The Kulka and Schlenger (1986) study is a prototypic investigation on the basis of having followed most of the major guidelines for conducting PTSD research. (Denny et al. [1987] recently provided a summary of these guidelines.) Kulka and Schlenger used ratings of combat experience and combat exposure with independent verification, measured for presence of traumas in addition to combat traumas, assessed presence of current stressors, controlled possibly confounding demographic and dispositional characteristics (e.g., socioeconomic status, classified for presence/absence of other Axis I disorders, assessed for possible secondary gains (i.e., compensation for symptom-reporting), controlled possible biases between PTSD symptom and combat exposure confound by independent verification of trauma experiences, and studied only Vietnam combat veterans.

Kulka and Schlenger found that the PTSD group was more seriously disturbed than the non-PTSD (no other Axis I disorder) group. The currently active PTSD group was more disturbed than the currently inactive PTSD group, the latter having reached criteria for PTSD in the past but becoming asymptomatic within a year of current testing. Those veterans meeting current PTSD criteria scored significantly higher on Scales F, K, 6 (Pa), and 7 (Pt) than those who did not currently meet PTSD criteria. Both past and present PTSD groups scored higher than the non-PTSD Axis I group on Scale 8. The PTSD group meeting criteria for another Axis I disorder was readily distinguishable from the non-PTSD group meeting criteria for another Axis I disorder, scoring higher on Scales F, 1 (Hs), 2 (D), 3 (Hy), 6 (Pa), 7 (Pt), 8 (Sc), 9 (Ma), and 0 (Si).

The results from this nationwide effort also suggest that PTSD is complicated by the co-occur-

**TABLE 7–3.   FREQUENCY OF ELEVATED MMPI CLINICAL SCALES
IN PATIENTS MEETING ONLY THE FIRST CRITERION OF PTSD**

Authors	N	Age	Clinical Scales (≥ 70 *T*-points)
World War II Veterans:			
Archibald et al. (1962)			
Combat	53	—	*2-3-1-7-8*
Noncombat	70	—	*2-7-3*
Sutker et al. (1986)			
Type I POWs	36	—	*2-1-7-8-3-6-0*
Type II POWs	19	—	*1-2-3*
Eberly et al. (1986)			
Europe POWs	285	—	*1-2*
Japan POWs	55	—	*1-2*
Korea POWs	15	—	Spike *1*
Non-POWs	113	—	*WNL*
Vietnam Veterans:			
Kulka & Schlenger (1986) [nonhospitalized][a]			
No Axis I Diagnosis	23	—	*WNL*
Past PTSD	9	—	Spike *4*
PTSD only	14	—	*2-8*
Axis I/No PTSD	14	—	*4-2*
Axis I & PTSD	57	—	*8-2-7-6-4-1-3*
Lumbry et al. (1972)			
[medical patients]			
Psychiatric	458	—	*8-7-2-4-6*
Noncombat	48	—	*WNL*
Penk et al. (1981)			
[with substance abuse disorders]			
Heavy combat	47	—	*8-4-2-7-9-1*
Light combat	38	—	*4-7-8-2*
Moya (1983)			
Combat	32	—	*8-2-4-7-1-3-9*
Penk et al. (1987)			
[with substance abuse disorders]			
Black, heavy combat	37	—	*8-4-2-7-1-6-9-3*
Black, light combat	43	—	*4-8-9*
White, heavy combat	82	—	*8-4-2-7-9-1-6*
White, light combat	89	—	*4-2-7-8*
Israeli Veterans			
Merbaum (1977)			
Hospitalized	14	—	*8-7-2-1-6-3-4*
One Year Later	14	—	*2-8-7-1-3-4-6*

[a]Samples for this study only met all DSM-III-R PTSD criteria.

rence of other Axis I disorders, only 20 percent of the cases turning out to be "pure" PTSD. The MMPI results also revealed that differences occurred primarily for those scales associated with coping by avoidance (Scales *8* [*Sc*] and *0* [*Si*]), somatization and psychophysiological reactivity (Scales *1* [*Hs*] and *3* [*Hy*], constant anxiety (Scale *7* [*Pt*]), and suspiciousness (Scale *6* [*Pa*]). The findings suggest that whereas one can readily differentiate pure PTSD from no psychological disturbance and co-occurence of PTSD with other Axis I disorders, it is more difficult to differentiate pure PTSD from other Axis I-diagnosed groups, at least when the subject population consists of all Vietnam combat veterans, since all groups have experienced life-threatening events. Such results are in keeping with a long tradition of MMPI research on traumatized groups, i.e., studies using the first criterion for PTSD—experiencing life-threatening events (Penk, Robinowitz, Roberts, Patterson, Dolan, & Atkins, 1981)—as well as with other recent studies that compared groups differing in all PTSD criteria (Keane, Wolfe, & Taylor, 1987). Results from these two lines of investigations corroborate findings by Kulka and Schlenger (1986) that findings empirically demonstrated less well by previous research have now been validated decisively in the National Vietnam Veterans Readjustment Study (NVVRS).

MMPI FINDINGS FROM STUDIES OF CLINICAL GROUPS MEETING ONLY THE FIRST CRITERION FOR PTSD (i.e., LIFE-THREATENING EVENTS)

Five studies have compared groups differing in situational exposure to life-threatening events (see Table 7–3 earlier). MMPI results confirm with less rigorously controlled studies what Kulka and Schlenger were later to establish with sophisticated experimental tactics. Archibald, Long, Miller, and Tuddenham (1962) found effects of combat were detectable 20 years after military experience in World War II combat veterans. Combat veterans were more elevated than noncombat veterans on Scales *F*, *1*, *2*, *3*, and *7*. The two groups were differentiated on 47 items; combat veterans 20 years after their war experiences were differentiated from noncombat veterans seeking treatment on the basis of items reflecting generalized anxiety and tension, complaints of disturbed sleep, nightmares, irritability, tension, forgetfulness, and reduced efficiency. Thus, Archibald et al. demonstrated that the MMPI can detect PTSD-like group differences many years after traumas have occurred.

Lumry, Cedarleaf, Wright, and Braatz (1972) reported an opposite finding: Vietnam combat veterans who were tested as medical patients obtained significantly lower MMPI profiles than psychiatric patients (see Table 7–3). This inconsistency would appear to arise more from the psychiatric/medical status of the patients in the Lumry et al. (1972) group comparison, rather than to dispute long-term effects of combat. As subsequent findings were to show (see Butler, Foy, Snodgrass, Hurwicz, & Goldfarb, 1986), Vietnam combat veterans who are medical patients usually obtain significantly lower profiles than Vietnam combat veterans with co-occurring psychiatric diagnoses (see Kulka & Schlenger, 1986, where PTSD with other psychiatric diagnoses and psychiatric groups in general have been found to obtain generally more elevated MMPI profiles than are found among medical patients).

Merbaum (1977) has published the only repeated-measures study to date. Israeli soldiers who were

psychologically incapacitated on the battlefield during the Yom Kippur war had elevated MMPI profiles both at the time of treatment during combat as well as 1 year later in civilian life. Such findings confirm prolonged effects of combat. Penk, Robinowitz, Roberts, Patterson, Dolan, and Atkins (1981), in a study controlling for many possible sources of demographic and motivational variables, clearly established MMPI differences as a function of the degrees of combat experience among substance users seeking treatment. Those Vietnam combat veterans who had heavy combat exposure demonstrated significantly higher autonomic reactivity (e.g., significantly higher Scale *1* scores) than did those veterans with light or infrequent combat exposure.

Moya (1983) reported pronounced elevations of MMPI group profiles of Vietnam combat veterans seen as part of the Vietnam Veterans Outreach program. Virtually no overlap occurred when Vietnam combat veterans seeking treatment in outpatient settings were compared with same-age cohorts who had never been in the military. Moya's study demonstrated that MMPI profile differences are readily shown when comparison groups consist of nontreatment-seeking samples. Such highly significant differences for patient-nonpatient comparisons further highlight the persisting, prolonged effects of exposure to life-threatening experiences for those studies comparing groups of patients differing only in the amount of combat (Table 7–3).

Sutker, Winstead, Goist, Malow, and Allain (1986) provide evidence against the notion that elevated MMPI group profiles support a homogeneous conceptualization of stress-induces disorders and PTSD. Additional arguments against homogeneity are directly implied by differences in profile elevations among psychiatric groups (cf. Kulka & Schlenger, 1986; Penk et al., 1981) where the former obtain much higher profiles (see Lumry et al., 1972). Sutker et al. (1986), in analyzing profiles of World War II former POWs who were tested routinely 40 years after their incarceration, obtained two MMPI profile types—both of which were elevated well above normal limits but the second of which indicated greater behavioral control. Differences in psychopathology were found to be directly related to trauma severity while incarcerated as a POW. Such results underscore the importance of quantifying degree of life-threatening circumstances as well as determining those dispositional and situational factors that produce "types" in stress-induced disorders.

Finally, Penk et al. (1987) provided evidence that ethnic and socioeconomic status interact in producing differences in MMPI profiles long after combat experiences. Among substance abusers seeking treatment, combat effects were found to be much stronger (as evidenced by significantly heavier exposure to combat than among black Vietnam combat veterans with light combat exposure). By comparison, white Vietnam combat veterans were more strongly affected by light combat experience than were black veterans, whereas black veterans were more strongly affected by heavy combat exposure than were white veterans. These ethnic differences were attributed to deleterious interactions of premilitary stress, speculated as greater among blacks who may have been exposed more to stressful experiences as a function of their minority group status. Although comparatively minor exposure to combat may have confirmed the views of blacks that life is treacherous and threatening, heavy combat was more overwhelming for blacks than for whites. These findings were linked directly to the frequent observation that better adjusted blacks are found more frequently among Substance Use Disorder groups than other kinds of psychiatric diagnostic groups (see Dahlstrom, Lachar, & Dahlstrom, 1986).

These MMPI results from help-seeking samples meeting the first criterion of PTSD confirm the notion that exposure to trauma is associated with elevated MMPI profiles, particularly on scales measuring avoidance, autonomic reactivity, and anxiety. These findings also generalize across generations from World War II to Vietnam combat veterans. In fact, Lumry et al. (1972) reported that Vietnam combat veterans were just as disturbed as their World War II and Korean counterparts. Moreover, MMPI profiles continue to be elevated long after exposure to combat has occurred (cf. Merbaum, 1977). Finally, differences in MMPI profile shape and elevation are indicated as a function of differences in psychiatric/medical classification of subjects, as well as differences in ethnic characteristics. The latter variable may be considered as a surrogate variable, involving differences in degrees of exposure to life-threatening experience and stress-related occurrences before, during, and after military service. Results of these preliminary attempts to assess effects of life-threatening trauma on MMPI profiles are a less compelling corroboration of subsequent research using more complete and comprehensive measures of PTSD diagnostic criteria.

MMPI FINDINGS FROM STUDIES OF CLINICAL GROUPS MEETING ALL DSM-III PTSD CRITERIA

Eight studies, in addition to Kulka and Schlenger's (1986) prototypic study, have assessed the full complement of PTSD criteria with the MMPI. Roberts et al. (1982), controlling for many possible dispositional and situational variables such as disability, socioeconomic status, age, and ethnicity, obtained striking profile differences between substance abusers with combat experience than substance abusers without combat experience (see Table 7–4). Combat veterans showed greater social alienation (Scale 8), more social introversion (Scale 0), greater naiveté about psychological symptoms (L), and higher emotional arousal (Scale 9). Not only did the PTSD veterans obtain significantly higher scale elevations, but they elevated scales that could be interpreted as indicative of at least two major PTSD criteria, i.e., generalized avoidance and generalized emotional reactivity. These findings were interpreted as demonstrating that PTSD may be expressed uniquely by type of co-occurring psychopathology. In cases where Substance Use Disorder and PTSD criteria are found together, it is possible that substance abuse represents an attempt to cope with disturbing traumatic memories (i.e., substance abuse may be a maladaptive form of coping designed to change autonomic arousal, maintain emotional numbing and social withdrawal, and reduce cues for traumatic memories).

Fairbank, Keane, and Malloy (1983) found their PTSD group significantly differed from psychiatric counterparts and a normal control group (see Table 7–4). They interpreted these differences primarily in terms of elevation rather than in pattern: both psychiatric groups obtained 2-8/8-2 profiles associated with anxiety, depression, agitation, sleep disturbance, somatic symptoms, fear of loss of control, guilt, and avoidance of close interpersonal contact.

These findings from a pilot study were then elaborated and cross-validated in a much larger effort involving both inpatient and outpatient psychiatric patients (Keane et al., 1984). Keane et al. (1984) also developed an MMPI PTSD scale.

TABLE 7–4. FREQUENCY OF ELEVATED MMPI CLINICAL SCALES IN PATIENTS MEETING ALL DSM-III PTSD CRITERIA

Males

Authors	N	Age	Clinical scales (≥ 70 T-points)	A	B	C	D	E	F	G	H	I
Vietnam Veterans:												
Burke & Meyer (1985)												
PTSD inpatient psychiatric	30	—	8-2-7-9-4-6-1-3	+	-	-	-	-	-	-	+	-
PTSD outpatient psychiatric	30	—	3	+	-	-	-	-	-	-	+	-
Butler et al. (1986)												
PTSD medical patients	16	—	2-8-7-1	+	+	-	+	+	-	+	+	-
Non-PTSD medical patients	18	—	WNL	+	+	-	+	+	-	+	+	-
Fairbanks et al. (1983)												
PTSD	12	—	8-2-1-7-4-3-6									
Psychiatric	12	—	2-8-4									
Normals	12	—	WNL									
Foy et al. (1984)												
PTSD	17	—	8-2-7-4-6-1-3	+	+	-	-	+	+	+	+	-
No PTSD	19	—	8-4-2	+	+	-	-	+	+	+	+	-
Hyer et al. (1987)												
PTSD	26	—	8-2-7-1-6-3-4	+	+	-	+	+	-	-	+	-
Combat/No PTSD	24	—	2-4-9-8	+	+	-	+	+	-	-	+	-
Noncombat	25	—	2-4-7-8-1	+	+	-	+	+	-	-	+	-
Keane et al. (1984)												
PTSD Psychiatric	100	—	6-2-8-1-7-3-4	+	+	-	-	+	+	+	+	-
Psychiatric	100	—	8-2-7-4-6-1-3	+	+	-	-	+	+	+	+	-
Query et al. (1986)												
PTSD POWs	17	—	2-1-8-7	+	+	-	+	+	-	-	+	-
Non-PTSD POWs	51	—	Spike 1	+	+	-	+	+	-	-	+	-
Roberts et al. (1981)												
[with Substance Abuse Disorder]												
PTSD	90	—	8-2-4-7-6-9-1-3	+	+	+	+	+	+	+	+	-
No PTSD	91	—	4-9	+	+	+	+	+	+	+	+	-

Item content and cross-validation of this scale are discussed below. Again, psychiatric patients with co-occurring PTSD scored significantly higher on the MMPI, a finding that was to be later substantiated by Kulka and Schlenger (1986). Keane et al. (1984) concluded that most of the differences between PTSD and other psychiatric illnesses could be contained in a decision rule for identifying PTSD based on Scale F higher than a T-score of 66, Scale 2 (D) higher than a T-score of 78, and Scale 8 (Sc) higher than a T-score of 79. This study demonstrated that patients with PTSD not only can be differentiated from other psychiatric patients but that the direction of difference is toward more avoidance ways of coping with problems. Finding such types of MMPI differences when comparing two very similar groups, except that one set of Vietnam combat veterans met PTSD as well as other Axis I disorders whereas the other set did not meet PTSD criteria but were classifiable for some other Axis I criteria, corroborate the views that: (1) the contributions of PTSD are a heightening of any pre-existing behavioral maladjustments (e.g., those who cope by avoidance, under stress cope by even greater avoidance of reminders about past traumas after enduring and surviving life-threatening events), and (2) there are unique symptom manifestations associated with PTSD but the direction of intensification is more likely to occur in those areas of special personal vulnerabilities. For example, if the same trauma occurred in two different people—one whose personal problems center on a need to validate consistently a sense of independence and the other whose primary concerns are to maintain emotional support from others—then, the effects of trauma are likely to be manifested differentially as a function of these two fundamental types of personality organization. In the first case, PTSD symptoms are likely to manifest through acting out and/or defiance of authority, and in the second case, PTSD is likely to appear through excessive clingingness and dependence in interpersonal interactions. The direction of MMPI differences in the Keane et al. (1986) study, when compared with the direction of MMPI differences in the Roberts et al. (1982) study, substantiates not only the lingering effects of trauma but also differential manifestations of PTSD as a function of differences in the personal adjustment among types of persons who are traumatized.

Foy, Sipprelle, Rueger, and Carroll (1984) reported MMPI findings among Vietnam combat veterans seeking treatment for psychiatric problems in California similar to those obtained by Keane et al. (1984) in Mississippi. Psychiatric patients with PTSD were distinguished from their non-PTSD counterparts by significantly higher scores on Scales 2 (D), 6 (Pa), 7 (Pt), and 8 (Sc). In addition, Foy et al. (1984) ruled out a relationship between premilitary adjustment variables and PTSD symptoms, but did posit that combat exposure differences accounted for PTSD symptoms.

Foy et al. (1984) interpreted their findings as demonstrating that the PTSD diagnosis was associated specifically with problems indicative of anxiety-based disorders, particularly generalized anxiety. Parenthetically, it is essential to note that both Keane et al. (1986) and Foy et al. (1984) limited their definition of "psychiatric patients" by excluding patients who met criteria for schizophrenia, psychoses, organic brain impairment, and substance use (see Table 7–4).

Only Burke and Mayer (1985) failed to find significantly elevated profiles for PTSD veterans when compared with psychiatric patients (see Table 7–4). This discrepancy is notable and requires explanation. First, it should be noted that both the PTSD and the psychiatric patient sample compared by Burke and Mayer (1985) obtained significantly elevated profiles (e.g., the PTSD group profile was elevated for 7 of 10 MMPI clinical scales). Next, it should be understood that Burke and Mayer compared an outpatient group of PTSD subjects with an "inpatient" group of psychiatric patients. Inpatient samples generally average higher on MMPI profiles than do outpatient samples, and this difference in hospitalization status may have affected profile elevation as well as the direction of differences, i.e., the inpatient psychiatric group scores significantly higher on Scales 6 (Pa) and F. If it can be demonstrated in future studies that profile elevations will indeed vary among PTSD groups as a function of differences in hospitalization status, with PTSD outpatients tending to evidence comparatively lower (but not necessarily unelevated) MMPI profiles, hospital status must be considered in profile interpretation.

Evidence that MMPI profile elevation will vary as a function of institutional status (and psycho-

pathologic functioning as well) is provided by Butler et al. (1986). Conducted among medical patients, the study by Butler et al. (1986) found PTSD Vietnam combat veterans yielded more elevated MMPI profiles than did their non-PTSD counterparts (see Table 7–4). However, severity of PTSD symptomatology was notably less than that observed by Foy et al. (1984) among psychiatric patients. Butler et al. (1986) concluded that a 2-8-7 codetype was more descriptive of their PTSD group of medical patients than the 8-2-7-6 profile found among psychiatric patients. The notable difference between the PTSD group profile among medical patients, when compared with psychiatric patients, also can be appreciated by noting that only 4 of 10 MMPI clinical scales averaged above a T-score of 70 for medical patients whereas 8 of 10 were elevated for psychiatric patients. This study confirmed expectations from earlier research that MMPI profile elevation and scatter for PTSD-positive Vietnam combat veterans is influenced by co-occurring psychopathologies and by institutional status.

Further corroborating the observation that MMPI profiles of PTSD groups are more elevated among psychiatric patients than among medical patients is the study recently published by Hyer, O'Leary, Saucer, Blount, Harrison, and Boudewyns (1986). Their study was conducted with groups of psychiatric inpatients, one group of Vietnam combat veterans meeting criteria for PTSD, a second group who did not meet PTSD criteria, and a third group of psychiatric inpatients who were not combat veterans and who presumably did not meet criteria for PTSD (see Table 7–4). Results for these samples, which were drawn in Georgia, were comparable with the findings obtained by Keane et al. (1984) in Mississippi and Foy et al. (1984) in California. Namely, the PTSD group scored significantly higher than both the non-PTSD combat and the noncombat-non-PTSD groups on Scales F, 1, 2, 3, 6, 7, and 8. The Hyer et al. study (1986) was conducted with a rich array of measures other than the MMPI (such as the Profile of Mood States, Rotter Locus of Control, etc.) and analyses were performed with multivariate statistics. Scales 2 (D) and 7 (Pt) were found to figure prominently in the best set of variables discriminating among the three groups. The PTSD group was differentiated with 92 percent accuracy, the combat group with 71 percent accuracy, and the noncombat group with 91 percent accuracy. Such findings underscore that the two variables, "PTSD" and "combat-experience" are similar but not equivalent, that effects of combat linger long after survival of life-threatening circumstances, and that both variables decidedly differentiate, among psychiatric patients, those patients with a history of trauma.

Such results generalize to World War II former POWs who were assessed routinely 40 years after their incarceration (Query, Megran, & McDonald, 1986). Whereas mean MMPI profiles were lower for World War II combat veterans than for Vietnam combat veterans, these differences in elevation were more likely to be attributable to the non-hospitalized status of the subjects rather than differences in combat experience or generational differences. That is, whereas subjects for the preceding seven studies were assessed within the first few weeks of seeking treatment for emotional difficulties, subjects in the Query et al. (1986) study were assessed as part of a nationwide survey of living former World War II POWs. Results evidence the familiar pattern of elevated profiles among those former POWs who met independently verified criteria for PTSD. The PTSD group scored significantly higher on scales *F*, *2*, *6*, *7*, *8*, and *0*. The non-PTSD former POW group obtained elevations only on Scales *1* and *2*. These findings confirm the importance of assessing for PTSD criteria among groups with a history of trauma but leave as yet unanswered the key question of why some trauma victims are symptomatic for PTSD but others are not.

MMPI PTSD SCALES

Research on PTSD scale development based on the MMPI is just beginning, despite the fact that a need for such tools has long existed and that the value of such scales has been demonstrated by earlier research using the MMPI (Archibald et al., 1962). Two scales are under development, one by Penk and his associates for studies of combat trauma among substance abusers seeking treatment (Penk et al.,1983) and the other by Keane and his associates for identifying PTSD among Vietnam combat veterans with PTSD (Keane et al., 1984). Both scales have been cross-validated by other investigators (e.g., Watson, Kucala, & Manifold, 1985). Keane's scale has achieved a greater range of applicability and utility. Denny et al. (1987) have provided a review of the PTSD scale literature.

The two scales were developed in quite different ways. Penk worked solely with substance abusers, focused only on combat and not PTSD, and used the entire 566-item pool of the MMPI, whereas Keane worked with psychiatric patients, carefully diagnosed presence of PTSD, and used the first 400 items of Form R. Nevertheless, the two scales have been found to correlate .65 (Watson et al., 1985), despite the fact that there is virtually no item overlap for the two scales. Keane's scale coincides more with current PTSD criteria, whereas factor studies of Penk's scale show a narrow concentration on avoidance maneuvers and autonomic reactivity (Penk et al., 1983). The preferred scale for clinical use at present, then, is the Keane scale.

Hit rates in cross-validating the Keane scale have ranged from 38 percent (Gayton, Burchstead, & Matthews, 1986) to 80 percent (Kulka & Schlenger, 1986). Overall, hit rates have averaged in the 70–75 percent range across seven studies that were conducted for purposes of independent cross-validation, which is considered to be a highly favorable rate of concordance across quite different subjects. Keane's PTSD scale for the MMPI has been shown to be effective in identifying PTSD across a variety of clinical settings (Watson et al., 1985; Vanderploeg, Sison, & Hickling, 1986; Hyer, Boudewyns, O'Leary, & Harrison, 1986; Cannon, Bell, Andrews, & Finkelstein, 1987; Blanchard, Wittrock, Kolb, & Gerardi, 1987). But perhaps the most compelling evidence is to be found in work reported by Kulka and Schlenger (1986), who actually compared the relative efficiency for a variety of scales: Keane's Mississippi Combat-Related PTSD scales (Keane, Caddell, & Taylor, 1988); the DIS PTSD scale (Robins, et al., & Helzer 1981); and the Impact of Event scale (Horowitz, 1976). The PTSD MMPI scale performed as well as these other scales, achieving a hit rate of 81.5 percent with a kappa of .605, a sensitivity of 90.1, and a specificity of 68.8 percent. These results are within the range of diagnostic accuracy found for instruments that have been designed to diagnose PTSD specifically (such as the Mississippi Combat-Related PTSD scales, for which sensitivity was 88.9 percent).

A clinically useful PTSD scale has been devised by Keane for work with Vietnam combat veterans. However, PTSD scales are not available for identification of persons evidencing PTSD symptoms for noncombat forms of trauma. Moreover, the predictive efficiency of Keane's scales is limited, as cross-validation attempts have shown (Denny et al., 1987). It is highly likely that the next generation of PTSD scales can only be improved in diagnostic sensitivity and specificity when levels of personality maturation are taken into account. It appears that a general PTSD scale or linear combination of clinical scales that would apply for all clinical groups will not be found. A re-examination of profile elevation in the Kulka and Schlenger (1986) study, or a perusal of group MMPI profiles in the studies by Roberts et al. (1982), Keane et al. (1984), and Butler et al. (1986), forces the obvious realization that PTSD is a disorder that can occur among a variety of different people at various levels of pretrauma adjustment. To expect that one scale can account for such a variety of people is to demand too much of any one instrument. The more likely solution in future PTSD scale development is the emergence of a family of PTSD scales, selected for application as a function of presence/absence of co-occurring disorders as well as by type of co-occurring disorder. Evidence in support of continuing this approach in PTSD scale development has been found by Penk and his associates (Penk et al., 1983) who, in studies of substance abusers, found quite different PTSD scales as a function of whether co-occurring schizophrenia was or was not classified with PTSD. Moreover, evidence that MMPI scale elevation in PTSD-non-PTSD comparisons is affected by such characteristics as ethnicity, hospitalization status, and extent of co-occurring psychopathology also presages several different kinds of PTSD indicators from the MMPI, rather than just one.

SUMMARY

A number of different directions for MMPI research on PTSD have already been suggested during the course of this review, such as the need to determine who is susceptible to PTSD following trauma; the need to settle issues of co-morbidity (e.g., how to distinguish between pre-existing symptoms and/or resultant signs of maladjustment from PTSD indicators); the need to establish incidence and prevalence, values that are likely to vary appreciably as a function of types of trauma, interacting social support, pretrauma abilities to cope effectively with stress; and the need to be consistent in diagnostic and treatment measures.

Two areas in this wide array of unfinished tasks emerge as topics of critical importance for the newly emerging subject of diagnostic PTSD research. One concerns PTSD treatment research using the MMPI and the other involves fabricated symptoms and malingering.

As yet, no study has been published on PTSD that can be classified as a controlled outcome study (cf. Fairbank & Nicholson [1987] for a comprehensive, updated review of the PTSD treatment literature). In fact, as the current review of PTSD research using the MMPI has shown, only one study has been published in which more than one administration of the MMPI occurred (Merbaum, 1977). This deficiency is notable for many reasons: e.g., we know nothing about the stability of PTSD symptomatology as measured by the MMPI in terms of either clinical/special scales or items; change norms for the MMPI have not been developed; and PTSD has not been validated by one key form of diagnostic validation, i.e., verifying veracity of a clinical entity by assessing treatment outcome responsivity. As quickly as possible, clinicians need to expand their research interests about PTSD to encompass PTSD treatment outcome studies as well; the MMPI, by virtue of its multiphasic personality assessment, is well suited for such endeavors.

In undertaking such an expansion of research into treatment outcome studies, clinical researchers must note that greater uniformity should be introduced when implementing an MMPI study. Not only would it be advisable to include other kinds of outcome measures (i.e., going beyond self-report symptomatology and assessing sensory, motor, neuroendocrine, cognitive, characterologic, and identity disturbances: see Brende & McCann, 1984), but investigators also should conform more to conventions already established in conducting MMPI research.

Most PTSD studies to date have not included adequate identifying demographic information, controlled for other Axis I (or Axis II) disorders, been concerned about MMPI profile validity, controlled for the potential effects of moderator variables, and amassed sample sizes large enough to warrant the kinds of multivariate analyses of covariance and multiple regression analyses that are needed for research on PTSD.

Future research must introduce greater uniformity in research tactics so that potentially confounding variables are controlled adequately and so that clinicians can compare findings across studies. PTSD research in general, as well as PTSD research with the MMPI, requires that clinical researchers pool their efforts in the form of cooperative studies so that uniformity in research methods are achieved. The fact that this current review is unable to note that any of the MMPI studies on PTSD dealt with MMPI profile validity issues is a sign that (1) the research is quite immature in its overall development, and (2) MMPI standards must be introduced immediately.

The second area of needed research concerns possible fabrication of PTSD symptoms. This issue is important because of possible secondary gains associated with PTSD. Any symptom has the potential for being positively rewarded in some way. PTSD is one of those disorders for which it is possible that a patient may try to make use of the condition as a way of obtaining financial or some other form of compensation. Patients who have been traumatized strongly feel, in some cases, that the responsible agent or agency should somehow pay for the outrage and horror that the patient has experienced. Particularly as our understanding of PTSD expands from the aftermath of adjustment for the Vietnam combat veteran to survivors of other nonwar forms of trauma, the likelihood that secondary gains will grow in importance is increasing.

As part of these cautions about the use of the MMPI in clinical studies of PTSD, the subject of fabricated symptoms is a vital one. The one study conducted to date on malingering (Fairbank et al., 1985) has demonstrated that those military personnel instructed to fabricate PTSD symptoms could still be readily distinguished from Vietnam combat veterans diagnosed as meeting PTSD criteria. However, Fallon, Harrison, and Boudewyns (1987) have classified a major segment of psychiatric patients seeking treatment, using methods developed by Greene (1980), as "overreporters" among their large sample of Vietnam combat veterans. However, Hyer, Keane, Caddell, and Taylor (1988) were not able to clarify whether secondary gain maneuvers accounted for such a large degree of overreporting, but their study documents a higher-than-average probability of obtaining invalid MMPI profiles among Vietnam combat veterans seeking treatment in VA medical centers.

Few of the methods developed for identifying PTSD have addressed this important issue about fabricating symptoms. The role of malingering is simply unexamined for such instruments as the Mississippi combat-related PTSD scale (Keane et al., 1988); the Impact of Events scale (Horowitz, 1976); the Diagnostic Interview Schedule (Robins & Helzer, 1982). Only in the case of the MMPI has an effort been made to assess effects of possible malingering and fabrication for secondary-gain purposes and the results of this one, pioneering study (Fairbank et al., 1985) has shown that appropriate use of the MMPI can attenuate effects of fabrication, at least among Vietnam combat veterans and Vietnam-Era military veterans.

The MMPI, alone among all PTSD assessment instruments developed to date, is the only psychometrically grounded test that contains methods for determining reliability and validity in symptom reporting. As a consequence, the MMPI maintains its premier position as the most favored instrument for use in both clinical evaluation of patients assesed for meeting PTSD criteria and in research studies designed to study PTSD. Whereas research about PTSD must be accom-

panied by many cautions, the one area that clinicians and researchers need not be cautious about is in the clinical utility of the MMPI for PTSD studies, providing, of course, clinicians and researchers make use of the many ways in which symptom reporting can be validated (see Greene, 1980).

REFERENCES

American Psychiatric Association. (1952). *Diagnostic and statistical manual of mental disorders* (1st ed.). Washington, D.C.: Author.

American Psychiatric Association. (1980). *Diagnostic and statistical manual of mental disorders* (3rd ed.). Washington, D.C.: Author.

American Psychiatric Association. (1987). *Diagnostic and statistical manual of mental disorders* (3rd ed., rev.). Washington, D.C.: Author.

Archibald, H.C., Long, D.M., Miller, C., & Tuddenham, R.D. (1962). Gross stress reaction in combat—A 15-year followup. *American Journal of Psychiatry, 119,* 317-322.

Blanchard, E.B., Wittrock, D., Kolb, L.C., & Gerardi, R.J. (1988). Cross-validation of an MMPI subscale for the assessment of combat-related Post-traumatic Stress Disorder. *Journal of Psychopathology and Behavioral Assessment, 1.*

Brende, J.O, & McCann, I.L. (1984). Regressive experiences in Vietnam veterans: Their relationship to war posttraumatic symptoms, and recovery. *Journal of Contemporary Psychotherapy, 14,* 57-75.

Brett, E. & Ostroff, R. (1985). Imagery and posttraumatic stress disorder: An overview. *American Journal of Psychiatry, 142,* 417-424.

Brett, E., Spitzer, R., & Williams, J. (in press). DSM-III-Revised criteria for Post-traumatic Stress Disorders. *American Journal of Psychiatry.*

Burke, H.R., & Mayer, S. (1985). The MMPI and Post-traumatic Stress syndrome in Vietnam era veterans. *Journal of Clinical Psychology, 41,* 152-156.

Butler, R.W., Foy, D.W., Snodgrass, L., Hurwicz, M.L., & Goldfarb, J. (1986). *Combat-related Post-traumatic stress disorder in nonpsychiatric Vietnam-era patients: Etiological, descriptive, and MMPI findings.* Paper presented at the 94th annual meeting of the American Psychological Association. Washington, D.C.

Card, J.J. (1987). Epidemiology of PTSD in a national cohort of Vietnam veterans. *Journal of Clinical Psychology, 43,* 6-17

Cannon, D.S., Bell, W.E., Andrews, R.H., & Finkelstein, A.S. (1987). Correspondence between MMPI PTSD measures and clinical diagnosis.*Journal of Personality Assessment, 51,* 517-521.

Dahlstrom, W.G., Lachar, D., & Dahlstrom, L.E. (1986). *MMPI patterns of American minorities.* Minneapolis: University of Minnesota Press.

Dahlstrom, W.G., & Butcher, J.N. (1987). The MMPI-AX (Adult Experimental Form). Minneapolis: University of Minnesota Press.

Denny, N., Robinowitz, R., & Penk, W.E. (1987). Conducting applied research on Vietnam combat-related Post-traumatic Stress Disorder. *Journal of Clinical Psychology, 43,* 56-66.

Dollard, J., & Miller, N.E. (1950). *Personality and psychotherapy.* New York: McGraw-Hill.

Eberly, R., Engdahl, B., Rinehart, S.J., & Braatz, G. (1986). *Psychological adjustment and health among former prisoners of war.* Paper presented at the 94th annual convention of the American Psychological Association, Washington, D.C.

Fairbank, J.A., Keane, T.M. & Malloy, P.F. (1983). Some preliminary data on the psychological characteristics of Vietnam veterans with PTSD. *Journal of Consulting and Clinical Psychology, 51*, 912-919.

Fairbanks, J.A., McCaffrey, R., & Keane, T.M. (1985). Psychometric detection of fabricated symptoms of PTSD. *American Journal of Psychiatry, 142*, 501-503.

Fairbank, J.A., & Nicholson, R.A. (1987). Theoretical and empirical issues in the treatment of Posttraumatic stress disorder in Vietnam veterans.*Journal of Clinical Psychology, 43*, 44-55.

Figley, C.R. (1978). *Stress disorders among Vietnam veterans.* New York: Brunner-Mazel.

Figley, C.R. (1985). *Trauma and its wake* (Vol. 1). New York: Brunner-Mazel.

Figley, C.R. (1986). *Trauma and its wake* (Vol. 2). New York: Brunner-Mazel.

Foy, D.W., Sipprelle, R.C., Rueger, D.B., & Carroll, E.M. (1984). Etiology of PTSD in Vietnam veterans: Analysis of premilitary, military, and combat exposure influences. *Journal of Consulting and Clinical Psychology, 52*, 79-87.

Foy, D.W., Carroll, E.M., & Donahoe, C.P. (1987). Etiological factors in the development of PTSD in clinical samples of Vietnam combat veterans. *Journal of Clinical Psychology, 43*, 17-27.

Freud, S., Ferenczi, S., Abraham, K., Simmel, E., & Jones, E. (1921). *Psychoanalysis and the war neurosis.* New York: International Psychoanalytic Press.

Gayton, W.F., Burchstead, G.N., & Matthews, G.R. (1986). An investigation of the utility of an MMPI Posttraumatic Stress Disorder subscale. *Journal of Clinical Psychology, 42*, 916-917.

Green, B.L., Grace, M.C., & Gleser, G.C. (1985). Identifying survivors at risk: Long-term impairment following the Beverly Hills Supper Club fire. *Journal of Consulting and Clinical Psychology, 57*, 672-678.

Greene, R. (1980). *The MMPI: An interpretive manual.* Philadelphia: Grune & Stratton.

Hathaway, S.R., & McKinley, J.C. (1951). *MMPI Manual for administration and scoring.* New York: Psychological Corporation.

Hathaway, S.R., & Meehl, P.E. (1951). *An atlas for the clinical use of the MMPI.* Minneapolis: University of Minnesota Press.

Horowitz, M.J. (1976). *Stress response syndromes.* New York: Aronson.

Hyer, L., Fallon, J.H., Harrison, W.R., & Boudewyns, P.A. (1987). MMPI overreporting by Vietnam combat veterans. *Journal of Clinical Psychology, 43*, 79-83.

Hyer, L., O'Leary, W.C., Saucer, R.T., Blount, J., Harrison, W.R., & Boudewyns, P.A. (1986). Inpatient diagnosis of posttraumatic stress disorder. *Journal of Consulting and Clinical Psychology, 54*, 698-702.

Hyer, L., Boudewyns, P.A., O'Leary, W.C., & Harrison, W.R. (1987). *Key determinants of the MMPI-PTSD subscale: Treatment considerations.* (Psychology Service, 116B, VA Medical Center, 2460 Wrightsboro Road, Augusta, Georgia 30910.)

Kardiner, A., & Spiegel, H. (1947). *War stress and neurotic illness.* New York: Hoeber.

Keane, T.M., Caddell, J.M., & Taylor, K. (1988). Mississippi scale for combat-related PTSD: Three studies in reliability and validity. *Journal of Consulting and Clinical Psychology, 56*, 85-90.

Keane, T.M., Malloy, P.F., & Fairbank, J.A. (1984). Empirical development of an MMPI subscale for the assessment of combat-related PTSD. *Journal of Consulting and Clinical Psychology, 52*, 888-891.

Keane, T.M., Scott, W.O., Chavoya, G.A., Lamparski, D.M., & Fairbank, J.A. (1985). Social support in Vietnam veterans with Posttraumatic Stress Disorder: A comparative analysis. *Journal of Consulting and Clinical Psychology, 53*, 95-102.

Keane, T.M., Taylor, K.L., & Penk, W.E. (1987). *Differentiating Post-traumatic Stress Disorder (PTSD) from Major Depression and Generalized Anxiety (GAD).* Manuscript submitted for publication. (Available from Psychology Service, 116-B, V.A. Medical Center, 150 South Huntington Avenue, Boston, Massachusetts 02130.)

Keane, T.M., Wolfe, J., & Taylor, K.L. (1987). PTSD Evidence for diagnostic validity and methods of psychological assessment. *Journal of Clinical Psychology, 43*, 32-43.

Keane, T.M., Zimering, R.T., & Caddell, J.M. (1985). A behavioral formulation of PTSD in Vietnam veterans. *Behavior Therapist, 8*, 9-12.

Kolb, L.C. (1984). The Post-traumatic Stress Disorders of combat: A subgroup with a conditioned emotional response. *Military Medicine, 149*, 237-253.

Kulka, R., & Schlenger, W. (1986). *The national needs assessment study of Vietnam veterans.* (Available from Research Triangle Institute, Division of Social Policy Research, Box 12194, Research Triangle Park, North Carolina 22709.)

Kulka, R., & Schlenger, W. (1987). *Performance on the Fairbank-Keane MMPI Scale and other self-report measures in identifying Post-traumatic Stress Disorder.* Paper presented at the 95th annual meeting of the American Psychological Association, New York City.

Lifton, R. (1979). *The broken connection.* New York: Simon & Schuster.

Lumry, G.K., Cedarleaf, C.B., Wright, M.S., & Braatz, G.A. (1972). Psychiatric disabilities of the Vietnam veteran: Review and implications for treatment. *Minnesota Medicine, 55, 1055-1057.*

Lyons, J.A. (in press). Post-traumatic stress disorder in children and adolescents: A review of the literature. *Journal of Developmental and Behavioral Pediatrics.*

Merbaum, M. (1977). Some personality characteristics of soldiers exposed to extreme war stress: A follow-up study of Post-hospital adjustment. *Journal of Clinical Psychology, 33*, 558-562.

Mowrer, O.H. (1960). *Learning theory and behavior.* New York: John Wiley and Sons.

Moya, E. (1983). *Personality assessment of Vietnam veterans and a cohort nonveteran group.* Paper presented at the 91st annual meeting of the American Psychological Association, New York.

Penk, W.E., Robinowitz, R., Roberts, W.R., Patterson, E.T., Dolan, M.P., & Atkins, H.G. (1981). Adjustment differences among male substance abusers varying in degree of combat experience in Vietnam. *Journal of Consulting and Clinical Psychology, 49*, 426-437.

Penk, W.E., Robinowitz, R., Cannon, D., Fowler, D.R., Bell, W.E., & Roberts, W.R. (1983). *Psychological assessment of combat-related Post-traumatic Stress Disorders among substance abusers entering treatment.* Paper presented at the VA Research Meeting on PTSD for Chiefs of Psychiatry and Psychology, Philadelphia and San Francisco.

Penk, W.E., Peck, R.F., Robinowitz, R., Bell, W., & Little, D.K. (1987). Coping and defending styles among Vietnam combat veterans seeking treatment for Post-traumatic Stress Disorder (PTSD) and Substance Use Disorder. In M. Galanter & E. Gotheil (Eds.), *Recent developments in alcoholism*, Vol. 6. New York: Plenum.

Penk, W.E., Bell, W., Robinowitz, R., Dolan, M., Black, J., Dorsett, D., & Noriega, L. (1988). Ethnic differences in personality adjustment of black and white male Vietnam combat veterans seeking treatment for substance abuse. In T. Miller (Ed.), *Primer on diagnosing and treating Vietnam combat-related Post-traumatic stress disorders* (pp. 475-500). New York: International Universities Press.

Query, W.T., Megran, J., & McDonald, G. (1986). Applying PTSD MMPI subscale to World War II POW veterans. *Journal of Clinical Psychology, 42*, 315-317.

Roberts, W.R., Penk, W.E., Gearing, M.L., Robinowitz, R., Dolan, M.P., & Patterson, E.T. (1982). Interpersonal problems of Vietnam combat veterans with symptoms of Posttraumatic Stress Disorder. *Journal of Abnormal Psychology, 91*, 444-450.

Robins, L.N., Helzer, J.E. Croughan, J.L., Williams, J.B.W., & Spitzer, R.L. (1981). *NIMH diagnostic interview schedule*, Version III. Rockville, MD: NIMH, Public Health Service (Publication no. ADM-T-4-3[5-81, 8-81]).

Rounsaville, B.J., Weissman, M.M., Wilbur, C.H., & Kleber, H.D. (1982). Pathways to opiate addiction: An evaluation of different antecedents. *British Journal of Psychiatry, 141*, 437-446.

Schnaier, J.A. (1986). A study of women Vietnam veterans and their mental health adjustment. In C.R. Figley (Ed.), *Trauma and its wake* (Vol. 2) (pp. 97-117). New York: Brunner-Mazel.

Schwartz, G. (1982). Testing the biopsychosocial model: The ultimate challenge facing behavioral medicine? *Journal of Consulting and Clinical Psychology, 50*, 1040-1053.

Spitzer, R.L., (1986, December). *DSM-III-R in development, third draft: Work group to revise DSM-III*. Washington, DC: American Psychiatric Association.

Spitzer, R.L. & Williams, J.B.W. (1986). *Structured clinical interview for DSM-III-R: Post-traumatic Stress Disorders (SCID-PTSD)*. (Available from Biometric Research Department, New York State Psychiatric Institute, 722 West 168th Street, New York, New York 10032).

Sutker, P.B., Winstead, D.K., Goist, K.C., Malow, R.M., & Allain, A.N. (1986). Psychopathology subtypes and symptom correlates among former prisoners of war. *Journal of Psychopathology and Behavioral Assessment, 8*, 89-101.

van der Kolk, B., Blitz, R., Burr, W., Sherry, S., & Hartman, E. (1984). Nightmares and trauma: Comparison of nightmares after combat with lifelong nightmares in veterans. *American Journal of Psychiatry, 141*, 187-190.

Vanderploeg, R., Sison, G.F.P., & Hickling, E.J. (1986). *A re-evaluation of the use of the MMPI in the assessment of combat-related post-traumatic stress disorders*. (Available from Edward J. Hickling, Psy. D., Psychology Service, 116-B, VA Medical Center, 113 Holland, Albany, NY 12208.)

Watson, C.G., Kucala, T., & Manifold, V. (1985). *A cross-validation of the Keane and Penk MMPI scales as measures of post-traumatic stress disorder*. (Available from Charles Watson, Ph.D., Associate Chief of Staff for Research, VA Medical Center, St. Cloud, Minnesota 56301).

Chapter 8

Neuropsychological Dysfunction

STEPHEN P. FARR and
PAULETTE W. MARTIN

OVERVIEW

The bulk of the literature concerning the MMPI and neuropsychological dysfunction has focused on the use of the MMPI in the differentiation of central nervous system (CNS) compromise or brain damage (BD) groups from either normal or psychiatric populations. These efforts have met with enough success to keep interest in the endeavor alive and with enough frustration to discourage primary adoption of any specific MMPI scale or index. Researchers have searched for BD indicators among the standard clinical scales and have attempted to develop keys or indices employing one or more of the standard scales for the identification of particular BD groups. Special and research scales for the identification of particular BD groups also have been developed. Each of these efforts has had its own host of problems and particular concerns.

Overall, the difficulties associated with this task bear on the efficacy of using the MMPI to identify:

1. BD in situations of mild neuropsychological impairment and psychiatric "good" functioning;
2. conditions where functioning obviously is compromised due to psychiatric disability and an organic component is suspected; or

3. conditions in which functioning clearly is compromised but not obviously characteristic of either organic or functional etiologies.

The last condition represents the one in which the ability of the MMPI to discriminate BD would be the most useful. It also represents the condition in which the task facing the MMPI is most difficult.

This chapter addresses two major questions. To what aspects of BD does the MMPI appear sensitive? Can the MMPI discriminate BD from a variety of other clinically meaningful patient groups (e.g., BD vs. schizophrenia, or BD vs. depression)? First, issues concerning the nature of BD must be reviewed to appreciate the definition of BD implicit in most MMPI literature. Then, the literature concerning the use of the MMPI in identifying BD or in discriminating BD individuals from non-BD individuals must be examined. This review employs a hit rate analysis and a common metric to facilitate comparison of the research findings.

CLINICAL POPULATION

To this point it has been assumed that, for the most part, BD represents a unitary construct. This assumption has several implications: (1) BD individuals, regardless of type and manner of CNS dysfunction, behave in a similar fashion (due to

THE MMPI: USE WITH
SPECIFIC POPULATIONS

© 1988 by Grune & Stratton.

ISBN 0-8089-1913-X

neuropsychological dysfunctions) and cope with similar issues of adaptation, regardless of age, gender, disease process, or other family and personal resources; (2) the underlying effects of BD are sufficient to override other nonpersonality-related variables such as coping style, time since injury, or residual resources represented by premorbid functional ability; and (3) different types of BD subjects can be grouped together and that, at least with regard to their MMPI performance, differences between BD individuals will not be observed.

The questionable validity of this assumption has been discussed widely and was reviewed recently by Farr, Greene, and Fisher-White (1986). BD is not a unitary construct. Since BD patients produce differential patterns of performance on standard neuropsychological batteries (cf. Meier, 1974; Boll, 1978), there is little reason to expect all BD individuals to produce the same pattern on the MMPI. Furthermore, even within subtypes of BD, individuals may not necessarily produce MMPI patterns that are typical and representative of their specific neuropsychological/neurologic diagnosis. These issues are not addressed in the majority of the research that purports to develop MMPI scales or indicators of BD or those studies that address the question of whether the MMPI is sensitive to a BD versus non-BD distinction. The clinically relevant issue of the relationship between subtypes of MMPI patterns and subtypes of BD may be, with the exception of the inevitable isolated investigation, a full generation beyond our present BD/MMPI research effort.

Typically, when investigators have explored the relationship between the MMPI and BD, BD groups have tended to represent patient groups with CNS compromise of an unspecified or mixed specific diagnosis or etiology. Buckholz (1984) observes that grouping or mixing individuals such as these is analogous to "treating all psychopathology as one category" (p. 698). This issue is not unique to this research area and it appears to reflect the focus of the investigator. Different categories of psychopathology typically are not mixed in research that explores personality assessment techniques such as the MMPI; they do appear grouped together in some areas of the neuropsychological literature where efforts are made to separate BD individuals from "psychiatric patients."   Conversely, in the neuropsychological literature, BD groups and their etiology tend to be

specified, while psychiatric groups frequently are presented as "mixed."

Grouping together all BD individuals is misleading not only because there are differences between subgroups, but also because pathophysiology, area of involvement, and moderator variables such as demographics may be very similar or quite different even within subgroups. For example, groups of stroke patients may represent a much more homogeneous pathophysiology or site of involvement than groups of patients with missile wounds or neoplasms. BD patients suffering from closed head injury may be more homogeneous than many BD groups in terms of demographic and moderator variables if their injury was associated with some aspect of risk-taking behavior. In the case of progressive dementias, such as Alzheimer's, the pathophysiology and demographics can be expected to be relatively consistent and homogeneous among samples.

Parsons and Prigatano (1978) and Heaton, Baade, and Johnson (1978) discussed the importance of moderator variables such as age, education, and gender within BD populations. Additional attention is warranted to the type of disease process, particularly with traumatic injuries and space-occupying lesions. Clinical history often is important in assessing the severity of the compromise, and these issues should be represented by variables coded as periods of consciousness, level of orientation, posttraumatic amnesia (PTA), time since injury, and other ancillary measures of impairment. Variables such as these may relate directly to communication and comprehension abilities required to complete the MMPI successfully. Premorbid personality characteristics also may confound the MMPI presentation of a BD group and obscure BD-related personality changes to which the MMPI would ordinarily be sensitive. For instance, if an individual with a Dysthymic Disorder suffers BD and demonstrates depressive features on the MMPI, is that pattern of item endorsement a consequence of the BD, the effort to cope with the presence of BD, a residual of the patient's premorbid personality pattern, or some combination of all of these factors?

To further complicate matters, the severity of impairment in a general or mixed "BD" group also may be relatively unrelated to type of BD or BD-specific diagnosis. The tables accompanying this chapter reflect, where possible, the exact terminology used to describe the comparison population in each study. In most cases, the exact nature of compromise among the BD groups was not specified. In cases where sample composition was specified, BD groups typically were "mixed" in terms of etiology. This situation serves to limit the possibility of determining the relationships that ideally would serve as a focus for this chapter. In this sense, even before this review is begun, there should be guarded optimism about whether clear conclusions can be made regarding the relation of BD to MMPI performance.

DMS-III-R

The revised third edition of the *Diagnostic and Statistical Manual of Mental Disorders* (DSM-III-R; American Psychiatric Association, 1987) distinguishes two major categories of neuropsychological dysfunction: Organic Mental Disorders and Organic Mental Syndromes. The term *Organic Mental Disorder* is used to denote an organic brain syndrome resulting from a known or presumed etiologic event. The designation of Organic Mental Syndrome is used in reference to a constellation of psychological or behavioral signs or symptoms that do not suggest specific etiology. *Organic Mental Syndromes* generally can be grouped into six categories: (1) Delirium and Dementia; (2) Amnestic Syndrome and Organic Hallucinosis; (3) Organic Delusional Syndrome, Organic Mood Syndrome, and Organic Anxiety Syndrome; (4) Organic Personality Syndrome; (5) Intoxication and Withdrawal; and (6) Organic Mental Syndrome Not Otherwise Specified. Each of these diagnostic entities can be specified following the monothetic and polythetic model of criterion identification in DSM-III-R.

In the case where a particular etiologic event is known or presumed, such as with cerebral vascular disorder or head trauma, an Organic Mental Disorder can be diagnosed using pathophysiologic processes included in the mental disorder section of the ICD-9-CM (United States Department of Health and Human Services, 1980). In some cases, specific etiologies of Organic Mental Disorders may appear within the context of physical disorders and conditions and, thus, are coded on Axis III. DSM-III-R recognizes that:

> Limitations in our knowledge, however, sometimes make it impossible to determine whether a particular mental disorder in a particular in-

dividual should be considered an Organic Mental Disorder (because it is due to brain dysfunction of *known* organic etiology) or whether it should be diagnosed as other than an Organic Mental Disorder (because it is more adequately accounted for as a response to psychological or social factors [as in Adjustment Disorder] or because the presence of a specific organic factor has not been established [as in Schizophrenia]). (1987, p. 98)

Organic Mental Disorders may occur at any age. Since they include a wide range of psychopathologic symptoms and organic etiologies, they are not characterized by any singular course. DSM-III-R notes that Organic Mental Disorders may be steadily or irregularly progressive, episodic, static, or rapidly or gradually resolving. These characteristics of Organic Mental Disorders, of course, relate to their underlying pathophysiology.

The DSM-III was introduced in 1980. Thus, within the present context, much of the literature concerning the MMPI and BD was concurrent with the earlier and substantially different DSM-I and DSM-II. The DSM-I designated organic brain syndromes as Acute or Chronic Brain Disorders, while DSM-II nomenclature makes the distinction between Psychosis Associated with Organic Brain Syndromes and Non-psychotic Organic Brain Syndromes (American Psychiatric Association, 1968). Even with newer studies, the manner in which groups are assigned and data are recorded render the DSM-III-R categorization of Organic Mental Disorders to be of limited utility in viewing and assessing the present literature.

PROTOTYPIC STUDY

The difficulties observed in the literature associated with appropriate group assignment, the conceptual treatment of BD as a unitary construct, and the creation of generic or mixed BD groups for purposes of study were discussed earlier. Because of these confounding factors, a single prototypic study illustrating all MMPI/BD research is not available. However, among the various approaches to the task, the use of the MMPI to discriminate BD from other patient groups represents the major effort in this area, and probably the most consistently reported of these studies focuses on development of special "BD" scales.

From a generic perspective, Clopton (1979) has discussed the issues and procedures accompanying these endeavors. Most typically, the MMPI is used as a dependent variable, while groups consisting of target and control patient populations are treated as independent variables. Each of the 566 MMPI items is analyzed in a 2 × 2 contingency table and frequencies are tabulated for each of the four cells. Using a test of statistical association such as the chi-square test, items sensitive to the target vs. control population differences can be identified.

Watson (1971) observed that most ability-oriented tests of BD were not useful in separating BD patients from schizophrenics since both groups produce very similar scores on many of the most popular techniques. Earlier investigations had compared MMPI profiles of hospitalized schizophrenics and organics and had reported that the means of the groups differed. Watson felt that it might be possible to use a personality-based measure to discriminate between groups, so he embarked on the task of developing a more convenient MMPI based measure for the BD/schizophrenic differential. The *Sc-O* Scale reflects the result of this effort. Watson administered the MMPI to 65 schizophrenics and 61 BD male patients under the age of 60. The BD group was composed of men whose history, laboratory, and clinical presentation were suggestive of BD. Sixty-five schizophrenic patients were screened and selected from clinical files. Significant age differences between groups were reported. Chi-square analyses were made on each MMPI item to identify which items were differentially endorsed by the BD patient and schizophrenic groups.

After the initial development of the *Sc-O* Scale, Watson attempted to refine his effort. He reasoned that he might be able to achieve equal or nearly equal levels of discrimination by using only the items at the highest level of significance, and he constructed three forms of the *Sc-O* Scale for further study. The first consisted of 80 items found to be significant at the .05 level. The second was constructed with the idea that weighting the items might enhance discriminative ability. Therefore, items significant at the .05, .01, .001, and .0001 levels were assigned weights of 1, 2, 3, and 4, respectively. The third and "short" form consisted of 30 items that were significant beyond the .01 level and were weighted as above. The initial sample was then scored on each version of the scale to determine optimal cutting scores and percentages of correct classification.

On cross-validation, these efforts led to limited success. Anticipating shrinkage, Watson cross-validated the three forms of the *Sc-O* Scale in two other settings and found that general medical and surgical organics and schizophrenics appeared to respond differently to the scales. He also noted that the scales may be gender-sensitive in that better discrimination was achieved among males. Finally, while the weighted forms performed more poorly than the unweighted forms, he found that cutting scores specific to the clinical setting would be required to achieve optimal discrimination.

Watson's effort reflects the strength and many of the difficulties inherent in an attempt to develop a special BD scale. He cross-validated the *Sc-O* Scale in more than a single setting to determine the degree of shrinkage and the need for locally specific cutoff scores. However, when Watson checked his initial samples for age, he found significant differences. Education, socioeconomic level, and other potential moderator variables are not specified in his original study. Since a particular scale, combination of scales, or markers may elevate in any number of populations for any number of reasons (associated or unassociated with the effect of BD), studies that do not clearly specify moderator variables must be viewed as providing information of limited utility.

The specifics of the chi-square analysis also remain unreported. Clopton (1979) observes that even with large numbers of subjects, expected cell frequencies may fall below five. The importance of this as a restriction has been debated, as has the effect of the experiment-wise confound created when serially comparing the 566 MMPI items for scale construction. Also, by virtue of their composition, individual MMPI items cannot be considered as uniformly independent. Watson's (1971) development of the *Sc-O* Scale is representative of the scale development literature as a whole in its failure to account for these issues.

STANDARD VALIDITY AND CLINICAL SCALES

In an extensive review of BD research, Mack (1979) classified the MMPI literature into two major areas and examined the MMPI as: a dependent variable to explore personality-related effects of neurologic compromise and adaptation, and an independent variable to predict diagnostic category. The latter approach will receive the greatest emphasis in this review. When using the MMPI as a dependent variable, research has typically focused on the individual standard clinical and validity scales in BD groups or the frequency of codetypes among various BD groups.

THE MMPI AS DEPENDENT VARIABLE

INDIVIDUAL VALIDITY AND CLINICAL SCALES

First, an examination of the traditional clinical and validity scales can be made. These data are summarized in terms of effect size scores to illustrate in a direct fashion the relative sensitivity of the standard scales to BD in comparison with available reference groups. In Table 8–1 effect

sizes were calculated following a modification of Cohen's (1977) formula:

$$(M1 - M2) / (((SD1^2 + SD2^2) / 2)^{1/2})$$

where:

M1 = mean of 1st distribution (BD or target group)

M2 = mean of 2nd distribution (control or comparison group)

SD1 = standard deviation of 1st distribution

SD2 = standard deviation of 2nd distribution.

Generally, a small magnitude of differences are associated with an effect size of .2, medium will be considered in the area of .5, and an effect size of .8 should be viewed as large. An effect size of .5 suggests that the means of the two groups are approximately one-half a standard deviation apart. A negative sign reflects a larger control group mean and a smaller BD mean, while positive effect size reflects the reverse relationship.

All effect sizes were calculated irrespective of actual scale levels, which means that differences

TABLE 8–1.   MMPI STANDARD VALIDITY AND CLINICAL SCALES

Study	Dx. Groups*	N Male	Female	Age	Edu-cation	A	B	C	D	E	F	G
Golden et al. (1979)	BD vs. schiz.		60	42.8	—	-	+	-	-	-	+	-
Holland, Levi, & Watson (1981)	BD vs. process schiz.	150		~41.9	~11.0	+	-	-	+	+	+	+
Holland & Watson (1980)	BD vs. process schiz.	170		~41.6	~11.1	-	+	-	-	+	+	+
Russell (1977)	BD vs. schiz.	95	5	~36.5	~11.4	+	-	-	+	-	+	-
Trifiletti (1982)	BD vs. mixed schiz.	20	21	~35.4	—	+	+	+	-	+	+	+
Weighted mean												
Holland & Watson (1980)	BD vs. reactive schiz.	160		~41.6	~11.1	-	+	-	-	+	+	+
Holland et al. (1981)	BD vs. reactive schiz.	146		~41.9	~11.0	+	-	-	+	+	+	+
Weighted mean												
Doehring & Reitan (1960)	BD aphasic vs. neurotic	34		~33.8	~10.4	+	-	-	-	-	+	+
Doehring & Reitan (1960)	BD nonaphasic vs. neurotic	34		~34.1	~10.7	+	-	-	-	-	+	+
Weighted mean												
Golden et al. (1979)	BD vs. hospitalized pain		60	42.8	—	-	+	-	-	-	+	-
Trifiletti (1982)	BD vs. depressed	16	28	~35.5	—	+	+	+	-	+	+	+
Wooten (1983b)	BD vs. non-BD	303	42	30.1	—	-	+	+	-	+	+	+
Dikmen & Reitan (1974)	Aphasic vs. nonaphasic BD	30		~33.4	~10.0	+	+	+	+	+	-	+
Matthews et al. (1977)	Ep vs. nonEp/BD (early)	26		~26.3	~10.7	-	+	-	+	-	-	+
Matthews et al. (1977)	Ep vs. nonEp/BD (late)	41		~28.8	~11.9	-	+	-	+	-	-	+
Meier & French (1965)	Bilateral vs. unilateral Ep	53		~28.1	—	-	+	-	-	-	-	-
Meier & French (1965)	Bitemporal independent vs. unilateral singular	33		~28.1	—	-	+	-	-	-	-	-

*Abbreviations: BD = brain-damaged patients; schiz. = schizophrenic patients; Ep = epileptic patients.

may reflect both normal range and clinically elevated comparisons. Thus, they do not account for the absolute magnitude of elevation or indicate elevations in abnormal range as opposed to normal range. The most sophisticated efforts using the MMPI to discriminate BD rest with multiscale or special scale techniques, and for that reason the purpose of this section is simply to identify which scale might be most sensitive and potentially useful when incorporated in other more complex applications. Following Cohen's (1977) suggestion that a magnitude of .5 be considered an intermediate effect size, only absolute values of .5 and greater will be consider for the current discussion.

As can be noted from Table 8–1, the majority of this research was conducted either with males or with gender unspecified. The majority of studies also made no assessment of profile validity before data analysis. The ratings in the Methodologic Issues columns follow conventions outlined in Chapter 1. As a specific BD type, epilepsy has received greater attention from MMPI researchers than any other single BD-associated diagnosis.

This literature will be discussed after examining BD related clinical and validity scale differences.

L Scale

Consistent differences on the L Scale were not present across studies comparing BD vs. schizophrenic (both process and reactive) patients, BD vs. depressed patients, or BD vs. normal individuals. Neurotic patients did score substantially higher than BD patients. These same differences did not appear when BD patients were compared with hospital pain patients. However, aphasic BD patients scored higher than nonaphasic BD patients on the L Scale.

F Scale

Large F Scale differences appeared in comparisons between BD and mixed or process schizophrenic patients, but not when BD patients were compared with reactive schizophrenic patients. BD patients in contrast to hospitalized

Comment	L	F	K	Hs	D	Hy	Pd	Mf	Pa	Pt	Sc	Ma	Si
Total Hit Rate >70%; 8, 6, & 4	0.09	-0.52	-0.18	0.07	-0.15	-0.17	-0.74	0.81	-0.57	-1.17	-0.68	-0.56	-0.43
	-0.29	-0.44	-0.10	-0.17	-0.36	-0.19	-0.30	-0.72	-0.39	-0.31	-0.44	-0.02	-0.42
Process schiz. high L,F,5,6, & 8	-0.10	-0.53	0.09	-0.12	-0.41	-0.12	-0.36	-0.72	-0.48	-0.50	-0.54	-0.22	-0.64
2-9, 9-2, & 1-3-9 absent	0.06	-1.11	0.41	-0.37	-0.53	-0.21	-0.69	-0.54	-1.27	-1.21	-1.32	-0.36	-0.93
Schiz. > pathology; BD older	0.88	-1.38	0.75	-0.33	-0.91	-0.15	-1.28	-0.65	-0.97	-1.60	-1.80	-0.90	-0.63
	.0	**-0.7**	**0.1**	**-0.2**	**-0.4**	**-0.2**	**-0.5**	**-0.5**	**-0.7**	**-0.7**	**-0.8**	**-0.3**	**-0.6**
BD low 2,3,4,5,7,& 8	-0.09	-0.10	-0.01	0.06	-0.41	-0.13	-0.21	-0.44	-0.08	-0.26	-0.12	0.24	-0.54
	-0.12	-0.25	-0.02	0.02	-0.46	-0.16	-0.18	-0.54	-0.12	-0.30	-0.23	0.24	-0.55
	-0.1	**-0.2**	**.0**	**.0**	**-0.4**	**-0.1**	**-0.2**	**-0.5**	**-0.1**	**-0.3**	**-0.2**	**0.2**	**-0.5**
BD and neurotic show similar	-1.12	-0.54	-0.45	0.54	0.28	0.23	-0.11	0.49	-0.38	0.11	-0.24	-0.27	—
personality disturbances	-1.05	0.40	-0.48	0.65	0.45	0.35	0.48	0.62	0.16	0.49	0.50	0.10	—
	-1.1	**-0.1**	**-0.5**	**0.6**	**0.4**	**0.3**	**0.2**	**0.6**	**-0.1**	**0.3**	**0.1**	**-0.1**	**—**
Total Hit Rate > 70%; 8 & 6	0.15	0.83	-0.04	0.53	0.52	0.66	0.43	0.43	0.81	-0.35	0.80	0.57	0.38
Schiz. > pathology; BD older	0.23	0.27	0.19	0.37	-0.72	-0.58	0.61	-0.80	0.34	0.83	0.45	0.38	0.17
Calculations from Table 8	0.05	0.20	-0.14	0.04	0.18	-0.04	0.06	0.04	0.04	0.21	0.23	0.05	0.17
Lesion location not matched	0.52	0.78	0.20	0.28	0.04	-0.18	1.14	-0.09	0.60	0.73	1.13	0.15	—
Onset: birth–5 yr	-0.66	-0.43	-0.49	-0.31	-0.39	-0.43	-0.93	—	-0.49	-0.01	-0.66	0.33	—
Onset: 17–50 yr	-0.48	0.41	-0.63	0.10	0.36	0.11	0.38	—	0.44	0.12	0.21	0.33	—
Temporal lobectomy patients	0.26	0.74	-0.55	0.49	0.51	0.17	0.37	-0.24	0.87	0.42	0.84	-0.31	—
Temporal lobectomy patients	-0.13	0.75	-0.41	0.06	0.98	0.66	1.17	-0.22	1.27	1.34	0.79	0.38	—

pain patients, and aphasic BD patients in contrast to nonaphasic BD patients, also elevated the *F* Scale.

K Scale

Doehring and Reitan (1960) found that neurotic patients demonstrated greater *K* Scale elevations than BD groups.

Scale 1 (Hs)

BD patients scored approximately one-half a standard deviation higher than neurotic or pain patients. Differences of reliable magnitude were not observed consistently between BD and schizophrenic patients, nor were they noted in the individual studies examining BD and depressed patients or BD and non-BD patients.

Scale 2 (D)

Trifiletti (1982) reported substantial differences on Scale *2* with the depressed group scoring higher than the BD group. Golden, Sweet, and Osmon (1979) reported that BD patients elevated Scale *2* approximately one-half a standard deviation above hospitalized pain patients. Reliable differences were not noted on this scale in any of the other patient groups (e.g., BD vs. schizophrenic, BD vs. non-BD, and aphasic vs. nonaphasic) that were tabulated.

Scale 3 (Hy)

Hospitalized pain patients scored lower and depressed patients scored higher on Scale *3* than BD patients. Substantial Scale *3* differences were not observed among the other groups of patients that appear in Table 8–1.

Scale 4 (Pd)

Differences on Scale *4* performance were observed in two comparisons. Overall, process schizophrenic patients and depressed patients scored higher than the BD patients. No differences were noted when BD and reactive schizophrenic patients were compared. Aphasic BD patients had higher mean scores than nonaphasic BD patients.

Scale 5 (Mf)

Somewhat surprisingly, a number of Scale *5* differences were noted. The schizophrenic (process and reactive) patients and depressed patents typically scored substantially higher than the BD patients on Scale *5*. The BD patients in turn scored higher than the neurotic patients.

Scale 6 (Pa)

"Mixed" or process schizophrenic groups scored higher than the BD group on Scale *6*. However, this same pattern was not observed when BD patients were compared with reactive schizophrenic patients. BD patients produced much higher elevations than pain patients. Finally, aphasic BD patients elevated Scale *6* at least one-half a standard deviation above nonaphasic BD patients.

Scale 7 (Pt)

Scale *7* appeared sensitive to comparisons between BD and process or mixed schizophrenic patients with the latter patients scoring higher. Substantial differences also were observed between BD patients and depressed patients, with the BD patients scoring higher. Aphasic BD patients elevated Scale *7* to a greater degree than nonaphasic BD patients.

Scale 8 (Sc)

A large effect size was observed on Scale *8* when BD groups were compared directly with process or mixed schizophrenic groups. The BD group produced significantly lower scale scores on Scale *8* than the schizophrenic groups. Large magnitude differences in the opposite direction were observed when BD and hospitalized pain patients were compared. Aphasic BD patients also elevated Scale *8* to a substantially greater degree than nonaphasic BD patients.

Scale 9 (Ma)

BD patients elevated Scale *9* to a greater degree than hospitalized pain patients. Consistent differences between BD patients and other comparison groups were not noted.

Scale 0 (Si)

Moderate effect sizes were observed when BD groups were compared with process and reactive schizophrenic groups, and both schizophrenic groups consistently scored above the BD groups. Comparisons among the other control groups were not reliable.

CODETYPES

Few studies presented data in a fashion that allowed direct comparison of the frequency of codetypes in BD groups (see Table 8–2). Infrequently occurring codetypes (< 5%) were not tabulated.

The most frequent codetypes seen in BD groups appear to involve some combination of Scale *2*. Scale *2* occurred in 13 codetypes and Scale *8* appeared in 9 codetypes. In addition to Scale *8*, Scale *2* appears in combination with Scales *1, 3, 4, 7,* and *9* in forming codetypes that, relative to many other possible combinations, occur frequently in BD groups. However, the *8-9/9-8* codetype appears to be the most frequently reported. Combinations inclusive of Scale *4* (*2-4/4-2, 3-4/4-3,* and *4-9/9-4*) or Scale *9* (*2-9/9-2, 4-9/9-4,* and *8-9/9-8*) also have been reported with relatively high frequencies in comparison with those seen among all possible codetypes.

The data summarized in Table 8–2 suggest that the clinical utility of codetypes for identification of and decision-making with regard to BD-related determinations may be rather limited. It is evident that even the most likely codetypes described above occur less than 11 percent of the time in a known BD group. At this base rate, the utility of any codetype to identify BD in an unknown clinical population will be limited, and there is little likelihood that a single codetype will yield a universally applicable MMPI description of BD.

Codetype triads also are depicted in Table 8–2. The combination of Scales *2, 3,* and *1,* and Scales *4, 8,* and *2,* appear most frequently in the work presented by Sand (1972). Wooten (1983b) noted that the *1-2-3* combination was seen in over 10 percent of his population of mixed neuropsychologically impaired patients. From the very limited triad codetype data that are available, Scales *2* or *8* appear in all the combinations presented.

SUMMARY

Tables 8–1 and 8–2 summarize the sensitivity of the standard validity and clinical scales and the frequency of codetypes occurring in various BD groups when the MMPI is considered as a dependent variable. While a great body of research appears to address this question, few studies present data in a fashion that meets even the minimum requirements for inclusion in the present tabular calculations. Table 8–1 required the reporting of means and standard deviations, while Table 8–2 required the reporting of frequency of codetype occurrence in the BD groups under consideration. That many studies had to be excluded is illustrative of the limitations of the current literature.

Several conclusions seem warranted based on the data presented in Tables 8–1 and 8–2. The standard clinical and validity scales appear differentially sensitive to BD-related issues. The lack of consistent pattern among these comparisons of BD groups with schizophrenic, pain, and neurotic groups suggests an issue of major importance. Namely, in considering the MMPI's ability to discriminate BD groups, the specific composition of the comparison group warrants specification. The actual degree to which the MMPI is directly sensitive to BD cannot be determined at this point. However, the fact that aphasic and nonaphasic BD groups performed differently on comparisons with each other suggests that all BD groups cannot be expected to produce similar MMPI profiles.

Table 8–2 also provides basic insight into the likelihood of any particular profile being associated with the presence of BD. Some codetypes do occur more frequently in BD than other groups. However, even common codetypes typically occur at frequencies below 10 percent and most certainly at levels below 15 percent.

EPILEPSY

As a BD diagnosis, epilepsy has received more attention than any of the other specific BD entities, and in examination of the MMPI/epilepsy literature we do not have to suffer the confound of "mixed" BD groups. For the most part this literature has been concerned with the appearance of epileptics on the MMPI rather than with distinguishing them from normals or other nonepileptic BD groups. However, another major issue addressed in the literature is the degree to which epilepsy is related to psychopathology and the MMPI's ability to discriminate epileptic groups from psychopathologic groups.

In viewing standard MMPI validity and clinical scale configurations, Klove and Doehring (1962)

TABLE 8–2. MMPI HIGH-POINT CODETYPES

Study	Dx. Groups	N Male	N Female	Age	Education	A	B	C	D	E	F	G
MMPI High-Point Pairs												
Holland et al. (1981)	Brain damaged	73		~41.95	~11.07	+	-	-	+	+	+	+
Greene & Farr (1986)	Closed head injury		36	—	—	-	+	+	-	+	+	+
Sand (1972)	Cerebrovascular non-normal profiles	56		>16	—	-	+	-	+	-	+	+
Sand (1972)	Trauma non-normal profiles	28		>16	—	-	+	-	+	-	+	+
Sand (1972)	CNS diseased non-normal profiles	19		>16	—	-	+	-	+	-	+	+
Wooten (1983b)	Mixed neuropsychologically impaired	303		~30.1	—	-	+	+	-	+	+	+
Hathaway & Meehl (1951)	Organic brain damage		52	—	—	+	+	-	-	-	-	-
MMPI High-Point Triads												
Sand (1972)	Cerebrovascular non-normal profiles	56		>16	—	-	+	-	+	-	+	+
Sand (1972)	Trauma non-normal profiles	28		>16	—	-	+	-	+	-	+	+
Sand (1972)	CNS diseased non-normal profiles	19		>16	—	-	+	-	+	-	+	+
Wooten (1983b)	Mixed neuropsychologically impaired	303		~30.1	—	-	+	+	-	+	+	+

and Matthews and Klove (1968) conclude that few if any differences should be expected between epileptics, nonepileptic controls, and mixed-BD patients without epilepsy. Matthews and Klove (1968) also note that when the MMPI performance of epileptics is compared with nonepileptic BD individuals, or when the performance of epileptics is compared with nonneurologic controls, no differences are seen. Multiple investigations (Hermann, Dikmen, Schwartz, & Karnes, 1982; Lewis, Lachar, Voelker, & Vidergar, 1984; Stevens, Milstein, & Goldstein, 1972; Lachar, Lewis, & Kupke, 1979; Hermann, Schwartz, Whitman, & Karnes, 1981; Hermann, Schwartz, Karnes, & Vahdat, 1980) also have failed to demonstrate MMPI-related differences between subtypes of epileptics in a variety contexts. Specific MMPI scale differences also are not seen if epileptics are compared with controls consisting of patients with primary "affective disturbances" and/or those who were hospitalized with primary organic complaints other than cerebral disease (Klove & Doehring, 1962). Matthews, Dikmen, and Harley (1977) compared early onset (birth to age 5) and late onset (age 17 to 50) major motor seizure epileptics with similar onset nonepileptic BD groups. Effect size comparisons in Table 8–1 do not suggest a consistent pattern between the two age of onset groups for the epilepsy vs. nonepilepsy/BD comparison.

Meier and French (1965) examined temporal lobe epileptics who had undergone temporal lobectomies for psychomotor seizures. Their findings appear in Table 8–1. For the study of MMPI-related differences, they classify their groups on two dimensions: (1) bilateral vs. unilateral preoperative electroencephalogram (EEG) abnormalities, and (2) preoperative independently arising bitemporal foci vs. a primary unilateral spike. As can be seen in Table 8–1, both comparisons yield notable differences on Scales *F*, *2*, *6*, and *8*; with the exception of Scale *8*, these differences are within the normal range. Additional differences are seen on Scale *K* in the bilateral vs. unilateral groups, while differences between the independent bitemporal and unilateral spike groups were observed on Scales *3*, *4*, and *7*. It is important to note that *all* individuals in this study experienced excision of the temporal lobe due to seizure activity that was severe and poorly controlled with anticonvulsant medication.

Hermann (1981) observed a relationship between psychopathology in epilepsy and neuropsychological deficit such that psychopathology seemed to increase as neuropsychological deficits became more severe. The Meier and French (1965) findings are from patients that should, as a result of neurosurgical intervention alone, demonstrate at least some neuropsychological compromise, even without the confound represented by surgical intervention. It may be that MMPI-related differences can be appreciated only in cases of extreme pathophysiology or between groups that demonstrate a profound clinical picture and are defined electrophysiologically.

Epilepsy has been associated clinically with psychiatric disturbance, and certainly the MMPI should be sensitive to any psychiatric aspect

1-2/2-1	1-3/3-1	2-3/3-2	2-4/4-2	2-7/7-2	2-8/8-2	2-9/9-2	3-4/4-3	4-9/9-4	7-8/8-7	8-9/9-8
	5.5%		6.8%		5.5%		5.5%	9.6%		9.6%
5.6%	5.6%				5.6%				5.6%	5.6%
								5.4%		
										7.1%
										5.3%
9.2%	8.3%	6.3%			6.3%			6.6%		10.6%
9.6%		5.7%	7.7%	6.7%		8.6%				

1-2-3	2-3-1/2-1-3	2-7-8	4-8-2	7-8-9
	5.4%			
			7.1%	
	10.5%		5.3%	
11.2%		6.6%		5.0%

of an epileptic presentation. A review of this literature suggests that when groups are matched, at least for some kinds of epileptics and particularly in the case of complex partial seizure disorders, MMPI elevations are evident. However, these elevations may represent the secondary effects of psychiatric disturbance rather than a BD-associated epilepsy phenomena (Hermann, Dikmen, & Wilensky, 1982; Meier & French, 1965). Mignone, Donnelly, and Sadowsky (1970) examined psychomotor and nonpsychomotor epileptics in order to illuminate previously reported relationships between epilepsy and a variety of psychiatric disturbances. Their subject pool allowed the examination of bilateral vs. unilateral temporal lobe EEG focus, and the presence or absence of generalized convulsive disorders. They concluded that with few exceptions there were no statistically significant findings on major MMPI scales. While none of their epileptic groups produced elevations of clinical magnitude (with the exception of Scale 5) the average scores for all scales among all epileptic groups were significantly higher than those of an independently derived control of college students reported in the literature. When Dikmen, Hermann, Wilensky, and Rainwater (1983) compared three groups of epileptic patients suffering from complex partial seizures, complex partial seizures with secondary generalization, and primary generalized convulsive seizures, MMPI differences were not noted among these groups based on seizure type. Differences did appear once the subject pool was partitioned on dimensions of psychiatric severity

and prior history of psychiatric presentation. These studies suggest that the presence of psychopathology, rather than the type of epilepsy per se, mediates the degree to which epileptics elevate the MMPI.

THE MMPI AS INDEPENDENT VARIABLE

The second major area of research in the literature employs the MMPI as an independent variable in facilitating the differentiation of BD from non-BD groups. This approach also uses the standard MMPI scales in the discrimination of BD groups from other target populations. In at least one case (Scale 8), discussions have appeared in the literature examining the utility of using a standard clinical scale as a BD indicator.

INDIVIDUAL VALIDITY AND CLINICAL SCALES

Table 8–3 summarizes the two validity and two clinical scales that have been reported in a manner that permits the calculation of hit rate type data. For the following series of tables charting hit rate data, sample sizes and base rates reflect parameters for the groups in the Diagnostic Groups column. The percentage of correct identification in both the BD group (sensitivity) and in the control group (specificity) are presented. *Po* reflects the likelihood that an individual scoring within the criterion

TABLE 8–3. MMPI VALIDITY AND CLINICAL SCALES

Scale Study	Dx. Groups*	N Male	N Female	Age	Edu- cation	A	B	C	D	E	F	G
F Scale												
Golden et al. (1979)	BD vs. schiz.	60		42.8	—	-	+	-	-	-	+	-
Graca et al. (1984)	Organic vs. schiz.		100	~49.9	—	-	-	-	-	+	+	-
Weighted mean												
Golden et al. (1979)	BD vs. hospitalized pain	60		42.8	—	-	+	-	-	-	+	-
L Scale												
Korman & Blumberg (1963)	Cerebral damage vs. cont.	80		~45.2	~9.8	+	+	-	+	+	+	+
Graca et al. (1984)	Organic vs. schiz.		100	~49.9	—	-	-	-	-	+	+	-
Scale *2*												
Watson et al. (1978)	BD vs. depressed	65		~47.4	~10.5	+	+	-	-	+	+	+
Scale *8*												
Ayers, Templer, & Ruff (1975)	Organic vs. schiz.	43		—	—	-	-	-	-	+	+	-
Carpenter & LeLieuvre (1981)	BD vs. schiz.		60	—	—	-	+	-	-	+	+	+
Graca et al. (1984)	Organic vs. schiz.		100	~49.9	—	-	-	-	-	+	+	-
Trifiletti (1982)	BD vs. mixed schiz.	20	21	~35.3	—	+	+	+	-	+	+	+
Weighted mean												
Sillitti (1982)	Organic vs. functional	33	33	~39.1	—	-	-	-	-	+	+	-

*Abbreviations: BD = brain-damaged patients; cont. = control patients; schiz. = schizophrenic patients.

range will be BD following Bayes' formula for the application of inverse probability (Meehl & Rosen, 1955):

$$Po = (P \times p1) / (P \times p1 + Q \times p2)$$

where:

P = Base rate of BD in the population
Q = Base rate of non-BD in the population
p1 = valid positive rate
p2 = false positive rate.

In contrast to a hit rate calculation, Po incorporates consideration of the false positive rate and the relative group base rates.

Given the level of interest associated with MMPI performance in BD individuals, the paucity of research on standard validity and clinical scales and codetypes that allow charting within a hit rate type framework is surprising. Scales *L*, *F*, *2*, and *8* all have received at least passing attention from investigators in this area.

L Scale

The data presented by Korman and Blumberg (1963) and Graca et al. (1984) suggest that the *L* Scale is more successful in identifying a control or reference population than the BD population per se. Employing optimal base rates, the ability of the *L* Scale to identify correctly the control medical

and psychiatric patient group in the Korman and Blumberg (1963) study at a rate of .80 contributes to an overall probability of correct classification (Po) of .71. The *L* Scale's difficulty identifying the BD group with only a .32 correct classification rate in the Graca et al. (1984) study yields an overall probability of correct classification rate at .53, which approximates chance levels.

F Scale

Golden, Sweet, and Osmon (1979) and Graca, Hutzell, Gaffney, and Whiddon (1984) have presented data concerning the ability of the *F* Scale to discriminate BD and schizophrenic groups within the context of examining several discriminative techniques in a side-by-side fashion. As with much of the literature, difficulties with methodology or at least the manner in which basic study parameters were reported appear to be present. In one study (Golden et al., 1979) the *F* Scale appeared to identify and classify correctly BD individuals with greater accuracy than control individuals, while Graca et al. (1984) reported rather equivocal levels of correct classification (BD, 56 percent; control, 60 percent). The two reported studies employed slightly different cutting scores, but both used an optimal 50/50 base rate. When the *F* Scale is examined in an attempt to separate BD from hospitalized pain patients

Comment	Cutting Score	Proportion Correct		Base Rate		Po
		BD	Control	BD	Control	
Controls significantly younger	60	0.80	0.56	50%	50%	0.65
	<67	0.56	0.60	50	50	0.58
						0.61
	50	0.72	0.67	50	50	0.69
Med. & psych. patient controls	6-7	0.48	0.80	50	50	0.71
Controls significantly younger	>6	0.32	0.72	50	50	0.53
BD group significantly less educated	31.5	0.96	0.64	62	38	0.81
BD or nonschiz. groups	36	0.60	0.61	35	65	0.40
T-score used for cutoff	<80	0.93	0.23	50	50	0.55
Controls significantly younger	<65	0.32	0.82	50	50	0.64
BD significantly older	<81	0.65	0.86	49	51	0.81
						0.60
Exp. > age; scale prorated	77	0.75	0.76	48	52	0.74

(Golden et al., 1979), classification rates similar to those noted above are achieved. Perhaps the most striking feature to be observed from Table 8–3 with regard to F Scale performance is the fact that a shift from schizophrenic to pain patients requires a shift in the cutting score of at least a full standard deviation to achieve optimal separation.

Scale 2 (D)

When Scale 2 is used to separate BD from depressed individuals, Watson, Davis, and Gasser (1978) reported quite acceptable levels of performance. Employing a raw cutting score of 31.5, it was apparent that BD individuals consistently scored below depressed individuals on Scale 2 and thus a quite acceptable 96 percent rate of correct identification was found. Paradoxically, the depressed patients were identified at a rate of 64 percent. In this case, as a result of the success in identifying BD individuals, the overall probability of correct classification was .81.

Scale 8 (Sc)

Scale 8 has received the most attention of the standard clinical scales with regard to its ability to discriminate BD from schizophrenic patient groups. Optimal cutting scores on Scale 8 appear to be between T-scores of 65 and 81, with the schizophrenic groups scoring higher than the BD group. Carpenter and LeLieuvre (1981) reported 93 percent correct identification of female BD patients using a cutting score of 80. Surprisingly, only 23 percent of the female schizophrenic group were identified correctly with the overall Po calculated at a rather modest .55. Scale 8 may perform as well on an organic vs. functional differential with identification of both the BD and the control group above .70 (Sillitti, 1982). The compiled data suggest that there is a risk, at least for mixed gender groups, that overall correct classification may be based more on Scale 8's ability to identify the comparison groups correctly than to identify BD groups.

HIGH-POINT PAIRS AND TRIADS

Table 8–4 reflects the efforts of Russell (1977), Graca et al. (1984), and Wooten (1983b) in exploring the utility of popularly accepted codetype combinations for the identification and classification of BD groups. Much has been written about some of these combinations in an informal or anecdotal manner, but few studies were noted that reported data in a fashion that would conform to the requirements of the hit rate analysis being used in this review.

TABLE 8–4. MMPI CODETYPE DISCRIMINATION

Codetype / Study	Dx. Groups*	N Male	N Female	Age	Education	A	B	C	D	E	F	G
9-2												
Graca et al. (1984)	Organic vs. schiz.	100	—	~49.9	—	-	-	-	-	+	+	-
Russell (1977)	BD vs. schiz.	95	5	~36.5	11.3	-	+	-	-	-	+	+
Wooten (1983b)	BD vs. non-BD pts.	303	42	30.1	—	-	+	+	-	+	+	+
1-3-9												
Graca et al. (1984)	Organic vs. schiz.	100	—	~49.9	—	-	-	-	-	+	+	-
Russell (1977)	BD vs. schiz.	95	5	~36.5	11.3	-	+	-	-	-	+	+
Wooten (1983b)	BD vs. non-BD	303	42	30.1	—	-	+	+	-	+	+	+
6-7-8 Psychotic Triad												
Graca et al. (1984)	Organic vs. schiz.	100	—	~49.9	—	-	-	-	-	+	+	-

*Abbreviations: BD = brain-damaged patients; schiz. = schizophrenic patients.

2-9/9-2

The *2-9/9-2* codetype received initial attention as a possible BD marker from Schwartz (1969). When the *9-2* codetype was cross-validated by Russell (1977) and Graca et al. (1984) as a discriminator for BD, both investigators found this indicator to be quite wanting. Zero percent correct classifications of BD were observed within the context of a BD or organic vs. schizophrenic differential. Wooten (1983b), in exploring this highpoint pair indicator in BD vs. non-BD patients, again reported practically nil levels of correct BD group classification. On the other hand, Russell (1977), Graca et al. (1984), and Wooten (1983b) reported high rates of comparison group classification accuracy (see Table 8–4). This may be due to the infrequency of occurrence of the *2-9/9-2* codetype in BD groups.

1-3-9

Gilberstadt and Duker (1965) popularized the *1-3-9* organic profile. This codetype performed poorly in discriminating BD groups from schizophrenic groups, with very low rates of correct classification for the BD groups (see Table 8–4). Where an overall *Po* can be calculated, its attractiveness is artifactual to the perfect identification of the schizophrenic control group. Wooten (1983b) found that the *1-3-9* codetype did not differentiate BD and non-BD patients.

6-7-8

Graca et al. (1984) examined the *6-7-8* "psychotic triad" as a possible differentiator of BD and schizophrenic patient groups. Their effort also appeared to yield findings worthy of only modest enthusiasm (see Table 8–4). Clearly, the schizophrenic control group had a much higher classification rate than the BD group. The *6-7-8* triad did not appear to be overly sensitive to particular characteristics of the BD group.

SUMMARY

In spite of the high degree of interest that the BD question has received, Tables 8–3 and 8–4 reflect the limited data that permit the construction of a hit rate type analysis of major validity and clinical scales and codetype combinations. Consequently, a rather cautious view must be taken regarding whether these MMPI measures can identify BD individuals and discriminate them from other likely reference groups.

Studies that did not confound gender (either all males or all females) appeared to have the highest correct identification percentages for the BD group when individual scales were examined. The majority of this work has contrasted BD and schizophrenic patient groups. While initially promising, high identification rates rarely are noted in both the target BD group and the comparison group. Consequently, the overall probability of correctly identifying BD in the majority of the dichotomous situations depicted in Table 8–3 were only an incremental improvement above chance.

The results appear even less promising when codetypes are tabulated. There is little overlap between the codetypes charted in Table 8–2 reflecting frequency of occurrence in BD groups and those charted in Table 8–4 reflecting BD classification and identification potential. Only the *2-9/9-2* codetype is found in both tables. Hathaway and Meehl (1951) reported a frequency of occurrence of 8.2 percent for the *2-9/9-2* codetype. Investigations by Russell (1977) and Graca et al. (1984) are in agreement in reporting 0 percent cor-

Comment	Cutting Score	Proportion Correct		Base Rate		Po
		BD	Control	BD	Control	
Controls significantly younger		0.00	1.00	50%	50%	—
		0.00	1.00	50	50	—
		0.02	0.95	61	39	0.42
Controls significantly younger		0.00	1.00	50	50	—
		0.06	1.00	50	50	1.00
		0.02	0.96	61	39	0.44
Controls significantly younger	<59	0.28	0.86	50	50	0.67

rect identification rates for the *2-9/9-2* pattern in their BD and schizophrenic studies. The frequency of occurrence of specific codetypes may be too low to form the basis for a scheme to discriminate BD from the comparison groups that are chosen most frequently for investigation.

KEY APPROACHES AND SPECIAL ORGANICITY SCALES

KEY APPROACHES

Acknowledging the shortcomings of employing individual MMPI scales in the identification of BD, several investigations have empirically sought to combine sensitive MMPI scales into serial "keys" in an effort to enhance discrimination. These efforts are charted in Table 8–5. For the most part they are based on individual scales or codetype combinations that were reviewed above and that demonstrated the most promise when studied individually. Three major efforts appear in the literature. Russell (1975) reflects the logic of a relatively complex key approach. Watson and Thomas (1968) employ an approach that combines Scales *2, 4, 5, 8,* and *9,* as opposed to a later effort by Watson and his colleagues which used a simpler combined index based on Scales *1* and *7* (Watson, Plemel, & Jacobs, 1978).

Russell Key

Russell (1975) applied the logic of the key approach that had received wide interest in the area of neuropsychological assessment and diagnosis (Russell, Neuringer, & Goldstein, 1970). His MMPI key was derived from an examination of BD and schizophrenia patient records. In noting

that the common pattern of BD on the MMPI is essentially that of a "reactive depression," his key was constructed to distinguish the reactive depression profile common in BD patients from a more disturbed schizophrenic profile. The validity scale configuration was incorporated in his profile since the inverted "V" validity scale was felt to be quite common among schizophrenics and relatively uncommon among BD. Because of this, his key is based entirely on validity scale and Scale *8* performance levels. Russell's (1975) key approach is as follows:

T-scores of *L* or *K* ≥ *F*	• Organic
T-scores of *L* and *K* < *F*	• Continue
Scale *8 T*-score ≥ 90	• Functional
Scale *8 T*-score < 60	• Organic
Scale *8 T*-score = 60-89	• Continue
T-score of *F* ≤ 60	• Organic
T-score of *F* > 60	• Continue
T-scores of *F* ≥ Scale *8*	• Organic or undiagnosed
T-scores of *F* < Scale *8*	• Functional or undiagnosed

In some sense, Russell's key acknowledges that schizophrenic profiles display greater pathology than those of BD nonschizophrenic individuals. Review of Table 8–5 suggests relatively consistent performance in identifying BD groups and relatively inconsistent performance in identifying comparison or control group membership. For males the percentages of correct identification of control/schizophrenic groups ranged between 20 percent (Golden et al., 1979) and 90 percent (Trifiletti, 1982). This inconsistency also affects the overall probability of correct classification rates (*Po*), which vary from .44 to .89. Particular weaknesses seem to appear in the correct identification of female schizophrenics (Carpenter & Le-Lieuvre, 1981) and hospitalized pain patients (Golden et al., 1979).

TABLE 8–5. KEY/CONFIGURAL APPROACHES

Approach Study	Dx. Groups*	N		Age	Edu- cation	Methodologic Issues						
		Male	Female			A	B	C	D	E	F	G
Russell Key (1975)												
Russell (1975)	BD vs. schiz.	95	5	~36.7	~11.3	+	-	+	+	+	+	-
Carpenter & LeLieuvre (1981)	Brain dysfunction vs. schiz.		60	—	—	-	+	-	-	+	+	+
Golden et al. (1979)	BD vs. schiz.	60		42.8	—	-	+	-	-	-	+	-
Graca et al. (1984)	Organic vs. schiz.	100		~49.9	—	-	-	-	-	+	+	-
Ryan & Souheaver (1977)	BD vs. mixed schiz.	40		~37.3	~12.1	+	+	-	-	+	+	-
Trifiletti (1982)	BD vs. mixed schiz.	20	21	~35.4	—	+	+	+	-	+	+	-
Sillitti (1982)	Organic vs. schiz.	33	33	~39.1	—	-	-	-	-	+	+	-
Weighted mean												
Trifiletti (1982)	BD vs. depressed	16	28	~35.5	—	+	+	+	-	+	+	-
Golden et al. (1979)	BD vs. hospitalized pain	60		42.8	—	-	+	-	-	-	+	-
Watson & Thomas (1968) Rule 4: ((D+Mf+Sc)-(Pd+Ma))<40=Organic												
Watson & Thomas (1968)	BD vs. schiz.	100		43.1	10.5	+	+	-	+	+	+	+
Watson & Thomas (1968)	BD vs. schiz.	52		—	—	-	-	-	-	+	+	+
Watson & Thomas (1968)	BD vs. schiz.	34		—	—	-	-	-	-	+	+	+
Watson & Thomas (1968)	BD vs. schiz.		22	—	—	-	-	-	-	+	+	+
Golden et al. (1979)	BD vs. schiz.	60		42.8	—	-	+	-	-	-	+	-
Graca et al. (1984)	Organic vs. schiz.	100		~49.9	—	-	-	-	-	+	+	-
Norton & Romano (1977)	Neurologic vs. married schiz.		28	~43.4	~11.3	-	+	-	-	+	+	-
Norton & Romano (1977)	Neurologic vs. unmarried schiz.		28	~42.7	~11.5	-	+	-	-	+	+	-
Sillitti (1982)	Organic vs. schiz.	33	33	~39.1	—	-	-	-	-	+	+	-
Weighted mean												
Carpenter & LeLieuvre (1981)	Brain dysfunction vs. schiz.		60	—	—	-	+	-	-	+	+	+
Golden et al. (1979)	BD vs. hospitalized pain	60		42.8	—	-	+	-	-	-	+	-
Norton & Romano (1977)	Neurologic vs. alcoholic		28	~44.1	~11.6	-	+	-	-	+	+	-
Norton & Romano (1977)	Neurologic vs. mixed psychiatric		28	~43.5	~11.4	-	+	-	-	+	+	-
Watson et al. (1978): *Hs - Pt* index												
Watson et al. (1978)	Organics vs. psychiatric inpatients		361	—	—	-	-	-	-	-	+	+
Wooten (1983a)	Organic vs. functional	303		30.1	—	-	-	-	-	+	+	-
Graca et al. (1984)	Organic vs. schiz.	100		~49.9	—	-	-	-	-	+	+	-

*Abbreviations: BD = brain-damaged patients; schiz. = schizophrenic patients.

Rule 4

Watson and Thomas (1968) attempted to test the efficacy of four MMPI interpretive rules in making the organic vs. schizophrenic distinction. All four indices provided levels of discriminative ability that appeared promising and suggested a need for further cross-validation. The first rule simply noted that if a peak on Scales *2, 5,* or *8* was obtained, a diagnosis of schizophrenia would be warranted. In contrast, a peak on Scale *4* or Scale *9* would indicate a diagnosis of organicity. The second rule stated that if more than one *T*-score exceeded 90, then the diagnosis should be schizophrenic—otherwise the diagnosis should be organic. The third and fourth rules were a combination of the first two rules. The third Rule was to apply first Rule 1 and then Rule 2 to the patients not diagnosed by Rule 1. The fourth rule is as follows:

$$((\text{Scales } 2 + 5 + 8) - (\text{Scales } 4 + 9)) < 40$$
$$= \text{Organic}$$

The fourth rule proved consistently to be the most effective and is presented in Tables 8–5 and 8–12 for comparison with other techniques. Watson and Thomas also noted the difficulties in discriminating between female BD and schizophrenic groups. Additionally, the Watson and Thomas Rule 4 appears to perform at chance levels or below in identifying hospitalized pain patients (Golden et al., 1979) and alcoholics (Norton & Romano, 1977).

Comment	Cutting Score	Proportion Correct		Base Rate		Po
		BD	Control	BD	Control	
Derivation study	—	0.72	0.80	50%	50%	0.78
38% of N unclassified		0.73	0.13	50	50	0.46
Russell Key		0.63	0.20	50	50	0.44
Russell Key		0.56	0.54	50	50	0.55
Modified Russell Key		0.80	0.85	50	50	0.84
Russell Key		0.85	0.90	49	51	0.89
Russell Key		0.59	0.32	48	52	0.44
						0.61
Russell Key		0.85	0.33	45	55	0.52
Russell Key		0.63	0.03	50	50	0.39
Derivation study: Rule 4	<40	0.86	0.52	50	50	0.64
Male cross-validation		0.77	0.65	50	50	0.69
Male cross-validation		0.76	0.82	50	50	0.81
Female cross-validation		0.36	0.55	50	50	0.44
		0.47	0.50	50	50	0.48
		0.60	0.54	50	50	0.57
Po estimated		0.93	0.50	50	50	0.65
Po estimated		0.93	0.86	50	50	0.87
		0.50	0.59	48	52	0.53
						0.61
Female cross-validation		0.07	0.80	50	50	0.25
		0.47	0.47	50	50	0.47
Po estimated		0.93	0.43	50	50	0.62
Po estimated		0.93	0.71	50	50	0.76
-1 to -15 scores overlap	>-1	0.60	0.69	9	92	0.16
note with extreme groups design excluding 9 to -15 prediction improves						
Patient groups are "mixed"	>-1	0.52	0.36	62	38	0.57
	>-4	0.60	0.62	50	50	0.61

Hs-Pt Index

Another approach to the development of a configural sign for differentiating BD from general psychiatric patients would be to examine all possible additive and subtractive, K-corrected T-score two scale combinations. Pursuing this tack, Watson, Plemel, and Jacobs (1978) found the Scale *1* minus Scale *7* comparison to be capable of separating BD from their psychiatric inpatient groups. Using the *Hs-Pt* Index these authors reported that a score of 10 or more suggests a three-to-one chance of BD, while a score of -16 or less suggests a nine-to-one chance of "functional" difficulty. At smaller absolute values, from their own data and from the replication data supplied by Wooten (1983a), correct prediction may become

quite tenuous. Indeed, Wooten reported that his findings when using a different patient sample did not support the use of the *Hs-Pt* Index. Graca et al. (1984) included the *Hs-Pt* Index in their comparison study of multiple MMPI techniques for the discrimination of BD. Using "organic" and schizophrenic groups, they reported a modest improvement over chance assignment in both the BD and comparison group.

Epilepsy Key

Hovey, Kooi, and Thomas (1959) developed a rather complex 14-sign profile analysis key for the discrimination of several epileptic patient group combinations, epileptic vs. neurotic, psychotic, or "personality problems"; paroxysmal EEG epileptics vs. nonparoxysmal EEG psychiatric patients and patients with nonparoxysmal EEGs. Using nonparametric techniques, these investigators compared composite group profiles. Fourteen pair and triad codetypes that separated groups were identified. They referred to triad codetypes as "*Vs*" and operationalized this configuration as the condition in which "any scale score was more than one full raw-score point below a straight line from a scale score to the left and to the right." Two-point codetypes were operationalized as the condition in which "a *T*-score on a scale was more than one full raw score point above a comparison scale score." The 14 codetypes were identified as follows:

1. *V* for Scales *2, 4, 9*
2. *V* for Scales *5, 6, 9*
3. Scale *9 > 6*
4. Scale *1 > 4*
5. Scale *9 > 4*
6. Scale *1 > 6*
7. Scale *4* is one of two lowest scores
8. *V* for Scales *1, 4, 5*
9. *V* for Scales *1, 4, 7*
10. *V* for Scales *3, 4, 9*
11. Scale *3 > 4*
12. Scale *7 > 8*
13. *V* for Scales *5, 6, 7*
14. *V* for Scales *3, 4, 5*

Cutting points were assigned on the basis of the number of criteria that profiles were able to meet. The greater the number of criteria, the greater the likelihood of epilepsy. Hovey et al. (1959) report that a cutting point of seven or more signs produced a 67 percent true-positive rate for epileptics and an 18 percent false-positive rate when psychiatric patients were used for comparison. With the exception of a epileptic vs. psychotic comparison, replication efforts by Jordan (1963) failed. This isolated success in discriminating epileptics proved to be due to the unique characteristics of the psychotic group. Jordan (1963) noted that the signs did statistically differentiate psychotics from neurotics at the 6, 7, and 8 sign cutting points.

SUMMARY

When faced with the BD vs. schizophrenic distinction, *Po* calculations from Table 8–5 suggest that all three measures (Russell's Key, the Watson & Thomas Rule 4, and the *Hs-Pt* Index) are roughly equivalent and perform at rates (*Po* = .61) that appear to be slightly above chance. Very different patterns of correct classification are noted in this same differential when female patients are studied in isolation. The Russell Key may demonstrate specific difficulty correctly identifying female schizophrenics (Carpenter & LeLieuvre, 1981), and the Watson and Thomas Rule 4 may show particular difficulty correctly identifying female BD patients (Watson & Thomas, 1968; Carpenter & LeLieuvre, 1981). Additionally, data from depressed (Trifiletti, 1982), hospitalized pain (Golden et al., 1979), and alcoholic patient groups (Norton & Romano, 1977) signal that overall performance of these three techniques may be sensitive to the specific comparison groups under consideration rather than exhibiting direct sensitivity to some aspect of BD per se.

SPECIAL ORGANICITY SCALES

An alternative approach to using established MMPI scales to identify BD would be to revert to item-level analysis and construct-specific BD-sensitive scales. MMPI research associated with the development of special BD scales has followed almost exclusively the model of treating the MMPI as a dependent variable for scale construction and as an independent variable for cross-validation. Since special scales have been developed to identify BD individuals, these also will be examined within the context of a hit rate type model. Tables 8–6 through 8–10 summarize these special scales. Several of the measures have different variants or versions, and for brevity only the most promising of the alternate versions appear in the tables. Because many studies also report incomplete data, classification percentages

TABLE 8–6.   CAUDALITY SCALE (Williams, 1952)

Study	Dx. Groups*	N Male	N Female	Age	Education	A	B	C	D	E	F	G
Williams (1952)	Caudal (T & P) vs. Frontal BD	116		36.4	—	-	-	-	-	-	-	na
Black & Black (1982)	Posterior vs. anterior lesions	58		~22.1	~11.9	+	+	-	+	+	+	na
Meier & French (1964)	Preoperative		40	—	—	-	+	-	-	-	+	na
Meier & French (1964)	Postoperative		39	—	—	-	+	-	-	-	+	na
Weighted mean						-	+	-	-	-	+	na

*Abbreviations: T&P = temporal and parietal; BD = brain-damaged patients.

and demographics were estimated on the basis of information presented.

In the vast majority of studies purporting to explore the development and cross-validation of special scales, the single greatest methodologic difficulty is a lack of attention to, or at least a lack of tendency to screen or to report, any consideration of patient profile validity. There is a frequent tendency to specify the basic subject parameters incompletely, sometimes omitting even reports of gender, age, and education. Certainly, when omissions of this nature occur, it then becomes impossible to consider the potential confounding effects that these moderator variables may bring to other aspects of the overall analysis.

Caudality Scale (Ca)

The earliest attempt to develop a brain-sensitive scale from the MMPI appeared with the work of Andersen and Hanvik (1950) and Friedman (1950). Extending the work of Friedman, Williams (1952) developed the Caudality Scale (Ca). For scale construction, Williams used 116 male patients with focal unilateral neurologic lesions. He divided the groups by lesion location (frontal or parietal/temporal) and attempted to identify MMPI items that discriminated between groups. After cross-validation 36 items that appeared to discriminate between the temporal and the frontal samples were identified; thus, scale performance was interpreted as being related to "caudality" in a broad sense rather than with parietofrontal localization specifically.

As can be seen from Table 8–6, only limited research exists on the Ca Scale. The derivation study (Williams, 1952), in comparing temporal and parietal with frontal patients, suggests an effective level of discrimination. This is a single and isolated finding, however, and the study is noted to have a broad range of methodologic difficulties. For example, the patient sample consists of only males of unknown educational level.

The Ca Scale is unique among the special BD scale efforts in that its research does not represent BD vs. non-BD or BD vs. "other" comparison groups. While the Ca Scale is of historical interest, the available literature suggests that the search for MMPI-related BD indicators must occur elsewhere.

CNS Scale

Hovey (1964) identified five items that he found to discriminate between BD and non-BD patients. This effort was the result of a two-step procedure. Following MMPI tradition, he initially identified items to discriminate BD empirically. His first scale was composed of 29 items that his brain-damaged group endorsed. On cross-validation, five appeared to retain discriminative ability. His findings suggested that a cutting score of 4 would correctly identify 50 percent of his CNS disease sample.

Hovey's 5-item CNS Scale for BD has received considerable interest in the two decades since it was initially presented (see Table 8–7). The bulk of this research compared BD patients with three specific diagnostic groups of patients: non-BD, some mixture of medical controls or somatic complaints, and psychiatric patients. Jortner (1965) also presented data that permit comparison between two groups with CNS dysfunction—a BD group and a group with multiple sclerosis (MS).

Among the three diagnostic group comparisons that can be compiled from the literature, the CNS Scale performs most poorly in the BD vs. non-BD class of study, at an intermediate level in the BD vs. medical patient comparison, and the best in the BD vs. psychiatric patient group of studies. The best levels of prediction across all patient comparison groups occurred in the identification of the control group. As can be seen in Table 8–7, the percentage of correct classification for the control groups ranged from .97 (Sillitti, 1982) to

| Comment | Cutting Score | Proportion Correct | | Base Rate | | Po |
		Ca	Control	Ca	Control	
Derivation study	>11	0.74	0.79	59%	41%	0.83
Missile wounds	>11	0.95	0.26	34	66	0.40
Quasi-experimental design	>8	0.78	—	100	0	—
Quasi-experimental design	>8	0.49	—	100	0	—
						0.47

TABLE 8–7.   CNS SCALE (Hovey, 1964)

Study	Dx. Groups†	N Male	Female	Age	Edu-cation	A	B	C	D	E	F	G
Hovey (1964)	BD vs. no CNS disease		126	—	—	-	-	-	-	+	+	na
Hovey (1964)	BD vs. no CNS disease		100	—	—	-	-	-	-	+	+	na
Maier & Abidin (1967)	Organic vs. nonorganic		146	~30.5	—	-	+	-	-	+	+	na
Marsh (1972)	Parkinsons vs. non-CNS	38	26	~58.8	~13.1	+	-	-	+	+	+	na
Siskind (1976)	BD vs. no demonstrable CNS dysfunc.	50		40.9	—	+	-	-	-	+	+	na
Siskind (1976)	BD vs. no demonstrable CNS dysfunc.		54	40.0	—	+	-	-	-	+	+	na
Weingold, Dawson, & Kael (1965)	Mixed BD vs. non-BD	53		—	—	-	+	-	-	+	+	na
Weighted mean												
Jortner (1965)	BD vs. peptic ulcer		50	—	—	-	-	-	+	+	+	na
Jortner (1965)	MS vs. peptic ulcer		50	—	—	-	-	-	+	+	+	na
Sand (1973)	BD vs. chronic pain		80	~44.2	~12.3	+	+	+	+	+	+	na
Sand (1973)	BD vs. cord		80	~37.5	~12.3	+	+	+	+	+	+	na
Upper & Seeman (1968)	Mixed BD vs. medical controls	44		—	—	-	-	-	-	+	+	na
Weighted mean												
Black (1974)	Brain damage vs. psychiatric	100		~21.9	~11.6	-	+	-	-	+	+	na
Dodge & Kolstoe (1971)	MS vs. conversion hysteria	9	18	~41.3	—	-	+	-	-	-	+	na
Graca et al. (1984)	Organic brain syndrome vs. schiz.	100		~49.9	—	-	-	-	-	+	+	na
Schwartz & Brown (1973)	Pseudoneurologic vs. MS	53	78	~40.6	—	-	+	-	+	+	+	na
Sillitti (1982)	Organic vs. functional	33	33	~39.1	—	-	-	-	-	+	+	na
Upper & Seeman (1968)	Mixed BD vs. paranoid schiz.	46		—	—	-	-	-	-	+	+	na
Weighted mean												
Jortner (1965)	BD vs. MS		50	—	—	-	-	-	+	+	+	na

*Estimated values.

†Abbreviations: BD = brain-damaged patients; CNS = central nervous system; exp = experimental; MS = multiple sclerosis patients; schiz. = schizophrenic patients; na = not applicable.

.55 (Sand, 1973), while the same percentages for the BD group ranged from .64 (Marsh, 1972; Jortner, 1965) to .10 (Graca et al., 1984). This tendency for the *CNS* scale to identify more accurately the control group is also characteristic of many of the special BD scales that have been derived from the MMPI. For this reason many of the authors examining the *CNS* Scale are cautious in recommending its use and are conservative in interpreting their own findings as having replicated the contention that there are five "brain-sensitive" items embedded in the MMPI.

Schizophrenic-Organic Scale (Sc-O)

Watson (1971) reasoned that since most ability-oriented tests of BD were not useful in separating organics and schizophrenics, the possibility that a personality measure such as the MMPI may be capable of separating these two groups warranted examination. Choosing 65 well-documented schizophrenics and 61 well-documented organics, he used item-analysis techniques to identify 80 items that appeared to separate the two groups at the $p < .05$ level or above. Of these items, 21, 7, and 2 respectively produced significant levels of

discrimination at $p < .01$, $p < .001$, and $p < .0001$. In addition to the original 80-item scale, Watson attempted to weight these items on the basis of their level of significance in the discrimination task, thus creating a weighted 80-item (long-form) scale. He also attempted to create a weighted short form of the *Sc-O* Scale by using the 30 items that demonstrated a significance level of $p < .01$ or better. The long, unweighted form is the most promising as an instrument for BD classification among the three *Sc-O* scales (Neuringer, Dombrowski, & Goldstein, 1975; Watson, 1971). Findings from the long, unweighted form of the scale are included in Table 8–8.

The bulk of research concerning the *Sc-O* Scale has dealt primarily with cross-validating the original scale of Watson (1971) and comparing the performance of BD vs. schizophrenics. At first glance, the *Sc-O* Scale appears to approach levels of some utility. Better scale performances were seen in comparing organic and schizophrenic patients than in comparing BD and other neurologic patient groups. Given the populations on which the scale was developed and its original purpose, this is hardly surprising. It does, however, serve to hint that other scales also may

Comment	Cutting Score	Proportion Correct		Base Rate		Po
		BD	Control	BD	Control	
Cross-validation	>3	—	—	53%	47%	—
2nd cross-validation	>3	>.50	0.86*	62	38	—
Considered raw K level	>3	0.21	—	47	53	—
Considered raw K level	>3	0.64	0.92	52	48	0.89
Flagged known BD	>3	0.15	0.86	26	74	0.29
Flagged known BD	>3	0.13	0.87	28	72	0.29
No psychiatric Dx	>3	0.28	0.72	52	47	0.53
						0.52
	>3	0.28	0.96	50	50	0.88
	>3	0.64	0.96	50	50	0.94
Mixed BD group	>3	0.13	0.55	50	50	0.22
Cord group significantly younger	>3	0.13	0.80	50	50	0.39
Statistically significantly different (p < .01)	>3	0.59	0.96	50	50	0.93
						0.60
	>3	0.24	0.88	50	50	0.67
One S lost	>3	0.29	0.67	54	46	0.50
Exp. > age than controls	>4	0.10	0.96	50	50	0.71
MS x disability rating	>3	0.44	0.77	53	47	0.69
Exp. > age; scale prorated	4	0.25	0.97	48	52	0.88
Statistically significantly different (p < .01)	>3	0.59	0.88	48	52	0.81
						0.72
MS pt. gr. not defined	>3	0.28	0.64	50	50	0.44

be quite specific in their application. However, for reasons that are not totally clear, the $Sc\text{-}O$ Scale appears to be particularly sensitive to gender effects. Indeed, a single attempt at cross-validation with female subjects (Watson, 1971) produced a discrepantly low identification rate. In part, this appears to be due to the loss of the Scale's ability to identify both female schizophrenics and organics. Two investigations, Sand (1973) and Golden et al. (1979), also examined the Scale's performance in discriminating BD patients from the other psychiatric patient groups. It is difficult to draw conclusions from these latter two studies in that the patterns of correct group classification appear to be sensitive to the same characteristic of the treatment or setting. For example, Sand's pain patients appear more similar, in terms of their $Sc\text{-}O$ Scale classification, to her cord patients than the pain patient groups reported by Golden et al. (1979).

For the most part, research on the $Sc\text{-}O$ Scale shares the methodologic characteristics and weaknesses of studies cited earlier in this chapter. Typically, the size of the sample under investigation and the adoption of a rather conventional design reflect major areas of strength and methodologic consistency through this portion of the literature. Almost without exception, delineation of basic subject parameters, the manner in which patient groups are established, and consideration of the role of moderator variables or the lack thereof reflect uniform weaknesses in these studies.

Psychiatric-Organic Scale (P-O)

Watson has been prolific in exploring the development of MMPI-based techniques for use as BD indicators. Feeling that his $Sc\text{-}O$ Scale failed to separate nonschizophrenic functional groups from BD groups, Watson and Plemel (1978) attempted to construct a scale to separate BD groups from patients suffering from general or all types of functional disorders. Watson and Plemel thus developed the Psychiatric-Organic (P-O) Scale. They identified 56 items ($p < .05$) that consistently differentiated 40 well-documented BD patients from 60 functional patients without evidence of organicity. Since it demonstrated overlap with all 13 of the standard MMPI scales and significantly correlated with all but Scales 1 and 3, Watson and Plemel felt that the P-O Scale reflected a wide range of psychopathology, and they hoped that it would differentiate general psychiatric patients without BD from BD patients. High scores on the P-O Scale should be associated with BD and low scores with functional psychopathology.

TABLE 8–8. *Sc-0* SCALE (Watson, 1971)

Study	Dx. Groups*	N Male	N Female	Age	Education	A	B	C	D	E	F	G
Watson (1971)	Organic vs. schiz.	126		~45.7	—	-	-	-	-	+	+	na
Watson (1971)	Chronic OBS vs. reactive schiz.	52		—	—	-	-	-	-	+	+	na
Watson (1971)	Organic vs. schiz.	34		~39.7	—	-	-	-	-	+	+	na
Watson (1971)	Organic vs. schiz.		22	—	—	-	-	-	-	+	+	na
Golden et al. (1979)	BD vs. schiz.	60		42.8	—	-	+	-	-	-	+	na
Graca et al. (1984)	OBS vs. schiz.		100	~49.9	—	-	-	-	-	+	+	na
Holland et al. (1975)	BD vs. schiz.	60		—	—	-	-	-	-	-	-	na
Neuringer et al. (1975)	BD vs. schiz.	94		<60	—	-	-	-	-	+	+	na
Watson (1973)	Organic vs. process schiz.	82		~38.5	~11.0	+	+	-	-	+	+	na
Weighted mean												
Sillitti (1982)	Organic vs. functional	33	33	~39.1	—	-	-	-	-	+	+	na
Golden et al. (1979)	BD vs. hospitalized pain	60		42.8	—	-	+	-	-	-	+	na
Sand (1973)	BD vs. pain		80	~44.3	~12.3	+	+	+	+	+	+	na
Sand (1973)	BD vs. cord		80	~37.5	~12.3	+	+	+	+	+	+	na
Weighted mean												
Ayers et al. (1975)	Nonschiz. vs. schiz.		43	—	—	-	-	-	-	+	+	na

*Abbreviations: ed = education; exp = experimental; Schiz. = schizophrenic patients; OBS = organic brain syndrome patients; BD = brain-damaged patients; cont. = controls; na = not applicable.

Table 8–9 examines *P-O* Scale performance and separates those studies comparing BD groups with "general functional" patients from those comparing BD groups with schizophrenic patients.

Even though the *P-O* Scale was not designed specifically to discriminate BD from schizophrenic individuals, the *Po* index performs as well as many of the other scales, including the *Sc-O* Scale. However, examination of the specific levels of group identification between BD and comparison patients suggests that this is a result of the level of identification of the comparison group. When the two studies examining BD and schizophrenic patients (Golden et al., 1979; Graca et al., 1984) are considered, the overall probability of correct classification (*Po*) is enhanced not by the *P-O* Scale's ability to discriminate BD but by its ability to identify the schizophrenic patients.

An examination of Table 8–9 also suggests that research with the *P-O* Scale shares common faults with much of the other research in the area. The majority of studies did not address the issue of profile validity, nor did they accommodate the potentially confounding effects of moderator variables in their groups. Several studies, including the derivation and cross-validation study (Watson & Plemel, 1978), used male subjects exclusively. No study ascertained the *P-O* Scale's ability to make the diagnostic discrimination using only female subjects. It was suggested previously that male and female subjects may be very different as far as special BD scale performance and the identification of BD is concerned.

TABLE 8–9. P-O SCALE (Watson & Plemel, 1978)

Study	Dx. Groups*	N Male	N Female	Age	Education	A	B	C	D	E	F	G
Watson & Plemel (1978)	Organic vs. mixed psychiatric	461		<60	—	-	+	-	-	+	+	na
Horton & Wilson (1981)	Organic vs. psychiatric	36	4	~58.0	~11.0	+	+	-	-	+	+	na
Sillitti (1982)	Organic vs. functional	33	33	~39.1	—	-	-	-	-	+	+	na
Watson, Gasser, Schaefer, Buranen, & Wold (1981)	Organic vs. mixed "functional"	180		~40.9	~11.9	+	+	-	+	+	+	na
Weighted mean												
Golden et al. (1979)	BD vs. schiz.	60		42.8	—	-	+	-	-	-	+	na
Graca et al. (1984)	OBS vs. schiz.		100	~49.9	—	-	-	-	-	+	+	na
Weighted mean												
Golden et al. (1979)	BD vs. hospitalized pain	60		42.8	—	-	+	-	-	-	+	na

*Abbreviations: Exp = experimental; na = not applicable; OBS = organic brain syndrome; schiz. = schizophrenic patients.

Comment	Cutting Score	Proportion Correct		Base Rate		Po
		BD	Control	BD	Control	
Age diff.; Ed. not cited	52.5	0.89	0.78	48%	52%	0.79
Houston cross-validation	52.5	0.77	0.65	50	50	0.69
BD significantly older than cont.	52.5	0.76	0.71	50	50	0.72
Anoka cross-validation	52.5	0.36	0.45	50	50	0.40
	—	0.53	0.73	50	50	0.66
Exp. > age than controls	>34	0.38	0.86	50	50	0.73
Data in Watson (1984)	—	0.67	0.63	50	50	0.64
Closest ind. replication	52.5	0.79	0.72	47	53	0.71
Data in Watson (1984)	52.5	0.57	0.69	28	72	0.42
						0.71
Exp. > age; scale prorated	33	0.40	0.88	48	52	0.75
	—	0.63	0.40	50	50	0.51
3 Sc-O versions failed	52.5	0.22	0.68	50	50	0.41
3 Sc-O versions failed	52.5	0.22	0.70	50	50	0.42
						0.44
BD or nonschiz. groups?	—	0.53	0.75	35	65	0.53

Pseudoneurologic Scale (PsN)

Shaw and Matthews (1965) attempted to develop a special MMPI scale to differentiate patients displaying pseudoneurologic symptomatology that would be suggestive, but not actually indicative of CNS dysfunction from patients whose symptoms are clearly attributable to BD. Using 100 subjects (50 BD and 50 pseudoneurologic patients), these investigators were able to identify and validate 17 items that appeared to discriminate these groups at the $p < .05$ level. The PsN Scale was keyed in a direction to load for pseudoneurologic rather than neurologic difficulty. As PsN Scale data are plotted in Table 8–10, the pseudoneurologic groups are charted as controls. This represents a reverse plotting to the design and keying of the PsN studies and PsN Scale; however, it allows a direct comparison with the other techniques discussed in this review.

Within the pseudoneurologic groups for which the PsN Scale was designed, overall Po ratings appear among the highest of the scales reviewed in this chapter and range from .67 to .91. Pantano and Schwartz's (1978) study, where base rates departed from the ideal 50/50, demonstrated a rather respectable Po of .79. The bulk of available research has been conducted as a direct comparison of groups for which the Scale was designed. In two studies (Graca et al., 1984; Sillitti, 1982) that examined the behavior of the scale in BD vs. schizophrenic patients, notable decreases in classification accuracy were seen.

Relative to other available special scales, the PsN Scale appears to function with a comparatively high percentage of correct classification in the patient groups for which it was designed, even when base rates depart from 50 percent. However, the PsN Scale has not apparently been evaluated

Comment	Cutting Score	Proportion Correct		Base Rate		Po
		BD	Control	BD	Control	
Derivation and cross-validation	27.5	0.77	0.52	15%	85%	0.22
	32.0	0.85	0.70	50	50	0.74
Exp. > age; scale prorated	23.0	0.63	0.65	48	52	0.62
Exp. > age & < IQ controls	29.5	0.73	0.65	17	83	0.30
						0.30
	—	0.57	0.77	50	50	0.71
Exp. > age than controls	>29	0.42	0.84	50	50	0.72
						0.72
	—	0.57	0.90	50	50	0.85

TABLE 8–10. *PsN* SCALE (Shaw & Matthews, 1965)

Study	Dx. Groups*	N Male	N Female	Age	Education	A	B	C	D	E	F	G
Shaw & Matthews (1965)	BD vs. pseudoneurologic	64		~31.2	~11.7	+	+	-	+	+	+	na
Shaw & Matthews (1965)	BD vs. pseudoneurologic	36		~29.5	~10.8	+	+	-	+	+	+	na
Dodge & Kolstoe (1971)	MS vs. conversion hysteria	9	18	~41.3	—	-	+	-	-	-	+	na
Pantano & Schwartz (1978)	Neurologic vs. pseudoneurologic	80		~39.7	—	+	+	-	+	+	+	na
Schwartz & Brown (1973)	MS vs. pseudoneurologic	53	78	~40.6	—	-	+	-	+	+	+	na
Schwartz & Brown (1973)	MS vs. pseudoneurologic	53	78	~40.6	—	-	+	-	+	+	+	na
Shaw (1966)	Epileptics vs. pseudoseizure	30		~27.0	—	-	-	-	-	-	+	na
Weighted mean												
Graca et al. (1984)	Organic brain syndrome vs. schiz.	100		~49.9	—	-	-	-	-	+	+	na
Sillitti (1982)	Organic vs. schiz.	33	33	~39.1	—	-	-	-	-	+	+	na
Weighted mean												

*Abbreviations: BD = brain-damaged patients; exp = experimental; MS = multiple sclerosis; schiz. = schizophrenic patients; na = not applicable.

across a wide variety of patient groups. There is a suggestion that the *PsN* Scale may be adversely affected by changing patient groups, particularly with respect to distinguishing BD patients from schizophrenic patients or perhaps other psychiatric patients. No specific attempt has been made to determine the role of gender differences as they relate to this scale's discriminative ability.

Epilepsy Scale (Ep)

Within the context of a complete psychological assessment Richards (1952) identified 56 MMPI items that in comparison with the MMPI standardization sample discriminated his military epileptics at the $p < .05$ level. In reviewing the content of the items endorsed by his "convulsive" sample, he reports that the epileptics "gave a picture of conscientiousness, competitiveness, and absence of humor. More of them worry about their health than do the normals, but fewer have financial and other worries." The *Ep* Scale generated limited interest, and only a single attempt at replication was located. Rosenman and Lucik (1970) attempted to replicate Richards' (1952) findings on a group of valid MMPI protocols from 16 epileptic and 16 BD state hospital patients. Their results did not support the use of the *Ep* Scale as a method for the differentiation of epileptic from nonepileptic controls.

The *Ep* scale does not appear to have been fully investigated since the derivation study was a composite of available military epileptics and a control group of normals derived from the literature. The replication study employed BD rather than normal controls. A successful replication test would require the use of appropriately matched epileptic and nonepileptic normal controls.

SUMMARY OF SPECIAL SCALES

The vast majority of studies attempting to develop BD screening techniques that rely on the MMPI have employed a direct group comparison technique. Reviewing the information in Tables 8–5 to 8–10, it is clear that the product of these efforts is highly sensitive to the context and specific circumstances in which they were derived.

Only limited attention has been given to the role of moderator variables by researchers in this area. The most systematic discussion of age, education, and intelligence as they affect special scale performance represents almost exclusively the effort of a single set of investigators examining the *Ca* and *P-O* Scales. For the most part these scales appear relatively insensitive to the effect of extraneous subject parameters. The *Ca* Scale does not demonstrate spurious effect related to age, education, or lateralization in BD groups (Horton, Lassen, & Wierinja, 1984). It may be sensitive to the effect of intelligence, since Horton, Timmons, and Golden (1982) report a negative correlation between *PIQ* scores and *Ca* scores in BD groups. This finding may reflect specific subject parameters as it was not seen on replication (Ryan & Robert, 1983). The *P-O* Scale likewise appears insensitive to the effects of education (Timmons & Horton, 1982), intelligence (Horton et al., 1982), and lateralization in BD groups (Horton, 1983). The *P-O* Scale may, however, demonstrate age effects with older BD patients showing higher *P-O* scores than younger BD patients (Horton & Timmons, 1982). When alcoholic patients were examined, *P-O* Scale age effects were not seen (Horton, Ivey, & Anilane, 1985).

One reason for the apparent lack of consistency between scales may be related to the issue that BD is not a unitary concept. However, in many circumstances these scales produced higher correct classification rates in control (nonBD) groups than in BD groups, which suggests that the MMPI is simply not particularly sensitive to the presence of BD. Thus, the empirical derivation of these scales reflects differences between target and comparison

Comment	Cutting Score	Proportion Correct		Base Rate		*Po*
		BD	Control	BD	Control	
Derivation study	>6	0.75	0.81	50%	50%	0.80
Cross-validation	>6	0.78	0.67	50	50	0.70
	>6	0.71	0.85	48	52	0.81
Exp. > age than controls	—	0.44	0.80	63	38	0.79
	>6	0.71	0.59	53	47	0.67
Extr. grps. on cutting score	< 4; >9	0.87	0.90	53	47	0.91
	>6	0.93	0.73	50	50	0.78
						0.78
Exp. > age than controls	<6	0.40	0.58	50	50	0.49
Exp. > age; scale prorated	>6	0.63	0.56	48	52	0.57
						0.52

groups that represent both the MMPI's sensitivity to psychiatric populations (from which samples are taken for comparison in BD studies) and idiosyncratic differences between BD and comparison groups in the studies in which BD scales are derived.

Item composition for each of the five special "generic" BD scales discussed earlier is illustrated in Table 8–11. Item numbers (Form G) are keyed to reflect a BD endorsement direction. A total of 171 items load on at least one of the five BD scales that have received major attention in the literature. Yet of this number, only 14 items (3, 38, 51, 95, 137, 159, 192, 212, 226, 274, 313, 389, 498, and 520) or 8 percent are repeated on more than one of the scales *and* are scored in the same direction. No single item is repeated on more than two of five scales, and 8 (5 percent) items (8, 163, 171, 180, 188, 253, 407, and 412) are actually keyed in opposite directions on different scales.

DIRECT COMPARISON OF AVAILABLE TECHNIQUES

Table 8–12 reflects the limited effort to contrast a variety of these techniques in a side-by-side fashion using identical BD/comparison groups. Three major comparison efforts are reported: Graca et al. (1984), Golden et al. (1979), and Sillitti (1982). Within each study the individual MMPI techniques for the identification of BD are presented in order of decreasing magnitude, first on the basis of the percentage of correct identification of BD subjects (sensitivity) and second on the basis of the *Po* calculation. All three studies made BD vs. schizophrenic comparisons. In addition, the Golden et al. (1979) study examined the ability of various MMPI techniques to discriminate BD patients from hospitalized pain patients.

Rates for the correct identification of BD patients range between .80 (Golden et al., 1979; *F* Scale) to .00 (Graca et al., 1984; high-point codes). Probability of correct classification rates ranged from .89 (Sillitti, 1982; Hovey's *CNS* Scale) to .44 (Golden et al., 1979; Russell Key).

When these techniques are compared across different studies, no single pattern of superiority of any one technique emerges. For instance, Graca et al. (1984) found that Watson and Thomas' Rule 4 appeared to be one of the stronger discriminative techniques. In the other two efforts investigating this technique (Golden et al., 1979; Sillitti, 1982), not only did Rule 4 fail to live up to the former study's rate of correct BD identification of .60 (*Po* = .57), but it also performed at a relatively weaker level in comparison with other commonly investigated measures such as the *P-O* Scale (Watson & Plemel, 1978) or the Russell Key. When considering the BD vs. schizophrenic distinction, the *P-O* Scale seemed to outperform the *Sc-O* Scale slightly across all three studies in ability to identify BD patients.

Certainly, there are isolated promising findings (i.e., .80 BD identification by the *F* Scale alone in the Golden et al. [1979] study), yet we have observed repeatedly that these findings are very sensitive to moderator variables associated with, among other things, the specific patient mixes in these studies. Frequently, the control group hit rate is greater than the BD group hit rate, which supports the contention that these measures, at least in some specific situations, tend to discriminate psychopathology rather than BD per se. Also, as seen previously in Table 8–1, when subtypes of schizophrenics were reported, quite different BD vs. schizophrenic patterns were noted between reactive and process schizophrenic groups. The inconsistent performance of these special scales,

TABLE 8–11. SPECIAL SCALE ITEM LOADING
(FORM G)

Item No.	P-O	Sc-O	Ca	PsN*	CNS	Item No.	P-O	Sc-O	Ca	PsN*	CNS	Item No.	P-O	Sc-O	Ca	Item No.	P-O	Sc-O	Ca
3	T			T		173				T		305	F			499			T
5		T				175				T		307	F			502		T	
7		F				176		T				308	F			507		T	
8			F	T		179	F					309		T		510	T		
9	F					180		F	T			310	T			511	F		
10					F	182				T		311	F			512			T
11		F				184		F				313		T	T	513			F
21	F					187	F					317	F			515		T	
23		F				188		F		T		325	F			520	T	T	
28			T			189				T		328		F		521		T	
38	F		F			190				T		329	T			523			F
39			T			191	F					338			T	531	F		
41	F					192	F				F	343			T	532		T	
46		F				195	F					344		F		537		T	
47			F			198	T					345		F		540	F		
51	F				F	205		F				347		T		544			T
56		F				207	T					354		F		549	F		T
57		F				212	F	F				357		F		551			T
61	F					217	F					361			T	553		F	
68			T			224	F					366	F			558		T	
69		F				225	F					372		T		559		F	
71		T				226	F	F				379	T			560			T
76			T			230				T		380		T		561		T	
77		F				236			T			385		F		562		T	
78		F				237				T		388		F					
80		T				238				F		389		T	T				
86	F					239			T			390		T					
90	F					242			F			394		T					
94			T			243				T		397	F						
95	T	T				248		F				401		T					
96	T					249		T				403		T					
106	F					253		T		F		407		T	F				
108				F		256		F				412		T	F				
114				F		260		F				416		F					
123		F				264	T					417		T					
129	F					266	F					420		F					
132	T					273			T			425	F						
133	T					274		F		F		450			F				
137	T	T				276		T				451		T					
142			T			277	T					468	F						
147			T			278		F				479		T					
149		F				279		F				480		F					
156	F					283		T				482	T						
158	F					284	F					488		T					
159			T		T	285		T				492		F					
163		T	F			286		F				494		F					
168	F					287	T					495		T					
170	T					288		F				497		T					
171		F			T	291		F				498	T	T					

*Keyed in BD direction.

even relative to each other, illustrates an important point: it simply may not be possible to select a single "most sensitive" index to BD. Finally, two of the studies charted in Table 8–12 base their results on all male samples, while Sillitti (1982) reported findings from both males and females. None of these direct comparison studies reported findings from an all female population.

FUTURE DIRECTIONS

The majority of the research reviewed here represented an attempt to employ or develop MMPI measures for the discrimination of BD. This effort was conducted under optimal conditions representing nearly equivalent base rates and the specification of dichotomous patient groups in a known setting. These conditions depart substantially from those that could be expected in an actual clinical situation. Even in these relatively ideal circumstances, success levels were noted that, for purposes of prediction, were only marginally above chance. Also, when empirically derived scale items are examined, as they were in Table 8–12, little item consistency across scales is noted. It may be that the MMPI simply does not contain an item pool that is sensitive to BD in any reliable fashion. Certainly, BD groups were not included among the psychiatric patient groups that participated in the original item selection studies. This issue will certainly overshadow additional research attempts in the area.

In spite of the fact that the ultimate utility of the MMPI as a technique for the measure of BD must be viewed with very guarded optimism, future research may be valuable if both BD and comparison groups are specified with greater precision than they have been in the past. Rates of correct classification must accompany the more conventional presentation of statistical significance. These studies frequently employ a large enough sample that a calculation of effect size may be more useful than a measure of significance in determining clinical utility, since as sample sizes increase the actual magnitude of difference necessary to produce a statistically significant finding may be relatively quite small and of limited clinical utility. Future research also should incorporate a validity screen or at the very least some report as to whether the profiles under consideration meet a criterion of minimal validity. Parameters of Scales

L, F, and K may not be equal to this task, and supplemental methods of examining profile validity and consistency of item endorsement may be particularly meaningful in BD patient groups (Greene, 1980, pp. 51–68). Finally, there is a strong suspicion that gender may be an important variable in questions concerning the behavior of the MMPI and BD groups. Future studies should be constructed and reported with an accommodation to the gender issue.

SUMMARY

A rather extensive literature has been tabulated in the above tables. Several questions can be raised regarding the efficacy of employing the MMPI for use with BD patients and the ability of the MMPI to contribute uniquely to the diagnostic identification of these individuals. First, can specific MMPI characteristics be of aid in identifying BD? Second, is the MMPI sensitive to BD directly? Third, do BD patient groups produce valid MMPI profiles? Fourth, can the MMPI provide clinical data on the emotional consequences of BD?

Can Specific MMPI Characteristics Be of Aid in Discriminating BD?

Identifying BD individuals clinically or with the MMPI is not necessarily difficult when the cases are relatively profound and/or the history of injury is clear. Application of an MMPI marker for BD is redundant if the patient demonstrates a .9 Halstead-Reitan Battery Impairment Index, a positive history of cerebrovascular compromise and a right hemiparesis, or some other compelling aspect of clinical presentation. In those situations, a technique such as the MMPI, which is primarily designed for the assessment of personality variables, may perform the task as well as a multitude of other more specialized instruments. For a screening technique to be truly effective, however, it must demonstrate differential discriminative ability in the equivocal clinical case.

Table 8–1 suggests that all scales are not equally sensitive to BD. Even when the standard clinical scales are employed, the magnitude of effect size differences varies substantially depending on what clinical group is used for comparison. For instance, it makes sense that if BD and depressed patients are compared, Scale 2 differences should separate the groups, even if some degree of depression is a secondary consequence of BD. Indeed, the MMPI has been useful historically in the BD vs. depression differential diagnosis, particularly since depression can be difficult to distinguish from BD on many neuropsychological measures. On the other hand, the large differences on Scale 5 would not be as easily predicted. Many investigators also have explored the behavior of

TABLE 8–12.   DIRECT COMPARISON OF PREVIOUSLY REVIEWED TECHNIQUES

Study	Dx. Groups*	N Male	N Female	Age	Edu-cation	A	B	C	D	E	F	G
Graca et al. (1984)	Organic brain syndrome vs. schiz.	100		49.9†	—	-	-	-	-	+	+	-
Golden et al. (1979)	BD vs. schiz.	60		42.8	—	-	+	-	-	-	+	-
Golden et al. (1979)	BD vs. hospitalized pain	60		42.8	—	-	+	-	-	-	+	-
Sillitti (1982)	Organic vs. schiz.	33	33	39.1†	—	-	-	-	-	+	+	-

*Abbreviations: BD = brain-damaged patients; schiz. = schizophrenic patients; unwghtd lng = unweighted long form.
†Age of groups significantly different.
§P-O Scale prorated from MMPI Form R, 399 items.
˝Sc-O Scale (unweighted long) prorated from MMPI Form R, 399 items.

the *F* Scale as an indicator of BD, and this scale has been incorporated into several techniques purporting to construct schemes to identify BD such as Russell's (1975) Key.

Despite differences of significant magnitude on some of the standard MMPI scales between BD and non-BD patient groups, these scale differences do not produce characteristic codetypes that could be used in a discrimination effort. While primary combinations of some Scales such as *2* or *8* seem more likely to occur in codetypes in the BD groups, the actual frequency of the most common code-types in the BD groups that have been reported is too low to be of much practical utility. The most frequently occurring codetype (*1-2-3*) occurred at a rate of 11.2 percent in Wooten's (1983b) mixed neuropsychologically impaired group. Among the most frequently reported codetypes, frequency rates range between only 5 and 10 percent.

It seems from this that the MMPI presentation of BD groups is likely to be quite varied. Related to

this is the observation that even in designated BD groups there is not any singular pattern or code-type that can be deemed as characteristic of BD. There are probably not specific MMPI characteristics that occur with enough frequency to be of aid in discriminating BD.

Is the MMPI Directly Sensitive to the Presence of BD?

The question of the MMPI's sensitivity to BD is closely related to the issue of whether BD is a unitary construct. If all BD patients are the same, then there may be consistent personality or other characteristics that are associated with BD and for which derived MMPI indices could demonstrate sensitivity. The presence of BD-specific characteristics such as these would serve to separate various types of BD from other "functional" psychiatric disturbances. If any or all of these characteristics were seen in a patterned or orderly fashion in BD,

Technique	Cutting Score	Proportion Correct		Bass Rate		Po
		BD	Control	BD	Control	
Hs-Pt Index (Watson)	>-4	0.60	0.62	50%	50%	0.61
Rule 4: (Watson & Thomas)	<40	0.60	0.54	50	50	0.57
F Scale (Golden)	<67	0.56	0.60	50	50	0.58
Russell Key (Russell)	—	0.56	0.54	50	50	0.55
P-O Scale (Watson & Plemel)	>29	0.42	0.84	50	50	0.72
PsN Scale (Shaw & Matthews)	<6	0.40	0.58	50	50	0.49
Sc-O Scale (Watson) unwghtd lng	>34	0.38	0.86	50	50	0.73
Sc Scale (Ayers)	<30	0.32	0.82	50	50	0.64
Sc Scale (Russell)	<65	0.32	0.82	50	50	0.64
L Scale (Korman & Blumberg)	>6	0.32	0.72	50	50	0.53
Psychotic triad (Holland)	<59	0.28	0.86	50	50	0.67
Hovey's Scale	>4	0.10	0.96	50	50	0.71
1-3-9 (Gilberstat & Duker)	—	0.00	1.00	50	50	—
1-9/9-1 (Webb)	—	0.00	1.00	50	50	—
2-9/9-2 (Webb)	—	0.00	1.00	50	50	—
2-9/9-2 (Schwartz)	—	0.00	1.00	50	50	—
F Scale	60	0.80	0.56	50	50	0.65
Russell Key (Russell)	—	0.63	0.20	50	50	0.44
P-O Scale (Watson & Plemel)	—	0.57	0.77	50	50	0.71
Sc-O Scale (Watson) unwghtd lng	—	0.53	0.73	50	50	0.66
Rule 4: (Watson & Thomas)	—	0.47	0.50	50	50	0.48
F Scale	50	0.72	0.67	50	50	0.69
Sc-O Scale (Watson) unwghtd lng	—	0.63	0.40	50	50	0.51
Russell Key (Russell)	—	0.63	0.03	50	50	0.39
P-O Scale (Watson & Plemel)	—	0.57	0.90	50	50	0.85
Rule 4: (Watson & Thomas)	—	0.47	0.47	50	50	0.47
Sc Scale	77	0.75	0.76	48	52	0.75
§*P-O* Scale (Watson & Plemel)	23	0.63	0.65	48	52	0.63
PsN Scale (Shaw & Matthews)	7	0.63	0.56	48	52	0.57
Russell Key (Russell)	—	0.59	0.32	48	52	0.45
Rule 4: (Watson & Thomas)	<45	0.50	0.59	48	52	0.53
//*Sc-O* Scale (Watson)	33	0.40	0.88	48	52	0.76
Hovey's Scale (Hovey)	4	0.25	0.97	48	52	0.89

or as a subset of characteristics that reliably appear associated with BD, then they might be used as indicators to flag the target BD groups. In this case, the MMPI should be able to identify the BD patient and BD as a construct directly, regardless of the population in which the patient with BD may be embedded.

The vast majority of the work presented here appears to make the implicit assumption that BD is a unitary construct in spite of ample evidence that different types of BD may be demonstrated in very different fashions. BD groups frequently represented mixes of different specific diagnoses, and often they were identified in the most generic fashion as "organics."

One overwhelming conclusion from the literature is that, to varying degrees, the BD vs. non-BD MMPI-based distinction is a result of the correct classification of the non-BD group. This artifact causes the MMPI to appear to be more sensitive to the generic BD comparisons than it actually is. This factor may have encouraged the proliferation of much of the research effort to identify an "engram" of BD-sensitive items embedded somewhere in the

MMPI. When the MMPI does appear capable of making the BD vs. non-BD distinction, it is operating within the context of very specific group comparisons, preselection factors, and optimal base rates.

Attempts to replicate the discriminative ability of a specific scale or index usually have met with limited success. Another aspect of this issue can be seen in Table 8–6. When similar groups are used for direct comparison of different discrimination techniques, optimal cutting scores for the same measures appear to fluctuate. Such outcomes serve to underscore the very specific study by study nature of these findings.

Another aspect of the replication issue from the standpoint of seeking specific individual items that are somehow sensitive to BD examination is illustrated in Table 8–12. Little consistency in the item composition between empirically derived BD scales was observed. If inherent characteristics of the MMPI were sensitive to BD, some uniformity in the empirical selection of items for special BD scales certainly should be present. Retrospectively, it could be argued that the MMPI should not be sensitive to BD since items of specific demonstrable sensitivity to BD were not included in the original item pool and as a construct BD does not display any singular and reliable psychopathologic covariant on which the MMPI can reliably key.

The final consideration regarding the utility of MMPI identification procedures for the discrimination of BD is also empirical and concerns the degree to which they can outperform the base rate. A great deal of effort has been expended on the development of various actuarial techniques to discriminate BD from non-BD groups (Tables 8–3 through 8–12). If the MMPI were directly sensitive to BD, then we would expect that a minimal decline in performance would occur on replication. While isolated (single study) successes of spectacular magnitude were noted, it appears that the best methods, on average, would be pressed to identify BD patients with a sensitivity level of 60 percent. Po levels can slightly run higher, but almost without exception, studies of this kind are making their test in the face of equal or near equal base rates. This, of course, is not a problem so long as the clinical sites in which these techniques are employed have nearly equivalent base rates; however, the likelihood of this distribution is, of course, low.

On the basis of presently available research, the MMPI does not seem to be sensitive to the characteristics of BD directly, at least as they appear in the generic or mixed BD groups that have been the most thoroughly investigated. Horton, Timmons, and Sloop (1983) compared age- and education-matched "old alcoholics" with cerebrovascular accident patients and matched "young alcoholics" with head trauma patients. They report P-O Scale differences in the young BD groups but no differences in the old groups, and they conclude that some BD subtypes may differ in the P-O Scale performance on the basis of BD subtype etiology. It is conceivable that the MMPI may be sensitive for some specific subtype of BD, but not for others. In considering epilepsy, the MMPI does not appear to be directly sensitive to BD characteristics but to the presence of psychiatric distress that can, but not necessarily does, accompany an epileptic clinical presentation.

Do BD Patient Groups Produce Valid MMPI Profiles?

Issues concerning the validity of the BD-endorsed MMPI profile are not easily addressed from the available literature. The overwhelming majority of work done to date neither reported nor acknowledged any consideration of the profiles' validity before analysis or group comparison was attempted. BD patients may generally not be capable of producing MMPI profiles that meet conventional validity considerations, or they may have a unique validity scale configuration. At least in the case of the F Scale, there is reason to suspect that BD groups are characteristically different than non-BD groups. In addition, it is clear that in certain BD vs. non-BD comparison situations, the K Scale, and perhaps to a much lesser degree the L Scale, also can reflect intergroup differences. Krug (1967) has reported that BD individuals gave discrepant responses to the 16 repeated questions in the MMPI. He concluded that there may be real questions regarding the overall reliability of MMPI endorsement for any of the items on the MMPI by BD groups. If BD profiles are demonstrating differential reliabilities of item endorsements, these could adversely impinge on the stability of the BD vs. non-BD discriminative capability.

On the basis of much of the present literature, the question of whether BD patients characteristically produce valid MMPI profiles must remain without a conclusive answer. Of different BD subgroups, some may and some may not produce valid profiles. Differences may appear when scales other than the conventional L, F, K Scale indices of validity are considered.

Can the MMPI Provide Clinical Data on the Emotional Consequences of BD?

Finally, of the other problems that have been considered in this chapter, the task of assessing BD-related emotional sequelae may be the easiest for the MMPI to achieve and the one for which it is best suited. As long as the emotional consequence of BD or cognitive decline is not different for MMPI purposes from emotional distress of a non-BD etiology, this question does not require the MMPI to be directly sensitive to BD. It may be that the MMPI is quite capable of demonstrating these effects.

We have seen previously that when the MMPI is asked to discriminate BD groups on the basis of many standard and derived measures, discriminative success frequently relates to the specific characteristics of the non-BD group. There are several ways to approach the question of whether the MMPI is sensitive to psychopathology independent of BD (i.e., if a BD individual elevates the MMPI so as to signal psychopathologic distress, can that profile be interpreted in the same manner as one that did not involve the presence of BD?). Holland, Lowenfeld, and Wadsworth (1975) note that the derived Sc-O Scale is "heavily weighted for severity of emotional disturbance" and should not be used with patients who are both BD and schizophrenic. They found that discriminative ability was lost when the degree of emotional disturbance was held constant between groups and argue that the Sc-O Scale should be restricted to use in groups whose diagnosis represents either BD or schizophrenia, but not both. The implications of these findings are important in considering the emotional consequences of BD. When BD and psychiatric problems are found to coexist, technology developed to identify BD fails because of the MMPI's sensitivity to the presence of psychopathology. It seems once again that the MMPI is sensitive to the presence of psychopathology, which may coexist with BD, and that it is not apparently sensitive to BD in the absence of psychopathology.

There may be a problem, however, if psychopathology antedates the occurrence of BD. In that case, testing a BD group for the presence of psychopathology may yield findings either because the MMPI is sensitive to the presence of premorbid psychopathologic condition, or because the MMPI is sensitive to the emotional consequences of BD-related compromise. This is precisely the condition reported by Dikmen et al. (1983) in studying the MMPI profiles of epileptics. They note that the MMPI was not sensitive to differences between patients of differing seizure type. When the same patient sample was regrouped on the basis of psychiatric history, however, clear MMPI differences between groups were observed in the expected direction.

Holland et al. (1975) report that special scale discrimination ability was lost when psychiatric history was taken into account. In the Dikmen et al. (1983) epilepsy study, accounting for history of psychopathology produced otherwise unseen group differences on the MMPI. In both cases, at least in terms of MMPI measures, BD and the presence of psychopathology appear to be independent.

If the MMPI remains sensitive to the presence of psychopathology independent of BD, and if there is not a uniform or necessary emotional response to BD, then the picture of codetype frequency in Table 8–2 can be easily explained. Codetypes containing Scales 2 and 8 were relatively common, but no one codetype appeared with enough reliability for BD related diagnostic utility. It may be that when the MMPI elevates in BD groups it is simply registering the distress of loss, accommodation, and adjustment that is part of the coping process. In addition, it also may be that BD groups exhibit a variety of premorbid psychopathologic findings. These patterns may take multiple forms, the variability of which is seen in Table 8–2.

The present literature can be interpreted as suggesting that the MMPI is sensitive to psychopathology independent of the presence of BD. This in turn implies that the MMPI may have the capacity to provide clinical data on the emotional consequences of BD. In some cases the MMPI may be sensitive to the emotional effects of BD, and in other cases MMPI findings in BD groups may reflect the presence of premorbid psychopathology. In order to clarify this issue, the presence of premorbid psychopathology must be accounted for in the BD groups being studied.

ACKNOWLEDGMENT

We wish to thank Dr. Pamela A. Farr for her comments and review of this manuscript.

REFERENCES

American Psychiatric Association. (1968). *Diagnostic and statistical manual of mental disorders* (2nd ed.). Washington, D.C.: Author.

American Psychiatric Association. (1987). *Diagnostic and statistical manual of mental disorders* (3rd ed., revised). Washington, D.C.: Author.

Andersen, A. L., & Hanvik, L. J. (1950). The psychometric localization of brain lesions: The differential effect of frontal and parietal lesions on MMPI profiles. *Journal of Clinical Psychology, 6,* 177–180.

Ayers, J., Templer, D. I., & Ruff, C. F. (1975). The MMPI in the differential diagnosis of organicity vs. schizophrenia: Empirical findings and a somewhat different perspective. *Journal of Clinical Psychology, 31,* 685–686.

Black, F. W. (1974). Use of the MMPI with patients with recent war-related head injuries. *Journal of Clinical Psychology, 30,* 571–573.

Black, F. W., & Black, I. L. (1982). Anterior-posterior locus of lesion and personality: Support for the caudality hypothesis. *Journal of Clinical Psychology, 38,* 468–477.

Boll, T. J. (1978). Diagnosing brain impairment. In B. B. Wolman (Ed.), *Clinical diagnosis of mental disorders: A handbook* (pp. 601–675). New York: Plenum.

Buckholz, D. (1984). Use of the MMPI with brain damaged psychiatric patients. *Clinical Psychology Review, 4,* 693–701.

Carpenter, C. B., & LeLieuvre, R. B. (1981). The effectiveness of three MMPI scoring keys in differentiating brain-damaged women from schizophrenic women. *Clinical Neuropsychology, 3 (4),* 18–20.

Clopton, J. R. (1979). Development of special MMPI scales. In C. S. Newmark (Ed.), *MMPI: Clinical and research trends.* (pp. 354–372). New York: Praeger.

Cohen, J. (1977). *Statistical power analysis for the behavioral sciences* (rev. ed.). San Diego: Academic Press.

Dikmen, S., Hermann, B. P., Wilensky, A. J., & Rainwater, G. (1983). Validity of the Minnesota Multiphasic Personality Inventory (MMPI) to psychopathology in patients with epilepsy. *Journal of Nervous and Mental Disease, 171,* 114–122.

Dikmen, S., & Reitan, R. M. (1974). MMPI correlates of dysphasic language disturbances. *Journal of Abnormal Psychology, 83,* 675–679.

Dodge, G. R., & Kolstoe, R. H. (1971). The MMPI in differentiating early multiple sclerosis and conversion hysteria. *Psychological Reports, 29,* 155–159.

Doehring, D. G., & Reitan, R. M. (1960). MMPI performance of aphasic and nonaphasic brain-damaged patients. *Journal of Clinical Psychology, 16,* 307–309.

Farr, S. P., Greene, R. L., & Fisher-White, S. (1986). Disease process, onset, and course and its relationship to neuropsychological performance. In S. B. Filskov & T. J. Boll (Eds.), *Handbook of clinical neuropsychology* (Vol. 2, pp. 213–253). New York: John Wiley and Sons.

Friedman, S. H. (1950). *Psychometric effects of frontal and parietal lobe brain damage.* Unpublished doctoral dissertation. University of Minnesota, Minneapolis.

Gilberstadt, H., & Duker, J. (1965). *A handbook for clinical and actuarial MMPI interpretation.* Philadelphia: W. B. Saunders.

Golden, C. J., Sweet, J. J., & Osman, D. C. (1979). The diagnosis of brain-damage by the MMPI: A comprehensive evaluation. *Journal of Personality Assessment, 43,* 138–142.

Graca, J., Hutzell, R. R., Gaffney, J. M., & Whiddon, M. (1984). A comparison of the effectiveness of MMPI indices in the discrimination of brain-damaged and schizophrenic patients. *Journal of Clinical Psychology, 40,* 427–431.

Greene, R. L. (1980). *The MMPI: An interpretive manual*. Philadelphia: Grune & Stratton.

Greene, R. L., & Farr, S. P., (1986, October). *MMPI correlates of closed head injury*. Paper presented at the Seventh Annual Traumatic Head Injury Conference, Braintree, MA.

Hathaway, S. R., & Meehl, P. E. (1951). *An atlas for the clinical use of the MMPI*. The University of Minnesota Press: Minneapolis.

Heaton, R. K., Baade, L. E., & Johnson, K. L. (1978). Neuropsychological test results associated with psychiatric disorders in adults. *Psychological Bulletin, 85*, 141–162.

Hermann, B. P. (1981). Deficits in neuropsychological functioning and psychopathology in persons with epilepsy: A rejected hypothesis revisited. *Epilepsia, 22*, 161–167.

Hermann, B. P., Dikmen, S., Schwartz, M. S., & Karnes, W. E. (1982). Interictal psychopathology in patients with ictal fear: A quantitative investigation. *Neurology, 32*, 7–11.

Hermann, B. P., Dikmen, S., & Wilensky, A. J. (1982). Increased psychopathology associated with multiple seizure types: Fact or artifact? *Epilepsia, 23*, 587–596.

Hermann, B. P., Schwartz, M. S., Karnes, W. E., & Vahdat, P. (1980). Psychopathology in Epilepsy: Relationship of seizure type to age at onset. *Epilepsia, 21*, 15–23.

Hermann, B. P., Schwartz, M. S., Whitman, S., & Karnes, W. E. (1981). Psychosis and Epilepsy: Seizure-type comparisons and high-risk variables. *Journal of Clinical Psychology, 37*, 714–721.

Holland, T. R., Levi, M., & Watson, C. G. (1981). MMPI basic scales vs. two-point codes in the discrimination of psychopathological groups. *Journal of Clinical Psychology, 37*, 394–396.

Holland, T. R., Lowenfeld, J., & Wadsworth, H. M. (1975). MMPI indices in the discrimination of brain-damaged and schizophrenic groups. *Journal of Consulting and Clinical Psychology, 43*, 426.

Holland, T. R., & Watson, C. G. (1980). Multivariate analysis of WAIS-MMPI relationships among brain-damaged, schizophrenic, neurotic, and alcoholic patients. *Journal of Clinical Psychology, 36*, 352–359.

Horton, A. M., Jr. (1983). Effects of lateralized brain damage on the Psychiatric-Organic (P-O) special scale of the MMPI. *Clinical Neuropsychology, 5*, 150.

Horton, A. M., Jr., Ivey, A., & Anilane, J. (1985). Effects of age on the Psychiatric-Organic (P-O) special scale of the Minnesota Multiphasic Personality Inventory (MMPI). *Clinical Gerontologist, 4*, 45–48.

Horton, A. M., Jr., Lassen, G., & Wierinja, R. (1984, October). *Age and education effects on the Caudality (Ca) scale of the Minnesota Multiphasic Personality Inventory (MMPI)*. Paper presented at the Fourth Annual Meeting of the National Academy of Neuropsychologists, San Diego.

Horton, A. M., Jr., & Timmons, M. (1982). Age effects on the Psychiatric-Organic (P-O) special scale of the Minnesota Multiphasic Personality Inventory (MMPI). *Clinical Neuropsychology, 4*, 108(abstract).

Horton, A. M., Jr., Timmons, M., & Golden C. J. (1982). How intelligent are organicity scales of the MMPI? *Clinical Neuropsychology, 4*, 170–171.

Horton, A. M., Jr., Timmons, M., & Sloop, E. W. (1983). Behavorial assessment of organic mental disorders: The role of the MMPI P-O Scale for subgroups of brain-damaged patients. *Clinical Neuropsychology, 5*, 43(abstract).

Horton, A. M., Jr., & Wilson, F. M. (1981). Cross-validation of the Psychiatric-organic (P-O) special scale of the MMPI in a VA domiciliary setting. *Clinical Neuropsychology, 3*, 1–3.

Hovey, H. B. (1964). Brain lesions and five MMPI items. *Journal of Consulting Psychology, 28*, 78–79.

Hovey, H. B., Kooi, K. A., & Thomas, M. H. (1959). MMPI profiles of epiletics. *Journal of Consulting Psychology, 23*, 155–159.

Jordan, E. J., Jr. (1963). MMPI profiles in epileptics: A further evaluation. *Journal of Consulting Psychology, 27*, 267–269.

Jortner, S. (1965). A test of Hovey's MMPI scale for CNS disorder. *Journal of Clinical Psychology, 21*, 285.

Klove, H., & Doehring, D. G. (1962). MMPI in epileptic groups with differential etiology. *Journal of Clinical Psychology, 18*, 149–153.

Korman, M., & Blumberg, S. (1963). Comparative efficiency of some tests of cerebral damage. *Journal of Consulting Psychology, 27*, 303–309.

Krug, R. S. (1967). MMPI response inconsistency of brain damaged individuals. *Journal of Clinical Psychology, 23*, 366.

Lachar, D., Lewis, R., & Kupke, T. (1979). MMPI in differentiation of temporal lobe and nontemporal lobe epilepsy: Investigation of three levels of test performance. *Journal of Consulting and Clinical Psychology, 47*, 186–188.

Lewis, R., Lachar, D., Voelker, S., & Vidergar, L. (1984). MMPI diagnosis of psychosis in epilepsy. *Journal of Clinical Neuropsychology, 6*, 224–228.

Mack, J. L. (1979). The MMPI and neurological dysfunction. In C. S. Newmark (Ed.), *MMPI: Clinical and research trends* (pp. 53–79). New York: Praeger.

Maier, L. R., & Abidin, R. R. (1967). Validation attempt of Hovey's five-item MMPI index for CNS disorders. *Journal of Consulting Psychology, 31*, 542.

Marsh, G. G. (1972). Parkinsonian patients' scores on Hovey's MMPI scale for CNS disorder. *Journal of Clinical Psychology, 28*, 529–530.

Matthews, C. G., Dikmen, S., & Harley, J. P. (1977). Age of onset and psychometric correlates of MMPI profiles in major motor epilepsy. *Diseases of the Nervous System, 38*, 173–176.

Matthews, C. G., & Klove, H. (1968). MMPI performances in major motor, psychomotor and mixed seizure classifications of known and unknown etiology. *Epilepsia, 9*, 43–53.

Meehl, P. E., & Rosen, A. (1955). Antecedent probability and the efficiency of signs, patterns, or cutting scores. *Psychological Bulletin, 52*, 194–216.

Meier, M. J. (1974). Some challenges for clinical neuropsychology. In R. M. Reitan & L. A. Davidson (Eds.), *Clinical Neuropsychology: Current status and applications* (pp. 289–323). New York: John Wiley and Sons.

Meier, M. J., & French, L. A. (1964). Caudality scale changes following unilateral temporal lobectomy. *Journal of Clinical Psychology, 20*, 464–467.

Meier, M. J., & French, L. A. (1965). Changes in MMPI scale scores and an index of psychopathology following unilateral temporal lobectomy for epilepsy. *Epilepsia, 6*, 263–273.

Mignone, R. J., Donnelly, E. F., & Sadowsky, D. (1970). Psychological and neurological comparisons of psychomotor epileptic patients. *Epilepsia, 11*, 345–359.

Neuringer, C., Dombrowski, P. S., & Goldstein, G. (1975). Cross-validation of an MMPI scale of differential diagnosis of brain damage from schizophrenia. *Journal of Clinical Psychology, 31*, 268–271.

Norton, J. C., & Romano, P. O. (1977). Validation of the Watson-Thomas rules for MMPI diagnosis. *Diseases of the Nervous System, 38*, 773–775.

Parsons, O. A., & Prigatano, G. P. (1978). Methodological considerations in clinical neuropsychological research. *Journal of Consulting and Clinical Psychology, 46*, 608–619.

Pantano, L. T., & Schwartz, M. L. (1978). Differentiation of neurologic and pseudo-neurologic patients with combined MMPI mini-mult and pseudo-neurologic scale. *Journal of Clinical Psychology, 34*, 56–60.

Richards, T. W. (1952). Personality of the convulsive patient in military service. *Psychological Monographs: General and Applied, 66*, 1–23.

Rosenman, M. F., & Lucik, T. W. (1970). A failure to replicate an epilepsy scale of the MMPI. *Journal of Clinical Psychology, 26*, 372.

Russell, E. W. (1975). Validation of a brain-damaged vs. schizophrenia MMPI key. *Journal of Clinical Psychology, 31*, 659–661.

Russell, E. W. (1977). MMPI profiles of brain-damaged and schizophrenic subjects. *Journal of Clinical Psychology, 33*, 190–193.

Russell, E. W., Neuringer, C. & Goldstein, G. (1970). *Assessment of brain damage: A neuropsychological key approach* (p.158). New York: Wiley.

Ryan, J. J. & Robert, J. A. (1983). Caudality scale correlates of WAIS IQs: A failure to replicate. *Clinical Neuropsychology, 5*, 161–162.

Ryan, J. J., & Souheaver, G. T. (1977). Further evidence that concerns the validity of an MMPI key for separation of brain-damaged and schizophrenic patients. *Journal of Clinical Psychology, 33*, 753–754.

Sand, P. L. (1972). MMPI profile characteristics in testable brain-damaged patients within several age/diagnostic categories. *Rehabilitation Psychology, 19*, 146–152.

Sand, P. L. (1973). Performance of medical patient groups with and without brain damage on the Hovey (O) and Watson (Sc-O) MMPI scales. *Journal of Clinical Psychology, 29*, 235–237.

Schwartz, M. S. (1969). "Organicity" and the MMPI 1-3-9 and 2-9 codes. *Proceedings of the 77th Annual Convention of the American Psychological Association, 4*, 519–520.

Schwartz, M. S., & Brown, J. R. (1973). MMPI differentiation of multiple sclerosis vs. pseudoneurologic patients. *Journal of Clinical Psychology, 29*, 471–474.

Shaw, D. J. (1966). Differential MMPI performance in pseudo-seizure epileptic and pseudo-neurologic groups. *Journal of Clinical Psychology, 22*, 271–275.

Shaw, D. J., & Matthews, C. G. (1965). Differential MMPI performance of brain-damaged vs. pseudo-neurologic groups. *Journal of Clinical Psychology, 21*, 405–408.

Siskind, G. (1976). Hovey's 5-item MMPI scale and psychiatric patients. *Journal of Clinical Psychology, 32*, 50.

Sillitti, J. (1982). MMPI-derived indicators of organic brain dysfunction. *Journal of Clinical Psychology, 38*, 601–605.

Stevens, J. R., Milstein, V., & Goldstein, S. (1972). Psychometric test performance in relation to psycho-pathology of epilepsy. *Archives of General Psychiatry, 26*, 532–538.

Timmons, M., & Horton, A. M., Jr. (1982). Effects of education on the Psychiatric-Organic (P-O) special scale of the MMPI. *Clinical Neuropsychology, 4*, 72–73.

Trifiletti, R. J. (1982). Differentiating brain damage from schizophrenia: A further test of Russell's MMPI key. *Journal of Clinical Psychology, 38*, 39–44.

United States Department of Health and Human Services. (1980). *The international classification of diseases: Clinical modification* (9th rev.). Washington, D.C.: Author.

Upper, D., & Seeman, W. (1968). Brain damage, schizophrenia and five MMPI items. *Journal of Clinical Psychology, 24*, 444.

Watson, C. G. (1971). An MMPI scale to separate brain-damaged from schizophrenic men. *Journal of Consulting and Clinical Psychology, 36*, 121–125.

Watson, C. G. (1973). A simple bivariate screening technique to separate NP hospital organics from other psychiatric groups. *Journal of Clinical Psychology, 29*, 448–450.

Watson, C. G. (1984). The Schizophrenia-Organicity (Sc-O) and Psychiatric-Organicity (P-O) MMPI scales: A review. *Journal of Clinical Psychology, 40*, 1008–1023.

Watson, C. G., Davis, W. E., & Gasser, B. (1978). The separation of organics from depressives with ability- and personality-based tests. *Journal of Clinical Psychology, 34*, 393–397.

Watson, C. G., Gasser, B., Schaefer, A., Buranen, C., & Wold, J. (1981). Separation of brain-damaged from psychiatric patients with ability and personality measures. *Journal of Clinical Psychology, 37*, 347–353.

Watson, C. G., & Plemel, D. (1978). An MMPI scale to separate brain-damaged from functional psychiatric patients in neuropsychiatric settings. *Journal of Consulting and Clinical Psychology, 46*, 1127–1132.

Watson, C. G., Plemel, D., & Jacobs, L. (1978). An MMPI sign to separate organic from functional psychiatric patients. *Journal of Clinical Psychology, 34*, 398–401.

Watson, C. G., & Thomas, R. W. (1968). MMPI profiles of brain-damaged and schizophrenic patients. *Perceptual and Motor Skills, 27*, 567–573.

Weingold, H. P., Dawson, J. G., & Kael, H. C. (1965). Further examination of Hovey's "index" for identification of brain lesions: Validation study. *Psychological Reports, 16*, 1098.

Williams, H. L. (1952). The development of a caudality scale for the MMPI. *Journal of Clinical Psychology, 8*, 293–297.

Wooten, A. J. (1983a). Failure of the Hs-Pt index to distinguish organic from functional patients. *Journal of Clinical Psychology, 39*, 551-554.

Wooten, A. J. (1983b). MMPI profiles among neuropsychology patients. *Journal of Clinical Psychology, 39*, 392–406.

Chapter 9

Child Abuse and Sexual Abuse

WILLIAM N. FRIEDRICH

OVERVIEW

The MMPI frequently is used in the assessment of adults who physically abuse or neglect their children. It also is used with incestuous parents and pedophilic adults. The MMPI often has been used rather naively to try to answer inappropriate questions such as, "Did this person abuse his/her child, and if so, will it happen again?" and "Does this person have the sex offender profile?" The individuals asking these questions ask for fact rather than probability, and have the impression that all sex offenders have similar elevations and configurations on the MMPI. The context for these evaluations is most often within a social service setting that is mandated to protect children and, if necessary, prosecute the adult offenders. Treatment considerations, in the usual sense, unfortunately are a secondary concern. However, the MMPI remains a very widely used measure in these cases, and with the ever-increasing number of cases each year, it will be relied on to provide information regarding likelihood of abuse, safety of the child, and treatment options.

Three types of child maltreatment are discussed in this chapter: physical abuse, physical neglect, and sexual abuse. In each of these categories are the offending parent or adult, the nonoffending parent, and the victim of maltreatment. MMPI data, although scant, exist for most of these groups (see Table 9–1).

Considerable problems exist in the MMPI research on these groups. First, defining physical abuse is a major difficulty. Physical abuse exists along a continuum, and jurisdictions differ widely in terms of who is prosecuted. Physical abuse frequently accompanies physical neglect, and thus different authors may create groups of subjects that combine primarily abusive with neglectful parents. Second, individuals who complete the MMPI as part of a court proceeding can and usually do differ significantly from individuals in a treatment setting. Studies in this area frequently report findings from samples of convenience and may combine court-referred with treatment samples. Finally, the median sample size in the studies reviewed is only 25 subjects, so generalizing to larger populations should be carried out cautiously. This chapter is useful not only as a review of this literature but also to the extent that it directs future, much-needed research in this area.

PHYSICAL ABUSE AND NEGLECT

Beginning in 1962 with the publication of a paper on the battered child (Kempe, Silverman, Steele, Droegemueller, & Silver, 1962), the physi-

TABLE 9–1. NUMBER OF RESEARCH STUDIES

| | | Nonoffending | |
	Offender	Parent	Victim
Abuse	13	1	0
Neglect	2	0	0
Sexual abuse	14	2	6

THE MMPI: USE WITH SPECIFIC POPULATIONS

ISBN 0-8089-1913-X

cal abuse of children has come to be viewed as a major public health problem. It is estimated that 800,000 abuse reports are filed each year and approximately 40 to 45 percent are substantiated, numbers that have been growing steadily each year (Friedrich & Wheeler, 1982).

The physical abuse of children is a heterogeneous phenomenon, however, and ranges across a wide variety of acts that vary in terms of planfulness, frequency, duration, intensity, and perpetrator's relationship to the child. A recent review of the literature on child-abusing parents (Friedrich & Wheeler, 1982) indicates that the abusing parent frequently was deprived or abused as a child, lacked accurate knowledge concerning child rearing, and allowed aggressive impulses to be expressed too freely. Also, socioeconomic stresses were neither a necessary nor sufficient cause of physical abuse (Friedrich & Wheeler, 1982).

A category that overlaps with physical abuse is physical neglect, where the parent fails to provide adequately the necessary food, clothing, shelter, supervision, and medical attention for the child. This physical neglect cannot be related simply to socioeconomic stresses. It is common to find parents who are both abusive and neglectful, and the research reviewed here frequently combines these groups rather than examining samples that are more "pure."

The revised third edition of the *Diagnostic and Statistical Manual of Mental Disorders* (DMS-III-R: American Psychiatric Association, 1987) does not contain a diagnostic code specific to physical abuse, although the clinical literature usually describes the physically abusive parents as impulse-ridden, aggressive, and undersocialized. Only a small percentage of these parents would receive a formal diagnosis of psychosis. More commonly, Axis II diagnoses, which include Borderline, Passive-Aggressive, and Mixed Personality Disorders, are made. Axis I diagnoses may include an Affective Disorder, Dissociative Disorder, Substance Use Disorders, and/or an Intermittent Explosive Disorder. No research exists that has formally diagnosed a large, random sample of physically abusive individuals. The little research that is available specific to physical neglect underscores the importance of Major Mood Disorders in this population, particularly major depression (Friedrich & Wheeler, 1982). Axis II diagnoses

similar to those seen in physical abuse would be expected to prevail. Neglectful parents also may be impaired cognitively, and some clinical evidence suggests that neglectful parents are less socialized than abusive parents (Polansky, Chalmers, Buttenweiser, & Williams, 1979).

Moderator variables, particularly socioeconomic stressors, have a large influence on the incidence of physical abuse and neglect. The available research, some of which is quite excellent, clearly indicates the important role of life stress in child abuse (Justice & Duncan, 1976). Pelton (1978) states that very clear evidence exists showing that physical abuse and neglect are not distributed proportionately among the total population, and that socioeconomic class variables are very important. Data from national studies indicate that < 10 percent of abusive parents have incomes that equal or exceed the median family income in the United States. The highest level of child maltreatment routinely is found in families living in the most extreme poverty.

Marital status and education level of the abusive parent are also important moderator variables. The majority of parents in the studies cited were not married and were not high school graduates. Number of children in the home, simply from a cumulative stress viewpoint, also must be examined.

The setting in which the parent is evaluated must be taken into consideration as well. Responses from a pretrial evaluation may be very different from those given as part of a treatment program that has assurances of confidentiality.

A "typical" patient in the studies described would be a younger-than-average mother with more than the average number of children who is single, underemployed or out of work, and receiving public assistance. This individual frequently will have a history of being abused or neglected herself. Abusive and neglectful fathers are not as common, primarily due to their absence in these families and to their reduced role in child rearing. Duration of contact with the child(ren), not the issue of mother vs. father, appears to be more important in deciding which parent abuses (Martin, 1983). This person would typically come into contact with the researcher/clinician as part of an evaluation requested by either a social service agency or the court.

DIFFERENTIAL DIAGNOSIS

Rather than diagnosis, what will be addressed here is simply categorization. If a researcher is truly interested in physical abuse alone, then great care must be taken to establish that physical neglect is not also ongoing. Usually this assessment is made by a protective services worker, and substantiation rates of abuse or neglect may vary from one worker or agency to another.

Although state guidelines at this time are relatively similar regarding what constitutes physical abuse, i.e., "physical injury initiated upon them by other than accidental means, or whose condition gives an indication of other serious abuse or maltreatment" (Helfer & Kempe, 1974, p. 235), parents whose abusive acts vary quite widely may be combined into a research sample based on the criteria of physical abuse documented by caseworkers' investigation (Friedrich, Tyler, & Clark, 1985).

The reader must appreciate, however, that conflict among definitions of child maltreatment abounds. Aber and Zigler (1981) outline at least four formal attempts to define physical abuse of children, ranging from narrow, restrictive definitions to broad definitions. The medical-diagnostic definition of "battered child" and the legal definition of "abused child" are examples of narrowly drawn definitions of physical abuse that are restricted to documentable instances of physical injury to the child. A sociologic definition is the broadest of the four definitions, including not only physical injury but also other types of abuse ranging from emotional abuse and sexual abuse of the child to the moral and legal problems of parental failure to provide an adequate physical environment. For research purposes, a narrow definition tends to be easier to operationalize and clarifies decision-making criteria. Since psychological testing is utilized usually in response to the medical or legal definition of a parent as abusive, MMPI research in this area would do best to use these narrow definitions in defining a research sample.

A great deal of misunderstanding continues to exist about the diference between physical abuse and physical neglect. Similar cases are differently categorized as either physical abuse or physical neglect on the basis of individual judgment, understanding, and experience of the so-cial service worker. The goal of protective services workers is to provide services and keep the family functioning, and accurate description of the full spectrum of physical abuse and physical neglect is needed only to the point that services can be provided. From a researcher's perspective, the study of a generic group of maltreating parents may be more valid than an attempt to create further, unreliable specificity regarding physical abuse vs. physical neglect.

PROTOTYPIC STUDY

Outlined here is the Friedrich et al. (1985) study that examined 14 physically abusive mothers, 13 physically neglectful mothers, and 15 low-income comparison mothers who did not have a social service history of either abuse or neglect. All parents were receiving social services, including financial assistance, from a county social service agency. The legal definition established by the state was used to define two groups of specifically abusive and specifically neglectful parents, all of whom had been investigated in the previous 12 months. From these two pools, random samples were drawn and matched with randomly drawn comparison mothers, nominated by the agency as having no abuse or neglect reports. Each mother was paid $10 and absolute confidentiality was assured and adhered to, so that greater validity of test results could be obtained. Babysitting and transportation to the test site also was provided. The parents were not significantly different with respect to age, income, education, and mean age of their children, but did differ on the number of children, with the comparison mothers averaging significantly fewer children.

Regrettably, for purposes of generalizing to other MMPI studies, the Mini-Mult (Kincannon, 1968) was utilized as part of a 2-hour test battery and psychophysiologic recording session. No validity inclusion criteria for the Mini-Mult were utilized, but the statistical data were analyzed using non-K-corrected raw scale scores. Univariate, as opposed to the more appropriate multivariate analysis of variance, was performed on each of the Mini-Mult scales between the three groups. Significant between-group differences ($p < .05$) were obtained on the Mini-Mult Scales F, Pd, and Sc. Control mothers differed significantly from both neglectful and abusive mothers on the Mini-Mult *Pd* scale, and from neglectful mothers on the Mini-Mult *Sc* scale.

When step-wise discriminant analysis was performed on the Mini-Mult scales in an effort to predict group membership, four variables—*Pd*, *Pa*, *L*, and *D*—contributed to optimal discrimination for an overall correct classification of 59.5 percent. The reader must be cautioned, however, that the sample sizes available for this analysis were not optimal and chance differences are probable. When the Mini-Mult scales, other personality measures, and the psychophysiologic recordings were utilized in a step-wise discriminant analysis, the *Pd* and *F* scales from the Mini-Mult contributed to the overall classification of 78.6 percent. This improvement in classification accuracy clearly suggested the greater utility of multidimensional assessment of physically abusive and neglectful parents.

For the purposes of this chapter, the original data were re-examined and two-point codetypes were established, with *4-8/8-4*, 4-6/6-4, and *4-9/9-4* as the most common codetypes for the abuse group, and *2-4/4-2*, *4-8/8-4*, and *2-8/8-2* as the most common for the neglect group. These differing codetypes would suggest greater frequency of depression in the neglect group, which would certainly be congruent with their neglectful behavior. The other measures used in this study clearly indicated that neglectful mothers were more poorly socialized, anxious, and hostile.

STANDARD VALIDITY AND CLINICAL SCALES

A central difficulty in the Friedrich et al. (1985) study, which is commonly seen in the other studies summarized in Table 9–2, is the small sample size. However, only mothers were utilized, and were not combined with fathers, a common practice in the studies reviewed here.

Stricter definitions of abuse and neglect were also adhered to rather than the more usual practice of combining both abusive and neglectful parents, e.g., "the case records of child abusers . . . who received psychological evaluations" (Furlong & Leton, 1977, p. 56), "fathers . . . and mothers identified positively for the injury or severe neglect of an identified, maltreated child" (Paulson, Schwemer, & Bendel, 1976, p. 559). In addition, the parents in the Friedrich et al. (1985) study were not evaluated as part of a social services evaluation, thus altering the demand characteristics and, it is hoped, reducing the defensiveness of the parents. For example, all of the parents in Paulson's series of studies (Paulson, Afifi, Thomason, & Chaleff, 1974; Paulson, Afifi, Chaleff, Liu, & Thomason, 1975a; Paulson, Afifi, Chaleff, Thomason, & Liu, 1975b; Paulson et al., 1976) were from the evaluation and treatment files of the Child Trauma Intervention Program. Parents in the studies by Beal, Melowski, and Hamilton (1984) and Gabinet (1979) were primarily referred to a training program by social service workers, and the parents in the studies by Wright (1970; 1976), Furlong and Leton (1977), and Kaleita and Wise (1976) were referred from court evaluations. Despite the fact that defensiveness could be expected in these circumstances, the modal validity scale profile in all of these studies was scale *F* > *L* > *K*, which seems counter to Wright's (1976) description of these parents as "sick but slick." Wright's abusive parents (N = 13 convicted abusers) did reveal less "bizarre" content on the

TABLE 9–2. FREQUENCY OF MMPI CODETYPES IN CHILD-ABUSING MOTHERS

Authors	N	Age	Codetype 2-4/4-2	2-8/8-2	3-4/4-3	4-6/6-4	4-8/8-4
Friedrich et al. (1985)	14	30	7.1		7.1	28.6	35.7
Friedrich et al. (1985)	13	29	38.5	15.4			38.5
Gabinet (1979)	22	18–35		9.1	13.6	9.1	18.2
Weighted Totals			22.2	11.4	11.1	16.7	28.6

Authors	Codetype 4-9/9-4	6-8/8-6	8-9/9-8	Total	Methodologic Issues A	B	C	D	E	F	G	H	I
Friedrich et al. (1985)	21.4			99.9	+	+	+	+	-	-	+	-	-
Friedrich et al. (1985)		7.7		100.1	+	+	+	+	-	-	+	-	-
Gabinet (1979)			9.1	9.1	68.2	+	-	+	-	-	-	+	-	-
Weighted Totals		8.6		85.7									

Rorschach than 13 matched controls, which he interpreted to mean that abusive parents could deliberately respond in a more socially desirable manner, i.e., "slick."

A final study illuminated the difficulties of using scales from the MMPI to discriminate child abusive from distressed parents (Plotkin, Twentyman, & Perri, 1982). They used Scales *F*, *4*, and *9*, separately and in combination, to discriminate 19 abusive parents from 35 comparison parents. Differences were noted on Scale *9* and the sum of Scales *F*, *4*, and *9*, with the abusive parents exhibiting more aggressiveness. Discriminant analysis could correctly classify 26 percent of the abusers, a disappointing result.

Despite these problems, some common findings do emerge. Neglectful parents appear to be more depressed and not as well socialized as abusive parents (see Table 9–2). For abusive parents significant elevations (*T* > 70) were reported for Scales *F*, *2*, *4*, *6*, and *8* (Gabinet, 1979), *4* and *8* (Griswold & Billingsley, 1969), and *9* (Paulson et al., 1974). However, rarely could the MMPI scales, by themselves, reliably differentiate between abusers and neglectors, or between maltreating parents and outpatient parents who were having child management difficulties. In addition, the number of normal limits profiles in many of the studies was quite high, even the majority in some cases (e.g., Wright, 1976).

An examination of Table 9–2 reveals the small sample sizes and routine methodologic problems. Samples are sometimes described very poorly, and exclusion criteria are not utilized, despite the likelihood of invalid profiles. These problems reflect the difficulties of research in this area, where psychological services are usually scant and mental health services are provided most commonly by case workers. However, understanding of physically abusive and physically neglectful parents will remain only tentative as long as convenience samples are used. It should be mandatory for future researchers to provide more complete subject descriptions, however, so that clinicians can better determine comparability/generalizability.

SPECIAL/RESEARCH SCALES

Paulson et al. (1975a;b) developed nine special MMPI scales to identify male and female abusers. He reported 80 to 100 percent discriminating ability within his sample of 30 abusing parents,

which was an extremely small sample given the number of analyses he performed. These scales were not cross-validated until later by independent studies (Beal et al., 1984; Furlong & Leton, 1977) with limited success. For example, Beal et al. (1984) found that Paulson's special scales misclassified abusers 50 to 68 percent of the time with their sample of 30 abusers and 12 control parents, and similar problems in misclassification were reported by Furlong and Leton (1977).

Paulson et al. (1976) contrasted the subscales for Scales *4* and *9*, as well as Megargee's (1966) Overcontrolled-Hostility (*OH*) scale, with a sample of 53 subjects (21 fathers and 32 mothers), identified as the principal abusers, and a psychiatric outpatient sample (46 fathers and 67 mothers). It was assumed, but never clearly reported, that education level and socioeconomic status of the groups were comparable. The special scales included subtle, obvious, and Harris and Lingoes subscales. Seven of the Scale *4* scales and seven of the eight Scale *9* scales revealed group differences, but the *OH* scale did not differ between the groups. Friedrich et al. (1985) utilized the Repression-Sensitization Scale in the study reported earlier, but failed to find significant differences between groups.

SUMMARY

The research reviewed certainly lacks definitiveness given the small and variable (regarding referral sources) samples. All too often, as indicated in Table 9–2, basic demographic information such as age, education, and socioeconomic level, and exact nature of the abuse or neglect would be reported in a cursory manner, if at all. This lack of basic demographic information adds to the difficulty in determining if any generalizability is possible.

Despite these deficiencies, abusive parents routinely differ from nonabusive parents on several MMPI Scales, including *4*, *8*, and *9*. That differences would exist on these scales is clinically sensible, but it is important to note, particularly for the practicing clinician, that while these differences may be statistically significant, they may fail to be clinically significant (*T* > 70).

The two studies that specifically examined the diversity inherent in a group of child-maltreating parents (Friedrich et al., 1985; Gabinet, 1979), revealed a variety of two-point codetypes. In the Friedrich et al. study, abusive parents were found to differ from neglectful parents in that neglectful parents had significantly higher scores than abusive mothers on Scales *2* and *4*.

Thus, it can be assumed that abusive parents have problems with anger, impulse control, and empathy. In addition, they appear to be heterogeneous in regard to previous history of abuse, frequency of abuse, severity of abuse, presence of physical neglect, and so on. However, the aforementioned characteristics are commonly found in any criminal sample or in samples of parents in crisis. In fact, Kaleita and Wise (1976) contrasted a sample of physically abusive parents to an assaultive (murder, manslaughter) but not child-abusive sample and to a nonviolent, but criminal group (larceny, burglary). They found "inherent limitations of the . . . MMPI to identify . . . subtle personality . . . factors which might distinguish the groups more clearly" (p. 182). This summary statement stemmed from the fact that few between-group differences could be reliably detected. Presumably, the same difficulties the MMPI has had in predicting violent and criminal behavior in previous studies are reflected in the findings of this review that the MMPI has difficulty predicting individual behavior regarding child maltreatment (Holland, Beckett, & Levi, 1981).

Consequently, if the need is to understand maltreating parents, the MMPI will assist in establishing personality characteristics and in guiding treatment, but parenting attitudes and behavior, a previous history of child abuse, and situational stress may go much farther in reliably discriminating abusing parents from nonabusing parents. Treatment recommendations also can be tailored much more specifically when a multidimensional assessment is performed, and when recommendations take into consideration both personality and parenting practices.

SEXUAL ABUSE

The sexual abuse of children is now recognized as a serious mental health problem, both because it is so widespread and because of increasing evidence of its traumatic effects. Large-scale surveys of nonclinical populations yield current estimates that the risk of victimization may be as high as 1 in 10 for boys and greater than 1 in 3 for girls (Herman, Russell, & Trocki, 1986).

Sexual abuse, like physical abuse and neglect, is defined not by a psychiatric diagnosis but by the nature of a traumatic event. And like physical abuse and neglect, sexual abuse is a phenomenon that is heterogeneous. For example, it varies widely from one child victim to the next in terms of the perpetrator's relationship to the child, duration of abuse, use of force, nature of the sexual acts, and the larger family context, e.g., whether other family members are supportive of the child. Male victims of sexual abuse more frequently are also victims of physical abuse in their home (Finkelhor, 1984) and

as a group would differ from female victims on that dimension alone.

Sexual abuse of children is usually divided into incestuous versus nonincestuous abuse. A common assumption is that not only should incestuous and nonincestuous offenders differ from each other on personality dimensions but their victims should also. The betrayal by a parent/relative is assumed to be greater, and thus the distress reflected in the child also would be greater (Finkelhor, 1984). Evidence for sexual abuse most often has to come from the child's self-report, since physical indications are frequently absent. Sexual abuse cases are placed on court dockets with ever-increasing frequency, which alters the characteristics of research samples considerably since sex offenders are more likely to be an incarcerated sample than is the case with physical abuse or neglect.

There are three categories of individuals within sexual abuse cases: the offender, the nonoffending parent, and the victim. The vast majority of offenders are male and appear to approach a somewhat more normal distribution with regard to age, education level, and socioeconomic status than do physically abusive parents. Yet offenders who sexually abuse children are quite heterogeneous with regard to offense characteristics, the use of physical force, and whether the assault was molestation or rape. Some offenders against children are preferential child molesters, or pedophiles, and others are not (Lanning, 1986). It is also true that a significant percentage of men who sexually assault children have committed other sex offenses in addition to the specific offense for which they were apprehended (Groth, 1979).

In addition to the usual important moderator variables of marital status, education level, and income, McGovern and Nevid (1986) identify "evaluation apprehension" as a critical variable to be examined. Evaluation apprehension is "an anxiety-toned concern about creating a favorable impression of oneself when the individual believes that he or she is being judged or evaluated" (McGovern & Nevid, 1986, p. 576). Consequently, the validity of self-reports by sex offenders should be of concern in both research and clinical settings, and failure to use strict criteria for MMPI validity seriously detracts from any conclusions drawn.

There is no "typical" sex offender. A somewhat typical offender, whose preference is children, would be an individual in his mid-30s who has a greater than average likelihood of at least one previous, sexually related or nonsexually related conviction. He has an increased likelihood of a history of sexual abuse himself. More often than not, he is unmarried at the time of the offense and is a high school graduate. A diagnosable psychiatric disorder may not be evident other than the paraphilia.

The nonoffending parent, usually the mother of the child, has been the subject of much clinical speculation but until recently, no empirical research. Nonoffending parents often are viewed as contributing to the abuse because of either their own pathology or an unresolved history of sexual abuse (Rist, 1979). This position has been debated vehemently with a strictly feminist perspective arguing that the responsibility is solely with the offender (Brownmiller, 1975). Given that a higher than expected percentage of mothers of sexually abused children have a history of victimization, simply the long-term effects of this history could be expected to show up on the MMPI. However, these parents are also remarkably heterogeneous, varying widely in their own history of abuse, response to the victimization of their child, and, in cases of incest, whether they cooperate fully with treatment and/or end the marriage. At the very least, these variables must be detailed in order to avoid inappropriately stereotyping the nonoffending parent of the sexually abused child.

The victim of sexual abuse has been the focus of several excellent studies, some involving the MMPI. The clinical description of adult patients with a history of childhood sexual abuse are consistent with a formulation of post-traumatic stress disorder that has become chronic and integrated into the victim's personality structure (Herman et al., 1986). Table 9–3 lists the criteria. Patients "frequently complain of chronic depression, anhedonia and inner deadness and may be driven periodically to seek relief in drugs and alcohol abuse, self-mutilation, and suicide attempts" (Herman et al., 1986, p. 1293). However, these authors also state that psychiatric patients with a history of sexual abuse do not provide a full picture of the potential range of adaptation and recovery in victimized children. It is unknown what proportion of abused children recover well and what proportion will go on to develop the chronic syndrome seen in adult patients. Again, this points to the fact that adolescent and adult victims of sexual abuse are a heterogeneous group and that a central variable that must be controlled in MMPI studies is the clinical vs. nonclinical status of the victims. Age is also a necessary variable to control with careful decision-making on the use of adult or adolescent norms on the MMPI and the combining of younger with older victims. Since the nature of the offense appears to be related to level and chronicity of pathology in the sex offender, these dimensions also must be explicated.

The typical victim is a patient in an outpatient treatment program whose abuse was relatively severe. Although educational attainments may be normally distributed, occupational status and intimate relational status may be compromised.

DIFFERENTIAL DIAGNOSIS

The DSM-III-R diagnoses most appropriate to this area are the following: pedophilia in the relatively infrequent case of the preferential child offender, and post-traumatic stress disorder in the case of the victim. Each of these is briefly summarized in Tables 9–3 and 7–1 (p. 199), respectively.

TABLE 9–3. DIAGNOSTIC CRITERIA FOR PEDOPHILIA

Diagnostic criteria for 302.20 Pedophilia

   A. Over a period of at least six months, recurrent intense sexual urges and sexually arousing fantasies involving sexual activity with a prepubescent child or children (generaly age 13 or younger).
   B. The person has acted on these urges, or is markedly distressed by them.
   C. The person is at least 16 years old and at least 5 years older than the child or children in A.

   Note: Do not include a late adolescent involved in an ongoing sexual relationship with a 12- or 13-year-old.

Specify: **same sex, opposite sex,** or **same and opposite sex.**

Specify if **limited to incest.**

Specify: **exclusive type** (attracted only to children), or **nonexclusive type.**

Note: From *Diagnostic and statistical manual of mental disorders (3rd ed. revised)* by American Psychiatric Association, 1987, Washington, D.C.: Author. Reprinted with permission.

The rationale for pedophilia is apparent; other Axis II disorders for this group, although disputed, when appropriate may include paranoid, at least for some incestuous fathers (Meiselman, 1978). The rationale for post-traumatic stress disorder is well-stated in Herman et al. (1986).

PROTOTYPIC STUDY

In this section, prototypic study is outlined that is applicable for offenders, nonoffending parents, and victims (Scott & Stone, 1986b). These researchers used the MMPI to study four groups of subjects from incestuous families: natural father offenders (n = 33), stepfather offenders (n = 25), nonparticipating mothers (n = 44), and daughter victims (n = 22). In addition, a total of 128 subjects were used in four control groups, matched on the variables of sex, age, race, education, and socioeconomic status. None of these individuals was from families in which incest had occurred and none was in treatment at the time of testing.

All experimental subjects were in psychotherapy groups at the time of testing, and in order to minimize the effects of crisis on their MMPI profiles, all had been in treatment for at least 5 weeks. The court had referred the various family members to the treatment program. In 42 percent of the cases, fondling alone was the type of contact, with the remaining 58 percent involving oral sex, intercourse, or some combination of fondling, oral sex, and intercourse.

Validity inclusion criteria of $F < 17$ (raw scores) or F from 17 to 22 and $F - K < 12$ were utilized, resulting in nine profiles excluded. The statistical data were analyzed using non-K-corrected raw scale scores, the recommended technique (Butcher & Tellegen, 1978).

Univariate, as opposed to the more appropriate multivariate, analysis of variance, was performed on each of the standard MMPI scales between the four experimental groups. To summarize, the daughter victims exhibited more psychopathology than the adult groups, stepfathers did not differ from natural fathers, and mothers seldom differed from both perpetrator groups.

Differences between each experimental group and its respective control group were examined by t-test. A more conservative alpha ($p < .01$) was utilized, given the large number of t-tests performed. Scales F and 4 for the incest family members were uniformly different from the controls. Additionally, natural fathers differed on Scales 6 and 0; stepfathers on Scales 2, 7, and 8; mothers on Scales 1, 2, 3, 6, 7, 8, and 0; and daughters on Scales K, 1, 2, 6, 7, 8, 9, and 0.

The next very useful series of analyses was the examination of codetype frequencies. Commonly seen codetypes in the natural fathers were *3-4/4-3* and *4-8/8-4*; in the stepfathers were *2-4/4-2* and *4-9/9-4*; in the mothers were *3-4/4-3*; and in the daughters were *4-8/8-4* and *8-9/9-8*.

The three groups of parents produced mean profiles in the normal range, while the mean profile for the daughters was significantly greater than the adults' on three Scales (F, 7, and 8). Both father groups, contrary to clinical opinion, were not significantly psychopathologic, which underscores the position that fewer than 10 percent of incestuous fathers exhibit specific mental illness (Meiselman, 1978). The normalcy of the mothers is striking, particularly since all had recently experienced major turmoil and familial disruption. The relatively high incidence of the *3-4/4-3* codetype may suggest dissociative phenomena, allowing the mother to be "emotionally absent," thus indirectly facilitating the incestuous activity.

The authors concluded that since the most evident psychopathology was in the daughter victims, speculation on whether it is psychopathology that produces incest or incest that produces psychopathology is in order. They also stated that for most individuals in the victim group, the psychological problems likely will continue into adulthood. Their commonly seen *4-8/8-4* and *8-9/9-8* codetypes are associated with highly malignant psychopathologic processes, and therapy with these individuals is very difficult.

A second excellent study that is worth some additional explication is the recent paper by Hall, Maiuro, Vitaliano, and Proctor (1986). In terms of sample size (n = 406), use of MMPI validity codes, statistical analyses, detailed information regarding the nature of each subject's offenses, this is the largest and best study of incarcerated child molesters of average or above-average intelligence. The authors attempted to determine whether there were MMPI differences for heterosexual vs. homosexual pedophiles, incest vs. nonincest, use of force, rape vs. molestation, and younger vs. older victims. Few, if any, clinically significant differences were found relating to offense type. However, the offender was the primary source of information relating to offense type. In addition, although Scales *2*, *4*, and *8* were significantly elevated in the mean profile of the sample, no single two-point codetype was predominant. The most common codetypes were *4-8/8-4* (7.1 percent), *7-8/8-7* (6.4 percent), *2-4/4-2* (6.1 percent), *4-9/9-4* (5.7 percent), and *4-5/5-4* (4.9 percent). No single codetype identified more than 7 percent of the sample. In addition, the *7-8/8-7* codetype would suggest greater anxiety and schizoidal and compulsive behaviors, whereas a *4-5/5-4* codetype would more likely reflect problems with sexual orientation and nonconformist behavioral difficulties.

Hall et al. (1986) concluded that their results clearly pointed to the heterogeneous nature of sex offenders against children. The authors' conservative conclusion was that the MMPI is of limited clinical utility in assessing and differentiating specific offense patterns among incarcerated populations of men who have sexually assaulted children. The fact that only 7 percent of the subjects had no clinical scale above a *T*-score of 70 does suggest, however, that the failure to find discriminations for offense type may be related to the limited range of the scores. The authors recommended the development of a multivariate approach that would yield greater discriminative power in developing subtypes of sexual offenders. Additional measures, including psychophysiologic recordings and sexual behavior interviews, should supplement measures such as the MMPI.

STANDARD VALIDITY AND CLINICAL SCALES

The finding of the significant elevations ($T >$ 70) on Scales *2*, *4*, and *8* in the Hall et al. (1986) study of incarcerated pedophiles is partially congruent with several other studies of child molesters (Table 9–4). For example, a sole elevation on Scale *4* was found in Panton's (1979) incarcerated sample of nonviolent child molesters, and elevations on Scales *4* and *8* were found for Armentrout and Hauer's (1978) inpatients, Panton's (1978) incarcerated child rapists, Swenson and Grimes' (1958) incarcerated offenders, McCreary's (1975) child molesters with at least one prior arrest, and Lanyon and Lutz's (1984) no-denial offenders, most of whom were child molesters. Elevations on Scales *4*, *7*, and *8* were noted in Kirkland and Bauer's (1982) outpatient offenders and Quinsey, Arnold, and Pruesse's (1980) psychiatric inpatient offenders.

Lanyon and Lutz (1984) used the MMPI to discriminate defensive from nondefensive felony sex offenders, the majority (80 percent) of whom were child molesters (Table 9–5). Only the nondefensive offenders had significant elevations (Scales *4* and *8*), whereas the partially defensive and defensive offender group (accounting for almost half of the sample) did not have any significant validity or clinical scale elevations. Using just the $L + K - F$ raw score validity index, group membership was predicted with 83 percent accuracy by discriminant function. The discriminant function rose to 89 per-

---

TABLE 9–4.   FREQUENCY OF MMPI CODETYPES IN CHILD SEXUAL ABUSERS

Authors	N	Age	Codetype				
			2-4/4-2	*2-8/8-2*	*3-4/4-3*	*4-6/6-4*	*4-8/8-4*
Hall et al. (1986)	348	36	6.1	4.4		3.4	7.1
Scott & Stone (1986b)	33	41	9.0		15.2		15.2
Scott & Stone (1986b)	29	41	20.7		6.9		3.4
Weighted Totals			7.4		11.3		7.5

Authors	Codetype				Methodologic Issues								
	4-9/9-4	*7-8/8-7*	*8-9/9-8*	Total	A	B	C	D	E	F	G	H	I
Hall et al (1986)	5.7	6.4	3.2	36.3	+	+	+	+	+	+	+	–	–
Scott & Stone (1986b)	9.0		3.0	51.4	+	+	+	+	+	–	+	–	–
Scott & Stone (1986b)	27.6		3.4	62.0	+	+	+	+	+	–	+	–	–
Weighted Totals	7.5		3.2	39.3									

TABLE 9–5.   FREQUENCY OF MMPI CODETYPES IN NONOFFENDING MOTHERS

Authors	N	Age	Codetype				
			2-4/4-2	2-8/8-2	3-4/4-3	4-6/6-4	4-8/8-4
Friedrich (in press)	37	30	9.1		18.2	15.6	3.0
Scott & Stone (1986b)	44	40	9.0		18.1		2.2
Weighted Totals			9.0		18.1		2.6

Authors	Codetype				Methodologic Issues								
	4-9/9-4	6-8/8-6	8-9/9-8	Total	A	B	C	D	E	F	G	H	I
Friedrich (in press)	3.0	6.1	6.1	61.1	+	+	+	+	+	-	+	-	-
Scott & Stone (1986b)	9.0		2.2	40.5	+	+	+	+	+	-	+	-	-
Weighted Totals	6.3		4.0	49.9									

cent when the MMPI clinical scales were added to the pool of predictor variables. The authors concluded that the validity scales were successful in identifying the denial seen in these men.

Several brief comments regarding research on victims is pertinent at this point. Scott and Stone's (1986b) psychotherapy sample clearly indicated significant psychopathology in the victims of incest, with a greater than average likelihood that these problems would persist into adulthood (Table 9–6). In fact, Scott and Stone (1986a) found adult victims to have significantly higher non-K-corrected T-scores than adolescent victims. In another excellent study, Tsai, Feldman-Summers, and Edgar (1979) assessed three groups of women. Two of the groups had a history of molestation during childhood, but only one group had sought psychotherapy. The third sample was neither a clinical group nor a molestation history group. The clinical-molestation group was significantly less well adjusted on the MMPI ($T > 70$ on Scales 4 and 8) than the other two groups, and the clinical-molestation group was also more prob-

lematic regarding psychosexual functioning. The clinical-molestation group did not differ from the nonclinical-molestation group on whether the molestation was incestuous, age at first molestation, or time elapsed to disclosure, but did differ on several variables related to duration, frequency, and severity of the molestation, with the clinical-molestation group being abused longer and more frequently and involving more attempts at vaginal intercourse. These results, obtained in a study of victims that has one of the largest and best controlled samples, certainly underscores the heterogeneity of molestation outcome.

SPECIAL/RESEARCH SCALES

The Pedophilic (Pe) scale was developed by Toobert, Bartelme, and Jones (1959) from a sample of 120 incarcerated pedophiles. It correctly identified 75 percent of pedophiles in a cross-validation sample. Panton (1978) reported significant differences on the Pe scale between adult

TABLE 9–6.   FREQUENCY OF MMPI CODETYPES IN WOMEN WHO WERE CHILD ABUSE VICTIMS

Authors	N	Age	Codetype				
			2-4/4-2	2-8/8-2	3-4/4-3	4-6/6-4	4-8/8-4
Scott & Stone (1986a)	27	17					22.2
Scott & Stone (1986a)	31	35					16.1
Scott & Stone (1986b)	22	18					22.7
Weighted Totals							20.0

Authors	Codetype				Methodologic Issues								
	4-9/9-4	6-8/8-6	8-9/9-8	Total	A	B	C	D	E	F	G	H	I
Scott & Stone (1986a)	3.7	14.8	29.6	70.3	+	+	-	+	+	-	+	-	-
Scott & Stone (1986a)	6.4	12.9	3.2	38.6	+	+	-	+	+	-	+	-	-
Scott & Stone (1986b)	4.5	36.4		63.6	+	+	+	+	+	-	+	-	-
Weighted Totals	5.0	20.0	15.5	56.2									

rapists, child rapists, and nonviolent child molesters, but did not find differences between incestuous fathers and nonviolent child molesters (Panton, 1979). No other research has been reported with this scale.

Only one paper that utilized any of the standard MMPI research scales was found. Quinsey et al. (1980) failed to find differences between child molesters and five other groups of incarcerated felons on the Scales *A*, *R*, *Es*, and *OH*. Finally, Atwood and Howell (1971), utilizing a sexual deviation scale derived from the MMPI (Marsh, Hilliard, & Liechti, 1955), were able to successfully identify 9 of 10 incarcerated pedophiles and did not misidentify any of the 10 comparison subjects (incarcerated felons).

SUMMARY

A far more extensive body of literature exists for sexual offenders against children than for child-abusing parents. Unfortunately, authors of the studies reviewed frequently were vague about critical demographic variables. Two recent high-quality papers (Hall et al. 1986; Scott & Stone, 1986b) have added considerably to our understanding of offenders, victims, and nonoffending parents. These studies also have illustrated how the MMPI can be useful, as well as its shortcomings. With the continued increase in the number of offenders and victims coming to the attention of both the legal and mental health systems, it is expected that continued input from the MMPI will be utilized in a variety of ways.

A common misconception about sex offenders against children is that there exists a "sex offender profile," and the degree to which an individual "fits" that profile relates to the degree of certainty a clinician has regarding likelihood of offense. The literature reviewed clearly illustrates that there is no such profile but that there are a number of frequently occurring codetypes. This diversity of codetypes reflects the diversity of sexual abuse and also the variety of offender types (Groth, 1979; Lanning, 1986). In addition, the information available to the researcher regarding the nature and number of offenses is certain to be affected by the fact that it is the offender or the child victim who is reporting, the latter frequently underreporting the events. External validation is rarely available, and there is no real solution to this dilemma. An offender will usually minimize any admission, and even when in treatment and being rewarded for candor, the true nature of the offenses often is not known. Future researchers must publish the various codetypes and attempt to identify more specifically the variety of codetypes that exists among offenders. Cluster analytic techniques may be very useful in further understanding this diversity.

What direction can be given to the clinician who is attempting to make decisions in this area, particularly regarding likelihood of abuse? The first suggestion is that while the MMPI is useful, it must not be any more than a component of an evaluation that also includes careful interviewing, other personality measures, and possibly physiologic measures, although their utility is still uncertain. Lanyon and Lutz (1984) illustrate that the demand characteristics of the evaluation and the degree of denial by the accused affect the profiles obtained on the MMPI. It is for these reasons that the circumstances surrounding the evaluation must be explicated very carefully in any future research.

The literature available on mothers of victims is scant, but both available studies indicate that they are more pathologic than comparison samples. A necessary step would be to determine to what degree this pathology reflects simply a previous history of abuse as opposed to some innate characteristic that "contributes to abuse." The MMPI cannot answer, as well as other measures, the quality of the parent-child relationship, a variable seemingly very central to further understanding how incest occurs in certain families.

Victim research, albeit quite good in comparison, also must examine outcome on measures more pertinent to psychosexual functioning and intimacy. By itself, the MMPI cannot illustrate the diversity of outcomes possible with victims, because the quality of intimate relations and psychosexual functioning can be assessed more directly with other measures (Tsai et al., 1979).

Finally, the MMPI, in conjunction with other measures and interview data, will continue to be of significance in the assessment of offenders, victims, and parents, as long as the user is aware of the heterogeneity of this phenomenon. For example, Lanyon (1986) recently made several pertinent recommendations to combine traditional psychological assessment with assessment tools that are specific to "legally relevant questions and behaviors" (p. 261). Combining the MMPI in a multivariate study with other measures could provide both the clinician and researcher much greater specificity regarding offenders, victims, and nonoffending parents alike.

REFERENCES

Aber, J.L., & Zigler, E. (1981). Developmental considerations in the definition of child maltreatment. In R. Rizley & D. Cicchetti (Eds.), *Developmental perspectives on child maltreatment: New Directions for Child Development* (No. 11, pp. 1-29). San Francisco: Jossey-Bass.

American Psychiatric Association. (1987). Diagnostic and statistical manual of mental disorders (3rd ed., revised). Washington, D.C.: Author.

Armentrout, J.A., & Hauer, A.L. (1978). MMPIs of rapists of adults, rapists of children, and non-rapist sex offenders. *Journal of Clinical Psychology, 34*, 330-332.

Atwood, R.W., & Howell, R.J. (1971). Pupillometric and personality test score differences of female aggressing pedophiliacs and normals. *Psychonomic Science, 22,* 115-116.

Beal, D., Melowski, F., & Hamilton, A. (1984). A cross-validation of Paulson's discriminant function-derived scales for identifying "at risk" child-abusive parents. *Suicide and Life-Threatening Behavior, 14,* 270-274.

Brownmiller, S. (1975). *Against our will: Men, women, and rape.* New York: Simon & Schuster.

Butcher, J.N., & Tellegen, A. (1978). Common methodological problems in MMPI research. *Journal of Consulting and Clinical Psychology, 46,* 620-628.

Cavallin, H. (1966). Incestuous fathers: A clinical report. *American Journal of Psychiatry, 122,* 1132-1138.

Finkelhor, D. (1984). *Child sexual abuse.* New York: Free Press.

Friedrich, W.N. (in press). Mothers of sexually abused children: An MMPI study. *Journal of Clinical Psychology.*

Friedrich, W.N., Tyler, J.D., & Clark, J.A. (1985). Personality and psychophysiological variables in abusive, neglectful, and low-income mothers. *Journal of Nervous and Mental Disorders, 173,* 1-12.

Friedrich, W.N., & Wheeler, K.K. (1982). The abusing parent revisited: A decade of psychological research. *Journal of Nervous and Mental Disease, 170,* 577-587.

Furlong, M.J., & Leton, D.A. (1977). The validity of MMPI scales to identify potential child abusers. *Journal of Clinical Child Psychology, 6,* 55-57.

Gabinet, L. (1979). MMPI profiles of high-risk and outpatient mothers. *Child Abuse and Neglect: An International Journal, 3,* 373-379.

Griswold, B.B., & Billingsley, A. (1969). Personality and social characteristics of low-income mothers who neglect or abuse their children (In Final Report: Grant No. PR11001R). Children's Bureau, Welfare Administration, U.S. Department of Health, Education, and Welfare, Washington, D.C.

Groth, N. (1979). *Men who rape.* New York: Plenum.

Hagenau, H.R. (1977). Parental attitudes, perceptions of parents and some personality characteristics of child abusing women. *Dissertation Abstracts International, 38,* 1402-143B. (University Microfilms No. 77-19, 971).

Hall, G.C.N., Maiuro, R.D., Vitaliano, P.P., & Proctor, W.C. (1986). The utility of the MMPI with men who have sexually assaulted children. *Journal of Consulting and Clinical Psychology, 54,* 493-496.

Helfer, R., & Kempe, C.H. (1974). *The battered child* (2nd ed.). Chicago: University of Chicago Press.

Herman, J., Russell, D., & Trocki, K. (1986). Long-term effects of incestuous abuse in childhood. *American Journal of Psychiatry, 143,* 1293-1296.

Holland, T.R., Beckett, G.E., & Levi, M. (1981). Intelligence, personality, and criminal violence: A multivariate analysis. *Journal of Consulting and Clinical Psychology, 49,* 106-111.

Justice, B., & Duncan, D. (1976). Life crisis as a precursor to child abuse. *Public Health Reports, 91,* 110-115.

Kaleita, T., & Wise, J.H. (1976). An MMPI comparison of child abusers with two groups of criminal offenders. *Clinical Proceedings, Children's Hospital National Medical Center, 32,* 180-184.

Kempe, C.H., Silverman, F.N., Steele, B.F., Droegemueller, W., & Silver, H.K. (1962). The battered child syndrome. *Journal of the American Medical Association, 181,* 17-24.

Kincannon, J.C. (1968). Prediction of the standard MMPI scale scores from items: The Mini-Mult. *Journal of Consulting and Clinical Psychology, 3,* 319-325.

Kirkland, K.D., & Bauer, C.A. (1982). MMPI traits of incestuous fathers. *Journal of Clinical Psychology, 38,* 645-649.

Langevin, R., Paitich, D., Freeman, R., Mann, K., & Handy, L. (1978). Personality characteristics and sexual anomalies in males. *Canadian Journal of Behavior Science, 10,* 222-238.

Lanning, K.V. (1986). *Child molesters: A behavioral analysis.* Washington, D.C.: National Center for Missing and Exploited Children.

Lanyon, R.I. (1986). Psychological assessment procedures in court-related settings. *Professional Psychology, 17,* 260-268.

Lanyon, R.I., & Lutz, R.W. (1984). MMPI discrimination of defensive and nondefensive felony sex offenders. *Journal of Consulting and Clinical Psychology, 52,* 841-843.

Mara, B.A. (1983). The MMPI as a psychometric measure of the pathological response to sexual abuse and a descriptive index for sexually abused female adolescents. *Dissertation Abstracts International, 44,* 2250B. (University Microfilms No. 83-22, 604).

Marsh, J.T., Hilliard, J., & Liechti, R. (1955). A sexual deviation scale for the MMPI. *Journal of Consulting Psychology, 19,* 55-59.

Martin, J. (1983). Maternal and paternal abuse of children. In D. Finkelhor, R.J. Gelles, G.T. Hotaling, & M.A. Strauss (Eds.), *The dark side of families* (pp. 293-304). Beverly Hills: Sage.

McCreary, C.P. (1975). Personality differences among child molesters. *Journal of Personality Assessment, 39,* 591-593.

McGovern, F.J, & Nevid, J.S. (1986). Evaluation apprehension on psychological inventories in a prison-based setting. *Journal of Consulting and Clinical Psychology, 54,* 576-578.

Megargee, E. (1966). Undercontrolled and overcontrolled personality types in extreme antisocial aggression. *Psychological Monographs, 80,* 1-29.

Meiselman, K.C. (1978). *Incest.* San Francisco: Jossey-Bass.

Meiselman, K.C. (1980). Personality characteristics of incest history psychotherapy patients: A research note. *Archives of Sexual Behavior, 9,* 195-197.

Panton, J.H. (1978). Personality differences appearing between rapists of adults, rapists of children, and nonviolent sexual molesters of female children. *Research Communications of Psychology and Psychiatry Behavior, 3,* 393-395.

Panton, J.H. (1979). MMPI profile configurations associated with incestuous and non-incestuous child molesting. *Psychological Reports, 45,* 335-338.

Paulson, M.J., Afifi, A.A., Chaleff, A., Liu, V.Y., & Thomason, M.L. (1975a). A discriminant function procedure for identifying abusing parents. *Suicide and Life Threatening Behavior, 5,* 104-114.

Paulson, M.J., Afifi, A.A., Chaleff, A., Thomason, M.L., & Liu, V.Y. (1975b). An MMPI scale for identifying "at risk" abusive parents. *Journal of Clinical Child Psychology, 4,* 22-24.

Paulson, M.J., Afifi, A.A., Thomason, M.L., & Chaleff, A. (1974). The MMPI: A descriptive measure of psychopathology in abusive parents. *Journal of Clinical Psychology, 30,* 387-390.

Paulson, M.J., Schwemer, G.T., & Bendel, R.B. (1976). Clinical application of the Pd, Ma, and (OH) experimental MMPI scales to further understanding of abusive parents. *Journal of Clinical Psychology, 32,* 558-564.

Pelton, L.H. (1978). Child abuse and neglect: The myth of classlessness. *American Journal of Orthopsychiatry, 48,* 608-617.

Plotkin, R.C., Twentyman, C.T., & Perri, M.G. (1982). The utility of a measure of aggression in differentiating abusing parents from other parents who are experiencing familial disturbance. *Journal of Clinical Psychology, 38,* 607-610.

Polansky, N.A., Chalmers, M.A., Buttenwieser, E., & Williams, D.P. (1979). Isolation of the neglectful family. *American Journal of Orthopsychiatry, 49,* 149-152.

Quinsey, V.L., Arnold, L.S., & Pruesse M. (1980). MMPI profiles of men referred for a pretrial psychiatric assessment as a function of offense type. *Journal of Clinical Psychology, 36*, 410-417.

Rist, K. (1979). Incest: Theoretical and clinical views. *American Journal of Orthopsychiatry, 49*, 680-691.

Roland, B.C., Zelhart, P.F., Cochran, S.W., & Funderburk, V.W. (1985). MMPI correlates of clinical women who report early sexual abuse. *Journal of Clinical Psychology, 41*, 763-766.

Scott, R.L., & Stone, D.A. (1986a). MMPI measures of psychological disturbance and adult victims of father-daughter incest. *Journal of Clinical Psychology, 42*, 251-259.

Scott, R.L., & Stone, D.A. (1986b). MMPI profile constellations in incest families. *Journal of Consulting and Clinical Psychology, 54*, 364-368.

Swenson, W.M., & Grimes, B.P. (1958). Characteristics of sex offenders admitted to a Minnesota State Hospital for presentence psychiatric investigation. *Psychiatric Quarterly Supplement, 31*, 110-123.

Toobert, S., Bartelme, K.F., & Jones, E.S. (1959). Some factors related to pedophila. *International Journal of Social Psychiatry, 4*, 272-279.

Tsai, M., Feldman-Summers, S., & Edgar, M. (1979). Childhood molestation: Variables related to differential impacts on psychosexual functioning in adult women. *Journal of Abnormal Psychology, 88*, 407-417.

Wright, L. (1970). Psychologic aspects of the battered child syndrome. *Southern Medical Journal, 58*, 56-60.

Wright, L. (1976). The "sick but slick" syndrome as a personality component of parents of battered children. *Journal of Clinical Psychology, 32*, 41-45.

Chapter 10

Issues in the Assessment of Adolescent Psychopathology

ROBERT P. ARCHER and
J. D. BALL

OVERVIEW

Given that this chapter is embedded within a text examining MMPI findings among special diagnostic groups, the curious reader may wonder whether adolescence is to be treated here as a "psychiatric disorder." For many of us, personal memories of our own adolescence might only substantiate the case for such a position. In fact, a recent Feiffer cartoon implied that if adolescence is a disease, it may be incurable (see Figure 10–1).

The authors do *not*, however, view adolescence as a pathologic condition. The topic of the assessment of psychopathology in adolescents is suited for inclusion in this text since adolescents are a special MMPI population, i.e., a group with unique characteristics and features that potentially may affect MMPI utilization. Many practitioners may be surprised to learn, however, that the empirical literature on MMPI usage with adolescents has been scarce in relation to massive MMPI research on adult respondents. Despite over 8,000 publications that have dealt with varying aspects of the MMPI (Butcher, 1985), recent reviews have found only 100 publications directly pertaining to the MMPI with adolescent respondents (Archer, 1987). Thus, the extensive clinical usage of the MMPI with adolescents has outpaced empirical guidance. While many of MMPI administration and interpretation practices standardly used with adults also may be applied profitably to adolescents, this chapter overviews those normative features and interpretive approaches unique to adolescents. Furthermore, this chapter discusses methods of maximizing the usefulness of the MMPI for adolescent assessment, treatment planning, and evaluation.

Consistent with the status of the MMPI among adult assessment instruments (Lubin, Larsen, Matarazzo, & Seever, 1985), the MMPI probably serves as the most widely used objective personality measure for adolescents in clinical settings (Archer, 1987). This popularity derives from both the unique capacity of the MMPI to generate meaningful clinical descriptions along a comprehensive array of dimensions, and the

THE MMPI: USE WITH
SPECIFIC POPULATIONS

ISBN   0-8089-1913-X

FEIFFER®

UNIVERSAL PRESS SYNDICATE

4400 Johnson Drive   Fairway, Kansas 66205   (913) 362-1523

FIGURE 10–1. Jules Feiffer (Copyright 1986). Reprinted with permission from Universal Press syndicate. All rights reserved.

nominal competition in this area offered by other objective personality measures. Competing instruments primarily include the Millon Adolescent Personality Inventory (MAPI: Millon, Green, & Meagher, 1977), the Personality Inventory for Children (PIC: Wirt, Lachar, Klinedinst, Seat, & Broen, 1982), and the Symptom Checklist-90-Revised (SCL-90-R: Derogatis, 1977). While these instruments have areas of unique strengths, each contains substantial limitations or weaknesses that have tended to restrict their usefulness for clinicians and researchers. The Millon Adolescent Personality Inventory is a theoretically promising instrument that has thus far received relatively little empirical evaluation. The PIC does not directly assess the adolescent's perceptions or responses, but depends instead on information provided about the child or adolescent by an adult, typically the child's mother. The SCL-90-R, while including adolescent norms, has received little empirical research in the evaluation of adolescent psychopathology.

DEVELOPMENTAL PERSPECTIVES OF ADOLESCENCE

Adolescence has long been recognized as a period of the life cycle about which much uncertainty prevails. This uncertainty is partially reflected in the continuing debate over whether adolescence constitutes a uniquely turbulent and stressful period of development. Before reviewing the storm and stress controversy, it may be helpful to recount the existing consensus regarding adolescent development.

Nearly all writers in this area concur that there are rapid physiologic and psychological changes that challenge adolescents' coping abilities. Significant physical changes in endocrinologic, biochemical, and physiologic processes contribute to a pubertal "growth spurt" that is often disconcerting to adolescent and parent alike. (e.g., Stone & Church, 1957). In addition, Piaget (1969) has detailed the adolescent's cognitive transition from the stages of concrete to formal operations.

The formal operations stage marks the development of the ability to reason abstractly and "think about thinking," which in turn often contributes to a preoccupation with examining the world as it *should* be or as it hypothetically *could* be (Elkind, 1974). Finally, psychological and socioemotional tasks include the development of an integrative and comprehensive self-concept or ego identity (Erikson, 1956), and the accomplishment of the adolescent's individualization from family (Rank, 1945; Blos, 1967). This latter process often is accompanied by a sharply increased self-reliance and identification with same-aged peers. While each of these changes is potentially dramatic when considered alone, their combined impact on adolescent behavior is particularly powerful. Futhermore, an individual's progress in each area may occur at varying times, making overall development more uneven and stressful.

THE STORM AND STRESS VIEW

G. Stanley Hall (1904), considered the father of child psychology in this country, was the first to formulate the *Sturm und Drang* or *Storm and Stress* model of adolescent development. This view, consistent with that of Anna Freud (1958), postulates that adolescence is *typically* accompanied by emotional upheavals and behavioral turbulence. In fact, Anna Freud expressed concern for adolescents who did not exhibit or express this turmoil, since she believed they were at greater risk to manifest adult forms of psychopathology. Blos (1962) also supported the storm and stress view by noting that adolescents often exhibit behaviors that resemble emotional illness or psychopathology. Modern object relations theorists (e.g., Masterson, 1968) account for this turmoil as stemming from an onrush of instinctual drives in puberty that in turn exacerbate any unresolved conflicts from mother-infant interactional patterns.

THE NORMALCY VIEW

In contrast to the turbulence view, other theorists have questioned the presumed inevitability of adolescent storm and stress. For example, Bandura (1964) argued, on the basis of interview data, that many adolescents establish more trusting and relaxed (rather than more conflictual) relationships with their parents during adolescence and that increased contact with peer groups is not necessarily a source of family tension. Bandura, working out of a social learning theory model, suggested that how adolescents respond to stress is more a function of prior learning experience than of age.

Muuss (1975) also related adolescent stress to specific cultural factors and to the rate of social change, suggesting that the modern phenomenon of rapid social change (Tofler, 1970) presents an additional challenge to today's adolescents. Other writers have drawn on the work of Margaret Mead (1928, 1930) to argue for cultural rather than age-determined adolescent turmoil (Balswick & Macrides, 1975).

On adolescent psychopathology, Weiner and Del Gaudio (1976) reviewed the literature and concluded that: (1) psychiatric symptoms are not a normative feature of adolescence; (2) boundaries between normal and abnormal adolescence can be drawn despite inherent difficulities; and (3) rather than "a passing phase," psychological disturbance during adolescence typically requires treatment for remission.

IMPLICATIONS OF DEVELOPMENTAL PERSPECTIVES ON MMPI INTERPRETATION

The view that adolescence is a unique and stormy period of marked and dramatic developmental change would suggest that adolescents can be expected to respond to the MMPI in a fashion that is measurably distinct from adult respondents. As Hathaway and Monachesi (1963) documented, this is in fact the case. For example, 74 percent of male adolescents endorse the MMPI item: "I am neither gaining nor losing weight" as being false. In contrast, 84 percent of adult men endorse this item as being true. While an adolescent endorsement in the false direction typically signifies the adolescent's rapid physiologic growth, an adult endorsement in this direction often suggests possible depressive symptomatology.

While there has been long-standing recognition that adolescents respond differently than adults to selected MMPI items, the decision over whether to use separate norms for adolescents has been less clear cut. If developmental processes for adolescents and adults are analogous (rather than dissimilar), and symptomatology displayed during adolescence is relatively enduring (rather than transient and age-determined), then adolescent responses on the MMPI can be best understood against a backdrop of adult norms. In contrast, if adolescence is a unique developmental period with a high base rate of aberrant and transient experiences and behaviors, then adolescents can be best understood when compared not with adults, but with other adolescents.

ADOLESCENT MMPI RESPONSES AND ADULT NORMS

When samples of MMPI responses for normal adolescents have been analyzed according to adult norms, typically employing the *K*-correction, mean profiles have usually been elevated on Scales *F, 4, 6, 7, 8,* and *9* (Ball, 1960; Baughman & Dahlstrom, 1968; Hathaway & Monachesi, 1961; Marks, Seeman, & Haller, 1974). Furthermore, when MMPI responses of adolescents in clinical settings are compared with adult norms, Scales reflecting serious psychopathology, such as *F, 4, 6,* and *8,* are typically elevated to a marked degree (Archer, 1984; Archer, White, & Orvin, 1979; Burke & Eichberg, 1972; Dudley, Mason, & Hughes, 1972; Ehrenworth & Archer, 1985; Klinge, Lachar, Grisell, & Berman, 1978; Klinge & Strauss, 1976; Mlott, 1972). This latter pattern has been consistent across both inpatient and outpatient samples and both male and female adolescents.

Archer (1984) has shown that norm conversion differences can range as large as 20 *T*-score points or greater when the same raw score values are plotted and contrasted against standard *K*-corrected adult norms and the age-appropriate adolescent norms published by Marks et al. (1974). These evaluation differences are also not simply the effects of *K*-corrections in adult profiles. The relative norm differences on Scales *F* and *4* are unaffected by *K*-corrections, and, even though Scales *7* and *8* are equally affected by K-corrections, only Scale *8* is dramatically elevated in adolescent profiles in contrast to adult norms.

Archer et al. (1979) provide typical findings when adolescents in psychiatric samples are viewed on adult norms. These authors examined 64 adolescent psychiatric inpatients with several objectives, including the description of mean MMPI admission profiles of males and females. Figure 10–2 shows the mean male and female profiles for this group of adolescent inpatients and

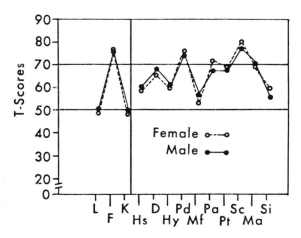

FIGURE 10–2. Mean MMPI profile for male and female adolescent inpatients using *K*-corrected adult norms. From Archer, R. P., White, J. L., & Orvin, G. H. [1979]. MMPI characteristics and correlates among adolescent psychiatric inpatients. *Journal of Clinical Psychology, 35,* 501. Copyright 1979 by the Journal of Clinical Psychology. Reprinted with permission.

displays the familiar Scales *F, 4, 6,* and *8* elevation patterns when adolescent responses are scored on adult norms. As shown in Figure 10–2, the MMPI profiles of male and female adolescent inpatients were highly similiar.

A number of studies also have shown that the use of adult norms with adolescents tends to produce high rates of false-positive errors for schizophrenic diagnoses (Archer, 1984; Chase, Chaffin, & Morrison, 1975; Ehrenworth, 1984; Gottesman & Fishman, 1961; Hathaway, Monachesi, & Salasin, 1970; Klinge et al., 1978; Klinge & Strauss, 1976). Chase et al. (1975), for example, found the false-positive rate for schizophrenia among adolescent inpatients, based on adult MMPI norms, to be 32.5 percent. Gottesman and Fishman (1961), in a study of normal adolescents, found that 63.5 percent of their subjects produced a "psychotic-like" profile when evaluated on adult MMPI norms.

These data support the popular perception that the adolescent life experience is turbulent in comparison with that of the adult. Compared with adult behavior, "typical" or high-frequency adolescent behaviors often *resemble* serious emotional disturbance and may be incorrectly seen as evidence of relatively enduring symptomatology.

In particular, adolescents show higher elevations on measures of confusion and psychological turmoil (Scale *F*), conflict with authority, impulsivity, and rebelliousness (Scale *4*), marked interpersonal oversensitivity (Scale *6*), and greater social alienation (Scale *8*). Gottesman and Fishman (1961) speculated that the typical adolescent MMPI elevations found when using adult norms are in response to the "normative crisis of adolescence," which bears a misleading resemblance to the "crisis of psychosis" manifested by adults.

ADOLESCENT RESPONSES
WITH ADOLESCENT NORMS

While the MMPI has been used for research and clinical purposes with adolescent respondents for over 40 years, the publication of adolescent norms did not occur until the 1970s. The relative delay in the creation of adolescent norms may be a result of hesitation and resistance to develop such a specialized norm set by the early researchers and theorists in this field.

Hathaway and Monachesi (1963) collected the largest MMPI data set ever obtained on adolescents when they administered the MMPI to 3971 Minnesotan ninth graders during a 1947–1948 school year and to 11,329 ninth graders across the state in 1954. Additionally, the MMPI was readministered to a sample of 3,856 of these children when they reached the twelfth grade in 1957. Their data continue to serve as the most comprehensive source of information concerning differences in frequencies of item endorsement between adolescents and adults. Specifically, Hathaway and Monachesi found that roughly 6 percent of the item pool for males and 9 percent of the item pool for females produced differences of 25 points or greater in the percentage of true responses when item endorsements were compared for adults and adolescents.

Correlates of adolescent single scale elevations encountered by Hathaway and Monachesi (1963) frequently were similiar to those found for adults. Elevations on Scale *4*, for example, were found commonly among adolescents and related to higher rates of delinquent behavior. However, much of the data produced by adolescents also appeared to involve scale correlates uniquely characteristic of adolescent respondents. Elevations on Scale *8*, for example, were found frequently in adolescents who produced no evidence of

schizophrenic symptomatology, either at the time of testing or in later follow-ups, but were of lower intelligence (boys) and experienced a higher rate of parental separation or divorce (girls).

Hathaway and Monachesi (1963) appeared to be well aware of the MMPI differences between adolescents and adults in their statement that

> Many young people show similarity to psychotic patients in their response patterns when contrasted to the data on neurotic scales indicating that symptoms of depression, physical complaint, and psychasthenia are less common in the adolescent. Maturation appears to lead the adolescent from a pattern of sociopathy or psychosis towards neurosis as an adult (1963, p. 39).

Despite awarness of these differences, these early researchers were disinclined to develop separate adolescent norms. In fact, they expressly noted, "We do not advocate the use of special juvenile norms with the MMPI, since to do so would arbitrarily erase much of the contrast between adolescents and adults" (1963, p. 39). Similarly, Dahlstrom and Welsh (1960) claimed that there would be a strong risk of obscuring significant clinical material for adolescent respondents if adolescent norms were used. They believed that adolescent psychopathologic symptoms could be of clinical significance even when such symptomatology occurred with high frequency in the adolescent population.

Marks et al. (1974) developed the first MMPI norms for adolescents based on selected subsamples of the Hathaway and Monachesi Minnesota data combined with additional samples of normal male and female adolescents from rural and urban settings in six states. These norms were grouped by sex and subdivided into four age categories: ≤ 14, 15, 16, 17, and 18. These normative data have served as the exclusive source of adolescent norms for over a decade and have been reprinted in Archer (1987), Dahlstrom, Welsh, and Dahlstrom (1972), Lachar (1974), and Greene (1980).

Marks et al. (1974) also were interested in the development of clinical correlates for commonly occurring MMPI codetypes in adolescents. However, they expressed the belief that the adult norms provided an appropriate basis of comparison for adolescent patients: "We are in basic agreement with the recommendation of Hathaway and Monachesi that one should view adolescent

MMPI scores against an adult norm background" (Marks et al., 1974, p. 137). However, they also provided an additional proposal that clinicians convert adolescent response patterns to both adult and adolescent norms and utilize the information derived from both norm sources. This recommendation has commonly been implemented as a "best fit" approach to adolescent MMPI interpretation, i.e., profiles scored on both norm sets are examined, and the profile most closely corresponding to the patient's symptomatology is stressed in interpretation. This recommendation has continued to be a widely accepted practice (e.g., Greene, 1980; Williams, 1986), although it lacks clear empirical support.

A series of recent reviews (Archer, 1984, 1987) have recommended that adolescent MMPI responses be evaluated exclusively in reference to adolescent age-appropriate norms. The grounds for this recommendation as presented by Archer (1987, in press) may be summarized based on the following observations: (1) as previously noted, when researchers have converted adolescent MMPI responses to adult norms, the resulting profiles have shown consistent patterns of marked clinical elevations in a manner that overemphasized antisocial and schizophrenic symptomatology in relation to known subject characteristics (Archer, 1984); (2) recent research by Ehrenworth and Archer (1985) has demonstrated that only 25 percent of adolescent inpatient profiles produced the same codetype (high-point pairs) on adolescent and adult norms; (3) research by Lachar, Klinge, and Grisell (1976) and by Wimbish (1984) has shown that the accuracy of adolescent MMPI interpretations based on adolescent norms, as judged by clinicians in blind ratings, is significantly greater than the accuracy of statements derived for adolescents based on adult norms; and (4) Archer (1984) has compared the factor analytic findings for adolescents on the MMPI clinical scales using adolescent and adult norms and has observed that the factor structure produced by adolescent norms is more congruent with the basic overall MMPI dimensions of psychopathology that have been found consistently in factor analytic studies of this instrument (Block, 1965; Butcher & Pancheri, 1976).

While the use of adult norms may cause substantial distortions in adolescent profiles, it is unfortunately true that use of adolescent norms also typically produces problems for MMPI interpreta-

tion. In particular, psychiatrically hospitalized adolescents have consistently produced subclinical (T-score of < 70) mean MMPI profiles when their responses have been analyzed based on adolescent norms (Archer, 1984; Archer, Ball, & Hunter, 1985; Archer, Stolberg, Gordon, & Goldman, 1986; Ehrenworth & Archer, 1985; Klinge et al., 1978; Klinge & Strauss, 1976; Lachar et al., 1976). Even when adolescents have been judged to be so severely disturbed that they require inpatient treatment, the difference between them and their better functioning peers is much smaller than is the case between normal and hospitalized adults. For example, Ehrenworth and Archer (1985) examined 66 adolescent inpatients to evaluate the validity of various MMPI codetype interpretations (to be discussed in more detail later). Figures 10–3 and 10–4 depict the mean MMPI profiles for males and females, respectively, using both adult K-corrected norms and adolescent norms. While the adult norm profiles show characteristic elevations indicative of serious psychopathology (e.g., Scales F, 4, and 8), adolescent norm profiles are subclinical for both male and females.

The use of traditional criterion (T-score of 70 or greater) for interpreting clinical level psychopathology would result in the judgment that most psychiatrically hospitalized adolescents are "nor-

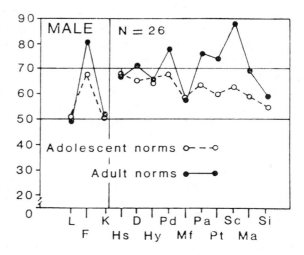

FIGURE 10–3. Mean MMPI profiles for male adolescent inpatients using adolescent and K-corrected adult norms. From Ehrenworth, N. V., & Archer, R. P. [1985]. A comparison of clinical accuracy ratings of interpretive approaches for adolescent MMPI responses. *Journal of Personality Assessment, 49,* 417–418. Copyright 1985 by Lawrence Erlbaum Associates. Reprinted with permission.

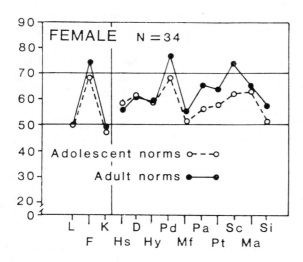

FIGURE 10–4. Mean MMPI profiles for female adolescent inpatients using adolescent and *K*-corrected adult norms. From Ehrenworth, N. V., & Archer, R. P. [1985]. A comparison of clinical accuracy ratings of interpretive approaches for adolescent MMPI responses. *Journal of Personality Assessment, 49,* 417–418. Copyright 1985 by Lawrence Erlbaum Associates. Reprinted with permission.

mal" when compared against adolescent MMPI norms. Some might argue that this high percentage of adolescents in treatment settings who produced within-normal limits MMPI profiles reflects adult intolerance for adolescent misbehavior, i.e., that these adolescents have been placed inappropriately in treatment. An alternative explanation, based on the current adolescent normative findings to be discussed in more detail later in this chapter, is that while the Marks et al. (1974) adolescent norms are better suited than adult norms to this population, traditional cut-off points for interpretive purposes are inappropriate. A significantly greater proportion of adolescents than adults (27 percent vs. 5 percent) produce normal range MMPI profiles on admission to inpatient facilities (Archer, 1987). Furthermore, 43 percent of the outpatient adolescents in this investigation were found to produce within-normal limits profiles on adolescent norms.

Adolescent profiles may yield greater information if clinicians are prepared to employ flexibility in their definition of clinical symptomatology with adolescent groups. Ehrenworth and Archer (1985) and Archer (1987) have recommended consideration of a *T*-score value of 65 in defining clinical range elevations for adolescents in clinical set-

tings. This recommendation is based on a view that the typical adolescent experiences sufficient psychological turbulence and distress such that even relatively minor deviations in the course of normal development may be sufficient to warrant psychiatric intervention and response. Thus, "subclinical" higher-range elevations (i.e., $T > 65$) on adolescent MMPI profiles may be significantly correlated with important clinical evidence of psychopathology.

STANDARD VALIDITY AND CLINICAL SCALES

VALIDITY SCALES

CANNOT SAY (?)

Ball and Carroll (1960) found that boys were more likely to omit "Cannot Say" items than girls and that omitted items tended to be related to religious beliefs, sexuality and bodily functions, and items that required the adolescent to be committal in areas in which they felt ambivalent. Hathaway and Monachesi (1963) also noted that items related to religion and sex were the most frequently omitted by adolescents. Generally, adolescent item omissions may be more closely associated with intellectual and reading limitations than with oppositional characteristics (Ball & Carroll, 1960).

T-score conversions are not currently available for adolescents on the "Cannot Say *(?)*" Scale, but some raw-score based interpretation guidelines may be suggested. Raw-score values within the range of 0–10 may be considered to represent a normal or expected range of omitted items. This level of item omissions is unlikely to significantly distort profile features or to affect the accuracy of MMPI interpretation (Clopton & Neuringer, 1977). Raw-score values of 11–30 on the "Cannot Say" Scale represent substantially more omissions than might be typically expected and often are produced by adolescents who are very indecisive or resistant. Distortions in profile elevation or configuration may occur, particularly if missing items are concentrated within a few scales. Adolescents who omit 31 or more items on the MMPI should be requested to complete the unanswered items or to retake the entire test. This range of "Cannot Say" Scale values is very likely to affect profile validity and often is produced by defiant or uncooperative adolescents or teenagers who are experiencing serious reading deficits or difficulties.

LIE (L)

The Lie Scale appears to be one of the MMPI indices that is relatively unaffected by the use of adolescent vs. adult norms in terms of T-score elevation differences (Archer, 1987). While there has been little research into the correlates of the L Scale among adolescents, elevations on this scale appear to bear similar meanings for both adult and adolescent respondents (Archer, 1987).

Low scores on the L Scale (T-score values < 46) may reflect an open, calm, and confident stance among normal adolescents and may indicate the presence of an "all true" response set or the over-reporting of psychopathology among psychiatrically disturbed teenagers. Moderate elevations in the range of T-score values of 61–70 may be related generally to tendencies toward conformity and the use of denial as a primary defense mechanism for adolescent respondents. Marked elevations with T-score values ≥ 70 may reflect an "all false" response set, the underreporting of psychopathology, or unsophisticated attempts by teenagers to present themselves in a highly favorable and "saintly" manner. Higher-range L Scale scores have been related to longer treatment durations among hospitalized adolescents (Archer et al., 1979).

FREQUENCY (F)

Significant F Scale elevation differences between adolescent and adult respondents have been found consistently. Higher adolescent elevations on the F Scale have been so commonplace that the Marks et al. (1974) recommendation of a raw-score validity criteria of 26 appears much more productive than the cut-off of $F > 16$ proposed by Meehl (1956). Archer (1984) recommended particular caution with the F Scale before a clinician concludes that a profile has been invalidated by an overreporting of psychopathology. He specifically suggested employing flexible F Scale validity criterion values, dependent on the degree of false negatives and false positives that the user is prepared to tolerate for a particular assessment task with a specific adolescent population.

Because T-score conversion values vary substantially as a function of age and sex on Scale F, interpretation guidelines may be most consistently undertaken in reference to raw-score values. Raw-score values of 4 or less on the F Scale may reflect very conventional life experiences among normal adolescents or may indicate an underreporting of psychopathology when produced by adolescents in psychiatric settings. At the other end of the F Scale range, raw score values of 16–25 represent marked elevations that should indicate that the validity characteristics of the adolescent profile are to be examined carefully. Valid profiles with F Scale values in this range most likely reflect serious psychopathology including severe behavioral problems and psychosis. Raw score values of 26 or greater on Scale F reflect extreme elevations on this measure. MMPI protocols with F scores in this range are very likely to be invalid. If overreporting of psychopathology, random, and all-true response sets may be ruled out, adolescents scoring in this range are likely to be severely disorganized or overtly psychotic.

DEFENSIVENESS (K)

The mean raw score K Scale values found in the Marks et al. (1974) adolescent sample and in the adult normative sample are nearly equivalent (Archer, 1987). The minimal research regarding the interpretive meaning of the K Scale in these populations also suggests few differences.

Markedly low elevations on the K Scale (T-score < 45) tend to be produced by adolescents who are offering a psychological "cry for help" in response to acute distress and who have limited coping resources and poor self-concepts. Scores in this range also may be related to overreporting of psychopathology by normal teenagers. In contrast, marked elevations on the K Scale (T-score > 65) often are produced by adults and adolescents who are defensive and resistant to psychological interpretations and interventions. In both the adolescent (Archer et al., 1979) and adult (Greene, 1980) literatures, high K Scale profiles have been linked to a poor prognosis for psychological intervention due to the respondents' refusal or inability to discuss psychological problem areas and consequent resistance to treatment efforts.

While the K-correction procedure with adult respondents has become a standard practice, the adolescent norms developed by Marks et al.

(1974) do not employ *K*-corrections. As noted earlier, this *K*-correction procedure difference cannot fully account for the different *T*-scores adolescents show when profiles on adult vs. adolescent norms. However, the absence of *K*-corrections for adolescent profiles presents a substantial problem for interpreters, and the empirical development of adolescent *K*-corrections is long overdue. Two separate adolescent norm projects are currently developing *K*-corrected *T*-score conversions for adolescents utilizing the standard weights employed for adults (i.e., Colligan & Offord, 1987; Gottesman, Hanson, Kroeker, & Briggs, 1987).

RESPONSE SET ISSUES

Archer, Gordon, and Kirchner (1987) recently offered data regarding characteristics of "all true" and "all false" adolescent response patterns, and these response set profiles on adolescent norms also are presented by Archer (in press). The "all true" response pattern is reflected by extremely low scores on Scales *L* and *K* and marked elevations on the *F* Scale. This pattern is associated with raw-score values of near zero for *L*

and *K* and a marked psychotic slope on Scales *6, 7, 8,* and *9.* If the special scales such as the Welsh Anxiety Factor (*A*: Welsh, 1956) and the MacAndrew Alcoholism Scale (*MAC*: MacAndrew, 1965) are scored, these scales also are elevated in high clinical ranges. The Welsh Repression Factor (*R*: Welsh, 1956) and the Ego Strength Scale (*Es*: Barron, 1953) would have markedly low values. These "all true" results are similar to those obtained from adults (Graham, 1987).

The characteristic "all false" profile pattern on adolescent norms produces extreme elevations on all validity scales and on the first three clinical scales (i.e., Scales *1, 2,* and *3*) or the "neurotic triad." When special scales are scored, an extreme elevation is also found for the *R* Scale. Again, these findings are similar to adult "all false" profiles as reported by Graham (1987) and Lachar (1974).

Figure 10–5 shows the Archer et al. (1987) findings for a random response pattern among adolescents. This configuration is characterized by moderate to marked elevations on the *F* Scale and moderate clinical elevations on the neurotic triad (i.e., Scales *1, 2,* and *3*) and on Scale *8.* Whenever adolescents complete the MMPI too quickly, a

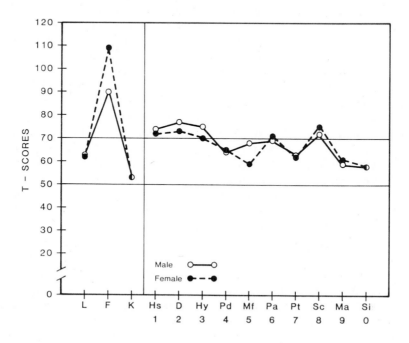

FIGURE 10–5. MMPI random porfiles 15 years old. From Archer, R. P., Gordon, R. A., & Kirchner, F. H. (1987). MMPI response set characteristics among adolescents. *Journal of Personality Assessment, 51,* 510. Copyright 1985 by Lawrence Erlbaum Associates. Reprinted with permission.

random response set should be suspected. While this profile is similar in mean elevation to the random set profile produced by adults, adolescent random profiles are significantly different in shape, rendering detection of random adolescent profiles more difficult.

Regarding the conscious or unconscious efforts to overreport symptomatology, prior comments regarding *F* Scale elevations in adolescent profiles are pertinent. As noted previously, $F > 25$ should raise marked suspicions of an overreporting profile but should not become an automatic criterion for classifying a profile as invalid. *T*-score elevations above 69 on the eight clinical scales (excluding Scales *5* and *0*) represent a "floating" profile that is also suggestive of overreporting of psychopathology in adolescent populations. Floating profiles were found to be much less common in an adolescent sample (1 percent) than in an adult psychiatric sample (13 percent) (Archer, 1987).

Archer et al. (1987) gave instructions to overreport psychopathology to a group of 94 high school students who were equally divided in terms of sex and race (black-white) and found the mean profile shown in Figure 10–6. This profile is similar to adult findings (Lachar, 1974; Graham, 1987) and shows a grossly exaggerated picture of symptomatology with a mean *F* Scale *T*-score value of 130 and clinical range elevations on all clinical scales except *5* and *0*. Thus, the adolescents in the Archer et al. (1987) sample were largely unable to offer a creditable or an undetectable overreporting response style. Clearly, the presence of both *F* Scale raw score > 25 and clinical range elevations on the eight clinical scales represent a particularly serious warning signal of a possible overreporting profile.

Another threat to MMPI profile validity occurs when adolescents consciously or unconsciously attempt to underreport symptomatology. Archer (1987) found that roughly 2 percent of adolescent inpatients and 1 percent of adolescent outpatients produced a characteristic underreporting profile in which there were *T*-score elevations on both *L* and *K* of 65 or greater and a classic "V" validity scale configuration (Archer, 1987). In addition, when adolescents with known and marked psychopathology (such as adolescent psychiatric inpatients) produce no MMPI clinical scales in excess of *T*-score values of 65, the possibility of a subtle underreporting of psychopathology should be considered.

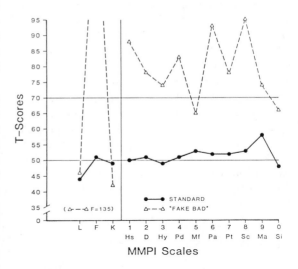

FIGURE 10–6. Normal adolescent MMPI profiles under standard and "fake bad" instructions. From Archer, R. P., Gordon, R. A., & Kirchner, F. H. (1987). MMPI response set characteristics among adolescents. *Journal of Personality Assessment, 51,* 511. Copyright 1985 by Lawrence Erlbaum Associates. Reprinted with permission.

Archer et al. (1987) gave instructions to underreport psychological symptoms to 22 adolescent psychiatric inpatients (10 female and 12 male). Two distinct profiles emerged as seen in Figure 10–7. One profile type, produced by eight subjects, was termed an "ineffective" profile. This profile was a poor simulation of normalcy and each adolescent in this group produced one or more clinical scales elevated at *T*-score values of ≥ 70. A second profile group, produced by 14 subjects, was termed an "effective" simulation of normalcy and all of these subjects produced clinical scale *T*-score values of < 70. Subjects in the ineffective group were significantly younger and tended to receive more serious psychiatric diagnoses. Perhaps more importantly, however, the high *F* Scale scores for this group would indicate that most of these respondents either failed to understand the instructional set or chose to be uncooperative and responded randomly. Subjects who effectively underreported symptoms were older, received less severe diagnoses, and produced lower scores on Scales *1* and *3* on their actual MMPI profiles given under standard conditions. There are slight elevations on Scales *L* and *K* even in the effective profile, although these validity scale elevations are well below the ranges reported by Graham (1987) for adults who were deliberately underreporting symptoms on the MMPI.

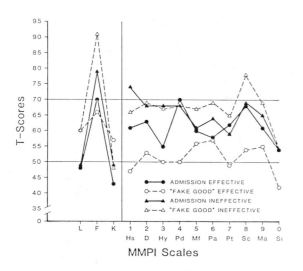

FIGURE 10–7. Mean admission and "fake good" MMPI profiles by simulation effectiveness. From Archer, R. P., Gordon, R. A., & Kirchner, F. H. (1987). MMPI response set characteristics among adolescents. *Journal of Personality Assessment, 51,* 513. Copyright 1985 by Lawrence Erlbaum Associates. Reprinted with permission.

CLINICAL SCALES

Research with the MMPI in adolescent populations has demonstrated the utility of the clinical scales for detecting specific diagnostic groups. The early research by Hathaway and Monachesi (1963) established a relationship between specific MMPI elevation patterns and the subsequent development of delinquency. Elevations on Scales *4, 8,* and *9,* singly or in combination, were associated with higher frequencies of delinquent behavior during follow-up periods of data collection. These scales were labeled as *excitatory* scales by Hathaway and Monachesi. In contrast, elevations on Scales *2, 5,* and *0* were associated with reduced rates of delinquent behavior and termed *suppressor* scales in reference to delinquent behaviors. These relationships held across both sexes and were, in fact, more marked for girls than for boys. Follow-up research has provided consistent support for these findings (e.g., Briggs, Wirt, & Johnson, 1961; Rempel, 1958; Wirt & Briggs, 1959). In particular, the findings by Briggs et al. (1961) and by Rempel (1958) have shown that the accuracy of prediction of delinquent behaviors is highest when MMPI data are combined with independent sources of demographic or social history data.

The major source of information concerning clinical correlates of adolescent MMPI response patterns was published by Marks et al. in 1974. This study has become very appropriately a classic in the MMPI literature, and its findings have been integrated into standard interpretive practice when using the MMPI with adolescents. The main sample from which Marks et al. developed adolescent codetype descriptors consisted of 834 teenagers receiving psychotherapy between the years 1965–1970. In acquiring this data set, the authors contacted 74 agencies in 30 states, ultimately involving 172 therapists who agreed to provide research data. The treatment sample consisted of adolescents between the ages of 12 and 18 inclusive, who had been involved in psychotherapy for a minimum of 10 therapy hours. Of the 172 psychotherapists who provided patient ratings, 116 were mental health professionals with at least 2 years of postgraduate experience.

Therapists completed an adjective checklist, a case data schedule, and a Q-sort inventory for each of their patients. In addition, each adolescent completed a variety of self-administered objective questionnaires covering topic areas such as attitude toward self, attitudes toward others, areas of primary conflict, and motivational needs. In total, a correlate pool was available to Marks et al. that consisted of 2,302 descriptors potentially relevant to adolescent development and symptomatology. From this pool, the authors selected 1,265 descriptors that occurred with sufficient frequency to permit data analysis and were judged to be clinically relevant for codetype analysis. In addition to the 1960s sample, Marks et al. collected further data in an adolescent sample consisting of 419 psychiatric patients in treatment at the Ohio State University Health Center during the period of 1970–1973.

Based on the combined data set, Marks and his colleagues were able to create narratives for 29 adolescent codetypes generated by at least 10 adolescents in each codetype. In contrast to prior research in the area, the investigation by Marks et al. presented clinicians with a meaningful set of clinical correlates for adolescent profiles based on clearly defined methodologic and statistical derivation procedures.

The relatively limited sample size employed by Marks et al. resulted in large variability in the number of subjects included in codetype analysis. For example, codetype descriptors were based on only 11 subjects for each of the following code-types: *1-6/6-1, 5-6/6-5, 5-0/0-5,* and *7-0/0-7.* In contrast, 94 subjects were employed in the *4-9/9-4* code and 60 subjects were employed in the *2-4/4-2.* In general, nearly 50 percent of the subjects employed by Marks et al. were assigned to high-point pair codetypes involving Scale *4* combinations. Only two studies (Ehrenworth & Archer, 1985; Wimbish, 1984) have examined the relative accuracy of the Marks et al. descriptors in contrast to codetype narrative descriptors for adult respondents (e.g., Graham, 1987; Greene, 1980). While Wimbish (1984) found the Marks et al. interpretive system to be superior to others, Ehrenworth and Archer (1985) obtained significantly lower accuracy ratings for the Marks et al. interpretive approach. However, all interpretive approaches in Ehrenworth and Archer (1985) were judged by clinicians to be less than "generally complete and accurate." Given the limitations of these studies (e.g., small samples in inpatient settings) and their contradictory results, there is still too little empirical evidence to judge the relative accuracy of the Marks et al. interpretive narratives.

Archer (1987) recently compared the adolescent codetype descriptors generated by the Marks et al. (1974) investigation with the codetype descriptors based on adult studies. He proposed that the Marks et al. sets of descriptors become increasingly more similar and consistent with the adult correlate literature in rough proportion to the relative sample sizes employed by Marks et al. in deriving a particular set of codetype descriptors. Specifically, it was noted that in the larger codetype samples (e.g., *4-9/9-4,*) the congruence between adolescent and adult correlate descriptors was highest. The greatest degree of discrepancies tended to occur for those codetypes developed by Marks et al. from more restricted sample sizes. Based on this observation, Archer (1987) suggested employing a clinical interpretive approach for adolescents that combines descriptors from adolescent and adult sources and stresses those descriptors that are congruent across the adult and adolescent literatures. Archer (1987) provided a series of adolescent codetype descriptors based on this interpretive principal in conjunction with integrating single scale correlate findings from Hathaway and Monachesi (1963) and other sources.

Until such time as further research on the accuracy of clinical correlates approaches is avail-

able, or until a new source of clinical correlate information for adolescent profiles has been developed, the interpretation of adolescent MMPI profiles appears to be best undertaken through the use of both the adult correlate literature as well as the specific adolescent codetype data provided by Marks et al. (1974).

In recent years, several research studies have examined the capacity of the MMPI to detect diagnostic or physiologic correlates employing adolescent norms. Archer et al. (1985), for example, employed adolescent norms for adolescent psychiatric inpatients in a demonstration of the utility of MMPI standard scales in detecting Borderline Personality Disorder. In this project, 146 adolescent inpatients (73 male and 73 female) were grouped by principal psychiatric diagnosis, as determined by an interdisciplinary treatment team at the patient's diagnostic staffing. This procedure led to five diagnostic groupings: (1) Borderline Personality Disorder, (2) Conduct Disorder, (3) Dysthymic Disorder, (4) other personality disorders, and (5) other diagnoses. Patients with Borderline Personality Disorder could be differentiated reliably from the four other diagnostic groups on the basis of MMPI scale *T*-score responses. Specifically, the Borderline group had significantly higher mean elevations than comparison groups on MMPI Scales *F, 1, 2, 4, 6, 7, 8,* and *9.* A stepwise discriminant analysis resulted in 82.1 percent accuracy in correctly classifying Borderline patients and 78 percent accuracy in identifying nonborderline patients. Furthermore, a recent unpublished study by Archer and Gordon (in press) has shown the ability of Scale *8* T-score elevations to differentiate schizophrenic from non-schizophrenic inpatient adolescents with an overall hit rate of roughly 70 percent. Finally, a recent study by Ball, Archer, Struve, Hunter, and Gordon (1987) compared MMPI responses of psychiatric inpatient males with either normal electroencephalograph (EEG) signals or a controversial 14 and 6 per second positive spike EEG pattern. The adolescents with the controversial EEG pattern showed significantly higher elevations on Scale *1.* This finding raises interesting questions about possible psychiatric symptomatology associated with this EEG signal. It also offers support for the cautionary note researchers have sounded throughout their work with adults concerning possible overinterpretations of Scale *1* as an index of hypochondriasis to the exclusion of actual physical disorder (e.g., Osborne, 1979; Prokop, 1986; Prokop, Bradley, Margolis, & Gentry, 1980; Watson & Buranen, 1979).

SPECIAL/RESEARCH SCALES

THE MACANDREW (MAC) SCALE

The *MAC* Scale (MacAndrew, 1965) is one of very few special research scales that have received empirical support for use with adolescents. Rathus, Fox, and Ortins (1980) administered a short form of the *MAC* Scale to 1,672 high school students and found *MAC* scores significantly related to marijuana use patterns as well as antisocial behaviors such as crimes against persons and property. Wolfson and Erbaugh (1984) compared *MAC* scores for four groups of adolescents: (1) normal high school students, (2) inpatient psychiatric patients without a significant history of substance abuse, (3) outpatient psychiatric patients without history of substance abuse, and (4) adolescents in residential treatment for drug abuse. The *MAC* successfully discriminated between these groups. MacAndrew (1979) has found *MAC* scores to successfully discriminate young (ages 16–21) alcohol-related male offenders from similar-age male college students and psychiatric outpatients with an overall accuracy rate of 82.1 percent using a cutoff score of 24. Other studies with adolescents have consistently shown *MAC* scores to be related to substance abuse among hospital or residential treatment samples (Klinge, 1983; Sutker, Moan, Goist, & Allain, 1984) and in a public school sample (Wisniewski, Glenwick, & Graham, 1985).

The optimal cutoff score in identifying substance abusers among adolescent respondents has not been established clearly. Current recommendations for adolescent *MAC* cutoff scores range from Wolfson and Erbaugh's (1984) suggestion of 24 for females and 26 for males to Archer's (1987) suggestion of 28 as a cutoff for both male and female adolescents. Archer's recommendation would appear to represent a conservative approach that will minimize false-positive errors in adolescent samples.

In recent studies with adult populations, Graham indicated that the *MAC* may be of limited utility in accurately identifying substance abuse within black samples. Specifically, Graham (1985)

and Graham and Mayo (1985) reported that an unacceptable high rate of false positives occurs when using standard cutoff points among black respondents. While these data have been based on investigations in adult populations, the findings are of sufficient importance to indicate substantial caution in attempting to interpret *MAC* scores of nonwhite adolescents until further research has been completed in this area.

ANXIETY (A), REPRESSION (R), AND EGO STRENGTH (Es) SCALES

There have been almost no empirical investigations of these special MMPI scales with adolescent respondents, but Welsh's Anxiety (*A*) and Repression (*R*) Scales and Barron's Ego Strength (*Es*) Scale have been so widely used with adults that they bear mention. Gottesman et al. (1987) recently developed adolescent normative information for these and other special scales based on their comprehensive analyses of the Minnesota "statewide" sample. In addition, Colligan and his colleagues (R. C. Colligan, personal communication, October, 1986) are currently developing *T*-score conversions for these scales based on their recent sample of roughly 1,300 adolescents in the Rochester, Minnesota, area. Typically, however, adult norms have been employed for the conversion of adolescent responses to these special scales due to the lack of published alternatives.

The use of adult special scale norms for adolescents is a problematic practice, representing an "interim" strategy until adolescent norms are available. In Archer's (1987) review of the Gottesman et al. (1987) adolescent normative data for special scales, the *R* and *MAC* Scales were particularly affected by differences between adult- and adolescent-based *T*-score conversion values. In general, a given raw-score value will convert to substantially higher *T*-score values in the Gottesman et al. (1987) adolescent norms for *R* Scale and substantially lower *T*-score values on the MAC, in contrast to adult *T*-score conversions. The Gottesman et al. normative data are limited to adolescents aged 15 and 18, and the generalizability of these findings to other age groupings is unknown.

Given that Welsh's (1956) *A* and *R* Scales have not been cross-validated on adolescents, their contribution to MMPI interpretation with adolescents is not supported by empirical data. However, their potential relevance may justify scoring these scales and comparing interpretive impressions with standard MMPI scale features and with the adolescent's clinical history (Archer, 1987). Typically, adolescents in clinical settings show a restricted range of values on these scales with *A* Scale *T*-scores between 60 and 75 on adult norm conversions and *R* Scale values between *T*-scores of 40 to 50 (Archer, 1987). Archer (1987) suggested that these findings may reflect the adolescent's propensity toward acting out rather than the use of neurotic styles of primary defense mechanism *(R)* and their typically elevated levels of distress at the time of treatment entrance *(A)*.

The *Es* Scale (Barron, 1953) also lacks cross-validation findings with adolescent samples. Reviews of the *Es* Scale in adult populations (Dahlstrom, Welsh, & Dahlstrom, 1975; Graham, 1987; Greene, 1980) have been mixed with respect to the ability of the *Es* Scale to assess available internal resources or to predict response to insight-oriented psychotherapeutic interventions. Use of the *Es* Scale is clearly controversial for both adults and adolescents. For the purposes of hypothesis generation, however, MMPI users might consider a *T*-score value < 50 as a signal that more supportive or behavioral interventions may be indicated during initial therapy stages unless a low *Es* score was produced by a respondent experiencing acute distress associated with a specific crisis event. In the latter case, the adolescent's *Es* score would be expected to increase rapidly as a function of crisis stabilization and such initial low *Es* values would not contraindicate insight therapies.

SUMMARY

Current Interpretive Strategies for Adolescent MMPIs

The MMPI can be used profitably with adolescents, but special caution needs to be exercised in light of the need for additional research with this population. There are ample data to suggest that adolescent responses should be evaluated through the use of adolescent norms. Clinical interpretation of adolescent MMPIs should capitalize on this empirical literature by using adolescent norms to convert raw scores to *T*-scores. Since the data regarding adolescent and adult codetype descriptors are less clear-cut with respect to which may be more accurate, the optimal interpretive strategy may be to consult both the adolescent and adult

codetype descriptors available from Marks et al. (1974) and various widely used adult "cookbooks" (Graham, 1987; Greene, 1980; Lachar, 1974), respectively. The descriptors selected for use would then be those that best matched the adolescent's history and clinical presentation. This strategy may prove superior to other commonly employed procedures such as those using adult norms in any way, those using adolescent norms and only adult codetype descriptors, or those using adolescent norms and only the Marks et al. adolescent codetypes.

Based on the available literature, adolescent MMPI users also would be advised to employ higher and more flexible *F* Scale validity cutoffs than for adult MMPIs. The earlier discussion of adult and adolescent response style differences show consistently higher *F* Scale values for adolescent respondents across a variety of normal and psychiatric settings. Similarly, adolescent MMPI users might consider experimenting with *T*-score cutoffs of 65 (rather than 70) for making clinical interpretations when adolescent responses have been converted to adolescent response norms. Finally, except for the *MAC* Scale, the use of MMPI special/research scales among adolescents lacks empirical support and warrants particular caution.

The available literature strongly indicates that the MMPI is well-suited for clinical evaluations and research investigations in adolescent populations. Our knowledge base for adolescents, however, is dramatically limited when compared with the thousands of studies that have been performed with the MMPI in adult samples. An awareness of these limitations would imply that the MMPI is best employed as a means of deriving an overall estimate and description of current psychopathology in adolescent respondents rather than in efforts to generate a specific diagnosis from the Diagnostic and Statistical Manual of Mental Disorders (DSM-III-R: American Psychiatric Association, 1987). While efforts at differential diagnosis can be usefully undertaken by use of the MMPI in conjunction with other psychometric instruments and interview and social history data, efforts to yield a definitive DSM-III-R diagnosis based exclusively on MMPI test findings are ill-advised. Furthermore, the researcher and clinician should remember that characteristics reported by adolescents may be relatively transient and unstable during this developmental period. Thus, caution should be exercised in interpreting adolescent MMPI profile features as indicative of long-standing personality characteristics.

Recommendations for Future Research

Research on the use of the MMPI with adolescents remains in its infancy. If adequate research attention is focused on gaining a better understanding of the MMPI with this age group, however, there are ample grounds to expect substantial advances over the next few years. There are numerous areas that should be systematically explored in future research efforts.

Research is needed, for example, to examine the optimal T-score elevation cutoff to employ in attempts to define psychopathology during adolescence. The current recommendations of experimentally utilizing a T-score value of ≥ 65 in defining clinical levels of symptomatology will require careful validation in order to establish the empirical utility of this approach in contrast to the traditional clinical cutoff of a T-score of 70 or above.

Second, as previously noted, the K-correction procedure that has been employed routinely for adults has not been developed in conjunction with adolescent norms. The development of an adolescent K-correction procedure would appear to be long overdue in terms of improving the clinical accuracy of adolescent MMPI interpretations. Research findings on the high rates of normal-range MMPI profiles among adolescents in clinical settings (Archer, 1987), for example, underscore the need for an effective K-correction procedure with adolescents. While research efforts are currently being geared to the application of the standard adult K-correction weights for new sets of adolescent norms (e.g., Gottesman et al., 1987; Colligan & Offord, 1987), research is needed to establish a unique K-correction procedure specifically designed for adolescent respondents. Development of such adolescent K-correction procedures would very likely result in much different weighting patterns than those used with adult respondents, possibly involving a different set of clinical scales (Heilbrun, 1963).

Finally, it is clear that while adolescents and adults characteristically respond to the MMPI in significantly different ways, there is little knowledge of why such differences occur. In particular, there is a lack of any recent item analyses of the differences between adult and adolescent respondents in a manner that would follow up the original item analyses conducted by Hathaway and Monachesi (1963). For example, the specific items in Scales F, 4, 6, or 8, that adolescents are currently endorsing with higher frequency and that generate their significantly higher raw-score mean values on these scales in comparison with adults have not been currently identified. Future research efforts analyzing adolescent response patterns at the item level are therefore, crucially needed.

There are currently several major research projects involving the MMPI and adolescents, reviewed in the following section, which may serve to generate answers to these and many other questions. After several decades of relative inattention, the use of the MMPI with adolescents has become a central focus for a variety of research approaches.

Current Research Projects

Two recent norm development projects are in progress for the use of the MMPI with adolescents.

At the Mayo Clinic Project, Colligan, Offord, and their colleagues have been working to develop contemporary adolescent norms and have produced preliminary raw-score findings (Colligan & Offord, 1987) on the basis of data collected from 1,315 adolescents in "mail-out" sampling procedures in Minnesota, Iowa, and Wisconsin. The publication of T-score conversion tables based on these data is expected to occur during 1988. The specific procedures employed by Colligan and Offord involved random sampling of nearly 12,000 households in an 8,000 square mile area surrounding Rochester, Minnesota. Telephone interviews were employed to identify households containing potential adolescent respondents between the ages of 13 and 17 years, inclusive, without histories of serious physical or psychiatric symptomatology. These procedures identified roughly 1,400 households with subjects in the desired age range who were subsequently mailed testing materials. Response rates were quite high in this mailout procedure; completed surveys were obtained for 81 to 85 percent of female adolescents and 67 to 79 percent of male adolescents across the various age groupings.

The contemporary adolescent MMPI mean raw scores found by Colligan and Offord are generally similar to the adolescent values reported by Marks et al. (1974), particularly in contrast to traditional adult normative values. Some differences are apparent, however, between the Colligan and Offord values and the adolescent norms of Marks et al. (1974). Specifically, mean raw-score data reported by Colligan and Offord tended to range up to five T-score points higher when selected clinical scales were plotted on the Marks et al. (1974) adolescent norms. Colligan and Offord (1987) suggested that clinicians plot adolescent MMPI profiles on both the traditional Marks et al. (1974) adolescent norms as well as the contemporary adolescent norms being developed at the Mayo clinic in order to evaluate more accurately the responses of adolescents.

Gottesman et al. (1987) also developed adolescent normative data based on responses from approximately 14,000 15-year-olds and 3,500 18-year-olds from the original Hathaway and Monachesi (1963) samples. At the time that Hathaway and Monachesi were conducting their research projects they did not have access to high-speed, large-capacity computers to analyze their massive data set. Therefore, much of the work of these authors was based on relatively small subsamples of their overall data pool. Gottesman et al. (1987) constructed adolescent norms based on comprehensive analyses of the 15,300 ninth-grade children tested in 1948 and 1954, and the 3,856 students retested in the twelfth grade during the 1956–1957 school year. A variety of exclusion criteria involving Scales $?$, L, and F, and chronologic age restrictions resulted in the exclusion of 1,066 15-year-olds and 182 18-year-olds from their data analyses. The authors employed a normalized *T*-score procedure in deriving their norms that is substantially different from the traditional linear transformation procedure utilized by Marks et al. (1974). Colligan, Osborne, and Offord (1980) argued in favor of this type of procedure, noting that since the degree of skewness and kurtosis in raw score distributions differed from scale to scale, a *T*-score of 70 derived from the traditional linear procedures has different meaning across scales. Furthermore, Colligan et al. (1980) noted that signficant skewness occurs for several MMPI scale distributions resulting in a tendency for traditonal *T*-score conversion procedures to produce values that overestimate the infrequency of a given raw score. Normalized vs. traditional conversion techniques have become a heated controversy in MMPI normative research. Colligan et al. (1980), Hsu (1984), Colligan, Osborne, and Offord (1984), and Hsu and Betman (1986) offer detailed discussions of the salient issues in this debate. Despite the inherent differences in the norm derivation procedures of Marks et al. (1974) and Gottesman et al. (1987), the mean raw-score values of both research groups are very similar. The rates of dispersion of scores away from the mean, however, are substantially different in the Gottesman et al. and Marks et al. data sets. Thus, the Gottesman et al. and Marks et al. norms should tend to produce different *T*-score values in samples of psychiatrically disturbed adolescents. While the Gottesman et al. data are based on MMPI responses of adolescents in the late 1940s and the 1950s, their current data are "new" in the sense of representing a complete analysis of all of the Minnesota adolescent sample, and in deriving both standard scale and numerous special scale norms from this data.

In addition to these two recent projects, the University of Minnesota is engaged in a complex and comprehensive effort termed the Restandardization Project. The goals of this effort are to derive not only contemporary adolescent and adult norms but also new test booklets that may eventually contain new and revised items in addition to the traditional item pool. As Butcher (1972) noted in an earlier publication, there have been a number of precipitants to this revision work. Many MMPI items have become dated in their content. At least 12 items are sexist in language and many others are worded awkwardly. After 40 years of research, some 50 items have been identified that do not contribute significantly to MMPI interpretation. Finally, the current MMPI item pool, while extensive, probably presents an inadequate sampling of items related to newer diagnostic categories, responses to therapeutic interventions, or symptomatology related to adolescent development.

In both the adolescent and adult experimental test forms, the initial 550 items of the MMPI item pool have been retained with relatively minor revisions affecting approximately 14 percent of these items to improve content clarity or item quality. Following the first 550 items, the adult and adolescent experimental forms each contain an additional and unique set of 154 new items such that different 704-item experimental test booklets were created for adults and adolescents. Items unique to the new adolescent form include a variety of statements specifically created because of their potential relevance to adolescent development and adolescent psychopathology. Thus, for example, new items were specifically designed to assess responses in the following areas: (1) negative peer group influences, (2) alcohol and drug abuse, (3) problems in relationships with parents, (4) school and achievement problems, (5) eating disorders, and (6) identity problems.

James Butcher, Grant Dahlstrom, John Graham, and Auke Tellegen have been advising the University of Minnesota Press on the restandardization efforts. Data collection for adult norms was completed in early 1986 in Seattle, San Diego, Minneapolis, Kent (Ohio), Philadelphia, and Norfolk (Virginia), and publication of the new adult norms is expected in 1989. Adolescent norms are projected to be available by 1990. Table 10–1 (modified from Archer, 1987) summarizes the major features of each current adolescent project, comparing these with the normative work by Marks et al. (1974). These current data collection efforts should provide, for the first time, a contemporary, national normative basis for using the MMPI with adolescents. Preliminary data from the University of Minnesota (Williams, Butcher, & Graham, 1986), the Mayo Clinic (Colligan & Offord, 1987), and a small exploratory study by Archer, Gordon, and Kirchner (1987) suggest that contemporary adolescent response patterns on the traditional item pool will represent refinements, rather than radical departures from the values reported by Marks et al. (1974). Each of the current adolescent projects eventually will serve to provide clinicians and researchers with new information concerning the MMPI response patterns of adolescents. Each effort has unique sets of strengths as well as limitations. Controlled research investigations also will be needed to evaluate the effects of these various normative values in relation to the ability to identify accurately defined sets of clinical and psychiatric disorders among adolescents.

The ultimate result of these substantial research efforts should be much greater clarity in the MMPI interpretation practices with adolescent respondents. As more and more research is brought to bear on these issues, substantially more straightforward interpretive approaches will be identified with commensurate reduction in the degree to which compensations must be made for current distortions or ambiguities in the un-

TABLE 10–1. SELECTED FEATURES OF CURRENT ADOLESCENT MMPI PROJECTS

Project Features	PROJECTS			
	Univ. of Minn. Press	Colligan & Offord	Gottesman et al.	Marks et al.
Sample sizes (males & females combined)	2,000 to 3,000 (projected)	1,315 (5 age groups)	15 yr olds = 12,953 18 yr olds = 3,492	1,806 (4 age groups)
Sample locations and dates	Multiple sites (locations to be determined)	3 mid-west states (1985–1986)	Minnesota (1947–1957)	Minnesota (1947–1954); Alabama, California, Kansas, Missouri, North Carolina, Ohio (1964–1965)
Age groupings for T-scores	Currently unknown	1 group (13-17)	15, 18	14, 15, 16, 17
T-score development procedure	Currently unknown	Normalized T-score (probable)	Normalized T-score	Linear transformation
Year of norm publication	1989–1990 (probable)	1988 (probable)	1987	1972 (Dahlstrom, Welsh, and Dahlstrom); 1974 (Marks, Seeman, and Haller)
Sampling procedure	Stratified random procedure; supervised group testing	Telephone contacts and mail-out procedures	Hathaway and Monachesi 9th and 12th grade Minnesota samples	Hathaway and Monachesi Minnesota samples combined with additional data
Exclusive criteria	To be determined	Presence of physical or psychiatric disorders	$F \geq 23$ $L \geq 10$ $? \geq 100$ Age cutoffs	Psychiatric treatment at time of testing (1964–1965).
MMPI form employed	Standard item pool (revised) plus experimental items	Standard	Standard	Standard
Selected unique features	National sampling including minority subjects; inclusion of experimental items; eventual products to include new norms and forms	Normalized T-score procedures; use of standard form with contemporary adolescents	Large sample size; data for 15 and 18 year olds; norms available for numerous special scales	Extensive research and clinical literature; availability of clinical correlate data in Marks et al. (1974)

Note: From Archer, R. P. (1987) *Using the MMPI with adolescents.* (pp. 192-193). Hillsdale, NJ: Lawrence Erlbaum Associates. Adapted by permission.

derstanding of adolescent psychopathology as assessed by the MMPI.

REFERENCES

American Psychiatric Association. (1987). *Diagnostic and statistical manual of mental disorders* (3rd ed, revised). Washington, D. C.: author.

Archer, R. P. (1987) *Using the MMPI with adolescents.* Hillsdale, NJ: Lawrence Erlbaum Associates.

Archer, R. P. (1984). Use of the MMPI with adolescents: A review of salient issues. *Clinical Psychology Review, 4,* 241–251.

Archer, R. P. (in press). Using the MMPI with adolescents: Overview and recommendations. In C. D. Spielberger & J. N. Butcher (Eds.), *Advances in personality assessment* (Vol. 7). Hillsdale, NJ: Lawrence Erlbaum Associates.

Archer, R. P., Ball, J. D., & Hunter, J. A. (1985). MMPI characteristics of borderline psychopathology in adolescent inpatients. *Journal of Personality Assessment, 49,* 47–55.

Archer, R. P., & Gordon, R. A. (1988). MMPI and Rorschach indices of schizophrenic and depressive diagnoses among adolescent inpatients. *Journal of Personality Assessment, 52,* 276–287.

Archer, R. P., Gordon, R. A., & Kirchner, F. H. (1987). MMPI response set characteristics among adolescents. *Journal of Personality Assessment, 51,* 506–516.

Archer, R. P., Stolberg, A. L., Gordon, R. A., & Goldman, W. R. (1986). Parent and child MMPI responses: Characteristics among families with adolescents in inpatient and outpatient settings. *Journal of Abnormal Child Psychology, 14,*181–190.

Archer, R. P., White, J. L., & Orvin, G. H. (1979). MMPI characteristics and correlates among adolescent psychiatric inpatients. *Journal of Clinical Psychology, 35,* 498–504.

Ball, J. C. (1960). Comparison of MMPI profile differences among negro-white adolescents. *Journal of Clinical Psychology, 16,* 304–307.

Ball, J. C., & Carroll, D. (1960). Analysis of MMPI Cannot Say scores in an adolescent populations. *Journal of Clinical Psychology, 16,* 30–31.

Ball, J. D., Archer, R. P., Struve, F. A., Hunter, J. A., & Gordon, R. A. (1987). MMPI correlates of a controversial EEG pattern among adolescent psychiatric patients. *Journal of Clinical Psychology, 43,* 708–714.

Balswick, J. O., & Macrides, C. (1975). Parental stimulus for adolescent rebellion. *Adolescence, 10,* 253–266.

Bandura, A. (1964). The stormy decade: Fact or fiction? *Psychology in the School, 1,* 224–231.

Barron, F. (1953). An ego-strength scale which predicts response to psychotherapy. *Journal of Consulting Psychology, 17,* 327–333.

Baughman, E. E., & Dahlstrom, W. G. (1968). *Negro and white children: A psychological study in the rural south.* San Diego: Academic Press.

Block, J. (1965). *The challenge of response sets: Unconfounding meaning, acquiescence, and social desirability in the MMPI.* New York: Appleton-Century-Crofts.

Blos, P. (1962). *On adolescence: A psychoanalytic interpretation.* New York: Free Press.

Blos, P. (1967). The second individuation process of adolescence. *The Psychoanalytic Study of the Child, 22,* 162–186.

Briggs, P. F., Wirt, R. D., & Johnson, R. (1961). An application of prediction tables to the study of delinquency. *Journal of Consulting Psychology, 25,* 46–50.

Burke, E. L., & Eichberg, M. A. (1972). Personality characteristics of adolescent users of dangerous drugs as indicated by the MMPI. *Journal of Nervous and Mental Disease, 154,* 291–298.

Butcher, J. N. (1972). (Ed.) *Objective personality assessment: Changing perspectives.* San Diego: Academic Press.

Butcher, J. N. (1985). Why use the MMPI? In J. N. Butcher & J. R. Graham (Eds.), *Clinical applications of the MMPI.* Minneapolis: University of Minnesota Department of Conferences.

Butcher, J. N., & Pancheri, P. (1976). *Handbook of cross-national research.* Minneapolis: University of Minnesota Press.

Chase, T. V., Chaffin, S., & Morrison, S. D. (1975). False positive adolescent MMPI profiles. *Adolescence, 10,* 507–519.

Clopton, J. R., & Neuringer, C. (1977). MMPI Cannot Say scores: Normative data and degree of profile distortion. *Journal of Personality Assessment, 41,* 511–513.

Colligan, R. C., & Offord, K. P. (1987). Today's adolescent and the MMPI: Patterns of MMPI responses from normal teenagers of the 80's. In R. P. Archer, *Using the MMPI with Adolescents* (pp. 215–240). Hillsdale, NJ: Lawrence Erlbaum Associates.

Colligan, R. C., Osborne, D., & Offord, K. P. (1980). Linear transformation and the interpretation of the MMPI *T* scores. *Journal of Clinical Psychology, 36,* 162–165.

Colligan, R. C., Osborne, D., & Offord, K. P. (1984). Normalizing transformations and the interpretation of MMPI *T* scores: A repy to Hsu. *Journal of Consulting and Clinical Psychology, 52,* 824–826.

Dahlstrom, W. G., & Welsh, G. S. (1960). *An MMPI handbook: A guide to use in clinical practice and research.* Minneapolis: University of Minnesota Press.

Dahlstrom, W. G., Welsh, G. S., & Dahlstrom L. E. (1972). *An MMPI handbook (Vol. I): Clinical interpretation.* Minneapolis: University of Minnesota Press.

Dahlstrom, W. G., Welsh, G. S., & Dahlstrom, L. E. (1975). *An MMPI handbook (Vol. II): Research applications.* Minneapolis: University of Minnesota Press.

Derogatis, L. R. (1977). *SCL-90-R: Administration, scoring and procedures manual.* Baltimore: Clinical Psychometric Research.

Dudley, H. K., Mason, M., & Hughes, R. (1972). The MMPI and adolescent patients in a state hospital. *Journal of Youth and Adolescence, 1,* 165–178.

Ehrenworth, N. V. (1984). *A comparison of the utility of interpretive approaches with adolescent MMPI profiles.* Unpublished doctoral dissertation, Virginia Consortium for Professional Psychology, Norfolk.

Ehrenworth, N. V., & Archer, R. P. (1985). A comparison of clinical accuracy ratings of interpretive approaches for adolescent MMPI responses. *Journal of Personality Assessment, 49,* 413–421.

Elkind, D. (1974). *Children and adolescents: Interpretive essays on Jean Piaget.* New York: Oxford University Press.

Erikson, E. H. (1956). The problem of ego identity. *The Journal of the American Psychoanalytic Association, 4,* 56–121.

Freud, A. (1958). Adolescence. *Psychoanalytic Study of the Child, 13,* 255–278.

Gottesman, I. I., & Fishman, D. B. (1961, September). *Adolescent psychometric personality: A phenotypic psychosis.* Paper presented at the annual meeting of the American Psychological Association, New York.

Gottesman, I. I., Hanson, D. R., Kroeker, T. A., & Briggs, P. F. (1987). New MMPI normative data and power-transformed *T*-score tables for the Hathaway-Monachesi Minnesota cohort of 14,019 fifteen-year-olds and 3,674 eighteen-year-olds. In R. P. Archer (Ed.), *Using the MMPI with adolescents* (pp. 241–297). Hillsdale, NJ: Lawrence Erlbaum Associates.

Graham, J. R. (1987), *The MMPI: A practical guide* (2nd ed.). New York: Oxford University Press.

Graham, J. R. (1985). Interpreting the MacAndrew alcoholism scale. In J. N. Butcher & J. R. Graham (Eds.), *Clinical applications of the MMPI.* Minneapolis: University of Minnesota Department of Conferences.

Graham, J. R., & Mayo, M. A. (1985, March). *A comparison of MMPI strategies for identifying black and white male alcoholics.* Paper presented at the 20th Annual Symposium on Recent Developments in the Use of the MMPI, Honolulu.

Greene, R. L. (1980). *The MMPI: An interpretive manual.* Philadelphia: Grune & Stratton.

Hall, G. S. (1904). *Adolescence: Its psychology and its relationship to physiology, anthropology, sociology, sex, crime, religion and education.* New York: Appleton.

Hathaway, S. R., & Monachesi, E. D. (1961). *An atlas of juvenile MMPI profiles.* Minneapolis: University of Minnesota Press.

Hathaway, S. R., & Monachesi, E. D. (1963). *Adolescent personality and behavior.* Minneapolis: University of Minnesota Press.

Hathaway, S. R., Monachesi, E. D., & Salasin, S. (1970). A follow-up study of MMPI high 8, schizoid children. In R. Roff & D. F. Rick (Eds.), *Life history research in psychopathology* (pp. 171–188). Minneapolis: University of Minnesota Press.

Heilbrun, A. B. (1963). Revision of the MMPI *K* correction procedure for improved detection of maladjustment in a normal college population. *Journal of Consulting Psychology, 27,* 161–165.

Hsu, L. M. (1984). MMPI *T* scores: Linear versus normalized. *Journal of Consulting and Clinical Psychology, 52,* 821–823.

Hsu, L. M., & Betman, J. A. (1986). MMPI *T* score conversion tables, 1957–1983. *Journal of Consulting and Clinical Psychology, 54,* 497–501.

Klinge, V. (1983). A comparison of parental and adolescent MMPIs as related to substance abuse. *The International Journal of the Addictions, 18,* 1179–1185.

Klinge, V., Lachar, D., Grisell, J., & Berman, W. (1978). Effects of scoring norms on adolescent psychiatric drug users' and nonusers' MMPI profiles. *Adolescence, 13,* 1–11.

Klinge, V., & Strauss, M. E. (1976). Effects of scoring norms on adolescent psychiatric patients' MMPI profiles. *Journal of Personality Assessment, 40,* 13–17.

Lachar, D. (1974). *The MMPI: Clinical assessment and automated interpretation.* Los Angeles: Western Psychological Services.

Lachar, D., Godowski, C. L., & Keegan, J. F. (1979). MMPI profiles of men alcoholics, drug addicts and psychiatric patients. *Journal of Studies on Alcohol, 40,* 45–56.

Lachar, D., Klinge, V., & Grisell, J. L. (1976). Relative accuracy of automated MMPI narratives generated from adult norm and adolescent norm profiles. *Journal of Consulting and Clinical Psychology, 44,* 20–24.

Lubin, B., Larsen, R. M., Matarazzo, J. D., & Seever, M. (1985). Psychological test usage patterns in five professional settings. *American Psychologist, 40* 857–861.

MacAndrew, C. (1965). The differentiation of male alcoholic outpatients from nonalcoholic psychiatric outpatients by means of the MMPI. *Quarterly Journal of Studies on Alcohol, 26,* 238–246,

MacAndrew, C. (1979). On the possibility of psychometric detection of persons prone to the abuse of alcohol and other substances. *Addictive Behaviors, 4,*11–20.

Marks, P. A., Seeman, W., & Haller, D. (1974). *The actuarial use of the MMPI with adolescents and adults.* Baltimore: Williams & Wilkins.

Masterson, J. F. (1968). The psychiatric significance of adolescent turmoil. *American Journal of Psychiatry, 124,* 1549–1554.

Mead, M. (1928). *Coming of age in Samoa.* New York: Morrow.

Mead, M. (1930). Adolescence in primitive and modern society. In V.F. Calverton & S. D. Schmalhausen (Eds.), *The new generation: A symposium* (pp. 169–188). New York: Macauley.

Meehl, P. E. (1956). Profile analysis of the MMPI in differential diagnosis. In G. S. Welsh & W. G. Dahlstrom (Eds.), *Basic readings on the MMPI in psychology and medicine* (pp. 292–297). Minneapolis: University of Minnesota Press.

Millon, T., Green, C. J., & Meagher, R. B. (1977). *Millon Adolescent Personality Inventory.* Minneapolis: National Computer Systems.

Mlott, S. R. (1972). Some significant relationships between adolescents and their parents as revealed by the MMPI. *Adolescence, 7,* 169–182.

Muuss, R. (1975). *Theories of adolescence.* New York: Random House.

Osborne, D. (1979). Use of the MMPI with medical patients. In J. N. Butcher (Ed.), *New developments in the use of the MMPI* (pp. 141–164). Minneapolis: University of Minnesota Press.

Piaget, J. (1969). The intellectual development of the adolescent. In G. Caplan & S. Lebovici (Eds.), *Adolescence: Psychosocial perspectives. New York: Basic Books.*

Prokop, C. L. (1986). Hysteria scale elevations in low back pain patients: A risk factor for misdiagnosis. *Journal of Consulting and Clinical Psychology, 54,* 558–562.

Prokop, C. K., Bradley, L. A., Margolis, R., & Gentry, W. D. (1980). Multivariate analysis of the MMPI profiles of patients with multiple pain complaints. *Journal of Personality Assessment, 44,* 246–252.

Rank, O. (1945). *Will therapy and truth and reality.* New York: Knopf.

Rathus, S. A., Fox, J. A., & Ortins, J. B. (1980). The MacAndrew Scale as a measure of substance abuse and delinquency among adolescents. *Journal of Clinical Psychology, 36,* 579–583.

Rempel, P. P. (1958). The use of multivariate statistical analysis of MMPI scores in the classification of delinquent and nondelinquent high school boys. *Journal of Consulting Psychology, 22,* 17–23.

Stone, L. J., & Church, J. (1957). Pubescence, puberty, and physical development. In L. J. Stone & J. Church (Eds.), *Childhood and adolescence* (pp. 75–85). New York: Random House.

Sutker, P. B., Moan, C. E., Goist, K. C., & Allain, A. N. (1984). MMPI subtypes and antisocial behaviors in adolescent alcohol and drug abusers. *Drug and Alcohol Dependence, 13,* 235–244.

Tofler, A. (1970). *Future shock.* New York: Random House.

Watson, C. G., & Buranen, C. (1979). The frequency and identification of false positive conversion reactions. *Journal of Nervous and Mental Diseases, 167,* 243–247.

Weiner, I. B., & Del Gaudio, A. C. (1976). Psychopathology in adolescence: An epidemiological study. *Archives of General Psychiatry, 33,* 187–193.

Welsh, G. S. (1956). Factor dimensions A and R. In G. S. Welsh & W. G. Dahlstrom (Eds.), *Basic readings on the MMPI in psychology and medicine* (pp. 264–281). Minneapolis: University of Minnesota Press.

Williams, C. L. (1986). MMPI profiles from adolescents: Interpretive strategies and treatment considerations. *Journal of Child and Adolescent Psychology, 3,* 179–193.

Williams, C. L., Butcher, J. N., & Graham, J. R. (1986, March). *Appropriate MMPI norms for adolescents: An old problem revisited.* Paper presented at the 21st Annual Symposium on Recent Developments in the Use of the MMPI, Clearwater, FL.

Wimbish, L. G. (1984). *The importance of appropriate norms for the computerized interpretation of adolescent MMPI profiles.* Unpublished doctoral dissertation, Ohio State University, Columbus, OH.

Wirt, R. D., & Briggs, P. F. (1959). Personality and environmental factors in the development of delinquency. *Psychological Monographs: General and Applied,* (1, 73 Whole No. 485).

Wirt, R. D., Lachar, D., Klinedinst, J. E., Seat, P. D., & Broen, W. E. (1982). *The Personality Inventory for Children (PIC), Revised Format.* Los Angeles: Western Psychological Services.

Wisniewski, N. M., Glenwick, D. S., & Graham, J. R. (1985). MacAndrew Scale and sociodemographic correlates of adolescent alcohol and drug use. *Addictive Behaviors, 10,* 55–67.

Wolfson, K. P., & Erbaugh, S. E. (1984). Adolescent responses to the MacAndrew Alcoholism Scale. *Journal of Consulting and Clinical Psychology, 52,* 625–630.

Chapter 11

Within-Normal-Limit Profiles

JANE C. DUCKWORTH and
WILLIAM D. BARLEY

OVERVIEW

Clinicians have noted the occurrence of within-normal-limit (WNL) profiles (usually all clinical scales below a T-score of 70) in clinical settings for many years. Since elevations on MMPI scales are interpreted to reflect psychopathology, it is a matter of concern when patients could be described as being asymptomatic because of WNL profiles. The K Scale (Meehl & Hathaway, 1946) was developed to correct for a tendency of some patients with psychiatric diagnoses to obtain WNL profiles, although the exact frequency of this problem was not then reported. Hathaway and Meehl (1951) reported that approximately 25 percent of patients hospitalized with psychiatric diagnoses produced WNL profiles.

Despite the occurrence of WNL profiles, relatively little attention was devoted to them in the MMPI literature for many years. Dahlstrom, Welsh, and Dahlstrom (1972) devoted the majority of their classic text to elevated scales and code-types, acknowledging lower elevations in only their brief sections describing "low scores" on each scale (undefined as to T-score range). This omission was to be expected given that the original purpose of the MMPI was to identify psychiatric problems on the basis of elevations of the clinical scales at T-scores of ≥ 70. Only in the last few years have WNL profiles been shown to

have diagnostic utility, partially as a result of the increase in the attempts to evaluate these profiles in the last 20 years. This interest in WNL profiles is apparent particularly in nonpsychiatric settings such as general hospitals, university counseling centers, and personnel agencies.

Since the MMPI was not designed to be a veridical self-report of behavioral tendencies (Meehl, 1945), correlates of MMPI items, scales, and profile configurations are determined empirically. Even though aspects of WNL MMPI profiles other than scale elevation, such as phase characteristics, have been investigated (Vestre & Klett, 1969), WNL profiles clearly pose interpretive problems. Yet, WNL profiles ought not to be ignored or casually assumed to indicate normalcy (Lachar, 1974a). Conversely, MMPI data on a contemporary normal population (Colligan, Osborne, Swenson, & Offord, 1984) revealed that normal individuals have higher mean scores (3–5 T-score points) than the original MMPI normative group. Females tended to produce these higher mean scores on Scales *1*, *2*, *7*, *8*, and *9*, while males scored higher on Scales *1*, *2*, *4*, *7*, *8*, and *9*. Colligan et al. (1984) suggested that a more conservative (less pathologically-oriented) approach to codetype interpretation may be needed in light of their data. Many of these scales, which have higher means in contemporary normal individuals, are the very scales reported as being elevated

THE MMPI: USE WITH
SPECIFIC POPULATIONS

© 1988 by Grune & Stratton.

above the *T*-score mean in psychiatric and non-psychiatric samples, yet still within normal limits. Thus, the correlates of WNL profiles should be determined empirically, just as the correlates of the traditional MMPI scale elevations and code-types have been.

DEFINITION

A WNL profile generally means a profile in which all clinical scale scores are below a *T*-score of 70. There are several exceptions to this definition, however. Elevations of Scales *L*, *F*, and *K* were sometimes part of the definition of WNL profiles in studies reviewed here. Scales *5* and *0* generally were excluded in early MMPI studies, and Scale *5* is sometimes excluded because both males and females are being studied. In some cases the actual scale elevations of profiles described as WNL have not been provided by researchers. Graham (1984b) noted that WNL profiles should have no *T*-scores below 40, either, but in this review only maximum elevations of scales have been considered in the definition of WNL profiles. Finally, some mean profiles resulting from averaging or cluster analysis that have *T*-scores of 70 or slightly higher are discussed here when they are of particular comparative interest.

SCOPE OF THIS REVIEW

Most of the research in this chapter was published after 1970, reflecting the increased interest in WNL profiles in the last few years. Several computer databases were searched initially, but it proved difficult to retrieve studies of WNL profiles, since "WNL" is rarely a descriptor or key word for studies involving these profiles. Other researchers (e.g., Kunce & Anderson, 1976) also have commented on this difficulty. Studies identified via this computer search then were used to identify additional pertinent publications, as was a volume-by-volume search of the most frequently cited journals in the literature on WNL profiles (i.e., *Journal of Consulting and Clinical*

Psychology, *Journal of Personality Assessment*, and *Journal of Clinical Psychology*). There may be gaps in the resulting coverage of this WNL literature. Hopefully, this chapter's focus on the usefulness of research on WNL profiles will increase interest in them and ease the task of future investigators.

Studies that used abbreviated forms of the MMPI were not included in this review. Examples of the 399-item version of Form R were included, since it provides responses to all of the standard validity and clinical scales.

This chapter is divided into two major sections, one addressing research on nonpsychiatric populations (those persons not identified by others or themselves as having psychiatric/psychological problems), and the other addressing WNL profiles found in psychiatric populations. Within each of these major sections there are subgroups of studies. For most of these subgroups, the research results have most commonly been reported as mean profiles with all of the inherent limitations of such data that were described in Chapter 1. Briefly, the use of simple averaging to produce a mean profile to describe an entire subject sample presents interpretive difficulties because, as noted by Butcher and Tellegen (1978), it is rarely reported how closely any of the individual profiles in the sample resembles the mean profile of the sample. It is possible that no individual in a given sample has a WNL profile, when the mean (average) profile is within normal limits. More interpretive weight can be given to the empirical correlates of mean profiles that result from cluster or factor analysis, because these profiles almost certainly represent more homogeneous profile groups than do simple average ones. However, most useful for interpreting a patient's or client's WNL profile are the relatively infrequently reported correlates of WNL profiles of individual patients or clients.

In the text of this review, subject samples and procedures are described sufficiently for broad comparison. Additional data regarding subject, characteristics, potential moderator variables, conditions of MMPI administration, and results can be found in Tables 11–1 and 11–3 to 11–12.

Studies of Nonpsychiatric Populations

GENERAL STUDIES

Few books or articles report general information and interpretation strategies for nonpsychiatric WNL profiles. Lanyon's *Handbook of MMPI Group Profiles* (1968) illustrates a number of WNL profiles: psychophysiologic and physical disorders (specifically medical disabilities and obesity), brain disorders (epilepsy, aphasia, and brain lesions), parents of disturbed children, student and occupational groups, racial and cultural groups, and miscellaneous groups (cerebral palsy, pregnancy, and Air Force officers under stress). Clinicians can compare a client's profile with a mean profile from a similar diagnostic group to see if the profiles are similar. It must be remembered, however, that the profiles reported in Lanyon's book are mean profiles with all the inherent dangers described in Chapter 1.

Greene (1980) and Duckworth and Anderson (1986) provide interpretations for moderate elevations (60 to 69 *T*-score points) as well as low points (<45 *T*-score points) on the standard validity and clinical scales. Duckworth and Anderson (1986) also give moderate elevation interpretations for Scales *A* (Anxiety), *R* (Repression), *Es* (Ego-strength), *Lb* (Low-back pain), *Dy* (Dependency), *Do* (Dominance), *Re* (Social Responsibility), *Pr* (Prejudice), *St* (Status), *Cn* (Control), and *Mac* (MacAndrew Alcoholism Scale).

In addition to these books, two book chapters and five articles have been found that cover the interpretation of WNL profiles. Kunce and Anderson (1976) and Kunce (1979) suggest that moderate level elevations of clinical scales may indicate adaptive, coping behavior instead of pathologic behavior, particularly in nonpsychiatric populations. They posit underlying dimensions for the 10 clinical scales. For example, the dimension underlying Scale 7 is hypothesized to be organization. Elevated scores on Scale 7 suggest rigid, compulsive, obsessive, ritualistic persons. However, these authors believe that more moderate elevations on Scale 7 are suggestive of methodical, systematic, organized, and convergent thinking persons.

King and Kelley (1977; Kelley & King, 1978) studied college counseling center clients who generate Spike 5 profiles (all clinical scales < 70 except for Scale 5) and WNL profiles with and without elevated *K* scale. (Many clinicians consider Scale 5 to be nonclinical. The Spike 5 profile, therefore, would be considered a WNL profile by these clinicians.) King and Kelley (1977) found that the men who had generated Spike 5 profiles were basically normal. The usual diagnosis for them was transient situational disturbance. The only consistent problem noted for these men was a history of infrequent or no dating. On the other hand, in their study of WNL profiles, Kelley and King (1978) found that these counseling center clients showed as much behavioral symptomatology and as many past adjustment problems as those with elevated profiles. It may be that if these clients with WNL profiles were compared with a psychiatric population, their symptomalogy and past adjustment problems would not be similar to a more disturbed population.

Graham and Tisdale (1983) and Graham and McCord (1985) studied the self-reports of college women with low scores on Scale 5 and the self-reports (adjective check lists) of college students with moderately elevated scores on MMPI clinical scales. These authors indicate that moderate elevations on clinical scales should be interpreted using negative descriptors since these corresponded to the students' description of themselves. This finding would seem to be contradictory to the study (King & Kelley, 1977) reported above, which showed college students with moderate elevations having adaptive behavior. Review of the negative descriptors of the Graham et al. studies, however, shows that the correlations between the descriptors and the scales were quite low, ranging from .22 to .48 with most being in the .20 and .30 ranges. In addition, the moderately elevated profiles were defined as those with T-scores of 75 and below. By going above T-scores of 70 to define their profiles, Graham et al. did not have individuals with moderately elevated profiles as these are typically defined.

In general then, persons with WNL profiles tend not to be grossly disturbed but may indeed be showing adaptive behavior even when the scales are moderately elevated between T-scores of 60 and 70.

NORMAL INDIVIDUALS

Prior to 1970, the majority of the studies on WNL profiles were with college and occupational groups: various college majors (Norman & Redlo, 1952; Clark, 1953; Hancock & Carter, 1954); college counselors (Cottle & Lewis, 1954); union business agents (Rosen & Rosen, 1957); future scientists (Kennedy, Nelson, Lindner, Turner, & Moon, 1960); gifted adolescents (Kennedy, 1962); and creative persons (Barron, 1969). These studies are discussed at length elsewhere (Kunce & Anderson, 1976). All of these studies showed mean WNL profiles.

Since 1970, a number of studies have been published on normal individuals. Kunce and Anderson's (1970) study of counselor-client similarity found that the clients who were agitated were referred to counselors who also were agitated, i.e., had higher scores on Scales 2 and 7 and lower scores on Es than their fellow counselors. These referrals were made by fellow counselors who presumably knew the personalities of the other counselors through professional contact with them. Kunce and Anderson concluded from these data that the clients were referred to counselors who were similar to them. It is important to note that the counselors who were "high" and "low" on these scales had T-scores of 53 on Scale 2, 60 on Scale 7, and 63 on Es. While these scales were higher and lower than the rest of the group of counselors, there is not much utility for calling counselors agitated on the basis of such moderate scores.

Jansen and Garvey (1973) studied clergymen doing their clinical internships in a state hospital and found that there was an inverse relationship between elevation on the MMPI and supervisor's evaluation of clinical competence. Those clergymen with higher MMPI elevations had lower evaluations. Again, however, the "higher" profiles were still within normal limits. Harrell and Harrell (1973) studied MBAs who reached general management early in their careers and found moderate elevations on the MMPI for those who did not advance so quickly, whereas those who did advance early had lower MMPI scales. No information is given on T-scores, however, so one is left wondering how high is moderate and exactly what the T-scores for the two groups were.

Lachar (1974b) found that those U.S. Air Force cadets with "significant pathology" on the MMPI (approximately 85 out of 1,402 subjects) had twice the drop-out rate, i.e., 24.7 percent, as those cadets without significant pathology (presumably WNL profiles), who had a 10.9 percent drop-out rate. Again, no T-scores were given for comparison. Saxe and Reiser (1976) studied three police applicant groups to see if they could differentiate between the selected and rejected applicants in each of these groups on the basis of their MMPI scores. All of the groups, although significantly different from each other on their MMPIs, had mean WNL profiles. In a refreshingly candid statement, the authors stated that

> although statistically significant differences have been found between the various applicant subgroups and the successful applicant group, these differences are too small in terms of traditional clinical standard scores to have meaningful utility in clinical differentiation of successful and unsuccessful police applicants (p. 424).

Several other MMPI studies also used normal subjects. Blaustein and Proctor (1977) evaluated active duty conscientious objectors; Evans (1977) used the MMPI to predict effective hotline workers; Wiens and Matarazzo (1977) correlated the MMPI with a group of neuropsychological measures in a group of normal male subjects; Kokosh (1978) looked at academic achievement; Bernstein (1980) predicted successful security guards; Cunningham and Strassberg (1981) investigated interpersonal disclosure; Wheatley and Ursano (1982) studied repatriated POWs; and Chodzko-Zajko and Ismail (1984) used men in an exercise program. All of these studies found WNL profiles and statistically but not clinically significant differences. Most of the differences reported between the various groups were less than half of a standard deviation (i.e., 5 T-score points).

In general, these studies showed that normal people have WNL profiles, which is to be expected. Another group of studies have examined normal individuals in various kinds of crises. Gayton et al. (1976) found that 26 of 50 women who requested abortions had WNL profiles. No information is given as to clinical differences, if any, between these subjects and those with abnormal MMPIs. Goldstein and Sappington (1977) looked at the MMPIs of students who eventually became heavy drug users. The 33 drug users and 33 peers who served as a control group both had WNL profiles. It would have been useful to know whether the MacAndrew Alcoholism Scale (MacAndrew, 1965) differentiated the two groups. This scale, derived from MMPI items, has been successful in identifying future alcoholics as early as entrance to college (Hoffmann, Loper, & Kammeier, 1974).

Dorr (1981) compared the MMPIs of a group of emotionally impaired physicians with an addicted group of physicians who were institutionalized for their addiction. The emotionally impaired doctors had WNL profiles, while the addicted physicians did not. Repko and Cooper (1983) and Pollack and Grainey (1984) studied workman's compensation and disability insurance cases, respectively. Only 17 percent of the workmen's compensation cases had WNL profiles, which is the first study reported in this section where a majority of the persons had elevated MMPIs. It would seem on the basis of this study that disability patients, in general, would have elevated MMPI profiles. However, when Pollack and Grainey (1984) divided the MMPIs of disability patients according to gender and status as a private or state patient, a very different picture emerged. The female private disability insurance cases had a WNL mean profile. On the other hand, the male private disability cases had two scales above T-scores of 70, Scale 1 at 77, and Scale 3 at 71, or the typical "conversion V" mean profile. For both men and women in the state disability group, which is similar to the workman's compensation group previously reported (Repko & Cooper, 1983), the MMPI profiles were highly elevated without the "conversion V." Thus, the workmen's compensation cases and state disability cases were very similar in having a high percentage of elevated profiles, whereas the private disability cases, in general, had lower MMPI profiles, especially the women who had a mean WNL profile. It would seem that when more homogeneous samples are drawn from a larger population, clinically significant differences in profiles may become apparent.

In summary, all of the studies but one (Repko & Cooper, 1983) of normal subjects and normal subjects under stress found that these people tend to have WNL MMPI profiles. It would be expected for normal individuals to have WNL profiles. However, it is somewhat unexpected for normal individuals who are currently experiencing stress also to have WNL profiles.

ADOLESCENTS AND THEIR PARENTS

The MMPIs of adolescent medical patients resemble those of adult medical patients, i.e., their mean profile is within normal limits (Colligan & Osborne, 1977). Colligan and Osborne studied the MMPIs of 659 girls and 534 boys between the ages of 15 and 19 who had been medical patients at the Mayo Clinic. They found that these adolescent medical patients were different from other adolescents in much the same way that adult medical patients are different from the general adult population. That is, these adolescent medical patients averaged higher scores on the neurotic triad (Scales 1, 2, and 3) than adolescents in general. These, of course, are the scales that reflect concern about physical problems and it makes sense that these scales are higher for medical patients. When chronic physical problems were studied, specifically cleft lip and palate and orthopedic disabilities, Harper and Richman (1978; Richman & Harper, 1980) found that the adolescents with cleft lip and palate had fewer personality adjustment problems as indicated on their MMPIs than the orthopedic Ss. The mean MMPI profile for the cleft palate group (15 males, 12 females) was WNL, whereas the orthopedic females ($N = 12$) elevated Scales 1 and 8 above T-scores of 70, and the orthopedic males ($N = 15$) elevated Scale 8 above T-scores of 70. The results of these studies suggest again the utility of looking at more homogeneous groupings of patients instead of averaging the MMPI scores of all medical cases together.

Monroe and Marks (1977) compared adolescent poor and good sleepers and found that both groups' MMPI mean profiles were within normal limits. A later study reported in the same article (Monroe & Marks, 1977) of the same population with larger samples looked at the percentages in each group that had at least one clinical scale above a T-score of 70; 79 percent of the poor sleepers had one or more clinical scale above a T-score of 70, whereas only 63 percent of the good sleepers had such elevations. When the codetypes were examined, Scales 1, 2, and 3 frequently were involved. Evaluating profiles with one or more clinical scales elevated above a T-score of 70 gave more clinically useful information than was obtained from only the mean profiles.

Parents of emotionally disturbed or chronically ill children also have been studied. Miller and Keirn (1978) and Anderson (1969) found that the parents of emotionally disturbed children had WNL mean profiles. Cairnes and Lansky (1980) found similar results for parents of children with a chronic illness. However, Smith, Burleigh, Sewell, and Krisak (1984) found that while emotionally disturbed adolescents' MMPI mean profile (using adolescent norms) was WNL, their mothers' mean profile was not WNL. The mothers of the 34 female adolescents had Scales F, 4, 7, and 8 above a T-score of 70, whereas the mothers of the 34 male adolescents had Scales 1, 4, 7, and 8 above a T-score of 70. Why this group of mothers should score so differently than the parents in the Miller and Keirn (1978) and Anderson (1969) studies is unclear. One possible explanation may be that these two studies were describing samples from different populations because of differences in the average IQ of the emotionally disturbed adolescents in the Miller and Keirn study (IQ, 103) and the Smith et al. study (IQ, 92). The parents in these two groups also may be different on intelligence and therefore not comparable.

In general then, when adolescents with medical problems, sleep difficulties, and emotional problems are studied, they have WNL profiles. When a specific medical problem is looked at, however, such may not be the case, which again illustrates the utility of using specific subgroups in a population as opposed to studying only a general population.

OBESITY AND BULIMIA

Research consistently has found that persons who are obese have WNL profiles (Crumpton, Wine, & Groot, 1966; McCall, 1973; Webb,

Phares, & Abram, 1976; Roback, McKee, Webb, Abramowitz, & Abramowitz, 1976a; Pomerantz, Greenberg, & Blackburn, 1977). Roback et al. (1976a) concluded on the basis of their study of obese persons that morbid obesity was not symptomatic of psychiatric dysfunction, although Webb et al. (1976) pointed out that mild emotional immaturity may be present.

When it comes to bulimia, however, such is not the case. Although the bulimic subjects of Williamson, Kelley, Davis, Ruggerio, and Blouin (1985) had a WNL profile, a comparison of the number of profiles that had clinical scales above a T-score of 70 of Scale 5 or below a T-score of 30 (considered pathologic by the authors) showed significant differences between the bulimics and the obese and normal subjects. Thirteen of the 15 bulimics had at least one clinical scale elevated above a T-score of 70 compared with 5 of the 15 obese and 5 of the 15 normal subjects. In addition, the bulimics were significantly higher on Scales 1, 2, and 3 than the obese and normal subjects. Hatsukami, Owen, Pyle, and Mitchell (1982) also found that bulimics had elevated mean profiles even though 19.2 percent of them did have WNL profiles. Thus, there seem to be clear differences between persons with obesity and bulimia on the MMPI. The obese persons, in general, have WNL profiles, whereas the majority of bulimic subjects tend to have at least one elevated clinical scale.

SEXUAL DIFFICULTIES

Persons with many types of sexual difficulties have been shown to have WNL mean MMPI profiles. Munjack and Staples (1976) studied women with sexual inhibition (frigidity). These female patients who were complaining primarily of sexual inhibition appeared to be identical to the normal control group on their mean MMPI profile.

The MMPIs for male sexual dysfunctions are more mixed, however. Munjack, Kanno, and Oziel (1978) and Munjack, Kanno, Staples, and Leonard (1980) studied 19 premature ejaculators and 16 retarded ejaculators and found that the premature ejaculators had a WNL profile, but the retarded ejaculators had Scales 4 and 5 above a T-score of 70. Munjack, Oziel, Kanno, Whipple, and Leonard (1981) and Marshall, Surridge, and Delva (1980) studied impotence in males. Munjack et al. (1981)

found that their private patients ($N = 33$) had a WNL mean profile, whereas the public clinic patients ($N = 20$) elevated on Scales *4* (T-score = 71) and *8* (T-score = 70.78). However, the private patients had a higher educational level and a higher proportion of whites (97 percent white private patients vs. 75 percent white public clinic patients). These demographic variables may account for the differences found between the two groups' MMPI profiles. Marshall et al. (1980) compared MMPI profiles of patients with organic impotence with MMPI profiles of patients with psychogenic impotence. The psychogenic patients' mean MMPI was within normal limits, but the organic patients' profile was elevated. They speculated that this difference was the result of the differing length of time the men had been impotent; the men with organic impotence had been impotent for a longer time period than the men with the psychogenic variety.

A series of studies have examined patients who were candidates for sex change operations. Finney, Brandsma, Tondow, and LeMaistre (1975), and Roback, McKee, Webb, Abramowitz, and Abramowitz (1976b) studied male-to-female transsexual subjects. In these studies, men had a WNL mean profile except for Scale *5*. An elevation above a T-score of 70 on Scale *5* is not always considered pathologic for men (Duckworth & Anderson, 1986; Greene, 1980). Roback et al. (1976b) and Rosen (1974) studied female-to-male transsexuals and also found that these subjects had a WNL profile except for Scale *5*.

These studies of persons with sexual difficulties indicate that the following groups have WNL mean profiles on the MMPI: women with sexual inhibition, men with premature ejaculation and those with psychogenic impotence, and male and female transsexuals. Those who show abnormal MMPIs are men with retarded ejaculation and those with organic impotence.

SLEEP PROBLEMS

Kales et al. (1980a, b, c) studied MMPI performance in people with various kinds of sleep problems. Individuals with nightmares (Kales et al., 1980b) were found to have a mean WNL profile, but 68 percent of these people had at least one clinical scale elevated above a T-score of 70, compared with 26 percent of the individuals

without nightmares. When people with night terrors were studied (Kales et al., 1980a), the mean profile was WNL but 73 percent of these individuals elevated at least one clinical scale compared with 28 percent of a normal control group. People with somnambulism (sleepwalking) (Kales et al., 1980c) also had a WNL mean profile and a greater percentage of profiles with elevated clinical scales (65 percent) compared with a control group (32 percent). Thus, for each of these sleep disorders (nightmares, night terrors, and somnambulism) there have been mean WNL profiles but also a significant number of individuals (ranging from 65 to 73 percent) who had at least one elevated scale.

When people with insomnia are studied, however, a different picture emerges. Instead of having mean WNL profiles, individuals with insomnia have a mean profile with elevations on one or more of the clinical scales, frequently Scale *2*. Kales' (1976) group of insomniacs elevated Scales *2* (T-scores = 74) and *5* (T-scores = 71 [for men]). Sixty percent (76 of 126) of the people studied had elevations above a T-score of 70 on Scale *2*. Roth, Kramer, and Lutz (1976) studied 54 insomniacs and found that 83 percent of them had clinical scale elevations, with 60 percent of these elevations on Scale *2*, 50 percent on Scale *1*, and 46 percent on Scale *3*. Shealy, Lowe, and Ritzler (1980), while giving no actual T-scores for their subjects with insomnia, reported that these people scored higher than those without insomnia on Scales *7, 2, 3, 1, 6, 8,* and *F*. However, when Zorick, Roth, Hartze, Piccione, and Stepanski (1981) divided their 84 individuals with insomnia into 10 different diagnostic categories such as nocturnal myclonia or restless leg syndrome, they found that people in only three of those categories had elevated mean profiles. Thus, in this study, it seemed that the type of insomnia rather than insomnia in general was correlated with psychological disturbance. Once again, dividing people into homogeneous subgroups yielded more clinically significant information.

In summary, findings concerning sleep disorders show that people who have nightmares, night terrors, and somnambulism have WNL mean MMPI profiles, but individuals with insomnia do not. In general, insomniacs tend to elevate on Scale *2*. However, some data indicate that only certain types of insomnia are associated with elevated MMPIs.

MEDICAL PROBLEMS

A survey of MMPI studies of 15 different medical disabilities shows that for 10 of the medical problems patients had WNL mean MMPIs: amytrophic lateral sclerosis (Peters, Swenson, & Mulder, 1978); asthma (Brown, 1982); left-hemisphere brain lesions (Dikman & Reitan, 1977; Gass & Russell, 1985); burns (Mlott, Lira, & Miller, 1977); dermatitis (Haynes, Wilson, Jaffe, & Britton, 1979); epilepsy (Matthews, Dikmen, & Harley, 1977); hyperthyroidism (MacCrimmon, Wallace, & Goldberg, 1979; Wallace, Mac-Crimmon, & Goldberg, 1980); multiple sclerosis (Davis, Osborne, Siemens, & Brown, 1971; Peyser, Edwards, & Poser, 1980; Marsh, Hirsch, and Leung, 1982); renal failure (Trieschmann & Sand, 1971); and rheumatic fever (Stehbens, Ehmke, & Wilson, 1982). Two studies within this group of WNL profiles merit additional comment. MacCrimmon et al. (1979) and Wallace et al. (1980) found that once their patients' hyperthyroidism was under control and the patients were eurothyroid, they did not differ from the control group. However, the patients with hyperthyroidism did have marked emotional disturbances on the MMPI when their thyroid functioning was not normal, and the degree of disturbance was related to the patients' level of excess thyroid hormones. The authors concluded that hyperthyroidism is primarily a physical illness that directly causes psychological disturbance.

As was mentioned before, Trieschmann and Sand (1971) found a WNL mean profile for their group of 83 patients who had renal failure. A closer look at these patients' MMPI profiles showed five profile types: a "neurotic" profile with Scales 1, 2, 3, and 7 above a T-score of 65 ($N = 29$), a "denial" profile with Scales 1 and 3 above a T-score of 65 ($N = 13$), a "depressed" profile (no scales given) ($N = 9$), a "schizoid" profile (no scales given) ($N = 8$), and a "manic-normal" profile (no scales given) ($N = 18$). What was not studied in this research was whether these various profile types may have had different responses to the disease or different treatment needs.

In five medical problems, elevated as well as WNL mean MMPI profiles were found: brain damage (Wooten, 1983); headache (Kudrow & Sutkus, 1979); heart disease (Gilberstadt & Sako, 1967; Lair & King, 1976; Shealy & Walker, 1978); hypoglycemia (Ford, Bray, & Swerdloff, 1976); and rheumatoid arthritis (Spergel, Erhlich, & Glass, 1978). In these studies, it seems that the most useful information was obtained when the patients with the disease in question were not studied as a general group but were divided into smaller, more homogeneous subgroups. The first two medical problems listed above exemplify the utility of such a procedure. Wooten (1983) found that 19.1 percent of 345 active duty military personnel with brain damage had WNL profiles and an additional 3.2 percent had WNL profiles except for one validity scale above a T-score of 70. When he grouped the patients more homogeneously and looked at the severity of the brain damage, however, he found that it was the mildly-to-moderately brain-damaged patients who had the WNL profiles, not the patients with the more severe brain damage.

The research on headache patients also shows the value of homogeneous subgroups. When headache patients were divided into types of headaches, Kudrow and Sutkus (1979) found quite different mean MMPIs. Male and female patients with migraine and cluster headaches had WNL profiles, as did the women who had scalp muscle contraction and combination headaches. Men with scalp muscle contraction and combination headaches and male and female patients with posttraumatic cephalgia and conversion cephalgia had elevated MMPI profiles. The authors developed a set of criteria based on the MMPIs of this first group of headache patients and correctly identified 75 percent of the males' and 67 percent of the females' headache types in a new group of headache sufferers.

Gilberstadt and Sako (1967) found that survivors of open heart surgery ($N = 53$) had considerably higher T-scores on Scales L and K than nonsurvivors ($N = 12$). They concluded that denial was an adaptive mechanism in this type of surgery. On the other hand, Lair and King (1976) found that women with high Scales 1 and 3 (also considered indicative of denial) were more likely to die as a result of their open heart surgery. When they used the rule, Scales 1 and 3 above a T-score of 70 plus Scale 6 above a T-score of 57, they correctly classified all of their expired female patients ($N = 4$) and included none of their survivor female patients ($N = 13$). It is not clear why denial seemed so detrimental for their female patients when it was predictive of survival for the Gilberstadt and Sako patients.

Ford et al. (1976) studied 18 reactive hypoglycemics and 12 people who thought they were hypoglycemic. They found that 12 of the 30 had WNL MMPI profiles. They found no MMPI differences between patients who were actually hypoglycemic and those who only thought they were. They concluded that their data did not support the hypothesis that the emotional distress experienced by hypoglycemic patients was due to their hypoglycemia. They further cautioned that one should not be too quick to ascribe a patient's symptoms as due to hypoglycemia because of the danger of overlooking a more serious illness. Their findings suggest that one serious illness that can be easily overlooked is depression.

Finally, Spergel et al. (1978) studied patients with rheumatoid arthritis. The 46 patients had a mean elevated profile with Scales *1* and *2* being the highest and Scales *0*, *6*, and *9* being the lowest. These authors point out that patients with this disease were not homogeneous in their MMPI profiles. However, they provide no data on the various profile configurations apparently found for this group of patients.

In summary, patients with some medical problems have WNL MMPI profiles, whereas for patients with other medical problems, specifically brain damage, headache, heart disease, hypoglycemia, and rheumatoid arthritis, this is not true. It is noteworthy, however, that when MMPI elevations are found for a group of patients with a medical problem, not all of these patients have the elevated profile. Only certain subgroups of patients have the MMPI elevations, whereas others do not. The most clinically useful MMPI information about a medical problem is found only when homogeneous subgroups are delineated and studied.

CHRONIC PAIN

This last section on WNL MMPI profiles of nonpsychiatric subjects is a good illustration of the clinical usefulness of dividing MMPIs into homogeneous subgroups on the basis of subject characteristics, subgroups of the medical problem, or MMPI profile codes. There have been many studies of patients with chronic pain and chronic low-back pain. Those studies conducted prior to 1979 are summarized by Adams, Heilbronn, Silk, Reider, and Blumer (1981). They reported that the

studies they reviewed showed that (1) no single feature or scale of the MMPI was likely to consistently differentiate functional from organic low-back pain; (2) the patient with chronic low-back pain had some degree of elevation on Scales *1*, *2*, and *3* and that the overall degree of elevation apparently increased as a function of the duration of pain, the number of surgeries, and the length of unemployment following the diagnosis; and (3) group differences on the MMPI did not translate to individual cases. Adams et al. (1981) speculated further that there may be reason to believe that people with other types of chronic pain would produce similar results. Their excellent article should be read for the complete analysis of the studies.

Table 11–1 summarizes the low-back pain research since 1979 as well as other chronic pain studies. Only the research involving WNL profiles will be commented on in this chapter. For information concerning other studies involving chronic pain see Chapter 2.

Hudgens (1979) worked with 24 chronic pain patients and their families. He taught the families to reward nonpain-oriented behavior on the part of the patients. Seventy-five percent of the patients were able to lead normally active and satisfactory lives at the end of the treatment. The six male patients had a *1-3* codetype at the beginning of the treatment and a Spike *2* at the end, but the women who improved (*N* = 12) had a WNL mean profile after treatment and an increase in their *Es* score. The women who did not improve (*N* = 6) also had a WNL profile after treatment, but there was not as big a change between their pre- and posttreatment profiles as there was for the women who were treated successfully, and their *Es* score did not go up after treatment. Thus, in this study, gender of the patient seemed to make a difference in response to the treatment.

Prokop, Bradley, Margolis, and Gentry (1980) studied multiple-pain patients and found profile groups similar to those described by Bradley, Prokop, Margolis, and Gentry (1978) for low-back pain patients. Three profile groups were found for men and four for women. One of the female groups and one of the male groups had a WNL mean profile. This study did not look at pain-related, behavioral correlates of the various MMPI profile groups, but Prokop et al. (1980) believed that the people in these two WNL profile groups denied any psychological conflicts and therefore

TABLE 11–1.   SUMMARY OF SELECTED MMPI STUDIES ON PATIENTS REPORTING BACK PAIN

Study	Pain	Duration	Profile	Methodologic Issues A B C D E F G	Comment
1. Hudgens (1979) 6 M, 18 F, $\bar{X}$ age = 46	Chronic	$\bar{X}$ = 4 yr	**Males** Pre = *1–3* Post = *2* and *Es* higher, *Lb* lower **Females** Pre = *1–3–2* Post = WNL and *Es, Lb* higher	+ + – – + + +	*Es* and *Lb* scales also reported. Stringent criteria for inclusion into study (had more motivated subjects?).
2. Prokop et al. (1980) 123 M, 221 F	Multiple (low back pain only Ss not included)	Not given	**Males** Four replicable subgroups, 1 WNL group (*N* = 30) **Females** Three replicable subgroups, 1 WNL group (*N* = 62)	– – – – + + +	Several (5) of the subgroups replicate those found by Bradley et al. (1978). Sophisticated statistical analysis used to determine subgroups. Cross-validated subgroups.
3. Roberts & Reinhardt (1980) 26 treated patients (81% F) 20 rejected patients (65% F) 12 patients who refused treatment (83% F)	Chronic	$\bar{X}$ = 9 yr for treated Ss	**Treated Ss** Pre = *1–3* Post = WNL increased *Es* scale	+ + – – – – –	No MMPI *T*-scores are given, just that scales were "higher" or "lower."
4. Long (1981) 22 successful surgery Ss (9M, 13 F) 22 nonsuccessful surgery Ss (16M, 6 F)	Low back pain	Not given	**Successful surgery Ss** $\bar{X}$ profile = WNL **Unsuccessful surgery Ss** $\bar{X}$ profile = Spike 1	+ + – – + + –	Profile configurations were predictive of surgery outcome. Ss with WNL, Spike *1*, *1–2–3* had successful surgery. Ss with Spike *3*, *1–3*, *1–3–4*, *4*, abnormal tended to have unsuccessful surgery.
5. Snyder & Power (1981) 141 Ss with unelevated profiles	Chronic pain	21–34 mo	5 subgroups of WNL profiles	– + – – + + –	No information on sex, SES, or education. Mean 5 scales given with no knowledge of sex of Ss.
6. Armentrout (1982) 240 M Ss	Chronic pain	Not given	3 subgroups 1 WNL (*N* = 61)	+ + – – + + +	The 3 subgroups are similar to those found for males by Bradley et al. (1978).
7. Leavitt & Garron (1982) 110 Ss 43 M, 67 F	Low back pain	$\bar{X}$ = 17.6– 22.1 mo	3 subgroups 1 WNL (*N* = 47)	+ + + + + – –	The higher the *K*-profile scores the more pain reported.

(Continues.)

TABLE 11–1. *(Continued.)*

Study	Pain	Duration	Profile	A B C D E F G	Comment
8. Naliboff, Cohen, & Yellen (1982)(1983) 74 LBP Ss 51 M, 23F 40 Migraine Ss 21 M, 19 F 40 Chronic illness Ss (hypertension or diabetes) 8 M, 32 F	Low back pain, migraine, chronic illness	$\bar{X}$ = 7.8–20.8 yr	LBP = *1–3* chronic illness & migraine = WNL	+ + - - + + -	Elevation on Scales *1* & *3* seems due to amount of chronic physical limitation.
9. McGill et al. (1983) 92 LBP Ss 46 M, 46 F	Low back pain	13–44 mo	7 subgroups 1 WNL (N = 25)	- + - - + + +	Replicated the subgroups reported by Bradley et al. (1978). Found different pain histories for the subgroups.
10. Hart (1984) 70 M Ss	Chronic pain	9 mo–12 yr	4 subgroups 1 WNL (N = 15)	- + - - + + -	Replicated the subgroups reported by Bradley et al. (1978).
11. McCreary (1985) 271 Ss 130 Ss (for cross validation) 40% M, 60% F	Low back pain	$\bar{X}$ = 3 yr	5 subgroups 2 WNL	+ + - - + + +	Replicated the subgroup reported by Bradley et al. (1978) but 2 WNL groups found. Sex differences found for prediction of outcome.

would have a higher probability of responding well to medical-surgical interventions. As seen in later studies (Armentrout, 1982; Leavitt & Garron, 1982; McGill, Lawlis, Selby, Mooney, & McCoy, 1983; McCreary, 1985), these predictions were accurate.

Roberts and Reinhardt (1980) treated 26 pain patients with behavioral management techniques. The patients had a mean WNL profile after treatment even though they had elevations on Scales *1* and *3* prior to treatment. In addition, 1 to 8 years posttreatment, 77 percent of the treated patients were leading normal lives without medication for pain compared with 3 percent of the patients who did not receive treatment. Roberts and Reinhardt concluded from these data that the abnormal MMPI profile commonly found in the chronic pain patient may be the result of the chronic pain and disability, the medication, the frustrations, and the abnormal lifestyle of the patient rather than an etiologic "cause" of the pain problem.

Long (1981) compared the preoperative MMPIs of chronic low-back pain patients who had successful surgery (N = 22) with patients who had unsuccessful surgery (N = 22). He found that the mean preoperative profiles were the same for the two groups except for a higher Scale *3* for the patients who had unsuccessful surgery. However, he found a strong relationship between profile codetypes and surgery outcome. His findings are shown in Table 11–2. Long concluded that the group mean MMPI profiles offered little to help understand the personality characteristics of the chronic pain patients or to predict response to surgery, whereas the MMPI codetypes were very useful.

Other WNL profiles also have been divided into codetypes that have meaningful behavioral correlates. Snyder and Power (1981) divided 141 WNL MMPIs of chronic pain patients into five codetypes. Group V was significantly different than the other four groups, which were not significantly different from each other. Group V had the lowest mean profile. The patients in this group (N = 12) were younger, had the shortest pain duration, had more specific pain foci, and were more likely to be outpatients than patients in the other groups.

Armentrout (1982) studied the MMPIs of chronic pain patients and replicated three of the seven Bradley et al. (1978) groups. In addition, his investigation of patient responses to a pain history questionnaire revealed that severity of pain and its

TABLE 11–2.   PRESURGERY MMPI PROFILE CODETYPES FOR PATIENTS WITH SUCCESSFUL AND UNSUCCESSFUL SURGERY

Profile Codetype	Total No. of Patients	Surgery Outcome	
		Success	Failure
No elevations (WNL)	12	12	0
3	2	2	0
1–2–3 (not a conversion V)	6	6	0
1	6	1	5
1–3	9	0	9
1–3–4	5	1	4
4	3	0	3
Abnormal (undefined)	1	0	1

impact on the patients' lives was the most severe for those with the highest MMPI scales and the least severe for those patients with the lowest MMPI scales. This latter codetype was WNL (61 of 240 patients). Three MMPI profile groups similar to the Bradley et al. (1978) groups also were found by Leavitt and Garron (1982) in their work with low-back pain patients. Again, the group (47 of 150 patients) with a WNL profile reported the least amount of pain of the three groups.

Naliboff, Cohen, and Yellen (1982) were interested in whether chronic pain patients scored differently on the MMPI than patients with other chronic illnesses. They looked at patients with low-back pain, migraine headaches, hypertension, and diabetes. They found that there was no common low-back pain MMPI profile pattern and hypothesized that elevations on the MMPI for chronic pain and chronic illness were the result of the emotional disturbance associated with chronic limitation and disruption of activity regardless of the illness involved. When the illness was not limiting or disrupting daily activities, their patients had a lower MMPI profile, typically WNL. Naliboff, Cohen, and Yellen (1983) reported that 29.4 percent of their low-back pain patients, 54.3 percent of their migraine headache patients, and 54.3 percent of their chronic illness patients had WNL MMPI profiles.

McGill et al. (1983) also replicated all seven of the Bradley et al. (1978) profile groups in their population of 46 male and 46 female low-back pain patients. Of these patients, 25 were in the WNL profile group, and they reported the shortest pain duration, the least amount of pain, the shortest vocational disability, and the least number of hospitalizations and surgeries. McGill et al. (1983) called these patients "pain copers" and predicted that they would respond positively to traditional medical management or to an operant conditioning program designed

to identify and reinforce positive coping styles. However, Bradley et al. (1978) did not see patients as positively as McGill et al. did, believing them to have denied their dependency problems.

Hart's (1984) study of 70 male chronic pain patients seems to reconcile these two different interpretations. He too found the subgroups originally defined by Bradley et al. (1978). Again, there was a WNL profile group of 15 patients. Hart found that the major characteristic of this group included an attempt to control unacceptable impulses through nonspecific physical complaints and/or uses of somatic disturbances to attract attention. These patients' interpersonal relationships were used for dependency gratification. The men's self-evaluations, however, tended to be positive and accurate. Thus, Hart (1984) found these men to have negative qualities similar to the Bradley et al. (1978) group (dependency) and positive qualities similar to the McGill et al. (1983) group (positive and accurate self-evaluations).

McCreary (1985) studied 271 low-back pain patients and found groups similar to Bradley et al. (1978). Three groups had elevated MMPI profiles and two had unelevated profiles (one more unelevated group than Bradley et al. [1978]). One of the unelevated groups had Scales 9, 1, 4, and 3 as the highest, while the other unelevated group had their highest scores on Scales 1, 2, and 3. These unelevated groups had the lowest pretreatment pain intensity and activity limitation scores of the MMPI profile subgroups. They also showed the greatest decrease in pain intensity from pretreatment to follow-up.

It is clear from the studies reviewed in this section on chronic pain that there are replicable MMPI subgroups of chronic pain patients and that the patients in these groups show different pretreatment histories and treatment outcomes. A WNL profile group has been found in all of the studies, and this group consistently has the best response to treatment.

Studies of Psychiatric and Correctional Populations

As shown in Tables 11–3 to 11–12, many studies of WNL MMPI profiles discussed in this section of the chapter failed to meet some basic methodologic criteria and/or did not report basic methodologic information. Consideration of potential confounding effects of moderator variables, adequacy of sample sizes for the statistical analyses, and specification of use of K-corrected vs. non-K-corrected MMPI T-scores were frequently lacking. These weaknesses should be kept in mind in the following discussion of these studies.

ADOLESCENT PSYCHIATRIC PATIENTS

WNL MMPI profiles are not at all uncommon among adolescent psychiatric patients when adolescent, non-K-corrected norms are used, as recommended by Archer (1987). Partially because of the frequency of WNL profiles, Archer further suggested that clinical interpretation of adolescent-normed profiles begin at T-scores of 65, at least for adolescents in psychiatric inpatient settings.

A few reports have compared the occurrence of WNL profiles among adolescents using adult vs. adolescent norms. Studying 12- to 17-year-old, mostly psychiatric inpatients of both sexes, Lachar, Klinge, and Grisell (1976) found a 25 percent frequency of WNL profiles (Scales *1-4* and *6-0* below a T-score of 70) using non-K-corrected, adolescent norms, and 9 percent using K-corrected, adult norms. Klinge, Lachar, Grisell, and Berman (1978) studied drug users and nonusers, ages 12 to 17, of both sexes, all of whom were psychiatric inpatients. Also using the above definition of a WNL profile, these authors found that 35 percent of the users and 22.5 percent of the nonusers had WNL profiles with adolescent, non-K-

corrected norms, and that 7.5 percent of the users and 10 percent of the nonusers had these profiles using K-corrected, adult norms. Archer (1987) reported that more adolescents than adults (26.6 vs. 5 percent) produced WNL profiles (apparently, all clinical scale T-scores < 70) on admission to inpatient psychiatric treatment, and he found that 43 percent of adolescents in a psychiatric outpatient sample obtained these profiles. A study of 22 male and female adolescent inpatients' deliberate ability to "fake good" on the MMPI found that those who produced profiles with no clinical scale T-scores above 70 tended to be older and to have less severe diagnoses than those who could not meet this WNL criterion (Archer, Gordon, & Kirchner, 1986). Archer (1987) concluded that higher levels of self-reported symptomatology are normative in adolescence, that adults and adolescents have different frequencies of endorsement of MMPI items, and that Marks, Seeman, and Haller's (1974) norms may have overestimated the frequency of pathologic item endorsements among adolescents. Archer (1987) also noted the effect of the absence of a K-correction procedure for adolescents on their production of WNL profiles.

FREQUENCY AND CORRELATES OF ADULTS' WNL PROFILES

WNL profiles obtained by individual patients and prisoners are reported in this section in terms of frequency and important empirical correlates when possible. When frequencies of MMPI profile or codetypes appear in the literature, however, WNL profiles are frequently not mentioned. It is then not clear whether they did not occur in the sample being studied or were somehow eliminated from consideration and, thus, not reported.

ALCOHOLICS (TABLE 11–3)

Lachar, Schooff, Keegan, and Gdowski (1978) reported 13 examples of WNL mean profiles obtained from alcoholics in various stages of illness and treatment, or not in treatment, and concluded that alcoholics have generated more WNL mean profiles than narcotic addicts or polydrug abusers. WNL mean profiles also occurred among primary (but not secondary) male and female, in- and outpatient alcoholics (Tarter, McBride, Buonpane, & Schneider, 1977) and among white and American Indian (but not Hispanic American) male alcoholics in a VA hospital (Page & Bozlee, 1982). Tarter et al.'s primary alcoholics retrospectively reported more symptoms of childhood minimal brain dysfunction; Page and Bozlee's three ethnic groups did not obviously differ on secondary diagnoses or other problems reported.

That individual alcoholics do produce WNL profiles has also been established. Krauthamer (1979) found that "few of the individual scores fell above 70" (p. 444) in a sample of alcoholic female inpatients at a private psychiatric clinic. Lachar, Gdowski, and Keegan (1979) obtained 11 percent WNL profiles in a sample of male inpatient alcoholics. Penk (1981) reported obtaining 14.97 percent WNL profiles in a group of in- and outpatient alcoholics (sex unspecified) at a VA medical center. Distinctive correlates of these profiles were not reported in these studies.

Several examples of WNL mean profiles resulting from clustering of alcoholics' MMPIs have been reported in recent years, often with data regarding important empirical correlates of these profiles. Three studies were found that reported relatively superior social, psychological, and physical functioning, less alcohol-related difficulty, or better prognosis for alcoholic patients in WNL profile clusters, compared with those in abnormal profile clusters. These studies were Donovan, Chaney, and O'Leary (1978), among male VA hospital alcoholic inpatients; Kline and Snyder (1985), in males and females from four inpatient alcohol treatment centers; and Svanum and Dallas (1981), among male and female alcoholic inpatients, 19 percent of whom were also polydrug abusers.

Eshbaugh, Tosi, and Hoyt (1978, 1980) cluster-analyzed MMPI scores of male and female alcoholic inpatients, respectively, and obtained correlates of more mixed valence for the males'

and females' WNL mean clusters. The males' two WNL mean clusters were associated with heavy drinking, and one also had hypomanic symptoms, but non-MMPI correlates of the abnormal profile mean clusters seemed at least as pathologic. The female alcoholic WNL mean cluster had good prognosis for symptomatic but not long-term behavior change and was associated with personality disorder diagnoses rather than neuroses. Another study (Conley, 1981) found two WNL mean profile clusters among males being discharged from inpatient alcoholic treatment; one had relatively poor treatment outcomes, and the other was indistinguishable from the other profile mean clusters in this regard.

Kline and Snyder (1985) reported that both their male and female WNL clusters were consistent with alcoholics' MMPI profile types previously reported in the literature. Thus, there is some consistency in regard to a subtype of alcoholics who may have WNL MMPI profiles and who may function somewhat better than other alcoholics.

OTHER SUBSTANCE ABUSERS (TABLE 11–4)

A review of previous research by Lachar et al. (1978) reported WNL mean profiles for samples of LSD users, polydrug abusers, and marijuana smokers. Penk, Fudge, Robinowitz, and Neman (1979) compared male veteran heroin, amphetamine, and barbiturate abusers (probably addicts) in inpatient treatment. The heroin users obtained a WNL mean profile, but no non-MMPI correlates were reported.

Cluster analysis was used by Eshbaugh, Dick, and Tosi (1982) on profiles of female, primarily narcotics users in residential and outpatient treatment. One of the clusters had a WNL mean profile and was labeled the "character disorder, passive-aggressive, passive type" on the basis of the MMPI. This cluster did not differ from the others in regard to type of treatment received.

Several studies have reported frequencies and some non-MMPI correlates of individuals' WNL MMPI profiles in drug-abuser samples. Sutker and Archer's (1979) review of MMPI characteristics of substance abusers noted that 5.5, 6, and 12 percent of three previously reported samples of opiate addicts had obtained WNL profiles. More recent studies have also reported frequencies of WNL profiles among heroin abusers: 10 percent among inpatient addicts (Lachar et al., 1979), 10.93 per-

TABLE 11–3.   WNL MMPI PROFILES IN ALCOHOLIC SAMPLES

Study	Age*	Sex	N	SES†/Race	Profile Characteristics	A	B	C	D	E	F	G	Comment
Tarter et al. (1977)					Group mean profiles: Primary alcoholics' was WNL	+	+	?	+	+	-	+	MMPI administered at least 10 days after admission; also after detoxification. "Primary" refers to severity.
Primary alcoholics	38.9	M	29	Middle & upper-middle									
		F	9										
Secondary alcoholics	48.0	M	20										
		F	8										
Psychiatric inpatient controls	32.3	M	22										
		F	27										
Nonpatient controls	31.6	M	20										
		F	7										
Page & Bozlee (1982)					Group mean profiles: Whites' and American Indians' were WNL.	+	-	+	+	-	+	+	MMPI administered at least 1 week after admission and detoxification.
Primary alcoholics	41.1	M	11	White									
	50.6	M	11	Hispanic									
	42.1	M	11	American Indian									
Conley (1981)					Alcoholic-type mean profiles: None of 4 WNL at admission. 2 WNL at discharge, with n = 31, 49.	+	-	?	+	+	-	-	Setting not clearly described. Profiles grouped according to MMPI literature. "Neurotic" and "classic alcoholic" types had WNL discharge profiles.
Primary alcoholics	42	M	337	Middle									
Donovan et al. (1978)					Alcoholic-type mean profiles: 2 of 4 WNL, with n = 14, 20.	+	-	?	-	+	-	+	MMPI administered about 10 days after admission and detoxification. Clustered according to Goldstein-Linden rules.
Alcohol addicts	46.2	M	102	?									
Eshbaugh et al. (1978)					Clustered mean profiles: 1 of 7 WNL; 1 almost WNL; with n = 18, 13, respectively.	+	-	?	-			-	Timing of administration not described.
Alcoholics	49	M	208	Primarily middle, 96% White									
Eshbaugh et al. (1980)					Clustered mean profiles: 1 of 5 WNL, with n = 24.	+	-	?	-			-	MMPI administered 7.9 days after admission and after detoxification.
Alcoholics	47.2	F	183	96% White									
Svanum & Dallas (1981)					Clustered mean profiles: 1 of 4 WNL, with n = 79.	+	-	?	+	+	+	+	MMPI administered usually in 2nd week to minimize toxic effects. 19% were also polydrug abusers. "Normal-limit acting-out type" had WNL profile.
Primary alcoholics	42.3	M	175	80% White, 20% Black; majority "blue collar"									
		F	32										
Kline & Snyder (1985)					Clustered mean profiles: 1 of 3 male and 1 of 3 female clusters were WNL, with n = 39, 22, respectively.	+	+	+	+	+	-	+	MMPI administered between 1 and 3 weeks after admission to control for withdrawal and hospitalization effects.
Alcoholics	40	M	188	60% White, 40% Black									
	41	F	112										
Krauthamer (1979)					Group mean profiles: Both WNL, with few individual scores above T = 70.	+	-	?				-	None drinking at time of testing.
Alcoholics	29–51	F	30	Middle & upper-middle; White									
Psychiatric inpatients		F	30										
Lachar et al. (1979)					Individual profile types:	+	-	+				+	Controls matched to each substance-abuser group on demographics. Timing of MMPI administration not described.
Alcoholics	42.2	M	65	51% Black	11%								
Heroin addicts	25.1	M	48	71% Black	10% — WNL								
Polydrug abusers	25.2	M	52	17% Black	2%								
Psychiatric patients	31.1	M	165	46% Black	15%								

(Continues.)

TABLE 11–3. *(Continued.)*

Study	Age*	Sex	N	SES†/Race	Profile Characteristics	Methodologic Issues§ A B C D E F G							Comment
Penk (1981)					Individual profile types:	-	-	?			-		Timing of MMPI administration not described. Ages of groups said to be similar.
Alcoholics	?	M	314	Black &	14.97%								
Heroin addicts	?	M	558	White	10.93%	WNL							
Polydrug abusers	?	M	307		9.12%								

*Mean median, or range.
†SES = socioeconomic status.
§"?" means information unavailable to reviewer. Blank space means data not pertinent to this review.

TABLE 11–4.   WNL MMPI PROFILES IN OTHER SUBSTANCE ABUSE SAMPLES

Study	Age*	Sex	N	SES†/Race	Profile Characteristics	Methodologic Issues§ A B C D E F G							Comment
Penk et al. (1979) Primary heroin abusers Primary amphetamine abusers Primary barbiturate abusers	23	M	144	White	Group mean profiles: Heroin abusers' was WNL.	+	+	?	+			+	MMPI administered during first week of admission.
Eshbaugh et al. (1982) Primarily narcotic abusers	26	F	178	Middle to lower; 50% White	Clustered mean profiles: 1 of 7 was WNL, with n = 17.	+	-	+	+	?	-	-	MMPI administered "after physiological stabilization from drug withdrawal". "Character disorder, passive-aggressive, passive type" had WNL profile.
Lachar et al. (1978) Polydrug abuser patients, N = 282 Polydrug abuser non-patients, N = 172	23.4 25.3	M F	288 166	White	Individual profile types: 13.8% 32.6%	+	-	+	+	+	+	+	MMPIs administered during first 10 days of treatment.
					WNL								
Keegan & Lachar (1979)					Individual profile types:	+	-	+	+	+	-	+	MMPI administered within first week of program with toxicity and withdrawal influences minimized.
Polydrug treatment "stayers"	25.8	M F	50 54	12% Black 88% White	11.5%								
Polydrug treatment "quitters"	25.0	M F	42 28	21% Black 79% White	1.4%	WNL							
Lachar et al. (1979) (See earlier entry)													
Penk (1981) (See earlier entry)													
Craig (1984) Heroin addicts	30	M	442	90% Black 7% White 3% Latino	Individual profile types: 2.3% WNL.	+	-	+				-	MMPI administered about 1 week after admission and detoxification. Used Marks et al. rules to classify profiles; found no normal K+ profiles.

*Mean or median.
†SES = socioeconomic status.
§"?" means information unavailable to reviewer. Blank space means data not pertinent to this review.

cent among male addicts in VA medical center in- or outpatient treatment (Penk, 1981), and (according to the Gilberstadt and Duker [1965] system) 2.3 percent among male, veteran addicts in in- or outpatient treatment (Craig, 1984). Non-MMPI correlates of the WNL profiles were not reported in these studies.

Among polydrug abusers, the following frequencies of WNL profiles have been reported: 13.8 percent of males and females from 13 treatment facilities, compared to 32.6 percent of non-patient polydrug abusers (Lachar et al., 1978), 11.5 percent of male and female polydrug abuse treatment program completers, compared with 1.4 percent of premature program terminators (Keegan & Lachar, 1979), 2 percent of inpatients (Lachar et al., 1979), and 9.12 percent of abusers in in- or outpatient treatment at a VA medical center (Penk, 1981). Some correlates of these WNL profiles are available: Lachar et al. (1978) found that patients with these profiles used fewer kinds of drugs than did other patients, and WNL profiles were proportionately more frequent among patients who preferred cocaine, marijuana, or hallucinogens to opiates or psychotropic drugs. As mentioned earlier (Keegan & Lachar, 1979), WNL profiles were more frequent at admission among abusers who went on to complete treatment than among those who did not. Furthermore, the authors suggested that treatment completers may have had less psychopathology, more internalized conflict, and less of a drug-abuse history than premature terminators.

These studies of WNL MMPI profiles among drug abusers suggest that polydrug abusers may produce more of these profiles than opiate and heroin addicts and that (although pertinent data are sparse) polydrug abusers who produce WNL profiles may function better in some ways than those whose MMPI profiles are abnormal.

PRISONERS (TABLE 11–5)

Lanyon (1968) presented examples of WNL and near-WNL mean profiles obtained by several groups of prisoners between the late 1940s and mid-1960s. More recent prison-group mean profiles have been reported, among male nonaddicts in a parish prison (Sutker, 1971), female murderers in state prisons (Sutker & Allain, 1979), white and Mexican-American short-term felons at

a state prison (Holland, 1979), and incestuous child molesters in a state prison (Panton, 1979).

Two of these studies (Sutker, 1971; Sutker & Allain, 1979) reported that their samples with WNL mean profiles had relatively less disturbance on their individual members' profiles, according to Meehl's (1956) MMPI profile classification system; the profiles of 50 percent of Sutker and Allain's female murderers were "normal" by this criterion. Other empirical correlates have been reported. Prisoner groups characterized by WNL mean profiles have shown possibly less deviant, but still illegal, sexual practices, compared with imprisoned nonincestuous child molesters (Panton, 1979) and relatively benign psychiatric and substance-abuse histories and later-onset arrest records, compared with imprisoned male murderers and/or female and male nonviolent criminals (Sutker & Allain, 1979). Furthermore, Blanchard, Bassett, and Koshland (1977) found that males at a county penal farm who had individual WNL profiles tended to have been older when first arrested and to have fewer previous arrests than did male prisoners with individual abnormal MMPI profiles suggestive of psychopathy.

On the other hand, Sutker and Allain's (1979) prisoner group with a WNL mean profile did not differ from other prisoner groups on many other social history variables, Holland's (1979) racially grouped prisoners with and without WNL mean profiles did not differ on socioeconomic indices, and Blanchard et al.'s (1977) interpretation of their prisoners' individual WNL profiles was complicated by an interaction of race (black or white) and profile type (WNL or psychopathic) in results on a behavioral measure of ability to delay gratification.

An example of a clustering procedure resulting in WNL mean MMPI profiles is the Megargee inmate typology (Megargee & Bohn, 1979). This much-studied, MMPI-based prisoner classification system was developed at a medium-security, federal correctional institution for males. The typology has 10 clusters, 2 of which (Easy and Item) have WNL mean profiles. They included 7 percent and 19 percent of prisoners, respectively, at the original site. In group Item, 40 percent of prisoners had no MMPI scales above a T-score of 70. On the many empirical correlates of these mean profiles reported by Megargee and Bohn (including criminal, academic, intellectual, social, developmental, family, educational, vocational,

TABLE 11–5. WNL MMPI PROFILES IN PRISON SAMPLES

Study	Age*	Sex	N	SES†/Race	Profile Characteristics	A	B	C	D	E	F	G	Comment
Sutker (1971)					Group mean profiles: Prisoners' was WNL.	+	+	+	+	-		+	Timing of MMPI administration not described.
Unincarcerated heroin addicts	27.07	M	40 }	?									
Nonaddict inmates	24.88	M	40 }										
Blanchard et al. (1977)					Group mean profiles: Groups defined by MMPI. 1 Black and 1 White group had WNL profile, with n = 31, 32, respectively.	+	+	?	-	+	+	-	MMPI administered within 10 days of incarceration. Black "psychopaths" and White "normals" had WNL mean profiles.
Misdemeanor and felony inmates	?	M }	64	Black									
			61	White									
Sutker & Allain (1979)					Group mean profiles: Only female murderers had WNL profile.	-	+	+	+	+	-	+	Subjects in prison at least 2 months prior to MMPI administration, to reduce initial prison stress effects. Groups said to be similar, but not quantitatively described, on many basic demographic variables.
I. Incarcerated murderers		F	22										
Incarcerated property and drug offenders	? }	F	40	?									
II. Incarcerated murderers		M	45										
Incarcerated property and drug offenders		M	61										
Holland (1979)					Group mean profiles: Hispanics' and Whites' were WNL.	+	+	?	+	+	+	+	Timing of MMPI administration not reported, but probably soon after incarceration.
Incarcerated short-term felons	26.07	M }	114	Hispanic									
			396	White									
			208	Black									
Panton (1979)					Group mean profiles: Incestuous molesters had WNL profile except for 4 = 70.3.	+	+	+	÷			+	Tested at or very soon after admission. Differences in molestation patterns not statistically analyzed.
Incarcerated incestuous child molesters	40.6	M }	35										
Incarcerated nonincestuous child molesters	30.8	M }	28	?									
Megargee & Bohn (1979)					Prisoner-type mean profiles: 2 of 10 (groups Item and Easy) had WNL profiles, with n = 225, 84, respectively.	+	+	+	+	-	-	+	Inmates were "youthful offenders." Profiles classified into types previously obtained by cluster analysis.
Medium-security federal inmates	?	M }	1164	64.7% White 34.4% Black 0.9% Other									

*Mean or median.
†SES = socioeconomic status.
§"?" means information unavailable to reviewer. Blank space means data not pertinent to this review.

interpersonal, institutional adjustment, and recidivism data), groups Item and Easy tended to function very well, were often the best ranked, and were often significantly better than other groups. For example, members of Item and Easy were less likely to be reincarcerated than were members of the other clusters. The Megargee inmate typology and its temporal stability have been examined with varying results at other penal institutions.

In general, these primarily mean-profile data suggest that prisoners who obtain WNL MMPI profiles may have more benign criminal and substance-abuse histories, less deviant histories of other kinds, better adjustments to incarceration, and a lower rate of recidivism.

OTHER LEGALLY INVOLVED GROUPS (TABLE 11–6)

Several studies have reported WNL mean profiles among legally involved groups referred by the courts for preplea or presentencing psychiatric evaluations or for treatment. These groups included males convicted of indecent exposure (McCreary, 1975), males and females convicted of minor assaultive and nonassaultive crimes, respectively (McCreary, 1976; T-scores on Scale 4 were approximately 70 for assaultive males and nonassaultive females), male indecent exposers (Rader, 1977), male exhibitionists and nonpedophile homosexuals (Langevin, Paitich, Freeman, Mann,

TABLE 11–6.   WNL MMPI PROFILES IN OTHER LEGALLY INVOLVED GROUPS

Study	Age*	Sex	N	SES†/Race	Profile Characteristics	Methodologic Issues§							Comment
						A	B	C	D	E	F	G	
McCreary (1975) Exhibitionists in pre-sentence evaluations:					Group mean profiles: Groups with none and 1–5 priors were WNL.	+	+	+	-		+		
No prior arrests	30	M	37 ⎫	74% White									
1–5 prior arrests	32	M	38 ⎬	11% Black									
6+ prior arrests	29	M	10 ⎭	8% Hispanic 1% Oriental									
McCreary (1976) Assaulters and non-assaulters in pre-sentence evaluations	31	75% M	450	65% White	Group mean profiles: All 4 sex X assaultiveness groups had WNL profiles, but assaultive males and nonassaultive females had 4 ~ 70.	+	+	+	-		+		Crimes were misdemeanors. Groups defined by behavior, not by charge.
Rader (1977) Preplea or pre-sentence evaluatees:					Group mean profiles: Exposers had WNL profile. All 3 groups may have had individual WNL profiles; exposers may have had the most.	+	+	+	-		+		Exposers considered less violent than other groups. Groups defined by behavior, not by charge.
Exposers	28.6	M	36 ⎫										
Rapists	26.3	M	47 ⎬ ?										
Assaulters	31.0	M	46 ⎭										
Langevin et al. (1978) Evaluatees at forensic clinic:					Group mean profiles: Exhibitionists had WNL profile. Homosexuals' was WNL except for 5.	-	+	?	+	+	-	+	
Exhibitionists			14										
Homosexuals			39										
Bisexuals			31										
Heterosexual pedophiles	≥18	M	29 ⎬ ?										
Homosexual pedophiles			22										
Transsexuals			46										
Incestuous molesters			27										
Multiple deviants			217										
Heterosexual nonpatients			?										
Rogers & Seman (1983) Accused murderers evaluated at foren-sic centers:					Group mean profiles: Insane treatment patients had WNL profile, and their individual profiles were less elevated.	-	+	+	-			-	Patients had been adjudicated as not guilty by reason of insanity and discharged from inpatient to outpatient treatment.
Sane evaluatees			40 ⎫										
Insane evaluatees	?	?	12 ⎬ ?										
Insane patients in treatment			25 ⎭										
Ray et al. (1983) First-offense shoplifters	25.68 ⎬	F	71 ⎬	58% Hispanic	Group mean profile was WNL.	+	+	?	-	+	+	-	
		M	23										
Anderson et al. (1979) Hospitalized sex offenders	31.03	M	88	69% White	Factored mean pro-files: 1 of 3 was WNL except 2 = 70, with n = 16.	+	+	?	+	+	-	-	Referred for pretrial evaluation or committed under sexual psychopath law.
Anderson & Holcomb (1983) Accused murderers in pretrial evaluation	26.7	M	110 ⎬	64% White 36% Black	Clustered mean profiles: 1 of 5 clusters had WNL profile, with n = 21.	+	+	?	+	+	-	-	Accused of premeditated murder.

*Mean, median, or range.
†SES = socioeconomic status.
§"?" means information unavailable to reviewer. Blank space means data not pertinent to this review.

& Handy, 1978; the homosexuals had a WNL mean profile except for Scale 5), outpatients previously judged not guilty of murder by reason of insanity (Rogers & Seman, 1983), and first-offender shoplifters of both sexes (Ray, Solomon, Doncaster, & Mellina, 1983). Two of these reports (Rader, 1977; Rogers & Seman, 1983) suggested that members of the groups with WNL mean profiles had more WNL individual profiles or generally less elevated individual profiles, respectively, than did comparison groups.

Empirical correlates, including group membership per se, reported for these WNL mean profiles suggest better adjustment for members of these groups than for some comparison groups. WNL mean profile groups had fewer previous arrests for indecent exposure, compared with other indecent exposers (McCreary, 1975); had committed non-violent crimes, compared with rapists and assaulters (Rader, 1977); had relatively masculine personalities and were relatively reserved according to results of the Sixteen Personality Factor Questionnaire (exhibitionists), compared with several other groups of sexually anomalous males, and were consistently distinguished from a control group of heterosexuals who had never been in treatment only by their increased femininity (homosexuals; Langevin et al., 1978); and had received extensive inpatient treatment and been discharged to outpatient status, compared with untreated evaluatees (Rogers & Seman, 1983). However, McCreary (1976) found that assaultive males and nonassaultive males and females obtained WNL mean profiles. Ray et al.'s (1983) shoplifters who went on to complete a psychoeducational treatment program, did not differ from the normative performance on a test of irrational beliefs, and scored in the "unsure" range of a self-concept index, but no comparison group was described.

Two studies used multivariate procedures to group pretrial evaluatees. Anderson, Kunce, and Rich (1979) factor analyzed MMPI profiles of male sex offenders and found one profile type to be within-normal-limits except for a T-score of 70 on Scale 2. These men had degraded their victims less and showed less symptomatology on the psychiatric hospital ward than did those in one of the other profile types, but they were also most likely to have a diagnosis of antisocial personality disorder, had a greater incidence of serious crime, and were less educated than persons in the other

groups. Anderson and Holcomb (1983) cluster analyzed MMPI scores of males charged with first-degree or capital murder. One cluster had a WNL mean profile and consistently favorable non-MMPI correlates compared with other clusters. These men had the highest rated IQs, were the most likely to have been employed at the time of their crime, were the least likely to have histories of drug or alcohol abuse, were the least suspicious and physically aggressive on the ward, and were the least likely to have killed using a handgun.

Again, there is evidence that relatively good functioning in some areas is associated with WNL MMPI average profiles, clusters, or individual profiles among persons in forensic psychiatric settings who are convicted or accused of criminal activity.

MOOD-DISORDER PATIENTS (Table 11–7)

Donnelly and colleagues (Donnelly, 1979; Donnelly & Murphy, 1973a, b; Donnelly, Murphy, & Goodwin, 1976; Donnelly, Murphy, Waldman, & Reynolds, 1976) cited depressed bipolar inpatients' WNL mean profiles as evidence of the effectiveness of defensive denial and overactivity in the production of socially desirable response sets, even during symptomatic depression. Donnelly and Murphy (1973a), Donnelly, Murphy, and Goodwin (1976), and Donnelly, Murphy, Waldman, and Reynolds (1976) compared unipolar and bipolar depressed inpatients of both sexes who were equally symptomatically depressed and found WNL mean profiles for the bipolar but not for the unipolar patients on admission to hospitals.

However, Lumry, Gottesman, and Tuason (1982, 1983) criticized the methodology of the Donnelly et al. studies and disputed the alleged normality of symptomatic bipolar depressives' MMPI profiles. Lumry et al. (1982) studied MMPIs of rigorously diagnosed bipolar patients of both sexes during manic, depressed, and euthymic phases of their illness. A WNL mean profile was obtained for the euthymic phase; but euthymics' individual profiles were not described. Abnormal mean profiles for the manic and depressed phases were obtained, and only 2 of 12 manic-phase profiles were within normal limits, as was 1 of 10 obtained during a depressed phase.

There is other evidence of the occurrence of individual WNL MMPI profiles in mood-disorder

TABLE 11–7.   WNL MMPI PROFILES IN MOOD-DISORDER PATIENTS

Study	Age*	Sex	N	SES†/Race	Profile Characteristics	Methodologic Issues§ A B C D E F G	Comment
Donnelly & Murphy (1973a)					Group mean profiles:	+ + ? + + - -	Patients drug-free during
Unipolar depressives	48	M	7		Bipolars' was WNL;		testing. Groups not different
		F	13	?	0 not reported.		in age.
Bipolar depressives	44	M	8				
		F	11				
Donnelly, Murphy, & Goodwin (1976)					Group mean profiles: Bipolars' was WNL	- + + + + - +	Patients drug-free during testing. Groups not different
Unipolar depressives, N = 17	?	M	11	?	at admission; both groups had WNL pro-		in age or race.
Bipolar depressives, N = 17		F	23		files at remission.		
Donnelly, Murphy, Wald-man & Reynolds (1976)					Group mean profiles: Bipolars' was WNL.		
Unipolar depressives, N = 34	?	M	28	?		- + + + -	Patients drug-free during testing. Groups not different
Bipolar depressives, N = 34		F	40				in age or race.
Lumry et al. (1982) Bipolar-disorder					Group mean and in-dividual profiles:	- + - - -	Most taking lithium and/or other drugs when tested.
patients	41.4	M	9	?	Mean profile for		MMPIs administered in
	42.0	F	13		euthymic phase was WNL (N = 12), but individual profiles were not reported. 2 of 12 manic-phase and 1 of 10 depressed-phase profiles were WNL.		manic, depressive, and/or euthymic phase of illness over 25-year period.
Silver et al. (1981)					Individual profiles:	- + - - -	MMPI completed at
Major, unipolar de-pressives, N = 24	58.6	F	13		8.3% were WNL; diagnoses not re-		admission.
		M	11		ported.		
Dysthymic-disorder patients, N = 24	60.7	F	11	?			
		M	13				
Winters et al. (1985)					Individual profile types:	- + ? - -	Marks et al. rules for normal K+ were used.
Major depressives	33.6	F	40		3.2% 3.2%		
		M	23				
Bipolar depressives	28.0	F	20		8.6% non- 0.0%	"K+	
		M	15	?	K+	nor-	
Bipolar manics	35.7	F	20		0.0% "nor- 2.7%	mal"	
		M	17		mal"		
Schizophrenics	27.5	F	20		2.9% 0.0%		
		M	14				
Davies et al. (1985)					Individual profile types:	? + ? ? ?	
Bipolar manics	?	?	101	?	17.8% WNL		
Schizophrenics			99		14.1%		

*Mean or median.

†SES = socioeconomic status.

§"?" means information unavailable to reviewer. Blank space means data not pertinent to this review.

patients. Silver, Isaacs, and Mansky (1981) found 8.3 percent WNL profiles in male and female major depressives and dysthymic-disorder patients. It is not clear whether these were inpatients or outpatients or which diagnostic group had the WNL profiles. Winters, Newmark, Lumry, Leach, and Weintraub (1985) studied inpatients of both sexes at a state, a private, and a medical school psychiatric facility. They found 3.2 percent normal $K+$ profiles (Marks et al., 1974) among patients with major depression, 0 percent among bipolar depressives, and 2.7 percent among bipolar manic patients. They also found 3.2 percent "normal" (not normal $K+$) profiles among the patients with major depression, 8.6 percent among the bipolar depressives, and 0 percent among the bipolar manics. Finally, Davies, Nichols, and Greene (1985) reported a frequency of 17.8 percent WNL profiles among a sample of bipolar manic patients. This codetype was the most frequent for that diagnostic group. Sex and inpatient vs. outpatient status were not given.

Lumry et al.'s (1982) study and their critique of Donnelly and colleagues' studies leave unclear the association, if any, of WNL MMPI profiles and relatively normal functioning among depressed bipolar inpatients. According to Lumry et al., a small number of WNL profiles occurred during symptomatic manic and depressive phases of the illness. Unfortunately, none of the other studies reviewed here that reported frequencies of in-

dividual WNL profiles among mood-disorder patients described any non-MMPI correlates of these profiles.

SCHIZOPHRENIC PATIENTS (Table 11–8)

Several researchers have reported frequencies of WNL profiles among schizophrenic inpatients. Gilberstadt (1971) found that approximately 18 percent of schizophrenics in his sample of VA hospital males obtained "low-ranging and normal-limits profiles" (p. 5). Caplan (1974) compared 30 schizophrenic VA hospital inpatients who had WNL MMPI profiles with 30 who had abnormal profiles that strongly suggested psychosis. Newmark, Gentry, Simpson, and Jones (1978) reported a 4.72 percent frequency of profiles "closely approximating" (p. 370) the normal $K+$ profile among male and female schizophrenics admitted to university or private inpatient psychiatric facilities. Davies et al. (1985) found a 14.5 percent frequency of WNL profiles among schizophrenic inpatients. This was the second most frequent codetype in their schizophrenic sample. Winters et al. (1985) did not find any normal $K+$ profiles but found 2.9 percent other WNL profiles among schizophrenic inpatients.

The Gilberstadt (1971) and Caplan (1974) studies suggest that schizophrenic inpatients with WNL profiles may have relatively acute psychotic symptoms, be more intelligent, and have less dis-

TABLE 11–8.   WNL MMPI PROFILES IN SCHIZOPHRENIC PATIENTS

Study	Age*	Sex	N	SES†/Race	Profile Characteristics	Methodologic Issues§ A B C D E F G	Comment
Gilberstadt (1971)	?	M	?	?	Individual profile types: About 18% had "low-ranging and normal-limits profiles".	- + ? - +	MMPI administered within 10 days of admission.
Caplan (1974)	?	M	60	?	Individual profile types: 1 of 2 groups had WNL profiles, with $N = 30$.	+ ? ? + ?	Groups defined by MMPI profiles.
Newmark, Gentry, Simpson, & Jones (1978)	24.5 }	F M	182 } 178	White	Individual profile types: 4.7% "closely approximated the normal $K+$ profile".	+ + - + -	MMPI administered 48–96 hours after admission. Marks et al. rules for normal $K+$ were used.
Winters et al. (1985) (See earlier entry)							

*Mean.
†SES = socioeconomic status.
§"?" means information unavailable to reviewer. Blank space means data not pertinent to this review.

turbed histories, but be less cooperative, compared with those with abnormal profiles. This suggestion is tentative, because of the sparsity of pertinent data.

BORDERLINE PERSONALITY DISORDERS

In light of the diagnostic interest in the Borderline Personality Disorder, it is noteworthy that WNL MMPI profiles among borderlines are extremely rare. Leach (1982) found no WNL profiles among male and female borderlines in a private psychiatric hospital. Gustin, Goodpaster, Sajadi, Pitts, LaBasse, and Snyder (1983) also found none among male borderline inpatients at a VA medical center. Vincent, Castillo, Hauser, Stuart, Zapata, Cohn, and O'Shanick (1983) found no Borderline Personality Disorder diagnoses in "false normal" profiles (all clinical scale T-scores below 70) obtained from male and female, private psychiatric in- and outpatients. Barley, Sabo, and Greene (1986) found only one patient with a Borderline Personality Disorder diagnosis among normal $K+$ and other WNL profiles of inpatients at a private psychiatric hospital, where the base rate of the diagnosis was 18 percent.

OTHER PSYCHIATRIC SAMPLES (Table 11–9)

Studies of a few other samples of patients in clinical settings have reported WNL mean profiles.

These included: nonpsychotic Air Force personnel referred for psychiatric evaluation (Anthony, 1971); full-time employed persons of both sexes in neuropsychological evaluation, compared with part-time or unemployed evaluatees (Heaton, Chelune, & Lehman, 1978); and behavior therapy patients of both sexes who were not experiencing unplanned distortions in mental imagery during systematic desensitization, compared with patients in the same setting who did have distorted imagery (Lanyon & May, 1979, study I). Eubanks, Hermecz, Patterson, Watts, Shehi, and Koplan (1985) cluster analyzed MMPI scores of male and female panic-disorder patients and obtained one cluster with a WNL mean profile and others with abnormal mean profiles. In addition to the above-mentioned favorable comparisons to other patient groups, the WNL group described by Heaton et al. (1978) had better scores on virtually all parts of an extensive neuropsychological test battery than did the unemployed group and did better on some of the tests than did the part-time employed group. The other studies did not report non-MMPI correlates of their WNL average or clustered mean profiles.

THE NORMAL $K+$ PROFILE (Table 11–10)

The normal $K+$ profile has been studied as a distinctive codetype. This WNL profile was 1 of 16

TABLE 11–9.   WNL MMPI PROFILES IN OTHER PSYCHIATRIC SAMPLES

Study	Age*	Sex	N	SES†/Race	Profile Characteristics	A	B	C	D	E	F	G	Comment
Anthony (1971) Nonpsychotic USAF patients	26	M	40	?	Group mean profile was WNL.	+	+	?	-			-	
Heaton et al. (1978) Neuropsychology evaluatees	37.7	F / M	84 / 297	?	Group mean profiles: Full-time employed evaluatees had WNL profile, with $n = 171$.	+	+	?	+	+	-	-	MMPI administered with neuropsychological assessment.
Lanyon & May (1979, St. I) Behavior therapy patients	27	F / M	12 / 13	?	Group mean profiles: Group without spontaneous distortion of mental imagery had WNL profile and few elevated profiles, with $n = 15$.	+	+	?	-			-	
Eubanks et al. (1985) Panic disorder patients	33.9	F / M	18 / 12	93% White 3% Black 3% Oriental	Clustered mean profiles: 1 of 3 clusters had WNL profile, with $n = 21$.	+	+	+	-		+		

*Mean or median.
†SES = socioeconomic status.
§"?" means information unavailable to reviewer. Blank space means data not pertinent to this review.

TABLE 11–10. NORMAL K+ MMPI PROFILES

Study	Age*	Sex	N	SES†/Race	Profile Characteristics	A	B	C	D	E	F	G	Comment
Marks & Seeman (1963) Psychiatric patients	43 46	F M	app. 320	White	Individual profile types: 1 of 16 types was WNL, "normal K+", 5.4% of sample.	+	-	-	+	-	-	+	Empirical correlates of code type derived from female inpatients.
Briggs et al. (1966) Psychiatric patients	?	F M	2875	?	Individual profile types: 6.8% had normal K+ using Marks & Seeman rules.	?		?	?			?	21.7% of sample classifiable by Marks & Seeman system. Normal K+ patients presumably inpatients.
Pauker (1966) Psychiatric inpatients	≥18	F	204	White	Individual profile types: At least 4.4% had normal K+ using Marks & Seeman rules.	-	-	?	-			-	Female inpatients only. 22% of sample classifiable as "complete hits". Profiles obtained 7 days or less after admission.
Gynther & Brilliant (1968) Psychiatric inpatients, N = 1155	32.9	F M	>434 >679	App. 75% White 25% Black	Individual profile type: Normal K+, 3.6%, N = 42, using Marks & Seeman rules.	+	-	?	+			-	Normal K+ only profile type classified.
Payne & Wiggins (1968) Psychiatric inpatients	?	F M	247 294	?	Individual profile types: 12.9% had normal K+ using Marks & Seeman rules		-	+	-			+	27% of sample classifiable.
Schultz, Gibeau, & Barry (1968) Psychiatric inpatients	18–65	F M	100 100	?	Individual profile types: 15.5% had normal K+ using Marks & Seeman rules.		-	+	-			-	23% of sample classifiable ("good fits").
Meikle & Gerritse (1970) Psychiatric inpatients N = 1068, and out- patients, N = 330.	35.8	F M	872 526	?	Individual profile types: 2.3% had normal K+ using Marks & Seeman rules.	+		?	-			-	MMPI administered within 7 days of admission. Normal K+ patients presumably inpatients. 16.8% of sample classifiable.
Owen (1970) University testing and counseling center clients Medical center patients State prison inmates	?	F M F M M	382 580 1041 696 1126	?	Individual profile types: 18.9% Normal K+ profiles, using Marks 7.0% & Seeman rules. 6.3%	-		?	-			-	23% of clients, 26% of patients, and 22% of inmates classifiable ("strict" condition). Subjects apparently not psychiatric inpatients.
Newmark et al. (1978) Psychiatric inpatients (See earlier entry)													
Craig (1984) In- and outpatient heroin addicts (See earlier entry)													
Winters et al. (1985) Psychiatric inpatients (See earlier entry)													

(Continues.)

TABLE 11–10. *(Continued.)*

Study	Age*	Sex	N	SES†/Race	Profile Characteristics	Methodologic Issues§ A B C D E F G	Comment
Barley et al. (1986)					Individual profile types: Base rate	+ - - + + - -	MMPI administered within 2 weeks of admission. K-corrections used. Only normal K+ and other WNL profiles classified.
Psychiatric inpatients N = 447					of normal K+ and of other WNL profiles in this setting was		
With normal K+ profiles	36	F	9	White	3.8% each. Used Marks et al. rules for		
		M	8		normal K+.		
With other WNL profiles	37	F	5				
		M	12				

*Mean, median, or range.
†SES = socioeconomic status.
§"?" means information unavailable to reviewer. Blank space means data not pertinent to this review.

codetypes identified and correlated with a large number of demographic, historical, and clinical variables by Marks and Seeman (1963) in the development of their actuarial MMPI codetype system. Marks et al. (1974) slightly relaxed the classification rules: (1) psychiatric inpatients only; (2) all clinical scales below a *T*-score of 70; (3) six or more clinical scales less than or equal to a *T*-score of 60; (4) Scales *L* and *K* higher than Scale *F*, with *F* below a *T*-score of 60; and (5) Scale *K* five or more *T*-points higher than Scale *F*.

FREQUENCY OF OCCURRENCE

Several researchers have reported the frequency of occurrence of the normal *K*+ profile, in terms of proportion of all MMPI profiles in their samples, classifiable and unclassifiable. Using the original Marks and Seeman (1963) classification rules, the frequency was 5.4 percent (Marks & Seeman, 1963), 6.8 percent (most frequent codetype; Briggs, Taylor, & Tellegen, 1966; described in Marks et al., 1974), at least 4.4 percent (Pauker, 1966), 3.6 percent (Gynther & Brilliant, 1968), 12.9 percent (most frequent codetype; Payne & Wiggins, 1968), 15.5 percent (most frequent codetype; Shultz, Gibeau, & Barry, 1968), and 2.3 percent (Meikle & Gerritse, 1970). Pauker's (1966) normal *K*+ subjects were female psychiatric inpatients only; all other normal *K*+ groups included male and female psychiatric inpatients. These studies took place in university medical center and general hospital psychiatric units, in a public mental health center, and in state hospitals. Also using the Marks and Seeman (1963) rules, Owen (1970) found 18.9 percent normal *K*+ profiles (most frequent codetype) in a university testing and counseling center, 7.0 percent (most frequent

codetype) in a university medical center outpatient facility, and 6.3 percent in a state prison. The university subjects were male and female; the prisoners were all males.

Using Marks et al.'s (1974) classification rules, Newmark et al. (1978) obtained a frequency of 4.7 percent "closely approximating" (p. 370) the normal *K*+ profile among male and female schizophrenics at university or private psychiatric inpatient facilities; Craig (1984) obtained no normal *K*+ profiles among male VA hospital in- and outpatient heroin addicts; Winters et al. (1985) obtained 1.8 percent among male and female schizophrenic, major depressive, and bipolar inpatients in state, private, and medical center psychiatric facilities; and Barley et al. (1986) found 3.8 percent normal *K*+ profiles among private psychiatric inpatients of both sexes.

Although originally studied among psychiatric inpatients only, the normal *K*+ profile is now known to occur in many clinical settings and in prison, among several diagnostic groups, and in both sexes. However, its original empirical correlates were derived from female psychiatric inpatients, and it is important to remember that more recently reported correlates were also derived only from psychiatric inpatient samples.

EMPIRICAL CORRELATES OF THE NORMAL *K*+ PROFILE

Marks and Seeman (1963) provided an extensive listing of the empirical correlates of this profile type, and Marks et al. (1974) presented these data in narrative form. As summarized by Greene (1980), this profile type was associated with shyness, anxiety, inhibition, and defensiveness about admitting psychological problems.

These patients avoided close relationships and were passively resistant. Their personalities had a schizoid component, often with perplexity and an incoherent stream of thought. They displayed paranoid features of suspicious fear and oversensitivity. Psychotic diagnoses were received by 48 percent of them, and 24 percent were diagnosed as having a chronic brain syndrome. They were significantly above average in intelligence, and over 60 percent of them were educated beyond high school.

At least four other studies have investigated empirical correlates of this codetype. Pauker's (1966) female psychiatric inpatients obtained personality disorder diagnoses more frequently than did the Marks and Seeman (1963) sample, although psychotic diagnoses were also very frequent in Pauker's sample. Gynther and Brilliant (1968) found proportionately fewer brain syndrome diagnoses in their normal K+ male and female inpatients, although they did obtain a 45 percent frequency of psychotic diagnoses. Their normal K+ patients did not differ in terms of education and IQ from a sample of patients in the same setting who did not have normal K+ profiles; this was at odds with Marks and Seeman's (1963) findings. Correlation of the normal K+ profile with many historical and clinical variables was investigated by Barley et al. (1986). Compared with base rates in their inpatient setting, these patients were less likely to have had chronic illnesses, to have attempted suicide prior to hospitalization, and to have somatic complaints. Their behavior and emotional state were more likely to be overactive, and their current hospitalization was shorter in length. They were also less likely to present psychosomatic symptoms than were inpatients with WNL profiles other than the normal K+. Normal K+ patients had a 47 percent probability of a psychotic diagnosis, but they had no brain disorder diagnoses, unlike the normal K+ patients of Marks and Seeman (1963) and Gynther and Brilliant (1968). Barley et al.'s (1986) normal K+ patients also appeared to differ from those of Marks and Seeman on many other variables.

Psychotic diagnoses consistently are highly probable with the normal K+ profile, at least among psychiatric inpatients, but these patients' symptoms may also be relatively acute and reversible. The normal K+ profile may have somewhat different correlates and different distinctive correlates in different clinical settings. Barley et al.

(1986) discussed demographic and methodologic factors that could account for the inconsistencies.

OTHER STUDIES OF WNL
MMPI PROFILES (Table 11–11)

Vestre and Klett (1969) studied MMPI profiles from persons admitted to a VA hospital during 1963. They obtained 10 percent WNL profiles (not including Scale 5). Patients with WNL profiles were less likely to be neurotic but were more likely to be committed than were patients with abnormal profiles. The WNL patients tended not to see themselves as requiring hospitalization, and adult situational reactions occurred more frequently in the WNL group, but there was also a 45 percent probability of a psychotic diagnosis in that group. Proportionately more patients in the WNL group had paranoid-type diagnoses, but this difference reached only the .10 level of significance. The two groups did not differ with respect to length of hospitalization, and of those patients discharged within 21 months following admission, the proportion from each MMPI profile group that had to return to the hospital was about the same.

Three kinds of WNL profiles were examined by Kelley and King (1978) among students of both sexes "seeking psychiatric treatment" (p. 695) at a university outpatient mental health center. Some students had all validity and clinical scales between T-scores of 30 and 70, inclusive, with Scale K below 65 ("WNL"); seven males had unelevated clinical scales with Scale K between 65 and 70 ("Hi-K"); and other students had unelevated clinical scales with Scale K above a T-score of 70 ("K+"; not the same as the normal K+ profile). The "WNL" group seemed to be either normally adjusted people who were experiencing transient emotional upsets or males who had currently remitted or residual schizophrenic disorders; these two subgroups' MMPI profiles could not be distinguished from each other. The "Hi-K" profile group seemed to be made up of psychologically intact but inhibited males who had marital problems of a sexual nature but no psychiatric disorder. Males in the "K+" group tended to be severely disturbed, with very high rates of bipolar manic disorder and psychotic symptoms; women in this profile group frequently presented with phobias, had no modal primary diagnosis, frequently had secondary diagnoses of hysterical neurosis, and were not psychotic.

TABLE 11–11. OTHER WNL MMPI PROFILES

Study	Age*	Sex	N	SES†/Race	Profile Characteristics	Methodologic Issues§ A B C D E F G							Comment
Vestre & Klett (1969)					Individual profile type: 15.6% of	-	-	+	-	+	-	-	MMPI administered at average of 4 days after
Psychiatric inpatients	?	?	256	?	profiles studied were WNL.								admission to hospital. Only profile type.
Kelley & King (1978)					Individual profile types: 11.6% of	+	-	?	+	-	-	-	Only WNL profiles classified.
University counseling center clients	22.0 22.6	F M	268} 282}	Almost all White	profiles were WNL with $K < 65$; 1.3% were WNL with K between 65 and 69 inclusive; 3.5% were WNL with $K \geq 70$.								
Vincent et al. (1983)					Individual profile types: 11.9% were	+	+	+	-		-		86% of sample inpatients; 14% outpatients.
Psychiatric in- and outpatients	38.6}	F M	141} 120}	94% White 6% Black	"false normal", i.e., no clinical scale > 70.								
Barley et al. (1986) Psychiatric inpatients (See earlier entry)													

*Mean or median.
†SES = socioeconomic status.
§"?" means information unavailable to reviewer. Blank space means data not pertinent to this review.

Vincent et al. (1983) examined diagnoses associated with WNL profiles and obtained a frequency of 11.9 percent among private psychiatric in- and outpatients of both sexes. The modal diagnosis for these patients was adjustment disorder with either depressed/anxious mood or mixed emotional features. Various mood disorders comprised the second most frequent diagnostic category. Of these WNL patients 40 percent had no personality disorder diagnosis. The authors concluded that "at least in this private setting a significant number of people who make a false-normal MMPI profile indeed may be coming in with minor adjustment problems" (Vincent et al., 1983, p. 841).

Barley et al. (1986) also examined empirical correlates of WNL profiles that had Scale K below a T-score of 56 and did not meet the criteria of the normal $K+$ codetype. Among male and female private psychiatric inpatients, these WNL profiles had a 3.8 percent frequency and, compared with the base rates in the hospital, were associated with less chronic disturbance, shorter current hospitalization, and fewer prior hospitalizations. These profiles were disproportionately likely to come from males. Many other variables did not differentiate these WNL patients from the hospital base rates.

These studies suggest that psychiatric and student mental health center patients who obtain WNL profiles may be less disturbed than persons with abnormal profiles, especially if the formers' test-taking approach is not defensive. Among these profiles is a relatively high frequency of situational or acute disorders. Inpatients studied by Vestre and Klett (1969) tended to be defensive and had a high probability of psychotic diagnoses, and Kelley and King's (1978) highly defensive males seemed to have been their most severely disturbed outpatients.

WNL PROFILES IN MEASUREMENT AND PREDICTION OF CHANGE
(Table 11–12)

Not surprisingly, one application of the MMPI has been in measurement and prediction of treatment completion and outcome. WNL profiles obtained under both simulated and actual assessment conditions have been used for this purpose.

WNL PROFILES OBTAINED UNDER ACTUAL ASSESSMENT CONDITIONS

A few authors investigating measurement and predictive properties of MMPIs obtained at admission to treatment or correctional programs have discussed WNL profiles. Forsyth (1965) correlated admission and discharge MMPI profiles of male

TABLE 11–12.   MEASUREMENT AND PREDICTION OF CHANGE

Study	Age*	Sex	N	SES†/Race	Profile Characteristics	Methodologic Issues§ A B C D E F G	Comment
Forsyth (1965) Psychiatric inpatients	?	?	96	20–30% Black	Group mean profiles: 1 of 3 groups ("acute psychotic") had WNL profile at admission and at discharge.	− + + − +	MMPI administered at beginning of treatment in hospital. Acute psychotics with poor outcomes had WNL mean profile at admission and discharge; those with good outcomes had WNL mean profile only at discharge.
Keegan & Lachar (1979) (See earlier entry)							
Megargee & Bohn (1979) (See earlier entry)							
Marks & Seeman (1963) (See earlier entry)							
Conley (1981) (See earlier entry)							
Grayson & Olinger (1957) Psychiatric inpatients	?	M	45	?	Individual profile type: 11.1% obtained "normal" profiles when simulating normalcy.	− − ? − ? + −	"Normal" profile not clearly defined. MMPI administered for simulation of normalcy 1 day after admission to hospital.
Rapaport (1958) Psychiatric in- and outpatients	?	?	48	?	Group mean profiles: WNL profile obtained under "ideal self" condition.	− − ? − −	69% outpatients, and 31% inpatients in military facility. 11 had no psychiatric diagnosis.
Marks & Seeman (1963) (See earlier entry)							
Newmark et al. (1983) Psychiatric in-patients	22.1	F M	83 58	White	Individual profile type: 18.4% simulated normal MMPIs.	+ + + + + + −	Normal MMPIs had all clinical scales ≤ 70 except 5. MMPI administered for simulation within about 3 days of admission.
Hunt (1948) Army inductees Navy court martial prisoners	?	M M	56 74	?	Individual profile types: 85% of 19 inductees and 32% of 68 prisoners who had non-normal "honest" profiles had "normal" profiles under "fake good" instructions.	+ + ? − +	All subjects in late adolescence or older. Profile called "normal" if no "personality" scale score exceeded 64 without K-correction. "Some" prisoners had "some degree of psychopathy."
Lawton & Kleban (1965) Short-term county prisoners	25	?	28	?	Individual profile types: 54% obtained 4 or 5 scores ≤ 70 under "fake low" instructions; 75% did under usual instructions.	− + + − −	Scores on other scales not reported. Most subjects' "fake low" profiles still appeared "sociopathic." IQ seemed unrelated to ability to suppress 4.

(Continues.)

TABLE 11–12.   *(Continued.)*

Study	Age*	Sex	N	SES†/Race	Profile Characteristics	Methodologic Issues§ A	B	C	D	E	F	G	Comment
Gendreau et al. (1973)					Group mean and individual profiles:	+		-	-			+	*0* not scored. IQ seemed to have little to do with successful faking.
Maximum security provincial prisoners	23.2	?	24	?	Mean profile was WNL under "faking good adjustment" set. 17% had any scales > 70 under this set; 79% did under "honest" set.								
Bennett (1970) State prisoners	?	?	32	?	Individual profiles: 34% produced profiles "without serious pathology" under "fake-good" instructions.	-		?	-	+	+	-	MMPI was administered "prerelease". "Without serious pathology" might not mean WNL.

*Mean or median.
†SES = socioeconomic status.
§"?" means information unavailable to reviewer. Blank space means data not pertinent to this review.

VA hospital inpatients with their treatment outcomes at 6 and 18 months after discharge. Acutely psychotic (as opposed to nonpsychotic and chronically psychotic) patients whose treatment outcomes were not good had a WNL mean profile with relatively high Scale *K* at admission and at discharge; those with good outcomes had a WNL mean profile at discharge only, and the validity scales did not suggest defensiveness. Several other studies, discussed previously in this chapter, also addressed prognosis associated with WNL clustered and individual MMPI profiles obtained at or shortly after admission to treatment programs or prison. Most of these found or predicted relatively or absolutely good prognosis in terms of length of hospitalization (Barley et al., 1986), symptom relief (Eshbaugh et al., 1980; Gilberstadt, 1971), completion of treatment (Keegan & Lachar, 1979), maintenance of treatment gains (Svanum & Dallas, 1981), and criminal recidivism (Megargee & Bohn, 1979). On the other hand, Vestre and Klett (1969) found no difference between inpatients with and without WNL profiles in terms of lengths of stay or later readmission. These clustered and individual MMPI profiles suggested a defensive approach to the test, according to Greene's criteria (1980), in only a few cases, i.e., Barley et al.'s (1986) normal *K*+ but not other WNL profiles, a small number of Gilberstadt's (1971) low-ranging or WNL profiles, and one of Megargee and Bohn's (1979) two WNL clusters.

Other investigators have examined the implications of WNL profiles obtained at the time of discharge from treatment programs. Stelmachers' *K*+ discharge profile was described by Lachar (1974a). This is apparently a low-ranging or WNL profile with an elevated Scale *K*. Lachar suggested that if this profile occurs on readministration of an MMPI or at about the time of discharge, following an admission MMPI indicative of more psychiatric disturbance and little defensiveness, it means significant reduction in psychiatric symptomatology and improved reality contact and mental control, primarily because of the increased defensiveness. A patient with this profile is considered unlikely to benefit from further treatment. Marks and Seeman (1963) presented mean discharge MMPI profiles for each of their 16 codetypes. Nine of these mean profiles were within normal limits, and none of these codetypes except the normal *K*+ had a WNL mean profile at admission. These WNL profiles are not obviously associated with better-rated response to treatment than are abnormal discharge profiles reported for other Marks et al. codetypes. Most of the WNL mean profiles suggest a defensive test-taking approach, on the average. Finally, Conley (1981) found that two of his alcoholic inpatient MMPI clusters ("neurotic" and "classic alcoholic" types) obtained WNL mean profiles at discharge. However, the "neurotic" type had a comparatively poor treatment outcome by 12 months following discharge, while the "classic alcoholics" were not very distinctive on this variable. Neither of these mean profiles appeared defensive.

WNL clustered and individual admission profiles, defensive or not, are often associated with various favorable outcomes. The prognostic picture with such MMPI profiles obtained at discharge from treatment is more mixed, and the role of defensiveness is not clear.

SIMULATED WNL PROFILES

Several researchers have attempted to predict treatment or prison outcomes from subjects' abilities to simulate normalcy on the MMPI. Patients' and prisoners' responses to ideal-self, very-good-adjustment, and similar instructional sets have been attributed to recognition of personal deviance as pathologic, to the ability to maintain a response set and to role-play, to empathy with well-functioning individuals, to regard for societal norms, and to the ability to maintain reality orientation. Such socially desirable response sets, as seen on the MMPI, have been hypothesized to enable patients and prisoners to function relatively better than their counterparts who lack them (Bennett, 1970; Grayson & Olinger, 1957; Hiner, Ogren, & Baxter, 1969; Lanyon, 1967; Lawton & Kleban, 1965).

Simulation of normalcy on the MMPI and its relationship to treatment outcome have been studied in psychiatric settings. Grayson and Olinger (1957) asked male inpatients in a VA hospital to answer the MMPI as a well-adjusted, nonhospitalized person would. Eleven percent simulated normalcy (not clearly defined as all clinical scale T-scores below 70). Simulation of normalcy on the MMPI was itself not related to relatively early discharge from the hospital, but degree of improvement on the MMPI by the time of the experimental administration was. Rapaport (1958) had military psychiatric in- and outpatients (sex unspecified) respond to the MMPI under ideal-self instructions. There was a significant tendency for subjects who were later successfully pursuing their service tours to have changed their MMPI scores more between an earlier, real-self administration and the later, ideal-self administration than had those who were prematurely separated from the service. The importance of a simulated WNL MMPI in these results was not reported.

Marks and Seeman (1963) presented mean "projected" discharge profiles for each of their 16 codetypes. The profiles resulted from instructions to "answer these [MMPI] items as you would expect to feel when you get out of the hospital"

(Marks et al., 1974; p. 11). It was Marks and his colleagues' impression that patients who could not project more normal discharge MMPI profiles did not improve and even became worse during treatment. These authors also felt that a WNL mean projected discharge profile is "a prognostically hopeful sign" (p. 101) for members of a codetype. The 2 of 16 codetypes that did not have a WNL mean projected discharge MMPI profile seem to have had relatively poor average treatment responses.

Finally, Newmark, Gentry, Whitt, McKee, and Wicker (1983) attempted to remedy methodologic flaws in the Grayson and Olinger (1957) and Rapaport (1958) studies by implementing more rigorous diagnostic criteria and outcome measurement. Newmark et al. had nonchronic male and female schizophrenics admitted to either a private or a university psychiatric inpatient facility respond to the MMPI as would a "normal, well-functioning adult" (1983, p. 438). The 18 percent of schizophrenic inpatients who simulated a WNL profile (with T-scores on all validity and clinical scales except Scale 5 at or below 70) had more favorable treatment outcomes (73 percent improved) than those whose simulated profiles were abnormal (44 percent improved). Acknowledging the possible complication of greater likelihood of marriage among the patients who successfully simulated normalcy, Newmark et al. concluded that "awareness of socially acceptable and approved behaviors thus appears to be a favorable prognostic sign in schizophrenia" (p. 440).

Other investigators have studied prisoners' ability to simulate normalcy on request. Male Navy court martial prisoners (Hunt, 1948), short-term county prisoners (sex unspecified; Lawton & Kleban, 1965), and prisoners at a provincial maximum security institution (sex unspecified; Gendreau, Irvine, & Knight, 1973) were asked to complete the MMPI under various fake-good instructional sets. These studies varied in the resulting frequencies of simulated WNL profiles, and it is difficult to compare their results directly because of idiosyncratic reporting practices. Gendreau et al. (1973) seem to have been most successful in getting prisoners to simulate normalcy on the MMPI, and these authors concluded that prisoners can simulate normalcy "fairly easily" (p. 192) when the instructions are concrete and specific.

Bennett (1970) correlated simulation of normalcy on the MMPI with postincarceration adjustment, speculating that prisoners who cannot or will not simulate such normalcy are more likely to have difficulty adjusting to life outside prison. Asking state prison inmates (sex unspecified, but probably male) to respond to the MMPI as would a normal citizen, he found that 34 percent produced profiles "without serious pathology" (Bennett, 1970, p. 30), according to a rating scheme that apparently did not require all clinical scales to be within normal limits. There was no relationship between simulation of normalcy and 6-month and 2-year parole adjustment.

Not surprisingly, many of these studies with psychiatric patients and prisoners reported that their simulations of normalcy on the MMPI clinical scales were accompanied by defensive mean validity scale patterns.

EXPLANATION OF WNL MMPI PROFILES

How does the MMPI "miss" in the fashion described in this review? How do patients and prisoners sometimes avoid the expected scale elevations?

DEFENSIVENESS

Several authors have suggested that WNL MMPI profiles occur under the standard instructional set because some persons taking the MMPI lacked insight and accurate self-appraisal or chose not to represent themselves accurately in their test responses. Gilberstadt (1971), Caplan (1974), and Vestre and Klett (1969) suggested that persons in clinical settings who do not see themselves as mentally ill or requiring hospitalization or do not view themselves primarily as psychiatric patients may obtain WNL profiles. Vestre and Klett (1969) mentioned extreme denial or even paranoia as explanations, and Donnelly and colleagues (e.g., Donnelly, 1979) maintained that bipolar depressive inpatients had sufficiently decreased self-awareness to enable them to adopt a socially desirable response set on the MMPI. Graham (1984b) indicated that the best practice is to consider WNL profiles in clinical settings as defensive.

It is clear that a defensive approach to the MMPI can result in a WNL profile. Dahlstrom et al. (1972) showed that elevations on Scales L and K have a suppressive effect on clinical scale elevations and that there is a roughly inverse relationship between the number of clinical scales in an MMPI profile higher than a T-score of 70 and scores on L and K. Graham (1984b) stated the converse, that WNL profiles are often associated with elevations on Scales L and/or K. Lachar (1974a) described a validity scale configuration in the shape of an inverted carat or "V," which was associated with "unduly lowered" (p. 106) clinical scale scores, and Greene (1980) identified a positively sloping L-F-K pattern associated with WNL clinical scales except for the possibility of an elevated Scale 5 among males. Of course, the various fake-good and ideal-self instructional sets used in research on simulation of normalcy on the MMPI and the sometimes defensive WNL profiles that result are another kind of evidence that a defensive test-taking set could be operating to produce WNL profiles under actual testing conditions.

However, with the exception of research on the normal K+ profile, only some of the studies reviewed here (e.g., Marks et al., 1974; Panton, 1979; Megargee & Bohn, 1979) clearly report a correlation of elevated validity Scales L and/or K with the clinical occurrence of WNL profiles. Most validity scale patterns reported for WNL mean MMPIs obtained under the standard instructional set do not appear to be defensive, and the very infrequent descriptions of validity scale patterns accompanying individuals' WNL profiles reported in these studies are equivocal on this point. Detection of a defensive test-taking set on the MMPI may require more than analysis of MMPI validity scales, as there is evidence (Gilberstadt, 1971; Graham, 1984b) that some evasive and mistrustful persons can produce WNL profiles without elevating Scales L and K.

RELATIVELY GOOD FUNCTIONING

The evidence reviewed here suggests that some persons in psychiatric and correctional settings who give WNL profiles function better psychologically than persons who obtain abnormal profiles in the same settings.

The paucity of reports of empirical correlates of individuals' WNL MMPI profiles is unfortunate, but the reported empirical correlates of WNL individual profiles and of the mean profiles resulting from cluster analyses frequently have indicated a relatively benign history, better clinical status, and superior prognosis. Furthermore, persons and groups giving WNL profiles are described infrequently as more dysfunctional than other individuals or groups of patients or prisoners. There are some exceptions to this general conclusion. The normal *K+* profile is reliably associated with a high probability of a psychotic diagnosis among psychiatric inpatients, even though Barley et al. (1986) also found it to be correlated with some areas of superior functioning. Vestre and Klett (1969) reached similar conclusions on both points in their sample of WNL profiles that may or may not have included normal *K+* profiles. Among Kelley and King's (1978) male college students seeking outpatient psychiatric aid at a counseling center, those with WNL profiles and very high scores on Scale *K* (above a *T*-score of 70) tended to be actively psychotic. Forsyth's (1965) acute psychotic inpatients with poor treatment outcomes had a defensive WNL mean MMPI profile at admission, while other acute psychotic inpatients did not. Thus, a defensive WNL MMPI profile in a psychiatric setting might mean relatively better functioning *or* psychosis.

Research on simulation of normalcy on the MMPI provides a second kind of evidence pertinent to the association of relatively good functioning and WNL profiles. The more recent research on simulation of normalcy, at least in psychiatric settings, suggests that patients who can simulate normalcy on the MMPI might have better treatment outcomes than those who cannot or will not (Marks et al., 1974; Newmark et al., 1983). The defensive and other personal attributes suggested as explanations for successful simulation of normalcy via the MMPI in clinical settings may be part of what constitutes better functioning.

INTERPRETATION OF WNL PROFILES IN PSYCHIATRIC AND CORRECTIONAL SETTINGS

Because of the many potential moderator variables occurring in research on which the following suggestions are based (e.g., Gearing, 1979), these are tentative guidelines for dealing with WNL MMPI profiles in psychiatric and prison settings.

INTERPRETATION OF DEFENSIVENESS

A defensive test-taking set is operative by definition in the normal *K+* profile, and other WNL MMPI profiles may also result from a patient's or prisoner's resistance to disclosure of his or her psychological life. Consequently, the possibility of a defensive response set should be considered. Butcher (1984), Gendreau et al. (1973), Greene (1980), and Grow, McVaugh, and Eno (1980) suggested and critiqued various methods for detection of this kind of response set in psychiatric, student counseling, and correctional settings. Their suggestions generally are based on individual validity scale elevations, validity scale patterns, or differential endorsements of subsets of the MMPI items. Once detected, the function of the defensive test-taking set must be ascertained. It may be correlated with a desirable ability to take roles and to empathize with healthy functioning, or it may mean that lip service is being paid to normalcy by persons who have no desire or ability to behave that way in nontest situations. Defensiveness and relatively healthy functioning may not always be mutually exclusive, but this relationship must be determined in each case.

ESTABLISHMENT OF LOCAL EMPIRICAL CORRELATES

While relatively good psychological functioning is frequently associated with WNL MMPI codetypes, such codetypes have few replicated, specific empirical correlates. The high frequency of psychotic diagnoses in the normal *K+* profile is one of these. Even in this well-defined codetype, many other potential correlates have not withstood attempts at cross-validation. Too little information about other WNL profiles is available for very specific interpretation of this kind of profile as a codetype. The advice of Gynther and Brilliant (1968) that clinicians should establish the empirical correlates of WNL profiles in their own settings is sound, especially if specific interpretive information is desired for WNL profiles as a codetype.

INTERPRETATION OF VALIDITY SCALE SCORES AND CONFIGURATIONS

Since defensive validity scale patterns may accompany WNL clinical scale scores, empirical correlates of validity scale elevations could be useful information. Butcher (1984) suggested that demographic variables and diagnoses are associated differentially with patterns of validity scale elevation in defensive profiles. For example, he suggested that persons with neurotic diagnoses are particularly likely to produce MMPI profiles with high Scales L and K, because moral virtuousness is part of the favorable self-image that these patients try to project. However, Sines, Baucom, and Gruba (1979) warned of the probability of psychosis in psychiatric inpatients with highly defensive validity scale patterns, even when the clinical scales themselves do not suggest psychosis. Gross (1959) discussed the validity scale configurations associated with good and poor behavioral control and social adjustment among male and female schizophrenic VA hospital patients. He found that a "V"-shaped validity scale pattern is likely to mean relatively less overt behavioral disturbance but variable adequacy of social adjustment. Also, relatively less overt behavioral disturbance was found among psychiatric inpatients with validity scale patterns with either large negative or very small mean $F - K$ differences compared with those with large positive mean $F - K$ differences (Post & Gasparikova-Krasnec, 1979). Greene (1980) and Duckworth and Anderson (1986) presented examples and some correlates of common validity scale patterns, including defensive ones that might be associated with WNL profiles. They also suggested interpretive statements for individual validity scales, including Scales L and K at various elevations.

INTERPRETATION OF INDIVIDUAL CLINICAL SCALES BELOW T-SCORES OF 70

Two sources for interpretive statements for individual clinical scales at T-scores below 70 are Greene (1980) and Duckworth and Anderson (1986). Lachar (1974a) indicated that WNL profiles in psychiatric settings could be handled by "overinterpreting" clinical scale T-scores in the range of 60 to 70. Butcher (1984) agreed, with some qualification. He said that this practice is most justified when validity scales indicate a defensive test-taking set, that personality descriptions rather than psychopathologic correlates are likely to apply to clinical scales in the range of 65–69 T-score points, and that if all clinical scales are between 60–64 T-score points, content scales

are better sources of personality description than are clinical scales. Graham (1984a) suggested that known correlates of MMPI codetypes can be used even when no clinical scale is above a T-score of 70, but, again, that personality descriptors are probably more applicable than the psychopathologic ones. Normative data suggest another qualification to the practice of "overinterpreting" WNL MMPI clinical scale scores. As noted earlier, Colligan et al. (1984) showed that today's normal, nonpatient subjects generally have higher mean scores on the MMPI clinical scales than did the original MMPI normative sample. Thus, some caution is called for in the application of personality and, perhaps especially, psychopathologic correlates to unelevated clinical scales.

A FINAL POINT

Lest this chapter conclude apparently smug in the conviction that a WNL MMPI profile must always mean concealed psychopathology or, at best, only relatively less psychopathology than a profile with elevated clinical scales, Lachar's (1974a) warning regarding the importance of base rates of normalcy in clinical settings bears repeating: "A within-normal-limits admission profile obtained in a setting with a variety of loosely defined referral sources may, indeed, correctly suggest an inappropriate admission" (p. 27).

ACKNOWLEDGMENT

The author (WDB) wants to thank Kimberly A. Storrs for preparation of part of the manuscript.

REFERENCES

Adams, K., Heilbronn, M., Silk, S., Reider, E., & Blumer, D. (1981). Use of the MMPI with patients who report chronic back pain. *Psychological Reports, 48,* 855–866.

Anderson, L. M. (1969). Personality characteristics of parents of neurotic, aggressive, and normal preadolescent boys. *Journal of Consulting and Clinical Psychology, 33,* 575–581.

Anderson, W. P., & Holcomb, W. R. (1983). Accused murderers: Five MMPI personality types. *Journal of Clinical Psychology, 39,* 761–768.

Anderson, W. P., Kunce, J. T., & Rich, B. (1979). Sex offenders: Three personality types. *Journal of Clinical Psychology, 35,* 671–676.

Anthony, N. (1971). Comparison of clients' standard, exaggerated, and matching MMPI profiles. *Journal of Consulting and Clinical Psychology, 36,* 100–103.

Archer, R. P. (1987). *Using the MMPI with adolescents.*

Hillsdale, NJ: Lawrence Erlbaum.

Archer, R. P., Gordon, R. A. & Kirchner, F. H. (1987). MMPI response set characteristics among adolescents. *Journal of Personality Assessment, 51,* 506–516.

Armentrout, D. (1982). Pain-patient MMPI subgroups: The psychological dimensions of pain. *Journal of Behavioral Medicine, 5,* 201–211.

Barley, W. D., Sabo, T. W., & Greene, R. L. (1986). Minnesota Multiphasic Personality Inventory normal *K+* and other un-elevated profiles. *Journal of Consulting and Clinical Psychology, 54,* 502–506.

Barron, F. (1969). *Creative persons and creative process.* New York: Holt, Rinehart & Winston.

Bennett, L. A. (1970). Test taking "insight" of prison inmates and subsequent parole adjustment. *Correctional Psychologist, 4,* 27–34.

Bernstein, I. H. (1980). Security guards' MMPI profiles: Some normative data. *Journal of Personality Assessment, 44,* 377–380.

Blanchard, E. B., Bassett, J. E., & Koshland, E. (1977). Psychopathy and delay of gratification. *Criminal Justice and Behavior, 4,* 265–271.

Blaustein, M., & Proctor, W. (1977). The active duty conscientious objector: A psychiatric-psychological evaluation. *Military Medicine, 142,* 619–621.

Bradley, L. A., Prokop, C. K., Margolis, R., & Gentry, W.D. (1978). Mulivariate analysis of the MMPI profiles of low back pain patients. *Journal of Behavioral Medicine, 1,* 253–272.

Briggs, P. F., Taylor, M., & Tellegen, A. (1966). *A study of the Marks and Seeman MMPI profile types as applied to a sample of 2,875 psychiatric patients* (Research Laboratories Rep. No. PR-66-5). Minneapolis: University of Minnesota, Department of Psychiatry.

Brown, E. (1982). Note on the relationship between nude figure drawings and the MMPI scales. *Journal of Personality Assessment, 46,* 370–371.

Butcher, J. N. (1984). Interpreting defensive profiles. In J. N. Butcher & J. R. Graham (Eds.), *Clinical applications of the MMPI. No. 3* (pp. 5–7). Minneapolis: University of Minnesota, Department of Professional Development and Conference Services, Continuing Education and Extension.

Butcher, J. N., & Tellegen, A. (1978). Common methodological problems in MMPI research. *Journal of Consulting and Clinical Psychology, 46,* 620–628.

Cairnes, N. U., & Lansky, S. B. (1980). MMPI indicators of stress and marital discord among parents of children with chronic illness. *Death Education, 4,* 29–40.

Caplan, A. S. (1974). Characteristics of patients hospitalized as psychotic obtaining normal limits MMPI profiles (Doctoral dissertation, University of Minnesota). *Dissertation Abstracts International,* 6088-B, Order No. 75-12,050.

Chodzko-Zajko, W., & Ismail, A. H. (1984). MMPI interscale relationships in middle-aged male Ss before and after an 8-month fitness program. *Journal of Clinical Psychology, 40,* 163–169.

Clark, J. H. (1953). The interpretation of the MMPI profiles of college students: A comparison by college major subject. *Journal of Clinical Psychology, 9,* 382–384.

Colligan, R. C., & Osborne, D. (1977). MMPI profiles from adolescent medical patients. *Journal of Clinical Psychology, 33,* 186–189.

Colligan, R. C., Osborne, D., Swenson, W. M., & Offord, K. (1984). The MMPI: Development of contemporary norms. *Journal of Clinical Psychology, 40,* 100–107.

Conley, J. J. (1981). An MMPI typology of male alcoholics: Admission, discharge, and outcome comparisons. *Journal of Personality Assessment, 45,* 33–39.

Cottle, W. C., & Lewis, W. W., Jr. (1954). Personality charac-teristics of counselors: II. Male counselor responses to the MMPI and GZTS. *Journal of Counseling Psychology, 1,* 27–30.

Craig, R. J. (1984). A comparison of MMPI profiles of heroin addicts based on multiple methods of classification. *Journal of Personality Assessment, 48,* 115–120.

Crumpton, E., Wine, D. B., & Groot, H. (1966). MMPI profiles of obese men and six other diagnostic categories. *Psychological Reports, 19,* 1110.

Cunningham, J., & Strassberg, D. (1981). Neuroticism and disclosure reciprocity. *Journal of Counseling Psychology, 28,* 455–458.

Dahlstrom, W. G., Welsh, G. S., & Dahlstrom, L. E. (1972). *An MMPI handbook. Vol. 1: Clinical interpretation* (rev. ed.). Minneapolis: University of Minnesota.

Davies, J., Nichols, D. S., & Greene, R. L. (1985, March). *A new schizophrenia scale for the MMPI.* Paper presented at the 20th Annual Symposium on Recent Advances in the Use of the MMPI, Honolulu.

Davis, L. J., Osborne, D., Siemens, P. J., & Brown, J. R. (1971). MMPI correlates with disability in multiple sclerosis. *Psychological Reports, 28,* 700–702.

Dikman, S., & Reitan, R. M. (1977). MMPI correlates of adaptive ability deficits in patients with brain lesions. *Journal of Nervous and Mental Disease, 165,* 247–254.

Donnelly, E. F. (1979). Adaptability in bipolar depressed groups. *Psychological Reports, 44,* 1252–1254.

Donnelly, E. F., & Murphy, D. L. (1973a). Primary affective disorder: MMPI differences between unipolar and bipolar depressed subjects. *Journal of Clinical Psychology, 29,* 303–306.

Donnelly, E. F., & Murphy, D. L. (1973b). Social desirability and bipolar affective disorder. *Journal of Consulting and Clinical Psychology, 41,* 469.

Donnelly, E. F., Murphy, D. L., & Goodwin, F. K. (1976). Cross-sectional and longitudinal comparisons of bipolar and unipolar depressed groups on the MMPI. *Journal of Consulting and Clinical Psychology, 44,* 233–237.

Donnelly, E. F., Murphy, D. L., Waldman, I. N., & Reynolds, T. D. (1976). MMPI differences between unipolar and bipolar depressed subjects: A replication. *Journal of Clinical Psychology, 32,* 610–612.

Donovan, D. M., Chaney, E. F., & O'Leary, M. R. (1978). Alcoholic MMPI subtypes: Relationship to drinking styles, benefits, and consequences. *Journal of Nervous and Mental Disease, 166,* 553–561.

Dorr, D. (1981). MMPI profiles of emotionally impaired physicians. *Journal of Clinical Psychology, 37,* 451–455.

Duckworth, J. C., & Anderson, W. P. (1986). *MMPI interpretation manual for counselors and clinicians* (3rd ed.). Muncie, IN: Accelerated Development.

Eshbaugh, D. M., Dick, K. V., & Tosi, D. J. (1982). Typological analysis of MMPI personality patterns of drug dependent females. *Journal of Personality Assessment, 46,* 488–494.

Eshbaugh, D. M., Tosi, D. J., & Hoyt, C. N. (1978). Some personality patterns and dimensions of male alcoholics: A multivariate description. *Journal of Personality Assessment, 42,* 409–417.

Eshbaugh, D. M., Tosi, D. J., & Hoyt, C. N. (1980). Women alcohlics: A typological description using the MMPI. *Journal of Studies on Alcohol, 41,* 310–317.

Eubanks, A. A., Hermecz, D. A., Patterson, W. M., Watts, D. C., Shehi, G.M., & Koplan, A. L. (1985, November). *MMPI profiles in patients with panic disorder.* Paper presented at the meeting of the Academy of Psychosomatic Medicine, San Francisco.

Evans, D. R. (1977). Use of the MMPI to predict effective hotline workers. *Journal of Clinical Psychology, 33,* 1113–1114.

Finney, J. C., Brandsma, J. M., Tondow, M., & Lemaistre, G. (1975). A study of transsexuals seeking gender reassignment. *American Journal of Psychiatry, 132,* 962–964.

Ford, C., Bray, G., & Swerdloff, R. (1976). A psychiatric study of patients referred with a diagnosis of hypoglycemia. *American Journal of Psychiatry, 133,* 290–294.

Forsyth, R. P., Jr. (1965). MMPI and demographic correlates of post-hospital adjustment in neuropsychiatric patients. *Psychological Reports, 16,* 355–366.

Gass, C. & Russell, E. (1985). MMPI correlates of verbal-intellectual deficits in patients with left hemisphere lesions. *Journal of Clinical Psychology, 41,* 664–670.

Gayton, W., Fogg, M. E., Tavormina, J., Bishop, J. S., Citrin, M. M., & Bassett, J. S. (1976). Comparison of the MMPI and mini-mult with women who request abortion. *Journal of Clinical Psychology, 32,* 648–650.

Gearing, M. L., II. (1979). The MMPI as a primary differentiator and predictor of behavior in prison: A methodological critique and review of the recent literature. *Psychological Bulletin, 86,* 929–963.

Gendreau, P., Irvine, M., & Knight, S. (1973). Evaluating response set styles on the MMPI with prisoners: Faking good adjustment and maladjustment. *Canadian Journal of Behavioral Science, 5,* 183–194.

Gilberstadt, H. (1971). *Comprehensive MMPI code book for males* (Veterans Adminstration Hospital, Minneapolis, MN, MMPI Research Laboratory). Washington, D.C.: U.S. Government Printing Office.

Gilberstadt, H., & Duker, J. (1965). *A handbook for clinical and actuarial MMPI interpretation.* Philadelphia: W.B. Saunders.

Gilberstadt, H., & Sako, Y. (1967). Intellectual and personality changes following open-heart surgery. *Archives of General Psychiatry, 16,* 210–214.

Goldstein, J., & Sappington, J. (1977). Personality characteristics of students who became heavy drug users: An MMPI study of an avant-garde. *American Journal of Drug and Alcohol Abuse, 4,* 401–412.

Graham, J. R. (1984a). What are code types? In J. N. Butcher and J. R. Graham (Eds.), *Clinical applications of the MMPI No. 4* (pp. 8–9). Minneapolis: University of Minnesota, Department of Professional Development and Conference Services, Continuing Education and Extension.

Graham, J. R. (1984b). Interpreting normal range profiles. In J. N. Butcher and J. R. Graham (Eds.), *Clinical applications of the MMPI. No. 17* (pp. 40–41). Minneapolis: University of Minnesota, Department of Professional Development and Conference Services, Continuing Education and Extension.

Graham, J. R. & McCord, G. (1985). Interpretation of moderately elevated MMPI scores for normal subjects. *Journal of Personality Assessment, 49,* 477–484.

Graham, J. R., & Tisdale M. (1983). *Interpretation of low scale 5 scores for women of high educational levels.* Paper presented at the 18th Annual Symposium on Recent Developments in the Use of the MMPI, St. Petersburg, FL.

Grayson, H. M., & Olinger, L. B. (1957). Simulation of "normalcy" by psychiatric patients on the MMPI. *Journal of Counseling Psychology, 21,* 73–77.

Greene, R. L. (1980). *The MMPI: An interpretive manual.* Philadelphia: Grune & Stratton.

Gross, L. R. (1959). MMPI L-F-K relationships with criteria of behavioral disturbance and social adjustment in a schizophrenic population. *Journal of Consulting Psychology, 23,* 319–323.

Grow, R., McVaugh, W., & Eno, T.D. (1980). Faking and the MMPI. *Journal of Clinical Psychology, 36,* 910–917.

Gustin, Q. L., Goodpaster, W. A., Sajadi, C., Pitts, W. M., Jr., LaBasse, D.L ., & Snyder, S. (1983). MMPI characteristics of the DSM-III borderline personality disorder. *Journal of*

Personality Assessment, 47, 50–59.

Gynther, M. D., & Brilliant, P. J. (1968). The MMPI K+ profile: A reexamination. *Journal of Consulting and Clinical Psychology, 32,* 616–617.

Hancock, J. W., & Carter, G. C.. (1954). Student personality traits and curriculae of enrollment. *Journal of Educational Research, 48,* 225–227.

Harper, D., & Richman, L. (1978). Personality profiles of physically impaired adolescents. *Journal of Clinical Psychology, 34,* 636–642.

Harrell, T. W., & Harrell, M. S. (1973). The personality of MBA's who reach general management early. *Personnel Psychology, 26,* 127–134.

Hart, R. (1984). Chronic pain: Replicated multivariate clustering of personality profiles. *Journal of Clinical Psychology, 40,* 129–133.

Hathaway, S. R., & Meehl, P. E. (1951). The Minnesota Multiphasic Personality Inventory. In *Military clinical psychology* (Department of the Army TM 8-242; Department of the Air Force AFM 160-45). Washington, D.C.: U.S. Government Printing Office.

Hatsukami, D., Owen, P., Pyle, R., & Mitchell, J. (1982). Similarities and differences on the MMPI between women with bulimia and women with alcohol or drug abuse problems. *Addictive Behavior, 7,* 435–439.

Haynes, S., Wilson, C., Jaffe, P., & Britton, B. (1979). Biofeedback treatment of atopic dermatitis: Controlled case studies of eight cases. *Biofeedback and Self-regulation, 4,* 195–209.

Heaton, R. K., Chelune, G. J., & Lehman, R. A. (1978). Using neuropsychological and personality tests to assess the likelihood of patient employment. *Journal of Nervous and Mental Disease, 166,* 408–416.

Hiner, D. L., Ogren, D. J., & Baxter, J. C. (1969). Ideal-self responding on the MMPI. *Journal of Projective Techniques and Personality Assessment, 33,* 389–396.

Hoffmann, H., Loper, R. G., & Kammeier, M. L. (1974). Identifying future alcoholics with MMPI alcoholism scales. *Quarterly Journal of Studies on Alcohol, 35,* 490–498.

Holland, T. R. (1979). Ethnic group differences in MMPI profile pattern and factorial structure among adult offenders. *Journal of Personality Assessment, 43,* 72–77.

Hudgens, A. (1979). Family-oriented treatment of chronic pain. *Journal of Marital and Family Therapy, 5,* 67–78.

Hunt, H. F. (1948). The effect of deliberate deception on Minnesota Multiphasic Personality Inventory performance. *Journal of Consulting Psychology, 12,* 396–402.

Jansen, D. G., & Garvey, F. J. (1973). High-, average, and low-rated clergymen in a state hospital clinical program. *Journal of Clinical Psychology, 29,* 89–92.

Kales, A., Caldwell, A. B., Preston, T. A., Healey, S., & Kales, J. D. (1976). Personality patterns in insomnia: Theoretical implications. *Archives of General Psychiatry, 33,* 1128–1134.

Kales, J. D., Kales, A., Soldatos, C. R., Caldwell, A., Charney, D., & Martin, E. D. (1980a). Night terrors: Clinical characteristics and personality patterns. *Archives of General Psychiatry, 37,* 1413–1417.

Kales, A., Soldatos, C. R., Caldwell, A., & Charney, D., Kales, J., Markel, D., & Cadieux, R (1980b). Nightmares: Clinical characteristics and personality patterns. *American Journal of Psychiatry, 137,* 1197–1201.

Kales, A., Soldatos, C., Caldwell, A., Kales, J., Humphrey, F. J., Charney, D., & Schweitzer, P. K. (1980c). Somnambulism: Clinical characteristics and personality patterns. *Archives of General Psychiatry, 37,* 1406–1410.

Keegan, J.F., & Lachar, D. (1979). The MMPI as a predictor of early termination from polydrug abuse treatment. *Journal of Personality Assessment, 43,* 379–384.

Kelley, C. K., & King, G. D. (1978). Behavioral correlates for within-normal-limit MMPI profiles with and without elevated *K* in students at a university mental health center. *Journal of Clinical Psychology, 34,* 695–699.

Kennedy, W. A. (1962). MMPI profiles of gifted adolescents. *Journal of Clinical Psychology, 18,* 148–149.

Kennedy, W. A., Nelson, W., Lindner, R., Turner, J., Moon, H. (1960). Psychological measurements of future scientists. *Psychological Reports, 7,* 515–517.

King, G., & Kelley, C. (1977). MMPI behavioral correlates of Spike-5 and two-point code types with Scale 5 as one elevation. *Journal of Clinical Psychology, 33,* 180–185.

Kline, R. B., & Snyder, D. K. (1985). Replicated MMPI subtypes for alcoholic men and women: Relationship to self-reported drinking behaviors. *Journal of Consulting and Clinical Psychology, 53,* 70–79.

Klinge, V., Lachar, D., Grisell, J., & Berman, W. (1978). Effects of scoring norms on adolescent psychiatric drug users' and nonusers' MMPI profiles. *Adolescence, 13,* 1–11.

Kokosh, J. (1978). Two-point MMPI code types and academic achievement: Replication and reanalysis. *Psychological Reports, 42,* 623–626.

Krauthamer, C. (1979). The personality of alcoholic middle-class women: A comparative study with the MMPI. *Journal of Clinical Psychology, 35,* 442–448.

Kudrow, L., & Sutkus, B. J. (1979). MMPI pattern specificity in primary headache disorders. *Headache, 19,* 18–24.

Kunce, J. T. (1979). MMPI scores and adaptive behaviors. In C. S. Newmark (Ed.), *MMPI clinical and research trends* (pp. 306-327). New York: Praeger.

Kunce, J. T., & Anderson, W. (1970). Counselor-client similarity and referral bias. *Journal of Counseling Psychology, 17,* 102–106.

Kunce, J. T., & Anderson, W. (1976). Normalizing the MMPI. *Journal of Clinical Psychology, 32,* 776–780.

Lachar, D. (1974a). *The MMPI: Clinical assessment and automated interpretation.* Los Angeles: Western Psychological Services.

Lachar, D.. (1974b). Prediction of early US Air Force cadet adaptation with the MMPI. *Journal of Counseling Psychology, 21,* 404–408.

Lachar, D., Gdowski, C. L., & Keegan, J.F. (1979). MMPI profiles of men alcoholics, drug addicts and psychiatric patients. *Journal of Studies on Alcohol, 48,* 45–56.

Lachar, D., Klinge, V., and Grisell, J. L. (1976). Relative accuracy of automated MMPI narratives generated from adult norm and adolescent norm profiles. *Journal of Consulting and Clinical Psychology, 44,* 20–24.

Lachar, D., Schoof, K., Keegan, J., & Gdowski, C. (1978). Dimensions of polydrug abuse: An MMPI study. In D.R. Wesson, A.S. Carlin, K.M. Adams, & G. Beschner (Eds.), *Polydrug abuse: The results of a national collaborative study* (pp. 149–180). San Diego: Academic Press.

Lair, C., & King, G. (1976). MMPI profile predictors for successful and expired open heart surgery patients. *Journal of Clinical Psychology, 32,* 51–54.

Langevin, R., Paitich, D., Freeman, R., Mann, K., & Handy, L. (1978). Personality characteristics and sexual anomalies in males. *Canadian Journal of Behavioral Science, 10,* 222–238.

Lanyon, R. I. (1967). Simulation of normal and psychopathic MMPI personality patterns. *Journal of Consulting Psychology, 31,* 94–97.

Lanyon, R. I. (1968). *A handbook of MMPI group profiles.* Minneapolis: University of Minnesota.

Lanyon, R. I., & May, A. C. (1979). Relationship between spontaneous imagery distortions and schizophrenic psychopathology. *Journal of Mental Imagery, 3,* 43–51.

Lawton, M. P., & Kleban, M. H. (1965). Prisoners' faking on the MMPI. *Journal of Clinical Psychology, 21,* 269–271.

Leach, K. A. (1982, August). *Borderline personality disorder and the MMPI.* Paper presented at the meeting of the American Psychological Association, Washington, D.C.

Leavitt, F., & Garron, D. (1982). Patterns of psychological disturbance and pain report in patients with low back pain. *Journal of Psychosomatic Research, 26,* 301–307.

Long, C. (1981). The relationship between surgical outcome and MMPI profiles in chronic pain patients. *Journal of Clinical Psychology, 37,* 744–749.

Lumry, A. E., Gottesman, I. I., & Tuason, V. B. (1982). MMPI state dependency during the course of bipolar psychosis. *Psychiatry Research, 7,* 59–67.

Lumry, A. E., Gottesman, I. I., & Tuason, V. B. (1983). The authors reply [Letter to the editor]. *Psychiatry Research, 9,* 357.

MacAndrew, C. (1965). The differentiation of male alcoholic outpatients from nonalcoholic psychiatric outpatients by means of the MMPI. *Quarterly Journal of Studies on Alcohol, 26,* 238–246.

MacCrimmon, D., Wallace, J., Goldberg, W., & Streiner, D. L. (1979). Emotional disturbance and cognitive deficits in hyperthyroidism. *Psychosomatic Medicine, 41,* 331–340.

Marks, P. A. & Seeman, W. (1963). *The actuarial description of abnormal personality.* Baltimore: Williams & Wilkins.

Marks, P. A., Seeman, W., & Haller, D. L. (1974). *The actuarial use of the MMPI with adolescents and adults.* Baltimore: Williams & Wilkins.

Marsh, G., Hirsch, S., & Leung, G. (1982). Use and misuse of the MMPI in multiple sclerosis. *Psychological Reports, 51,* 1127–1134.

Marshall, P., Surridge, D., & Delva, N. (1980). Differentiation of organic and psychogenic impotence on the basis of MMPI decision rules. *Journal of Consulting and Clinical Psychology, 48,* 407–408.

Matthews, C., Dikman, S., & Harley, P. (1977). Age of onset and psychometric correlates of MMPI profiles in major motor epilepsy. *Diseases of the Nervous System, 38,* 173–176.

McCall, R. J. (1973). MMPI factors that differentiate remediably from irremediably obese women. *Journal of Community Psychology, 1,* 34–36.

McCreary, C. P. (1975). Personality profiles of persons convicted of indecent exposure. *Journal of Clinical Psychology, 31,* 260–262.

McCreary, C. P. (1976). Trait and type differences among male and female assaultive and nonassaultive offenders. *Journal of Personality Assessment, 40,* 617–621.

McCreary, C. P. (1985). Empirically derived MMPI profile clusters and characteristics of low back pain patients. *Journal of Consulting and Clinical Psychology, 53,* 558–560.

McGill, J., Lawlis, G. F., Selby, D., Mooney, V., & McCoy, C. E. (1983). The relationship of MMPI profile clusters to pain behaviors. *Journal of Behavioral Medicine, 6,* 77–92.

Meehl, P. E. (1945). The dynamics of "structured" personality tests. *Journal of Clinical Psychology, 1,* 296–303.

Meehl, P. E. (1956). Profile analysis of the MMPI in differential diagnosis. In G.S. Welsh & W.G. Dahlstrom (Eds.), *Basic readings in the MMPI in psychology and medicine.* Minneapolis: University of Minnesota.

Meehl, P. E., & Hathaway, S. R. (1946). The *K* factor as a suppressor variable in the Minnesota Multiphasic Personality Inventory. *Journal of Applied Psychology, 30,* 525–564.

Megargee, E., & Bohn, M. (1979). *Classifying criminal offenders.* Beverly Hills, CA: Sage.

Meikle, S., & Gerritse, R. (1970). MMPI "cookbook" pattern frequencies in a psychiatric unit. *Journal of Clinical Psychology, 26,* 82–84.

Miller, W., & Keirn, W. (1978). Personality measurement in parents of retarded and emotionally disturbed children: A replication. *Journal of Clinical Psychology*, *34*, 686–690.

Mlott, S. R., Lira, F. T., & Miller, W. C. (1977). Psychological assessment of the burn patient. *Journal of Clinical Psychology*, *33*, 425–430.

Monroe, L., & Marks, P. (1977). MMPI differences between adolescent poor and good sleepers. *Journal of Consulting and Clinical Psychology*, *45*, 151–152.

Munjack, D., Kanno, P., & Oziel, L. J. (1978). Ejaculatory disorders: Some psychometric data. *Psychological Reports*, *43*, 783–787.

Munjack, D., Kanno, P., Staples, F., & Leonard, M. (1980). Some psychometric data on ejaculatory disorders: A further note. *Psychological Reports*, *46*, 1047–1050.

Munjack, D., Oziel, L. J., Kanno, P., Whipple, K., & Leonard, M. (1981). Psychological characteristics of males with secondary erectile failure. *Archives of Sexual Behavior*, *10*, 123–131.

Munjack, D., & Staples, F. (1976). Psychological characteristics of women with sexual inhibition (frigidity) in sex clinics. *Journal of Nervous and Mental Disease*, *163*, 117–123.

Naliboff, B., Cohen, M., & Yellen, A. (1982). Does the MMPI differentiate chronic illness from chronic pain. *Pain*, *13*, 333–341.

Naliboff, B., Cohen, M., & Yellen, A. (1983). Frequency of MMPI profile types in three chronic illness populations. *Journal of Clinical Psychology*, *39*, 843–847.

Newmark, C. S., Gentry, L., Simpson, M., & Jones, T. (1978). MMPI criteria for diagnosing schizophrenia. *Journal of Personality Assessment*, *42*, 366–373.

Newmark, C. S., Gentry, L., Whitt, J. K., McKee, D. C., & Wicker, C. (1983). Simulating normal MMPI profiles as a favourable prognostic sign in schizophrenia. *Australian Journal of Psychology*, *35*, 433–444.

Norman, R. D., & Redlo, M. (1952). MMPI personality patterns for various college major groups. *Journal of Applied Psychology*, *36*, 404–409.

Owen, D. R. (1970). Classification of MMPI profiles from non-psychiatric populations using two cookbook systems. *Journal of Clinical Psychology*, *26*, 79–82.

Page, R. D., & Bozlee, S. (1982). A cross-cultural MMPI comparison of alcoholics. *Psychological Reports*, *50*, 639–646.

Panton, J. H. (1979). MMPI profile configurations associated with incestuous and non-incestuous child molesting. *Psychological Reports*, *45*, 335–338.

Pauker, J. D. (1966). Identification of MMPI profile types in a female, inpatient, psychiatric setting using the Marks and Seeman rules. *Journal of Consulting Psychology*, *30*, 90.

Payne, F. D., & Wiggins, J. S. (1968). Effects of rule relaxation and system combination on classification rates in two MMPI "cookbook" systems. *Journal of Consulting and Clinical Psychology*, *32*, 734–736.

Penk, W. E. (1981). *Assessing the substance abuser with the MMPI* (Clinical notes on the MMPI, No. 7). Nutley, NJ: Roche Psychiatric Service Institute.

Penk, W. E., Fudge, J. W., Robinowitz, R., & Neman, R. S. (1979). Personality characteristics of compulsive heroin, amphetamine, and barbiturate users. *Journal of Consulting and Clinical Psychology*, *47*, 583–585.

Peters, P., Swenson, W., & Mulder, D. (1978). Is there a characteristic personality profile in amyotrophic lateral sclerosis?: A MMPI study. *Archives of Neurology*, *35*, 321–322.

Peyser, J. M., Edwards, K. R., & Poser, C. (1980). Psychological profiles in patients with MS: A preliminary investigation. *Archives of Neurology*, *37*, 437–440.

Pollack, D., & Grainey, T. (1984). A comparison of MMPI profiles for state and private disability insurance applicants. *Journal of Personality Assessment*, *48*, 121–125.

Pomerantz, A., Greenberg, I., & Blackburn, G. (1977). MMPI profiles of obese men and women. *Psychological Reports*, *41*, 731–734.

Post, R. D., & Gasparikova-Krasnec, M. (1979). MMPI validity scales and behavioral disturbance in psychiatric inpatients. *Journal of Personality Assessment*, *43*, 155–159.

Prokop, C., Bradley, L., Margolis, R., & Gentry, D. (1980). Multivariate analysis of the MMPI profiles of patients with multiple pain complaints. *Journal of Personality Assessment*, *44*, 246–252.

Rader, C. M. (1977). MMPI profile types of exposers, rapists, and assaulters in a court services population. *Journal of Consulting and Clinical Psychology*, *45*, 61–69.

Rapaport, G. M. (1958). "Ideal self" instructions, MMPI profile changes, and the prediction of clinical improvement. *Journal of Consulting Psychology*, *22*, 459–463.

Ray, J. B., Solomon, G. S., Doncaster, M. G., & Mellina, R. (1983). First offender adult shoplifters: A preliminary profile. *Journal of Clinical Psychology*, *39*, 769–770.

Repko, G., & Cooper, R. (1983). A study of the average worker's compensation case. *Journal of Clinical Psychology*, *39*, 287–295.

Richman, L., & Harper, D. (1980). Personality profiles of physically impaired young adults. *Journal of Clinical Psychology*, *36*, 668–671.

Roback, H. B., McKee, E., Webb, W., Abramowitz, C. B., & Abramowitz, S. I. (1976a). Comparative psychiatric status of male applicants for sexual reassignment surgery, jejunoileal bypass surgery, and psychiatric outpatient treatment. *Journal of Sex Research*, *14*, 32–36.

Roback, H. B., McKee, E., Webb, W., Abramowitz, C. B., & Abramowitz, S. I. (1976b). Psychopathology in female sex-change applicants and two help-seeking controls. *Journal of Abnormal Psychology*, *85*, 430–432.

Roberts, A., & Reinhardt, L. (1980). The behavioral management of chronic pain: Long-term follow-up with comparison groups. *Pain*, *8*, 151–162.

Rogers, R., & Seman, W. (1983). Murder and criminal responsibility: An examination of MMPI profiles. *Behavioral Sciences and the Law*, *1*, 89–95.

Rosen, A. (1974). Brief report of MMPI characteristics of sexual deviation. *Psychological Reports*, *35*, 73–74.

Rosen, H., & Rosen, R. A. (1957). Personality variables and role in a union business agent group. *Journal of Applied Psychology*, *41*, 131–136.

Roth, T., Kramer, M., & Lutz, R. (1976). The nature of insomnia: A descriptive summary of a sleep clinic population. *Comprehensive Psychiatry*, *17*, 217–220.

Saxe, S. J., & Reiser, M. (1976). A comparison of three police applicant groups using the MMPI. *Journal of Police Science and Administration*, *4*, 419–425.

Shealy, A., & Walker, D. (1978). MMPI prediction of intellectual changes following cardiac surgery. *Journal of Nervous and Mental Disease*, *166*, 263–267.

Shealy, R. C., Lowe, J. D., & Ritzler, B. A. (1980). Sleep onset insomnia: Personality characteristics and treatment outcome. *Journal of Consulting and Clinical Psychology*, *48*, 659–661.

Shultz, T. D., Gibeau, P. J., & Barry, S. M. (1968). Utility of MMPI "cookbooks". *Journal of Clinical Psychology*, *24*, 430–433.

Silver, R. J., Isaacs, K., & Mansky, P. (1981). MMPI correlates of affective disorders. *Journal of Clinical Psychology*, *37*, 836–839.

Sines, L. K., Baucom, D. H., & Gruba, G. H. (1979). A validity scale sign calling for caution in the interpretation of MMPIs among psychiatric inpatients. *Journal of Personality Assessment*, *43*, 604–607.

Smith, P., Burleigh, R., Sewell, W., & Krisak, J. (1984). Correlation between the MMPI profiles of emotionally disturbed adolescents and their mothers. *Adolescence, 19,* 31–38.

Snyder, D., & Power, D. (1981). Empirical descriptors of unelevated MMPI profiles among chronic pain patients: A typological approach. *Journal of Clinical Psychology, 37,* 602–607.

Spergel, P., Erhlich, G., & Glass, D. (1978). The rheumatoid arthritic personality: A psychodiagnostic myth. *Psychosomatics, 19,* 79–87.

Stehbens, J., Ehmke, D., & Wilson, B. (1982). MMPI profiles of rheumatic fever adolescents and adults. *Journal of Clinical Psychology, 38,* 592–596.

Sutker, P. B. (1971). Personality differences and sociopathy in heroin addicts and nonaddict prisoners. *Journal of Abnormal Psychology, 78,* 247–251.

Sutker, P. B., & Allain, A. N. (1979). MMPI studies of extreme criminal violence in incarcerated women and men. In C.S. Newmark (Ed.), *MMPI: Clinical and research trends* (pp. 167–197). New York: Praeger.

Sutker, P. B., & Archer, R. P. (1979). MMPI characteristics of opiate addicts, alcoholics, and other drug abusers. In C.S. Newmark (Ed.), *MMPI: Clinical and research trends* (pp. 105–148). New York: Praeger.

Svanum, S., & Dallas, C. L. (1981). Alcoholic MMPI types and their relationship to patient characteristics, polydrug abuse, and abstinence following treatment. *Journal of Personality Assessment, 45,* 278–287.

Tarter, R. E., McBride, H., Buonpane, N., & Schneider, D. W. (1977). Differentiation of alcoholics: Childhood history of minimal brain dysfunction, family history, and drinking pattern. *Archives of General Psychiatry, 34,* 761–768.

Trieschmann, R., & Sand, P. (1971). WAIS and MMPI correlates of increasing renal failure in adult medical patients. *Psychological Reports, 29,* 1251–1262.

Vestre, N. D., & Klett, W. G. (1969). *Admissions to a neuropsychiatric hospital with "normal" MMPI profiles.* Paper presented at the meeting of the American Psychological Association, Miami.

Vincent, K. R., Castillo, I., Hauser, R. I., Stuart, H. J., Zapata, J. A., Cohn, C. K., & O'Shanick, G. J. (1983). MMPI code types and DSM-III diagnoses. *Journal of Clinical Psychology, 39,* 829–842.

Wallace, J., MacCrimmon, D., & Goldberg, W. (1980). Acute hyperthyroidism: Cognitive and emotional correlates. *Journal of Abnormal Psychology, 89,* 519–527.

Webb, W., Phares, R., & Abram, H. (1976). Jejunoileal bypass procedures in morbid obesity: Preoperative psychological findings. *Journal of Clinical Psychology, 32,* 82–85.

Wheatley, R., & Ursano, R. (1982). Serial personality evaluations of repatriated US Air Force Southeast Asia POWs. *Aviation, Space, and Environmental Medicine, 53,* 251–257.

Wiens, A., & Matarazzo, J. (1977). WAIS and MMPI correlates of the Halstead-Reitan neuropsychology battery in normal male subjects. *Journal of Nervous and Mental Disease, 164,* 112–121.

Williamson, D. A., Kelley, M. L., Davis, C. J., Ruggerio, L., & Blouin, D. C. (1985). Psychopathology of eating disorders: A controlled comparison of bulimic, obese, and normal subjects. *Journal of Consulting and Clinical Psychology, 53,* 161–166.

Winters, K. D., Newmark, C. S., Lumry, A. E., Leach, K., & Weintraub, S. (1985). MMPI codetypes characteristic of DSM-III schizophrenics, depressives, and bipolars. *Journal of Clinical Psychology, 41,* 382–386.

Wooten, A. (1983). MMPI profiles among neuropsychology patients. *Journal of Clinical Psychology, 39,* 392–406.

Zorick, F., Roth, T., Hartze, K., & Piccione, P. M., & Stepanski, E. J.(1981). Evaluation and diagnosis of persistent insomnia. *American Journal of Psychiatry, 138,* 769–773.

Chapter 12

Summary

ROGER L. GREENE

After reviewing the use of the MMPI with specific populations, several concluding remarks can be made. The reader should be aware by now that there is *not* a specific MMPI codetype that is characteristic of any population, although it is clear that some codetypes are more frequent than others. This chapter summarizes the frequency with which various codetypes are seen in these specific populations, discusses the research that has been reviewed, and makes some suggestions for future work in this area.

CODETYPE FREQUENCIES AS A FUNCTION OF POPULATION

One method of examining the frequencies with which the various codetypes are encountered involves comparing the most frequent codetypes in each population. Such comparisons begin to provide some data on which codetypes are more likely to be seen in which populations and whether such occurrences are specific to that population or characteristic of most clinical samples. Tables 12–1 and 12–2 summarize the frequencies with which the various codetypes are encountered in men and women, respectively. These Tables are a compilation of the codetype tables for the specific populations from the earlier chapters. Studies that did not report their data by gender or combined their data for men and women have been included in Table 12–1. Several general comments seems warranted before the specific data in these Tables are summarized. First, investigators infrequently reported codetype data that can be summarized.

They tended either to report a group profile for their patients (the attendant problems of such profiles were reviewed in Chapter 1), or not to provide any type of summary data for how their patients performed on the MMPI. If additional criteria were imposed such as validity of the codetypes, these tables would be essentially void. Second, the few populations that can be included in Table 12–2 relative to Table 12–1 illustrate how infrequently investigators either have analyzed or reported their codetype data by gender. Since gender is one of the moderator variables that is most likely to be considered in psychological research, it should be apparent that other moderator variables such as education, socioeconomic class, and so on rarely are examined. The potential effects of these variables also represent issues that must be addressed in future MMPI research. Finally, the almost total absence of data on whole populations is hard to understand given the long history of clinical usage of the MMPI. The reader could compare the Table of Contents with the diagnostic categories of *DSM-III-R* to get some idea of the populations that essentially have not been studied with the MMPI. For example, MMPI studies of Anxiety and Paranoid Disorders rarely are reported.

Despite these inherent limitations, there do seem to be a number of conclusions that can be made based on these data. First, clinical populations tend to elevate the appropriate clinical scale among their most frequent codetypes, which attests to the construct validity of the MMPI. For example, schizophrenics tend to have Scale *8 (Sc)* as one of the scales within their most frequent

THE MMPI: USE WITH
SPECIFIC POPULATIONS

© 1988 by Grune & Stratton.

ISBN   0-8089-1913-X
All rights reserved.

TABLE 12–1.   FREQUENCY OF MMPI CODETYPES FOR MEN BY POPULATION*

Authors	Codetype									
	1-2/2-1	1-3/3-1	2-4/4-2	2-7/7-2	2-8/8-2	3-4/4-3	4-6/6-4	4-8/8-4	4-9/9-4	6-8/8-6
General Psychiatric (Hedlund & Won Cho, 1979)	4.9	2.3	7.7	4.8	5.5	1.4	3.1	7.3	6.4	7.2
General Medical† (Colligan, 1986)	14.7	17.9	3.4	9.3	4.3	1.4	0.5	1.5	1.3	1.3
Schizophrenia (Table 3–2, p. 61)			5.7		8.3		5.4	7.8		14.0
Affective Disorders:										
Depressed										
Minor (Table 4–3, p. 91)		6.8	7.6	12.2	7.2	4.8		5.6		5.9
Major (Table 4–3, p. 91)	9.6	4.0	5.5	16.5	11.3	6.0	5.4	6.2	6.0	8.7
Manic (Table 4–7, p. 94)							8.0	7.4	16.5	8.0
Personality Disorders										
Borderline (Table 5–2, p. 117)				25.0	26.3			18.6		16.4
Substance Abuse										
Alcoholic (Table 6–6, p. 169)	6.5	2.9	15.3	8.1	3.8	3.4	2.1	3.8	8.5	1.3
Polydrug (Table 6–16, p. 187)			13.1	5.5	7.4	4.3	5.1	10.8	16.8	11.0
Child Sexual Abusers (Table 9–4, p. 255)			7.4			11.3		7.5	7.5	

(Continues.)

TABLE 12–1.   *(Continued.)*

| Authors | Codetype | | |
	7-8/8-7	8-9/9-8	Totals
General Psychiatric (Hedlund & Won Cho, 1979)	5.6	3.6	47.7
General Medical† (Colligan, 1986)	2.3	1.3	59.2
Schizophrenia (Table 3–2, p. 61)	6.4	6.1	58.2
Affective Disorders:			
Depressed			
Minor (Table 4–3, p. 91)			48.9
Major (Table 4–3, p. 91)	8.9	17.0	56.8
Manic (Table 4–7, p. 94)		18.8	51.1
Personality Disorders			
Borderline (Table 5–2, p. 117)	10.3		66.8
Substance Abuse			
Alcoholic (Table 6–6, p. 169)	3.1	2.4	57.5
Polydrug (Table 6–16, p. 187)	9.4	14.5	75.3
Child Sexual Abusers (Table 9–4, p. 255)		3.2	39.3

*Samples that did not indicate whether their patients were male or female and samples that did not report their data by gender have been included in this Table.

†These patients were referred for a psychiatric evaluation so they represent a subset of medical patients.

codetypes (*2-8/8-2*, *4-8/8-4*, and *6-8/8-6*). Similarly, depressed patients tend to elevate Scale 2 (*D*) within their frequent codetypes (*2-7/7-2* and *2-8/8-2*). Second, these frequently occurring codetypes, that contain the clinical scale that is most appropriate for a specific clinical sample, still do not occur in over one-quarter of the patients. The most frequent codetypes in Tables 12–1 and 12–2 appear to be a function of the limited number of samples and sample sizes within a given population (e.g., Borderline Personality Disorders and the various types of Child Abuse). As samples get larger within any population, the codetypes become more heterogeneous and the frequency of any specific codetype decreases. Generally, the most frequent codetypes within a given population occur no more than 15–20 percent of the time, and most codetypes are found less than 10 percent of the time. Third, the 24 codetypes that are summarized in Tables 12–1 and 12–2 represent 53.3 percent (24/45) of the possible MMPI codetypes and account for approximately one-half to two-thirds of these populations. Again, the heterogeneity of codetypes that are to be found in any clinical population should be evident. Fourth, if the frequencies of codetypes for general psychiatric patients (Hedlund & Won Cho, 1979) and medical patients referred for a psychiatric evaluation (Colligan, 1986) are

used as a baseline, it does appear that some codetypes do occur more frequently in specific populations. Before making these comparisons, however, it should be noted that there are differences with which the various codetypes occur in these two samples. Codetypes involving the neurotic triad (*1-2/2-1*, *1-3/3-1*, *2-7/7-2*) are much more frequent in the medical sample while codetypes involving the psychotic tetrad (*4-8/8-4*, *6-8/8-6*, and *7-8/8-7*) are more frequent in the psychiatric sample.

Table 12–3 summarizes by gender those codetypes that occur more than 10 percent of the time in specific populations. It should be readily apparent that there are few gender differences in the frequencies with which these codetypes are found. This conclusion must be tempered, however, by the fact that these comparisons can only be made in substance abuse/dependence populations. Most of the frequently occurring codetypes in Table 12–3 are to be expected within the specific population and again they reflect the construct validity of the MMPI. That is, it should not come as a surprise that *2-7/7-2* codetypes are found frequently in depressed patients and *6-8/8-6* codetypes in schizophrenic patients. It is somewhat unusual that *8-9/9-8* codetypes occur frequently in patients with major depressive disorders and manic disorders. The fre-

TABLE 12–2. FREQUENCY OF MMPI CODETYPES FOR WOMEN BY POPULATION*

Authors	Codetype				
	1-2/2-1	1-3/3-1	2-4/4-2	2-7/7-2	2-8/8-2
General Psychiatric (Hedlund & Won Cho, 1979)	1.9	3.8	5.3	3.8	4.7
General Medical† (Colligan, 1986)	6.1	28.3	3.4	5.1	2.8
Substance Abuse					
Alcoholic (Table 6–6, p. 169)	2.9	2.7	14.8	9.4	5.2
Polydrug (Table 6–16, p. 187)	5.0	1.6	14.2	2.3	5.2
Child-Abusing Mothers (Table 9–2, p. 249)			22.2		11.4
Nonoffending Mothers (Table 9–5, p. 255)			9.0		
Child Abuse Victims (Table 9–6, p. 255)					

Authors	Codetype				
	3-4/4-3	4-6/6-4	4-8/8-4	4-9/9-4	6-8/8-6
General Psychiatric (Hedlund & Won Cho, 1979)	3.1	6.5	8.8	5.1	9.6
General Medical† (Colligan, 1986)	2.3	1.5	1.9	1.2	1.3
Substance Abuse					
Alcoholic (Table 6–6, p. 169)	7.6	5.4	6.9	6.2	1.5
Polydrug (Table 6–16, p. 187)	0.8	3.3	11.7	22.7	4.7
Child-Abusing Mothers (Table 9–2, p. 249)	11.1	16.7	28.6		8.6
Nonoffending Mothers (Table 9–5, p. 255)	18.1		2.6	6.3	
Child Abuse Victims (Table 9–6, p. 255)			20.0		

Authors	Codetype		
	7-8/8-7	8-9/9-8	Totals
General Psychiatric (Hedlund & Won Cho, 1979)	4.2	3.5	47.5
General Medical† (Colligan, 1986)	1.6	0.8	56.3
Substance Abuse			
Alcoholic (Table 6–6, p. 169)	2.3	2.7	63.8
Polydrug (Table 6–16, p. 187)	3.5	6.8	75.8
Child-Abusing Mothers (Table 9–2, p. 249)			85.7
Nonoffending Mothers (Table 9–5, p. 255)		4.0	49.9
Child Abuse Victims (Table 9–6, p. 255)		15.5	56.2

*Samples that did not indicate whether their patients were male or female and samples that did not report their data by gender were included in Table 12–1.

†These patients were referred for a psychiatric evaluation so they represent a subset of medical patients.

TABLE 12–3.   CODETYPES WITH FREQUENCIES GREATER THAN 10 PERCENT BY POPULATION

		Population									
		Mood			Substance Abuse			Child-Abusing Mothers	Child Sexual Abusers	Non-Offending Parents	Child Abuse Victims
		Depression					Border-line				
Codetype	Schizophrenic	Minor	Major	Manic	Alcohol	Polydrug					
2-4/4-2											
men					15.3%	13.1%					
women					14.8	14.2		22.2%			
2-7/7-2		12.2%	16.5%				25.0%				
2-8/8-2											
men			11.3				26.3				
women								11.4			
3-4/4-3								11.1	11.3%	18.1%	
4-6/6-4								16.7			
4-8/8-4											
men	14.0%					10.8	18.6				
women						11.7		28.6			20.0%
4-9/9-4											
men				16.5		16.8					
women						22.7					
6-8/8-6											
men	14.0					11.0	16.4				
women											20.0
7-8/8-7							10.3				
8-9/9-8											
men			17.0	18.8		14.5					
women											15.5

quent occurrence of codetypes within the psychotic tetrad in polydrug patients also would not be expected. It is possible that this latter finding reflects inadequate attention to validity considerations with the patients still being toxic when evaluated. In any respect, these latter two findings are worthy of further investigation.

Finally, it appears that those codetypes that occur less than 10 percent of the time are not specific to any given population (see Tables 12–1 and 12–2). For example, 4-6/6-4 codetypes occur from 0.5 to 8.0 percent of the time with no apparent pattern in the populations represented in Tables 12–1 and 12–2 except for their occurrence in child abusing mothers, which was based on a combined sample of 36 women. Similar conclusions can be drawn for 7-8/8-7 codetypes, although 7-8/8-7 codetypes are found rather frequently in all of the populations summarized in Tables 12–1 and 12–2. Further research is needed to determine whether these less frequently occurring codetypes and the codetypes not represented in these Tables are specific to any population.

RESEARCH ISSUES

Despite almost four decades of MMPI research, there still are a number of basic issues that have not been addressed. Since these issues have been raised repeatedly, their need to be considered in future research will not be belabored. A quick perusal of the ratings on the methodologic issues within each chapter will demonstrate the work that needs to be done in future MMPI research. Clearly, researchers and journal editors need to be sure that such issues are included in designing, implementing, and reporting future studies. The failure to consider the role of moderator variables such as ethnicity, education, social class, and so on must be corrected. The reader could review the methodologic issues discussed in Chapter 1 or Butcher and Tellegen (1978) to realize the issues that need to be considered in future research with the MMPI.

FUTURE DIRECTIONS

As MMPI research continues in the coming years, it can be hoped that investigators are sensitive to the multitude of issues that have been raised repeatedly throughout this text. Well conceptualized and well designed research can only further our understanding of the performance of the MMPI within any specific population. Also, investigators should rest assured that there is still sufficient work to be done with the MMPI in almost any population that they might want to consider.

REFERENCES

Butcher, J. N., & Tellegen, A. (1978). Common methodological problems in MMPI research. *Journal of Consulting and Clinical Psychology, 46,* 620–628.

Colligan, R. C. (1986). [MMPI data for medical patients referred for a psychiatric evaluation]. Unpublished raw data.

Hedlund, J. H. & Won Cho, D. (1979). [MMPI data research tape for Missouri Department of Mental Health patients]. Unpublished raw data.

Index

Note: Page numbers followed by the letter *f* refer to figures.
Page numbers followed by the letter *t* refer to tables.